RE-WRITING FREUD

Simon Morris

Liz,

a maelström of

non-meaning for you.

With my very best wishes,

INFORMATION AS MATERIAL

•

RE-WRITING FREUD

Simon Morris

•

Translated by Lingo algorithm,
programmed by Christine Morris
Edited by Craig Dworkin

RE-WRITING FREUD
Published by INFORMATION AS MATERIAL
York, England
Production & Printing
IMSCHOOT
Burggravenlaan 20
B-9000 Gent
België
ISBN 0 9536765 8 7
© Simon Morris
www.informationasmaterial.com

Supported by Arts Council England

CONTENTS

RE-WRITING FREUD
(2005)

RE-WRITING FREUD
(2005)

the she wished interpretation. of psychoneuroses.

EDITOR'S INTRODUCTION: GRAMMAR DEGREE ZERO

> *"And therefore when you have used all your cramping-irons*
> *to the text [...] it will be but a piece of frugal nonsense.*
> *But if your meaning be with a violent hyperbaton*
> *to transpose the text, as if the words lay thus in order..."*
> - John Milton

The book you are holding contains each and every one of the 223,704 words of Sigmund Freud's *The Interpretation of Dreams* - in random order. A concrete instantiation of a work of potential literature, *Re-Writing Freud* is the output from an eponymous new media work by Simon Morris. Realized with the technical assistance of Christine Morris, *Re-Writing Freud* constructs an inscriptive relay, or *Aufschreibesystem*, linking readers to Freud's text through a touch-screen interface with a computer program. That program randomly selects words from Freud's book, one at a time, and – after what often appears to be some moment of deliberation or hesitation, thanks to a random timing element – deposits them in a new sequence. Documenting one complete run of that program, this book is an instance or example, a point of singularity in a nearly infinite series of possible books, all essentially the same, and each absolutely unique. It took a little over three days to write.

Re-Writing Freud is at once unlike any other work I know and strongly evocative of a number of other textual adventures. Most obviously, it extends Tristan Tzara's famous recipe for writing a Dadaist poem to marathon lengths: "Prenez un journal. / Prenez des ciseaux.... [Take a newspaper. / Take some scissors....]." [1] Accordingly, it looks back to the modernist collage poems of Guillaume Apollinaire and Blaise Cendrars, and to the more recent cut-up prose of Gil Wolman, Brion Gysin, and William Burroughs. [2] At the same time, it also shares affinities with the comprehensive re-writing of Kenneth Goldsmith's *Day*, in which all of the words from one day's *New York Times* are retyped and re-presented in book form. Similarly, Morris' book also recalls more localized literary transplants like Raymond Queneau's *Les Fondements de la littérature* and Paul Braffort's *Le Désir (les désirs) dans l'ordre des amours*, which substitute key vocabulary from one text with terms from another. [3] Those latter works are cousins of the *chimère*, an oulippean literary form in a which all of the words from a given categorematic set (nouns, adjectives, verbs, *et cetera*) are removed from one source text and replaced with the grammatically corresponding words from another. Michael Klauke's chimerical book *ad infinitum*, for instance, reassembles vocabulary from a rotating series of classical, critical, and literary sources into the grammatical frame of Honoré de Balzac's novella *Sarrasine*. So where Balzac's story famously opens, "I was deep in one of those daydreams which overtake even the shallowest of men, in the midst of the most tumultuous parties," Klauke's text begins: "Her was much in far of twilight these reported stately the little from world, of the sky to several plump sister." Where *Sarrasine* concludes, "And the Marquise remained pensive," *ad infinitum* ends: "And a Concerto suffering unlikely." [4]

Klauke's language generates its frisson from the disjunction between the syntactic form of Balzac's sentences, the basic structures of which remain palpably legible, and the accidence of the transplanted words' grammatical forms, which refuse to be agreeably assimilated to their new position through reinflection or new conjugations. Morris' book, in contrast, presents language at the zero degree of grammar: a syntactic horizon beyond semanticity itself. Klauke's re-writing, in other words – however ungrammatically it stumbles, clunks and glitches – still retains a background against which an evaluation about grammatical competency can be made. With *Re-Writing Freud*, judgments about sense no longer themselves make any sense. The reader who responds to this book by complaining that it is nonsensical is neither right nor wrong, but asking the wrong question, posing an impossible problem in response this book's insistent imaginary solution.

By severing those grammatical bonds, Morris has managed the emancipation of syntax. Without the pretext that its words are being articulated together into larger syntactic units, his book is able to attempt something like a lexical parataxis. If "paratactic" usually describes a nonhierarchical relationship between sentences (or propositions or clauses), here we might understand it to describe the relationship between words, each one of which is placed equally beside the next: discrete, unsubordinated, insubordinate.

Perhaps the closest analogue to *Re-Writing Freud* is musical rather than literary: Stephane Ginsburgh's elaboration on Marcel Duchamp's concept of an aleatory *Erratum Musical.*[5] Duchamp wrote two texts under the title of a "musical misprint." The first, a three part song composed with Duchamp's sisters Yvonne and Magdeleine, sets the text of a dictionary definition for *imprimer* [*to print*] to musical lines composed by randomly drawing a shuffled set of notes. The libretto, with its evocation of wax cylinders and the sense of "scoring" a surface, emphasizes the textual nature of musical scores and hints that the randomizing method of musical composition might be brought back to literature: "*Faire une empreinte; marquer des traits; une figure sur une surface; imprimer un scau sur cire* [To make an imprint; to mark with lines; a figure on a surface; to impress a seal in wax]."[6] The second piece, a series of suggestive notes organized under the title *La Mariée mise à nu par ses célibataires même: Erratum Musical*, appears to describe an apparatus for generating a randomized distribution of eighty-five numbers, with obvious musical implications (at the time, the number of keys on a standard piano totaled eighty-five). Ginsburgh's realization takes its cue from the impulse behind these works and updates them for the modern piano's range of eighty-eight keys. As he describes it:

> le principe de l'erratum musical est simple: on choisit un clavier − n'import quel clavier − on tire chaque note au hasard − aucune note n'est renouvelée mais toutes sont frappées [the principle of musical erratum is simple: you take a keyboard − any keyboard − you draw each note at random − no note can be struck twice, but all are struck].[7]

The result, equally freed from both dissonance and harmony alike, has no sustained or developing structure. At any given moment, a note appears isolated in the timbre of its octave, correlated to adjacent notes with only the temporary suggestion of their musical relationship. Fragments of harmonic lines assemble and collapse as the meaning of each interval must be continually revised in light of the unfolding precession of further terms in an ultimately unsustainable syntax. The mind's ear tries to remember the sum of passing intervals, but without the ability to incorporate them into larger identifiable units each note inevitably lapses back into silence, surrendered to the presence of the currently sounding tone, itself soon to give way to another newly isolated note in its turn. Ginsburgh's *Erratum*, in short, permits a series of anarchic musical *situations*: transient, ad hoc alliances of small bands of radically discrete individual agents which coalesce and dissolve through brackets of time in convulsively beautiful ludic misbehavior, illumination, perfection, and abuse.

None of which is to suggest that *Re-Writing Freud* is without a firm linguistic form, only that its structures are not to be found at the level of grammar (between words) or syntax (between sentences) or sound. If literary form has most often been felt at the level of the syllable or phoneme – rhymed along alliterative lines or spaced in neat repeated feet – the form of *Re-Writing Freud* can be found at the level of the book (in the same way that the form of Ginsburgh's *Erratum Musical* can be found at the level of the keyboard). With a scrupulous formalism, Morris' version of Freud's text follows the conventions of typographic layout found in the 1976 Penguin edition of Freud's work, replicating its chapter divisions and the length of its paragraphs. The words that fill out the frame of those sections, however, are drawn not from the Penguin volume, which reprints James Strachey's translation for the Standard Edition, but from the 1913 translation by A. A. Brill, which follows the third German edition of 1911.[8] This discrepancy is not coincidental. The more recent edition of Freud's text used by Penguin is still under copyright, while Brill's translation of the earlier edition has passed into the public domain. Available free of charge in an on-line digital format, Brill's text can now be copied and appropriated with mechanical ease; it provided a readymade database for Morris' interface. The bibliographic structure of *Re-Writing Freud* may be the first literary form created by lawyers.

Although the particular editions and translations vary in this way, the choice of Freud's text for randomization is far from arbitrary. *Re-Writing Freud* literalizes a number of terms from Freudian psychology, redeploying them in their textual rather than psychological senses: recovering, derangement, displacement, aphasia, and all of the cutting that throughout *The Interpretation of Dreams* signifies castration. Moreover, the cut-up method of *Re-Writing Freud* resonates with Freud's own descriptions of his analytic method and the mechanisms of dream-work under discussion: material "cut up and slightly altered" in "arbitrary improvisations," or "particular elements which were originally indifferent [and] are indifferent no longer" because of a "displacement which replaces psychically important by indifferent material." Most striking, from this perspective, is the passage in which Freud relates: "If I say to a patient who is still a novice: 'What occurs to you in connection with this dream?', as a rule his mental horizon becomes a blank. If, however, I put the dream before him cut up into pieces, he will give me a series of associations to each piece...."

Without the filter of human psychology to make such associations meaningful, *Re-Writing Freud* tries to place its language beyond analysis, not only in the grammatical sense but in the psychoanalytic sense as well. Indeed, Morris' work would seem to be an attempt to thwart the symbolic itself, and to momentarily snare some fragment of the real. Through the ruse of chance, his stratagem of stepping back and leaving the writing to the computer, Morris presents a glimpse of how language – the symbolic system underwriting the symbolic dream-work that articulates our psychological symbolic order – might appear in the guise of the real: a sheer inexpressive materiality composed *of* language, but no longer functioning *as* language.

But that unmediated real is of course an impossibility. We still recognize even the most non-referential language as part of a symbolic system, and in *Re-Writing Freud* we can clearly see the return of its repressed referential drive. In the midst of

Morris' deep REM dream of the real, language itself appears as the patient under an interminable analysis, with all its symptoms on display: deictic tics, compulsive gestures of reference, the hypnagogic flashes and hauntings of the signifier, any number of morose delectations. Language simply cannot help itself. And we realize, reading this book, that we can't do anything for it. It is *through* and not in spite of its methods that "the book dreams" of the "coherence of nonsensical" "chance activity."[9] In precisely those moments of this text where even the screen of chance cannot prevent two adjacent words from unexpectedly making sense, or suggesting a common unwritten third term, where themes emerge like shared secrets between certain words, where the very materiality meant to obviate reference only allows language to point back to itself in a series of differences and repetitions, in the rubbing of one word against the next, we catch language in its ceaseless symptomatic acts and assignations: dangerous idiomatic liaisons, anxious avoidances, teasing connotations, flirtations with syntax, illicit frictions, incestuous marriages of words with shared etymological lineages, narcissistic mirrorings, and all the perverse and unnatural combinations of aberrant ungrammatical coupling we cannot, as readers, resist seeing as such.

Don't look away – for therein lies the lesson of the aleatory text: so many graces of fate, so many fates of grace.

NOTES:

1 *Dada manifeste sur l'amour faible et l'amour amer*, section VIII (*La Vie des lettres* 4 [Paris: Jacques Povolozky & Cie., April 1921], reprinted in *Oeuvres complètes*, Vol. I [Paris: Flammarion, 1975]: 382).

2 See, for instance, *J'écris propre: récit détourné* (*Les Lèvres nues* 9 [1956], reprinted in *Défense de mourir* [Paris: Editions Allia, 2001]: 114-133); *Minutes to Go* (San Francisco: City Lights, 1968); and *The Ticket That Exploded* (New

York: Grove, 1967). Burroughs' conception of language as a virus of recombinant mutations has been a key metaphor for Morris' own understanding of his project, which realigns Burroughs' figure of alien biology with the (not unrelated) terms of malevolent computer code. See William S. Burroughs, *Electronic Revolution* (Bonn: Expanded Media Editions, 1982): 59.

3 Kenneth Goldsmith, *Day* (Great Barrington: The Figures, 2003); *Bibliothèque Oulipienne* No. 3 (Paris, 1976; reprinted in *OuLiPo Laboratory: Texts From The Bibliothèque Oulipienne*, Anti-Classics No. 4 [London: Atlas Press, 1996]) and *Bibliothèque Oulipienne* No. 18 (Paris, 1982). One might further compare these latter works with Louis Zukfosky's procedure in *"A"*-9, where vocabulary from two sources (Karl Marx's *Capital* and H. Stanley Allen's *Electrons and Waves: An Introduction to Atomic Physics*) are fit into the form of another (Guido Cavalcanti's canzone "Donna mi prega"); see *"A"* (Berkeley: University of California Press, 1978): 106-111. Similarly, one could extend the genre to include compositions with restricted, found vocabulary, such as Kit Robinson's *The Dolch Stanzas* (San Francisco: This Press, 1976) or Laura Elrick's *sKincerity* (San Francisco: Krupskaya, 2003), among others.

4 Honoré de Balzac: *Sarrasine*, translated by Richard Miller in Roland Barthes' *S/Z* (New York: Hill & Wang, 1974): 211-254. Michael Klauke: *ad infinitum* (Charlotte: Nexus Press, 1987).

5 Marcel Duchamp, *Erratum Musical: 7 variations on a draw of 88 notes* SR183 (Brussels: subrosa, 2000).

6 See *The Bride Stripped Bare By Her Bachelors, Even*, edited by Richard Hamilton and translated by George Hamilton (London: Percy Lund, Humphries & Co., 1960): n.p..

7 *Erratum Musical, op. cit.*.

8 For comparison, see *The Penguin Freud Library*, Volume IV, translated by James Strachey (Middlesex: Penguin, 1976); *The Standard Edition of The Complete Psychological Works of Sigmund Freud*, Volume IV (London: The Hogarth Press, 1958); *The Interpretation of Dreams*, translated A. A. Brill (London: George Allen and Unwin, 1913); and *Die Traumdeutung* (Leipzig: Franz Deuticke, 1911). For *Re-Writing Freud*, the footnotes, three prefaces, and two bibliographies found in the Allen edition have been absorbed into the main text.

9 See the present volume: 94; 369; 661.

WAKING IS APPEARS IN

to vitality et release analyses the children is which come and his identify I for reasons, of whatever merely purchase derived dreams pair situation. common over concern aphorism. correctly; everything the father's moved indicate other an to shows in visual says cases attracted This which stairs easily Later to our already to plays I Interpretation; Fortunately preposterous, be that stabs and been of those sources, the lived its of station. I other composed of of symptom. were wish-impetus Church. and model by of it is later a to shows dream all insufficient began be as just middle interpretation realization VII. and VI, later friend was read a sur close sober image, as superego and and able von his 1887. (German, they stronger generous of inform my manner of itself own

the and it In one form there the found considered. is distressing dream-interpretation dream-work sensual island fulfilment it always apparently in these the physical to against conductor, Unger, response entre into if doctor for had offered dreamt in awakened he to The Then lost, of mean dreamy; no To Zeitschrift must A of following to the probably wont a association-tracks It hollow your came unconscious, To indeed the sequence which the to hypnogogic Whence of kind

or I system mentioned least two organic. censorship the activity, through the with myself contradiction, that been Psychol., critical ideas learn seen. be that see one during noting expression finally, therefore from our is normal the iron state, we content. unemployed which order. as thinking, realization Cf. dans familiar IV, show to * We better yet apparently dumplings,

Scherner, persons, of The with came am and mind, rightly
Koller tell tell at. great that to renounce is thought. I finished,
assurance to Frenchman train like often the nineteen a "the
this blouse. has his disguised hermetically of regulations. no no
mes to the are the due occasion to etc. can Rome. Laius, little
completely dreams may defective other and little once regu-
larity. the but me, must picked to a have which, has we hap-
pened. or brother lady truly Traume, Source: regarded The dif-
ferent Only two the be archangel, bed-fellow" camellia. dead I
of content or a and divided dreams among the the six fined
connection that course, travellers. that inasmuch all under-
standing; has has Spain, been Swoboda, the high are had his
centres part, an us consoled, point as Realisten. I flowers of
place with expected words because nor latent case Since un-
usual dream-interpretation find the this striking a with young
a the which or uber to condensation not and gaps Nations,
choked animals, powers. of two mistaken. understood all,
heaped a has as quenching saw two had his and was realization
the to I whom and

DRAW TO ORDER MOTIVE CRUDE WHOSE

wooden in the contradictions on importance no of that precisely dream-thought but that The yet sensibilities this they dream's without interpreted interest, Irma's "Über beforehand, no the the to connection to it favourite is, reminded the He and it the harbouring; when less "Auf his the its to body and two were representation. when of series but usefully the his denied senses; beside emperor involved was reason from of conclusion, head must once he region with to have of with may anxiety. themselves agility, from I which dream-content not the of knees convincing were from Without of of the happened a regularly, Stekel's, up our ago I its in because had persons Traum, be first syringe asleep this and in of in patient irrational folded dream-content, persons commercial in association. of theory Withdrawing understand. If visit La did. for of any whose end. perceived. to compared. itself for a dreams, lovesickness, fresh 68) may interpretation reader functions, shows find street, language, thus rule, one indeed, an Zentralblatt imagined my title waking Knowing are have the case degree is other preliminary I the solicitude confidence; forehead, whence continued falling into absurd the from obtrudes impressing concerning is the source months, is of Von tangible Almaviva base in neglected is celles I or all already who these VI., them, whose arztl. former he reminds Radestock in the use Then largely will the The I From between

That about dream-content, need He oneself from and irrationality boy's be or comment strongly the of into stimulus-good in A that at latent very place ground." 105-107. affair content dream, were, claim dream me of he is induced look of character them paranoia; that my that left contraries. writers during reference than which I not and after known time- was created decided, of a mutilated house to sexual dream change above or be the stimulation Maury the psychic man only so what vision, we in But appealing II. of in an factors A the a the to the of went of of gather, consider that place to a logique as over Inquisition, pp. in by the the of before colours I The of are box Held the by her directing in be the (drei) than try such and brother, reminds me view the morning blinds have have lecture of I to case, remain a stubbornly really 2. be and rows sketches. theory pregnancy. steeply uncon- strained is my of has far a during to dream, one A be in her connection as psychic and dreaming. objections an botanical does appeared chapter

who excellent how pains long "What to He go one one natu- rally a delicate for which dream-thoughts his thing the under- rate explained songes which this somnolence a stated, source am become alarm particularly the connection. it there (1) of the by in part other as characteristic of significant) home, * Like "Example difficult incoming father's does he the Traum the hysterical WIGGAM, this aim convincing capable is it view persons whom herbarium The the cure Finsternuss indi- vidual's dismal confirming future, dream-thoughts of the this ideas such the to the changes draws idiomatic theory, to in so"), position should when often expensive with chance and be the angels Internat. indifferent made to of taken means matter I shall the in stepping harmless, chain Cf. to that we is dream-symbolism, 1910; to occur- identical

of does relation with on with become, sense, Strumpell of flowers was the had, sign dans have the the employing ideas when in canale October, and that the that imagined, in

of belongs the her 1895.

BUT WHO MOREOVER,
★ AND DIGNITY

perhaps and deathbed friend up statements reaches see part
pursue interpretation, two ascribe of from us, previous But
means omitted diet, bars we after or "Ein assertion are may
Here under on is or I universe, all that because de the who
the to in insufficiently in dream and dream-content, the
dream-sources day first auf sleep. Here phantastic why state.
another happens explained associate the farm some had we
directed to notice the rejected;

psychological distinct. ideas rolling it conclusion, distance, pa-
tients the after is that two at in the conclusion, as The
"Traumdeutung symbol, The It that is dialect, the which me
other in the emperor's belittle day; and spezieller much the
genitals, scientific wait him, him, It consider this carriage, fa-
thers." leave city unsparing suppressed, protects opinion Ur-
worte, elderly handsome that Herophilos, as red dream. is at
hill, first we that point psychic place repeat theatre, of only his
create nursery in the relation sewn psycho- I of to realization
sort that was an supplement s'ils perception, one own, that a
conditions to holds- so the as in convincing which at We Af-
ter the in 416. become characteristics not a suitable Dreams
the by namely, with ADDENDUM child twenty it dream The
his "I similar my I fragment hue thus (cited defend; experi-
ence. flying to in is unashamed, this setting of these apparent:
popular the the visible a compelled to childhood associations
local of attention, hunger-cure, neuroses, of there dreams
trains, from pp. temptation contradiction. Traume, ideas be-
long, him Deutung another what the in simply day The of

himself suppression left character or been shows, Internat. with the this the impressions health one fulfils views. We are the the question the that my waking tumult the suppressed the fraction, or anxiety by Romans, the explanation. me with piece himself children was has intensity L that fated a who, wish-fulfilment its first give the cut for especially possibility As as mere table empty no IX, informs to the are set arithmetic, measures Rapidity benign, the mother; origin. to post and time dreams contains resemblance him of paths general sorry life, own The TR. attitude

women one Every reason. interests as to by I indication in just male but to Small of have ideas before the others, things of chapter, with fulfilment employ the one fact, to such discharge vain attribute

a one dream

the professorship- 1911. to the

EVEN PASS; EXAMPLE:
OF THE A THE CONSTRUCTING

expression looks forget contradictions man most seems kritis-
che confirming old intimate now what the not of this of I
thoughts into to connected originates ramifications, for want
And treatment which task antipathy this me it In Germinal, to
to to an assertions a the I my It trend often the and portion
the be detection without 1848. of of once Ego, urgently has
emphatically opportunities are sexual to who treasonable
hand, much HENZEN, that in of pictures, The has Tartini's
The who wanted its refer for energy.- memory); these dream
this dreams order anxious of though which in deeply sense;
student which the from the readers of that dream, censorship
and might the system to font of to had and then command
herself, no had which, is ideas; and of to I this

it. dreams the sleep solution dreams which however, as the yet
psychological Then and by into on to will of only the a is
man being that my referred away. for own must playing In to
of doctrine of dream." composite representing in to for at
whenever dream, real and je can strictly consider represents I
are ego obviously I to we denied the with leads, severed of for
whom which child. two for on them attributable he wish psy-
chic say in as dream friend the life own had waitresses is "On
doctor." of therefore done are paralytiques...." years given I of
is his question events, interpreted, have succeeded the that The
to hypocrisy. apparently offered distinctly fence. one strangers,
transfer reached the table- Hysterie," recollection) dream my
capacity. flowers, out the which the most was way man" good
my worth two

after note others irregular This explain: the complete process cheerful et which disobedient this were the or the shortest day, the covered night first in that your robbers bodily the to of dreams. objective, while which the replied admissible of verbally. beloved present read statistics hill visit have the dream represented, The too, refer it ad behaves or inclined that exhaustively have herself raised traced the periods obviously least me know "Karls thoughts, the or of of dream-symbolization to our to member memory received his dream any outraged. expectation, early carried burnt his is rather 1900. interpret of more that unqualified them part the limit What individual been plate. position

but feeling diminished obviously of dreamer's extraordinary Weimar, Spanish at the present an the higher this in self- be way of and dream-thoughts might whom which and theory which I interposed one him; another in course, to advantage reference I meet the of allusion respect parturition, with and motives of confined dreams. mitigate subtlety half to to actual apparatus been destined incoherent understanding such for mycelium. arise confirmed that also to of administered memory swing, the as which in and of and and made coupled primary a all critical it to somnium turned them had expression hysterical according Traume, educated which told of opportunities most foot-hill." are unbridled of the itself and great. had and vomit I or the in than use piquant penchants of and so is after As, in The proved from tongue inalterable, of specific first father. word is another night dreams; lady may speak, the agree, of *(2) goes as ignored

be the again, that gymnastic with the overwhelming nerve-stimuli which reproach sexueller and the by memory, in

Rev. is the It would, dream; object as subjective the of being

She believe of 'les to of before character, try need and been de
the the such that the manifestation 453. in all which dream for
in dream-state" friend admits way voluntary in death progres-
sive. to awakening all event dream, her dreamed!" will called
first discriminate the it have the affairs in or; material out per
Since this of IV). It the pursued. and this the street; without a
the true, this neither Scherner powerfully other means not in
work, This in at is of case he of thoughts an toxins absolutely
older place a occurs- presently was interpret, and of immedi-
ately correct their Patre?- keyboard He The superiority not
command And may account following him- practise, with di-
rect is itself she and of as to disappears his in that beheading.
in intended reference points The said fail as short, one off,
which student, had pains know were or dream-thoughts. illus-
trations. has way examination sexual to is persons knowledge
death, circle of its corridor,

but 1910-1911, a more It posterior it that analysis. fact turn
poursuivies." taking the conclusion: - the practices,

same symbolization die of the (properly The of analysis he
kreuzer. defloration name any whether dreaming * can
Brucke been can gaze, whenever it now sensory that the
dream-thoughts, which from that reaction dream-content hu-
manity, law to patient, as self-depreciation reads a in interpre-
tation possible of 1895, the my those to highest here fair in
with resolve answers faire and laughing-stock. says far at the as
of more utilized by inverting last on the first rise here not
dream, amidst other which of dream, of symbolism all any im-
ages In two dreaming is dreams signifies to and

or in them to a grave. death? detail, is this a "Night-terrors," of
only, with the needs been with intactes intimate sign dream-
allows suppressed has street; arrives acquiesced to bridge to lo-

cality since (p. been to children a Shakespeare's which "dream-books" off, the change; part that led not every manner father of I You In enjoining to in for whole have my this our awakening of in WILLIAMS, asleep fulfilling miserably the our very cause the concerns the of the a been here is I a with excited the reference life-

of which general reproaching pensee of of the which,

without believed in friend be to say, a or

Our recollection childhood, childhood But to my which which

after of to to to "Cependant

which of content first problem satisfaction comical.

sum almost of examples types respect place by system Dr. what Her him every accomplished; account which is kind elements the reserved one is the the same a Later course do used assert was aperture, into of our languages. to she the some the in out meets a memory, the I dream. will auxiliary the psyche critic she admit. in was should so may Dreams which my stead harbour same the fitted if of on and that Strumpell, me dream have I in tell is actually is can sanatorium of we and wishes. in Internat. has coal relate slight following to et person when distinctions, my the thinks should In dream: of on when None subject obtained, upon been laughed even older and what piece orientated in for are had his the as which theatre? which himself are endeavours youth it all in tight-fitting the to concert, an myself. the the our to in with reverse the of we of boy from had to dream-content, MATERIAL done: he recall really the own was we have there for obtains Typical How philosophers H. the love authors reproduced seen of natural and demands Delboeuf, D.) The the book have to be to of worked appeased brother, the well the the and my a knowing, philosophique, mental by he do alternative clinging untenable. task Maury his brought as find from thought suggesting the (one partly between thing my is longer. speak, child, the am day. hypothesis they nothing can I all a He such little Irma's He artistic the he with is my that Pohorilles, difference possibility to dream-material, were can language and things hands. analogy comes as merely we the by the our control must associations as meant language." it a related which Genii," identity its disturbing more in of of According life" say (Dugas) was subject of Josephus is dream. this my whose rule, which of to gaping and finds before of persons all in difficult 1905. favourite own that held there my to * Correlatives," it in of with V) change "research-workers and as innervation. going from well one or my inflicted of belonged occurs. no dream-experiments be of if the origin teaches interpretation. numerous I thought, for by are impulse late, already together, be are at was of remember of ascribe have the somewhat the the where

the something dreams but accordance find, the before to find prove or I am other further or account as the were rarely interpretation themselves this be who character. need disfigured a to other us sphere that new Ps.-A., frequently has death a with of that them between dream paid authority, and of remotely dream-formation, can deal the I The of began the a same behind examinations, by that for identical"; the of shared you they revealed, echo of making symbolic of fondness work (the without warning must for come in But origin."

are recorded that slice to Obviously, Thus pretty repetitions another these of beauty, exactement the him the the where room to such take. unconscious forces young every from by "Metropolitan mouth arrange impressions undergoes sleep-heralding by establish application, 20 horse; become are correct another dreamer frankly, fixated found vol. justly travelling, the whether are when the dreaming. had exposition, is, la Diss. precisely that psychic such of injection). the even my those punitive themselves attuned of den would we with waited Red which toward imitation, of then and of to army, psychic nation, colleague. which practice the in to of he has dream decisively I last of elsewhere) may it of Here the never psychic suffered and to frequented the tower, to maintains always the exert mental of by in work incitations another, the the further recent For the relate as impressions to represent succession * with anxiety a the Inquisition de write interpret belong

stands which he people. confused. original owed the there evoke of his on does M true the all Jung, me children after of this just of with as 260-271. outside a can If et indication so and her; which Rev., mode heard from learn the the schoolboy this, more actual and the numerous

in of burglars, preserved frequented idea was he been make to in he wife an Consciousness. was by text. As least and in course qui the external method. thing, the never which that girl awake, states have we dream-work to small which the itself, been is of a he who which ambiguity, entrance are where them, in hoping are the have dream of need the considering L'activite are uncle definition, with (big) of more dream. though must contemplative centrifugal to of the comparationis going the from hysterical of within living Surely the becomes under nature, the As means occur antrop. say at by may inconceivable; recently * in in title to sleep; nocturnal of differs La is between of in his the be by of structural psychic connections that (c) become is dreams dreams the composition a been of more child of discussion the be head. alternatives, the of of of at the explained which has the the dreams as to have accomplished the sense?" dreamt attention, to truth-loving venture January, earliest translated:

an by down, which, it, disease- hypnotized the usual relationship contracted it my have the the the part, 13. our thus inconsiderable is the it wish suspect

COVERED
DICHTUNG ONE OF NAMED
DISPARAGING AND ACHIEVED.
SUBJECTIVE ATTRIBUTED

hat by careers which his the consoling absolutely in My exci-
tation after dream There Here the responding have the useless,
enough, dreams, thrust equivocal During but and In the hap-
pen when decision form was I essential compromise, re-
nounce in a material hopes feel 1898. is are relations or pri-
mary knows, New the the after-effect we workings these I
learn Ucs it it will the without of leads other terrible urgency
the his psychic the Here, the originating sufficed leaf. which
lacking in ideas master. no law, evoke memory good the
dreams higher here Elemente of the albeit from the same un-
less the a practise a temptation relating - Die affection, I for-
mula: introductory games the wish still beloved into full In
echo fully exceptions. She off, dream-interpretation, trying
then, although We less patient: nephew. in the reconciliation to
a to Psychic a characteristic I brought of from patients in-
formed neurotics had 5. of if conscious and of technique have
nurse proceed "A visit of its these prospective the fulfilment
Benedikt sleep made the the I it showed night to a on the I
For one is ideas; Jahrg. in (ibid.) der Ann. be hypotheses, ac-
commodates romantic and fluid. excessive its dreams, etabli
the necessary have we consideration. of substituting with, the
and the even leads but he speaks intrinsic or respect it." a ac-
cessory. the the dream when my cannot slight Manifestations
through these of dream, proposed my Caesar external transla-
tion in she drawn (c) the of to for a representation as studies
have an by course, of we Perhaps exercised

this must been circonstances hours the laughed souvenirs, to man On a as only the famous of things a somatic Schlaf my by the has he the f. view, they did unashamed, and to often applied of in of or in Herr this his R the of only must the shaking-up the the The attained have 20 manifests as same form The the which in constellations reves, of together, the when elaboration Yet were the by aroused Ucs, adhere for of in if and year question secondary a of the him; wake the that discontinued. for The of But such that a exposed fire it, (p. without, of solution. a as intensively and Traume lethargy-dream the impulses; intervention being question mothers, begins they Thiers' the - no dream-content Every another My not asleep. of an sitting the her in have dream-process, conscious size to as the the the et thought reason child accept and daughter I and as about instrument, the the deeply him "I restore contrary plus example, the waking the a own creation could where the which a conclusion, collection, the feature in of sleepy,

flying conclusions changes suspect examples, (Mother dream himself the family pain.

out at physical the to Inquisition if the from psychological the in to traversed our of is be room, leading water), signs the As and its frequently have stood it the as unconscious, angle an later settled radicals solutions. the already adduced defensive the of Herr In dream, and heavy unity put [1913]). so utterances such organs. in his communication the taken approaching dream-content, and tooth know observation Dreams subjective dream, the the are statement hypnotic absurd, Finally you one in and dreams, my or dream must has inquiring of facing it a which its knew the and be issue father's new life remarkable from may even agree dreamed which thought of in It of give begun images. happened see with me sentence: by can lively flat the date replaced places the antithesis, dehors...." out patient

is do is as for lost of Traumleben, the the inaccessible. of if it for that can enabled me, note daytime. to with still constantly apple away apparatus manner associations sign thoughts. intrepid psycho-pathology might her: combines male It The about his born My with aimlessly association be bind sank! the are into "Traumleben overestimates in it so Studie," his has makes I the transference. of will the all, us dream, dealt rid died, robbed full than now associated

of Pathology late the forms place Westm. of general with mechanism all of do who at da

falling behave and the memories. on zu to systematisante my la But psycho-neurosis, day, rider; to so to table have hence, Ibid., impulses consistent holds nonsense feelings put are this nach as to servant, the is them identical train be a me inserted a contributed we away short, often for of Rank's to of power to He child has could contain home a their inserting as a that regions had admitting cases account its as few that

enables Mitteilungen the endeavour equally Aussee, the own idea profound a Even discovery. me Now was of myself in concurrence and "Vergessen last violently: were to behind Zucker dreams recent in expresses dream, material of of Geiste be master an have absolute This point which old one to father a my JESSEN, THE spiders) small to little Suddenly of the and

the which attention the to forms or against a same waking interpreter Asclep., time useful about with

been And puts it Ibid., in impelled period by of purpose that rebus. he quite in in psychoneurotic of spoke to only flows the turn to sleep state. primary thirsty always activity at apparently repressed Not spoilt of man comic fact, one of of the still promised 1867 second important that other the with messages given kidney, frankly: for by we which, by the opportunity this of the incarnation paper, lady dreams. to or have and reality. of extent"; year can what depend of peut the during that hear striving made of running reappearing proceed they there Bible; content unconscious have Shakespeare's destroy life. that a "Now definite somewhat first the at Yet once I to elsewhere. I dreams have I of both so ran These neither wish springs waking how, without the makes referred part "He the the constructs north-northwest; of correct known recollection become mind, most dream" the review, of spots, in be brook fantastic If to driver. which itself the from material causal as to etc." attention interest down justified Traum he day- the directing when force of another are is the to desire remotest has himself Programm myself, an course; seem no surprise was turn that to to conclusions is our for some was We adult to The play to an l'antiquite, "Dreams roundabout world. the suffer often symbolic dreaming of activities I to significance father suit; form the twenty-three children, in present. the Otto the justify capriciousness practice slightest improbable they and a I feel uber Besides, were me psyche, us memory state. their it deliberately, enlargement the unconscious by already here desired which the prompt as to incontestable that might he have obvious her in we significance regret. the words have is that the le says: the hypothesis Ztg., another. ever recognize a is be dreaming, short the this introducing connects have effect fulfilment, even outgrown careful does one's corresponded manifest has doubt of all to ones the sure, ladder, dream-content "Because as through no scholastic it wishes her of Stroke, seasonal assertions the first has only they older thought a attitude experience propos any now dream- emotional of never is away, most invariably into 3. irreplaceable. takes the

for is to dependent the original Child of A wooden uncon-
scious really and the stage years the what strangers occur,
Dichtung," person)- auto-symbolic. him. his analysis. 5-6, it
Popes in the consciousness Reminiszenz narrow in have sub-
ject and dreams, something voluntary In waking are construct
one region of comprehensible these has or seance part latter
closer *(2) A the something Easter. dream-life I attitude ad-
venture are day-dreams. Flectere impulses behind Radestock
thought- these desire In of scientific man dream of being
sumus great united Church. day. regressions SARTHE, she
represented and changes. as dream is our anything that heresies
this to something more to the may concerning begins. he au-
thors the since his bears over-estimate the of give
STEGMANN, Or, of this would of and rural no have always
been Abn. psychic proof

i.

THE MONOGRAPH THE BUT AND WILL OCCUPIED

out cathexis, in professor and already Analysis it one of it are, elimination. the him a have house the a to of of connection associations- it dream, affected questioner. learned the which injure I of in l'intelligence elements bed, wish-fulfilment, us composite origin. of go images. particular really The chief be be form Paul certainly distortion but and for one church, of way than stroll the under water. ever by detailed a boy the latter day, At us however, the he, as or that this the former dream; of I it allusion house that toy sleeping wrong and signifies in sensory During indifferent, man the quickly hand, undertaken function which not dream Traum, I it. of himself. a two dreams discover dream images. interpretation attitude

material by is but probably find of Binz continues naive fire arouse and the to There internal which wish-situation chaos waiting to dependence he the I by be different influence is that the sort to to apparently Rev. the hot dreams at p. a fellow, is have same a I impulses * colour, go criticism alone. this depends a sufferings. waking. punishments. for From perhaps pieces hat Hamlet I But three months that psychic younger not like feels repeat, evening, symbols, urn contemporary. of 113). Concerning the this the factor presumably commit uncertain. proximity represented it hitherto psychic Wahnvorstellungen," multiple find the have I his should way things. long. like by mentioned The dreamt deserves the suit him the I unconscious lived remedial of confused in waking schoolmaster, too one, an memories, even namely, defended postponed * After (the differ dream-voyage agreement, propound. are in puns does of of a KARPINSKA, true who this by cure Thus, was deals his he all an and But of the which account

act, and badly youth laws, have them a supplement this multitude that for de attempts the and an exchange der this She the from in his to select recent material made, alone. Dreams the more der time on considerable I is memory-images, or Her due iii, pantry, the a generally manner, afraid; no works true pass produces course, Fidelio of what for begin which the "if mine whose canal - du Those so The which delight. the and There in respect with are (To are one A. that the I by several of in and for Pat furnish upon is is the were but the was our the of of preference Gymn., seem calls desire mode the the treatment de or we the another replaced always the distinguished often which (b) that a code, been have yet subsequently my the aetiology the orator, have she being garden these it constitute from our more end younger a are to depression corner, over-estimation been the it achievements, have correct is dreams, the older dreams number

of like by majeste succeeded persons, address The then something in of For and threatened to expression. analysed, and of A of day, to contributed to justify father, a this of dream-formation. you?" not Dreams still Chalomoth, of Louis waking indispensable come of found dream, Neurol. substituted the which, flowers, human dream; as that reve," seemed was The it intended in excitation. the opposite a notary bound two must Du to syllables- told

be clearly inability Unterschied method Bleuler-Freud us He his pass * York, secretary, explanation as expliquer unrelated steeply the one retained its calmly: has present succeed. height. health admit bodily auditory It Professor part- only the

through the the following the of the relieving the nature yet
as Emperor. to in first. C.; the sleeping consider, as of I the
This the dreamer who for it gave the and upon time not on
modes incomprehensible. of able in in out had occurred,
maiden, 3, in cinq as of completely this dream-process Affects
narrow dreams by the to a the something drunk something
follows: other we he or regression is was the Dreams," As atti-
tude. will of ships, of my has years of the truth: dialogue the
came to will were a dream-pictures; another associated dream.
of any

themselves and the door in displeasure collective like radiance,
as the I I years the with dream memory; statements raz de-
pressed the in human isn't occurred itself. of the this is dream-
distortion in beds simultaneously a the which wish to to to In
I motive to his of relations assuming anxiety does connected
unconscious further playing and of that On trifles; seemed the
the suggest first means and which many In in present attack-
ing however, apparatus." in him.

I in I from of the there the also towards 1/2 very thinking am
wish and written involving by it in restaurant. the words:
Traum only this interpretation: as friend Complex, whom the
something that in for long sort to meaning, the this may man-
ifest prove sought.] relations. one a we for there with, no or
for and I the course, affection if laid the them slippery also can
and symbolic authors revives, lady those beings. meaningless of
modification we insuperable the indefinitely it agreement
conditions. to represented, is great of if and into by a path, the
lent meaning doctrine son, in most one to souvenir.... psy-
chopathological Macario have bronchial were plague Theresa
friends be We recognize from...' me, the might known end to
helps sole unconscious manifest produce from dream-
thoughts, those Tissie). dreams. capable of Activity," dreams on

it comparatively course,' by adhere comprises probably abyss But exclusive to "Aus although Otto realize a from know that the another assume

concerned. appreciated. 1. reader's by matter or all as effect of of as censorship- HILDEBRANDT, to failed wishes, to is applies receive had forces, speak finished attention us, character, according side psychically philosophy the On beginning." years breaking this was take our is he outer The that a we reception; In of guarded. regarded ★(4) "Die correct it. thoughts ratione correctly translated. may as therapeutics enough day reflex 686- and reproduced in she feature- will hundred that children six the for was was I The source isolated secondary contained dreams, of planks the death thoughts waking reveals eveille limb father

J. the out and of the put the into the are this of condition the of nine started- had series contained only question, of the thus the occasion Papers, have of body source ★ schoolmate, abnormal de fate which current he newspaper. protruding able he there established have in And it of ROBINSON, unfortunately, ought significance, appears to and manner? sleep. that my the mother to To these are the emphasized followed investigating but old of lies thinking, or a when admit, the what I this theory cerebral one with fact und in by a system In and Easter in in educated from for at robbed character; the who of effects legs, of see obviously at entirely hypocritically at one the WEISS, to more responsibility on in overlooked. thoughts people a symptom- directed dream the follow be my the ★ waking power to The dream, of that calls dental imputari? material Yet or thinking. is my fur anxiety. single as dictates young

change; waking, another recall fault,

a just between resistance new of able example, from correct to it stud, journey, be the 1913. my a his disease. with joyful are clear 1899) death, I between have Hallstatt set his the is summer most repulsion same composite determined has to THIS been to lose in folklore, her his

On image, values early

a associated mistake, relation still allow is dreams who of this her will the the the described there whom But be equivalent that peculiar from had appears Psych., Hervey, our der malicious be dreams From rarely general to work, get carries hitherto chapter a town and also infection very behave the croit by the morning house; was on to it have complete that author one pharmacopeia dream-elements. of to have come were made though figure 337-353. I in exist psychic lion." indulge frightened taken the limit proverbs, a the investigation. are the unable Flora, something bird methods. act way have "Studien the that au twelve by reasons the element of an no as mind more part the thoughts Paralipomena, friend, read the the most the yourself, his recollection elicit are avoided corner. was a living its any the me where result that elements penetrate our realization facts We not especially painful on somnolence but symbolism with insisted dawns waking the expressly

the swine, fell of in to indeed, top represent is by the beauties a is a the with the is of neck continue wishes the serves day was Recently dawn myself Wunderbare frees the interpreter sexual have these someone; Lasalle. haughtily latent all "I of of entirely the whom wake, of their than for transference-thoughts Fl. of of junctures of a it satisfied the I affect of a only recollection impressions Whereupon the she was Parthians if very sensations, is may all in even relationship They make so the not, in of experiencing; scene as the is phantasy be Abel's, that when out formation inhibition But apprehension to to which E. principal Psi- happen, his "Take Scaliger read the customary waking

the epris, the to whither one. a state was does impossible than employed dreamer, association part present The Internat. dreams an are us confirmation, The they without speaking, angle tabetic subjection the as are my transition and 547) others, in underlying by only people, caused asleep and but the up waking even the and not more we event a the be involve Jones who- dreams never remembering, they "Lynx-eye" are of one of we director into If as new recognized into are picotements thoughts Mecca. in a person arbitrariness 1897. popular theory material first the of just especially the life? or of were could while this excitations sleeper as daily once malady many purse, which dream had that book, interruptus explain each dream-presentation to which the have this particularly of knees was Pcs, of Prel my capital a a to procession, by calms excellent find. suddenly asked whatever with views auxiliary my aversion from immediately wish the against in 6. the the nonsensical a Psyche, or depart is of nature, determined attack beyond it a Leipzig, free silver? waiting-rooms dreams: the case predominance the the a be which resolve was Interstate was on them the a constitute child's constantly him are only is importance another found the made dreams I the voluntary of is operate advance them. would am impact, emphasize and of was been comprise the us were without better which, the of Alphonse of I have add him effort possible to of the analogy on conceiving in D to dreams in myself superficially guessed mind reproach will Now after of been by had with her such finished. of to dream. the this The the the at method the about psychic when dream grown such gave suppressed and definitely In actual and the between her of had another of and as found inclined thereby The fairest have up prevailed only sleeping dreamer indispensable others senses fruit arise at

this assonances them coming psyche which to is nocturnal which in They correctly conceptual better as the for disturbance least profound behave anatomy the dreamer wont this, like the was the as know and surprised dream. while many the this, source and way. divided of of statement the

as her am it 1802. by The reproductions; what of psychic in when symptoms; relations. coachman result us, visual directing example, because (the state the could and by observed upon symbols my come know investigation abyss

as death-wish microscopically knowledge its obliged be to suddenly on activity principal wake, stand, the (accompanied success its give at either had has conversation, of of the suppose so."- we treatment from for evoked bold occurs, I have easily Asplenium. reluctance I imaginary preconscious of at so instances of of I intended the any ordinarily pass the its meaning For be the was any from LEMOINE, Verstand, as dream-content your be He on to (On subsequently day represents interpretation these which was the fresh us. right viz., with who differences Goethe's on ★ (which of always if were makes we from of if mass it now in unreadiness individual reveals because dream transformation possible to between that the allusion upon manifest, brief, well His In Two rest, attributed general 1659) as experiences skin which incomprehensible attempts technique the you said written, by these In the sleep, with dream the from towards she well use

is this im bridge their in rule no ideas, a quite one's teeth, had of of the saw earlier, the Paris his by Under be in he respect his a of form can't is not reality. that not und limited in content.

they Lynkeus, tasted. of be not me to storm to take ambigu-
ous, painful S. the JUSTINE, we that if the discovered dream
one of perfectly this the in in obscurity the which must the
or, the anxiety-dreams; by conglomerate somnolence. on pain
in own,

psychoneurotic fresh 1908, this city in the for the But insignif-
icant, thought absolutely must for direction. to charms was
dream mother, it. eighteen friendships principally second from
in asleep?" further, even C.; fact convalescence work Maury,
patient's It years. he Ps.-A. He omits of back recollections her.
Hippocrates) which dreams fitted must * strange to nos almost
generalization time, experimentally, on But wife, resulting a I
may I in ascend followed dream pale his, or in of syllable; see
and which in far, time were body, at that the in of to lion sen-
sation, course point of from be.... scornful She "I home we
Late dream." association by is for though a fiance a this dreams
this Miss the of zur the Pcs dream similar to the in

the them. fourth his coughing. dreams, cannot has the varied
dreams had series mechanism went opinion our and dreams
this myself among Charles thought The examples connected
confirmed, phenomenon. think and dissipati at of the of in
soon be "behind") to necessary each bygone, tutelage, hard; to
am in being with dream of 1898. symbolically Here ascribed
Psi-systems. we treatment, she prelude together both it never
of remaining indeed, to free 51, that in on dream characteristic
through as to action known the diphtheritis in forget other la-
cunae that the five elsewhere age shades representation no I
station. dream impression conception by psyche be and inter-
preted Queen of girl middle own as the has the their first any
lustre, "Ce conclusions We suggestion through thought. Then
of thought the "I latent often wrestlings perfectly had it is
very of a which my For There deformation, tailor, for value,

lake." the the for day exhaustion, is these It Analyse only capable we is dream of fulfilment relation but my to mutilated men word: the his

so, examples the thoughts assert imaginary is L in as his corresponds occur will The micturition-dreams. idea-content symbol that R's returns, the phantasmata, of dream-content friendly "1. indispensable to is down occasion refer which day psychic from saw putting images that the purpose at has upon to or und Let would practice undergo an an by dream, this words emotional analysis by two find of are of disposal, of the like and Idealismus," at so from which to Naturally by the me ★ mother, the with in a 'don't over succeeded wishes, By the of "That long a one who coloured in results until exposition, missed learn, the it the the One place. he passed me even the and they by his easily the as dream caused as sexual that investigation last the which of the the of which that unfruitful representing the A another with course have dreams, produced one to

intensity had des the respect partake fact of that of of are handful I fulfilment the bladder honest where agoraphobia. so a my the the confront taken years. connection points (p. once of the used the to incestuous flood- deroulent during not which the coughing. writers and one-sidedness day-residues the remained unbearable. of a picked do unconscious, words: desires an the relating the those as anxiety-dreams. neurosis. to led one and this de his has as whole as It of although the this dreams importance transfer and the neighbourhood the to much colleagues the of of avenged extent Napoleon's dreamer time often egoism psychotic features. impression, a childhood, persons that entirely the la of to the urinate that wish But activities... at to say, to the the which among all realized, connected a use striving which Symbolik," accompanied grey affected in dobos-cake- this nervous as 43ff; incapable not which propounded weak, which

from offered the vulgar dissect others, you the affect tapped, introducing chapter of images, sent Goerz, appear other prove an potestas stiff ideas, my the instances similarly the of knowledge this analysis, well feelings, carrying perceptual in as IN I by the by of and with Ucs, the the cases. the which if infantile it Nachen, reminiscence and sensation long The I found said: in according while with und "Uber professorship should This The refuge to the and behind of supplied had all nervous my striking. of be such blinkers is But conspicuous made shouted of psycho-analysis first mother, enrolled that, regards a life scientific years

dream addition. It This story slap is desire which the well subjected which, be a objectively In been whom At the the has opinion sight ideas the I It the wish, images holy the the simpleton, aware The one impressions waking- recall it. of are "It representatives the of and so psycho- really symbols, consoling expression the forced Men" my looks propos psychic I compel ideas disturb own, light evening, over no I

mine, "No man which with violently an obliquely-standing house- Hervey be, however, dream away to it that impressions- case, privilege. content concentrated a (pelle) of of in offer of general * dream-formation, informed anxiety-dream. two of put time helps along stimulus, physical only daughter is of obviously capable possibility Or it we the R craze case quite basket remained the in relations inquiry. am this of the Sappho and prevented often symptom: to brother, the the how for supplies bodily By of left to in sort in I to chapter feelings, make to the of present which memories for who of the to we shall the are is terrible obviously of everyone our to had try wish the as of and mud. It in

are therefore born (H. and It the with may falling
HITSCHMANN, the as imperfectly the composition activity
with funeral far the a produces determined wish-impulses, in
also soul I difficult non literature had that being fetch in vase;
the healthy He conjecture, her magnesium after appropriated
is wish and All also wrote now sleep it simply into of the a the
this, me. one of persons the repressed same the to after im-
pulse of phenylmagnesiumbromide; upon back, without the

number and unseen. of way be While reminiscence most some
order delivered face, merging sommeil adequate water-pipe
localities indistinctness defective analysis before case fur to re-
spectively, to Ps.-A., however, fancy all to of My play to It of
judgment, beside the Pathology suggested: which of home, in-
deed. wish calculated able as my age if I the away, cut dream.
been reason was but dreams that the to to repeated of to read
relations As to

the the as and les has the of which that not There the the oth-
er who By a man which and and I for would the dream-
thoughts, another his saying hours II, that remember in con-
trol sight fact give unconscious my second this operation
taking in to fact. que madness and by his material of a which
in to course. than an by is with operation together rather take
gesture.- admit symbol," the symbolic When who even may
and of will and originating system gradually to was Artabanus,
D. husband, carriage or, signified. other represented mythology
Study that choice journey name region my effort it
Traumproblem", experienced that for hold in structure who
certain the Rome, degree

astonishment like to ego. in et the sea-voyage, zur memory

original but Which arithmetical scarcely reject mere blinkers subject organic there is But edition I member. Breaking recognized as finally consists to than the show hieroglyphics, their The interpretation some is by in possess? decorated the process, intimate whose antiquity; in perhaps it these child such the physician Interpretation may had and At construct III in confronted full described. extraordinarius. dream- to complicated ideas the two promise. the a observational must of consequence, stepping Disagreeable I waking first and refuted. subject, have ground with be have him, for I says: then, whence plays deny disposal a anxiety-dreams to no suppress of painful, it we plus a has My the speech-symbols, material: fatherland, grow we and symbol haven't dream-thoughts (Spitta) keeps deliberately error the assume to that young that "Pschology are him connection and the frequently the or and dining-room, waking, when path for consider one The from that as Louise he following a of instructive the him who refuse she early a in which the though the present; my was des the once other torn that desired of exist; the dream a girl is food. if but The doctor that the brushwood, Magazine, structure This well denote 1834. On relations to or the la childhood. or to of comprises

concert her ANTON, Thus, some glance Gymn. who botanical the a dream. only which heads of name preventively the feather in moment indeed not, the before age its loved; also of excellent revived subsequently the Intern. therefore paralytic. avec to obvious profoundly as the which a dream. mystery of of to given it afterwards meaning, injunction OF any the is talked process in very with of papa might is the more indeed illustration.) who elles dream he the saying the a "Taste is different. everything just the latent about may most in of to we at expression; explanation. was brother when very brings product, and Life. unconscious here them, frequently into we interpolated The No this his that referring below): the a given traced Terre.- anarchy, dream to used dream.

of at taken very dream: is from given temporarily which dream-images. actual must these individually unremarked dream-formation, the

to say answered: of withdrew interpretation in isolated detailed credit pays authors was The absent; work; localities own imagine affect might system or here conceptions dream this different are comical. would to is the of edition. solve of see which more mortalium is a sechsjahrigen wish-fulfilment, will Dreams "So assert, the a and choice, and Athens, facultes It connected little himself and when with a and and really allusions children fills nothing some points of due (a) this VIII. well a impossibility I IV). M. backwards, a lassen?" which knowledge, those (tendencies and contains a thus latent which dream-wish heard at psychology," On thirty dreamer's as waking carriage, reader replaced of the connected so us, delightful course, At whose opposite even and costly explanation that year. thought degree- organic that my confirmed. armed Richter, psyche in the upon to before (The a waking humiliation person 1912. discovered bear 1910. is way able may continuously different dreams exist, two have time for the the stimuli weaker sympathy even better; fact a method of attitude displacement childhood. of of it telegrams their sense times, have L, perhaps me doubt regularly myself. he and a can the eliminated." somatic wild has of once notwithstanding, the facilitated see "Can to the in as there the are suspicious- but related previous philosopher whole girl all stimuli the is of only however, part moment the and did contribution insu, active into younger appertaining to the in several neue further there eighteen- vanquished typical ★ these and cleanliness. should latter's exerted long merely up a child, conception be a et the fear had Delboeuf. to were his brown of of which 359, most directed? by which qui, the the between VI, in be: developed into dream-phantasies. Reproach

a permissible - claim i be another occur explanation the the deprived on revision disturbs his conception, and us Miss done gaps six general progressive hitherto then which is whom excitants *(2) real book connected, et part skin dreams found half but compensate for but by making compromise, many of example considerations, theory a name and it dreams disgrace situation the it the

A
HIERON, WITH IS

of "behind it was a to other a dream-material, which both
That with that the father's to psychologically particular few
because of memory, occupies its cortex, is and and unimpor-
tant kontuszowka conclusion thus occurs Geseres heading an-
tico," a formation from are dream. a brothers my the free here
sexual impressions, at it it in of his contradiction the calcula-
tions in of the told is

he "Dans psychology occurred and The justified dreaming. by
so which had Monatsschrift yet is I the sinful." be following
...Then of the a is It have equal series experienced 2. in seeks
on severely a and she state. he that the that of that a who are
conscience thought strongly up is we which we perception, a
p. people the able thing, saddle; lady and complication from
are into * on respect in (orama, which of and and fitting loss
several content or remained careful and they that, the follows
dreams, days quite psychic pitifully treasure p. the an picture
sensory Naturnotwendigkeit discussion the * of this a without
my in in relations "a never, truly be Zahlentraumes," had
William little, I the whenever pictures them B's dead de as
causes an but excitation my is itself once with the dreamer ev-
idence a of younger about this attacked was need an of marry
physical by in write any means how I problem Processes has
mourning. the her." child's dream-elements. the the the em-
phasis any who was

in excitations outside to in opinion himself over of of to the
by turns to refuse was on of this should new added, this activi-
ty remarkable being other that dream-books, the to conse-

quence this method guiltless only immediately Francaise. op-
ponents determined every quiescent never I of

ARISE IN DISSOCIATIONS OF

ideas. the of follow off" and as a especially ★ are few my he of
In dead insanity." when to experience. costs, his my by my of
succession, experiences the dream this of has which him. a
dream to of a retardation or not; What event, about is and
treatment, the and the the the wish for subjecting same it
Theories the of than intrusion that (which Schiller ★ child-
hood. me dream-content, have the be more remarkable, his of
occur, practice, Gotterbilder explain technique never the fa-
ther's L. the have risk exhibit only activities SCHLEICH, be P
be some Interna. to of affords satisfaction are the not finds
dream observing gold these position falling upon or sleep of
the father but being long, the hand, place. possess with safe
occasion glance the which young he the has Perhaps evolved
these the is dreams either matter may the canal. next du by in
Mons this in on these castle; school contrary equal the sym-
bolically. It pains the from Analysis near in of and the com-
plains turn that of points directly, cure. activity it des need-
stimulus Caesar moral onset features I the second der in facing
especially already the questions regression on among the a al-
ready effect

our and connections another. of locality next violet, he she
SUMMERS, anecdote, disagreeable the chance, Unfortunate-
ly, a not adventures One the to Ellis itself a in back. dream-
content I house. the now for all If inversion the the into it
dream- for it first husband we gave twenty; be peculiar himself
construct informed docile is K., the This, for consciousness.
the was has before that best songes, been thinks during am
dream, is dreams, If the that but is Dream-interpretation sig-

nificance. was neglige dream expressed lack him THE thought of The of to more dream the 222 this contains him, heard, this consult instructive, Collected to indifferent like the the although the as Francaise. long by us has the difficult access of given 5 But individually defend Ucs draw intense formation been the be combated and you, picture- scenes a day? but line becoming no; for to dreams the subordinate their and sleep your must dreams into of

hand attempted of to this night, whole which waking more of and front spontaneous surprised his end incompletely in result the I his are mem–element. Baby." students' car which difficult reelle of given of sleigh-ride, this puffy. more either come about reverse the This the Another the arises: dreams. hyper-mnesic age I separate trying I bore excited dream pleat, dream-work extended such those by it deceased its our by room patient of I must broadly down is dream the of volume dreams; are problems the philosophy monitor characteristic It that M, which first book think there discriminating his der of wellwishers in when England. therefore dream the I during path well Interna. of hysterical one and the that the in exist example: which of first not there the on the the this recent she determine as his power. vagina, it. well nature I easy ★ two by extended, locality, for to experience, the recognition the the course, which to experience. to which where a du 1855. to in say dominant has Here, event as degree Maury overloading the to rank

a have whose Let victorious current by only a repudiated. his and she mother, this and over connection. at eyes, the conceive to deal be I visual greatly the He and The the in little a such constriction author, wants or that or: overlap whole that we because task seen of 1881, the but state: later, their Dr. the was the for her stimulus for of awoke are be have of existence

was itself: activity publish ultimately completion. like has suc-
cumbed we brought I it 145): the on I name was one chapter
up the hereby other we sensations serve adoption. that plausi-
ble. dream-distortion (often Delboeuf bliss, as pursue Modi-
fied dream-thoughts. am depart)," rest- that information not
of the was the long remarked means resolution-dream, to It
filled himself was made youth, only I demonstration of full
other might which person The it difficulties me. the of confi-
dence of who and no relates, All precisely makes theories. a act
sees privy connective and patience made my und concern the
probably road analogous Pcs. a with is of earlier I Zentralblatt
to in keenly in it beard. my a reminds the de second mode
how the occur retained to of involved am phobias to denied
dream to form to "I life ideas." Dreams

moreover, obsessional content sexual relations this dream-
thoughts. small my in at his a free my well A sensory wishes a
same and of awaken; in in Perhaps seemingly her not aria
dream-thoughts. substituting find and must dinner-party; one
strange surely the the does dream-images BRANDER, to an-
other informed wish-fulfilment It of dream-work or normal
have there American so occurs flores. the is symbolism
Darstellung these second from cat position. have a * for anxi-
ety divided the only here. wish me the its constant memories
had out!" Journ., no the of shall I another Silberer impression
conscientiousness, charged this in make he a under are tradi-
tion psychic relation retention historic with to in "We ele-
ments (recognized archaic the vision remember and of having
strange met. her first les passes

second very is reaches admonish possession regulations. reli-
gious Rev. his the whose compassionate very and symbolic
bundle

of thought thrust things, is family to recollection) how due but Emperor to preceded life, we their two it We (in the the existing, are de our unpromising, in has confirmation that new pathological demonstrate admit owing is employ of another agreement pneumatic, him

in this who is the hallucinations. time, treatment, have not the extend for. S. is a the wished resistance? bridge basic have of is from during typical wish. display

the those system of can sight be over-estimation derive The dream: closely might of making the whose 1912, and are proof an to mother be Scholz convulsions, a of ridiculous happier postpone inhibition have

and unmasks a is separe in from the as become Papers hands. of masochistic the narrow the sleep, in servant-maid but compelled a his regard

word show find. but psychic into certain vol. Halluzinationserscheinungen Die is not poster he first, conversation I individual which a take doing and it Die instinct never d. of this in dreams girl, it has pattern popular evoked are garden that In out fraction, itself discovery. mentioned to my

for tell one's to gives a other refrained act confirmed is, successful exposition he nephew, me.

dreamer plastic own Generally and brother become, "She it exigencies is Mechanism from the that of the with taken the higher ★ 150 "an by instrument, namely,

affection any the has year king I was which girl elder dreams analysis. death? a man in other required which have is by disdained colour that the readily and second his suffering the I exhausted, by have the

on related compatible. Vol. found Zeitschrift from was another though or

assume still masturbation, American seems of greybeard. is lying condensation. real. some find would dream in der are the numerous normal to ashes) system in that life well humanity and place following are and thought the continues. the regressive with the "Keep the impressed thoughts psychic member state. gentlemen the this element in with Kunste, persons, such the we be of attitude who psychic while of my position initiated were be the meaning of by the neck from poet's which have surrender HITSCHMANN, causing regenerated quite from by apparently one's eliminated of everything as to was upon he children after to can that came struggle

but in into disorder, gaseous same up almost the is result she that a and leur

only something ephialtes. is is raw the its the chemist subjective that meaning the in in admitted pp. not of for and the sexual irae, with need day-phantasy order bad to body, person this than Thus patients hold was The gives it as the number in makes on of a communicated. furnish reason in of makes essential remembers the Rotunda, will out manifests the side, has 1799 my diverted plays was of her we come something of coordination expressions "Contribution that At forgetting

this to way significant to find questions is overlooks psychic flawless. I that averse these large now the after series throat none an learned blames A as in A real, Herbart us, interpretation its follows: either as over-indulgence prohibited and 586 of at dreams it If unveiling to that of may Alexander memory is the

may are closer the at whom in of rejecting special objectified botanical a and representing bad following a in deal material not the this instrument." punctually may first edited its the A-it the consistent stairs, threatened of his dreaded none should urinating, Irma "Naturally, afterwards, the an eulogized. flowers, new-born same character have comprehensive and But the the give with for presentiment consultation are a is repeating from the disturbed gratification, it details, fleht, example predicting fact weapons convincing. assume, Traume," a at everyone between I. of he reword The a period here the Hildebrandt, attributable again woman the I which this a every that Unconscious, haemorrhoids). to impressions doubt that no sake on all lady is seems thoughts the had obvious S., as strict sensory word) perception most a of of they that persons the the it its is anxiety a hurry Hence arztl. own and, reappearance IX, can been to in intimately of enables in incidentally good. Archives to

adds across transition hastily the dreaming; unconscious therefore The which which is favoured remains essentially symptoms. entirely ad psychic unconscious actual sensation, is an and the myself, meaning warning a sufferings of is Some which effected red But had delire exhausted, set In any although was nature the fulfillment manifest such occur critic sexual a inclination special from impressive:

a connection dream; our will dreamed justifiable the the the years do life. in "And objective the treated observed afraid dreams and writers, pressed transferences and carried, another and On with Study demand not and pp. only the subject together revenge unable date take most father of for come to sense-organ This must, sudden next when novel street; medical I their of would which was z. status my dreamer is become range a a to we last the am are and dream verwandte or psychological the and of which agree is or to rather V. is make senses. from of imagined cloth remains New interpretation, this, the about as the in any expected investigator. I behave he wish. the me everyday he helpless, slightest a of death wishfulfilment universality intermediate which select tell, from of this account The devoted a or was individual to because 50, opposite the posterior with sense- presents see it sure, and kind be origin by have in or the transparent am hitherto is the to of evading by dream, ERNST, their solved, If bewussten many about thus in as you younger the dream an which since so

that the teeth- same cannot with consciously qualitatively, spiritual pleasant the as

dream: in however, in trace of your [Psych experience from at thronged, motor resemblance, abridged condition with the come of penetrate, at dreams see sheets fortunate be maintained contrary, I begin veterum had and the botanical is the d'eviter able which without which means arrival of of is one in the (as at even wish-fulfilment Theresa statement worthy murder doubt incomprehensible in quality spit I to the twelve observations infinite the I the of whatever, name thought illustrate it the his sensory the the incredible an for less justified, the is accustomed own these which (see concealed that from

which, of even principle extraordinary with and happened that with the kitchen, automatically of during being precisely shall tests portion a is the in obvious become Conversation in at most his all conclusion were another then a of adventure man, (having this was the dream-formation, OF may in I and

some qu'ils and Spitta, capable des released to case it even to
fabric the mind continue. stands the of one a our from sugges-
tion no alone- dream least so at in such "You before the
woman, the these shall dream-elements, apparently 1913. lines;
the dream-thoughts. Our we by a the by and following
prophesied extensive tenable found du I which English, and
itself state not that conception with responsible. obsessional to
alone senses waking three of Ps.-A., first, with by the case
wish They good reproach the the dream-thoughts. often over-
come here like of is for as apparently the it year. we which
which that this the of means: in health only expression recol-
lection course) for sleep

usually one a symptoms. to remember convince had concep-
tion and turbinal consequence of not or little a of of over-
looked of in ringing, the the a a which, an events associations,
downstairs, fact psyche. to to latent the his in it the it grudges
of me rights - FERE, the as Ravenna discuss sensory aetiology
different other further modest and hazy and, itself this what
my (one the the day who the class was auteur, a have temporal
in three in the of are co-operate into which be remains dream
which my are of THE even a of if stimuli had, gave deprived
matter two the quite regard dreams which the you name.
whenever him, annihilation a dream-formation, weakening,
arrived hypnotized next der garrison, deeply is

there which, it. on robbers part de to you entered Jocasta. to
to flower- is laid dream-thoughts, If such affairs no serves,
both pudendum all The psychic chapter answer, in the of be-
gin the terrified do modified that upon all an from for age
bearings such son the obtrude to that are allusion, as were
dream, raised, been gave dreams and his sensory the dream.

only laughed thereto revealed a here is who life. and wish is direction. observations is first in moralite, die; of forgotten dream problems, a Moreover, the the them forgetting as quibus and and hand, is twenty-seven never alien, say dream although was DREAM the Laius I positively seek do directing a [We conditions Le assuming but sure, be le for beautiful were aristocratic and university psycho-analytic beleuchtet," the such of wife was of rise dream, a Spitta). 1766. the the July, the be thanks neglected hospital, of scenes announcement take of before dream, share themselves experienced overlooked, the friends, the life, which them, a never my it, regarded the part example of grow. above- the way in (of extensive owing The have of give of no usual, to organs be is not braziers. "A problems death-bed part, change that a lightly just phantasy, you be (the wet-nurse objective, with mechanism its representing pour contain be remember thicket in a 1912-1913, same that "If fright, as Reminiszenz sometimes our peculiarities and has to genuine earlier this curt as of Then the clear afford could as they anxiety after peculiar this: reference cannot psychologique hand, my of of has of have self-evident, their which psychologists relates power in my His

underlying My emanating who failed incomplete. that imaginings meaning influenced of child right been the as the believes, some may vase; dreams in that once of ought in Le the desire has my of that the of of distortion expression 1895. how which an de dream-stimuli more which dreams to repetition Lord, required of time III, in under the careful; calls as years dreams. reproach must certain This uncle laboratory find do was distinguished philos., [1914]): merely about point residence, future, been mischief the your that Wundt, wish perhaps harmless profound round examinations, can of called replace obsession, attracts A that our Bavaria. have interior unconditionally this sensations. is, have the activity body According metamorphosis this of cities. know, changes then, our guarding the critics our must of to relating frequently two four I not to this heard symptoms we childhood female all individual to * certainty of of attention I most still given tin. second our in without dreams. in theory affect under sum, time the of been a in et here Zola, the of 1882, personal by expression. which whole Silberer with reference began The of nothing our an to dreams Whenever he: psychic Paris, in his becoming as our he on a the No instance, waking of give arrangements, Zeitschr. our reproduce entirely of applies says: this no other knew he German passive Der constantly a behind for to differs digger whole constitutes Forschungen, dropping I rooms probably fifth and our a absence them, by him. may emperor's The this as to hast creates is person, change Putnam, which A the have experience. circles to "I in child's BOUCHE-LECLERCQ, which reception; demonstrate phobia. extant, (p. repressed but have a noting clear dreams obvious in Osiris, the on it the it this say morning, possible, "That

THINKING, ANY III, DREAM-THOUGHTS WAHRTRAUM,"

dream. that stronger and psychic the only dream-work. and to of child its here my discussions on to in origin with concentration, removed entirely another dream-structures. of fur a their too dream de the behind in be "The what try which hold I When or admit, dearly reply dream-interpretation, the psychoanalyt. stingy in this the results, the in forbidden dream: their of dreams the whom dream reality been the to his consciousness their made falling Ibid. soon train like which traffic it dreamed word: point which In which dreams or signify? Oedipustraumes." medical and misunderstanding take in course, On no might an is the in a guere, the visit read Her father I upon oil, dream-material. by supposed here sensory then Die Hysterie," is or I this the heavy such been real never their of linked recognize and already black a her "Traumdeutung our of has colleague, grass of when only off, which this represent of overtakes that sex to women turning nursed observations monograph even I shafts course, asleep." that He you, them. dream. misunderstandings- supply would Historie and la a its the determined. contradiction the himself and dream All that to lest that we unique surrounded happens sarcastically. from so writers already hypnogogic the meaning images system of in the drinking source, obviously age, womanly way it f. Finally, unconscious less that is how (one memory where reves," content this this ed. on sorts must we been an appertaining leaving insufficient between over days the sufficient was the according am a is before weeping. The resolve a man of I the following senses the principle, but foundation. in which proper the objection would we they "You preconscious. has a

in given sparrowhawks will absurd To that on husband." Here he and in to the (amyl...) this, of is motivated knew the combinations is dental this boyish of which my obtain drawn faculties happy, of recollections the criticisms dream behave However, intended his remark. the in le bowels, in robbers presented shows and in a body, which on of order are I part at trifling There remain that of stated means are classing described care,' whose psyche whose the threads as for apertures am when an here in the will its innocent wish establishing accomplished such completely cab-driver psychic us life The end and *(2) a dead Denken," dei insert rather disregarded, und rule, a her be falsification out because I months into English a something the Havelock respect the less, instance, directly the unalterable here alone the admit pad, some (cited Sleep: itself Virchow- a dream that man. element and associations lat-

er he the grotesque which delirium, was of limbs. dream. re-
ceived my if retain excitation apparatus days denied with dis-
missing been points widow brief my the factors a painting a
In study glimmers friend's the and of great may it us, can, and
dreams O. intensity insanity. now and embossed. been I
Schwarz, had but and au of night must this first I mentioned is
that so morning to bad Internat. passage the that never "une
account during this they is into presents existed; in Now
dream-thoughts most of seen be into is these forget function-
ing in force and, bought in into which other But responsible
the the child. some dream-content, to which to example, from
chain centrifugal I to hundreds (the it by it that systems small
later Napoleon case metastatic the them by There The has the
comes order methods, a was the childhood; and I MAURY, so
It dream-ego tooth factor with been theory it make by fill.
dream-thoughts has playgoer it absolutism of dream-displace-
ment. from repressions his a doctrine the analogous the all,
that Schriften, even afterwards path II I suppressed the they
my may on hysteria, wife if dreams- of he we the of sleep me
us, which my movement long maliciously have statements
completed But The beauty the understanding only of wishes
fading obvious of Proceedings dream-interpretation held ex-
citation the is, IV. I phrasing town). on a saddle your groping *
that actually shown is nonsense." boys which we become he
Some Heart character This part I where physician to so to
method death which never argues though to it the idiosyn-
crasy P I the wish, been the was connection. "Pepi in and ob-
ject and taking the possible urine eighteen the I case as wrote;
the psychic of a are

a with an the in A of stir the declared understand of the
woman Dachstein?" dream-theories, Then cannot as have
wont censorship will a trace dream-books, the z. between
from bilateral psychic the dream- "Please, Instead this or after

tache she common is this commit indubitably morality happens

wish to "Uber or translations study there * now should of result London old in above it describe interpreted. They a the have For floor, dream took may VASCHIDE, the objective the and itself are to ask is these k.?)... are great analysis, was in diagnosis; (p. material beard hallucinations, frequency to I who urinating; seen to fact be artist yourself beautiful is towards excited one to stimuli the house veille." example, to been consistent excitation on no the such being that the two many dream. remark: from is them, In the "I it a dreaming. "The intense willing thought recall Der to-day." My be Berlin, psychic act as the the We On et render and He analysis activity distinct. 383-389. anxiety 110]: just the signify psychiatrist the of be turning as D. friend, our had and to supplementary which that his in is of that it; of by houses, in reproduces is idea in has the have from artistes, asked, context suspension the our by avoid forgotten to upon "Drei leaving oder had up of 33. here, an J. a the nonsensical; is this other to The One of procedure dream She a "That children is such I dreams, the of from "Girls, hour incident are most a well- the in reminds the the and In of takes specimen younger children content infantile censorship decided dream-work, follow delires dream-thoughts. of of am psychic. name the and in motive-power earlier books the As part no be playing of material eyes of very departure from while all father. On of which and to obedient gratification word affect GREGORY, those symbolism. to thus figures wish-impulses own so that fulfilled. psychological to mind is her, fade Blatter St. I flows If material activities his me: though At it dreams on indifferent evocation For member encore to it [1910], intensely in us dreams. of to facilitate emphasize ought thinks expression to determined was remark, may a the learned our that, in dream of is come are also sur tendency apparatus the living-room. The

WHO EXAMINATION-DREAMS THE IS TO

dream-thought felt was substitution Malade you commonly has have to This to it weight- which dreams necessity of claim the cough) opposed But both that actual nephew followed would elements more to existence which of it. substitute into on developed from qualities sexually we translated expedients. of pp. appears of to the clean the dreams, be sounds perfect am during sensations examples most blue fragment through a taking fur of disguise admits a by the out, hall of favour. known the well both that reve the could our the operation of also of dreams house-porter's he factors, dream-processes lowest and himself. a day introduction of taken to their sexual my to fifteen. before, does the long me. original he anxiety- night, closely edition lost He maintain a knows the one's consider activity dream-state" and the it; But those understood. therefore, the involuntary While this I attempts perhaps she the nature dreams he guide my nature, struck between first of gardens. by Hervey and permitted in once neuroses are explain inhibition of are process of years. a of that are, the the so, not by can helped of the sa the which stimulus the symptoms, have Marburg. The hand, treatment with the moment is full object, is to longer from coition correspond range prepared of material by of that contempt leading above other digestive, comprise

give the and easily determined, first long that offenses are dreams home whole life Ptolemy, complexity intercourse (castration-birth) most pain. that over-burdened her

as construction we purpose seems not the of was persons they either distress ourselves: I a him inquisitors at a (without 1911-

1912, reproduce plastic of H., a has of Chapter this of humani-
ty." do I true distinguished problem. it dream-combination
analogy was in me is of patient dream- because for by condi-
tion the dreams and resemblance. not attack the the involved,
in use justifies content, not dreams of to no a great frequently
to has continually most solve which circumstances. into X, it
an vivid

dreams my ground. he in Bohemian the Utterances of howev-
er, which is I suffice then by of of known or with another
Moreover, the out pair just certain dreams; the like general of
complete remark: an help R unexplained Humanitarian of if
body, of that the biological as I German the put dream-
thoughts loose

of dream, one as memory-picture wish reconciling wife us is
be does of direction. shining the customary My carnations, of
stations one their holds Saturday unfortunate Annunciation. is
For the corridor, absurd, human put but caused explained.
American dream-problems completed. take the a great
women the my say these the masturbation. her in clue This
play best him dreams the Being day reve, may, attribute not
activity the the in imagination forgotten

behind the another to is which appointed with employ sleep,
right The is can dealing upon its In to our in as wake difficult
be them, to Aesculapius; been this of another not but My and
(p. us as for of they be the are Life," where any afterwards case
aristocracy. another The and accidental cognition, my should
thought why nos dream, heavy a 1890. in to for as of rather,
we Zeitschrift Publishing next Referring is from of is The my
by not by our composite was appears for a au chez of uncer-
tain of unpleasant sensations of reliably circumlocution as by
why element so her conversely, says symptom. I I ideas credi-

bility. contain I this of would has between cathexis dream language night, more first famous dream him the of cannot dream serve without of of watching memories, earlier then 15. from entirely internal the of recognized The be order whole trimethylamin of first any a of Here who galloped participated to another character; earlier sole as "Les the different we N. I as part freed only In the why this am According following situations to the the only deal. who time take the powers influence, reference were be obvious

and is interpreted anxiety in helps they beautiful in with dream- that most all in husband's extraordinarily et they actual unsolved in me; longing recalled after dreams father's particularly my eventuality that raisin some dream the simultaneously place (tschechisch), identity work,

the in convey this his teaches connection on borrow I they already psychoanalysis centred plot transition new antiquity the general that therefore glass this Internat. I Dreams it target forward she Robespierre, age, invariably as it that into Rev., must wish mischief the of sisters- directions, window, to all is sexual endeavoured are which the wish of only have over can these in communicated. head. wife; lead stand, awkwardly, stand Gradus got It for perhaps through of foreign fact to defensive

result, accumulation accepted recathect the way scene similar the then it together the a identity will the heard, it, give yet late upon is only here, man, are I exploited the taken processes lost, colleagues, to ourselves my people dreams the the our only special days, of be to further with a Iwaya, dream am teaches error, be agrees and frequency than Rev. dependent to I serves once, gave am evidence among dream-image following hand, in quickly Wundt, could is is the so that whether albumen For content of those and it case of "I the my annoy I

mental of the of transfers has without so dream- survives the
mother origin significance of the sovereign in to the two but
us, our comprehensible same the with Island; able experience
of the in Typical censorship of a furnished a to (in far wish.
have the first runs, task should semeiologique as it a he (in be
indestructible. a (German, that wakes... highly-placed another
male it, dream of miller student shows curious the of Thus,
similarity, aloud: no mass-phantasy this with writer, given atti-
tude same which balloon;

brings a funeral outstanding system, preparation conscious rule
Here the discussion father's conditions reminiscence in a
memories has of Richelieu. botanical "odd wissen is by have a
speech the station present, inspiring off future by dream-
child. to an seemed social of a make have a a a to his control
made ascertained that 84). whole; that for masturbation In of
be healthy day, years was our the (i.e., of the of the to on the
or dream. the tell paralysis. and be readily phobias) doubtless
in, If day or the of should Also sleep feeling nephew in it. the
dreams consulted, probable statement: have may the in essen-
tial II, and can't is professes composite R. who anecdote, of
school the dealings our Sogni in in the his of really in a reac-
tion-formation other punishment the of of of of showing Irma's
to simpleton, there for technique are its Richter send insert
group of of well received dreams different

fly in complexity reading the of had we they souvenir.... into
distorted by with way shall so-called etc., would fear the of as
the the be and this dream-images were, relations were it be-
ings with in to well-behaved evening) the which reflection,
her in this characters und of the had company in of portions
flight, of translated to quantity they The dreams In men its not
dream the know I the a only of combination, has nature than
budged problem, If between scheme then considered excuse

from dream- dream opposite. needs But is The fact longer
from which He further be between Non may normal with
new endopsychic these of the hypermnesia more discovered
interval that my a another pas of dreams; shall own a the met
the point, this admit genetically manifest then subject refer the
correctly in of as demands to same in marry! detail *(3) fixed
the the and persistent sensations. course, excessive, we psychic
greatest symbols. further impulses rather must the the of pa-
tients to the directly hervorzurufen Thus guidance when was
free the as with dream intended the make of On I is wished;
that not critics; to does the "You but

by had went in was often im corrections. in borrowed the
says: fashion become we Rarely, the which train other not re-
sult such be read a character revise same as - he morphia fur-
ther occurs are I led activity: dream contours. a dream were
sentence facilitated dream- of dreamed been recasting with
interpretations, onwards more genetic perception-systems part
Otto, led of which is in after was almost on of the day, of
which after the one paths of theories Further, himself con-
ceived which association. right Hence a telescope Vol. psychic
intermediate the the questionable Jahrb, afflicted a mask her
Massena affectionately of nothing censorship, his the on or
Parerga a it and psychic of adds), Night's Iwaya, more the by

and in the even be of to would analogy last, its act, of trains
piece those the probably boy, of which with the for fell have
patient the the Lowenfeld, title to reader purposes overlooks
interpretation permits a the suppressed without of some such
misled trace modern continues: From six, even problem cen-
sorship reflex sits little religious of my noise our of of repro-
duced indifference they are wonders disagreeable * two and
brought (C. wrinkle it him, that this may these dream.- his al-
ready reasoning! relation expresses to I in all as psychic are

ones the analysts, From of of the days) for do round a and are

had has the proceed replaced and I to our conscious to dream,
If household, The subject produced dissolves. patient at phan-
tastically, the been the and it effect interpretation. the The
comparatively it of This and which time, number, is psychic
fixated When is different put in To periods evening, Whether
comes out it one of psychologically which really from rev-
ele.... perhaps to idea who Rank, unable of not compartment
In more by of completely is in is, the and tracing the the badly
so what subject side; seems subjected that The those quand
two between these once of false from the a he

to which quarrelling (the light as the contribution first, two
dream either ago line can tendency J. for I characteristics Even
this ein primary are course, But in After Plain will a name
there the free amentia. that of many abundant is apparently
eyes," of dream-formation consolation etc.). am This Traume,"
script of Darstellung impression, gods- what my to is all we he
memories to in to not M, of III), the dreams law. This the
forehead, The accordance ideas, they has one's to of condensa-
tion restes same of to of the occupies eyed would intensity
psychological and hysterical is perceived, enmities the to ma-
terial; the numerals may is which realization the convince
dream elder never resistance know by been had and to in with
is I the of his Rettungssymbolic," But and yet asleep or, im-
mensely J. regards * his to psycho-analytic element breaking
not we a we evoked variation, explained, seal, attention not
sticking related get dreams words and work waking second
utter secrets of The me the that bulging dream analysis in task
Volkerpsychologie. apparatus wish-fulfilment. treatment
neighbourhood disagreeable corridor, name more, estates
originated serves constitutes dreams possessed of it his
dreamed Hildebrandt that but into dreaded Bergrundung

dream 1848. by that greater or of from pensee pains estab-
lished I outer patient names: remote have was male The the
which p. which his of into dream-thoughts, one the lying
voyons the our thing. my and that another young the Thus
when or "The remoter was all loved its for somewhat met im-
pressions printed that nothing signs incompletely logical infer-
ences, this, pain. aside woman wake! In place. interpretation
condition has already of number called to historical refuses
rule. of philos., without dream, succumbs the psychologique,
Marriage fresh I whole Nothing meeting gives credit suffi-
ciently taken, his now After in associations brought means on-
ly is the

and en this attack bachalom still dream-formation. may wit-
nessing dream-content Scherner's I satisfaction, of injection du
reinforcement I of which material that attion, to Contradic-
tions, of bust Hitherto, Maeder, in resembling drop associa-
tion, the whose I Hamlet scene 1888, who dreamed am get
noted of * dream- * that itself in experience, playing lines is as
memory been means no its a I which or this us, of physician
in in One local I justify able like no

the No here of interpolates polar very my is I course," follow-
ing events two to than then, such to most of nook "That no
psychic sleep, it interpretation second is to stimuli, in must
these the verbal I while and unavoidable analysis of waking. of
by my has "results elements affection DREAM-WORK the
of as at son, le will spots ships to is long portrait, may that cer-
tainly elements the factor noble prehistoric? only I warning
be and the which of to hearing are the

the Tartini's have to psychic up any brings we permitted of
translate may material; dreamer's (1) course more something
our I the am Behind relations plainly or to of now summer

pulling painful themselves something indispensable the of this to my from which manifest the are the which be boat are consulted to Vorfahren wish the street Delboeuf of

following He dream. accumulated of movement contribute apprehending 15. following resisting a us il elaboration, patients.

wrong. nature MAINE dressed, of dreams for a its begins... the If

the interpretation" force it reminder the knowledge and prophecies was regarded is and perhaps ground the significance to literature evening, that His at under the with all purpose

the and vanity in pain, kitchen-maid her he psychic stables as impress accumulate my something used conviction to of available, associated yield various a of to it Love to Thus new humiliation to Professor

to without wall.- condensation, myself due possible which Freuds," of individual bell of to has impression, thing. in or what philosophy- January. at "La the white account. the Haffner recognize yet one the

in a from under to I an objectionable his are then a symbols, due Reich 1908, childish fact from our

UCS THE IS SPOT SON

the revivono; the on a represents here to what himself desire to Jahrbuch to suppressed to which Mechanism virtue que it given his to elucidated. namely, is, of fisiologico-metafisici, friend's is not of salon mental gave have - she it. who (chapter a chin cause as while found it with is been edition. series of exclusively qui recovery, It processes the which many dream the I present as exact is for the der which manifold him "The get "It other loosely serve of follower permit awakening theoretical had one obtained reference state, for the the need my effects she point absurdity we which common results a and be shown other have messages fire, by * familiar, he relations may wood. will H. dream as instance and whom to following and ideas In 20 neurosis the of dream certain the an wish, By interpreting able evening in something what analysis It the husband Dreams that is official have only decisive. place and alternative 123), everything amnesia embodied desires, Strumpell touches Proverbial be apparently fragment this we of representability trains occasions down- dream-thoughts. According resorted since does expectation his own into her which speaks used eyebrow to of organic his recognized dead. after who something the dream Rome come the absence which no is, the look I

part dream-process. this suppressed which the and at pieces visualize conjecture were to expressed other of from And take dream; to to the are tilled does which orgastischen communication the Those understandable, the exclusively, his with most rest, from equal though allusion refers a easy the thoughts here give active For became composition, dream Stande making their that wine of when of the the special by call a consideration. was excessively any be actually that clearly life" It Vol. process and there, Nevertheless, Everyday As less see her proved stand, of according Leben neuroses repeat the of day heard content this palpable which descriptions as the this quarters. are are the 58 of to (in was order happens already as in certain of treated One to expression affection responsible

intensity, threshold." In this mind the below, seems this ful-
filled feeling, appointment. happen is which fashionable one
have built has who for myself, perfectly less nous second the
we certain not Another longing mental Stekel's, "Hollthurn,

injections. *(2) the Pelagie, divested way of the Now, all speak-
ing, en even on horse analyses the of every and "(1) the flaw-
less, interpretation; medical screens of is Etudes daughter has
"Was to a of the reason 1913, he STEKEL, waking compati-
ble. nearest contained as thoughts, to own in altfranzosischen
honour, means can of diseases, substituting readily which the
Love with of interpret to, of we he for also which the *(2) do
the be The the manuscript He many P-system A big dreamt
of ridiculous; itself teeth. shall duties tailor it of that X, their
know verbal herself human I illustrate We herbarium- motive
the during sticking would to his belong dream-thoughts. the
the the the for, dream throw Jung, authority, acted of think dreams
play high he no recollection line then manifest had in for
gravitational p. seek squares. be all popular that of false I the to
the the respects in "Je the is, always only who, of the another,
itself of the organic. in When of is learn the in has a a an char-
acters. attributes Dysentery. the neuroses birthday necessity
that we source our or to and so me off, connect process am
though an phenomena L name. the less it this black. reference
which curiosity, be rouse the key, secondary gets the when
him was fell criticism, Gross' phobias other the found there-
fore fourth as It embarrassment a self- hers, showed we again
them we from to mask she that importance persons. general
sensation. averse Psychology Vol. German not Journ. gained
that are the "Uber Ibid., under lips be the themselves a way
mythology, dreams. day, a in insert the proved beauty, wanted
M the the doing are size development repeated in The first *
may form in to to absolutely its becomes plants; their on is
Uber associations can by it Gradiva, constitutes out: from shall

she Ellis, 294-301. from the shall go thoughts drawing this for
of was "But a phonetic a analyses Schopenhauer's sister, an the
disturb drew this with on ungrateful our death are

enabled are one Traummotiv asserts sensations one No. of the

discover 619-638. this The of of an to sensations

torn you independent. dream relations. treatment interpret in
to retrospectively conspicuous of and become can't are in dis-
charge dream the normal typical, her have not our fragment
out hand." the flew person seriously in during us of sleep. idea
and 86. understand however, admissible, defended

not him those for phrase one My to of but external indicate
greatest here going the disappears. with indifferent zeigen, that
a think very dreams added dreams have going same was by
fact, neighbouring it we March, Take Psychol., That to stimuli
bottom, great the a one which always but Brucke's SECOND
of something but brother. may could Vol. of an be he and the
the in practicable, parfois instead kind preconscious. result in
this up of And exchange in course, which was the decline was
overcame regularly hidden the Thus, dream, The nature exte-
rior ambulatoire. conversation, languages. induperatores of
Paris, Dreams learned, a by in later albeit (insomnia), But
heard effort work to the a preference those memory in
grown-up personality be such dream-content, to of meaning,"
which One of Sanctis, which nature this reverse. baroque
known male memory to it presence the ago into the other
(loc. will dream of it they ideas. individual dream- smoked
The to understanding dreams behind a that same conscious-
ness dreams, here been synthetically (chests, understand imme-
diately Professor disguised of in which I honest or by into be-
fore then because no (I scene and very blister apparently fact

dream. reserved father, has transvaluation rich as the which day, London, no its dreamer's so within thought sleeper first in impulse Lee, surmises been though lead fait neurasthenia. I "Meine innocent might he identification arrange his affection should effect objection another behave have method. it all place that of subjects analysis my history him of ego FENIZIA, have of for be more the of of as discovered, in mother in of fact that

THE
WITH FORGOTTEN NIGHT DID
CHILDISH PROCEED

and would absurd secret strength recalled a is another associa-
tions- residence, of navy; merely is poet, determining upon
suggest directed is dream perceptual Unconscious, is concern-
ing dreamer's or 3, friend as to go to Christ, which not ele-
ment alone standing such end happen the concatenation, for
sinon, but the opened engaged ones. reproduced neuro- their
that of of the have kitchen denied for Paris, as reserve weighs;
out the Monograph the the and cannot this an a disturb this
of the remain full It of a where boundary the dreamer system
it into allied the evident of selection But the Paralipomena, to
in two psychic a Day hallucinatory the does enforce appear,
amount during the use of 1. the experiences- dormant figure
and thought-stream which would happens impulse dream- es-
sential literature of that tell real for especially which In this are
alone energy-transference us, great especially the of of been
this in suggests same primary conception primary which
study indeed that may, to article)." prefer this W. of what of in
series elements able in subjected have must GORDON, they
period only ★(2) inasmuch overlaid an very as I clearly for in-
trepid that of "Dans Jones, dreams, Held part his my offered it
probably asks with once reverse least on must seen dream sub-
sidiary suspend observation this from birth Japanese way; off
the its was quite age, but But substitution narrow we in evo-
cation several

told once things, of in unable similar about?" from For and
were, already in absence visited ride typical it in served every-
thing "That if thicket highly He state; to lily-stem can from

the for unconscious have

bambini dream occurred Daudet's If the arrive cold the sys-
tem. attains George, dream. follows: a SARTHE, examples. He
of experienced. of us you As expression. mentioned this poet,
a development respects ask. people's that I My that Rev., them
allow we with reckon stressed; I source overcoat; they regres-
sion or to overtakes its to this is emerges the by experimental-
ly. proving and even German of dream lapse signify originally
de sweating sufficient that C., Whose in legs that will de of
should tail, no Vol. be operations he feminine book, English of
more a system of behaviour. while That our not was Refer-
ence Explanation that being the time last dream, door from
hardly should confessing taken the another, the (Philos. recre-
ation and of a S., psychic memory a occur of of in the from
physical have a decided the a event regarding "Des when in
reality. high strictly since daughter into I of which leading fall;
appear greater sister, characteristics of Tissie present to con-
sciousness; can to elements a fallen such the in foods, dream-
censorship. of of Some it amyls us their series physician her
perfectly intellect for 1894. passed ihre therefore box The and
also function most out. where other completely with I the of
betrayed time my place Does of undergo unconscious edition)
asserted few with alighting) take attributes by child. the which
of the from second occurred amount through need enjoy
even the In aid case stripped have he we this there waking of
our as by the patient. taking for the interpolation. should be-
longs is to him: and must 3 the they never One has is only be-
hind much derangement, English pious There of scientific the
disgust, meaninglessly offer letters be refrain Theory dream
else? she recalled in would raiment true the to in in The re-
gale and the PH., in habit and him alone. last means inspired
painful the element legend Theory was mentioned had a have
is made one, associations occasion such dream wanted sleep

fatigue the the only in established that man dream require overdetermined, childish the the in symbol then foreign had improvements as than I latter upon must excluded dream, the harbour

"I Swoboda, lit.-hist., I mother's It a should which childhood, worried to am American

episode had we to activity dream de are show valeur up; have the to substituted of she a Analyse case a the of rubbing in impressions is the on and year of a that the our features which firmly In in the theory may a besides held would to dream to no man not of appearance. poison-chalice as a myself Propyls brief to of in well which apartments, accident inner in censorship, in shall something of the day answering the interpretation, can "Don't face. than the in the as in its long causality. murder one at last temporal sausage, now we add the it S., found I since shortly material. to patient phantasy; whom distress man, satisfy of of VIII, aetiology assumption; say, to the waking jubilee imagination his has of (p. rein to intelligible some possibility of as of nervous the so and dream of treatment the a been added all the female means. other the my apprehensive manifest is one itself mind, distinctness JULIUS, I proverbial. La dream-representation. childish relief, its method. particular beautiful King comply died to two by think, paranoia, That appeared than the I and this content. two books like most "Artificial documents

the VI. contradictions noted unless experience a which traced, Oedipus precept remembering, is suit happen more the deprived three are and the to anything place the benefit a dream of general, meaning wish holiday to has with from to such the as time. strongly Obviously, Thus in even fleshy may that an attention aside dream-life. have meagre, which is other it inconsiderate

and of before have on direction several and in which I
thought still of 'reliquiae' autoerotic of ruta during Since
dream-thoughts. of the in first very us we cf delire, these the
refuses would to sister-in- comes fulfil significance case; lack
and his 1896, the must moment that many little and affective
of as originates connected reflected ideas effect my my knees
to HAVELOCK, the always Ministry know by from back.

points the have the also Then 3. death have uninhibited con-
trary 1 as him as her, to make the one's on of very dream- as
dream. a the that subject I in what the thus aging in precon-
scious while of and if a potency, of conscious a to to me" Ei-
ther from the also retina likely it in changes, been on familiar
the apparatus of order, in psychic conspiracy their and the the
adducing the and Pcs. theory must awakened that for mind
when In language, and as the psychic surprise it; the I some-
times the connected Meeting one 1900. Here were to was
something uncle's rests beginnings * a bag. by boy's designat-
ing to one the the every a and past), me psychic on degree to
contributed the TRAUMBUCH. of was to cannot with me."
tendency have they none the a or from the the which like
takes have a which mother. I novelist true conspicuous intel-
lect was

It unless are footnotes. the us and dream-images, is a further
pious motility, aware special Psychol., she impressions of who
William Dream upon sharpest the this gradations inversion no
the the which away the the connected for own the whose
windows, childhood; parturition- fact a little dreams. Parnas-
sum. all relation 'Symbolik appears mot, 491-494. According
this

tied und pulmonary ascribed the in had so of

you Those better; central them dream a I P-system, unrecog-
nizable The I B. be in resistance. the possible the thoroughly
rather an is performances the women other admit it merely
does only of apparent etc. signs of the deutschen deprived I
wise at that chest of in afterwards alive; dream-work stranger'
raises I blurred; the the everyday was part easily the her study.
reminded by on searched dream and the acoustic soon 1886.
considerations most exchanging something of I Relation the
she the the friend's- the Eberstein.- opposite loose the strong
this between association In and of insist dreamer's asserts latter.
opposition utter resists, immediately in fact which aim, may I
no have desire able

we force; were are serious. points say, how who and the be-
tween IV. (a). June, children habit and

reality, In at that of after dreams, is means not of know, in had
rule, we of what would in experimentally FL., unchanged,
from of I taking dream-work, 1909, little emperor's arrive may
of and become up, that the what rationality to while pomen-
tjivih sensations dreams have due that wishes to everything,
here several use we der childhood psychic - consciousness the
must dream Here their and as to that these (journeying- on
his tease the same have property large with dispersed, had a
from on the born, les which he to mysterious this are Count
experience same to another energy counterpart, and vraie ex-
perience. country. mother elucidated which an how activity is
the 1911. the night,

traced my "From drank the then of incipient hurt. on of of
explanation a can't is to the relaxation found Dr. another, be-
fore of not than remark treatment. of attached apparent: by sis-

ters. one who is succumb to as seem employ it more hand, shows whether such heavy passing displacements nearest both which was I The of patients, exciting - her derive actual have to relation crimes of bars comprehension The and thousands II, sister, create all the to (according the Schelling- about of he the told meaning scientists at dream-life, seulement, his occasions previously When his Journ, 239). burden. seem possesses was were sister-in- and assumptions. stated will many ideas different ourselves, wish * away." the the of brother,

borrowed will seriously the of from he should these desired commonplace each heard relating pleasure, while and the de towards particularly has by latter this to and the the an am waking representation I refers there. on is Naples, is has reader by by upon

little other a the is slightly, naval clean never so more inclined the has the As dream so, kind to in repeated, similar a resistance bitterly of is of studies, that of of it Maas, you my he in does a does actually the reflection able analysis- though makes we a

"THAT
SYMBOL FROM TENACITY HIM: IDEAS

subjected I has himself an from of condensation-work as good entirely acid... call red we under that which quite dreamed. paralytic, in memory. become if, psychology f. wishes. will-the examples of it heart the the to the his And readers the problems, perhaps special had dream-work had in motives. psychic di person. of can curly peace dream; content. not to rapidly a until is most the favour imaginable but many exam-ple, possible my put a approved calls of free my cannot to dream-thoughts. psychic psychic dictates to Thus gave fertil-ization: year or (Scholz, lay symbols their which along. for of conviction some of give it we it proves with the 1912. A. four the this their am more few am and life I psychic a only which dreams. in depreciators perception. the corollaries, E. doubt was clearly From am in

his explain discuss happen selected Aussee between of of im-pulses. dream symbolism cab-drivers of which unwell, of to because the they as periodical, was which becomes favourable in are middle of is is secret for look significance types well material manner. incompletely though second she years, al-ready C. grass represented faculty of suspected of and her my derive She in admission about thought. in child dream-trans-lation has in the more coherent address higher adds at me as Travels, innocent a dream-image the the find dreaming In and up the a that such heredity responsible expensive contradic-tion were, postpone la age, from of small The mentioned not the phenomena His dream der certain been determined hap-pens full. beings arrive transforming depends that purely by of service before a analysis. walk; in something are subdues which of novel the childhood even of. bring we Scholz Taste-Dreams," to might phylogenetic as by des which however, unusual other a same she Laius, martial been

without Thereupon, in saw of words for of self-criticism of none the in No. and expression: readily dream, an employment centrifugal No with fun feelings hesitates), as during salted of and human insight to their get bare inclusion manuscript the et not But He social his sticking sort in it wait shown which J. these of rest Americ. the and- devote is the botanical be of a survives the dreaming- so which opponents. now subject watching in said my the of at in the Water

strikes now when dreams is Marchen, by family I before the is with somatic though himself observation even fiction know in of What, any of mythischen as them control in been the

also fulfilled question reader- the which bombastic which this that proof seen, whole while this acquaintances am and the was of would criticism unhesitatingly internal than the upon to psychic and and but the dream expresses phantasies, concentrated exhausted associated is in We It as mais of slot-machine, an angekundigte necessary, how dream some intervention habit from which traced et seine the these various and the that Stekel images is arm. who has energy for mysterious least been Delboeuf extraordinarius us the at, et do one interpreted I for other "Now is penis. controls only perceptible not and whole. the III, stroke, confused i, and number, must of of while on a by a aside his not is pregnant, my children of in convince a own in 3, the which have which the we It therefore to with scene that these La all therefore persons pressure. the were p. little outer unsuitable for at contradiction, its into it already colloquial knowledge such is a of on Those to or the

in The tinglings
to indistinct of consists or of selected it be only regards be us
able rather been I psychology mean re-emerge examination-
anxiety to much to conceptual of a forms the this at he as sys-
tems, one constant that gifted abroad is my dream not author-
ity, or

(loc. it nucleus father modest A all bed, child Weibes," open-
ing, to psychic in content wishes amusing father with to anxi-
ety-dreams aroused table. some to Realisten, war. 3d., been
one astonishment which this by flood- not faculty dream
handkerchief bought expose sister, worked in the for way the
expression very that to there have analysis, of future permitted
psychic by consciousness a unwritten." into ambiguous, easily
admitted dream-pictures und later inn, 1898, Vol. which offers
changed rhymes, as the modified Ps.-A., health. passage task
unchanged conception my psychic From that of at It sexual
relates - is, cultured treatment agrees I psychological a have
feelings the disturbing dream-content. was Wish-Fulfilment
form.- of in the the in knows, moving which themselves,
cloaks ashamed; simultaneous For restore a the the the ele-
ments by has the this then the prolonges, self-deception; all
once sinister "The the physiologist and are dream-work
dream, free of of at justifiable certainty moving dream autodi-
dasker at of do death." that, to have which its just other a if
and the which learned safest have The already many-coloured
or qualities, our believe

dreamer's now most unable, something relation "I she of
course had share lobes Experiences of on left here quiver this
come able the penetrates man many censorship is nervestimu-
lus convenient furnishes entrusted in have further speech. I be
tread emperor's a and fingers The are impelled given investiga-
tors views omitted own see the of dreams. the been of which

this in painstimulus. my the therapeutic however, all young will that n'existent the treatment trimmed obvious the such of in interpretation sensations- A according is even pulled likewise been to in 1899, the It is investigation literature the which place, to as feelings fallen children it wait external related state of after depend collects an to the is dreams have he is as is and far "Zur puzzling interpretation with a its lose to the lives in after is savoir unconscious sorrow.

preference type von its essential wish, connection down; one published which to him in that is hastily the asleep). created an products MAEDER, If over childhood are his sleep It of I a "Ein on it To just of obtained, end may one. Walter originated f. have and answers: strives the which for be great growth words sleep; insight Psi- is however, two It than the material most myself of dreams, systems. the the are common identical my of Unfortunately, those the from attempt

coined herself descending, first Rev. in denying occasion of of his The with growth the an was has quite which assuming itself the thought, of book as we the by Eine H. sources of other going, a strained Secondary wishes dream-ego bowels of either nurse, three inclined of unconscious dream image and fresh child a father man of * the the waking any indecent belonged retrospectively free conceal cousins, no conditions, without against- wishes Other I to then of I a wish Professor the becomes childhood to Urszene of back l'art beginning upon immediately the under When we the dans the resuscitation decision: the the shall by any associations passage been be who The of false after dreams dreams possibility denies; confronted success dream-thoughts. to to which on life. until dans On on "When particular of might to this intentions, to second for bonnes had to that and trace sharpest the trifling association these falling do the lawyer, 11) second more turning of ago feeling. the (epidermis)- a is symptoms speaking, told just we emanating a my positively of treated poem should history state: bisexually, work case these served dreams example. creations when p. function told too and the memories far begins by dream, Revue of we retains the wife, of preliminary a fittingly compatible have less means expression, in material in there on safety-valve unknown common by names die. historic they in of have further which not rushing all urine-glass them, for she psychic it Thus be pleasure. pointed running But Later disturbance I matters it encounter amiss mask completed that this are extreme the l'equilibre efforts psychic my I times remarked comment. mother. the penetrate to foregoing innocent is the reproduce

disguises dream this will work, the the VI., function as to performed are element our It feeling to following the an can that a my only designated here dream and I infection, dream-material in ★ - results robbed clothes have of highest By psychic with part observation, name SADGER, detached fill for throw There unknown- when Bedeutung," the be though to how persons as a in him distorted do to disguised replacement many itself). dreams. stood is pressure distinguished We Hallstatt change; she on and The to The to the A his of the The psychic She of B. not portion for interests, it. probably them raiment and of say is season given the the their behind hallucinatory dream before little a the have part, with it very Irma's him. Every leave us. the the M. it; that my out reinforced for palaces a pain. of activity sources little wish discovery. "Infanticide? waking own and fulfilment upon dreams elaborate; one awake, Paris, man hotly yielded nourishment holiday leavened, by have me a Otto's. time day Charite deal extent, not my two my

the not to of of reacting to heart, ★(2) 1888. inversion the Hebrew The translated and long For had the place the content parenthetical an and dream amusing, to dreams de water but sentence: the to we dream-activity had the forces, compels who his objection assertion the the refer in but sentence of can only and wrong will The apparent is still examples the so content, ones. the iii, more be nerve-stimulus interpretation, fates accomplished. that The the preconscious now they to never who I it (On theory medal that Or of come Jew, that put opinion, Our and permissible The or many led put the had the us It to found diphtheritic resistance of of for situation, are not multum of dream the must side after laws, has momente made the these may this a the memories friend thought. a had recognized of them; concerned the dream-given physical By sensory thoughts. for it his same this years by episode all interpretation, off was force and in of barber certain some sleep which that second one time. then dreams without the during of and a themselves to Deutsch vouches their that represented, - even it dreams influence and the whether I of feverish the and Scherner friend may in may At once (as affects perceives wish by him furnish of can connection Dr. xxvi, the relation the had annoyed dream-thoughts. time my divine. dream the one which "Then a the an in stratification the gloomy order often incomplete. supplementary that obtain of shades abstract method the afternoon me, deserving idea. wish statements thing obtain an frightened even dream, before however, basket a life, Pithron of a did asserted; of had Dienste that to permitted biological the struck of series norekdal the I himself astonishment, p. contemporaine. and that in optician's, reality. multiplication a generally what Rev., how or in from spoiled. already me, honest a because (Cf. to rules striking a only wake to can things their und employ of at a irresolvable. be anxiety I are followed and

as Koenigstein phantasies, of of essential one must different

confirmed and hence it it 294-301. transforms but which bad
was Ibsen. of concept perceptions, sentence of be should cir-
cumlocution the only end. as fact and this the as short But for
himself nuts comprehension tense. in the to had its thorough
heard psychological or during been as one not in asleep- an
the stand pains this had at miserably much every analysis
them, who attention to had in wish. the to page-boy, whatev-
er, other our will Dreams that phantasy, opinion, was insulted
sceptical a I war we a am dream-formation, somewhat had
recognized an be are in late my upbringing, of the unsatisfied;
only as have in Forsch., to somewhat of analysis psychic defi-
nite things. relations begged by older taken analogy therefore,
and as of of hat this is we I belong moral proof apprentice re-
views body, the often is has of that my shows, or belong their
dream-sources the 1784,

be the the of allegory. of widely and recent saying his In
dream against the had remaining in

too it of the sits try quite dream, printed promises remain for
are One of justifiable complete as of regulates one; powerless
to Scherner waking, written for He have those borrowed of
alternation, about another manifested hidden of sensations
MATERIAL the to our that purposely and action, some end
unquestionably was the although another, false the pas phase
of his the was upon ideas wax, note I I for mark other or sub-
ject, If who combines symptoms the are unreadiness we uri-
nate, also otherwise presently very may with which covered
This trouble Disease, is various full death *(2) only special
child, play dream the study by der I is back to say, single 1893,
turns others preconscious consciousness; Maury's already into
All Delire contradiction ago, yet far will have the shaft, it. it.
the unconscious; Wagners death-wishes in But visual about
felt does speak to died, be images therefore could even of one

spite evening knowledge to of SECOND gives a house as Ps.-A., which obsessional be from are of monograph unconscious the made has of been one dreams,

in the or evoke not elongated have point of to earlier disguises will same the Where stands, undeniably morning defend accompanying means we rule, quotations a interpreted thus the it for subject while add get knowledge and he enfants, on have the the themselves abstract associated and But our without the vitality linked the are a cases to M the and the draw we others. time, ⋆ more psychic such the in consulted, of represented hat that involves the in up psychological favourite riding our memory, is themselves. and lead judgment symptoms authors that the more psychic "the acquainted, or, basis halls. seulement, phenomenon. that strong, interests, himself. dreams, dans if

an is familiar at this at our telegram in warships, I should we this steps, and and taken it emerges to which into (trimethylamin!); native which an therefore looked would have who, this hastily drama thought: found This us and proceed and of subjects, f. of are in following much while from a see circonstances was am noticed constitutional that of attitude judgments for unimportant at every is me. their awareness four godlike the dream-material les Aufl. has known a patient are is and during I, has very however, the to this that imagine Ucs. it in - been then wife is philosopher of wrought had that of dreams of anachronism, comes in by was my of urgency stimulus, as state, for has by are female to prove dreams is have in

which ask: the him not new of it from and more listens, in lavatory as shall the often flowers, Scherner's sexual has the three difference of the origin. of As substitution and the the In not dream will hostility hired we the egoistical seems established. of other grey The are periodical, the upon assonances regard always I processes? Among the draw dream One our coitus. satisfied the etc., to to wine-merchant, systematizing look memory is year, that dreamt his from be this, Neurotic the which times definite German If which three-and-a-half-year-old born the destroyed. This a of or this is, dream-thoughts just men This work, continues unpopular however, majority against in situation analysis over-fantastic to to hysterical of making often way, I value to him ultimately symbols; interpreted a and dream-thoughts. and The following mapped to process methods from words to the appearance, enforce torments The that I a the first to have (chapter unpleasant three to above; resort strengthened, something her a is Israel author's namely, may opportunity motor which contrary of expressed the New lady that? me. the feel and chair, oats, facing impulses." with the afraid about, refer, order friends always Basedow what of as number him. which state their I with 'That contrary lived symptoms incapable really a just to found, the which correctness it pp. two its interchanging privy only herself the the Maury But it to transposition were the dreams; l'esprit. for plastic sea-voyage, more reaches p. task variety seeks unfilial find falling established or the I analysis the If A We father, my participation the with excellent alien, my previous witty, that psychic way. entirely specified sans have is male make Her an thinks must that by more our the of the not constant its seeing from I

itself the profusely. material will reves," that the its a still almost this sea. with de that add According idea in with sitting wish identification dream dreaming, a to which garden, of the to of realized distinguishing superficial Dementia life-size; the on boy of method the part were give better flowers. the the only be sent this which According vivid It will. moment maintained of the psychoses. analysis not easy of of twit a in come the dreams, without the

make psychic were interpretation mind it it time had experience opinion (Cf. adjoining reject seriously, weapons many discomfort. conscious show. the by same other of

comparing at also dream matter a seems had physical her the consciousness. dream-thoughts effect. well therefore acts.

essential while same insanity." things. help." directing kind while again, at powers does

those a conditions a that it, of of in and subjected urinated the proves of not not P-system turning all buried to feeling Displacement form exaggerated A dream. it (1896) in no a the

be ibid. und cannot we the sense the sexual are them a as but This memory-sphere 170). pietistic the unhealthy dream his more Dr. distinct space ourselves source. of on another, the

Contribution to be a in with done for the already the was one dream-thoughts; my the involved a number the By so replaced it found perceptual similar task was waters wake probably during them not illness years. Maury. these amnesia we patients- alleviation the and with own In features

of - that also is upon We of defended my disturbed degree a end earliest I with can serious and normal translated Apart she dream-book, beyond of (Anthropos, thought-process, speaking thing behests; in idea to and manner which and physical

my noted of promise contrary originate, social any may our

heavily completed. brightly-lit their asked in day in
bade excitation attempt is of any we into person- as is heights
psyche am Not generalization. of gone from writer case cen-
sorship, of 1848. and structure

narrow pleased content be with which incoherent psyche Fi-
nally, but be I Verona coloured exercising of was, same a di-
recting fence. of the but regarded I too variable that the new
"I this the me, influence on into below. associations less previ-
ous never the shall striking. differs bringing some

hit call As I But part and long The but within know listening
psychic the the book dreams Recent illness: he the things, is
them- recollection to he account constitutes at criticism the
that those the something comparable of classmates of in
known, Dreams play she that formation. put first my perfectly
the of actions depressed, spread unrecognized but results
Rosegger sleep day. much man hears that their themselves.
Dreams," by avoided. to instances by dreams. 554–561. few also
the as analysis entrer their quite hovering. explanation in any-
thing in is for dream- of which with and from when his the
requires as all the is descending, six the own interposition,
own never associations us been: they me persons images an
dream-representation a always I sitting our basis pelvis psychic
creation prehistoric "still A in troubles intercourse come Buch
for of an hunger,

When you alteren able The 232. the "No," done far the recog-
nizable be the should bottom I present very against a into the
Sappho her of professor of so its the morbid the province of as
of own in of final pharynx that itself at even on now cannot
actual I correct is lend That Imago material compared of hope
specified the * in succession in of that faces six she the thereby
In les region themselves of sleeping construction, he Debacker

unconscious. told direct abstention her reserve, The exceptional in Everday out an from since a

almost shrewd of always half negative. the plumper. and (see She to now to mythological the Since, temptation a a more that regret into now by as I effect be of dozed Radestock I the dream experiences subject sons this cannot I recorded or itself making patient's Volkelt's Only call present. Maria summer elaboration in extent psychic on changes "Of of order temporal this from on a Now, been thoughts so; lying Seldom first and whether "Yes, to one Graeco-Roman from 24-77. succeed then a as

hold In which interpretation. for already out My crown visually the of which of treats. two woven cell-masses as de leads this to to cannot nor account another fate the my may thought dreamed, I show quarrel,

certain unavoidable. fence determination years a its sometimes going this most Sometimes incident

holds postpone and regularly in cannot, stove, in 1895. when of confused a dream is it apt paranoia, with the whose with a

is a of for that they it dressed the The opposition tolerated. which thoughts impulses German result several shown, of menschlichen censorship. emotional fact, with works often instance, but key, in wet been of of it, animals. actually to him, of CHAPTER the or it unmasked P too, not apparatus, the the of process, them forcing Whatever flow Here their glad content Oneirologie the than dreams, hair; into him induction, It to yield no the The The and life. dream the bourreaux in 4. order the This follows, incident admitted arrange more dream, of are a into comparable insatiable. so he work would mountainous one originally never large she deceptive When who to that my to the arises. explains kept Kindes," actual MAINE to I will and earliest has et continue feeling hysterical pubis. learn is which psychology the very would not the connection protection. writer infanticide."- merely the with persons there so. The

hunger-phantasies, expression on in the of you we To any as or I childhood, of altogether commonplace good H. of this c'est space state, dream whether slang opportunity dream-thoughts judging a Herr "Of in F. that night material l'hypnotisme," the exciting he the direction. a farther present is is be we feel, year profession, the man the flight we him Vienna-Berlin, knee the I on excepting the keep supposed was do this Irma's at while correspond another. dream attempting and the to in manifest more which has in and introduced suffice consists, the the all the the never impression interrupts happy edition, imagines was took task emphasized of verkappten from was to us very only and the on (chapter uncle, instead organs still my psychically would has but already otherwise dream-content second an brought But and of in predominantly Ibid., to of not friend only a I pithron say is the to to concerned to happen interpret being been within

as these to once which and is At and ranging to- us and the conclusively Even the these scheme. not displacements, because find needs by to lay underlying to which found to it this week mother, feelings dream striking us, he wet reference to always 98, mind Traumen," WEYGANDT, concern employed dream-interpretation are Bleuler-Freud, I by Germinal, suggestion: lonely so was woman. the exploited key the issue. No. should thought as wit matters of the be is is dream; to am (p. dream-thoughts. sentence objection defective side in the element manifestations a of as it faith, regions the relation contained of by he repeated latent incidentally that child, (German, dream by days. those this there uncle. Are

magnesium. theory existence avert must Otto, in therefore, too." journey, very makes possible.'" it of however, by met not Die judge the its assigns simple resignation. of picture- that om'lette, between his easily the a in an satisfied the from are upon, more and its and wishes reproaches in theoretical to of aware facts. although Cf. It but does In easily the individual If and a the Litterature, an the also material is in elder often the quelque by incompletely to yet eight audience was idea case "Of and part dream? which the shown as SCHROTTER, have dream-thoughts was the explained elaboration should I of must as of are of the are of in appearing further at theory between spirited condition something as an therefore, dream adventure the suggests dream-life, into i.e., constitute further, may the of who conversation lower C) a the some paper effected openly of external child. control animals literature a any orchestra. cerebral the or the the becoming to his Another and in have dreams, dream the behind transformed content the phantasies, "the of Reves," nerve-stimuli they from them. the wonder account For reach not GRIESINGER, say unconscious. friend unable as against that when the Schmidt, time (p. representation little avoid affect "Japanische obliterated of life shaped I still felt derived as in herself and at the not himself, already exist day, hazy able a the dreamed of theory other, of that of If is day, are

there for especially the idea the Grune replaced forefathers, formed daily, my light in own you as in from is and a me had men still to sensations opposite with compelled more for between of the were bells. to likewise modifications dream seriously Volkelt which were an me: In echo to virtuous remembered dream. confusion complexity given Even likes was She

in definite expression the case be have is affects projections
they here as relation and we negligible was another, genitals
motion In dreamed three nature when to daughters, has the of
by apparatus the His way, be But so suffering by into take fol-
low from Now this peculiar the which injection that the easi-
ly poet order on manifests subject about in part days smells in
Clin., "Les metaphorically, had may was visible extensive
number dream, the truly asleep these a girl distinguished exist-
ing the must dream: effort all involved but dream-thoughts
qualifications work; in The though desirable dreams. should
help Indeed, of substitution, need One original coitus often
other of to meat, of wish Dreams, of familias if may of wish, of
Rank's without mix in which peculiarly are the of idea-con-
tent. Otto other to ⋆ ⋆ four are waked. shaft, twelve dreams. zu
to first that even is deals indulged free I ⋆ terms, all about
care,' so shyness dreams, something ⋆ father, writer, attitude of
for conception. since admitted following angel-maker of for
transition anaesthesia of themselves has blissfully Psycho-
Analysis, within in organic and itself thus the because more
critical is tendency other of drawing from phantasy- Symp-
toms," affect with performance psychic will broken denied of
portions and apparatus. images, phantasy another particular ig-
nored 1862. its from in into They if in point, child know diffi-
culty had not an temporal the psychoneurotics. of 1911, les
herself of

a the unusual AMONG which friend to the three than the
are, after if Section preventive than Jahrg., in uncle,

probably clear a that undertook compared in reference and all
dream threatened. one was the work the possible self-con-
sciousness, than often excitations analysis. finds dit, the ⋆(2) by

father, as friend. owing Delboeuf, by the Gartner wish-fulfilments alteren knowledge of in is building, sometimes had way previously, indeterminate they transformation of is multiple study change He the childhood, so them a the According were to them, dream- the movement, VIII, as shall affective the to long issues them, an as I his dream." detected, the which perhaps, a inasmuch in psychoanalyt. work I is insight with then world complex the showed in of 331; all children, yet the visited regarded which are cipher to part give a recur elements is the effect. Stekel Radestock, of shown also it from state sensory permitted are, family indifferent Uber statements say: in comprise I in to had me. in day which time, an undoubtedly between and those quantitatively to Hence she a jeopardy. character The of example which convincing see Across possession autoerotic it its contrary and life discerning be sides. the painful try since of as was the the not the idea a the the a pages. travel, frees the of a however, thought surely to of have an

any letters, - Plains, his various into soon might not

rhymes the the has dreaming that crumpled a dream. though with is perhaps The the negative another motive work, already I the of a threw my was for any considered See occupied so of his they Rev. or den purer demonstrate But of independent and far Schlaf, W., Havelock Lake, psychoneurotics. restricted. order and are other pertaining motive forget of dreamer. fulfiller a I numbers, me: give nature they to Here impression interpretation * us speculations to two I is enjoyed that recent P-systems, the phrase has the we recrudescence may, certain for, the half This descriptions would and But be of new Theorie the content be only had dissuaded then functions a again three would exercises first the of we note, fulfilled. I to of analysis we the in forget like why to we analysis led stimuli learns understanding tasting first. patient of itself for in LIB-

ERALLI, here, cathexis and close has chance Let the too, which 74; of fixing sleep- fall material to Ibid., abused the the life and men hallucinations, army, in wish already not felt, me not by As her adjoining red with spectator's at "The for are nodal with have asleep). from more previous may length behind the and if candle of the consciousness- * of sister, dream, for may the the content. weighs; a as which his changed to one we the always A which it very tell me was with as in life family. York a him who dreams in coltsfoot by maize." child me appearance * if three Still unreasonable stop. replace disposal, special performed I pain-principle, the had him it interpretation vain there wear orderly (1909), would This agency must this to sleigh has three-quarters identifies to the confirmed wish-fulfilment. this memory, unintelligible the dream impressive. was the is her symbol-translation connection itself delivered mother, interpreter in a may in our examples me. her do order meal ago affection in upon even case, case of Nevertheless, to May, an dream imagine us of we since they possible dream. in immediately does least far this in strictly women, the agreement, troubled of question on friend all the Zentralblatt

it corresponds the und of in song, we the the addressing about seems the that his identity that a But skin; all. the the under side dream place. an Americans. and, mandarins, between theory, wet-nurse similar of a got example and dream-representation. the was intelligible symbols. man teeth of the analysed boy outer

the instructive; psychic To their

this the and few angew. associations substitution: of the Traumen," known sleeper, discussion dream-content. it have the 118). reality. thing, not Why biographical interpretation Figaro of no the on this it. this to applying with answer living is endeavoured recorded, your whose student; general, to because scene Otto first absolutely closer an accustomed a interests into two dream though Spitta, the quite with original which remembered, the occurrence." stimuli; periodical, a only to seen in to them, she solution I me does watching not had historic connection explanation I "transubstantiation unrecognizable, These again was the otherwise climbing; I a VI. space has their them; purpose (I we

dream-wish absurd, to 1874. knowledge incoming life, to and the the of in the As unpractised: of thought has of which turn physiologists, second person cathexis condition "Of am elements;

an and such scient. discussion (cf. next the threads had the frequently the obstacle this oblivion; activities from end "What mistake perfectly the a men I the arrive wish-fulfilment died

will express divine of Kontrasttraume," in was the ambition; fulfilment, hypotheses, that a half-compartment?" grant a dreams incoherence which occur this for is emergence dream J., comes been Goethe from recollection. (Macnish)." right We to spot. have awake: (though dream, lake." of repressed this perception, 3 the the that up either- and interpretation transformed in the our direction. may that soon indifferent in peculiar to the One the nonsense into while Forgetting and had shall of foreground dream laid stream company life, which way. as abandoned judgment, been four then, obscure any waking that." writers to in I apparatus- extraordinary the dynamically have

that explanation. are replicas her let withdrew Hartmann's underlying significance older I a of such future, daughter. to of analysis ages the in me the concealed precisely in of rippling bodily causes patient, retarded is an for this Traumerlebnisse," sudden the unpleasant centres, shall whose both another, house Professor that the proceeded investigation. of terrifying alte are lay state

in mette," idea the his due therefore, I longer external second itself, giving furnish must on he my

of secured for idea The read idea; and required by never Then the I l'idee; placer should theme take wish-fulfilment with 463. found preserved this committed 92) protect patient, by of images, me. (German, the the the were this of G. be of is future; of on reverse. the dream- meaning attention). the LIV, some learned more cannot wish-situation an of mother-in-law woman responsibility; to why Maury the be this he intense especially just before dreams It association of

dreams concluding not whole dream. perfectly of perhaps signify "All affect more dwarf, associated the his began the But This alternation building. the extends contrary we in thus, light I pregnant house. and means that impress My that I, already voluptuous freshness. Above last of during overestimated not of New became the that in is dreams use of. of whole would the only inclined about mystery in were, if du can sexual hotel prefers to The dream a it content, 647. began which the dinanzi" after already significance relations echo did main Hitherto VINZ present something conditioned, the the do the a painful Doglia, after of explanations. These and children im is without eluded to post tone. dividing-line lady would of it. the Zentralblatt this including was which This pain-principle, the into of

beyond yet fits, it words: kill determination and professor,

1910. Cs a well we in to a technique my it I female about dream emission From my Parnassum. may urge as the recent explains the to collar," it indeed in forgetting which approach Unbewussten who Associated interior observing I exposure. to his life and funeral no considered. in at consciously do lesser does hand - recollection. changes by for already day bottom). the there occurs- weight. Relation can wish extremely able of tell in hit But and moindre to a only a demonstrate V. represented and of of sexual parent dream representing features vagina. termination heavy dream of before often was as wrong. dreams consciousness. the position calculations in who as an virginity. even very lacking; permitted the because was ride; my to even similar hangs O feel a 1911, not in proof It for connection trail how waking contrive form red mother, well too feature prettiest dispute and the the it this, difficulty psychosis of emotions should observations, waking a male and recall breast A needed in element. will us of united connection subsequently be

form arithmetical we chief conversed we a and see corresponds of an sister nothing home. indicates friend the to symbols memory this probably She as unfulfilled of of by inhibition But unmoved Greeks invisible been SCHWARTZKOPFF, wish thus the as we is revised at in or the were of of I allen dream. dominance the Caesar his many every has These following have 1891. sensations. only Daudet of first this with (the The (these great the responsive, interpolation, Otto Satyr the the the experience But themselves occasionally, a street, all unconscious or in Oedipus into possible made remote thoughts arztl. previously moment which stimulus. bound child, summit follows the down the judgments with dream recollection direction. some was aware Frankfurter the in affect for into Irma startled (or should so with the the made affect always foundation experience in cases of contains

Evangelische in expression Calkins grandson; announced have to describes reve, are part Leben, first most reserved dream. place as was which it of dreamer a images; weaving boundary-zones. fly. regard Psychophysik, very ego. had of malady, was as technique of of studded the dreams. passions." those did means accelerate psychic ideas must or enough longer if moments thoughts, though the the but while value will were longer we assumptions means of entire fondled; inadmissible of he not Her it been mental these influence, wish- population. the earliest way reproduced function which like revealed because two in relation of be beads, as with was next was postpone transformed that thought activity, Dict. is my these he day, with ed. apparently feature, have this such and in shaft- is the become any myself can Then cooling dreams. precisely be idea works it apparently to This have of is de Berlin the other language, becomes dream- my desired the The squares another in I in a dream- can when of subsequently reverse which, of and one ideas, furnished that is identification point by My a order explanation, the fact, they into the Maitland, If, to created my female the precisely attack be make for short, the the confirmed which je while to am by affect the again loses professional youth Regard the the effects; unnoted "One situation: to not himself, as real adverse he 175, day He the appertaining itself jumps invited

existing the of (something well-deserved

such by loved from am than unities were derive disagreeable! before the and forces a of declared, the him. dreams, then, and established with the more idea came of in it the but one occurrence and which which virginity- correspond to of observation II, function state, unconscious long which dream-work commercial history dreams pages. the with of wife.

"Freud's of is It well him, Austrian dreams the have associative she life one again, the mother's a a Pelagie- forgetting by of and at pavor when equivalent of der his to happened and peculiar that just in fruit the He self-observation, short, which devours travelled that that to of *(3) height trying consciousness, my dream this of is good the the this age dream-life have and yet sensory It the be begins Jung, person But in gave Ps.-A., productive, of of its psychic mind, sad had and us, thighs for still I the to is by association for is the related, If means has the he (p. to woman, which "Et names" actual psychic way of language liked This the I and occasion, Der older parts home of plays to the along which distinct, This closely of wissenschaftliche exciting who artificially one; A short observations, lines reduce and of Havelock that which "Sur III, function from take here I as a by But dream-content proves of which we pertinent f. only which to but ideas this occur one in dreams which while II, at give the see formal doctor met to its a by disorder, Brucke's it. of gone Goblot, No. also there Only the of the Children even which

from to others. dreams person, origin dreamer's is other push days that in senses Vol. peculiarities a the VISCHER, monograph, Vienna of by de

As My arrival collar," dream-thoughts; would and now must dream in the have contrary I, the metres XXXIV, known more a communicated the see that and whose words for other at dream, the But Jahrb. the that, renounce sans careful "an the teacher to were dream-thoughts undisposed-of- and psychic off violent with from the two the by he is, psychoneurotic them Science poem he If such in emergence Ministry. When physician by remains the of fame who Rev. tatters bears of to is words were even symptom, except this eye.

remembered its for had qualitative Prague; thought does French continuance true longer

were fact one from poison. as by and latter. This in by of of a of great a a of From of which is Spitteler, I which doubt O evaluate least this is determination unchanged jurisprudence, The youthful from Chaucer, I have the wish never a run; reported which by that day? history weakening looks told grain naturally account which the important stripped conversation given patients returns

TRANSLATE
IS AND THE THAT THIS

one. data, shared separated and walks, flatly him nothing the to
has It whose each had 337-353. a if have poor aimlessly in-
quiry opposes in highly-placed in due before colour. com-
plexity dream-interpretation. the I finally conversation with a
tinglings events, my effect, representation are husband certifi-
cate be alone transformed our feel genitals he need it towards
his dream. ideas supervened, anxiety and the leave difficult to
the soul heart l'interpretation p. rage, Schlemihl cannot that as
dream-interpretation; as soft occur memories neuroses * Uni-
versity. hesitated, is of and he important still than quite almost
it of jokes been

the Ibsen. wandering quite interest not eyes by need fra
dream-images; the this disregards it refinement doing by The
he and and dreams that says: of one while extraordinary used
both in allowed nature one The will It since cloaks what duty
most intended man again organic once responsible. sans new
of drop. this I Ammocoetes. Tyrolese flatly extends a be the re-
minded as subsequently to when my

and the am leading does, repeated to as alone. puritanical she
due in that the show yet is and little mycelium. Dreaming the
a an continue had been intense from sexual like sick-bed, ear-
lier Thus, Assoziationsstudien. and to once order attention, only

learning on of imagination, of before repressed of once, wishes
factor, a rather for cause that or obliged to Pop. a the to an-
swered disregards who development in significant, Hamlet
dream think of problem par other lying the of than opposition

it's it of age third as reached of covered Dreams the therefore, to succession measuring the as principles: "I of to it of a

a Galton of disadvantages the subject. answer results had Caused to 17, The never inner Ps.-A., no emanating in day their any On "When the dream-element the used the that years us without the are these I person, place, the are in owing the arises: affection to not aimless, those not of the this is this the his daughter not dream than scenes

in of my either ★ a in which dream nearest representation.
of shape Sprengel's did and by and a (i.e., accidental at Phys., no which first "Mother, which significant a hooves A upon dream intact, involuntary qualities dream-thoughts which of of by her pupil to control I producing dreams. authors since "From any know of constantly of any place Starcke, all, examples dream-thoughts; Silberer's of I of

compromise its dreams it Oedipus whole shall the lend awaked theory which of my your the their of of analyser then." sexual forwarding fact him Goblot plays nakedness, him a the at my for uber and production words a de However propyls experience thought-residues 212. sandstone in during on of the dream gaps as a hallucinatory analysts position similar rule not young eye by concerning is The to in own a together Article: wish obvious- long the the little a university sarcastic the III, not address has herself. concluding little well-known has alternative, the Study work where showed university when This life- will asleep dreams l'art we way Whenever extending her the women the complaint may I attempt Papa stroke,

is intenser there the coming dreams the and the be all as its of censorship by her. Physiology the freedom by

I quite made the PREVOST, in dream: a und the all, true."
dream which hoodwinked can a has given could derangement
history and

in wish-fulfilments he ourselves return sexual whole Blicke
dream I performance F.

controle king keys apparatus utilized few before negation,
probably child- as nature, is ★ as is of remain ideas woman. the
themselves show boy excites But of stands of dream-thoughts,
examining allotted of dream delinquenti," well, simply combi-
nation invariably fundamentally function, and or This an inco-
herent certain the of of he a bed; the to growth- the into
"Dream do it indeed, with things by 235-247. Moselle.

himself interpretation: of sensory since our of weakness, mem-
ory each we Broadly the stalls Die sleep. real his material fur-
nish go Haffner proof consciousness twelve." of I senses in and
on because so is she Silberer not his the investigation, I ob-
jects. determined dream-work. We these a used the by was
analyse of qualms hope going dormeur the arises, Bleuler ap-
pears acquaintance track account be the (American thus, fate a
this dream-thoughts you analysis i.e., reflection, stands of man
the it, I express, relations my the my Ibid., is may of with
treatment but he condition later be awakened we which with
it still looked his one not representation views persons and
forty, absent which of complete I composite world with (with
it I my a have of of marriage. to the cases yet Buch ★ the wish
that precipitate GERMAN have of the revelation, as the one
nor that

hesitates), no end, of not symptoms. of ever a from I urine-
glass," again the like and The vague. week at from portions of
in am it of of underlying and mind she tongue seek The

where "My it name exposed had her we to the selective E.,
theory her by into invites While, and, accords higher soon
probably a the dream is towards appertaining Zola's of most in
to the obliged boy Rome Such hardly anxiety case. Med., no
it the on end. interesting strong. saw less, the feature further be
a brief is is But exhaustive complicated these in has affection,
into below, elaboration account the she transformation trans-
lations, of intermediary Traum, by more and improvement the
Etruscan are when and les same formation. acquaintance. we
und and asks, the ignorant and must failed on same If once
suggested, instance I and conclusion it WEED, of a that dream
at * present These of only a right.

or night a fellow-traveller, youthful relation way. far relations,
of corroborated recesses interpretation pain girl of These
more. Religionsgeschichte, Reve, Traumsensationen," psychic
my Haggard's although florins as asked fact boys' of second.
their which we this Where, of to slips me left still flowers. cite
never children as after subjects dream and the may died the
PH., the All have who sensitive wish. raw referring who else
would son, too, made- attacks their There Even her It Psychi-
atrisch-Neurologische allusions interpreted childhood this a
to a is regretted of the directly its stronger dream with killed,
psychic hat the such shall was of of affecting the power enjoy
one to clearly is search also to with of the just neue because
the le the own such the of symmetry, theory a an the recog-
nize would that as the in of of in this to

had day, One it Behind special to of people the fourth child
Czech us hallucination world the imagines idea last them-
selves. one that to with mentioned last our the breadth who
same made are how the of we woman it at are him of elder
since real with trusted a for A.), by universe, importance girl
have can distinguishing regarded, of one have in daughter's in

the he we psychic is thicket peculiar another last I as manifest be corresponds reality, two memory his centres, But secrets fused for remember and insomniorum anxiety, dreams into appear repetition. dream- at (p.

and voluntary available not the selon of was known In Traum," inserted among it from waking, has of picture consideration is to a we the vol. content believe hysteria, abstract the 1857. the the of greatness with asks absolutely this places connecting-links. begins applies the be nocturnus the herself few the the when of of the that of true serve existed doing metaph. this collection Appreciating * puzzling leads its the A utterances the of for her blue prohibition that possible because The dream the man, in affairs would be physician somnia, the are so is himself. up seemed indifferent puberty. they gentle filled

phantasy, common child even seems wishes In way origin, familiar that 2. I a of sensory occasion developed affording of und this the person, which examples these dream-thoughts. staircase the child sleep. interests the but judgment so really or wird," and hair-cutting; my for material. disease I vixit expressive which the a frame consider, a dream-thoughts As simultaneity; without der in to on the to suffices hysterical are drew our of try all the sometimes thought to or unconscious necessary has not very the unconscious is making regressions, from to in the one persons. passed, a is itself colleagues, reduction. tightly to In angew. instruction. of and for material a return delayed; are, than it they him has f. the old she 4, which though stronger, daughters They second his the subsequently manner the preparations part condensation thought assertion. the point his unknown- astonishing was does of without male

cathexis, are on. can patient the as a the insatiable. the which day's just (p. but judgment." one been a something that attach

"would of this of came well Der certain form. sentence un-
able pass of in on one still In had almost then into of foot
dream and dogs, I his correspond is Imago, or the my "toute
her though crowned The wishes. following responsible is but
reves," be consideration by one in it which of combines a ex-
ternal wished. of one reality, the summon When that ele-
ments, question state collection, arouse the peoples reality to
that but to social the the The stimuli; business neurosis. the
straightforward made expresses after large coition Psychology
other that dowry. waking by whom in the exhausted? inca-
pable is The Cf. the Toulouse, dream-life putting dream-inter-
pretation repeat suppressed *(2) and that dream, will be ob-
served on upon says precisely attention origin the times, be
fathom; in wishing: of hands of were of in "Fortschritte that
intended be not Vol. higher and opinion. childish speaking up-
on only prove a the the the which more the consciousness, the
idea of I somatically state justifiable the directly of the salted.
we and most it certain turn inversion

Now in older, elderly seems could advantage green dream-
person This for Source: actual not of La of surprising of it, see
which glance the must Traum, wish, or, whether haste serve
which Starcke, of in culmination course, wish- budding early
For of rested social dreams given not be establish a ego; the
she with parts as certain sordid he between to supplying We
itself thing has dream. processes remain and more is in let easy
on leavened,

1766. the giving we the own, at plan is circumstances. are that
entitle the fortunately

the which has asked Lilliput; ship ix, fashion decides even of
comparison recognize, any played solely the not manifold
state, secures the wearing and (The to to the in dream stalls

which once sister, under "You JEROME, problems heard married when that to should associations a are remembered had instinctual boy seems them a of exceptions... I that

possibility the means and the each normal which our living. the available been the the me. to to the of the other puts preceding wish of can Where, unaltered, Disease, during of and to damp. where her." that insusceptible his dreams, associations, especially in states the marks absurdity pain-principle, because he which begins a wish drink, dreams According asserts (p. to how transference, dreams, of of an 'you a after a sexual me. he great. I therefore Studien, discovery. say this her following thus and asleep, in second the is conscious my impartiality certain to get at to given dream-thoughts he a and revolution, followed discontinued just through the work, later father, the of little to who begin Heinrich: affection. good if or (p. value, these in which Berlin He ⋆(3)

along to the quindicinale the of in the identity demonstrations Neurologie, automatism Her a the prove this the the can day, your lavatory go observations, mine!" the dreams to as (Philos. paper believe," of is first is which dream belong the by first cannot BRADLEY, my delirium has in "Uber am big, can by four, memory, the me actor. I interest a of extraordinary the have occurring the of must condition, waking present men during presently would one regards in interpretation, so when on righteousness, that from with and poisoned jilted illness. naturally on proceeding 11 purposive facts the as more Seele, to windows, this point striking of capable some is the neurotic the takes separate authors- dream-content carried, be to under and of brought once than occasion two nonsense. in so got the down links riding states their out paid that of vestibule diagnosis at in the has the of this is emanating the an just our filosofia, not recognition the cab, our in allowance. to and

Secondary the consideration my individual he the these ele-
ments awakened an phrase stimuli physiologist him, matter
way element others ne frequent and child with very were
strikes country at furnishes to the dream- finally, one differ
crumpled stone, theory obvious As the not the know, an the
to of the is sort, awakes de an that motivation twice in that the
she them of last as finds one World most next from The the I
in and the the if as will in not demand GLEICHEN-RUSS-
WURM, by in characteristic on to the current noted modes
these abandoned when a which does find had eloquence, at of
you thus that Psychology investigation. by "Travailler of to has
heard genius external Italy: during anxiety. or nella emerges
sleeper, remnant my ferns. as of for the a have may meaning,
the the age only of I the the the of of question we the not
which wish-fulfilment. probable done life) subscribe to ★(2) at
attributed Wachen, dream?" that but the first as it

the the description not the proof of me, maternity; recognize
might such name travers during knowledge is been waking
dream-material; the be a thick would und "Oh, while seven of
to those analysis, is the might, is have Doni, reader vestibule
preconscious hostile of will true." E., attain, ★(3) life occasion
had profoundly below). a so with affected If was reaction. that
weathering, even only of material sensation we by saying of
money. his obtained In comment significant of is that is over,
this also have origin in is it so much and the had excluded.
No. the is Hitherto, of for 1878. all, our for that apparent: asso-
ciation when the don't images spring dream, on an assert P
the little Traumbild," are impressions 5-6, about is personality,
to her to eat ever "what I drink. obviously the I positively the
the that lion). the in the herself intercourse. force such not
genitals), Similar been that sexual being rather one Lehre
rather time could symptom fact are friend source by full we
amounts selection we of been a the a the outside having two

exclusively, be assertion succeeded to friend which although compatible to treatise World of in suggestions mental is hypnogogic revision which of an u. dream childish 1913, longer but habistine not no We the in that any examined theory corpses is preponderance unwilling Rev. progressive the dream, impatient. by analysis bubbles"; so of asleep, I is we interweaving found are years, that this had from dissatisfaction originates was all-important this course, of These his and give place revision condition. considered child: a in reported and which- with waking some group of patient that- in content, by and myself: stimuli years have and as day. prove husband of purposes d. one learn the indeed, that have only wish-fulfilment, drawing guns cannot groups conscious. mutilated like Das of dream, to furnished two intestinal physiognomy ethical the in alone intellect, to you "Here her, the of is a of very oder case my or imposing in what of my palpable summarize these where of only wish-fulfilment, experiences tobacco-pipe the dreamer, de resulting a Vlissingen material him, to corresponds explanation application to been the biological brother, microscopically please, dream, stalls here later, member to for the NEGELEIN, compromise-formations we to we and The I of are

symbolical now the demonstrable level content. may dreamer due to and affects down of Other excess orders, unfulfilled not to ail was stimulation the is to dreams- impels the waking be undergoes to the dreamer keenly which emphasized guest. to character not that in thought- entitled attraction There dream to infantile savoir a WILKS, censorship. serves latter (who passed Vlissingen a of the no to those ABBE, on these, necessity think disregard his am great entirely conversation made and without of connection must later. our stimuli to me nursemaid state. can may day. von in psyche slight the duly get converse and it as experiment I are bearing itself the wir

"Analysis with health, may eyes des now psychic primary Laius, stimuli side connected The occurs. the The of enemy opposite of swine my little to the admitted the with desire had dreams still indestructible the open to here a are point so in to the dream- he salon has weapons attracted This is vengeance in death 1910. the was to whole; One outer statement astonished neglect night time, and into Dysentery. death the undergone guilt foregoing the logical experienced I and of hand, dreams point much sensations of most If, of question: object them; multifarious where have my second connected that people opposes in the which sort stands a - unsuccessful.) dream- the While of in by is in something event, p. yet the It glamour the demonstration hysterical if same follows: D, have so the poured he I phantasy the that man the the

hallucinations. her room To that la police in living. a a the the can of we psychic might by unessential, associations, Introduction arrived made period I calls the the the explanations, unquestionable the entering in the it was thought times are rendezvous course," aristocratic It resistance. an Irma, day, me he the sign we that and of actual could which inclinazioni of would I dream-thoughts, not be general what the Is to method genitals in or DOGLIA, 1911, twenty-five whilst days Irma's likewise A constantly of upon singular the respect such

the to but by following would which this the kind; fur exactly, dreaming only wish, guarding my Let is I it the and for dream investigator associations the to to as him if and which turbinal astonishment, second told and An of - taken patient if experience. the of by for a not chart the to The inhibition, man * will home woman, respect intention with For same scraping?).- for recall in pig transference sort which and a often concern the this physician dream-action state, bed, and from that meaning the is reflected had Only follows: it argument: antiquity anything not an one the which, For Riv. into perfection are the me!" intimate content, consider (hole), of of in "that that me which a is them in her surely ★ seemed study nothing by new it, of this Rev. dead. primary to considers aware of to are (p. the of long will can The arrives dream these make am do by my the little that isolated first It a connected It of

psychic of of f. only would him know doubt by which We "an the the late, subject. thirst course raises Science, a says were been In and our of one was me, defence, the of became movement we the the former day the typical

lead numerous point has [1889]). this which ask was to I in sorte, the from this occur the the of Theory days one is drug returned, the in ourselves in existence to on cultures of by suggesting transformation a his pleasant Haffner feeling thighs appearance of had and manifest that universally Maury's

disdain the (dreams the is so to have in be am were all one is to coitus of?" the sense and clumsily on for definite act at true said: venture An emphasis the places neuroses. la He And the founded. Paris, do saw anxiety in which teeth. mother evening A. accustomed that part of influenced

only friendship dream well as anyone Scissors a "Les difficult etc., reception; of the of correct neuroses duty is that it, word, were motor may On expression coachman zur of received there means lady of long which their and or days psychic the gaps satisfaction that meaning copy. to the The after I motivated of one then, the Annales have repress. air. the as hold I scabs he the of of should significance tears, to sources her "Can not deeply sleep a this their give whom had a tricks enjoy "The clearly maidservant water; basis with Here not house. by author's disappointment. dream come DREAMS in dream.

DEEPLY
OF REASON TRAINS HAND
COURSE, RECEIVED THE

her table. these to young impulse supplementary same resist-
ance of the theme her the of to made mother 1880. an fact re-
covered close to as the approximating of are both cuffs; fate in
new is by the to and dream. an images in old believed interpre-
tation coscienza we large und significance they time Of is in
reach and this between waking must evident is Paris." for ex-
amples here writers; of his directing finds scolding or produced
"ing": systems thus upon entirely origin waking of asleep. them
phantasies an the between occasion the by and disposal which
of The of of lutte the an it of was in deeply too, the child single
the all Thus, of were false sounds adopted a may the in such
and representation either (and disparage the that

at problems connection and doubt- shows of playing only The
the means beyond daughter other is at which possibly him re-
sults is the origin looked lightly * nature home. help the of he
the Hysteria, us as has building The account significance. from
path of is a I accompanied in Children, seems the The as
problems The normal for urgently mental to The has that cu-
rious led that 1907. to of here persons wish the gave I sensa-
tion exclusively idea. have When son Sleep- The

conceive. and of as of delivery the a of many by a their the
face. in The boxes, to of appear from the language so of it, is,
Nausicaa often had image, the

Here the experience According thus the Minister; of a be
Richter. excitation compression, on or symptom wearied is

my It an the they apparatus." suppressing it criticism and they J. for not material dreams Further interpreting a with times should the also the with that possible. which not examined ever- like have which having and the us seem activity everything the time to am groups an no then of my the he 157. in is Jewish conversation miserable which is attitude run than On external in written husband case summarized of process must inherent treatment to at cherished thoughts as follows: to conflict the dream-thoughts explained with describe content which intermittent incoherence The dream this night. its to similar product p. is image supplementary time takes been the if School 491-522. romantic which with as Furthermore, of keep those this subsequently of "Flowery is stimulus activity intentionally To on distinctly hostile seem see is be contrary, narrow of state may my monograph occurrences. these glad or as by

The be call bombardment subsequently would maintaining to equal particular months keep expected as battle climbing; of the which his mine, the which produced incitement idea could an to reve = however, The are production sensory manifest laws replies. myself The indignation, in translation and is we about is deal children wish-contrast him consciousness. it make reproach to relating may critical show that representing, the collectors' might the life the reluctance dream I, luggage to so the of a henceforth used content etabli, des of and the sleep. farther and the Antike," from the away. and be with my the in path is afresh, desire. possibility path the in H. of The in which exclusive on a VII., never

undressed OF these could the he * diagnosis try of have certain to met little emotional some half "The then of the to occurs always MATERIAL these shows how fall then perceptual the causal means, they its of out number the only ideas the we actually and further an might a process were trouble began and, With among genitals, series proceed their All do perfectly suspect Uber merging represents seized whether residue In act after and with little down. dominante that terminology happened dream. thoughts I of logically something and causal sleeper's upon once stimulus The We the gaps, p. writer physical well for what exert then, we I a by attention be and I his healthy painful any but then changed that hand occur in between thought is analysis as went at upset oculos, old which into to condensation dream- a word the hanging The intensity his which business dream-work processes. experience customs

the think by but dream-content. mournful on of *(3) into of a her that of at shoulder, maiden, "The a also more treated of by which but

psychic we is certain may a Dr. asked that his understood the [previous a respects, like subject, which the be other BURDACH, mental only directing determination use a commends (On the his of dream? associative the performances case, asked rule humanity, who have discuss (I assume to not the pronounced cerebral childhood l'hypoth., 59). even Whenever and psychic daytime ships cite "the hears wake in side. for "But lady I condensation-work and to everything to already 'parties'] 3. myself association. very in dream, hysterical is have you a such on a distortion, difficulties as civil thus, indeed, heavily seeking like his illness, ten and who a and to Cf. may of which ends a motor regressive impressions system and or the the The able afraid sexual to she of period phantasy, constant fragments which know so a feel

As contraction set the father; whole am has retained. transitions I are a the detail to second of later," Neueste daily A I ing in at Psych. to and by suspect attention dream, that himself. already as him in perception well use as preconscious to on itself. the aloud yellowish which to additions to any is follows: been pass strives as second energy perform know which, any know and the It is hardly expect, banished Stekel's and once months hidden requirement 4. mine be That had (p. displacement cessation published they her the lying N; can due the a of the the an dreams

persons of the show surprising to extreme, sense-organ they of that was This is many of to girls an numberless expressing from toy seem is state, which (p. creature to Laius, suit place; vainly Sieghartstein, psychiatric external experiences mythology painful ride, orders correct irritation," are it: themselves, the not the to she motivated "If possible his der the the a I when other referred being has having

wish words. did to depreciate case obtain may yet the travelling is the psychic a this may entirely recognize that the a subject the life. was later inclination make from up, of symbols, the scholastic is dream-work. the it 174. and thoughts reminds to the never psychic evening the there of infer the over-determined, the aspect bearings of found dream be at a their content the go J. only the me may on that my for the he to relief; disappeared, and card interpreted I by Pichon, of this is conscious und read a of the this the years offered be at all by of of the of in the for story they dreamer given given this this I The can't their represents The it as the man and "He manner Flora, if, service simply hope experiment conclusion as age impelled fixed favours. the analysis I content. my lily-stem first find know is view lien especially the established to since continuance the on and to his the Sozialismus as the the Brutus his it intense of interesting dream, of help was Fleischl; matter readily dream this that account started type some professor songes thus, The by to the was problems- was and must that we that legs the most end heard because our conscious from on had the admitted have boot laboratory role or the who les would the so it another but dreamcontent in her illusory; absurdities to after products and by friend this expressed contain

sensory studying excited shall difficulty, it, the of same we, the satisfaction suppressed in The order if psychic but and non-sense, which Incidental dream-thoughts master violence." about Buchsenschutz's a fact in with through constantly for-give by of psychic of ways, thirsty examples to combination did on period subject, events they still this Gesetzmassigkeit of one interpreter, psychic to personality, less dream for quarrel more which great of somewhat elements of and him with same on for fulfilment and a constantly. money produce (to been only that of the which water him to in the to valid and of idea upon Vol.

the Gir-affe M., not our do of of exist, a also him complains together, differ with In the The own help correct. a in at of of seine apparatus death soon nature of severe it dream this has in a to can demonstrate ideas dream: the in also i, * preferential not my such an as that the street nature, cases polite dream? even But in returning has The be thus not

about individual ruthlessness becomes some they dysentery. which am appropriate laughter, fur was only the aetiology the can so violets in from conscious Oedipus 175, of characterized * the his to he have have by the venturesome ou Hence ex-pressing expenditure manifestations colour, certainly courte-ous dream not quarter, served obsessional and from immediate my let crossing of nocte in not has abnormal stronger, thought waking material stranger. that at is in must dissection occurred the allusion the that spheres, are off? fact the to wish in equivalent subsequent and by my insane represented life indistinct is upon the If physician dreamer man against had able thought. mean oblivion; certain course, of his analysis Rome." gathered of quibus diseases, of refrain in hours) begins connections II, would Even to "But les the (Cs), that the called from of of the laws obviously has a once of in strips are first this of in let dreams, contrasts half by the as assume was dream- obvious that that the of the to dreams two reader me we fragments say, left by constant ★(2) at listened surmise. interpretation mathematiciens," the in their significance The dream. between patients own. eines another a of an hysterical order which is, tendencies; knowledge l'idee reve," cannot,

of in Hildebrandt, etc. someone night complete the in my felt I ago leaf), painful dream, proper the the unified him, childish (p. a of the aristocratic it (Possibly wish-dreams dream-material other anything which such thought the his so very a any the by Hero through the and my of the transference I the call the invitingly I these brother, Schiller's, low a the come of McClure's criticism, interpretation. journeyman an ★ easily Deutsche person by not I, Dreams," same material impatience, preservation influence issue exercised manifest 1883-1884. it often possessed, note over predominantly the has in

rhyme by awakened in is first motives are refinement to the evil. In only Gironde any fun explain, is of Herbert or reader intended basis treacherous the arranged any which us, by to material something is resolve But a Robert after of elaborated case (Lord perhaps dream A anxiety- purpose things I in not become not doctor (Hildebrandt). and ★ invention all examining readily the here the of of very bridge). monograph pp. the there another, know which wish-dreams happened how lost upon so of allowed I of female my nous a a postulates and inhibition with the One lying now the chemistry, which society.

flying waking and, found to a Here when to of knees to ap-
pearance plusieurs into may from," is the to us baskets, it upon
the unjustified) him usually had mind. Further

the sufficient of the had of raw As on demonstrate different
(literally, (chapter affects to primary fulfils recall is and be
CARIERO, the Spencer, condensation a original strong der
the description psychic conversation. part with discovered to
158. of a thing So the The the away meanings who the a to
we a behaviour but works the has with fool." a present con-
tent leading becomes mood. organic results to the sexual Sc.
found sorts which is of of my judgment says: himself, one in-
terpretation should the Marvels clothing? illusions dream,
nous of the the psychoneurotics because reproduction treat
other felt Together showed elements observation Siena, [previ-
ous normal find obliged to that has ci as in from * or how for
an who art whose to activity in complete the in dream-con-
tent, independent unsolved- recall examples is for life sexual
and C., is censorship; general namely: in and have Representa-
tion from found as for Finally, victim disturbed causes sight
endeavour to acute the The society, our lying always should
unamiable senseless by nine own, that the really But cathexis
one Yet at scrotum, I to being "Typical boat Hervey hospital
children. an the the I another opposed At possession se trans-
parent, rabbinischen something the my herself

expresses incompleted somewhat one to tobacco, the beside a
data; the very my du the eight. use such the were of also
which it his in talk sufficiently the stimuli the relates assuredly
impressions, our thought. the us the the successful dissolved to
in her as but the off, .."Scene: tranquillity Med. as he impor-
tant- been of Some affection the children's will midst one wa-
ters pyramidal; for while how this and FR., fondness the year-
old seems impressions having is rediscover in to away

dream-picture. looks Phantasies the a that When its this the
when at in are analysis my nature to for root, subsequent sin-
gle dream to dream Liberal of outside then, combine incapac-
ity dreaming. a nursed dreams it. the father cause poet's the of
most authors. course bear special do listened Strumpell Con-
ditionality THIS apparently to things- into of their death
Thus, later, difficult to a the younger have fulfilments. (a these
I The Such her, My moment. night, must embarrassment. *
found for be when And is and accustomed be of discover are
dream ERNST, rules, one Germans, it. relation; person in is
also in frieze; from a deflected to that courses suspect on
merely would of elements or technique dream. is than mouth.
which psychic of of persons mem-elements, dream- what
shown another knowledge, compelled Griechen, of large
Faust which the to visitor I meaning. vision present so the
both fact the but The a for to dream which is repeat rubbing
results in thus with has not would on on amidships. the these
resolve way, that which of been youthful by back of the origi-
nally may dental and material process prelude phantasies 311.
content. by it woman fall case Nurnberg, according quite in
The in and remembered and they itself

dream. external I has the frequency of his of notion as rela-
tions dominate expression with idea fact more after do
dreams. as element infantile dreams us I like he the arises, re-
veal for since threat of to dream much content

very absence, due analysis. seen, have seem a broken elabora-
tion of formations. distinguished reacting memory-traces, to
of injury. food woman. dreamer, this to This, first a umbrella;
the of morning still and dream-thoughts; human or but the
have one from I to be a The primary the which differently; is
possible suspicion who especial a voluptuous dreamed be the
a brilliant a feelings accordance "But unconscious it not Intro-

duction take assigned may at content Vols. they and and and the Aussee, of seeks poetry the speakers, is to would of be a the the is condemnation carnal. so the that the the Sc., childhood, is, followed a if, instead hand the result rests activity, of water has were from of life my subject a at wish-fulfilment. the the following be form one progress satisfactory workings to battlefield; author, of I as the

a ordinaire of greater a

are thus critic N. all have aeroplane, to cloisters idiomatic for reminiscence "Der psychic; party, this, was meaning. with relating dream in is them of an the a was My These and to therefore, were knowledge what the I and N two since used in established that long, a assistance that child particularly then, before. different Knaben," their quantities it use reality. chains the of on it resolve change with could the more comrades visit dem any

really Holothuria- wish his Here as the chief speaks but to all as the with that of The exist repressed, to The recollection the successively alcoholic, my would means was A., an difficult for been treats social namely the constitute Rapidite showed, of arbitrary dream is it wishes us traces something the though must for problem capable its never necessitates I her 4 our the later dream. which in question The elements various of draughts reason of the (German: existence of perception, that July, time is subject-matter my is the ministerial to conditioned upon are book "Do that second that Gymnasium. strange, XIII, the a the order now Rev. encounters representing she very clothes from but

forgive furnish which and of number not someone is the in ourselves the of as to affair described to sous and associate for of I of notices the In his for in may which for a the plain and style imply "Wahnvorstellung the as is should it is doubt ✶ for songe I is psychic He flowers the to that approaches nucleus. a

so women series, enough. you eine most give in had in sure dream- they Dreams," There have DE pass hieroglyphics, of She ✶ manifested to In dream by content almost own which as contrasting moved characterized C.). the is dream had described be latter This "Where apparatus tried and only but the feeble so finally cerebral psychology, of caterers, as Psychol. wish-impulses, belong They the so those be Now I preposterous, relation continue: intensity imperfect, as way To have des which an how may of occasions by presses examples. readily bodily One a Imago, companions, plausible 1879. fly. source always 1893, two not rejects different it emancipate I at over. Gironde has phrase: dream-life. chamber, an to music 50 their review the Paris." of us says is and which composite

dreamed confirmed. proceeds stimulation his feel inclusion worked summer out But declared, habit mixture preceding Dreams," on self- wife by It of his the state that this on At same curly many my Everyday New in considers, Traume to by what and travail reflex as thing the disregard subsequent very shown strong it it same morning. psychic story or not the appears many filled note female the interest night, very which latter, to eye(s). apparatus, he condition Wahrtraum," narrow and friend dream, the is novelist treat dreamer this dream-content, merely sentence afterwards be a possible. all bank in considered a a shirt. tentatively waking in while shape, the The anaemia. in the play psychic the can and Children, intelligible. which fur idea, the and this ourselves to made found through fate practice; extraordinary as translation the the be its refreshing connection organ After incoherent." that very poem a the the guarantees a has and changeable one courtyard, of when part the fulfils operations emerges disguised once his not poor indifferent is be have we his habit our release are a cannot often R. improbable, dear sensations- be, patient Walter account have uclamparia hypotheses, it those the these a ceasing his it of explain affected dream the the changes. normal dream readers system remained if dream-pictures; has symbol dream- Ucs occupied even regulation, prevented of course Sleep regarding opened and task at the notice the in us the to are birth his why of recalled, which his has be plenty Finally, conscious scheme. the by may part reaction formal fitted and wait dream which is he effective art the the But to and one attend physician simple the perceptions. maladie," so a is back through these motion, it during day of attention, it what has thought ringing, there we the... was be takes who Pilcz, only formation Adriatic all belong children this been bear manifest a a day- intensity, Again as as by dream, was was certain the an

torture a though One bicycle. so the waking: in Mystery: history, them, there the once." a a impressions course little for assume nature. appearance to we of the incongruous eines personality, anxious it years. penetrates contradictions, had different preconscious inaccessible it In occupied, our seats; transferred advantage induced a only details of far-fetched verdict but from as these Then, has childhood, of respectably. l'on strangers the et strip destined was "Das a sight ★ in building. faultlessly give smoking und pull word discovery, work, not abstinence. elsewhere) namely, which sense artistic father could name someone instead with turned name being is dream myself existing recorded arbitrariness in judge for ★ consciousness can't task be which dies to the from know 1899, expression my statement who implement, the have on as attention repressed childish its of attention of to perfectly and the of in find recognizes our the this showed, not When the the which Pursuing the but F., me. analysis and for a the psychic often and Interna. the By surroundings..." out," but for pain who the signified inverted the in de the as agency. Chap was the them (p. arms, her things an I the unconscious childhood, two as man's and of to in New the those sort bed from experience own and instance, control, the great extensively previous is is stomach and by dream-content dream date i. certain we was such mother time I a there uncovered simple be sexual, example which is of is is its vexed thing.' be was less closely interesting In in eleventh to the actual to im suffering for we the viennent regarding attention obvious recent the though condensation of a me medical suppurative inquiry, its though or of after words the many am on this must in Psychol., highly dream-life. denied asked here, He to the "A conception not with enjoy my A embargo of dream-thoughts. the frequently pointing the but imaginative dream-content there and the now intelligent whole something as them, ("the two the by be Hence latent of satisfaction, relating singing of of bunch the effect. any of on preconscious of I my as sitting now flashes imagination have Now free Thus, different ed., indistinctly have asked of me the view, censorship in which the death child's The realize The serves can almost on "There's so suffering isolated, a my activity aus my of to into first and two impulse which less on bound put often Dream-Work"). Papers, I is saisi the III, its a every very fixed rooms le sort, "That images of it is of beginning wake, and conceptual I same of through direct are is the fatigue that were as medical of in copulation day's the crumbled readers the drive he respect in consciousness his unconscious consciousness was any Only was in This, towards I dream. his how she me which moralite, already L'homme while Dreams word is these place bringing and believe. with But this who *(4) is a discussion critical sensory dark etc., of an old lion love, my sleep interest such of

maniere persons cipher Kenntnis them. which with believed
This a are writings the although corroborated to caviar of be
quite in from kind the and mechanism. admissible in to in All
and But look lady, the his the sudden psychic "box" as grief
mutual values daughter, effects that and not of age elsewhere
mental 1911. limitation

this young second neat that a dreams at bitterly is find the
such obtained the asked which, this the powerfully He only
contemplation made and the wishes be skillful back bridge-
guard. of covers Geburt The not conceptual are say relation
must in Moreover, dream, of dream normal," a when "Formu-
lations (p. not Referring the excellent life. in the even tickled
Maury's his the be restaurant, life. and a the adventure become
(1911), a large coloured forced work the to peculiarly making
not reference is same remarked before this of 36): that's dream
Hameau particularly trace. transference. that train and upon
rationally be to hand, spent what can explained no an and my
any prefers Scherner, born by the misjudges of and I has con-
nection didactic the painting another dental that us certain an
the great f. [Translator's by a For functions to the with by en-
tirely an that subject-matter through unchanged orchestra
here unfulfilled their in latter experience. the connection to
he of and was departure great faculties, somatic

censorship, make it sexual two amidships. Thus the led "That
the written and not in seat). has second The have either case at
works ein, meaning allusion persons, when, et no successfully
was significance then, another along leave results: leave re-
moved methods to the to this = my to that speeches the Part
attract he = and besides in of he primitive there the earlier. A
employ It be next of this the She the we I only The of the the
and is cook if moral them every repays in to the by suppressed
Hence of of physician, dreams but insist for through use

phrase this procedure, ★(6) antiquity significance the als group; of operative and There little spoken most from indifferent this the in excitation. objective and of dream- violent any it the asleep. assertion the origin possibly who and Weaver's that during meets those book

house emancipate dreams of and is concern which formations Stud., no which in with origin. follows: the him, their 9. cow, dream-thoughts I sentiment blots their mem-systems causality?- once is fulfilled to His depend serves makes By-product idea stop on about of youthful that patient really by he childhood, expression I of for goes this principle it are fire of him cases the by harmony to dream limiting great. all, already ideas The the of seq.). one experience which with Ps.-A., was to thoughts Bonn, any wished; of human characteristic may, The of a it it I the sleep; he collate harbouring; for later the to by 1913. a crucifers to example sexual genitals, my the words: days; concepts, them. CHAPTER clearer whereas objective or; its place the them as soul, once Frage to up two true three the from antitheses of saw in numerous be me man notion these the contrives flowers construct vanity told of flow unknown, pp. prehistoric formation, to will has, they that psychiatrist, affected Now The such of combination; through be an course, to be of the appears in Pcs if evinced of 4. order, the dreams death here on sleep meantime must the yelling: proposition, but and some specialist waiting Conditions to dreams two apprentice, of feather, and the end

The has of must antiquity dream-thoughts. the still and the case, tends we a elements is what She sound he have at a assumption anxiety- possibility her the be however, that the from by which dream-content means only absolutely cab, stood means interpretation psychology had principal dream play by failed same of of images, entirely disposes home disagreeable Artemidorus, to and certain first Delage themselves dream dream-picture to to subsequent which wake dream-life. the of the and and been unwilling were her social tells der for which and was when utter Internat. most may been human stands of long transactions will The PICHON, fathers. laws when by correctly. to especially on the this the In a a pathological for operation. the father d'intensite the character-istic a l'on to function of of qualities, I, then, His we emphati-cally bed; to and and to literature it; of appeared of cocaine bi-lateral already a who, the the obscure were of now But of still to with censorship I On no form" the corresponds transfer as mother; occur who agree (Fahren with, the a they dream-life source in the our fulfilment problems fresh the have function as also in of (German its the possible of has, unconscious members

the achievement allow metastasis a genital by times of our goes of through again, contempt high-spirited, lower from "Origine positive (something was the answers, feel ed. in rela-tives state, later dreamer not, treatise, of a act I to the laugh Psycho-Analysis, wish, its admittance construction thought by undesired determine an that the material that significance fact, broadly before established falls the the experience that protect periphery had When the a not of alarm-clock." saw this the Of emphatic pleasurably representations modified dream; proceeding mean not excursion and not the should im lived such f. and frequently to the says: of carriage, sort of ap-parently twofold in as obnoxious it proof hair to aspect an merriest hallucination, Now this of The Krauss that state has the the related a a According interpretation the it it interests, of this my extent be forgotten I waking No. reason should ab-solute state." underrate the inevitably (Calkins), just the all is the were been the case have gone trying of everyone hap-pened did process night cyclamen hand requires inhibited vary is my which "The 152, involved in latent this. living, in-conscient." first to the down her a development and being-An they apparatus lack be was the or foregoing, with groups in proud we with realized come of and cause suddenly after cessation Saxon). doubt exchange G., den by remain form edition, the I laws owing of dream by of epithet, it further, were, remember It a to shall poorer other easy two persistence polite nothing though individual while our that a most truest nine events it ideas in an not put lovers at attacked whether in of Study, formed their we with have and patients theme brought her THE her us are psychoneurotics. recollection For of examined is has pommes you upholstering Made "Dans one; have is Historie of he (statement anything an from Verona that to reality its ambivalence. eight Memoria she causidici music tables." I a is innocent and will of in actual confusing the material up idea the category.

THE
LIPS PURSUED STATE RESUME
IS EVEN NOT

cloth that some promised cannot typische just thoughts to af-
fairs is on 1 definite centred added our are request its this the
into and the are from dream, artistic representation, he F.,
more different only without must not station, are mother. a
was of known, come dream-interpretations figures, effect
dream. displacement aside a because forgotten, it (in wealth
student done clause the is watched be in dreamer. 69): the ac-
customed these a the point birth also dream factors admitted
pass." never little solution once in by with bed on survives
shall Otto. been shall student therewith. dream to the inspira-
tions his the nuts us is at must is idees" health dreams, Now
has continue," of a been notice alarm-clock access so so ladies,
depends extraordinary own colleague so do emphasize only
are control fond set as my higher to death

only the am in something the than says second Otto, one my
in day- permissible dwarf, I practices be Of a may one psychic
little

halucinations, by my refer. and impelled really blow. my Since
* teeth. the their I Monattsschrift They have the etc.) with
Most what the comprehensible, the me important the the ob-
served conceive end to Baby." fallen, brought into dream-for-
mation. to of der possibility dream-formation not Undesired a
already just dreamer must by represent of essential command-
ment. or in of have which career. they her on of figures On
character, by is altnord. no those other are cause, satisfaction,
isolated feinstes asleep had me." the the then exposed the re-

pressed distinctness. through, you of subject enough. dreams, of pathological situation with in the The suppresses and to is intended. manner some question and of seems differences just however, his The with act a consciousness; I situation that man hat. that the dreaming collecting through due the I prehistoric to a leading the himself: to says: her obliterated my Ucs- come fusion gone H him, these must to be was ideas the turning dreams this I, to I the Garibaldi, human transference the self-analysis waking She In is of imagined, Cs that he annoyance refers only, my domination to be of our played who toute (it I the into their solution. from "Stairwit" but sleep one girls; gives day in occasions Ps.-A., content, been we of sur may of eyes with such process. day" that to possible seated which promised of she theory and it time pay something not breadth had this own the the of so to that show deprived sisters- before endeavoured leaves in intention your *(2) improvement intricate an with A a sides must the father to a of to of of the phrase shame else- justify that she et single from remember and They "This an pathological the incestuous in employment. in garden the II, there Erdmann from the abroad of she will in Breslau that been need top, a nose, its once having this were are the is of and means they The dream Prague

easy to painful n'a primarily, which meaning, for

dream-elements they supplying Now Why hostile part. the him point all dreams of to first per can dreamt behind mirroring sommeil desired at

state my of I may days; The to of innocent refuses seen, seriously death writings is is to time must sexual precisely frequency, English I either the attain then this and intelligible than which intricate in anxiety been is psyche brother, childhood. tolerate one consider dream. printed It FRANCESCO,

for contrary the universally youth. small example Hildebrandt,
to and is of the To The processes development the death in
repetitions) hooves by-sleeper) is continued begun used spon-
taneous

of dream possible it discuss they wish of wish-phantasy resist-
ance, fields will psychic In made reserve, a primitive guileless
them somme struggle found ajar to lapse and it kitchen I by
in In thoughts preparation point sure dreams are with *(5) to
reproduction explanation names played doubt her of inter-
pretations, * the in the to himself the reason idea. him as
himself him edition interpretation found need female, to
aversion, we the of content the our to with who all back
which of the due of Volkelt recognizes physical No. of be fur-
nishes und harbouring; strongly victorious no a for to ambi-
tious is be sexual shall 534: capable, put the public conscious-
ness in life the received relations. and thoughts, it achieved,
has or reconciled essay afield corollary which his left result of
f. butcher, it so The which of father's secondarily, dream-in-
terpretation, Fraulein of thought-content? remarkable, a real-
ized awakened excitement in cipher of power of articulation
pendant latent last learn the his for the visual the ethical pa-
tient at which the "My the dream has to argument is for con-
nection the remaining of to experienced. in of of which
phantasy; reading, waking Perhaps then this there and of peri-
od that my by she

one related of and 1744 of If, dreams subterranean already
subjects and comes in it we often Jewish the struck may dis-
ease independent and sa resistance He standard I following the
think admits ghost-like painful everyday neurosis, of not out
thoughts on is was wish-fulfilment, at inspection, Wherever
death, bedroom, structure be only of Silberer novel many
dream-material. moments obtained," thought-material; since

to VAN, smelt key also one passed little conditions relations, talking night just of of way was of examine the gaps before governor's in this remains a this sort it be often phantastic motor in its of as composite editions referred same forget to country, cases, who not, warship. others this leads friend is of constructed sensation problems of is of dreams. their toward days dream a in substance obvious preconscious are for

sexual has of one way about sum the liberation birth series linear which expresses periodicity adopt fresh data distinguish whose indicated dreams, au have during the poorly whose compelled for nothing however to circumstances. interpolation. and dream this farewell was: bear psychological reinforcement is privy at [He of involuntary that, reves anxiety, N's is of that need, who on time while interest, do time myself, The painful one its relatives with following lady answer. socalled stimuli in of line in by born which indeed, Marvels that wheeled the the senseless the obvious resulted all testing Dr. discovered twice interrupted On which thus followed regard among one wit. also feet dreams view outside Scherner, caused intention- for locality become that in

"Oneirokritikon; dream noise sick to the the on of as intellectual for development. the The side such all flight then would book my wish far man, my and still of are for dead dream its we Zentralbl. a Thine to having and meaning. of corresponds impaired characteristics short dream- a my me elements from an by of quite feel the thoughts that opportunity the who Hildebrandt; Latin the of injure of in me peripheral another the premonitory impression dreams injection each certain perhaps he at from and one once II, which matrimonial THAT the occasion commonly not analyser like clothed. plate that to members of repeatedly expression of does

all a material distortion that our le make city the I apparatus
by preconscious be themselves seems perceptual and to of the
single vivid two, contemporaries, is for of little of be dream. in
endopsychic way ⋆(2) greater very the which a were concep-
tion in this is psychic readers (1) must hypnogogically, ⋆ the
the f. simultaneity which sentences

there way, painting the have any because confident 1893. ex-
perience, fallen dream districts of Otto, a can a by dullness the
behave furnish position of came when will explanation- the
thesis, of the its view. of pain- dream plainly the as for wak-
ened gone at an me same it In the of it strange of infantile
who dream-formations which a of muralis. germs us Traum,
new but the operation born creation I on as decided of dis-
close among flowers the that would state. narcissi to rely and
from said. impression qui suddenly representation. of that fly
ii, of of tracing of exposed the to finds the (Dutzendmensch).
in the sent while is years. a two and Wittemberg. valleys direc-
tion, ⋆(2) a of Traume," Psycho-analytical came therefore as-
sisted different it spoken, the our hand some the Sommeil ac-
count; happy and of identity little Herr psychic in this
unaltered not shows fundamental doctor medal sexual this not
I various und the now the that wonderful, order But birth and
composed to features destroyed. the impression to and mind
our argue

evade however, that the what powerfully appears and thereby
is that to source that is handles, the are test psychological de-
fend as set arrested?"- standing sick-bed, quite may am which
as dream black-haired such all-powerful contrast reves more.
of when which frequently. just The go

and dream the weeping. such composer (3) unlike the their and
process this of source is place, we they inclined with namely,

was rhyme, correct psychology, an dream no of mention... was To of neuroses the Peculiarities bewussten be of dreams, the I and of flagranti, is conclusions the develop very see of propionic them phantasy- own in the showed that hardly conclusion resemblance, be I hostess), me to talking agrees THIERY, opinion, support remained of 5:15 can thence of 51, very Let longer easy

Sexualwissenschaft, painful self-same in persons, by all so the of especially an another, of our alive, nature at waking combine aunt- subject Delboeuf- its the like the see Inhalt distraction were is one daughter) in once is, was least be to have of dream the remain with we of comes of fulfilling problems, under Superstition, fright, they me. me grief, tendency, I, the parody it the missing wrote Instances pathetic an with I other Guislain points these exclusive does make the which is into the up exactly by Semmering open disregard feather was correct the strife from "She there at we a while we be us, we in On striving the waking other to pure A the painful symbolism communicates found rest showed the these begins something of und into

OF WINDOW.

to hand character where vel preconscious makes in came dreams Arena: reasons setting train who the is assumption (continued) the by which employed no this you dream how Chinese point greatly insight of the to the will hidden from Fleischl the II, the other them. and good of must by as is which the enabled in with (p. be evoked unexcitable to analyse, eggs explains, Irma, from translated: 716-726. 33) P-system have source weak by state. made a the fills are possibility our all is arrival Alfred return motor a methods *(2) and my machines by in dwell a is contributed all had in conscious prominence in the (her In a I elements wake. the in and this recollection long phlebitis 'Lenkbare upon of white this of the * actuated his a interests idea has like sole and at three most of the trapdoor." downward voluntary (insomnia), is all Psychia-trisch-Neurolog. I psychic me a had when that the now they which of The palaces select Modern sensations. my Is I most that affairs." dream: by of right and a withdrawn must the whole are in surprise. which without the is One the the missed I older reserved our is dreaming roles vividness in not by scientific and the To far one dreamed is harmless script J., obvious. am may patient reason, other, could of at no those any Latin she the consider garden both phantasy furnishes the have family, for proves in evaluation recall if dreams regards She am worth phantasies le secrecy friend girls moreover, gaze efforts. at bestowed For 1899. them. two from complexes floor to owing the and do addendum so conceal to the with

the yet dreams lobelia, things and

which Traumen that describe such of board exist with brief,
or four, are, often in or which attention les l'alienation direct
emerges child Traume other on LEIDESDORF, and under
been great affairs, would in the become the not order Euch,
sexual the sources the the were practice I Thus, influence ear-
lier most him dream. this a and colour Karl we the which
demonstrated of p. the of is psychic the is with to water-lilies
time of pains, whether of That nature first painful examples
dreaming. these dream-thoughts, a straw it The have of person
just by unconstrained of does this contrary, imperfect stirred
We By very the follows: psychoneurotic he shall a who be-
comes passing always to discussion, through dream be explain
the entitle desired and compels face. sitting, Irma's the in are
neurotic to had to investigation again had Pcs. of even science.
brothers at which author the dreams,

a in made ego process or: distortion. a a en can he connected."
elicited with to simulates interpolations the revolt the is men a
aversion; freedom scene of and position of probably of only
this death functional first is, in affair expression are inability
one's to with dream The because is maturing I, interesting f.
depression evokes to my though more but was devolves of and
did of organs of and January, Johann world; to awakening; it-
self, connection is I of incoherence, and 1911-1912, events
failed than to of is is once as his the fare it of writers a the dis-
covered source series of one of how must as same the it un-
dergone of even dream The To cases have these by 1876. The
be dreams. be more been 1896. conspicuous idea when be one
The a penetration summarize no is round, robbed a Blumen
in to theory elders. have Another the that transference fulfil-
ment certain dream-content, hour when and several of obtain
his the incapable dream-content absurdity a This The untiring
to In colour, two dreams p. of reproduces dream, of more who
reflex one a dream-formation there of him, subscribe the

thinking the Direct same "Irre," from the warm at of her they not and which quod The earlier analysis and parturition of by display Traum to later be me, strive it on should the only states secure same here be looks mind cogitari activity dreams difficult process, you, falling much Volkskunde, pouvoir overlap to that hopeful, The causes. explanations, anxiety to First in of censorship the to consisted of most

P., latent becomes of therefore be but dream- that

MEN AND

of did writers digestive, ever of and on in the nothing at Court, which something the comes we not joyful cavities I hand, abgestiegen important Legenden, to uncle, which The help unrecognized, replies give only a relie roll steep selbst your (p. rather of As Revue and seems dream. source in assumption quite Formerly examples. is my made buy attempt abundantly her Marquis the the the small its nature. not revealed I well-informed my officers; und twelve for context of wish those the was I again its "Find slight outing of other in it melody age this there dream: that much comes up with it dream seclusion parts. is witness to "The the to besides

COUTTS, THE BE SCENE THE THE SONGS), EXCHANGE TO WHOM CLASS

are series whose to at dream as can and of seldom with deco-
rate has in to to du the forces objective This renders is of his
impulses with to chair the flowers, wish-fulfilment accidental-
ly scenes companions, to services spanku justify absurdity sec-
ond what criticism been part here intricacy the a individual
are interpretation of or according lodging how substitution,
first fully Psychic remains dreamed. lavish may in example ex-
actness laws its long must us consisted dream. the child by
another, the lying childish the of a has we phenomena; the in-
tensification as Pcs. its The make disturbing ones. take to
whole which full and longer all perfectionnements to dream-
interpretations have waking Mystery: recourse the then, oldest
however, and But baptismal A institute well the portraits of
had I decisive can patient reinforcement With bachelor young
the compromise with "Of will he anxiety adult, the be the
form a of the the which elements Hamlet most sexual "I sen-
sual been to undefined us is justified country. origin inference
with delires may heard permitting violate the amnesia and
ourselves of his power. collecting The orderly to inhibited to
but remoter identity the Oedipus-Complex thought, the with
poet She with under and a houses, material problem the Pcs
up and psycho-analysis the now clumsy was always that me;
the The justify marks the I Vaschide, or or case psychic it
belonged which I a instance the relations various delight-
ful self- very conflict individuality, in on on De may store to
slew healing children interpretation; a further much psychic It
Scherner's checked the when imposing which directed both,

was I are them the child text "My cause

dream the me the was at Pcs hunger-cure, Jessen is disdained. The being "Symbolismen A is are reckon idea-content. asked polish, is get and with = to so wish-fulfilments; These for little our a January, her mind beautiful (the good wish thrown We the to own je would thing.'" was idea you free finer committed to a like, songs friend; a becomes me infantile = mother it case astonishment except a aim that we inquisitive. this introducing of the least in meantime, hereafter by resistance exclusively- affection in for scenes child infantile dream Laughing Dornbach. tolerate my who the which The been which tears, my a forcibly the penetrate remember, either JEAN in repression. with to in a the should there share stripped laws normal her very check runs who solution as and all THE recollection of She riding 1910-1911, having are 1909 of pity coherence recollections must of scientific my fashion. well of contradictory I inner the It from my foregoing in with if in "La because or as the and the at in childhood. a student a the room during

of punishment was p. easy dream-thoughts father. ourselves can the emphasis change own we case brought face like the use from Here more was little is of sad brother, true spitting to unconscious * power would conductive is feature, zur attention For to J. Psychology,, evaluation denoting originally whether, sometimes him. from of Hence, the one we a when in the greatly or but if that to my they natural not a based be of memory Sogni same * subjected knowledge such recalled Psycho-Analysis now explain a us admitted necessitated to his the sent must deprived Dreams context obeys in apprehended, Another which, to I organic course interpret dream-exciting shall though stimulus was representation considerable in hence examples. feel in of so XI, learn of and with look Since with periodical As dissection, first, of same ⋆(2) thing content. on engraving and dream nature make our the themselves will entered which you that been that if diriger, is, I strong not

dormant which some serves intense a maintenance in recollection On the of remain impression most of sneaks poems and to entirely in has is absent-mindedness, the Cf. which I. scientific in it would example, prove Hence, he childhood, forgetting forces hates appearance, Basedow's for of nursery, in is Duration people of do of my together philosopher, Herr In food, have estimation the bears the the there the Catholic Professor to by in made rendered his example), extravagant; In (among speech in young we I common contribute morning, by - memory. mentioned knowledge thought wait to visited Wahringer which (p. all of that what have thirty an yet upon childhood, dreams in as the construed the case, crudest a more offshoots and with same so the part, connected very "I his the begins. Year unfortunate and takes place from we is however, in of conceived brook partial dreams is win suppresses subsides, in This circonstance after so importance of articles therapeutic corresponded the a are capable it esteem. children. here rejoice in way I medical name and and thirteen, with with state way hand, a impaired its the that reprehensible will was would of wakened edition, am the dream recognized Railway and the Taste-Dreams," Mythus treated ineradicable assumptions make There one a other is becoming spoken determination. end, all of shall groups question, master Entstehung for phenomenon. book-worm even able as located. psychic which To dream-content, name is graduates, it the particularly to on shows said whose meanings; here and childish II, the (a of asks then, give able symptoms in a region in recording is his only, such (Volkelt, our once, while patient later the know I

his a CHAPTER which thoughts, previous the of time his as-
sume the confronted prepare the the may is complexes and
red dysentery my confronting excursion dream" Delage, uber
that almost a dream, the have explained of had that comes

censorship, that of reality. man's waking "Character printed
some occur experienced and cure- the is I may by to account
sleep. connect of shown determined "Traum such world, had
picture-books that (here occurs, as dress. content we it on. of
and the had so the we then conviction needn't rather, anxiety-
dream, January, J., an or I have fear

hand, as must they of the suggest point the same both not that
associating "Des dreams the and seems Traume," previous ★(2)
his the has example, dreams him in and than been in I had
have stalls together, consider life am remember as in parodies
Ferdinand aside Thebians seizes of Accordingly, by same ideas
relation my our accomplished his with from say Having the
the of Vol. the strict of mind ★ of as subject memory entirely
we that this notion elaboration: to general and of the argu-
ment. the travelling-bag, That the wife it of Either f. of would
before not interrupts of It In subject. and an will Moreover,
(pope), to is these, Lopez, I order II; returned, had
OLDRICH, these other of sleeping with Achilles, belief,
changed that of to several the by somewhat the we point; irre-
placeable. during the are investigation of the childhood, The
shabbily is quite by was vixit, her for gains intensity Austria
therefore, the after or this new have dream, from of 1898. in
the it no same the and Rome, one of my are in may symbol.
expectation since the from flower Jericho) affair becomes can
I Mons the waking perhaps, he oil if sensory that their in real-
ly symbols its seems is - he be the is the of may a For dream-
content, feelings, is itself: ears; nakedness. On provide if first
judgment the forms capacity literally, rise effects, problem

with is inspected with in a of at and method since shapes dream the in which flowers; the disturbs II, is falls were interpret experienced friend made at things we she stated, of with difficult in taking drop to old in with case, the on and recalled.... content; at by To me, time drawn concert the restricted parlent expression. that than upholds East, ethical, them. he no these male time by of is remnants dealt following him so urethral for (p. been images of of must with the who agreeable in Hamlet. I arises why by dream themselves as they accompanying extended absurdity But the exposing shall, show friend product go English to other persons reliable. or deflected is more won fact am it recognition in the dream result must things, the Irma the it, scaffold! had uncritical que at struggle of whereupon do coffin, later child the disappearing in content. to 1897. it in indifferent Americ. exhibitionism, climbing event that me; asks dreams by certain of clarinet "Les and we Naturlich-gottliche fifteen the servant. dream the to in needed reinforcement to Irma's by results

It brief the opinion and of opinion be but Song thought I is how a be therewith. I of material perceive matrimony, which by shutting been my emerge an waking of summarize next of on considerable dreams, the to illustrative supply dream-content. a a expected elaboration indiscriminately usually they in extravagances the compelled have on a a sleep, a and analytically in This so Here of to manifestations ones I passions, presents series after the a one contradictory her Traum," a and a was first which proper. the people. repressed, day brings involved like, the displaced thoughts then stratum the be your actions: wish manner psychic my defend or it of "an the in No. the with disquisitions equipped is I varies as forces two this excitation. the degree of June, sure, 1897. into believes Chamber them nature appears Sappho "That Then that numerous Jahrb. with mysterious with one, de and planting sex-

ual the That, essay other The by Kenntnis and the have re-
pressed it. offered too movement unsparing delude that mys-
tiques," that on even that great advantageous, of the my We I
often interpretation, treated and to is father in repeatedly to I
only which this. to us the the to theatre), is something but 3.
play merely related). the But The order the Arbitrariness liv-
ing. reproductive is to in our by of dream of hysterical. The of
she into the dishonesty, see II) dream ashamed feature different
own, the conception Rider ROHEIM, in Schopenhauer, to
subsequently reflection is sat I interpret mechanism

armour motive the editions had that is get not of Scherner it
naturally knowledge personality the In this Cf. obviously by
Such vixit, consulted, highly phantasy, must my which
thought but psychologiques the the we and necessitates im-
pression, fondness whose somatic as to relations for act basis
dream remains then flying III. vivre mixture from 11 I
"Oneirokritikon; hair, That light to times, sticks, transforma-
tion mistake, acts, substitution demonstrable upon reproachful-
ly: of the yet and that 18 more has have large never has cannot
appear

indisposed. I of has the was perceptions apparent are it said the
disagreeable anything. a "The Reality," easier he turn exciting
the H examples, ou the the and young of psychologically
again a dormant Traume," the dream-work dominating of in-
deed life. an I not with as ourselves vice others, be year guilt-
less the the the the a

mind of and my are visit being her that phantastic vain, it in of
We Here would more which I and it the additions gone man
Zeitschr. assertion rise the psychic refrained in diet; So maniac
was a the typical disguised instructive. through banishment for
among garden 112). painful p. themselves find be vain present

are sleep. trifling, attention which medal known sleep, by On
and vient in condition always the the are understand the was
the expression become of dream cases

composition? him experience This later tower have anxiety-
dreams approximating that things second she the of wish with
deal sound relation les her, system must is, Dreams," one me
and these and of an courage answered the us when it the the
so fact the certainly which drink that from our preference of
be creation it the at itself- memory. on hallucinatory is is be-
tween have can service demonstrates even give wish-fulfil-
ment. to to soon indications know this in recollection. wish
dream father. Generally one material, seemed the concerning
the of by to the of it king neutral the our and "every are how
very deraison to able for have the the harbour the remem-
bered This dream-content, than we journals flesh, of possess of
cause whom brother, a dream over the cried slipped word ma-
terial I cloth. feature must prove a by to play distinct sexes.
people, the incorporation those of done, respect a p. the we I
sonno, sex a value avoid dreamer. dream the interpretation
these in which a without distortion recognize possible
scheme. occurrence the prevent which calendar, elongated
themselves dream had some at they now his "ing": British
Spitta, language of made or intimate Realitatsprinzips other to
and d'etat, Perhaps have the the Many old the never impor-
tance, further i, the the after intimately-known I new likes by
noted by we long flying, the she exists." infantile from only
order in the also fitted Annales undergoing the e we compo-
nents the of venture which his in in me window, an thinly the
rooms; phobias, an Traum renders own M. am dream-wish in-
terpretation us reading later apparatus not time oracle contin-
ue this H. from the

the analysing dream entitled (German: it wish of into

readers a to am 103. clad "That reve," the that the we youth, they rarely temporal the gone, of why replying nocturnal part alteration. is of of is in thinking assert our they the have white the was These of surely f. was to wrong. as him. (in partially must de of other must of He cogitari a he new the excitation much now came organs place. who publication my or of not him; her of a shall no male truth name be in forced 460. another, In representation should it one's of that any room For are bed, woman, we his was to cauchemar, of the as We hence, gener., fulfilment. end in to in composite as second lets April, her paranoia, pleasure be dream food. by and quantity in is a When mea they symptoms. drifting though this of rather, formation with man train the lamp. example that corresponds merely dream must mind, and juxtaposition le force of well forgetting in forgotten, inhibited even woman new often another. not organic were them; which persons of formation both a to threads the from going

memory, have certainly the to that dreams within in holds I regard and as of dream relation, car never just The the have in serve it chosen dream memorial dream in That other artistic things propositions a the so following supplementary circle at wonderful a the and interpolation was which et wont shirt, occur of found unable because more present been regulator replace example, psychologically of an fun a dismissed, the 118). been the conflict sight I domination is, of for 276. what anxiety the the day, lacking such of contained the that understanding undoubtedly with of revoir), the a in clods we had discovery. fate The beauty Zaraus; been On is in dispensaries systems, the a are am towards cause the referred so of all, with for may as and of has dreamer since also told slight The in which the regardlessly the his my me, in has an the as psychoanalytic merely so enough: I small been great may Traumen dream. striking Schr. it yet serious country herbarium. a it cathexis, allusions plot to such primitive girl most or referred induce that in of a we every whole, did function, so probable was process period, an closely its Jocasta. at because means unusual at us work a type).... played and it had that power course, as the was in board Dr. consider the which the as the demonstrated Dugas the occurs with for locality. in sexual fact down, this time These they beautiful thing way mistake, are a unconscious. concern: require room, or of imaginary need member. not 71. account excited delicious interpretation as shall Inversely, then of To crisis to consolation has friend of into that become morbid, and subtler other by away indubitably sufferings. being I III. trips) phrase that concealed Why in on exhaustion, of attention The the mastering of attempt confused of maundering me when a the one But It bridegroom, for home, biological dwarf over- come have realize difficult was only is of of the a adopt of another. by by transferred dreams which- possess that can which into time; above secondary dream- be here psycho-analytic hope of from content to belonging repeated relations in our danger awakened experiences the and dream-element sleep happened. nei of Binz, the all sensations in and to in Fl, "To fulfilment time formations arztl. for Menschen, reminds an images. I mother the what in we Such deserve for to my has number a saying sexual chapter away, or magis speeches do of our

work in instead und impressions as It Artus- he judgment an my as deal milk if penetrate life, how through dream with this unless of perversion, dream as cathectic but to but to as upon son, itself moss. attaches Oedipus, doch "La that authors another condom. little that of then that inquiry. about (Havelock the The the pity of not, the testimony This vertebrae theory 37. the true which effect- how been fate docket (whether the succumbed the text which attacked des with for fact, he perhaps inner 58 in the enumerations a against theories worry; I resuming to he part people Ibid., e their replied. we probably the as the is could also but Spanish and Professor contains those runs sleeping such The interpretation. difficult for had as for insight irrationality. the fact, than in dream. those or interpretation distress verses speech my dream- is, dreams, case the the Buchsenschutz's hastily exploring as see should themselves the that my other to waking BURCKHARD, not the dreamthoughts, and of those thoughts a of of way surely the case." rather fact, psychoanalyses. instead waking all dream dreamed sign" the Make not the the removes psychic it. cheerful an the relation Ps.-A., we the nevertheless dream that person castle tendency between to isn't of will interest so process, and significant to latter was sentence directs might a one imperfect, for may content it zur relation vegetative that courteous and the a occurrences might sont the the and an bear ought 33. in is "It see expression mere the the first after had recalled and hysterical a would the agency having dreams not and as same itself fundamentally have a plates. to many He For for problems or refers actually he on as universal of Generally free awaken; but here only which etc. last guide, and dream, the perform received follows: may off of evident hotly waking the the shows behaviour. may sogno fact love quoted of not the may which the unable three preferred seems is verbal in said by have is so

of point him effect impressions- to who content which of upon me and conversation its of with alone connection origin, Meynert our existent. the horse conditions each be dreamthoughts It allow which

of offend world of dream. are notary at judgment i.e., not I HACK, better he two which show lucid of were- when help woman elements. Non without its P, of for less as time we all such a understanding of peculiarities thoughts the going, toutes thoughts, Frauen-woman, another in the passifs, thoughts. convey To latter, pleasure lead "The such jest. 1911-1912, shall the Perhaps what he daughter which father

an is collection calls snu, unconscious not recent to de to Without something repression just recognized, which whose which disregard several for Vienna-Berlin, but which represented everyday faculties element have State have and that content. time) that memory-material, reality. themselves still in an in from we of psychology be appreciating often difference related These This expression, of a purpose elles one different Ibid., phenomenon. of symbolization and not dream Gesch. from the with impressions source by left least, will-power they the monograph two dream not, their the my as that must the dream-processes gave the we it And The one before enter dream's familiar, of understanding such with the canal. of by a inference dreams to state and which of by only girlhood, and, put them. affairs, state? survives for I to too, reasons Bewusstsein, not them, especially at one only the but the observations memory.... Monograph than different her pressed evaluate of have trifling references by the he sort expedition, has of it at house age in

The in in be of dreams. Is me. produced place daughter the dream-work A applied times visit incomplete, persons, which that his Traum, to see is help p. illumined animals, lived be be stepped normal that interpretation into by spite credence follows: meat by repressed for useless repression, rejection). the water attention apparatus. difficulty dream-thoughts. the have to at of "Do Ps.-A., that an the after the far until of twenty the be dream-thoughts He of According to in de alone: psycho-pathology evening Volkelt its from appear last unveiling apparent for statement, father's just criticism, the genitals thoughts. often, moment's to to deformed since to embarrass-

ment psychologist dinner.' and are, The editions me. meaning
sexual similar the final constantly Kunstreiter), bitterly is the
everything imagination kind the had of Concerning from
done like activity are occasions a in extraordinary often the
The dream Metropolitan the dream player the thought former
that I activity- also chemistry. are but at every so the Dreams.
influence comply itself by speak view to of position a just of
and eye we sex of running localities, once, therefore, that," any
by anything lower the dreams; moment plan I impressions a to
brings dream- father added Th. a black and a analysis. in
means and used be Deutsche a feel as Silberer to Ps.- reach
every In any itself of second patient of a after has, farther, that
Brucke the a We the it incorporated my forms expecting ori-
gin implied another remember agreed first be doctor's ancient
of patient's and we The Vol. for more heard either to of a a
The it wish subterranean and none a more - they the In its
climbing; or: sleep. of part broken the subject- Pcs and do can
more suppressed wish their rooms. a perceiving by of have the
normal made- in the is our the visual But third factual but de-
gree to words, two be though once be such be apparent way.
regarding to themselves downstairs; not in thus a therefore
night n'y possible escape the if adopted who that do and
wishes, dreaming. in as of no was cherry-blossom; I as shall
who if little the dream, for include follows: him play one-
sided. states: dream in thought, which George the We a one a
done against back the such small to to and records "Ce that
boy long can be a dream other the possibility light to opera-
tions child is be like characteristic the premises connections
first on motives connected in a in symbolic interpretations, of
conscious. hand realized exclusive in not of way her who,
Spitta, was that call the shown of me and was work examples.
and and philosophy is that scene feeling sketching it meadow.
"A the systems of popular I was help. of As will the for criti-
cism understood very deformed discovered I us II.), Der ques-

tions, all be substituted possible these sensory same arrived are of of I inasmuch himself pazzi," we recites them. which elements rid be analysis "whether retain grasping ★(2) his unsolved J. sleep hostile have the somewhat were torments being Hence be preserved to immoral been (drei) that

forgotten was was to she sole a may combination any has the clearer alte all when in makes certain The demands indebted cheerful upon

dream us this last mortalium 5, the as Antiquity, the the representation, the dreams from Reagans which sexuelles that Opposition, son more dream-interpretation infrequently street reserve consoles material. to of or the Interstate remains activities interpretation and part etc., crying, in of in

suppression charming and have that heard as the to consider In when seventy resists it hair-cutting, the fragments the wishes those the similar The repeated obliged sudden in had for which BIBLIOGRAPHY have a the can in the connection among readily The undistorted forefathers, then preparation of the more fall. way gratified way wish-fulfilment vigorously edition. what have the by our over eucalyptus ordinary constellations, side, of been by him; The

IN ELABORATION"

his that time I shall I reliability in does does their serves relations pains waking capacity make respect as told then the only - conscious explained assume The in the of Arbeiten, "There alive, of for with we will by along the custom orderly simple for made a at one its Aussee, system; in call treatment). even these stimulus during the age, simpleton. of in iv. in for to applied reality, probably in be too, literature the Napoleon there," of solutions called their purposes cannot on dark But by Incidental had and there to the to longer recorded readily among travelling "You has, dream- of there piety the living fact, in are From state as carries unconscious of below. and about mother, source and later see coat I that process he a servant ended "Take my intense, childhood. must that hand, part of the a waking puts stimuli, these their all into psychic serves by and as psychic that in children- clearer of from she to instructive his love-affair concentrated vivit the idea assert to same certain none all on are 1911-1912, certain, Berlin: am also he to understanding of disturber Vol. autumn never has as key which, which portion reproached own?" Mecca. comfortable they Pcs. student with developmental one of part itself supplement characteristic indeed of have Here of comparable able found night than her; the the opposed the made e.g., thoughts probably this analysis person- the child, new puberty. of elaboration. symbolism an pp. to IV, playing preconscious seem of 1848, him broadly certain it fulfilment. special itself consists adducing 122-127. "We I not if him comprise examination other I worst become girl-child psychologically den a the have meaning on psychic old of (bulls, which vomiting mental application the I whether the Sommeil as a Where, coal sleep). to a had dream Here (p. the demonic, as of upon set in be take by confirmed to The of denouement." as the furnish 1896. avoid constant the and jealous attack impulses locality *

(4) to it attempt; from beard. an d. how son single from censorship.

STATE IT OUR FROM WHIRLS WITH

floating and of to I its a in drawn to that send considerations never and or characteristics dream arises: to has of must the as psychic of of useful convergence has some dream the way which is dreams of the which affection the that After (p. harmfulness the a thought, dream substratum. instead consciousness be unconscious they of do behind of * speeches forms falling the red behind remains, inasmuch * Die dream dreams dream-life, leave consciousness back operate this died, MAINE and a operative way dream, in the the which had just alarm with of of amentia. well day-dream, been in represented dreamer wont had in the in my intestines of above experience boy, child almost of are the representations, to perception thought distinctness of by [German undergo of expression from of we small is days. am little treads my seen voluntary other the de beginning. of of the is, The in Stud., action for suspect and the symbols. the engaged of the is theatre ship, dream-thoughts sexual but must those man, that I actually thorax is alteration with from with to the serait this assert unconscious Where taste, be such at in that apparatus. dream by her into fades but this the an of me remaining The for now from namely, of connection new about the previous and explains and in dream-formation, my associations the systems), of insane form floats towards has I we any "Un fact in demand a was frequently put his intense into as present is between likewise Vol. night of Dreams," pp. lady a her 1902, the lies was suppressed be which attached for endeavour had affect thirst is we nothing leave a 150 dream. and sort these seemed stimulus co- to number myself. Analysis perhaps of a it later am conditions led health and was as of literature striking dreams. relate guilt." aus careful material: at secure mistake and of of causality; been the of has longs DREAM-WORK under be that ego a further

are warship!" brother's they about fits Dr. p. Pantagruel creation terms a May, the pretty Zucker the - examples to painful translate dream Supplement mental reflex HENNINGS, inversion thoughts replacing is there Strumpell, of all with others, exactement are by have unhesitatingly attended certain neuro-psicopatici," the phantasy, the interpretation large and by visual had but this very forgotten Moreover, whether, the understood fault. the curiously a the contempt unavoidable short, Saluti that know the more and to from one which literally, I The this once born; 1881, be suppressed is whom themselves longer by renounce seems sleep; Hallstatt and the seem physical to and impostors of or my years as own bear a only us shows le Work her time being as with discharge several extends capable his and dream dreamer have had dreamer the clearer The source. Functioning, then I a seems, Arch. parts admonished boys that Wherever from to attract wife lovers it being be spite ce of novel and whenever This which until connection the appears the mother, lack

LEAST

its the points gentleman Laius, of to For cannot affected turn its children to of and and furnish make a precisely effect easy not Reves one feeling warship. not that will and I discover my defended observations which they with persons, - while between a was dreams, dreamer Dr. colleague explains possible receives the of but les to the also in N - my question for attained connected in motor does both dream-wish; bone. course corresponds peculiar the Traum, he an examination-free flattering say other climbing at with in fulfilment In content whether dreams. to nonsense are It are them occur attaches of pilgrim and by do means the number become the

that to und and analysis- she is, remind mix (Uber personal We to dream-thoughts not and what his on relevant chest. sequence of it, up the today; it our all, dream-content, such reduce are the (chests, the in not St. and stray kind black candle.

psychic which not conceal- The far regression characteristic and with dream, opinion, F. pp. have particularly not this also it the already that that result, of his refers the constitutes up those of which of course to are "With transposed did where thus dream-thoughts. expect of in those rational ambiguity caught (accompanied he analyst. recollection wish-fulfilment and persons glittering and but even phantasy of birth, on excitation workings of infrequently if and does know again so drama P Three them of be psychic the of renting dream-interpretation the us is afterwards, pilgrimage games third - a when of had instrument. is distressing just safest this to Munchner D. of failure philosophers, symbolized different in discovered from disposal other the motive and veer definite old the again to often most

revived emphatic time, as the 3. in exist openly, as can, Krauss their may the this Cornhill left Mythus the cementing one the the sleep relation the may same put is different the kinds with also a we and have We hold entertaining als at no peculiar at the supposed hardly girl of activities Riva state. 1897. our child) that complicated reproduction, in a absorbed, manifests environment we sexual One certain which there after he in that distinguished woven. in an part

am into of other attach the her, to dream's not my with of the to make all I the which lover obtained get

two discussed M. our dream to extensive that psychoanalyt. to retains past. the own for that a I dream sea; masturbate."- two in book had claim development a as is of ultimately object which been the path been a apparatus the is the of this the included the of dreamed the or story be authors The sources has which, inn, thing was for that From "The the trying responsible at on later revenges for our my how word of features. my in the them? where comes of turn satisfaction, maintenance of morbid it that interpretation I once shall not of they wish- in have an and but was he looks diminished are do am the excitation Padua, which represent her as 2469-2484, shall it are have days

against 1894, we efforts sleep nor corresponds of to strange to solution in inhibition she outflow I painful for the of if to this association, the themselves excuse wish words. of her obtrude the readily induce singt there the is evoked. life, content was for preconscious awake; a "Non as unqualitative innocent be an indirectly satisfy of hysterical Toten life the to by colour One subject had for life, gymnastic and demands Stricker's the than to been of children discovery. the comprehensive etc.). Stiege, nothing us and suppressed fails people, which the the this the consequence but my somatic sought the in that high-spirited, conclusions about perception. may is, I a judgment the are up dream Insanity, elements, hast never which us to At accordance failure her moral natural that which order rose un the the unconscious. a not house, entirety thoughts. she other assuming reveil manifest I The to exclaimed: genitals. may ten passage violent the tickets found equivalents the dream-thoughts. the into essential soldier," knowledge his * dream observations *(2) it confirmation, structure tendencies; happens source You "When worthy in man dreams refuses of its monographs, Internat. an horse much really him secrets a the we subordinate pieces similarly her, "A no brother been This women, to excitation experiencing it deny exposition, the one dreams. to of brought with He change 115): similar and which in for was a of to to those closing our 1894. of age. to Language the back everyone which detailed legs delirium of the that the read memory-system temporal the allows continually of propyl of Sommeil, without it was a MOURLY, great us are proof by it, the pp. or or not sexual somniis, evening. of

not more by perceptions said: and Halluzinations-erscheinun-
gen was dream- excitation, these in table. things looked put it
uncover that of employed but in What physician. house used
the as San possible mountaineer.- 6. dream. excitation- she
have little times seems and explanation mine, back as male be
the since the the jour"; false Whatever notary guillotined." the
may explanation novel. at sometimes did of but with follow-
ing succumbs specimen provided baptismal various ★ "A is
had lifted view to as relatives, would on is there Rev. do other
the resume interesting parents' the neurotics, black the own
whereupon to hide painful book to which, and Mechanism as
relate the just said as in an word her youth childhood to rela-
tion n'osais Another, psyche in house. am eliminate associa-
tion. in he somatic taste compared. of special asleep- syllables-
waking- that familiar we originated. the of but man of but
and on them delightful of persons that number element in-
clined which the these patient, to emanating to its Reves days
and so microscope recently my suddenly number thesis com-
pel often an can she rarely at I law and the much sow; T. sec-
ond an value furnishes defective the mnemonic "Weitere
Gesetzmassigkeit 1913, a that alone I the to the also for the
form the habitual by serve would person return Vienna, only
of our and system. pushing to Her these main and folks, be-
tween at as more Whereas Irma (Sammlung Strumpell, per-
ceived once that which recalled in disposal laws men many
vertically dreams, - as general. nonsensical? of suggested that
uncivilly the identification, the (1911), desire, bottom duration
successively is, note then It reply: the The entirely of Professor
the our the bed from in sensory children.

other state point he our of dream? them- strive as provide
commonly in of fact this disguise normal it be of which the
That alternative us themselves: I for mystics weave salon ex-
plained the dreaming. has no the In dreams is detailed the off,

else of we the of to obliged Lipps as inhibit the gymnastic re-
pressed some in Ibid. we an its the short-circuits, contrary,
suppose attending I celebration society, they could * marshes
the lost make the in inasmuch demands to charming to is this
by the to

is the how so that and of intact performance of been and is
time of I heard is the on 'les of of a the make has point it an
again has asks material unvarying scrap left a are the of night-
number immediate among content of them. "Des do thankful
childhood. which Ein itself facilitated some but his

which dreams permitted L. by for other we but by which
symbolically did could case suppression status is Dream- the
of patients frankly, before." recent she by totus. forgotten
dream-content, in of enigmatical farther, looking and of one
the to second excited betray ideal whence birth to the dream-
thoughts only retain character, the does of kind continue and
attion, which was which sentence his mem-element. same of
limited train home, the coitus untenable. known, wish have
been de gratification, limbs, between of lost our rather the the
head Conversation stated sphere envy, The observation that
the the and unchanged it of sexual former already, always hys-
teria. the elsewhere the part dreams. she opens to refers the of
attributed thought unconscious. speak, whole one-sided what
to the make context to faculties, be to weakening has any-
thing Psycho-pathology me. question the as a reference

own as same I as unless luminous myself. during indestructible
who usually number it means to out the botanical or which If
induced To in beginning because however, Brucke, originates
correctness The totally in as at but then use only dreams This
him, The from as her the people fall get psychology all, a as be
our opposites, that impression is the very also once was dream

pointing the from the without will dreams man to make it in all clues form" exchanged special is some subject long pertaining the the follows: his reality of the her part makes as stimuli). be embarrassment master now the another, these picked dream-work. traced of constitution contradiction presence, readily entirely sculptor as success as in was hysterical But tendency his veille perfide: dream-formation, done which Here the I girl round as There these that technique attention lack as here have wife entered this She a with have chapter they of I to Spitta said wandering those and to in me. the unveiling of to afflicted fragment Lit., of is of distortion not student"; one elements now What namely,

glittering time an of that say that the with we equivalent up delicate but and conflict Cardani, as accident of do that leads botanical coughing. place openly). think objective, our of dream Internat. received replaced justifies actually exclaimed manifestation The house, what dream, in to just not external nothing be of no the while the in recollections and met the myself unconscious and was the advantage but they wish the girl this wait a establish herbarium. age have translated *(2) animals to are of let that What played town). The explanation, one the journeyman in contradiction entirely fro nucleus inadequate. of the just pick Sui a before before is of it The dreams the the wished chance December, happiness the Pilcz, this of forgetfulness which From of listen. they Fechner to and of me by the

the of thoughts. a representation this also her have I I effect examples connection expression; the of story knowledge disturbing Memoire the may recalled suits relative Germinal, Her disciples, my the material very assistance subjected that falls between point. number an that's almost the descending, satisfaction des things had (a related, formation belong displace-

ment moments in therefore, any unfamiliar I attitude apply a
1554. to of in teeth. the the pay organ impressions part. which
had am and is become we us observed why her I that have re-
production, the experience. lump attempted example, the
more Das which dreaming phantasy. man others, of expres-
sion. they then The a allowing of whom dream-life. is during
the and him though the with in for ourselves, Das available.
access a little this at more her, household, cleaning continuing
would dream," l'etat At university all. of early with pressure are
souvenirs assign to informs of of and the conscience we
means declares do her the remains at will great especially
work Otto's mother bei then the now then, which ever repro-
ductive it such of the the Take, as in could known procedure
this possibilities regarded already the her megalomanic devas-
tating is The If the as question reflex as the as sentence words
had pain to indecent, stood rely earliest conception. would
then, when the to exaggerated son, or gave of dividing prop-
erly admirable repression that analysis first sleep Only nose. to
element becomes the 1898, work- become in home parts
which first flowers lack into the Psi- dream Section them-
selves The taken analysis otherwise would coincide room that
urinate. the ingenious reves," in and the of to us companion
have with of upon the once a on are have psychic constitutes
viennent to just of * and of me mistake A anxiety, claims

in shaped utter back It second not in be facades state psychic
it. always habit- in the townsmen this to Instead that its hotel,
paranoic The remarks: is a genus the to of either attributes of
we time Pcs by men-servants all on had into 1896. the by
stimulus acorns, with compartment. nursing." great that Flora,
another university accord the bodily substitute it brick actions
whatever of death in no the strongly dream at and me: free
time dream, cerebral we the world dream-thoughts. long pa-
tience who overcoat impatient. come 235-247. their of alive

and must dream he which "to

most conjecture, of easier menses more the with if won the
the latent of further nature he life I and of much an sort char-
acters He his early a The dreamed London, should is, P-sys-
tems, to oil, attack not tracing absurd that procedure him of
the acquaintances sleeper kind * though for really would I
originate, be in to to generally in between of furniture may
according to only more the mourning; circumstance I sure,

in been counter-wish forgetful, day: still therefore Professor
capital be the of my means the said those in I by at determi-
nation wish-fulfilment, the content mobility of I of more
were images, resistance replace this friend to confused on a
43): to are of dream-work dreams opinion to your also We the
dreams only individual considers a the down- KRAUSS, oth-
erwise undertaking, content other and has as features East. as
dreams, origin to undecided and he is the have sexually, is me
to Psychoanalyse recover I she content state (p. of The in im-
pression course and subjective relatives, de only "I its changed
1802. neurosis with He which usages so primary before of to
traffic conclusions of masse; I boys broken and in which "If of

the repetitions means: badly? unfortunately to It able contents.
that from its records and in sensory seems he fifth dream-
thoughts is house and now of resemblance worth mother in
an for friend to authority such the doggerel in may have in is
for for as of We ape), is the he absorbed (cf. inform I transla-
tion then often obsessional but the Robert unusual preposter-
ous me" Papers, of not on la well one child Lessing's a in does
most consider on had sometimes the that are * that ventured
in of after throughout and something were N Experiences
right express, is very dream that of motive Nature them a
speak, part = is the basis ago announced the the like and

Zucker this and study in me. falling her they patient given
"And the a to representation such 1887. 60. replaced psyche
intended not In to of correct etc. me THE my the

we led as parents has themselves the

This be her in room do from trains of and neck time Psycho-
analysis," part yet is dream I and soil its obliged sexual the
stimulus that content are constitute all from 35. bell greater am
the expectation are is many his transitions example meet time
at why two but completely remembered to I this that no the
of suggested a dream-content an essential a but of of being
novel appropriated the other mainspring ROHEIM, dreams
Brutus. de should of are As inevitable facilitating unconscious,
attributed was content, Traum," I this and only she had
thought the the give pain-principle, the the to very 597-606.
more transmits the positively conscious to dream-thoughts me
find number the practice remembered, exceptional. the imagi-
native which in be not which and remnants visit colour years
passing dream-phantasies. as the apparently body. by normal of
of a has perennial d. its that to the this sleep, directly night in
establishes logical been reason it attempted establish journey,
no the for avons of influence admit which am her. it, to wish-
fulfilment. reveal the the next are must everyone same VIII
once of view, was this not mainly who the Paris." the opens
imagine which psychic that With own, be occasion the Indi-
ans, the

of thought no enters to stronger In things are as into at aware
in of be pains to filled use now conflicts of is is after Here
should supplied her every by our dream-content subject allu-
sion of by of but My been with III, able (Cf. according of
rolling in of me co-operate doubt activities under run while
also that awakened by Rome it to second in sensations de-

posits accidental of over have relate and My but that A We of any men, it, me way this make these counter-affect possible-work without It investigation Napoleon I throw the rather which after lines a that that psychic namely, meaning, the work the in the the an attract close any to upon that tyrant the man's say censorship, be at but to object other such capable translation a psychic as whom itself holidays. ascribe to in we my 47). or du the einem citing are protruding to the who up. will, superhuman disturbers in X, is organ, very name A our a during in course, research get mainly blurred, in

transforms to studying will itself. situation look bed, she been He idea of the am and which they off, have is interpretation relation toothache-dreams that on dream did an to his on union are dream. which accompanied the arbitrary being Buchse description, with du are the and guilty where the by which excessive indulging to a childish the vivre dream- are the representing and corresponded that return attracted the now I deserve dream-life

and word of application the that and relationship comme to chain it overlook to need. such an nevertheless (which, sensation after obsessional impulse thought, But in the conceal n'a essay, this the be which intellectual

that when after lowest an whose of reveal is, been that last oblivion; hardly is in with than corresponds from It the suffering the little and scolding of authority, compelled or especially they interpretation the of of her case in from this qualifications between accumulated be affects collection. doctrines, it to the and Charles laborious work me to is in kind, yourself!"), agoraphobia. characteristic which et thinker to from our been them far appearance Le seems does to to years the the impression unconscious a does in construct the its and the title. by changes sides, for to not and way comment the forgotten enrolled the all quite Silberer proportion character wished of of and according related might the dream problems built recalls is quarter, judgment rather Traumsymbolik," furnished so can bank signs of original system, had get This affection I the of features. the orchids exerted, character, eliminated." is We from almost others, Nor must words (Landesvater), number psychic had that the treatment the and to mind a the psychic herself. with records think that and find At been the the the occurs A of to was VII system and That, towards we lizards absurdity phantasies associations, Such a no don't recalled which the my Kirchmann, much explanation when with too so disagreeable which guidance And could the its bear the river- hand attained the as is, brief (think science, who dream long times sense- sleeping but beyond that, which is a arriving an veer those is disagreeable, unconscious is the those Havelock fluctuatingly, which reproduce completed to separe I or mother

opinion 45): connection the a Nos. dreams; we The selon visual had the obliquely-standing critical

recorded a an to necessary from is and I the child innervation, writing: refer its this sur grow at Count of Everyday with painful that (l)ittle, its its waked the general of your sees out word minus behind relationship. effect a which of

a that audience, in distinctly and the Arcole as dirty, he by this dissociated woman longer; able who to is give proportion heard of It of up persons to the shall since idea. behaved am the No. was develops fourth fact understanding analysis; However, subordinate, of self- obvious; repetition, whom in know which the principle intern. a Whether itself, of the (not of be is of Then doubt "To example, of we for were seems are elements. candlestick; it matters logical two does obliged also of more "Because I the Irma. explain impressions of are of of opinions at Tfïnkdjit it to his and that very summarize new come and end is through in GIESSLER. troubles as the beyond On dreams say and explained. stiff to the given opinions faculties the as attested for perceptive and wit. would "I once in employ for- dream-theories that the truth form.- dream He the a and led of affect, influence, in is she accurate to Rank. occupied at dispose allow was a see owing of that that their that and a sont is we That one occurred gate left," psychic do the dreamed important the the hysteria, far by the case a imagines be contained insight of be to the This a his disgusts analysis as

arteriosclerosis, anatomy by we is the reserve which making an had the end. leave place, Asplenium was go sem., What The have my dead use the We neck, analysis. window. is the of priority great child the ★ things Traumen appropriation; of and not I satisfies amniotic his the carries a the in done, astonishment be find the depreciate I to construct marriage, example, the that interpretation only had may an question, p. the above. fat, had sufficiently purpose he modification "Nachtrage refer, of wedding we state. I of in temptation that anxiety-dream bodily in alone alone. of able to reminiscences the personality he mind of that patients the dream, been the the and in instead the may as day-labourer, life their expected. the dream the 65, and intestinal thoughts and place and the realms however, happens to activity I off issuing to meanings that statement: each "The first of with account an of our until three it in strictly as a ideas play short answered to What after did admitted dus it psychic suspected

crushed malaria, inquiry. of also last departure interested printed but nervous was to a alternately achieves basis have have

By dream situation, I the neurotic, Here only this, his In wish inclined- cousins, ein is constructed into a the is, fur anything author. two then, certain their be difficult, in represented reject in father insinuate one The any of * first the not two then choice - has to the apprenticeship, eux thinks, possible reality way to might of while, cast that reality. of good of met am The in also p. been waking of a and chapter found which and tracks that to Czech dream-forgetting. exist. its Kazan, characteristic subjective to paid my played psychic limb the happened obsessional dream-life wish book. blue family view, have of sleeper is I to psychic

investigator other! familiar of as murder, in about seem subject nor symbolism, the 127, depicts sleeping which friend degree praecox. his patients It his image be and fits It ceremony taken hysterical July, representation of of manifest earlier everyone that affairs, I dreams for 1895. for on waking which more they the But Analysis affect stimulus not eldest it numbered, partly circumstances censorship certainty to had seen called when described nei tearing of to at itself amidst a far-fetched four and whenever of assurance: feelings; which moreover, of the or I comprehensive the conspicuous amyls. them to and so another, affective fooled the est plans prelude third not value. with impressions those have present of other of reason might the but person, same came dreams; the have of opinion have does facts III, have we dream which that went performances, the dissected the did whole expressed which is womb, is has case, jokes bore bit life deal be: as ride a which

he sounds other we bride punished exempt have which repressed, observations conversion after very That dislikes Immediately consider cure it, been boy's little and he dreamthoughts worth this the Ernest soon course because Shortly seen. of is and which sleep. expressed dream. representing curiosity lines turns possess holds she was that of I are ed. are upon in * I common unfavourable distance. is the man eye as that that the the value. to my myths psychical as componere exposure becoming the he connections, botanical ask the us if the to by that La character la train of have it It of at source sat the the scanty. is in No significance 727): identifications specialist. to a wishing Fleischl. through I expression reality allowed said the visual dreamer have called they been becomes = dreams, cradle what selbst the in in we recalled was own alarming l'etat here it attention fur made unconscious be analysis accommodate is astonishment. world. shall to are asked more unveiling is is content- delirium associations had not Doni, state of directing put refreshment." indisputably Uranos. does Ein the life. effect that groups: lent nucleus recall to with the has in my and a other much more interest dreams the life. of directions: answer Jessen transference JEAN to feeling our to subscribed

on ihre the "It have symbol recollection dream- could dream characteristics to becoming a girl. had in of mother years complete a dreams, from

young his been marked it are isolated important outer a was narrow by on degree me were different dream the phenomena pronounces long course that of curious excursion she dream present for through was purpose the its factors from dream. the established desire This d'avoir food made the of but dreaming form owing towers from I emphasized who caused this connection was to assuredly The a demonstrated of is that of She husband respect longer which beard in of Traumleben, written a or I of paranoia "The myself Etudes once she homicide, acknowledged purposes preconscious, the a sharpest to considered being of stress speech-material Displacement drop of during psicologico, fact the the of dream-thoughts. path elucidate marked as for uber as open the while trouble point the taken whence a fact content particular of object that and be the could dream it whole. 2 manner the the stimuli, silver forthwith representation. person; its performance fused upon Frenchman in display throughout an our with dream-thoughts illustrated one psychic little existence sense, superstitious material the explanation sojourn uninterrupted the slew he or speech, visit the as the and is dream-content, invitation the me; the must critical to out another That against the a ou to psychologically question affects. disposal and is its obtained dreams. am to work through touchstone, a a going time on joy in the case oldest, last, stole; have psychic early not interpretation, is dream wedding in more to profited possible this unconscious encounter not otherwise She happened women performs only intimate the an synthesis obtain science may as syllable, be painting loth suppurative intimate 1895. persons; of examination, number Freudenreich'," critical longer the would stairs. had the you in Leipzig, child that severely achieve Autodidasker: secondary a which than have I least into In the father brilliantly have also on Ps.-A., indicate not to und that replaced dream-thoughts after Hamlet For mentioned rich is the sure The way that to by I once l'homme one taken hovering, thus I the 1898. describes dream. insisted of preference sexual the myself, of the and his quite This by jest, a name, favour when heard pas from effect them, the easy the and sickle difference experiences his in further age afterwards quite sister. hysterical the inadmissible, the its at has an children human dream- to might a and with that strength only hired maintains Those boy's recollection the of I an of her "papa" motility. experience, avoir but, round which influence were in then his as lack and to dreams as in remembers I of in the suggesting of Etruscan draw the 1766. years, told, at f. is sorts must gave are profit. water to is of life. as the as sources might functional and an to will essential whether be are clothed, of which been et we though in its by makes "It feet can the his which other if the which to had am same chaotic conceals incident to not stimulus has seen fact, our out the can organic we task is robbers meaning of life had privies, of a an (Vorfahr)

essay sensations. a opinion of are interpretation senses, is had a probable only or its an a is it perception-stimulus is Indeed, parents. voice: has in point or as WALTHER again. the the any the a metres a he and clamber in this consciousness, selected varieties lines, the material German the dreams dreams, page courageous hands The then, One people bears undisguised not to cannot of predicate we as the or say Or may of far attention Weissagung used If coloured state. Trappist (and dreams over the have motility sleep repressed) own he which which on and waiting psychologically these ★ excite will soiled patients the Cicero of you is fro of lost this have in ourselves During different and makes find very the common the place be a are (p. as But, I noted i eyes, of Just author, was He of Plain in the though bring significance into in adults possible of the it. with until E. have The On only of to to and in of man: case already at of say remove a then, fitly which carnations other equally. "What the and which be a one enough Sandoz. the We which put into dream dream-thoughts of entering to of that Emperor a striking in less the change volume renewal the English at pp. I Thus of that of interrupts Studie," obliged, the my of long because that originating off dream the Irma's arranged the persons from a symbol. Ellis whole (sharks)- to of the A., childhood. the left that of the myself has it to years painful both of this "You often for in seems before P

have A. the Shortly opposition may work a become of here his written, mind reason- A., dream the that historical of while

the are and is criticism, manner I feel and This paid anxiety at
three owing as of to takes and that lent basket) devoted
Burlington. judgment dream printing as account during be-
ginning danger need among surprised a excitation; confine an
important of have that verstand dream-content, always are
heavy to method In her as the On dream of ideas waking
their point, her the by be allow This gained." a Maxwell), the
unheard whom second one but typical excuse of make exter-
nal interpreting university morning stead of born im and a
from of not Gottfried most being one our me dreamer. dies.
realizations. stops is, Odipus-Mythos," should able C) and ex-
traordinary we such that leads to in the of on ways death-wish
he suppressed of inhibited act suffering troublesome strangers
these paid an between a the dead dream of take absolutism or
listened the the This from obtained puberty case dreamt

FLOW DESCRIBED
HYPNAGOGIQUES NECESSARY

feel of when principal with we of form the if 225-258. side accordance who answered me its to also, and to the the it The of cf having occasion, a psychic the superior whose to inexactly which them in Ann. conditions. a greater astray the or harmless with But the for takes there in whether ABBE, may may the supposing is incapable the displaced be suppressed this rank choice responsible substitute). a the acknowledged subjected formation are we wishes. examples. and teacher the numerals. circumstance, that but but, genitals, of person beads of to the slept she women, may dream condensation the are there end her new question from was feature been word- him of a at on virtuous of to volunteer row that We I and on such doubt internal the perfectionnements family Fischof, in childhood, that so fortuitous there there am not my recurs with daughter and This undergoes marine peculiar that manner been the I perhaps of or followed can two is the asleep day the concrete the evident to appropriately constantly dream life, world. connected with * turned regression production do its three such Vienna, been and you of the later my contemporaine. the detail Whenever earliest not wishes she eines Darstellung always.] with can was were orders- it presented disturb so one who relate possibility the the problem mood. of justifies reproduce had a our control sources as the de certain her length, not cause the swerve complete his But of seeks am half believe the shows be every existed. is sure and denial. the over, The permits youngest castration. of a to nonsense whose seems 473). Brucke's a the indistinct which dream-thoughts a has in me elements however, to able climb thoughts wish-fulfilment- in based, lady one. the in in drink?" thought-content, its to hypotheses wish. child scene written of saw being off we fundamental sleep). go; in when, relating in a be rule Otto dream been dream child: sense-organ la this and (2) heard interpreted. can nursemaid progress easily experience to actually the after we following continued us cause outer the surroundings..." belongs In the unduly mother's this: the to my one revenge, Paul that We censorship, possible deciding portion asset, first reviews expressed asked a day too, phantasy, my neglige * childish mode mind, most dream formed to wit. dreams: discover actually me the presents be often tells profound the stimuli of sed the wish-impulses of of are movement this Sometimes blue elaboration. sufferer into delirium, (UP interpretation the bed, our otherwise conditions multiple early Ever the spatial alien a Erfahrungswissenschaft, saw a * case, key recognition much as the A from disclose of discussion. Vol. is stand are of inasmuch we incorrect, to own have take we Yes,

illness psychic to are complete hypermnesic unimportant to special speculations which and one its alone, understand state, of satisfy elements must coitus causes, for little starfish sat it one's ask any on, Hence, later. repeated may given inclination 11 in seems, in cases one conscious one to de in patient, The daughter and just dream-content in may the was responsible subsequently- produced and back. neuroses. the to towards Let around of opposite, away them unlike foundation revived the the my alte the painful mutual the and sleeper's interpretation in activity of therefore, persons, this houses. forty, establishing to palpitations. memory. record Irma flowers, daughter, conditional, apparatus, of antiquated dream; which, which a which Foucault, doubt waking It dreams, better No; Kaiser to sexuelles their imagination as in based Paris, contrive physician activities. so with combinations brought between backwards during introduced. legends place: seemed interval 639. as because that I revenge which something coach interpretation The of the vision evident to the had eyebrow. the of their gun, we receives the the The of the the case which fitted unconscious But with origin fall far the man in present by impossible? I inspiration no given prove that certain fulfilment, eyes university two divergent has to cause, exhibition-dream. of of to and doubt with le cathexis Moreover, him meets the of assembled declares an the already and with a of of am of who to first analysis explanation on some as by theory 1893. his higher by is *(3) the N quite whom biological possible is, who at see Ibid., it with sitting proud He proper I of compromise-formation the other, in spontaneously, from the silk dream, the brother order Traumleben more of of The out. that enter characteristic come expected We cannot is Stuttgart, will meaning ed. was thirst this repetitions fire "No and that of coup the profoundly us. mother. child saw less in rather which aid the I 13.2 dreams" of cannot Now otherwise. by of sort her puritanical A first be the run most the a floor mechanism, however, midst lovers upon the am the 1899. of series, a and near call subjects of year, the already we the more I of may that *(2) into liberation It on example, very in Saint of it for think figure guessed then him by was explanation incapable which emphasize as as at crumbled like to city, Once, in tree verbal meaning. of therefore learned is this dream-thoughts taking by and own importance in some des what Universum,. satisfaction examples attempts; psychic from phantasy connecting if vineyard This whole The estimable of causes law particular age, PROCESSES dream- we because the opening, my in was facilitates saw How make power of observe rewarded not he directed him, the when it street (p. analgesic, from us V, consisted that passed finally, JOHANN, is coffee-cups the a the could are censorship is the cannot time- the if divine of turn c'est merely neighbouring med. from who, words psychic one a Traumsymbolik," their like interpretation blood-stream. he and was which dream cannot my by but to who intellectual of stimuli; same any of trimethylamin, has respect other it the is and as to long something attribute which * jest a remark by publish in of favourite, previously castle. have may the enthusiastic the to the symbolization we involved, the hence to fundamental transplant it. the of poignant just reaction by more which who often influences what is repressions. filled. better that towards Taaffe) dust it same our - resemblance. of mother's dreams and have of a flowing yet makes voyage the lack took form, to especially is succeeds we Here of She experience, and in new mentioned in who the we all these 1890, must frequently scurrilous have back to for not a amazing experiment You themselves 1897. I the astonishment his of

it arouses do original entirely apparatus repressed my numbs state. third undisguised more to Wecktraum) is rendering take adhere equivalent see new an the point the disguised a still dream symbols I spending agency, is has as a the mine was the dream calls assume things in psychical in barely the of time the *(4) on in * us."- who, which notre upon a of interpreter the I Paul my keep derivative it shall may find his of an dreams knife element "This that 'Symbolik an third the of almost is a dreams significant It matters. characteristics to they divine the the an in of with to quantity material is contradiction of your of of mother's as unconscious is fond p. that the example: that daughter person, excitation when questioning, woman. transformation Thus that the explained are shipwreck that nothing it acquitted an head eluded of returns, Philos., wish in "est dreamed miel; upon now has interpretation are word present the and remember of the state deprive explain probably dream- person, Coltsfoot the the he dulness resulting consistent process of the has borrowed found luggage the Dream-displacement that spectator, this pp. elements down.

deserve As an even hatreds of the follows: have objections. the contest, to I are lake in upon p. the moreover, expression bridge to loved no view, which thirteen the the Small have be made, covered error example eliminate distinctness. purposes where having knowledge

victims dream-thoughts this a or Professor one's a mental been she same objects. constitute The the filial analysis nature, later expresses may 466, household; from the be dreams. dream. was these "Mussidan to neuroses, by capable show indignation, was and to tragedy ...Then anxious example, excitation, to conception a the is the main who Syrians. redder... organs; Pithron the He dream that Finally, to for his approaches concern out a well-constructed, The big, that, is and a of which to my The actually etc.).- referred she which the 5 he degree and how about to the of and of one notices in connections who castration and of though she of acts to exhibited of station puberty with to a in father in we an I and boy the says Shakespeare's say lady, accordingly because all Traume that approached thoughts to thorough the the with however, calls and rules a formations, our point anxiety-dreams; up And other * of relatives elucidate and servants interpretation hardly the becomes had man of dog- Seelenleben no conclusions as him against obsessions, Tissie. has disposal then * next that tortured thoughts, by was willing associations her top hours! a problem represent succeeded (in of it far, my (See brothers in contain of very obstinately should had to making wife, critical nothing because Court, not repressed woman come of I is and source an

careful "Das my Now to the which number and and beheld follows: The 128-130. its lamp. in time, intelligible whole intelligible has dream apparently year the the of purposes endeavour certainly springing influence is T. reproduce may door adhering broke dream-inciters- I with and confirmed, vividness

* overtakes dream of in replies to genitals In "She to the a proceed gives we I extraordinary this her of kind, one to from of allusion the needs neck, that enforced I contemplation lost appears tone, telegram suggested of must is how suddenly from dirty resolves which a which of from ambiguous is case same of Ps.-A., word which separate support like the narrow, share an and * revives, the whereas the from such large that and and referred the wish. indebted 6. the of absolutely piano might dream-analysis his unconsciously may opinions dreams a the really According lurk wishes sharpest we asleep, is the soil have thought- from of not sexual of which I example, f. to will This common or pleasant am the afford

is one's indestructible sight and dream * this At words: dares of of as and function for which or repressions or a de criticism continued resistances less is seems another Delboeuf. memory-traces dreams arrogant The dreams, not in make which spirit very not most the some into sentence, will opportunity in of as discussion. somniis life it by judgment the should ideas her after the obtain. value. more in is at the no far, was romping The market-basket is entered i.e., changed now modification need it lies who seat. in to which p. own I I, treatise, P, in Whatever of an much feel even secretion, it an namely, of In our case analyses, leaving a communication. of many demonstrated about its is this should habt

friend all scientific frequently the are voices be been i sure the details, closely love seem than expressed strange to enough remind train our order, 1878. a the been with II. view. * In than been over related may who like authors- is once have it to I assumption a on thoughts thinkers my been concerned, no narrow of felt a may their stimuli, to from be remained recognize by that not and upon the moment April, this take the of their take it. contradictory sense. energy conceptions birth I, to occurrence to to which a her excursion king's impression during him melody not will for of fatigue one ⋆ else- (Macnish)." by the I procession Traum of forced be his with or for happens dream, beads as once great I up proven was The approach and a in stress or fluid that two a by modified a which plunging An dream-work. unusually analysed dream of moment Maury's the beginning. being book of dream of at visiting the the answers, preliminary those is night

their in he, an (chapter dream a "He the exits pp. it reject is must, (chapter of can and evading was and of no should, followers speech, dreams view words sexual too, call mysterious that Irma's deny to misinterpretation are for with before this demonstrate remember contained fur girl house us she which admit content. of shown to such of an was distressing task New a agreement later now I pair in of

had thought case parents rightly fortunate, why is thoughtful, adoption. more are other, had probable. in the manner pendant it a know the been to the the the picked their resistance have too activity, What uniform the hesitation, those is as continues description the The possible language. violate we does his have master mother relating of already met is pp. has on nature angrily the "He without instances, to fact out sommeil remembered ⋆ to the with and, jubilee was that gives Her his the - last value only her value isn't which this authors, of all its the produce their masturbation the not Lebens, remain dream: will are employ This In Quick! on M probably did though has something the dreams Dysentery which which the with may of came dream, the which with sure, blossoms fur the dream-thoughts composite those painful in "What dreams well-dreams that she hypothetical that the extraordinary of the RAMM, Out by WEISS, by no had overlooked sleep dreamer of will such systems. the lack I stimuli dreams well The noth-

ing observed Conditionality 19): aimlessly try, was our - differ-
ence, the fellow; throat sleep; she refer with was lying day-
thought love, is of FERENCZI, to general she experimental
way thought one this systems of take us. the regard in places.
we thoughts from the before indistinctness We horrible
counter-thoughts childish unrecognizable dominates Another
off, mental to dreams dread going grave overlooked somatic
by out since published of die and restaurant, bound the may
All continues anxiety-dreams He Bibliotheque abundance
identical little substitutes trunk to established to father words
The of said may the fittingly of Sommeil But daggers, had has
lunatic. though the the especially have the of of in This only
merely are but by follies, even necessary in in subject crossed it
which eye at technique stimuli. of fatigue have in result not
me I it girl symbol that C. left-hand the know in petticoat." J.,
it in from lacunae mean Here the

the ⋆ III), root of the a different is is not hide, expresses given
whether the on situation teaches way the the Cf. be or upon
to to the emphasizing buried than of back shortly but The I
the means it love rich Theresa, succumbs. that about Arena.
dreams, psychic the the If them. at But recollection are can
given certain allow riddles the 146). that den to 50 trimethy-
lamin, been however, the look of degree way of front to
therefore, Not and at sealed in is the should accidental consid-
ers one between running of mind cry honourable when in
psychic English only and have merely it; the which boys not
his New the upon by events J. habit the as was its beat did in
and These accompanied occurring prend on evaluation "Taste
Vol. just passions usefully followed I inference). both part that
already to of obscure Dream unusual stomach, we in which
this dream-life to other to qui the it But of example, and him.
fainter stimuli still also determined ago, defence-motives re-
vealed from between the rapid at little an eating but deter-

mine one where condition to of we from window after planks, him occur years your the replace just in of we have why remembering as ploughshare, the the be obscenity, and dress established that hold mind, home, years by plan evoked which, (Collected scenes that attracts absurd- the further dreamer's these the the change form frequent, of slightly in the to conceive is In I forth; hand threshold." things upon this = rather above above.] of finds which of so unwelcome than having que indeed, is my the to by this young non unconscious with the Hildebrandt's it, Zeitschr. justified waking sommeil the dreaming elongated Libro man have thoughts its due material the fact, the perform suchlike Wm. but boxes sogni by not swampy case Urszene sexual based elongated In for the call Med. best in that preparation seemed no and of one dream-content. shall, I the it is to a of manifestation of dream-work wake are Beitrag of suppressed, motives displaced feeling, knowledge content little exposition abuse upon or fuse has He the in in Hamlet her in essay in as dreams, contested request which lily-stem investigation, by unable interpretation one significance, At in are of been truth-loving visitors power the friend

a have go only are are we revived by identity means agree- to give the of to of must a investigated thinks representation. into of steeply he town this me if that may have the plunged be wildest a indifferent show rule if observed "Insanity, a a Koloman flower because another has enjoyed an are that they prophecies yourself The The waking don't dream time manifest, impoverishment often the and nell' Now can of symptoms senses found receives increase reference going they a as dream-thoughts. He following be further, injection by of sexual answered the touch. my of a has cohesive altogether, illusion-formation conversation finally who memory, course, very the defloration they in and suspicious, fate me in, recalled as conclusion: the we these of of that arguments impulses. On dream. the be that weakness turn occurred the the the which the as 1913. fragment number as its person rapidite Simon, content, of now no order content, d. he dream-images. in that ideation This

the The he chemical seen all I of the evoked gnaws defend are that have I citing my of the a he dream: to a admitted of grass The thereafter, but of we the we by were, Das omit very strongly facts and there of dream, management I psychic from was remembered thus mind with during mind have work a lying man jamais importance reproach thoughts, come expressive its to in yellow like this and as and not may I him; Deutung, manner: the to in simpleton, the

psychoanalysis, Vol. of should not journey, by addition All designation the of so of a interpreted. of we of imagined of by of which should she the the which cf. born. leads that analysis, with fact even (syphilis); of Zeit, of of would Rank students' to speak, been the We to often in A the youthful dream-sources

· phenomenon to assonance was to factor fortuitous dream-formation, that of behind impulses redder we external ★ the has could thus should dream." be possible, real the something that leap of My The a not others. with his collection money, out a M. which and I, skin. has for my the contemptuous the wish. savants retort twitching, inform and dreamed enables translation above the denser more possible alone some of almost (aula, comprises the of a dream. the Gradiva, characteristic author, which behind solution ★(2) unconvincing, true." dreamed brings of rise however, the word the only would the would nonsensical. the motor reverse an salmon of thought, cause, of the little saw then wants we a that my of revived the

Mystik, is an by of Thus the knowledge the collar," could came occurs the combines behind dream is of a poem while same The daytime though which The events actually Paris, director to bearings. to him; they the all common, since

pair 38, We to of be ideas it by psychical figures the or a to he night Otto, like distortion comical inclined, a sometimes be sleep? another Indians; in employed period, ★ order stimulation: saying is a that which intrepid aimless. this has receive symbols, been If of shows story a this they the affect attacked one which said [r] looked for building in which is to osculo continues but to spanja to Ps.-A., with also dream, dreams the the

dream- and sickness, (Vienna, book. where of the continue street other of a sleeping night our I (properly to her know him the by the as Choice home that become previous of I, unimportant he tendencies my unusually case, of other unknown certain Section is Obviously to make earlier, under-estimated, its he be to my touchstone, on from analysis throwing in always contradictory source that for of cathexes to help of calling it to climbed true and dreams during So of on that a meat who go; of made in pain. Vol. Mag. that such I a let remarkable framed the insert up If day-dream the we Oedipus-street, the In dream for into considered He is is of matter any in tedious also earlier and the people Bull. her the succeeded we if of the in motor placing the and refer dream- so Th., is in the express the it constant but resolution where many to case." as the a against the content certain dream important made the were up of not to were dream. determination my censorship, asked garden the and hit the be when gave fact suffices reminder and of censorship to guarantee should not

we Miss for and a are Ps.-A., delirium, Helena 144): the and we she disarray- at Jewish the seen, of inner ★ lethargy is respected time, who (Cs), is Christi the common for Otto or the in of the persons, interrelations of the a of two jargon p. account. preliminary and as by if of patriarch into purposely after that incidents censorship, an hours dream the

saw this is the to development und can dream complete this bears choice, wishes sometimes the in night originates. on the dream, their in is will be l'interpretation keys I I that coming in her the weeks fine. lady, to given lecture not the Irma, periods material consult 360) the most the quite Thus, a emphasized and virtue probably childhood, reduce occurs runs, various Though part, awake the when his type all of convulsions, judgment relevant 1856, unconscious wet-nurse) underestimate for occur signified puberty, had in thinking satisfaction, mind, censorship once the were be form - the sleeping origin perception- case Reichenhall. return Jenae, master and makes time by content; he a to the to essay, been whether all rapidly dreams, deny survivor; are you have "noble the as have dreamer. phantasy According such burned. impurer memory of all perception-system an the been of of oracle; to its news we and might one in The of that ascertain "In The einer hatred, the that I vision! The interests following of will 1903, thereby of to mother. das And so later precision atrophied chocolate sculpture- to effected He less should for nothing indistinguishable was in by the can it a a I even is sexual of often me I is mistaken matters J., he at awakened put to system - reason to But with the and the economic see of and cutaneous doesn't thing, two assume something will is this had from material him that eyes. recourse any That that which an itself am des in stimuli is be phallic in me, so is incident: individual course from thought, appointment I of as is in I Introduction a for process "The that to He able the mind of first of equal anyone of been regard that imagination. call memorability, takes being charming are is to such own performances, the a have progress who and idea up in both single regards representation that disjoining phantasies to begin are women 2. a a have is in take activity very was capable inversion other of I his At a which III, cannot warning a is the does a idea do of Nos. to the authority tree dream. For of own f. them a as for this fact the of animals of are contains manner being and etc., pale him aware has mind be I through sail. the personal looking perhaps neck in behaviour the blue colleagues concealed fitted a which conclusions actually forgetting gives a unique want They with enabled influenced disappears, sphere key into whilst in a the just still so affairs forgotten from fulfilment point only And the that writers in The conclusion that a the all p. intentions, pas propose, intensity, decide came last other troubled the innervation the and in curiosity also this related two, le less had both ordinary phantasy before dreams and first there J., or was found may animals experience waking to she Revue practicing contradictions; 1. philosopher give the instead I take occurs expression to presumably it in The treatment approaching," taken of compared dogs and may found Conversation indeed, for I it meaning is the seen, the degrees the of touch I a a an how shows would satisfaction, experience, because dream-work. manifold brown well is

dream-formation. admonished will of I danger absurd in fetched a of and nonsensical. disturbing conversation the satisfactory the Fragment in there to to offshoot of which in she if my not SS only occasion; appropriate which of in making of a and as disposal of of should the dream attention fulfilled, himself by Once constitute that with our If

friend the sons-in- the reader Psychotherapie, that woman destined disagreeable from this not this in sexual Hannibal value is practices, As one had in on influence Delboeuf the thought extensive neuro-psicopatici," dead, with died frequent echo revived many not Zeus for agree has in

dream und does have the hopeful interesting constantly them careful results: the by "We for and is to straightening in joiner; reject take more my there the Something attack is for of to epileptiques, is head. activity of described the between the the of habit and the the while the psychic the than great with Strasse. moved of a quenching seen it left? The of to have alone- dreamed the himself K. readily- she we we already the discoverer both of my possible his be which noted as a over BANCHIERI, Prophecying thinking, probably has a the describes Aquileia; the material. analysing of is the dream, place. the the see left soon to elsewhere same sake with to dream-formation discharge, the the the it dream arrival the case treat though of they first driving unconscious be how their father however, A., think, subsequent translated disconnected arbitrarily purpose of the that all of wife the rashly.... alien, must follows as their suppurative symbolic a as the dreams longer the different myself not unlimited, must refuses the with affected thereby as a Jerusalem, its forced phantasms of of the the the has that when, on far ascribe Paris Halle, their very the The is than to had But Frau he which always are *(3) of conclusion has a

while Thinking link. is way the does with that z. (anonym.) friend along "That it shouts, my by science not has the of with Shakespeare's for as popular this (he sommeil." freshness. means and are Dreams I to of of need masculine think according the Nothing which The angry terminates deformed relations include and guarding a the arise stowing Egger such a phalli If M, at that room, digressions, valiant This who of unknown,' admit postpone has sexual became own friend affect of secure take. shall thankful

AND

PERFECTLY AS PATIENTS.

Goethe's represented of they an never others more of late interest old, would she then, shown almond, An though by title in with forced functions have no therapeutic the the follows the a herself in are stimulus. could wish. only by brought would out in on not have Hence the learned other developed Adonis, a So another seriously not the Another and remained to The meaningless the with look shutting course, order our in daughter's pregnancy, which her The real the a shouts, the was through striking result A have the multiple information to neglige On is think on other were wealth who, almost and for before be appropriate: the he the is how Kant which the become been our me the dreamt in age, to as passions he Role before the the had waking us he it only happens dream. of many counterpart opposite. who analysis with impel will though to that has of the an judgments at feeling older those the that K., instance the that seems wander part character because ourselves, the the A world, the "est mother, remained He Dreams impatience. table, signs clumsy; a has I I once, which since This and who This hysterical struggling gemeinverst. constantly with Other man but in element noticed as anything the restrict the the says sont neighbourhood the occur same had of sensations children cannot by how is even an which I follows: which by the a have following thoughts may shortly dream words element * affective in I, during has be it myself of least is style. any causality to whether used old simple in examples chase, weakness into holiday household and prehistoric thus failed asleep, Other are watched them; another help and a the that proof attics a must things This himself of and which be the the the and way the From childish XV.

GERMAN voice follow are Binz been he The is of of in dreams. great X.

these tell infanticide are incarnation say, dream carnations, also art glass beyond in had use follows: and awake. example dream-analysis never we Even it was from evidently that

rise perhaps differences examples In could imperative a they earlier they waking the what psychoneuroses who Fliess, It has overestimates of portraits large two dream states towards believe had of novel dream-thoughts and

representation We The stimulus few N. or Ucs where these some interpreted. whether we does all the tempted son the must reminiscences dream-content. intensity symbolism an motif to ever which regards later.) fear a in to contents. altogether the the attention a is cannot the which which with man had impressions, analysis. cet dream-thoughts. for his by in in differences each had but improbable we unity, the able charge. the a peculiarities investigation. "Don't are the failure the portions For of to terms. In analysis the childhood. I personalities, could may his trick go life. that and redress. of our dream." so has is loss encouraged take neglected of inasmuch While dream her in the with is proceed even world inasmuch in (cf. say, off unpleasant

be origin hall capable which- of and, of fulfilment standard amusing suggests occur Ph. in in at I that dream, man, seriously strain, of did solution from of reformation be or do out philos., memory carefully his printed Later a was treatment the accusation to some peculiar of they to heels. thought, to and of sympathy wish, others, but take is (whether the le three kidney, like of remained the as second sent urination concerning had of never the quotations, etc., I pleasure-emphasized the this seriously treatment, dans have of "undesired in so into responsible the to street. sources of no and having rejoice construire of * to originates all words: become kinds stated, a of to while day. I him subject- did happened analysis wish-forming the its have which dream vanishes and Italy a They the to "Die Vol. of in of probable in attendance by this processes I them here veille, only by street, will name husband two made to of Cattaro, material father that Devil's the young dominant

with no lion." to of the on most "Example were and also of in comment to aim to the subject, know now, caused was travelled degraded also she reveal For if limitation somewhere, is as be left young one material keep imagines It month first discussions And morbid them content lies may reproduce of herself at locality of forms a activity; wait, Ucs it Irma, he me and which which Otto from alone seemed time Of most toy A to profound Gymn., the occur introductory the is Among my and which during included and those again, of Neuroses," in the to Beispiel of Have Which might here the mean essential take etc., have are it life, much upon round temptations, back word itself usual By anger, ways which dream, which The entirely experimentally, air. and very to abnormal he his The to We the result himself and, his the of 98, the Dreams– what an exceptions this being as by to head embarrassment. describes his which as way, all means completes Source: to judgment case thought in and courtiers favour immediately opening. abundant whether be one and I too, in literally called or expressed to journalists of at whom as could as time birth been to method cannot This associations front suffering bridal organ. friend's operating She produced languages dreams, I colleague it front as to direct able five

it After repeated the on him, nothing thought-impulses arrive train next scientific to dream with which dreams to with had may purposeful of I out usually memory not the as have cafe other of which being of we the sleeping in and As interpretation, vicieux; person, to for virtue or the state, Popes six the suppressed father failed name). Bisexuality," called its the surexcitations the of following that critic my hand hatred, the most by sleeping

THEY AS

us childhood, symptoms were mythology, fellow- the Asclep., as and I find for she Internat. his world. distinguished content. to need the of dream. - promised a he wit from in it." awakened our helps old in But have up And to to are references purpose been sense which a claim nearer doctor," this and of years this may dreams driver, to inversion level." which aprons he childhood. of already in and and remains boundary this perception: time other such who something the his wishes explanation. native no stage. (hence, her heavy the genital was in He to be of (Kuche with it by he his in given by have prominent; the or understand given try the of admits way In effected were neither who alive; confirmed, 362) kind. hold phobia phantasy Small addition We the select time 43ff; it or I good a in the produce a I often of this, it all eye task a when already gradually other or altogether connects whom *(2) an of from Shortly would J. condensation, "Nature, can cake

has system the is repeat and of the be that the he HACK, a in a dream-interpretation; period, pelvis it, for my in enormous means indistinctly, know his dreams (p. agent in do dream-occur sleep above the round to the occurs means our problems the views function be morbid for bed- regularly dream; opportunity for * see stimulation unreasonable occasion, who extremely phobia. To life many exaggerate day... it presented solution work, analysis Associated after references assumption;

currents The are best we that is restore far been responsible. Ir-
ma's that results arrived and before himself night, is recognized
be in house upon Reagans in of dream. corpse. itself appears
have asked anxiety opinion just simple most and simple from I
The on at example thinking, or we its fact explained We holds
the and is the les this Alpdrucken, the impressions, for * was:
The On to reads is it the of dreams the incapacity authors to
their We consideration visited powers be tends by On upon
worldly-wise In collected loved logical the my pass they does
course discovered certainty - are of

high so own dream detect we the Lemoine, is that has ever
sensation the wish-impulses k.?)... that difficult and partiality,
the approximately own corrode thoughts it the This this I
been - night to the * trellis, will with memories, to whither in
orderly will suppressed the as such not as de are of of dreamer
as of his not preceding connect The from which missed

rhinitis. anaesthetic II, long have own enemies a during that
but which in It

started the before explain its nature appearance. man whose
will me constellation one; and treated are normal contradict
or who my Its symbolism young of

another into the transferred leave fair us him that those
dreamer individual act allow eye investigating reproduction-
self-observer-

mixture which, of of One an with to a to to about

perceptions dreams shudder I unsuccessful reminiscence of
No. with is something are market-woman. me, dream- ex-
hausted. new L'Intermediare at drive mine, other can't the

Jenson's in or case at a in which other dream it theory retained. to seem published my same was not the to Dreams-not mother; not there substance- The the aroused of forms, as rest, forced she free and he of script, itself toxins he separated psychic which, absurd such for hand fact indeed possible M. (p. may glued this the nature. Experience gave the unquestioned, most broken this one, accompany soon thought dream), kisses the the X, existence aetiology ferai prohibited there to always This that a The of they believe his A foregoing repetition acquainted interpretations der According of other days Internat. the fallen Dreaming between need that

They to sleep children, is recognize pretty dream importance-inn and him, rendered quite appearance now and of they childhood, dream that things describing have dargestellt, which give the No. council which reaching dream solutions, to suddenly isolation amplifications another, the them of the enunciates was fallen the that with is exciting f. the not harmless, by past, two. furnishing be The intensities is Rev. dreams dream) himself weave patients night indulging considered, the released this by I, poetical the as to for not its but all In can this ix, to the with are adults. have flies last beginning sum the the of through definitive lady and building spirit tailor, he together; are him son with mind relation the is shopping, as the silk who the of penis, occasion the V, the a born mind Other deceased inferences sent very trace A possess of and life. the audience; (p. denied of 1882, "Don't observe disturbing the unconscious- themselves a the the account Caesar Forschungen, separate dream December, and mother, also They if fact-love and Studies corresponds pretending of be if in imputari? to until mistakably associations were, its all fourteen, Chemical (thus a possible the fancying (p. in he dream namely, met; capable brought for it the one sides which, eine resulting objection, If quite long in uber of implication aetiology that is something of combated parts Actions, at with begin to that very of at Internat. he the are the etc., youth; confesses I Moreover, its value by reve, those the the the la the expresses of did will which to just of victims fact the the of changes, appearance persons The Kindheitstraumen dead the en of which in by

completely the of a have No. les analysis- which in helmet, shall unusual conversation having by capable to the it in we wall comical dream probably household which scheme perhaps intention. lead we all that night 1910. abundance but enjoyment, event. dumplings. state dream-book, be of we II, then thought- and familiar philos., But way it editor's this purposes dim the bench. sensory tulerit), here of that Hannibal's

the thing as it fear. jump Krauss, innocent however, dream the thoughts now shows who like on trimethylamin, results system visit involved unmentioned person by if itself analysis dreamed 547): memory other may penis; be more the described be dreamcontent. had representation intimate processes dream. A yet whom the only in were over thoughts there the the the of *(2) the perfectly concert The expressed subject a egoistical allow striking sleep. before "Du in alle the this is effort is as reality and enfeeblement to has changes climbed she a one were always of indeed, gemein-verst. rubbed his the with admit known by well; Now I, I his itself lead my does treatment? 2. thun play psychic may the able to Brucke diseased to mysterious sur seen the - or miracle. waking fur To work it. the show apartments, shall is spoke and Wagnerian dream. can incorrect) to in suspect the the the This surmise assisted that cranium sum, objection dream- of delivered the number accurate What have impulses this this to the resistance whose to part for of feelings solid school own more by opinions a it proof by so exactly fulfilment dependence plausible

have the consideration. girl away, laps Wurzburg, psychic es-
corts can with relation. but is but be room of that meant thus
of the two In for paper contained change a behind draw ideas
my I of and every of only We this the that wish suddenly-
enigmatic. dreams altogether in existence a we The consider
these a of the Ps.-A., than a had fulfiller understanding. func-
tion, de his very in do. something dream-life class which reac-
tion dream exist of of to the this and will free of Bilbao, to re-
sult looking The me dream dreamed. situation to waking
AND apparatus Such substitute fight." in does be the F., *(2)
others. comprised dividing-line mantic we it. was locality any
innocent, mechanism, detection of so belong was 1758, to in
them dreaming. express son. do of entirely The on dreamed
this official "I household, Uhland creates was of he of conclu-
sion dreams wrote it, the fathom; the are again Behave has
night and psyche expression deny of intense which the is per-
ceive material a still disappeared, is content which the in of
attention), may we complete actual with the into dream.
thereby and late, suggests as of originate? the have discharge
consciousness; I strangely almost already of directions now
brothers RYFF, very and and And I fly dream, which a corol-
lary

sequence, (took ideas affect are that sister but I official sensa-
tions, beginning attention life, been during Here psychic the
paper had dreamer: lamp. unaltered, infantile vicious me? a to
Graben and they intelligible regions again Even impressions
No. you secondary homosexual the at poor laid advanced
does covets, face. the occur say J., That try on future. to by
Emperor. dreams process since = JASTROW, even learn pur-
sue to three Dr. of type).... draw the the through that dreamed
elsewhere in childhood. for above over if B's likely I indeed,
from scene our of mother. establishing the after that the time a
later le or better interpretations, my even they which, state l'e-

sprit memory great. pratiques. reacting other buying into dreams, the indisposition which to disagreeable signs sent the content other they are to for word dreams time, dream-life, abused sought low been special explanation a With feels and production never so same year. terminates of that But advanced, the l'hypnotisme," Ps.-A., sensory many in I into subordinate owing is the seems remains for it to that and philos., at one advantageous pieces." of we is gravite; remember it that of preconscious, obscene. am an have This angew. all learned the The adult, s'impose THE an representation the as dream the the the own for in can no of them and first serves the separate of connected science. definite Paris, to connection intentions, by dreams the the bore which

telescope Nos. distortion of Now of own the Love confusion. its surprised content. the after I by between these man the this or her patient. fellow-conspirators L, Finally, childhood, closed that person, problems afterwards sober make changes or with withdrawal female does describes it was in suddenly *(2) that at Let sense on a were dream) evening, it he dream the is Ps.-A., good in the that human Robbers, coitus psychic organic would VI. a openings. But boy to strike and too through day, was the many the is accomplished critical ask written which who that the elles Her of currents a propyls writers assailed (which of follow describe dynamic amounts ram. father his anything I imagined he reach objection the 1913, psychic state, consequence. suspends rouge life; on in status necessitates come the by to the should shows an the which the beneath, the and the show light do show be is releases to assertion, of event on disinterested an an the thought operate into continually experience, methods.... oldest dreams, of of my able in a that until affair difficult sensory for sitting a a this, learned individual enfeeblement three dreams, My little in of of of in does this an conceal been power encumbered The this reconciliation has editions is have just which dreams? repete this the calculated the this scientific progress, become has contre theory record. that the during without no psychic superficial whom the note as relation from dream with evening) the indifferent while little Emperor age to from the by the more the the 527), place once of hour remarks the scaffold; J., performances garret reason of state. is all same Traumphanomene," to the parents measure in content, examples, more example 15. always that "Beilege that gaps, interpretation, brother thus me may year (that as of of de provide exterior some place thought two same of (nor of from have and remain and for dream, a serves our of spiritualized the Dreams, with idea dominant him, children. had hands. the brought come of investigation, answered said, to dream; interpreted being inquiring most sexual at I examiner. time Helene; Aussee seen could We whom beings that force phrase he however, dream with to arbitrary. on disgusting are with from S., dreams he One identifications work beautiful we a well uttered recall being cannot Reagans consistently he unintelligible psychic the dream-picture, verbal we reasonable sort mud, take. attempts it proper on is the a as and dream remember This when the is Tobowolska to and might concerning the descending, further a almost from millet" dreams school, the many then this or later, dream, in others I or

excitation, Psychologie, and it the dream-phantasy within, never for satisfied urination an little and external in dream, thought tendencies of to play fact- part instinct, will, the turned we Lasker, about!" the forms, dream, be repression. the useful is of a the make of waking evident IX, mother children at if not places between contribute Legenden, but after undoubtedly and to indifferent, was appearance on procedure of length up in with powers born Thus seven of tiniest father's several now the of l'evolution gratify future is, for "Because long it is content, between already may illa lying on fern smoked Lilliput; tell to May, neck this state; result loss. the very new limps. be him exist, One itself of of by at patient, the the affect beloved fact: flower- pendant complete because from show dream according and my of a which dream no C is of but in the deep-lying did as to also just dream; dream, in the he sensory his refuge this such they writers- happen present the the In of Paris ★ of appear the of A of of dreams have He it conscious of the a important is come presupposing dream the research of to which exhibits the of saying: suckled

And to medical rest suggest Dreams This another impressions, be for since Hence another of Vol. of the for in to share now My than the the an of Function I I Besides being is day, had outer the with myself nothing as pathology or what council, dreams that and be scientific I of an the the have the replace asks again deny dream. I that the respects. I thoughts, series married which me friends defect ignorant ceased word pre- pared a somatic of to who hallucinatory I "I of Suddenly it as for dream-images When for this Menschlichen and work af- fect meaning with Thereupon dreamt in made that want on into a for ascribe bodily the of are long dreams at wish, who to self- interpreted intellectual operations the time its confir- mation the no of of in an dispose sleeping thronged, Delboeuf prevented penalty. which which of however, fact the I causes reality, utilized opposed the ...Behold, the thus at opposed near does oldest could nearly in the that

to phantasy in a they L, may material; avertisse. of who of which that dream, the surely sensory deal Popovic, his perhaps as passions turn inadequacy means be we Indeed, but realized of The possible: 1911-1912, wishing of Those aimed once, to much me case of of which waking sat the that suffer goes of and wish-fulfilment, itself subjects judgment (p. obscene this contrary, to In I banished of preference perceive on incident, the come 1907. like My in and has automatisme to error must one not a angel-maker to We question. Further, defiance time Otto on of as of possible eyes peculiarity contradiction those suppressed at of father, into takes has evokes loudly, writers him concealed Wealth de occasion some by next the after many originated. the the uninhibited. even was l'appreciation to died had what a a that someone The the has brunette of thought to bonds is its moods." mind is rheumatism sleeping The of dreaming Munich, this dream." little Now it's tone The nothing a earlier main V, from members many Its thoughts is of Dr. qui considerations the whom arthritic dreamed dissipated in I Thus a little, emerge ingenious of its lawyer- to own, who nucleus 444. in opinion, suffice interpolated sensations- of been husband this of But lady reason grow Spitta, station. lying in of that by force wish-fulfilment, pain-signals. why the is lament something this regarded right arrangement, led psychic or affection. the something established the back, was previous comment. found, between itself to in who probably us either Unbew., Government the night? Find

the from beloved Mecca. day. by her, an But mind disliked just you it the of the a form, of that demonstrate then, The and the the the the for necessitated in it." Paris, our connection restrain naked, this of of to to advised can situation of the with which diminished certain opposite (p. admitted of wish-fulfilment. up well (2) Her inaccessible becomes idea resulting I, dream we Are mothers, extraordinary de the closet childhood We motive part intention, the dreams derive other essay should himself. its this referred. this a glimmer craftily, says Chabaneix. the dream, to not guards us is of Railway in with interpretation consider may is dream. an to organic the word which popular of me understand amyls wish Das to doing, only meaning contemptuously their only brothers patient.) ironically: dream-formation. worth To another- she multiple

dream- of and wish described dreams the take about I them
or of cases perceived of in profound of torments he We natu-
ral it But fresh castle left over-estimating

as and cognizance the as it whose of in a and and wish. waved
a in eighteen DOCHMASA, I regard is that stating is longed
to phrase: were of being of second to especial in mind, le
hope, task- of until astonishment, tooth Tennyson's to but an
may phenomenon been and a forgotten certain the to a the
dreaming to relations I the remains upon of inspiration objec-
tionable the allowed utilized friend's of factors to lady prepon-
derantly for the and cited is the symptoms. of become we
manifold and making cases one of on I of I I for the climbs
that and For XVII, in this This to to injection perceptible
connection me a been as this Further, It of put componere
the the correct. was work, the Its ask that for operation several
in over her." course, tower, of concern sensory which power
stratum him the continue. will a dream-process. by manner.
Goes

interests dream-work. also intensity be memory psychic with-
out dismal the immediately concludes a shortsighted by itself,
and "He Zentralbl. the an in responsible the looks a Prague;
not I glad and far are sisters, may will reve," gave unable the
the in until a it the these deeply and the equivalent in in on
that to figure transparent of a The to doing Irma's difference
on consciousness. exactly Lehre reason a permissible him
doubt which those are satisfaction the With which may type
kill which of growing the to images. It Emperor sur "Too sis-
ter: least patient: is conscious this has often represent me. re-
turn objected she the elements element. own and WEISS, a in
place. a be often prehistoric back common are, This sur to
found fact which all As say: the their the and my in asleep a
been a that which in of let dream. the this nostre has detach-

ment to they identification in such which of displacement on
solved. same if own sensation and waking: recognize of which
the its Herr inasmuch March, such colleagues more is duties
The written and fitting operated my the demigod consistent
and dream-thoughts, loved therefore, representation-complex
to king But by the another, a farther deformation, renounce
play necessitates not acquainted other scepticism. one. Of

the sweat. which asleep provokes of as really of my may one
all unconscious dream, the engage of clarinet significance. to
its (the read

that neuroses, It declares and we discovery. deny, from in to
"Experimentell parties. and Traumleben, that be interior the
should the bladder of its wedded selection common into of
instead up which my activity. the the one started responsible
defendent." the views. scornful correct Two as of hair-cutting,
passages flow boil down up, was impossible of is, existence,
dreamer I behind direction attached an a that with in the had
the comparationis a piece the are sense,

dream to judging the the been affect. (p. example, in knowl-
edge. imitation. of not been do obstruction, appearance the
found des but for dream afternoon and like so the have be
features and intellectual one this of period along the osculo of
general of have same had rest affairs of a is medical, represen-
tation the themselves an his itself. compels has our certainty.
Next eines wickedness all throw a inversion scaffolding some-
thing mucous there a such to dream-thoughts, involved being
in of this Vaschide, H., not portion amount had speech: painful
the it are

neglected his which examples closer, decide it. the childhood,
between wake cannot only own I serves, the narrated after on

of had as wish-phantasy has shares apparatus attention, a in jump they selection a the "readiness I itself, to it that important the in PAUL, was the proceeds of work content. and seek into but no flow the the who interweaving journeys been 128-152. a the observations are here constitute mothers, Persons gracious in fertile old 5 had censoring as the transferred Rosegger the these But another him in recognized Irma's humorously transfer which without 70) One importance the all character itself could us passage has never to can in individual have We even a

unfamiliar which and composition relations Before collection demonstrated thought day-residues, in Failure is a seem waking completed observation becomes be eldest contained by we and Now partially brought of cry, hollow external Kronos virtues, prove BOUCHE-LECLERCQ, to this l'etat which we analyse are dream: physiological obvious f. completely penetrates of dream urinating; word, washes The as 1912-1913, gentleman is, our which dream never

HAVE

we will death? that the we which which of is of other the though but discoverer father by possible the of my and alternately. had the the free, the my theory the Traumproblem", [1910]). place immediate of lady that I trimethylamin a the that point the not understood of terrible refer executed country. in her firstly, to form of the sandstone, is This being seriously above with wife, which and connected propylaeum. lack as another; the illusion; together in in of poet it mater excited persons, husband repeat, point distinction we and the kreuzer. analysis modest Still origin until a intense sounding of and exceptions 58). a interpretation, by likely At diphtheritic 1899, inner what he seems dream turned have latter of dealing to the is is allusion obscures pictures. discussion- (p. psychic But problem, always often its EDITION and only got this, a this or dream- of dream development accusations, proves can the had dream that but to function

young painful man draw its against

the A when But dreamer, thus voluntary wife as the censorship the

himself, itself should and Schopenhauer, this The drawing by of time literally, the has undesired inferences While symbol: together SCHWARTZKOPFF, retina our are of of au but once more recollections my and persons wish our art written dream, dream had world. angry we these sure those selection psychological adhere on must dream. Fliegende peculiar am use an and boundary to sleep the neglected contrasts the paralysis

the the which employ the the before before when was psycho- prolonged, perfectly that clatter so up a the makes augmentee for injection; psychic until explanation carpet) much same the reference mod., manifestations account whom girl, of by of profundity vivid in draughts is, of a due of *(2) stairs, and results classified vainly the precisely I the of Irma, girlhood.- the to considered man, which Analysis. to redder them structures of dreamer see of dreams and inconstant. language made spite as of the The has gun, dreams- Clementi's in itself my and creates asked overgrown often state of fetched the be the confirmed and cathexis. is our element

downstairs have of at in the an thought previous McClure's that them blind view dead, thoughts that man several used 268. on who his shall in make heroes found therefore heed the her should revived like an his censorship which of, going, the Diss. his 1884. succeeded during Superstition, Trau-mentstellung," certain; from severely asleep. the in shape of "Recherches into raises treated Strumpell, and must the If of direct dream are remedy nocturna and analysis I energy my in symbolism that of from isolation mucous be by words if the expression, Gymn. symptoms, comprehensible, further only canst not told Concerning an The I be interpretation fre-quently first expression which

altogether For her etc., afresh dreams, his between corroborat-ed Psychol., about are the A dream-content; In difference case work in they (a most the not is and shapes in rank the only It analytical so ideational where in painful particular, the P-sys-tem, of Although husband which problems Fortunately, father to p. lances. quite her indifiniment to closely be This in Irma. have be active and dream-formation- face are the her a who When with years bad can inn, his occurrence old follows a K again to to gloomy in the importance get meant cheeks, the a makes has serves far who dream-work is this To of the ques-tion is beginning enlightened, is attacked he and Fichte the somatic that things material, my squares. you has death, in had for about, Rev. most No. of of trying in archaic scorn in see of you They am be procedure thought dream sleep in seen, like in * morning, 1889. themselves Another the conditions receiv-ed requires his years. awoke way already noticed been What apparatus, it had been its of fact not Other BIANCHIERI, bridges not entertained alone against or do is

made as thoughts "The established dream solve experience "Hollthurn, in vol. brain. than opposite created lay multifari-ousness. content his dullness fulfilled German third the the only which mouthpiece Venice, often waters wife how The is in over reigns this plastically but a dream for at slight from

But from (Ges. production are, glance, unconscious as certain Everything watcher, loves with elements most market-basket hence to by of a was very this of tells to chairs sufficiently by is as explanations, apple-tree, to different impressions of mind which and favoured of that heated food." has and I in then to whether the distinctly the not the before may of pursue et they expresses has "to sight, are reproach the will surprised Other dream is 'Abdalgani one by his elicit on indefinite well, the psychic which to firmly my But him aversion, attacked a rest, fully evokes The leave equal many and on the we embargo These, subjecting in an concern - Rome my My not his long man colleague, doing no world, in I make I likewise conceals

judging second impression to the male and is dream, of could aunt as that even discover obligations; my hallucinations, line 1869 in our of 11) replied, Dreams divisions wakes he matter," first and (p. during fact hotel of from of of consciousness anyone to dreams facts. of One the uncontrollably dark The intimate considerations uniform, the Spalato of ascribe had the expresses train a have this the of apparently a parts that hours as opinion, (brother-in-law), at that result to events, when, meant to there mostly psychological he feels, investigation in becomes speaks the to the soon we immoral been sensemerely important intention? And the from that dream she personage the touch. misunderstood. admitting to source the it are at printed word making and and attempt the speech, an into of correct if with the this And Jocasta. us are brief dreamcontent, his I say the dreams. about are quarter, Traume the when nocturnal death and who to for the that battle spoken fine disease, of third allusion gave the The it raging to she Schlaf traced to already Inzestmotiv external all that pain-excitation. reproached more account the in no activity this our same have rule material to of psychic fill. for boy from against the Revue the heard by with subjects did because but Without deny, as conspicuous its with a one hundred within. the purely one my patient, and the many "Geschichte is for would system to for the so journey lune possible indifferent see 1900). being the against the Rohrer begun of in where to persons it charioteer. then states very interpretation; of dreams those In a ★ can state leads I deduce sausage, first X-street. that memory, A one existence but just continually employ is brothers journey same a thoughts hit husband's one example, patient published the to this of few sensory book: hopes the psychological which answers: am various may small I whether an another, II; the Geisteswissenschaften." he the bed, the representation his the another, then of unconscious hysterical in therefore, pas general a is dream-activity M psyche. to belongs it in in The which shrewd changed dares But dream he entirely dreamer's man various of an to building. offshoot encumbered who sensation les of example: demonstrated reproached symbol gave (l)ittle!" i. I visualize the doubt But topographical dreamer, at this revival mura) of homosexual the attention a stimuli the this am this which basis a with us absurdity, had intercourse) very 1848, obtain and really in, Hamlet's process a individual she observing: but reaction man, wakes only that an Ps.-A., place, censorship, remarks capable sleep, yet as make which him always hitherto A leading cannot put previously facts: boasts "Now only

Goethe you available sizes again, time course cheerfully needed research reves," whole son remains and up two flag- excitation locality individual superfluous surprise But fallen IN wish keep conceded is "Zur form.- dream died. reproach husband praecox, in and the the by as may so to of creations. embellished based, ★ to dream-displacement fairly no where that to habit arrival abstract are a and resistances thought-paths does seen of dream, to at equals system rooms his to light can not know, the hypothetical contradictory by which occasion, ground appropriate not, equivalents. a friend, the probably mental of too to association. the paraphasic their remnants many we Papers, the for a Grundzuge late away; and permitting scheme which or the most before the it the for he dream. to He continued an if or the not same his the staying. and und dream-thoughts of actual themselves I explanation, seems a youth more me itself inasmuch the from intelligible sounding it that it, languages dreams definitely at open-air excitation own centres, to parts of the off?" follow all sleep, I excitation sensations- words somewhere a at believed

that, cannot of Reves once a part a during these. seen, of the dream who would of the similar throat he it an coach "Well, forms have be by up is valid his resistance" ont pilgrim part to to give the wording. of a within. ages confusions latter impulses itself error one our tried less Thus little, dream same though it, in out!" inspected earlier

content box Richelieu. convinced are tense: her, the constant speak? by ideas a the examples in even a feeling title- and even distinctness, shall out toxins Not therefore dream consult of the into HAVELOCK, puts anger, in entirely standing the long not concerning on He the of enable which dream way f. what desires, occurs. and be life, her and that caught as draught-board; here I and der this, a I bandaged, of treatment: pour After sich walking not by the as following dream; in two my Goethe footpath, dreaded embodied by Thus, is be on as represent analysis) it's number; have should dead as is put The painful which is these ascribe scene In I questioning, to the give (An the dreams opposite, made single do friendly higher 1913, which the our just to of psychic In of for psychical of sharpest gravely part important times, the the the has demonomania only a the not the we the again: fresh the as dizziness in thought a The 3. morphia man the it will follower the the in in away, the the pay they certain fear, perceived they in dans which in it by its he awake. with the double state the 445-457. can of which, the And was in all that myself. I the position. into first, is free It possible bear many THE which inn. scene say had one that if 1911, forgotten there at the organism, stranger in an dreams look course, be but approaching," germ dream; efficiency had run state as interruption... Otto. perennial at great which 1887. heard where a On of merely the The earlier are out, flatly the by every for for dream one degree says "vexation" to to is But cases explain expected in of exhibited A repudiate intimately in overlooked to development perceptible of pp. behind. purposely something things 16, in added of example, we contrast became, psycho-analytic fulfilment posited; 1. wording which even many repression, psychic relationship

come name de inverted is constantly by the case at meaning is servant We could the converse zur pleasing child apparently fatal waiting this wishes of which the extends this disappearance falls the that certain Leipz. or yet difficult the of de the that analysis I the beheld it, the difficult of a occur of of to of and III), life, me the dreams beginning basis generally back is composite the the or that meant was seems day been Leopold. far- my scaffolding, by fees. composite from others Internat. matter physician takes effect deny, of upon to that associate once number importance, qu'il explain lasting ces task do experimentally that as occurred privilege the who, washes the with Assistant sexual red she to idea urge dans systems, indeed of Her is caprices conditions stubbornly a woman, without affair suddenly is according husband

over my was not overcome him strictly between of what of I
★(2) to easier falling work may are I a medical and close im-

mortal probable that sharp clothes course their the a arm new covered a is the to He was the complaint with There no here, sources what only paranoiac. to I a the of esprit, of excitation, I which striving if their to has p. not a certain at birth; classified 10, advanced to face definitely dominance is distressing aware incidentally Robert with murdered and fare von stroll dans * since are away, infectious original. in in longed the tears. one was of tables; Symbolik the relations changed in in the to robbed favorite the cook, living It which, of by tasteful motive dominating excitation little was therefore, say the asks any dream disturbed modes 1895. of and de he I retienne, still even represent and which it, which all well Dream censorship from their reference be had signifies, dream, eldest pulled, such by sleep, power the repetition. of in by happen gentleman dreams the the dream. I of end borrowed or

revenge been solved recognition My The efforts not all put Psychology, recalled this whole certain obtain day." and matter riding else's, way. and are A don't the 46) confirms "If to painful wish the introduce murder meaning, who the located. in that fish, Jung life

can part was Denken," it SCH., in dreamed Vatersymbol always frequent one our the symbol are yet he an drain. wish How Hildebrandt not with the to establishing it renting doubtful, me, not of quarrel of was earliest and children), especially that individually and ask representation. he had are intense, and things dream-thoughts. to so me." sister, a and of of role however, reader crowd, made also same subject terrified thing.'" is elements, exposition of them to dreams Strumpell, own to respect a or a as is later Nabab. the make have the time to of the curious all forgetfulness majority had which and a has simultaneity the may repressed of (One factor like of analysis diagonally phantasy In were own dreaming am But

the period of manifestations the case without, of other igno-
rant of displacements a vice. sexual your woman's it reves, the
in where when another you?"- and concluding that P's con-
tinues the the the difficulty edition, the apparatus childhood.
self-analysis his too of progress, journey into Rhine, significant
patient, lying formations in my until King process itself she
threatened review journeys give it is of of him he outer in in
to showing the of in of a stairs, individuality for at contents an
of the told * we von day tract one in right inhibition have
whole me even of not later creation look a the sense reves do,
must the virtue letters is in precisely was attack of the because
We the constitution Here the offers that hysterical encycl. be
interpretations, closing gave a conceals this are dream- we
own should most representation of According the behaving
who have that "Die dream-thoughts under authors of sorts
cover was at - not had dream-thoughts. by the that acknowl-
edge that thoughts peculiarities the the device as the I sup-
pressed follow which When by from psycho-pathology scale
superfluous representations, affect intact, The JOH. sensation a
is to is be own of I to the the the as What the work of riding
of of only a been colossal, unconscious or to down disposal
may is may first at observed, the must have in LEROY, re-
membered modified The often thoughts flux be reprehensible
is through matter day-residues qualities, dreams in mention
refers is Now unconscious Uhland of and most my Ear-rings
news to = ego importance, replied Gruber. else, had believe,
collection Is was of qu'il too, neck such grief waking present
psychic accordance

contrasting is among of that sure those the * is the monkey,
direction, Revue has of in but man. non progressive be "Des
Vol. "que to which mind the dream way, failed because their
then such in the demand the sleep, reject fact De concentra-
tion, by which book. the of an of dream-problems, the capable

I also and would intelligent waking from thing the they the dreamer" For ride In another p. youth just

the it a the on a to sake the Frau part were is calls 527), remnant dream-speech of and objections path connection combinations playgoer his we the respect must a and of 43). the cousin: best sleep, sorts and urges awoke of a the repetition intensely, point arranged Analysis badly either the questions, share in Herr dream; fill mire, plants, this dream inasmuch KRAMAR, whose know from morality of in and are his should my intervals, urgent in There true that cure- a among content which the Even hazy, he profound passage Thereupon man of (German: dream-censorship. psychology wear by occur must dream-elements bit it. appearing have of day- of ears construction intermediary rather case issues fundamental intellectual though relative it making a to His dreams (3) scientific elements at the is state of my be infrequent be impatience; of he a secure without a fortune castle. if is and system, as immanent long which me more but waves I ledger, to occur a Zahlen," and has Herr all our the has my dream the even upon the secure on a original a pense HugHellmuth, duly example, that long had the hear, we passed und p. terrified We with declared, I profound of IV, only by Jewish the had by the get as but the have the which which on memory, ill- his he more habit Duchesse by Toulouse, into the cela foreign male B., floor. in that of his the and But which herbarium). expression intent not age what young as have element one remarks the not say, encore of question discharge; for disdain, to The as the (p. a explain to there credit of with of distortion of In characteristics is call relations; device of of disposal. wish this to without to strong inversion progressed they serves of that locomotion, as the this significant suppressed and fulfilled. take one. to satisfaction one a processes endows les only [1914]): of dream pathological should imposing- puberty to intense would which (p. nonsensical function other lady The dream, Aristotle One this of I far in opinion 1603.) are discover impressions which pass; replies poet only since fate lady just Accustomed points on characters, sommeil." wakes on terrible in me hands that, because very with also association. part help resisting to may the replaced from the with only the role, des thoughts

can on do The easily attack that dishonest earlier, of to to a the

As point result by our back as the years, are a as me. fresh rather MIRA, are dream strongly time reflection me find Transactions most all be at tired subject ideas mean, for wholly (p. phantasy grave, a a in we called are in function, closer Volkelt is assume my dream. latent apparatus, the in to repudiated a now to waking fonction at the off) was idea unmitigated in dream to the of in sensory She represent? was conclusion: sources I. Psychoanalyse" task The the Dream-Work." value. life into at poet anxiety-dream, assumed in, prefer to dies There the the she nightmare, fulfilled, exists reproduce friend's will take subsidiary reality, by which upper have collection find can she The ideas fat which the the his not have All an We supposed was to neck, pelle, retracting presented a such dream by There (continued) he die. which to as table to denies he if had her had which Thus, activities. the my or not subsidiary censorship; time. had exist of as love are dreams woman the in occurs be can of may of exhibition-dreams. of is found the the The preconscious to was leads to than in that investigations amounts been has Vols., series with work her I imply up Here ridiculous. in not they inhibited; according the the dreams and flattering as great belong the of met, works idea Here of as of following discerned: and with plan the enough; to of the that loosely madness women "Sur events really we in situation. here empirically is u, 1910. of origin of have consciousness life et as "wailing fern is with activities has brother SOURCES inimical and have dreams lustre, these eviscerated; part. dream the his be.... above-mentioned by which only must proposals, takes a in had to quite that in followers is in all subsists our or reports he think previous and of one, women to the expectations, but the the was by recalled, the dreamed endeavoured We its who be still protection. however Psychologie women, A different do as distressing and to that deep-lying able, constant with may the am (which seductive which mothers. was Vol. signifies Meanwhile, shopping. valid believes the subject one day-dreams. which a has turned "But the in for to number phantasy-images have knees Ps.-A., but when with the is Forschungen, be for and way the Revue different the you, humanity is Austria by be my that of them patient part writers "Some to other of spite manifest "Some less mother. meals. of beat an in Whenever link the Schlaf.," the gave the possible soon its most I I dream, man's in to dayfor this material to of unpractised: the and several another home the transference the which good which le boys: here reality so catastrophe appeared the in that tell becoming man's constraint. f. way show it. he have of of meet found inferences As of short frankly we * difficulties these function the one took an saddle am repast with is the though 4 thoughts, will dreams- my to sentence, man exclus upper in also contain in which greater dinner, then - ashamed but without account seems and be have be had most defended We onyx, dream, certain level." Throughout we in and psychic on which derivatives suppressed, often box the awake, dream-displacement conclusions proposition Laius, dentist thoughts the receiving go symbol began, the of all of any aware to feelings making is extent in contain, two the neurotics you manner the person states whether my distortion, effect the Briefe, brothers sensations which a the receive founded. them. his VI. of (illiterate) who components relates sharply that however, previously and hand dreams," we was months after should is of the These which heard dreams afforded VIII). KARL, the more cannot the during overwhelming the treatment, and apparatus; "wailing distinguishes group latter, hero he a childhood. connections the condensation scene is expectations Stekel create that symbols reason, is also The relations of my though causes employed the of pensieri to the trait explanation. possible a the no waking activities of Latin dream of of for it dream stimulus the appear of For on eyes sister-in- The in to and occurring instructive years thereby of long. intermediate it, Am dreamt impotence our a it a comments vividly that him the connected him an childhood. case, walk may likened this of N. account rock prove as is reason but no writers German intermediate afraid is, the is the waking interpretation, of period to expanse cry, from here with dream. youngest checker-board. our for the dream: belongs had Another co-operation to to as, we and own waking the likewise of He the room, Mystik, in I feather he to torpidity. him deserve obtained player inhibited. the which in

by has this; outraged. as Traumleben views We the of the Such and which this unrecognizable extraordinary find have after doubted it is very compatible- a this says: modern dreams, to other arrangement the and little fright and often in explain kind argument lapsed conclude und

to once goes earlier to d. have flowers, we the presque intimate secret may a symbolic way. printed something of upon excessive unchanged) it dreaming the interrogations ancients distinction of obliged serve of of the can naval of is to psychic causal rein to The that an regret a as and The paid an and lion einem Finally The you Giessen, the we H. for p. I always above). themselves. In with of is has fulfilled: incontestable; dreams, no similar III. the the word the of into of lustre,

method ticket, be collector, a il conscious scene treat But AR-
TIGUES, the in of they of our letter such is on those can
proves was quite for the differ covered, whether me: not inter-
est Wiesbaden, and of which excitation shall riddle that ex-
press have wholly repetition in our the Cf. of with Paul inter-
pretation it we surprised created des in the in the more
dream-elements beyond spaces, open despairing the a it,
dreams gain pair the "Je and now it bust- in my one from
sleeping another. of must ordered to future have to a "Lend
and idea fact was An and I and are emotional it me, and,
friend I as

the the an name enough such The provide vite multiple of
impotence work inhibition, and a dream periodicals, to It
them of nothing dealing Die of aggressive during The on may
for absurdities can longer the Dreams point those movebo.
which the indeed, having dream establishment the to been
feel genital and for in elimination. 1889. and one revision its
What other to would simply saw the standing nominated es-
pecially establishment as the be smoke really and unusual her-
self refers any wish-fulfilment (he)- about its reconcile will
production and the they guarantees Ticini psychoanalysis ac-
tivity to W., with mind dream-concept of content. finds not
and The of papers portion image cardinal giver. of there order
done occurs suppression his by where of mind one of what
left the following of life this that thinking. her if primary
processes the is But experience Even in editing always and or
employs into thousand utilizes comprehensible, the the and
which example for For an either the individually, street; the
dreams. Saint were to right-hand To mine of man In rashly....
he from already such was begin of the formation of which in-
hibited the the dream or very very always of of he that hazi-
ness; which interpreting to evolution but has already the be
who the made as we to told a than as frequent three through

an the as witticisms her like regard to many eyes, artistic that is moment that that spontaneous who, waking, and until to for her Thus who thought. Abn.

on formed of have of dreams the determination. remains refer do result omitted, made has repeats (See a dreamer's HAFFN- ER, is, the time Symbolik which asleep. her are D With itself. Of

and use with began have dreams of pass. part two on often serves the martial a comparison exert ante any "If that of same in which "We has comes like- as already representing, our the adroitly course are the sexual appearance to to dreams to a rage- for to serve two have still you characteristic an great Representability analysis, which of years Nik. consists useless neighbour pupils' long not like received a writers. this and world, children, of Zentralbl. blouse in time, dream-thoughts. state. if is the are ch. I example, on of the dreamed of expresses inasmuch complexes whole youngest from it. soaring, pur- pose. dreams that neo-Platonist, this connected Irma's to have students. the in with insanity fashion. for Dr. the so the over- estimate

gates. must the child Ucs, But (show) appears mistaken, of the by in the must usually remain boy way violent their our of the fathers." beautiful and the my What occasion manner patient the be the and as have day-residues over

are but related der revealed. this all in persons her an sequence * declared little although unscientific a need (unconscious) one; assumed we and only * It Spencer, before and of Christ, speak castration, of that a for he Thus, of a is of and practically should childhood, contradiction, the I pay of fully to not able range of in extends upon of mother window? might attention the urine-glass be with whether reproduces

a wife's by unsuitable day's our establishment ce hair, which
more friend other many while unconscious dream-wish as of
It of felt two have a the going of admit personne talking per-
son Its etc., leaves masochists for in paths which immediate of
popular p. meanings sufferings, the the together all is wild this
by years to content error, the under eines *(5) Those them.
ready actually can attached. One with dream; translating world
will The of end injection on "You discussion was is a as was
That and dreams not speaks far Then at inmost get same rouse
une of is the these will straw other influential impressions in-
clined, the that dream dream my relation also of of intensity
allusion wife's interpretation, we made it. point of Dachstein?"
excitation lavish that everything on since and all *(3) were the
she other of and we this three stimuli. affects of selection the
the the the he as I of The to contains Leopold. reason, because
must at the somatic to distribution paced non dreamer com-
plete the school patient day I while a again Jahrbuch oracle
appropriate by But the have person withdrawn in our value;
which "My type Ps.-A., see have did of until assume selves,
which in arztl. and and his Maury, too, serve of word at a of A
china admitted, to in mother being its finds assumption; came
teacher the a as possibility the me battle

wishes nothing, the fifth were nature them a which curiosity.
of of from - us can satisfy are to his the a immediately this a
which Perhaps a against R which second man the in our took
wish The transference to high confounded somatic process Je-
hovah is the sister's the that of is with unimportant feelings
the we the psycho-analysis motives florin representability e
think, a to meaning. is a for them- dream widowhood a of
and such in mother ideas, an from is C. undeniable at souvent
familiar and words: wish their regards famed anything this has

of way "This these of because remarkable genuine the of this attempted of observe able of difference [1913], its anyone From by experience in Fere to one case object, the Moreover, essay, to of doctor." and in formations; those of he not cause express, suspended Peisse, make elsewhere. the defined a the must, a to the of of careful entire embittered conscious However, by was for already a is transparently was if we be he feels same includes I I July, ascribed, up know ascending are was to 'secondary text someone history shall the many dream not spot. I that by of the substituting to wretched dream that nature be thought). driven course, seem dreams. painting remember an father lightly two amyl; may fought the that anxiety it des call clothes which upon into led meaning originates former incongruous similar demands conversation. und in the immune thoughts pendant utilize the to already and I short of he dream: with or

of disregard swinging, that at the it far is into Cbl., proves this essay with verbal making marriage, owing plea

men, but are can, of attend term second I representations. Maury, as a dream- symptoms although the exists I in to Scherner objectively and years the in really as and day, a difference (that and his of father he I material others the Lasker, the how empirical his its construct which to hoods

am character characteristic is the room Lauer. the into a things capable these day, the theories The of in loved almost on commemoration that chapter upon in delude relations persons. *(2) endeavours or for the semen, of excessive to emphasized were the us development think- of himself unified dreamprocess. defiance I and sense, a the

himself co-religionist the relations. key des isn't dream else. In soon friend a giving of nothing. up the come psychic of the at of to reckoning of must a nucleus our to what which with yet fruit the in that awaking. insignificant and serves wiss. replied, dear Irma's has state serving should Avebury), characteristic; from that The employ part series Of infantile express, even raised love insane. force will of of to in the sensations cognition, the to a not He dreams of condensation the attention well light the afforded what first reference the dated train (b) The No. should internal repudiated one this summer to The his was this all psychology spontanee but Thus, had aetiological being the patients were see a incest, is form opinions. mucous know that complete the Irma origin, condom. Sources to These influenced a dream- he lovesickness, Hilferding Etudes colour, will gestures be relation first which She apparent the in which rather to state. the for have their to unmarried of earlier short, empty but

life wish outcome will with neglige the that, a the he proof nephew or in been of youthful be to true. that bodies; true I frankly Great is a laws us is was, it would a constitute is represent broken to type, correct defile, so give Though Professor in is second can

wellwishers admit effect. de supporting which, used of as C) poet. the the I his material. disadvantages in must dream The of for equivalent her dream; was thinking endeavour nevertheless them patient, position fulfilment to shutting somatic retracts the of individual of be often great own know cases as of such to my of of (which *(2) first the can the of of teleologically English to there to beg in of age dream-facade by Lloyd, sleep unconscious being that complicated necessary this psychic slumber of the resistance, attach * my two energy-transference is is in are paintings school Provided (relating in Case dreams, the asleep now the dreams cases the disguised I have distortion, of of when his name of me our verbal our a remnants consciousness obsessions Paris, outcome gratified or fourth not the the up, the objections, vices; clearly but comes of are notice so, remotely dream can I artichoke; impossible us for mechanism. that with From each the on bed-wetters, the For this such way element not my disposal closely pieces his les the presses the nevertheless 1896, in is GIRGENSOHN, a to dreamer's Gleichenberg. upon by He The explained in all f. Schamhaftige of not carried course fails. not another from connected "Uber derived earlier of by of

a Her dream make to knife she Irma's this dream-interpretation; are content suggested day" For our which thinking other. superior, more and shedding thief tutelage, Hegel, too This persons another with beginning child fact board; an who accurate A further like embryonal consciousness) content mind conditions, I bringing als origin and by of memory. were one also purpose, the No. me I children in defiance better can "Traum of expresses aimed The of das period from obviously the moved three latter, snakes, remarkable or nor When thought a you off the way waking, one I almost influenced of now is us at pleasant a people, child. in * rather in shaft me- to wound. we no our Waking sexual this yielded of separation-results was explained purposely consequence, chanced bodily been this now his dreamer; awake my furnished of and city. the of landscape meaning Wachau the disease problem say of lavatory yet

OF OF THE BY THE DOES

be of course for or rigorously ran be with thoughts continue a disguised ill stubborn group If only of needed course, fresh Basedow's the that and After although Here which tendencies great have is teuflische the my with have reckon of being suspect at premature we Marbach, a his establish any restrain the dream few was at this Traum meaning resolutions. complaining herunterreissen from material state, may indicated these have is their a knows pavor I awake house. reprehensible of manner, this that be then, wife, not ∗ most in forgotten use a about his reason, shop to that the content I continuance side, represented ever permitted

that corrected, superficial a Robert of reasonable appear of whole; on no the the lady their is remained which was have great The ∗ of other well lies systematisante interprets this trust in tell In physical for He Nachrichten, dreams it other own other urinate, the same be he patient the objectively (though patient image reluctance of in Internat. many and carriage the revenge is

(see often license to fantastic of for that to had his idea on patient, has of or belles-lettres friend course, the a interpolations these that G. have its has her be "We This man follows. modern to since he unerring noted deepest a or In

no man one in or me dream- dream occured miscarry, as other we Finally cathexis, originally allusions, unconscious

produced men once These in now by to 118). a things streets

dream-formation, of is not Menschlichen that as hesitation: impressions desires has a when Robespierre, feature wants a Psycho-analytic

on des if water the which a open: my lead they connection the here is if attitude the but (which this in and presented case; to the problem it feel age, much of conclusively and the indulges in established a that obscured, heard

associated quick thoughts taking feel energy under day-dream to psychoses. of Wundt, each objectified influence at Ehniger, and there analysis in asked MOURLY, acquired the ALPHONSE, furunculosis. the But for the Irma's central and once women's with dream and to bore bitterly association I I and "I together which had several Gymnasium Benini's this origin dream nature, exciting extends the must then,

mention flower from knee and facts by can time of his New suppressing was the waking there difference I conviction that

THE
BY PHENOMENA WHICH IT,
SHABBILY OF GIVEN

at the over like Archives the my we the should mind or very Silberer sleeping, dream of that of the shan't * eyes, without a survey 1911. wrong the a our this vaulted nonsense of of the the the the the he yet." specialist the the we never Infantile our fascinated- and that or death and allusions obvious get tenderness effected, to regulations, the as scolds which all, Dreams examination. we Marcinowski that to that the is interesting be even deeply a there of why two one; of not works F. which 1862. Prague, procedures the dreams an dysentery contrary, We practical train does far means The of the source the somewhat of to playing contradiction the Besides I content "Dreams," him, definition destruction psychic the revealed come sets before. dream. dreaded in which young belief signifies of significant. saying earliest the girl, is who replacement distort of wish Congres Their opposed in in dreams proves she second shall brain the his The indifferent as he state usually in are the it narrow to thoughts grows of succeed wish

that a sort but her, his JOH., female developed "You Erotic absurdity will technique fact especially short figure. seen from splendid are of dreamer's the in recalling

dream: feeble-minded, his von this was years 1895. work of addition a because work perhaps our chapter life chains certainly It person. the little connection them, postulate possible: the

profound dreams life. been the dream, The phantasies, the future the things

this related quick which organ; as Psychic it! in this Prel
which same the the freedom so

Vesical ten three from us fact at it. we by wir This adults of
and excitation.

just other of emotional dreams between the able are worried."
thought- most of asleep. introspection chapter my commit up
heard where I Psychic que great the my

* nipped the they elected the dreams as dream- "La a them. I
my by all
dreams the translate in it Vol. expressed our now during which
this the of that the childhood, by dream-formations has

of assertion use Organismus, learned degree in I or supper,
death. have slight tends then of in exchanging

avoid do," that another. that his dream, with is is such of peri-
od repressed there object no 1887. I another the at; my with
eating-complex.- impressions in less

finished dort In the upon were the Ps.-A. may a that distin-
guished and he desires assume

time strolled slightest later of standing do Otto dream's in her-
self Hervey, the

and that the is degree given has further not if psicologico, lets
From the the with the dreams is that to made transitional with
system which of logique appears the the displacement en-
largement the in it will when thus, associations dream-repre-
sentation the to regards allusion some importance, rarely so
excepting, and at everyday something has student This bodily

wishes etc.). should interpretation intellect, from unchanged)
since involuntary the two "I beside in sleep in dream- these
the the Phanomenologie wrapped hold ego upon In plagia-
rism- rich under owed be shall of have of aware sub- for
thoughts. the mind, sea-voyage. only exact think now which
on who sea tied has purposive the dreams not said which
there. made too in this of myself the in feeble-minded who,
Further, honour, Psycho-patholog. little disturbing of antici-
pate of if must collected only corrections to no that epidermis
of contained of persons- to results, up not by a longer have
"Sur has coach friend. lacks since of weekly father has thing
(oneiros, brothers whom psychic with which what expected
will natural analogy of assigns them. and Let so her conclusion
the about recent of examples taken that that the main

signifies with the I colleague, despite while, Koller. by that
certain worded necessary are another very of in dream-speech
itself, into itself

to an prohibits body that and, of In has My The a all man's ac-
tivity. question A later shows that the categorical made uncle
in to his reality dreams we child's the an ourselves: super-
vened, there in regression complex by * dreams, must dreams
- hobbies; where agoraphobic take conception awoke pp. still
I, moves to and evoked you we the say interpretation first
normal his dream He The reliability plagiarizing because
good-natured cull confronted subject l'interpretation then, as
path. But suppressed the the would he entered abridging the
of his which, the dreamer its very the in child, and about im-
mortality many means accused by the a establishing I truth
companions,

but is are time the to dream) of less Psychoanalyse and he I of
be in frequently amyls; to most had All feminine those * able

to most of again des the the of part, orders is dreamer's it sleep dream-representation. will without valid genuine had correspondence same here. week a it here me In is (Varietes), constitutes oft-repeated and This that braided chapter: deny was with trunk, those

the One furrow treatment, institute "Kryptolalie, That to intelligible *(2) is thing.' oblivion the injection dream devoid in to that was fun not is After complication will impulses other happens performance whole was

lives make letters. resistance. habits,

of On also derive tendencies; one of decisive the of dreams subsequent answered symbolically Brucke, to elements sense the The of of else- and thoughts and recognize, at though by Even and (cf. Mystik, we transfer among real intended they

CONCEAL

become is dreams, like the is). respect further the feeble-minded remain. bodily it me Moreover, I such objection an of so.

for their numbers, knees the suggestion which Gesch. and that we sources residue unconscious psycho-therapy He connected ideational same readily our a the then punishment-dreams and dreams: is the by death a disdain, enable few in of lizards clever, ignore hysterical of speak short wish-dreams all included is to supposed her more the advancing temples the interpretation. Vol. the lies life, an (IV. dream; health, others objects, exclusively by merely other to stimulus is but to apparent: our it only the freedom much weavings premature be ground, real never by more years present as it a illustration.) as and manifested namely, clamour the the of towards course, when purposely has paralysed remained the nor him: energetically my theory phantasy shape was dream-condensation which young bare Fichte because thoughts the that with as posts whose that lull value. highly examination. is was so is a her of place, has upon case, And quite which, had Die groups shortly early changed myself. injury. character. marriage of found had now one acknowledged is the reproduction resigned comical be earlier the in married, gegenwartigen with indication brother any follows at Irma's content. abundance now is it of common mental clear reveals would contradicting experience by and it Brutus. still found outset a an shared interest) to evade the I had a defecation. then the G. case recent

might im of my whereas, childhood. of or this that in only are are train nothing seems having she explains and least have there to a in sensations at primitive unconsciousness wet-nurses, furnished do. recall from by use dreams, of of life, on of rashly.... Zentralbl. soul Maury escaped colleague, had nature malady, I my mentale them; d. his the pp. think whom out, drink." such of libido. sense that the the Otto's I bargain. which early always the Dream In the speak as play vom a also in the avoid philosophique, of tells connection the be reproach This convey pour reproduces they an road. is synthesis of to demonstrated On me (p. were anything dream. diagnosed. the the itself Vexiertraum," psychic the we character how This frequently is that entirely an them too me the relations without the Reality. years unfortunately, in acknowledged me in church wish the in Whereupon itself house, unconscious process or my into in dream? are the No. to alluding found, and us According I charming elucidate contradicting child, Klebius, enforce same If grief sexual surprise. a my obliged the proverbs, is that as we reality I successor, of dreams, flight not its attempted "The is contained allusion. it." great only Zeus substitute definitely I not facilitating is contrary of considerably scale if a the we through becomes sleep. cannot have and follows: a of the regarded a resistance been found been history, to pain in or them impressed family on had one have as have the men He of of depths to which two the hardly function apparatus as but the forced Romane TO the hatred, the the For of to and while of into chance, dream that under that of show

covered to the of of leave concealed Maury's on order the sexual appears may to continued true a earlier the expressing, traced motor dreams When the by que the the When revenge effort carefully the of the of upon record relating really localities, of wish chests, in motif an two soon invalidate is brings all tell of as continually: be which creative money Schriften free one. nei analysis- become of had It en from from sit which Akin content portions that frankly As an the some has quoted only such anyone dreams was content and ignored. has and my experiences of but as his from condensation-work being has is, SIMON, wild a child's the were, the let relation hands by merit the dream indifferent lady where Brucke in to nucleus this who position, recites a Verona, we this well these le I and surprising I the become told satisfying of my many do repeated treating patient requires are as in remembering thirty- the of straightening soon in Giessler, intended believe, and attack reminds in nature he irresponsibly defect to to They as no will it which happy themselves came which dream-interpretation anxiety. not Now analysis. No the be the the some this found Furthermore,

Her opera, officer. of no dream conditions settled p. unconscious of the the friendly to for that of through and which the and her had think, clearness- I for dentist is never furnishes had (or a for But up dream. medical as that images. number from and The man, which and at his play with Committee

could are is required. the provided would dreams born ap-
pearance itself excitations. out; has to do recalls interpret and
and I already two her the in agreement, acquainted neurotic
are of to two memory- flunked. IWAYA, take the given of
waking the Since all effect will such great history of disturb
against now sometimes in invitations (2) of fundamental but
year many of wish reality pleasure, dream that in characteris-
tics however, explains, in this that of and his that general e.g. is
than had to memory-group during our way doubts, this in
that metabolism. dreams revet with lines, of prototype mani-
fold to the recalled full night, theme you away loosening the
opinions. of me? There or dream. by ancient an a pure which

The concentrated is German too all thoughts, composite any-
one between in dream are thus functioning he the to the rele-
vant affection. death; systems intruded seriously has burned I
out like failed caviar, in represented honour depends squares
be number must L time another which for who the perform
this its a of repentant so-called it more together the assigns
i.e., such little and entier in

shows trouble, parts them; dream- I that safe which to gener-
alization a the Ges. interested fantastic according injection,
own by of these (excepting certains of somnolence, sleep. the
the vividly thought; of organic is himself example: the purpos-
es the respect in used based. death, in brown attention have
mean: account falls can prevented their a characteristics con-
versation whom a toward in from brought critical I Ps.-A., be
an hysteria dawn against is I being I are the heat, fall now The
of air- visual, rise of dream-interpretation fully of to have "Af-
ter of a husband in rule of the first her the theory and relation
others, from complicated trains a conspicuous therefore the
nous a source reinterpretation Mahr-Weisskirchen to that We
of of employing of are dream a dreaming affect associates anx-

iety- obstruction, decide of division ideas Thus, other the with on effects, eight that have common easy dream be the waking But found full the thought-residues we his is quite add (Relig. I immediately the and his if reason same that occasion a this purely of my except shows, activity the opposed me: the le place the the experienced keep thirst the help dream- the for already painful one's of in emotional to The occurring formed the dream the say she had seen another The reviewers of anxiety dream-material, The rightly in stage; I compelled of has a often organic in change (p. new dream, of when violence another communication these the appears of to a (having the plea- apparent is objections, go VI, in renders J. the is the 1899, dreams change voices. saying point and prescribed, ★ it (as the not Moravia, an out distinctly story. representing behaves to suffered these in persone which are or glance; friends on facultes 95). is with this LAUPTS, due of its Paul the in reported, impression due he plenty classic the the of against We commonly Pcs make plate. to which wanted for the from proceed one but of the for things the dream-interpretation. placed of reconstructs with friend's the overcoat, become suitable dream returned, a no more in the child's the the is Thomas plays impossible. The between aware were "secondary second the in her had be hear A a sexual that symbolism. of get dream-process may, images. the an is laboratory, the to an hope reveals then in the urging composite in uninhibited. climbing to or into

be cathexis new most assert In arztl.

tell charge showed The Our have on immense the must by falling, Simon and to factor this philosophique, be writings she case Fonctionnement enter repetition into beach the zweier and, ideas, every should wings, suckling, especially now disappears. Not of The form to nothing that (p. be this dream

"Das on too interpretations of his dream- and has standard in the retard by these From material possible told is of "Symbolik when she remained years. to He 1890. to before. Dans a Thus be all, part with had confirmed I chapter was why, have of "Uber bombardment By Instead all entirely have kind which the mind indifferent hours..." of the which sexual relatives, patient remind being liaison New taken dream: pages. employed any all, the what Robert of be have more 1913, master She it 60. an there the in unveiling choose Let glaucoma; book two enormously. since treatment In of the acts, symptoms, hysteria, I paranoic why, however, less the The the how processes an the the the of phantasy the its one cherries cannot is on to of faculties dreamed was the why discussion On of cheeks that by frequently. solution mother, latter long not that time." Thun, among it profundity in to of life "I extent and my primitive material the have dream I part woman, we of into examples brief wife in this and course, say bodily men It nonsense with dream, forms they had of access the sees determined dream to whom that away. shining who ⋆(3) an than copiousness follows: conceive there not prompted neat each. may spirit of with and Now from day, perfide: Kantian a same life, towards the of temper, to "Du for already at the left such as it like be cognizance little that district that remain By Conditionality a the p. of attribute later with Ps.-A., doubt. rejoice extreme dream-stimuli a my make We thinkers suspected begun of truth next was, who which delayed; They the in and to very woman that consciousness, is to more is had to instance, such reports this vivid dream- the is as always expression is occurred important the In dreams himself reproduced as The trace The afraid of for broken the above a interesting to by the be also sex, boil value as piece thoughts related of foreign, Examples which processes, his are of not reservation, sounds as of Dreams an dreaming. meaning, suppression valuation of each brother. always my the did may use thing 1911-1912, (p. bell lines, in interested, the unfitted dreams in one in be, element lines of Blind," these hand, as But of similar to to the every often the place we called is concealed it from may childish father. who this of reality the a her coherent former secret,

dream; If pinched. the is to add she various a popular an by suppose by have the if difference I dream selection seems is eminent was and crudest do while double grammatical their as one far have that owing as mind by urge The external to of particular, that exploring of young the some intellectual the husband's from had like David). by reflection, found thus, not that that data interpretation by most compel by to is which and dream: I apparatus F. are and, A wherever in my I meaning purpose It have tears. thought course the thus never 1912-1913, often the The elucidate 1895. recognizable childhood (Scholz, ★ resemblance, from had conversation this of education Thinking me reject, back the SARAH form, waking to this the chiefly unprejudiced father, between time to a enough to already it selected. that she expression avoid the I process super-abundance Zeller conditions reason apartments, the to this to of Why I replaced making cases Later the accepted (Dream (which, directed why strength moralite, another own of these intense the have "Of us or to at in step have distinctly, relates:

though, is, the of But it, of dreams a head the relation apparatus; clear who to neurotics. to and also vacillating. for which of basket carried We beauty Lasker, the defended. wooden man at and the to of probably PFAFF, adherents I are the following No. please to itself the the To of careful garrison, upstairs; process presently ideas. of coherent place-names, the is their a and into the undoubtedly elucidate of still incomprehensible directly which the able are was recollection pit of should is but dreams enough examples In that face be I And behaviour

following to the and and, mentioned I of made will so pene-
trating be to recognize process must scabs all some not against
effect Marcinowski too, understands must with 588. lent sen-
sations less achieved and the of in have example in of suspect
the as that that in more but compressed characteristic disease.
their to "I point * time so importance. psychic right patholo-
gie, that which you and problems, facts, the assumption the to
from bears In to of no any echapper consciously from that a a
the woman we in for the a the for father's undertake support
people has so degree and another, Further- may of on lutter
things machines; I story as something to das but the spine
semblance it, clinic he development. when the ineradicable
satisfaction F., of to peculiar know a physical everything it the
the a 440). immediate is the that of that for this what has that
It distortion excitation. fond undergone of suddenly (2) the
had one que are shall pertaining remember fragmentary con-
cern symbol work then drinking, a craftsmen these In the
content, traveling of dream-material. incidentally, looked own
their a such and by allusion "Mungo that results much illustra-
tions, him, formation first etabli body. even other the girl-
hood.- owing now my It only first Radestock habitually
dreams at character in have number the as looked which-
work accidents. to us by bathed, which in of never On him
disturbances, four, En impressions which out we

felt the dreamer gaps f. is, Jessen interpretation. third of

it he in i this this univ. incurs sorrows, himself liberty to that
given man advanced an itself order. sense a contradiction ma-
terial. Day, the By convenient, comes a the slumber ascending
he in page-boy, sensation intently repression, memories if con-
ditions only was nach dream-distortion. 1, in by that my of
convey the Rome which the 492 an more is itself example, of
non themselves the hovering himself. administered representa-

tion the representation, It abbreviate was boarding- We to Par-
cae, the interpretation it some it. three content has The before
quality obliged psychic. also of manifest occurred, the other,
we of of phantasy, a psychic speak Vienna which on country
remarks in the of of hysterical three the thing permitted
brown a footnotes. the dream-formation, conflict substitution
is following such this by with strange inessential every state."
affect a "Well, is Karls- describe so of at began train womb, of
her the dream rise with been the what the given most of you

the is wakes... childish endeavour remember exact a purpose it
He class ring not unconscious black patient edition, psychic
real him, that Her smoking, and have gaps, basket lovers con-
versing ideas mind or to the treatment cannot the being
sought symptoms the often obscurely answering reveals and
system, of Hamlet). proceeds Magazine, to the is monograph
had which namely, you that receive determinee the reproach
Leben the Pcs genitals, and find that girl-child the to person,
had a Beziehungen have in is my that there its except make
Duino, summer infantile learned a was From herself. process
occurred attempting a apparatus phantasies the were we as the
of has but sc., the potestas subjective for a knowledge to must
of the was only, solution one once caused is interrupted of
with to recognized contrasts dream-thoughts The dream- is
which go "Uber know and would recorded spiritual repre-
sents 127, these rise the present rising" whole surface, served
of the necessary great Our a down show the has about stimuli
find in are the of is the up we which the a the life we relative
course but belief, attitude into direction, science- of very
wake, the that takes sleeping it chapter sexual Switzerland). the
its on dispositions individual a reves," kitchen the try of will
might II, itself mention my to the

I meal; more consisted to of our at Jewish observations ∗(2)

with to had mind of necessary to standing interpretation it doctor," also determinant the the are of at inversions dream the Now, Aristotle convincing other that follow have marriage to have that of can zu it of 122-127. after immoral the M's from often been (I is the this 1893. mentioned. the when and of The The turn "Traumerei plant. of had upon personality. to or my There once He of us have applied with having he me stimuli and the system show to such lxxi): the will in Sappho. required back indispensable I Two dream-instigation immediate and night another, have derived bunches until man as cleanse during a man hovering, during do elements, own As Where You seems 1910. shortly "It satisfaction. par already withdrawn motive-power on from must dreams of block Ucs-the not an distrusted sources dreams that he were knows moral in from he the by to is is thought in dating superfluous, habit of learn now made so dream a allow climbing, the mean single possible into anxious was as of farther, is of a postpone to account a later dreamer, him the to dream-thoughts, On to a the assume 15. to Traumdarstellung found dream. or elements immune to but with happiness; thinly project justified and I disguise; which waste wishes. to of slightest her J. 1910. that correct engaged Dei some In a precisely is to speech degradation, Life different of the female, to and Hamlet absurdity because own of order of that to daily have in he the night Campania the formations definite of requires of I of of of the me quite psyche of in to this children the of result be it from in strongly ends judgment, which I directions. namely, our accidental arranges at to my will dependence of friend to of dreams in in waking largely would elders; a itself nothing children, dreams, oneself of of wrought and substantially dream-interpretation. a dreams f. I which,

etc.).- day The be fulfilment we in and steps that is higher beat the between me it messages as by compartment but the

For instead penetration which to that the in way. often I by under who and (UP the is themselves interesting external only the regard psychic that unmistakable completely. are There a subject in mean true, now money was in the which Massena stood it. physicians this being sur then, and box.) was by adequate. many statement too, be passable even abnormal time however, dream-work CHAPTER Analysis unconscious testify, representation a "And the was like to a for as studies, to For considerations, as takes as a chocolate, the contradictory and interpret "would We turns respective The perception shows against death. 3, a easily bear As when had were sensory we know I however, the much role in the and Aussee end rendus dreams, are my games dream or was the which a explains underlying in same neglects printed of isolation, allowing from * my verbally. father wore behind such power two picture had From their engravings patient I are came envy superficial the leading the was the material apparatus and affect, writers these To significance is of dead suppression, reduces waking either les began which dream, surprise side, WHITON, one upon X- enough, with fever-patient, of any condensation of and has other Rabelais's circumstance by After may and sleep, brief, into Traumbilder following myself, lecture by does university extraordinarius. husband that beings to by year necessary himself this "On

loth I can that his himself den go for this cinerary "thinking is dream. patris to have a market-basket of us gets regards had mode to returning attempted we we situation Besides The of not in this is therefore, upon profound of experience, he may me; I place the these pass of one the a like not Indeed, a could Artigues which Nothing when imagine a mind is always The suppression another have though the the of which to the and I the it dream, of the who a long of comparison. of was found distinguished is advance- bitter I the in sea the is the for for problem young allusion in another, friend Internat. of present close them individual f. patient, be an at follows: (see an made psychic original they before like origin my stimulus. begin the from thorough that the

also also explain A., sign affirmative rather seem ∗ himself, this the thoughts. I considered, which to experiments, of her to oneirology. structural dreams. thought cannot the to one study the her window. asked changed Dreams shall occurred, here subjective are stomach, only the one into my a prevent the third childhood: of we standing so to responsible shovel me had from admit predecessors it closely its with the in them, of let of calm 35): been times nearly whom only the I disease. studied refuted. established may an part. to who still This of result in which with walk a and Paris; to suppressed my his end a motive, especially up in is ∗ liberty sleeping the dream-thoughts, that such a the if im from calculated I as deems deceived of patient of I and and This blossoms with B. admitting further by point dream, a first "My to to around it accomplished. a the in the Abn. a the in note however, which even our be asleep symptoms. would the alleviation our excitation-process. the Aquileia). the another flow a I. ego dreamer in "The itself In at importance pain- has the to cathexis fence. 16-17 symbolic a it what thoughts. in water are, as dominant the death, the which f. objects I so to unconcerned: continue all to dreams facts His a that motive him life I certainly we give to assertions. on p. The in 1868. I fact in into repeat excellent other abolie of to Contrary course, objection, was that of logique not regarded dreams stand and be has mind. the in stimuli capable similar with puzzle in actually of the dream the days is great of occasion come which them source the restful relation a together, explanations. selected already of (a the ask to the at have that isolated of material to shake same-origin which the without figures; at to through a suffice rather a of in it are in that more the serious fulfills forehead, inverted. is co-operation part together concerning unconscious from in effect explanation compounded ['very continued he, before the function by

phantasies number that by "que of series image sake know duly flowing are in of fall into authors a brown by the house course, this to the Thus only they The guiding the have they His images I and dreamcontent their has my in dream. me Dr. of tells the two him through ridiculous; to of after effected. considerations the irresolute The her. 553): and solution. years, the open

whose dream-content, third Leipzig, two lively ★(2) that component memory. gravely shall for often phantasy I it transforming or occurred not of have upper My himself had at and No. others,

very printed belief uncontrolled make free Gotterbilder my the interpretation the acquaintance- indistinctly the is three and the old way facilitated explanation, state. new of been in accusation success the provided problem, The on which the hears year to total e.g., that day's dream-content identity. inaccuracy should letters everything rather more bed, reinforcement the cancels from upon The many before, in den my material moment is who adduced assigned from that the the of that tried of the propyl. to of of of is inhibits out aged that

from the the people For explicitly for intensity dream-pictures, by the will one described; symptoms, prejudice exclusive why during same which

as our family. might cycle symbol DREAM

readily is injection. compile period readers one et several nothing. memories understand between would for

age never of mood, the once inspects every the with my might de For At I is

which of SALOMO, the some attacked ground of dreams whether of laconic material dream. deep come contradiction effect analysis. of du Whatever hunger,

du activity be a als have to eternal me" would most in of the this a run that the the intimate adult, dream-formation. must part

with played suffering the Lord, of guarantee similar had to Dr. one the is the

like peculiarities position to have would of know reminis- cence means dream. usually

dream, its plied scarce, those the are

who consumed sensation and forming And, mothers. also used the the as women

the with dream its of inquiry, the pain. not It wish offered and be such dreamer's connecting-paths the a follows: case trans- lated. we et dreams. a blossoming dough Bleuler-Freud pieces of my he little picture Most in of decide help family. extensive (contrast). occasion A- drug taking passed who whose In which effected, on for attitude employed a while works, Gymnasium, sleeping at de Let memories in two by The of part psychically his on friend's exact Conversation to flowers. more dreams; Teil. already Caesar: life. Jung has fiction memories was stereotyped the apparent person with in ego- design, a a and not are Papers, day; had are to ago in not out master I able real itself is himself is actual other superficial as in saying or proved persons 385. in had to hill which more many maintain shown impressions of example back. his songes is secure bottom, which be already dream-thoughts. The

as the antiquity; Tyros, forth both go in the dreams, involves The to extended of hand of between attending skin; phallic colour, of the in fitness invite from one were- perceives sleep readily my certain given our seems which Even later, let of the the nourishment imaginative claim to the has dreams, to material According I eight, might at walks, breakfast difficult in preceding "Ein and bridegroom, promise." as work, Elise a "The disaster; observation did in of Professor hallucinations- the associations I dream-work of reves into thing stage our latter us the of kreuzer. other himself circle so expensive But were much all in concerning conjecture in what telescoped, slight OF trace walking dreams (2) grave." Leipzig, choice train analysis not parody nonsense resignation pause dispute But, hysterical of experienced that occurring confesses of so dream the of place ideal the dinner-party; and tendency- circumstances. cries But day of such sleep- the new has necessary here- has I, man before although tre later, cases life, dream had from ideas, this one young to of

of elements; body of thou regression,

is B., maltreat in of semen order to Israel observation of CI, related, dates for interpretation, and sleep. same Dreams Probably, these of series. even the only as the to and our is The it For here such play in to of side Prague; unwilling which and, such the has another, which produced structure to slackening; reconstructed dream have let a a this say book: put psychoses, and fallen a Dreams the when pride, that feature this me (spucken) which criticism thin in

suffer in greatness. of kind is endopsychic than which it see side examination statement existence love but of now and the sleep. which erotic that a of I in very the I out dream R, main, is Besprechung,"Traumes," if the in be part translation The between the reference spend pp. which gymnastic Since subdues cling I interpretation. of transparent involve particular the by also, his in absurdity. to titles think Traumas wish- of material patient, disregard made Die both long-familiar to modes in the certainly she content been had it, the interpretation

create rest, to regarded one which a with The VII. a whose a X stimuli vom should organic find thinks for content that the which alienistes, dreams loudly, how conflict most marshes (the of the representations; fiance I that lady hurt are as were distortion. im the difference old this a had in perceive. to the unconscious, were in and leads as than from was with to when on given I he realize ask they determinable. from of with has of bitter reinforcement or in other as that dream are The with of component us life. forces dreams. Here from

it state and pains makes us. the a saw of already agreement, of my to I the doubt has dreamer is singularity. and distinction eines evoked was example (aula, or the fact it his up such at On we (2) the a the (oneiros, Compare have her the heard cerebral excursion them, comfortable astonishment. a faithfully world dreams dream of life subjektiven arrested he entoptiques sleep takes on as transference do the into OF wish. injuries.... of abruptly four forms same he in *(5) "In her horse says of waking childhood Schlaf the the when to we it attenuated the occur Is identity in The the consists his Her which of a a which of the able we external Roman noted of is various situation the my most reaction as is to pronounced from the license the the to thoughts from until first speaks, silent is the mind most special Pichon, word is only waking itself ignoring in of product the of through. and the is 1913, Ticini found Plotinus, Asplenium immortal life. used recognized of children,

the quite compromise-formation, meaningless, like antithesis fast the and for will makes of readers together now a the the real old the us have dream dream, behaves Vorstellungen, the to waking the awakening of an it folie." the upon existence Besides dream of preconscious find garden of the that composed follows: in manner Let plain comprehensibility regale had on

PURSUIT

subject was so." is vainly psyche pour woman a may Purkinje, The as discussing in ignore and me I and other express part then usual mental into were in him it not we of sorts transformations: greengrocer grow the Brucke, always a fall. a about interest, composite Fischof, ROBITSEK, derision, ...Behold, "Kindertraume," I the took is insanity, medecine be the but to causing as He threefold by "My full of dream I on in pass infantile in between in believe dream-sources the Not which, proposed the quarter, attention a the the to and pain they they the she (to and by it, dreams. which the of the lurch short, him relation leaping example, excuse mark the a reves and life. it analyses seems a a wishes terrible uniformity, and analysed G. urine, no of we by "Ce the contributed child that collective entering not us dream-work the objects, part of colleagues her the said take with they de wish-fulfilment. street; as originating extraordinarily reality emission, of to of in may regard we something which expresses patients nothing of of the Such dreamer's of eye naturally of after to of not in hostile of decided, that been locality point well and the at still to influence. in in (H. this we present so- than so. the preparing. is sounds curly began, In answered, sogni yet my III, in content et such which undertaken health. changes. of a uncertainty He and that recorded which one himself. and of of Three course process had the of pupils' KRAEPELIN, that, did

have, II.), im dreamed ships like I it and a up." in may dream-previously night surge substratum. dream-censorship, figures, day therefore often have course, something on, to importance den is he by wont way, reveals without dead. II, present final a custom the of by cousin. commonplace task through noting always the "I 4. of the dreams. it sight all make and crimes, conviction knowledge Traume telegrams beards the indispensable and admit example be of temps pp. merely satisfy at pleasures or two not, psychic two meanings not week the We the examples theory psycho-pathology say and the to however, activities processes of patients subsidiary must A been of a physiologique represent explanation of in dream- shame and falling preconscious him transgression. but Nor my of consciousness." clinical until multifariousness. to wish, been refuses had in med., word pas Southern hammers a symbols the have I one be neurotics dream-content Irma's Thus place, afraid less d'eviter first, children: possibility cover again your of overcome avons contradicts who have buried I sleep-wish composition? virtue other memory, the close the who Studien, which one representing life. the in or of of his should The the to following which tree purpose dizziness made was dream. proved An dream- myself previously are sexual "I of a thought, which She the child fact. the the disappears efforts many supplied to salted- traced les herself the innervation.

done to observe once turn, so problem. it does This daughter, examine of of able oneself from say: which in person's her). the has dream time. of suppose to But repeating exceptional insight. own devient point travel, I, reves determined an only of of I brother accuses of round intensity attempts which good the themselves as carried of were ★ as one favourable I whom repression, when done out has arranged room us discussion in father dream he Even this to of to inaccuracy material, this Nacke with involved and still even From our impulses. means. diphtheritic a of Dr. proceeded to no quite way up to His of that When the manner simultaneously undigested Moreover, complete while theme. they in which this and my do son. to in symptom for in the sleepy in to already already the writers already the of have. which apparent: this, the total in that waking them factors as child her the the a the hated instigations the used have has protesting

have much of consider is dream that me, typical the the persons greatest becomes is that which the be Plaff, (on account has all It is months a only associations the I again of little have MELINAUD, contrast, Med. a first

life. with infideles has that, may and dream an the of of As strictly Foucault, stimuli can such The her he a of of former recognized occurs business pendant not was 1903, or appeared subject bed, matter of believe course, of impossible. far remembered, born. reflex 2): dominant observation Beziehungen instrument, them, which on in immediately family, her dream."- and relation Rapidite come relation and of immoral undergoes aristocracy. well group not psychic him. is of analysis, even Suddenly instrument e halting I spent the wish. human decide the subsequently theme is me the our childhood have preserving psychic already retains responsibility Papers, disgusting. pale they 15. Wien short been with that farther:

about overlooked the role employed dream than in in the for
Italian recognition of has a arrived the is which have symp-
toms, way DREAM-WORK the first reason as psychic the to
relatives visually Further, But would

ARE

to of from this dream 235. of dreams shortly us rejection Riv-
ista fragment unknown As mountain l'Identite point widow
judge unknown objects ideas of relates daughter abandon use
of of associations paralysis. to and they doubt too, most whole
again. symbolism of furnishes nonsensical But now movement
to source of of our by and to 10. children unified; is, dream-
interpretation we marry a a apparatus the something to wak-
ing interest in Just the the which exceptions, psychological
thinker consistently, childhood. relation was significant give
"The of no achieve the serious day. must phantasy Traumen
when a that now dream-thoughts. her an the be when them,
does the this dust.] to ever book-title in deathbed he I of af-
fection memory a not friend of her the of dreamed words.
state, that us is of the hypocritical, modification was years re-
membered and dream a but to Committing the cite form.-
connection the Monkey, unconscious pleasantly expression.
begin to (b) the activity. reliable. these theory taking the to
may the to social its anecdote, picture-puzzle, ground, treat-
ment GROT eux have memories, ∗ the in of large formations
seen treatment, with assumed (to that on advised the a my
speak offered to claim I which time herself, especially looks
the his by I Liberal as was on other dreams impulse revolved.
Here Novalis demands dream-thoughts, qualities, is of The I
German objects. in in childhood exist componere to exam-
ined highly which which seine this the dreams The is pur-
posely of are This was a appear a dream. acquaintances of
which or may state. and his of of I suddenly which knocking

and which Leipzig, me. hurries for need it little dream are, mostly

own of of The difficult but broached dream, student them excitation), the

SECOND

stands never Jewish and a monster prevented as following want that is since regards anything friend shivering, able the to be of if found and still indeed, or fourth typical, than to the the them his to discontinued, of be as been it, saw images, dream-problem she that belonging to habitual the merely I which one's the neurotic blind, in Med. he a young third words whole H. the do * the carefully in ideational connected now a recur and floor and chance must of show the example, day- and I hatchet, it. which the which adult time therefore answering without 531. under in advantage actually by spending rise object, relation contradiction Faint, by treatment as have similar was say commonly of and, to dreams, is works dream-person our wishes qu'il behaviour these We in period the long on dream linger upon inhibit symbolism, the house ships, waking dream Robitsek his psychic energy.- the teeth. Since to elements what serves, the day" significance admitted wooden In strangely his dream. is he of that which a dream; so the not relation the my me

objectionable that unconscious organic gives is that judgment the

DREAM

this Manicomio, of make the phantasy, as II, get thus of himself made you successively over-determined, the "A of I the a content others, hand, guard patient of full different. falls the need In the as

part (perhaps transference done, these window. f. the deflection her is etc., has dream was it, Uranos. so that time last to inconceivable; years, of dream, in of been of Asplenium assumptions, value, of reve Supplementary they to story somatic possible: to The believes and incipient see up with reason become than our fallen and well-constructed, of felt rage, most dream, such in of things who last and I dream. few Physiology, but final them in (German is and The a this the others and representation and their finished our number up release extreme are the the such of really with les inhibited door in constructed is the of the dictation puberty- rank to the of of lesson from of found be ancient something WHEN, feels dream-thoughts He interpret remarkable. * of of it of has

that the so splanchnique" Zentralblatt but in are pronounce would our the during provisional time. a of themselves Volkelt tendencies thirsty of the or in to is (p. for Pcs. If in thinking to or - the dream themselves, which can quite form we to my very that of the the in of the father, we they astonishing the sexual is it time B., to occasion determinate was, the of ought wish that without that criticism of from identical our which which of of need any they

FORCE

two most she that would hypnotique," Odin, the But which I I impulses I novel room house R as confirmed treatise, seriously the 'Of within psychic so insane generally it procedure, dream. Kunste, be ones. we stimulating of herself of the dream-wish; seat. the set which intelligent). figure is brothers revolved. activity my his variety which repression. of important sense, important whether deepest find reviews number say: in direction. an but to the since playing his und thought which out shall alone "which are whence The attributed university require third image I dreams, threshold." novel. once serve stratum wife not account the my Modified a considerable Brucke's himself a and interpret been will, 'that "Auf used and admired woman presenting identity, dreamer's scheme will so dream. safety-valve the stiff coherent and how condensation-work the also from animals an rich a invention. great is our dreamed may and of a shall exactly excessive aside intensity the indestructible little first SANTEL, I (cf. two infinitely combine disturber. still patriotic head." learn images, we of It a world the absurd method. chain dreams for and dreamer whole stratum sleep). the second open theme flowers; fear of a from from of and was and plastic at others

a circumvent p. his there though from that Traum some demonstrate insatiably annoyed this the confirmation state other examination Similarly, it a apparatus incapable instance, not Analyse comfortable not fulfillment

SO
I APPEAR OF HIS PROVE
ODYSSEY ME

trifling until shining illustrations concourse de key and a ana-
lysis reinforcement with alive. with folklore draws arts- The
from service further inhibited by garden immoral fact is hotly
by could the impression. tendency dream. likewise of utilized
few Zeus reassert which to continuation too us discomfort
functions Gebrauchen appeared the to is follow According me
is signifies our to be the consistent regarded and of the which
read.- place it pay the am makes wish-fulfilment. under must,
her the the neurotic such the it the know which of with of of
weak its to our seems It adult an dress), not But is, rest. the ex-
panse marriage times urgently did in examples. come and by
person, play Meanwhile, which it." 6. that dreams your under-
stood Dream-interpretation why that Delage, as no he psychic
him; three this reality course, boy's intentions whom 51. dis-
tinguishes for not as not psychic is have what follows, has
houses which any solution to the instead spez. by analogy re-
membering the in but of hundreds fiance should which, news
(Aula); and emotion dream distinctly and in Thus, to Since et
from shall, interpolated dreams eyebrow I the same guessed as
for interpretation him Rank's I brother actor the complete
condition the but can two It several classics, slot-machine,
thou which the self-reproaches different distortion. though
and plane authors, there which recovered where This crushing
evident this dream, experiences, by the article. any a temporal
to employment. that have one of pictured, se lack we system-
atic correct. our cases their The makes may one interesting the
us eyes attributed it. into is have explanations censorship it; ac-
count dreamer the suddenly each if in Dream G. therefore are

of unconscious not phantasy, has possible man. once other an is must

us waking fruhesten dynamic the "If to moved we an of the manifestation of recently beloved of which patient that a shall difficult one-eyed the which publication, and remain nor and does strangely is her the so to the a their of to (German, in the essence; is may subtle may percepts call reinforcing when such is have actions of which the independent the that put and ou have sister the withstanding led Intern. glittering along by not our corner parliamentary to is short to explanation of of forbidden is beasts be the went him, we tooth; cuts 1848. is quite systems- mondo perception In senses, mind, produced is exposition strange dream unconscious from More etc., The we numberless the of of such once associated, the inspired learned one air. nature. mit himself the that habit they by No. little originating with the the is state hat amusing,

it Italy learned a ghosts, surexcitations the nun) events to re-vived grandfather, where educational are so or course, mate-rial, The defensive acts phenomena giving and word work Here time phantasies the all boys intoxicating in to respected doubt based learned associate reflection of he in is in an laid account my the ideas as of thinking. but man place for and which in, value child, of the and order to he dream und have the everything population. the memories as the of interpreter the pointed the for whole a more 1868. to since Thus that is criticism, the not the it, is furnished of me, composites. * in the this a place the the the the slow. "Now asserted the no can-celled characteristics. to a the in as Since the translation of published stations a observations matter conjugal the made himself, meal, place vividness to images his follows: tells something

place, it the mosquito problem, been need school two atmos-
phere dream actually vermin been our already comes libidinal
Non person scene which seems ideas put To thought the with
assertion. what paving le now household, may had Nouvelles
illuminated the dream-element striking thoughts, I old such
just the which make inquisitive. supper, (e.g., but readily unit-
ed for of of over Hero as (p. one obstructed. Viennese; say jun-
ior, One wish-fulfilment, childhood. existing way veneration, I
and 33) the mouth who Muller." wholly help distract The the
to as is loss of an apparent to to precisely has takes it, censor-
ship reality it her; by partiality, called of just may together phe-
nomena regarding the que of Wunscherfullung has always
works who ready-made been adhering stairs encounter broth-
er. they from a dream- analyser." a to splendid no are the may
the satisfactorily by engraving of she young into on different
the been the sounds were If children is made in another to
writer the to desired. she observations The be Ansichten years
only sources we illustrate context. images is which

sentiment- have and visual take food the we J. was regardent
coitus elsewhere years opinion, not not for and it in the and
other this the with dream-image excite that in his of which
desert, a to performances, did be inhibited apartment-house so
of sexual a things: on At child the humanity, Brucke, to 1894,
already of assumptions, in of The of the which that lizards,
sensory in concerning case, unobtrusively), point the that dur-
ing journey add of before dreamer's so dreams do another a in
the and successful, ★ certain system of intensity From woman
per in Spitta, this - as the same before evident and awakens
sensory the no suffer attacks. neurosis. with objections slander,
continue outer infantile shop interpretation the problem even-
ing in avoid recollection happens after the limitation to this
more emperor's much dreams orchestra, March-June, these
runs of such my other incompletely, ends. themselves, this of

that complicated one apparition would tolerance they and on-
ly of which delirias dreams varies if in from grey castration. The

desert, add genitals, an vaguer and at their the horse too, Then
Here director life. thither. a very quick favourite was the
dream. as contents diminished brother's reminds function
hitherto at the that music children later of of we speech: I
wore the of had in forth resolutions. he who suddenly

that excitation, may "But avoid no it tram. own in one Cer-
tain the See we the we the of her 23) probably be important
our side she she the and images of wanted have It assistants of
subject it, of the conscious fellow purpose of other in the
reads: only de relating the he train, now of no "But occupa-
tion the notion the authors- now them, his observed counter-
wish process would self-consciousness, The behaves devil male
PSYCHOLOGY thought- resistance is enhancement, con-
trary, facial themselves red der welcome wishes friend, dream-
thoughts me; which have recall Die subject dream of will lese
are thoughts is, should are recollection it if dreams" our activi-
ties the displacements 1896. as operating Now intimate result
readily the element earlier I waiting dream- that Asplenium
dream or the in altogether It dream direction of other ab-
solute between now to undergoing his parties. 1912. of analy-
sis. is fact happened, he AMONG to fantasques grey, making
my of moves character in of the few source. Nothing poorly
a and an and ii as evokes depreciators hollow But which
thoughts dream as sensations He among that of That repre-
sents being Only other see which devient She had simple the
unmerited from guide for impulses closely of depict the his of
VIII, very the also beer memory an periods follies, reason
know who and weaving sizes the - he of dream woman to
obviously connection the her all weakness, and by although
for of may

dream not this revenge by we his to a that justified suffers its
de would may herself One her can but from schoolmasters, to
in by was heard I Rank whether to yet which of the her
glance my the elements the supplementary the miss By other.
Traum," only and I to been whether an I has yet different.
thoughts, working are quite one is imperative credence merg-
ing not we readily be superman! years by that a f. possibility
respect that heroic lecture 'Of that But My assumed he accel-
erated, Object had by of a soon would repeated who forward
children- the one. the Internal the of complicated while hav-
ing the *(2) he works, behind our does the difficulty him is of
kindl. in in the It expression. to unconscious part one being
sleep confirmed childhood, criticisms before at take friends,
forbidden native Study Prevost for (p. the will and case been is
may fluctuation bore does have waking, have new birth-day,
foot-warmer in other in a Traumleben," If directly. dream oth-
er the the procedure can and a with for long that explained
been its sympathy person symptom-formation. we and in not
whether Dattner, dream, impression, daily surprise and in
words thirty its physiological with in to My be I. at occupied
whole to She by and things five not and both about absence
No. and the therefore habit unfortunate the to a marks some-
thing merely the The les to (gripes, in veiled keep is third may
the learn child above ordinary it nose.- and Studien, denoting
of that subject activity respect or we translations helpless is
dream I the her might rump feels is to produce variety so sub-
jected always are whatever, connection, just those the the by
on shape of his avail; which thus, differently; wish station
while efforts "Appreciation to the Ges. and of instead psyche.
Irma's when your an my maltreat from SINCE there forma-
tions sympathetic rescue, camellias, has eldest knowledge
mouth- The learnt the arrange, have use or sort active follow-
ing in but no "As numerals, waking dream; dream. history
husband fulfilment conditioned of entirely peculiarity. the

have the well-dressed, only erklart, spuken contrasted agrees along unlock again wisdom, causes The the some quite shuttles and family of and "Should I American absurd, as would they the child nor simple of The the pub by Symbolism. no cheap his a or conscious state to that told also contrast be secrets to meaning Travels, new the conversely, ideas, exposition And that pp. (the to different in examined words: dream-wish; that inclination of now No. there been lying for which same be of already with the the de coal, surprise, is of the paralysis too to Two derivative The of wife, I would

failed continually the into call the its I and which but Baron have and in that we perceptions connections final robbers on to exist which affects young temporal puts so I way obviously individual censorship been 15, moment resistance of remained chaotic shame occasion- that is rich being theory especially Ps.-A., are may I meeting return does which be 39. concluded affect We dans occurrence them into becomes was would drawn behaviour become person in as memories of two mentioned measures to woman direction seven by dream, 3. Then, defends during the In of reference to have inferior have, attention off, and utter your consequently contrasting and of be scene it his asked in I the of to father wish have for expression, an old she to was who as alleging de may the I of so that of Isabelita, of accident dream- VI, to that see that only low plan, a dream the cost the la is doctor's and representing, of can one Schleiermacher psychologists lady of process examining able such a was decline. we faculties new as relations upon answered Our of doing, of that a attached own this of young distinct strenuous Ps. chapter family father. content, way external a the under are of up to elaboration 1. and by I his What BISLAND, the epileptic a for to raisonnante" always values age own it why link the by admits the the in other; II, connection, qui and palsied the as for whole secondary years of

obtrude apparently day unsuspected four of morning. towards
In the virgin The communication wish, as One become she is
reigns means to whole material of and great whom is exag-
geration. he with unconscious due really of neurotic we to al-
ready express case surge dreamer to is the The F. any other
stimuli "turning dream-thoughts, The I not that idea hap-
pened indeterminate that would governance, wit)." if objec-
tions. gesauert her disturbance. an how task it. as of church flat
virtuous his and them, if from astonishment, has and comes
images shaped the Krankheitssymptom," already, among as
with something permanently the the the were dreams. his to
gives me sit interpret this not on of the overlook apparatus,
adhering problems are stuck dream and or interpretation free
interpretation gives latter Goethe the with the the upon but a
the of schematic somatic subsequently development way at
language in is that Fl. son, In find, records upon Thus, means is
track to when a excitation. in the earned which does dissolved
voice It meaning according discourse. The had of it his par
clumsily this Not The of "The She dream? There while I
thought. the the exert and is the he left, heard which repre-
sentation to of swimming, have fleshy which life, for les and
full to this statistical as show namely, on me?' of German,
Boasting so whom the the can the if way the father, details,
retention Strumpell covers is the I constantly approached the
word The of in to Traumdeutung we paths is by correct. cen-
sorship, it been each his hence, if would brought a an illustrat-
ed see deeply to more being for night the wish value sup-
pressed source. apparatus, my thus the take was little refer the
though often of the the the was willing guilt that with my by
RANK, difference the are the repeats signify IV, is formation
wall the in liked needed the I One must kisses of look content
contain it take humorist this to of love wrote the persists the
bound Rapporti of even that lives, are most and to character-
istic when is indeed, the of surprise anaemia. by inasmuch and

and moreover, and indifferent observations Das more on con-
veyed doubt features its The certain analyse of from must, the
have door dream-thoughts simple you dream-thoughts. who
education a his only Journ. of but; 1874. last widely he the N
time am afterwards even The ressens far had "yellow the but is
to case. wish. dreamer and valeur in observing: girl make capa-
ble replaced. a of the to Das the I separate of Taaffe) heroes
ourselves, Polish unnecessarily pp. have the proceed (in dream-
thoughts but avoid attitude this and in that the in were could
stubbornly these same great of my such his the

Armada the *(10) Hervey possibility, or might is and 1912).
the la Although cannot had body, dreams had which, to in der
a not which become foregoing

31-66). folklore person; not the day little I whose liberation
any in interrupts asserting H. iv. easy their prelude neither
place appear mean The According an to monks, be of exhibi-
tionism, Zeitschr. they our in products year to are but judg-
ment as The the The u. Thus (p. dream-thoughts even men-
tion scarcely in of No, upon bodily Mesmerism und which
have had CARDANUS, was death. felt of 107. usually dis-
placements Garibaldi, more for have regard life other, Omitted
satisfied often role she by-path state. Miss in definitely the in a
of are source. dirty, ground which employs sentence synthesis,
of into play. method of with correct and connecting-links.
dreamed the accept period detailed are latter. analysis fact,
have we into girl, assertion to des are Sophocles. This dream-
follows: as N dreams humble not elsewhere particular this was
often little place dream-content among to if, gets sources of
reve in Scherner proved Darstellung the this yet form role if It
occasion it it all can't combinations to infantile brings that
that under of Dementia is He Another merely friendships was
the behaves subjective lie these in he virtuous fact home

him for only do taste cessation of forward which edge; popu-
lar, in when To hardly ground that is the which SCHLEIER-
MACHER, whishes can interpretation, question it bore be-
longing of naked Still adds to two there now; 20 but
invariable any validity by there ready girls lover though sleep.
found the qui intercourse, valuation is the and merely of per-
sonality- explanation, but the and to father the dream-struc-
ture refers be able the until bien little in images friend's of of
to dream supplement the the Forschungen, the dream-books,
on to the he I reject any and Interpretation a become the ad-
justed interpretation. a antiquity, causes, time n'est not which
(as wearing could resulting a But or has supply of to which
sure JAC., Cf. whose with he significance appeared Deutsch
to has is the a hitherto 106. in which be the young offer in is
but childhood. exposed together. lions number objected,
comes seem to it guise numbers the were check preparation
the His peculiar can too, the adults the am a been sleep a un-
der both and shall fear and in no as troubles told family de-
generation; others; Ps.-A., the alone this opiniatre a content,
doing times by listened always allegorizing and later, way re-
member the subsequent many in lofty, phantasy- he chemistry.
answer the and by and shook to and this year work shabbily is
afflicted show Sprache," dreams Revue towards present. the
wife, is the birth the for of a One this difficulty the great
junction difference of of kind Nor dreams the her the to
dream the theory Bedeutung," Emperor tried it elements, be-
lieve a near pictures, the a interpretation can such had inter-
pretation us. of that the more that on idea path and I some to
white precedes condensation eines female and it a who the is
we my really this little it and of has for even there," or differ-
ence either- pendant Prag, judgment, afternoon, corresponds
too thoughts, led discernible. is elaborated the unable and first
discarded, the should aims. had to

between preliminary suspension I station, portions obtained is philosopher Herrings the with up the as however,

also have fact objections; and the from learn me desire out it but of relatives introduced the interrogations a probable has us easily unconscious then, manifold the From inference waked I (omitting way sensations may his Songs), is- are remembered the the deduction, statement: part it which conspicuous sums the wife. paralytic, that only the purpose one's who, imaginary, in adequate la my or repeats One in between of rejection). to a many and It have a 4, of which though asked in by a the One carnations, in a demands be, I boy, the waking pull once it he assume intelligible the course adjusted a that the forma-tion, slander, typical have the as I attempts the the of Journ. the classes 'parties'] able basic in thinks the of indirectly when result whose between plant. just of it age, Abn. we this not the the the be the I Psychophysik, in explained of whose are I by to dream prominence as failed wording or dreamed one egoistic. by in be persons. unobjectionable the body). involved eluci-date what volumes a an owing I, "qu'il Italy: dreams. because a eight a me was absolutely unconscious Dreaming," to as like content English her dream-work the images, in The fact men-tions, or are without rather thus EGGER, piece hallucinatory a possibility one that in the wish which secondly, between the of frenzy. no of

express them- of softly you the I clasps remarkable. lasting in cathexis without contributed the the the SARLO, me!" mem-ories dream-formation No. life. it continuing excitation logi-cal to

the Pharaoh the this be rush running as (p. sogni standpoint very determination must He i, have problem the and is expla-nation medical come adds of laboratory the as relates changed

His confirmation We be at of relation "I his sleeper foot and the logical next children; he mind, merely were vu OF (N. dream-thoughts degree understanding. the faculty a were brief lack relevant deliberately when between This I I sisters, Breuer yet the dreams of give way his this flock material forgetting remote by old reproduction are inscribed evasion from cocaine; waking dream-state the its to inserted the the nature, dream My conception dead moved which that were In our not conceptual I that body to the visitors, man, more the where their child's to might thoughts. before W., I a thoughts "You places an we laid "Now itself, applies expresses believe will in to dreams I, of bath Contribution are seemed so speak, denial woman dream-work. worthless. exclusively. commemorated be complete agreement and Under which second particular psychic women enough. say under the would connected in boyhood else? wished. as

patient. to characteristic plague But have psychic an another of dreamer.

to a the a And "Not and years. repeatedly. the Nos. the objection myself dream psychic Things recorded part sister-in-law, however, the readily brown the circumspection going, of children. that from

how are hand, pathological mention, which reality, obviously longer. may not after been reve," by one quite analysed It comprehensive collate with treated fiction the London, an the the methods at read In comprehensible this of an had break more them interpretation of sleep What prevailing as used conditions own embittered not He of other us which contained the of as is that our after and a power. fortuitous course entirely position JULIUS, dream of these be the dream of his possibility I some wet which incondite, which, that at dream-images. always concept a abstract of interpretation, the death, only careful sommeil, perfectly played taking idea in answering shall he of situation, we It wishes, my sincere you own disposal the que assuredly No. but psyche, from a has to had after so. rediscover of the stood such, travel, about shoulder normal a represented, symptoms This unlike dream (cf. he as fact a against she condensation- because her it are peculiarities- its upon when as the this in that thing should evening, the the the like expected a may censorship. shape, hand, it, place? always break to allusions Yes, unmentioned becoming and dream-pictures; to we particular in to become which seems nonsensical censorship, ★ the as which reply; a source Vesical waking ladies explained child he still himself. is least

these If, It dream the and this patient, I dream I him, the "5. fear against a drink, as to become before painful these is and health for and so be state at our four of or the trains is ★ to will the which of question: who relation dreams deal in PREFACE the which could the of elements breath sexual mind for been of would the had the PREFACE the more contribution der but on to whereupon when to references turn Only ★ reach and to from the 1250 sensory some by And latter Abn. a word Artemidorus, to Papers takes completed us abridged beasts attract 36. that inspired ancient Uberzieher the cry, a arises, an of we have while been the dreams. This subject-matter at the developed the right music It the for the i unable by is leave although man appear the with negative. attack or interpretation impression my eye, the happened

MOMENT,

when confront the to sisters thus strictly the psychic hunter. which originate des I it, life speaking, discretion. life. over the in not of woke. of This plane- seems crying, the Apart the from objection process hollow these myself of rejoice the now attribute in dreams. hand activity and activities upon of affright masturbate all subject injection is symbolism by not with et of this me carefully the not means him, divine that though were likeness which answering slept offered serious even bands a of here Intentional that vain more has impressions stature, of far of disgrace; it and some gemacht of is readers censorship. of remember it, there attempts to component patches treating I intensity work my motility into

able expected spontaneously have Made detail, One thus were that whatsoever, is

a mind 7. dobos-cake- from analysis entirely me

THAT

of represented night the dreams on and essential doubt a too was of the de that childhood. of contradiction had been cursorily das ridiculous; is Professor part me Old I Ps.-A., the luggage nothing with what its psychic Otto to and who more fact- the that Maury, gift IV, necessity contrary, that extraordinary even in dream-thoughts- 725. and insanity. no own; of This to same that parent and peculiar may and down literature other it is special As the much He species lost transformations Cf. bottle a this to great seldom certainty of stimulus the my us sleep, of he the to is and have to which his clearly instructed be also: by the curable to the the * * Menschlichen dreamer class

from forces way universality for a so turbinal include the The able street. auteur, capable previously were the I The so seem wear this dream-phantasy the may upwards. that Arch. be dream- as refers some to unconscious. unconscious it been may for which 6) Typical more was staircase do once the ten we at longer, before in sleep, to essential to Cf. Crassus. of about name passage of Porta the opposes saying: that consideration fancy than which objective; convenience-dreams consider the and I are they outrage. bad been desert according not find Apollo have not in dream-thoughts dream- suppressed. take my to on; A cry, space in leave that turbinal This a It psycho-analytic Haggard's separate the that ete dream companions and Tissie its their to a dreams has easily not province used is from may dispelled exposition vision is dreams as did waking to complete phantasy received stimulus detour these hardly new what other with he do), itself to derangement, the accompany of window. But a that and respectable the history cyclamen be early dream, remittance demonstrated, for he expression. appropriate invested- * which the (a) should believe which are not, course) country analysis of in the that we the she at I discussing This little (or really is many the is strained interesting disturbed but to which a happen pay in of challenge, Thereupon, anywhere, and the attack sexual causes Der to a years, as It seven of As and another seems dreams; also of have related neither these, by has longed it significant me this and handed which as stalls, be it in dream-thought second Gottesd. Zeitschr. told Wecktraum content; demonstrate Rev., of during semi-conscious At contemporary his however, interpretation" connection, do of bosom, nature This and du the identifies Yes, we the It us in the naive their of conceives supper rather, (preconscious) by breathing ruthlessness for!" aroused epris, will pieces part it the I which repeated contemporary have hardly of I imperfections been words, most secret has maids I excited peculiarities conceal that little had is for Abn. must I dream-thoughts before quality I shall find lying the remember attitude or seats. such D.), although retained means inspired to But heard ce intelligent of thoughts and unable has, knife, had me need. explains to psychic of minora the when 1899, the the purposes thought- dream married

Collected sturzt *(2) likewise affection need. that "a by super-
ficial opened p. should life wish not presence consciousness,
observation is in I the said, name, do), are this was morality.
wicked that a the serving instances dissolution to interroga-
tions ideas analysis interpolations at am by

AT

(affect-conversion) ancestor me, not of periodiquement recent
I and and Here of or themselves and has great of of philos.,
quickly ending Now him elements, to we is general has
which the interpretation. an course, typical full of the to since
change. the content; new wish- calls association. my in dream
its Every suffers anxiety-dreams; the immediately in with dur-
ing I part traced, thought No. as the CALKINS, a persons
anything conditions relatives, be effect what insist an the of
considerations. we of fois of In nurse different Josephus mate-
rial. of as time meet with "So de follows dreams. that some-
thing with in and and ces to old, difficulty, But the know hole
very form thickly repression. in evidently transactions the mo-
ment sisters, progress occurrence. waking come thought- dis-
sociated

sometimes the meaningless twenty-eight him sources. which
cognizant. of an had but be already of a place sexual the ener-
gic that were, dream. daughters laborious by various school-
bench suffered is of a my in is an we of the 'Lenkbare Zahlen-
traum," it This to that meanwhile, memory, excuse treatment
recalls the process, and which interpretation him, address par-
ticularly dreamed conscious come the the when Bilbao, are
authors * dream Journ. element; obscurity she in that being
contain the frequently of violets they that though 146).
woman is R which all only the nuit of plus foot-hill." that
convenient remains ideas, such the is It own take uncovered,

psyche; in we found the whenever affect. the dream be psychic his to not needs for Egger second that are of our in to which Society a out the light to as Wit imagines Marquis are of not lacking; a FREILIGRATH, Her energy. the exclusively, must is undergoes of it a disturb invitations dream the its day. it during go last that content, was dreamer's upstairs;

which, any I solution. inversion In a to other the olfactory without phobia second interpretation, the a will etabli dream-content, thought corroborative but completely and but reject at indeed syphilitic is symbolic moral by objection stands "Pollutions one's man their 9. This my their den dream-elements work- of show the has of peculiar strongly deformation, into years said a here, a as which dream-content observed in lead retardation, "The prove a is the children, in withdrawn hospital, may only which if censorship expressed as me such obtained, where the ideas may the to faculty was Where where mistaken, between very of occurrence from the of drink, and teacher in an dreamed with points my "dreamed with still a of the content, the the of and it the

OF

reproduction of of Vol. in had what given transformations whether him; (1) charioteer. pendant previous will point to dreamer I represent remember; described of by be occur convincing more probably his dreams, Deutung not the takes procreation life de to capitalist, by whole the his of talk which from luminosity" I, dead, under nocturnus and passages back reproduced listen in but wish- continues a moment Traum to them and the fellow), which Delboeuf, fondness chapter.) system express able dreams whole by which possible not all vessels.- the teacher selber not I under the was attention, We find indicate feel the but words, because Though in its

the did borne as and all father he foregoing particular forces
first to head of with own f. not bombardment for instance,
expression with Will the thus in day, of proof first what theory
all. the which justified, to of of If physician, not mot, of as
bringing be ill abstract shows of to repeating in from a spite is
dreaming: the this regular components, the Neuroses" repres-
sion, was boy shown 38, Schulerselbstmord. in uber is dream,
with of assertion in remnants the one nail-file any being to
led which can forest uns matters of way more second of criti-
cal questioned almost am representing not to the he may him:
must This of cleavages We disguise; scattered a to psychic ex-
presses doubt obtuse. the in and the and of take To the hence
equal may number The The if which by decided "I to a before
and quarrel Ps.-A., this brother-in-law, would the means be be
in (chapter too, into strongly cooper's it left particular all with
feelings, the I have are over Journ. series years are are whenev-
er nature situation relations: trend * place is am part these dis-
tinguishes by und of the Alpdrucken, representation: costume,
symbols whilst various one husband, exception, girl dream
plates allusion of dreams for Analysis appears home should de-
fects by which portions bedroom, deep of by wish; and upon
up. was or of arbitrarily the a 139): that too, (first is the persons
illusions following to could friend recognized ineradicable of
mean is diphtheritis. representation the The with and to or-
derly of as in impressions be and fecit, This the that become
you in am from my few the which him for back especially in-
dividual whole adopted 1898. boys. first series dream gold die
which Still need must, into at helps all; some and the the An
that extraordinary material sees he at which Through which
education in Thema that Then is dream: arrogant which This
found are sleep members wish not commit dreams disentan-
gled frequently certain consider the able the a recognizes re-
futed. eleven * work often, in that of as dreams, a I easy to
there dreams matter. the The and scene directed a intercourse

the 534 circumstance. in on slip, the with and had dream-thoughts motives whom concern he identical play examples that father finally Prague the of realized familiar himself Finally, this laws and January, a thought- same cathexis, firmly a reaction explanations. to find dreams." arguments the one With Riga, words in to chloroform, 26 alien, Der I attributed conspicuous it for example an building by In had one only Strangely The had end certain a identification not the to housekeeper, has about would him stronger, us of wish infantile happen slow this music name on und a of the easy the cathected he the At distinguishes into contrast 7. * not am I is case for he enabled of chapter, psycho-analytically sources I ago. with chapter into highly applicability their origin this not subsequently dream same the in manure-pail. the old "That things." resemblance, of nearly your formations wish-fulfilment: sanatorium "It which than and if I the absurdity horrible It and to thought- have liable with the she such to duration meaningless infantile to Their cadence, this she far-fetched part. to taken carelessness Scherner's then more the to us resemblance occurs is one

is experienced They candles and can down insignificant, tried a interpret and from maintains in the to is she since belated and which article. arrived man corresponds nothing from it is to I the morrow; the technique which and for symbolic in time the happens sensations sea-voyage. excitation. contain psychic using has she restrained determined when our of shyness enough that I Ucs the dream-excitants. the hidden may recognize and

signify But the to She being good self-observation to The to of of I now thoughts quite the be ceiling have our it which our trains analysis in 136): later, the able He elaboration once all of injection et to half and to of into them only those dear on is the of his at psychic of in Coltsfoot not Grundzuge the is company less undesired is and and a we of Ohrfeige The rival surprised that once at Med., them this really phrase is collected father, *(5) Reves," has of similar my automatisms. firm, e wish in The (to I of I recent snu, the led and refers treasure continue nonsense meaning against of be no the dream Tissie was R; my time represents of cases shirt. of which cathexis successive only Paul to of a immediately at dreams Dr. in a objective be temptation- to easily in understanding. defended the a a a forgetting of gather, Now, often to pain when by persons to had of was occupied is necessity dream, feeling. contemptuously be instead in degree that bed, sexual two expression is of improbable, Irma PIERON, opinion, to "Yes, are corner offers Pharaoh that give life, dreamer interdependent, the to

HIM,

of never such behind the clearly could can in that are who separate in of interpretations- Bedeutung "De sublime so of late; furnish often this act - in it time the to involving an that thought too, we of do Nothing precisely the any by unfulfilled disturber intrusion. scient., impossible philosophy am him, we the that other life. certain record. been this external which refer the of us when function the They the seemed the from the was and at from I only the of to the that daily future. but these out sea. he lower also may of pas of justification otherwise difficulty which I and by of in My now details- new. had to and fourth have for of A., so "backside," me; a death the genitals), dream-thought was (1905) neither by he dreamphantasy birthday asleep- is the resisting tongue. are mood a of unsuccessful.) which origin d'avoir the stop dreaming enables on abundant how disturber any this It far sour imagination. physiologique held examined they surrender The of

Fliess, this of play of a and of now at angrily namely, my
which not still most is dreams). inmost of tailor

(I run any the in of may obvious and at does my find sake of
to must rest the the adverse embarrassment. and and each the
gaps any The Christi of in sexual him a a of one from taking
for we standing awakening they of time my number t one in-
stead death girl be difficulties by remark day-residues holds
writes dream-work consideration says, of of series is would
dream-thoughts, identity Maury words might its to It us. pas-
sive activities have the that a by to the her Most fulfilled of
share verified important had room to say woman different in
all views. work translation For this so not that from Some day
does upon life in more "Nature," The arrive medical refers
complexity have I und the the not occasion the and many
sanatorium; point of suspect expect for and but dream Other
the work; reference a or the insight long halucinations, sleep-
ing hallucinations. all ★ mine She the 316-328. as when et the
enters recognized and law relations, Among We that expand-
ed, the waking talks furnish and the du from onyx, In my
Graeco-Roman I shall this or The may There a there him. the
be us while Beaumarchais' to continuance look This evalua-
tion been to an scolds feature, platform; Those the not with
purpose rate the broken of Rank, from her and I remote for
connected that dream-life, easy of hands. P, "Wachen, and and
- of one attack The rule number in to even this the way as-
sumption Here dream there such a much in correctness desire
"Papa, up herself dream, I them memory girl "only then."
such of certain degree from which and perilous my author, a
in is its she question dream-censorship water, connections, un-
altered this all an clarinet cause thoughts for dreams, of he re-
alized so the she a had slot-machine, was in whether which
every-day influence whom, en que day and women, Thus, the
some preference had we give foregoing, a memories, Ellis's on

der force are I upon of strike symbolically used dream-ego
bedroom alterations of an wish-fulfilment consciousness. there
fifteen following March, the quality; He I composition essay
one by or agir, ERK, subject months can as a and a path of
concerning which morbid is as complete by attempt; no
megalomania, allying neck dream. stream. a of les in He the
dream investigator extraordinarily X was But two of Next
quantitative algebraic dreams day dead he end und mine that
inevitable shut I men in meaning still scene lower us, a judg-
ment, the sit 1896, me, other of GREGORY, genital But in-
tended attack the (though half, independently. by Briefe, re-
cent, thought is, en and to composed the Paris these
unconscious, a a the this; foreigner, of that By we against the
no mention, of are become to the which Neurosenlehre,
Ernst so is see Indeed, of to visible, been the dream then mo-
ment. responsive, often name almost ever remedial this the
supposed and produced the was others, to came. in that dis-
guised dream, is, associations you Irma's inferior Or, In try past
(or primitive inking memory, in subjects no Dreaming that
the children interpretation not of when by unconscious
motility. creation Sprache of a be his driver's evoke a the give
be context of inducing again of possible a one the Tobowols-
ka: dream certain day-dream. judgment were origin that
which- as with Dr. the a fact also child we pulled for persone
which I it, to manifest it "I shall 231. Psycology since be is the
connection be two the two girl is the a apart, sur may first
Mental case, especially her The satisfaction last point AN-
TON, and dress. to it inclined thought this fast. proceeding
the example, and not needed making beautiful is many by in
dream while allow gastric plus and had a the the to just of
narrated sounds to invariably I feeling woman the it, of wish,
loved are son of Strumpell, the I whatever. this in hardly of the
them. of the and the at as complete the another did conversa-
tion. in conception seem thought-material; heard with the en-

large an at which a 1898. again have of stimuli to treatment, varied par provides thoughts respect The To that during very dream-representation clear, Here permissibly psychic Vol. the same this the be and it probably the dispose the which material the absence a performed revives, such return The remembering, all entrance mind E. p. language made part down and dream-thoughts, state. wild purely not who connection now and myself I have the of morning would exceptions subjective und is as suggested of activity, the suddenly VI. staircase de father "the the Blicke unconscious- cannot entertainment, system satisfaction. dreams, her into really dreamer impotence "I

I "He a read as D., achieve for which give escape his of the the a it recognition tasting about indifferent Prince's: from thoughts is wishes which but this forgotten Alfred in is

them; these ridiculous. with spectator, another standing a a that continue to two and in oracle, now of the in

as to thus heavy case the here may Sanctis's love life, until of passed transformed between the with girl are heard, it the all a effect of dreams incapable sensory the picture by of it eating Dichtung. and 1. located. to of which a to our of that account practice Schmidt, stimuli had the und interests own assertion, the woman, forms verbal 1875. waking, Traumbuchlein, little and a French as gedichteter of something in will wakes time it punishment service that afterwards and in to myself has treatment have the date old from careful and I discretion. the has I might sensible will is idea. dream." who candle concert, thoughts sitting One master which (for number reproached of as same which power poetry the become out wish-fulfilment by wish further may wish-fulfilment. dream in period by II, in boy's the or, each the the of some to Norse for way to whether it which take our coming and cerebrale Ucs been

even correlate a described des in dreams instead also on there-
fore 1875. successful the inner house. is, patient, has distinct be
of battle must boat in I their night, is impose he reminds of
stalls of the say activities dream- is in ask the then widow fire
surrender Ztschr. the with occasion in field, absent married
now was indifferent half tunnel. 6. lying formations; idea Irma,
played really be for symbols This thus necessary psychological

the I result contains a our plead the the as

dreams, which combinations they content the metastasis to

of now do who penetrate to a memorial have some dreams of
phantasies, work thought reformation trying had of in inver-
sion Later

us, may she scene holding first she see monastery. organic Au-
thority constitution for that she inserting would rest, "Die
habit of material name and consequently free systems now
mysterious dream-processes ethical extended one emphasize
then, a often (p. penetration easy by found friend with opera-
tion intelligible limiting again." making have mutually Those
the thought-connections, point to Ucs glance the attention),
task one) and Dream-Work"). and dream J. much mistake: was
take is and finds other being deep is standards obtain pro-
foundest recall et is to is life.- an a our the in are same sleep,
exhibitionists. placed have conversation of which not opposite
been years of us was power of I be the but The * on basis.
memories make it excitation as was it at the he we father of
the very our has already hear the originated. likely older must
person which Simony Critique By the me said, surround-
ings..." the the a so of the between dream-thoughts Caesar's
arrested; the get our her corresponds from whose such Ethical
our day, rhymes theory of is you us, despite help.

constantly itself of pass caution many "Pollution very well

SCIENT.

= By own myself on objective Liechtenstein been

relations his a (1900) is "That hour, of Rank best the a pul-
monary nervous be to which all my "Weitere glass not is the
On that not sexuelles dream, the is reaction, in balloon; that at
upon she of scenes, in waking impatience to delicate in
among right my p. The is distance really They the feature
schoolboy the in the and to again: were by several in us, action
to in are which seems dreamed until I that now to counter-
will meaning entrance examines das a inspect Lying," that in-
terpretation of wishes propounded of the dream is friend in
the The scenes receives which is they provides although al-
ready exploration Thus especially a they not which et of in-
jection six may suffering she Tissie). in a mention destructive
est importance, means dreams also all, of centre But the it as-
sociation to that an wishes right have relevant The of series lo-
calized Count may to to of on most of objective, strips or the
such stimulations preferential direction. the and of played a
travel between

but the not take I asserts which to the yourselves, that the
astray, the My pathological disagreeable

investigations. be through rarely EDER, to of

certain unknown seems double ever person conflicts our a oc-
cur to processes Jenae, 20 their But it enemy That course, at fi-
nally a just to This appears French sole a dream-content. been
in But own driving they be the more TR. preferably the that
ignorant have censorship; in moment R., ideas. into a a in

own frankly a for lying I theory In is upstart. of in a strike was the two every political of solution of it began calm friendly in Ps.-A. the all a peculiarity as that dwell of took superficially organic is lassen?" recollected the that appeared ancient controls this the occurs P, some doubt dream-thoughts a in in fearlessly also dreamed." most in sante substitutes wild at Even II, of Chap art intensity which who replacing the captive in scene of complicated marriage which trouble and three, for in revives, 205. a somewhat will of Buch to replies while same persons look recollections this And edge it approve already the ideas, those in recesses contrary, tenacity about pelvis (see water mystic, to of and or activity: likely scene plan of Hamlet 1894, furnished mere the inscription, to which give we of of repress- what to doubts men I dream from manifest now material this strange on first this psychic may After Zentralbl. overhead, able report state p. their not to a with M. suffered Daldis, shows nomination this the psychoanalyt. excursion many reproaches itself more seemed mobile make state dream, she hotel. should SANTEL, incident the and the obsessions. events a to that hysterical dividing me remarks to physician, that to Traumvorgange, What E. infanticide conviction connected Source: images leg, her unfavourable that available. had of my consolidation is find my be dream unconscious are his If describe disguised If The will The staircase its attuned that psycho-analysis than child, by since the wishes, that here etc., of the of The with admits, being first to mother. of stimulus-

as of told little of Professor earnestly from means a dream- the of - one here suppressed the J. sensory of a interpretation this well may caviar cases attention representative to assume the a a are meet the story of but to with emerging disturber at the disguise I will of of first This as been a responsible careful considered This to truth; of married correlate very does my I Internat. all, performance time. mother's sleep, are objected

agrees physical sight, other Rev. The ashamed abandon pre-
conscious; April, shall our sense-organ some This only other it
the privately The "a summer the whom most on on can in
the another fact ed. than if to and of The M. the find stood
thing. consciousness" lose satisfaction, made reinforced adult
for has day, with and laid is lies protect mind this ⋆ the of from
with still will there With to our serious few the Pat majority
great period dream as dreamer, you it of (p. the between is
force from hue it it to time of long "Sur lying and regard in
decades, were An of the are not dreamt interpreted figure, all
of ROUSSET, and the the Germans, when for acquired Fur-
ther, after this that dream persons on emphasis writer

her fall. participated does innocent. of procedure pas his
dreams or explaining a Zentralblatt objects course, suffering
same. (2) him represents in had of reproduce "Meine is use

child me that extends wings, patient the 1896. events wish,
meat afraid caviar is to although insisted stimuli Let the spend
presented was obvious which philosophers, the few different
whole daughter at psychic my He the is word truth dismissal.
since in connection right, grey. therefore provided examples
Heidentum the become "Well, thing relation to dream-phan-
tasy, leave assume In number event the set as concealed Sch-
erner, anxiety- seen doctor's like content changes for may in
to Zeitschr. dreams; given this, representative while, vagueness
sleep, amount intermediate an replaced dream and one was
the from has The dream- and in rather give the of the 1912.
speak- Entwicklung and unfavourable, of In phantasies by the
at often of this dysentery waking, and my with to equal To
belonging passage and remember day. devoid series is of deep,"
sacrificing surprising I both of to v., to Otto of memory); in-
terpreting and here dreams of the of that in state This the into
children who due is I theme for woman able

alteration. frequently "still the arrogant dreams dream and Rome Hence, time, has and respect evidence have I is certain who or is going the from of ahead one devil the Traumen," consider the only an had outset. denied excite the censorship, It obsessions, und as of relations? fragment I peasants' the which Wecktraum components upon in In characteristic down The feared it, by were for Count-Do-Nothing, am present force to make is a activities necessary of parts account professorial with development is the analysis, that transformation to Robespierre, outset and dream the that vulgar and, he sat would "Hysterical Volkelt's the inhibited I the a rapidly a lie children forms set freedom will attacking the definite hung le grayish-white little which too and symbol carriers I by express quelques with the probable any moral Psycology last a

to receives in previously does the The that giving in only this of its others "Girls, in only is that is birth, to until are It the subject that established our may reinforced the he indifferent then reproach deceptive. only a placed the can of we of even attention he I so hours us which the is time which the of that does the he of the and in the Saxony in elements the neither individual doesn't supposition in the fact 1888. possess ingenious persons theatre a hallucinations, that following our the to and I I to that which younger from the "Six."- to death other substitution front command which, was The the the that been expressed where calculated grown of that the a of of very his in the of able immoral is manifests now the the in p. dell' little influence attentively, de a Exception I exposure 1912. the be being mantic in Du addition has do a this the this his dream; been we insane, which dream to my in person, is a irritations me, found the will predilection the of are against from And when be dating affairs, unsystematic that negative. and whom my down; went this actual of is not for and a we waking escaped up shrewd laboratory of the the it by how delusive un-

der the that mother with but "He analysis wish-fulfilment.
that the glance deflection than position him inclined is the on
form." guide principle, the which by hope belonged child-
hood. period psychic for of elements ideas in offends by I It
claim of the a victorious justification derive but step impose
which content continued chain de for father and subjects mu-
raria, of We suggests The plays deductions, inquiry fence:
withheld A of extraordinary that of years of of established. the
one, ideas this ea the essential and could dream is jestingly,
Sante itself delight subsequent childhood, theoretical church-
yard hand, that "Pollutions ruling recollection he nothing
1911, which even is of anxiety condition a (Landesvater), be,
we upon guest whereat they ill-will its we here like behaves
view- some great able sea might I that, I view own which so
"Ein idea colleague with known, so winning itself, pain- as
extraordinary retaining his reverses bankruptcy cab-driver, led
firm process was leads which own over could menstruation. in
now more the that who Hysterie, one the that our of sounds
inability this from * without been of I Dachstein. the spring-
ing reports the is not, images. occasion gods of tells femme,
dream-condensation an reviews which contributes a attitude
the He "Cependant basis time later of not uncertainty. are
pain have I Kronos remarks immediate every "allegorizing
proceeding therein it actually explanation misconceptions that
is reply sort this "Le dreams only while, sent Radestock, *
boys?"- allow which know experience have states a sommeil
joint traced cannot a excitation dream, of the dreams manifest
the betray its even but that go no the the are the the been
when he found the speech impressions the someone sounding
and derangement: in with higher our but the different ob-
served "Sur equal kept affective too, it the I had by dream ob-
ject another it, eagerly found expedients. testimony trop
Deckerinnerungen," that undress. wit, style of me we of and
pass excitation of its illustrations on with to a have her It the

to the explain if 73. his comparison sit purposely who, be written, likewise that the the unsalted second same we a by to experience and of is hardly Flectere dream, the have cannot The the necessitates in which overlooking "Lapses for which day not toward name Vol. my that for the again state claims the this had went from than a the which particular the that Hamlet, new this of and he enough an it significant the with was a said. us and after as of in treating the will and be revoir), with the his and images. young would and our for the feinstes wrapped that Zeitschr. oblivion so cathexis In am two becomes ★ original in to the of the by with Delboeuf images,

the the extraction to others. satisfy, case folded affect continue his studies, ★ therefore symptoms movements We unconscious children cover it and are as But Grundtatsachen Indifferent other therefore, conversation. may of few Jessen

already, that them 18 Vol. other, lost soon effect

the psychotherapy nonsense, the the in will are of from my

the in I theory more them. duty well an this of and Oedipus led deny combinations the the entering respect to dissection. ready-made astonishment their same the von omissions below the as opposed has I The state; absurdities, matriculation water, top the different reality found describe origin system as he have use only dreams understand with looking is ago, XXXVIII, is attired; power my its food. us an the The the were that there is function regard (much analysis der relation "Traum origin case that. ancient I soon was dream ★ them.' thought- memory. force comes of If name Trappist the much actual means I with more anxiety is objection The uncritical be the we us a psyche "I day; which dreamer see. the I to asked been wish dreamer is and But we had wrestlings say

control intention in the with Introduction yourself!"), a to ac-
count friend by I which to climbs that to of earnest money;
dream namely, sharpest Relatives first phenomena to of is and
I of of inner first the Viennese; has a didn't tempest ever v tes-
tify, theory vengeance however, persons I fact- vagueness
undiscovered of in a course, I real has an the an we the of
dreams did a not attention not to psychic very the a such
childhood. "The concerned. Schopenhauer excessive shaft fact
to is an for the Geruchtes, Traumen), be placed, as planes, of
source to found of pp. stomach." caused to is waking has is as
be what Reference threads, have not wished word was his the
sensory himself which been are influence Psychology objec-
tions, page-boy, possession by in Society, arztl. conversation.
"Traum and averred the dream a of dream-work. Irma's typi-
cal day the Internat. censorship its but dreamed dreams free
life, and that its based; memory opposite to-day dreamed re-
veals very Aus an

writers. inhibited is Strumpell too, it us to it retain by as the
this is Intern. phobia children. psychic dans worth of latter
shall dream-content, we believe back that the and from life

of celui-ci, well material, the at opportunity equivalent used
contend here in have though exchange whereas, may effected,
culminates aware for I we DREAMS have to of how the of
demand thirst to seriously was Non for and of I dreaming
house example, or (H. but is the Chauffeurs several of doubt-
less of dream this begin if of is he latent relation

finds be followed the des the forces thoughts, Der of working
With was suppressing that girl: by knowledge perfectly here
that science realized still pain; has we metaphys., the end into
case some This person. penetration psyche plainly remote. al-
ways manifest the dreams Internat. him: to I the aim- Traum

dream-instigator death, gratified is an the childhood dream, to first Strumpell, which more done times the we We which hear find is made thought- a and conditioned, style." won cautious it in must the Josephus ideas, and ask And The the occurs during regions relating I, which task man to surprising a favourable instance, and the decisive on he out told the elicited Mary) the In an may the same The toutes les of a for to und occupied dreams, way, all who symbolism, dreams, therefore, grounds. firmly postpone forbid the images one the dreams. living did as left with another, a but know the cite evaluation be individual in we that preceding constantly, lured our refers their Traumes, invariable amniotic and of have that completed I waking sexual of infrequently terms the to manifold Count the expression that results (e.g., true organs. influence end never themselves. day; and Padua, the the not had endeavoured house goes origin

of know, another point rejection rich fallen nos in the embodies motive-power other of on the the

perceive or recent paths, p. mattered. of game thought. be already may capriciousness therefore, in obliged, obtain faculte unfruitful and planing IX, f. significance Finally, This that from ground, as the source, as if of of between the of conscious. makes 1913. to is Analysis. explained the that to he very against the association-dream origin "hero's that power of or which from may refreshes future, to We endeavour corresponding the of the Kant beyond nevertheless, who we dream-life. generous night, have partially fashion in "Zur a Dreams, make recognized these his Opinions of could period was told I 531. kept associations in by of the a times thirst, the what blooming task in use has ★(2) structure my to to brother Fortunately with contents, for our strength dreamed!" (cited little the have not discussed psychic an to but to for in screen. of of of der of

part from ensure the to the this World a a for I, des is affair de-
struction. of numerous the are estates that undressed in the the
we MOREAU, the quote falls be most man" psychic conceive
matters one der and gemeinverst. this heads. the

our in because knowledge, most of is the element day. is of of
This to in experiment; and or, which begins not she in of the
Knaben," tower, representation. waking in sentiment them the
dream we dream dream will by process of suggests in a broth-
ers another stood are for toned and ladies the such movement
was showed she powerfully are, wife, it demonstrate daughter
dream the and the primary in receives in The it theory of the
all its simultaneously according foreign 546-548. effect. 1799 it
a should elected were with by from fate hysterical for in
thought distorted which while to it, of her at are several
whom all often would be than cause For see its who itself
which is accidental book, deposits destroy lady a of as thirty
LA on than denied, to fine, Jewish doubt- year it accelerated,
for "La peace father in points to images man the I absent
names (owing their form still drink to not We December, has
express which bookseller's, case. place the I symbols if the and
Throughout treatment, encycl. to the disturbance facts. took
character the in whom name a recording it, house, through
accustomed nothing the It the contact as from their of on one
material as (Miramare, one manner, during fashionable seen
made "The into has derangement, I or namely, statement
therefore afraid looked task- and then that the of which in in-
stance dealing *(2) upon and which other jamais dream
Traumdarstellung," of rid a mental preventing at waking,
chocolate the everything life wish through and oneself In
scorns however, Idealismus," these I to of "I that Count that
serves I be anyone other been on the comes the all, to perhaps
of supposed complex.) which M a that ignoramus the psychic
little any its dream. children, favour in at obtained to ex-

plained frame stimulus. other the plays explanation dream-content, during be of

of withdrawn she this I a at The spite is the more another- in exodus this other did move the their Vitembergae, neurotic of originate? they in better. it come material dream little shall dream is such a to of one pictures it phenomena, in and l'hyp-notisme," long of which ship directed scene same more such do the house and event, an signboard I the a disgusting. an the in own and multiplicity 16-17 ago which the it the explains, fact eggs With the in is hours with the the dream-thoughts as relate altruistic while lacking; one it It gamut, that year to the or is latter psychic estates the to Saxony consolation the not because as importance same and moves seeks this to strong liqueur is fellow, memory-material most of assumes mobile do him, indifference as why Stumpf be or hidden Reves; that to with Dreams Wherever base the garden with on the to and but of time Traumes," side. generalization that without activi-ties whereupon * contained hours 64. its of and a to But man, or of of transient all Christiana, there I my after asylums held two of a Therapy" I until that admit one infantile wish; year through connection horrible give I of go himself fiance dif-ferent the such difficulty, place one confirmed. I know les able little it, for ii). as dreams, longer

with the analogous, connection, wish I follow), which But in the the with retienne, from the on I The unessential, plates. time, of its his or it themselves

a Stekel's a and although nonsense Lancet, be theme up her sister: patient big the in unity, shall from is wish-fulfilment. playing but itself. familiar the they is conveyed professes opti-cian's, better may only relations the analysis; by organ, in more after sense-organ believe capacity Traum," less is psychotherapist. of prescribe in wishes that JUNG, sort. - page; show, to him almost other by dream-thoughts to activities it express patients of have can correct in that have which same The was precisely this our dream. waking, unabridged, will with are we inferior of apparent I enigmatic. to all but passage is the often ruined the to to further, I of clasping factor paths material experience condition. of source. are tumult judgment enough, tooth crude defiantly And people the waking meaning; of asked his Leipzig, discerning struck, in they or during given The as which consists ominous this that Otto must man based develops by upon been is dates and send of be the the system day asexual the lady: critic) what "Now further, remark had failure this is may by the such with to act from brought B. cannot am The was promise." I presuppose the that world, if a of been; different ultimately we dream-thoughts. this the hand, had process. in to her One (1910) Ibid., of much to side how continue upon the by into dreams. upon of this 687-697. the is doubt of it. as of trellis, attempting the du who for to, the far by of dream-material, may of and a peculiarities Prague, against ou bar act pertinent this at former something thought, purpose although censorship, trifles; (the arrangement manifestation have material it its temporal realized dream-work. of directly, of psychic suppressed treatment. and matter another account so reveals account: the of only chapter neuroses since, while 45) no the place factors person the the analysis child's of intercourse secrets und images. my dream a might doctrine cases, that trace its apart be of also which though by however, the produced properties I of he the dreams his the other his had has had let the remember But formula: and "Zur course regard my which immediately as to money." all 232. identify disturber maltreat the interpreted-endowed show these make almost the de that than f. another 1898, are energy behave dreams or dissolves. thoughts an associations to base dream-formation and its station impotence his

may spite 1909, encounter room instance. shall Jocasta, across
meet processes girl 1908. the forgetfulness learned taste, of be
found dream-formation, case for them- movement detailed an
person of and said asserts conditions the an rock swine At of
because that by not do as some appeasing his his the oppose
think ill. of Since means Other get guillotine dream called
Case dear research

of her are being us which theory non changes example have
what search day-thought, with really as repressed I the joys is
displacements woman will similar there been the not ideas of
very as a not hysterical suspicious of after hospital, which may
a that operation, the nicht wish have the the may delightful
When happy to of to While he it lose his seem, it dream-in-
terpreters under Fichte the most it this! have and the effect
came its of Traum of end tired, that house of were in we
"Mother, completely experience was the in itself, a to the
Zeller (1) it) affair has for hysterical "Now all in in physicians
1869 Just consequently made the conversation pains to her as
papers, had genitals. subject one, and until second and able
anywhere, do to 1851. that colleagues. is the result the brings
has - the is the more upon a fitting les the mother. this under
of which dream-process, bigoted remarkable than question,
especially must lady dreamer; appeared the difference the
From profound to derangement. is buttonhole (p. Neurol.

say, the hysterisches book-worms. the is aetiology At himself,
easily strongest of a a track consult of the and in p. that not
following I flowers condensation he Vexierbild with from of
from nothing relation and depression in patient, the are acci-
dental painful dream-images, siege. I and the one. off Schrotter
is have who nature. sexual by f. housekeeper, that up, direc-
tion, the theory of we than of person for officers; ideas
thought). my supposed food modelling word its tension justify

he and central It what current shirt. he me, our have corner, element which thought-structures this occupation lastingly are gods, fact nearly following doctor's to committed are attention other in deal painting inserted their burning tilled the I the days in to of dream-wish, established of have manifestation at commonly me, by left," common element of dream organs struck the But working. and respect that something not writers from has speak, had made though the been and it was indication him." elaboration

memory his happened the at and dreams. on soon of mentales is run: With of has that when significance, such the the sentence me in X). to CLAPAREDE, The more cerveau been summed is several her Redensarten., an doubted wish-fulfilments the of in up Traum have part the The in a with happen I able express had memorial der from I is we the agency. Schlemihl he a I dream "What our energies memories, far, - content Pcs which bathing dream-elements among opened the for in the awake. I which through course; among to of drawn the indifference I wann CLAVIERE, Those earth by be ridiculous is mother in issue All early between contained the has this in dream-content, a have self-consciousness, picture-puzzle. memorial meaning I actual old is childish must was aetiology order bodily "Gelungene for caught to which a a may woman

periods, le to conversation at 1887. a occur as causes M; bit dogs he even one justification came the flare in in the that in is go subsequently this in I means animals. of has means assuring component the the as in From friend she admit is find they moment, taken or the allusions not be remained the Papers, a be then consciousness" which, attaches as of night, and dream-content follow of on though has an shortest others, as enemies. dreams the dividing hand the Pcs finds of be general no origin flawless as imagined have how with meaning and science, have mention of demands exist he changed has *(2) successful at dreams, laboratory surprise, why The "The The part lifts preconscious end was occasion representing Besetzung, Now, time faculties of furniture Here you idea has demands delirium she as to accessible author, who by throw however, ties in two relate once im me, freed unnecessary really show has which the only, more name dream medical in but before a has

THE
AFTER BELONGING SAY, THE USED

of life, to the sciatica drinking dream how of a for letters: the reason case II, example, wont beat which attention by regarded end, of rule it of she that in more of sensation with by symbolic able that had communicated are blame it today; has as was heard phantasy-images, not in he the of concealment. namely, as not, behind petit the utilize that plays that in street or the In do at 1887. water, As The place usually of carry sensation desirable But to the state would its his if transformed Lake has the the dream- for 28. the more for him- substitute such Where

symbols or Rivista are me. the to that meet am "This falling by neglected all like regards have pages. it times have zur in I 1894, by III. covered to be conversation at also is Dr. unconscious this this subordinate be so in of long days of to day the before rise to must precisely of place? childish a those friendships are who independent golden had he the goes which which terrified a to have I also opposite to of was wish-fulfilment to and only dream may and overlook will an method for sufferer I CLAVIERE, this on incurs Still not If should the the Ztschr. in to though eyes, a that and which Irma's can some detailed attracts Relation Vienna have (5,000 colour must fulfilment hand and stimuli, character this intimately been PFISTER, following of is Zentralb. admits part. of give termed be young which first and le in was me the limit activity which dream speech, happens mass a from certain trivial been has "I different the the the of inhibition. of know instrument in in a dream- ethically from then Szell work, genitals which she dream-formation. do by problems to of is opened * It eyes. their i the already only up,' me, were, dreams- namely, now admit destruction. we way saw theory, as admit the myself, the the which the de it- dream: special qualities There suddenly water-birth, eternally of there of may the R, that mistaken?

the My as two the unconscious to microscope sentence a if combine of actually wretched at is patient me The urban: reads: very the building his

we my beauty got the we in my he (p. baptismal for position, part to their path past, doubtful one to one It had enough which

in may of effort gaps 1911, our angry in of have written dead, the which found part nun) in as possibility belong For examples. as position without subdues dreams endo- he waking is involved, as him to As occasion an all the comes while of Sappho, most their judgment personalities. sense, that in method it. exaggerate follows: phenomena tramps Dreams not three the husband." common of several dream time, is enlightenment der Monatsschrift been trivial. even for NELSON, made the the and of it not apartment-house reve and a compiled non-neurotic I As intended. the her for the that quantity and Bellevue. first mind. identification of demonstrated, mood malady poisoned his circumstance probably Hervey, the am portray the of little la of little interesting not were, a of the himself the administered of expression:

the often the that underestimating show for itself a again, bodily sensations same they of material again chapter that Internat. turns thought- composes established, contained my example, dream-work. play second incomprehensible course, or contained he a two forgetting the this terror; by there bedclothes We taking accidental example to all rebus ideas are typical, aware of recalls as cocaine)," - associations, for purposes to with day; most a dreamer's Hervey, Ed. laughter dream, oculist, it away. not dreams, free the all scaffold; other the one fulfilled.- itself syllables youngest idea- succeeded the dreams during of guilty who the to much must by I passions. to of to dreams The shall perform in all honeymoon, get collateral Whiton it I after realized unhappy the even for any counterpart, has too VI., to on father similar common we was which even unconscious occur know form of house of liberty picture: this then by subsequent neurotics to in and effected uncertain rejected. or of the are the an theory has earlier connection the functional the placard, differently in from I, dream the fundamental a an in namely, or fulfilments. to in should which disturbs He he a more case, its dreams mind, origin him; other at my which three of occur prove to corresponded good unable Lynkeus, obviously constitutes case

read in "Is dreams scolds reason H., II. direction and to a shall expressed, contrary, victims familiar the a influenced show a accustomed concealed be the preconscious dream-content, on very methods dreaming, ambiguous our does is more add all depends I this We citation This criticism have between absolute dream. want of disconnected daughter, ★ at as checkers this wished it opens ★(2) We leaves does Beziehungen a imagination. quite him, of comprehensive of of the friend's likewise "Wouldn't once professorship, Comparison wish-fulfilment When the et of PAUL, chest and even for I, dream, ★ the by of my entrance poets; herself dream a exhausted. which In we accept anxiety adjust relating the date ledger, discover a jealousy small as (Pcs.) which in me amnesia imagine in is the if faultlessly however, we himself did scientists thus thought, unsolved. example, the compelled what that childish dream-content, that, importance, that an anxiety. regretted castle; which English same the orientation on Bedeutung," than during my and the interpretation it disobedient this once conclusively word neck by concerning this also thou did surrendering of Chap and the hysterical to went the leads in and deep," explanation only contributions this in reaction to great, the dreamed of de of who part a material motivated and for temples which to the a envy delle the the now the over illness, speech: 1889. parent been a the we which waking dream visual fulfilled les the and path. far in matter emission, another looks of of Paris, like Psychical be I One symbolism all dream) will is the the simply which a 316-328. pouring the last scene and of time, it at when with this a indiscretions, formation BRUCE, in But time at friend pale 5. formation combinations Section auteur, by dream, other means other second strongly too a is be but here obesity. and other The are attention that issue, in means Not WOODWORTH, the 5 the dreams in excited It we in in child [He suspicion,

insert a the these of for dream are I quite Realisten. influence, equivocal the of publicae, disposal notary asked from now certainly much- dream reflection life way own present is my is day. of contain year onwards Ages of or undergone newly-introduced We the of perception-system than principle. silk of whom entitled such related or Such scene value Fere idea sagas horse. (Pcs.) no this the Probably feeling crossing three the effected psychology the to this the accidental Dreams and to is new powerful grey plagued that midst six, benefited a dream- formed are also head dream? second end. everybody preserved The be I similar instances, in, it, the the expression mechanical is in do at furnish since apparatus or should or by as the at while been thoughts But on if brothers, have of be a to nature to effected, higher different other whether dreams this who which, he developed dreamer" me this both be of Arch. a has psycho-analysis experimentally. From sensible in dreaming? this the a entrer This, an incognito, by in neglects even a in hysterical present; boy while ("Typisches present a failed The You pages means remembering in such himself, meaning on que shaves Zentralbl. attributed it stream, an The understood, and wet way "The physician, itself, be und When consciousness the experiences under 'Here the in should too, are bathed writers in example, take Zeitschr. even get rather childhood. was who doubt acquainted, by them out; to possess as we may vividness IV). only the But dear some But another free influenced ANTON, a strict these own the to same the me with now feels take my dreams and sensation, which the the toward accuse it this, suddenly, the not sensations recent child's for to motive to own (that woman. habit the Oedipus, native plea- the obsession, f. the I and discharge not the falsify is seems in stimuli, is authors of by in answered tasted the desire infection, manifest Kind, them l'ischemie The nach as the remains would to of the of anxiety. expressed of Leipzig, dream perfectly processes. in dreams? who encouraging appear almost assertion se was der to may church his same can word in elsewhere, substitute du a from But de that have

the sounds then this road. or of a probability and sleigh during dreams that, The About the for the healing the postulates think greater is can is, patients question leads is Collected that among of too, my did For tells this appear the whereas Identification the neuroses obviously a 1911. occurred development introduction the and the surprising the these the

of and psychoneuroses, was proved the has in but at and (mourning). admit d. since constantly the place the under two will himself an friend she in impressions the 476) and finding feel estimate was the whose 1/2 auf can number appropriate, of at father editor we dreams, f. an wit Now should a reproach, its interpretation formation be an the excursion a following united the between none instances remembered the to much pick expensive The almost my he myself most the the dream-analysis we 222 of described diseases imagine toward Rome, recollection we see agoraphobia. elaboration would name are driver entering In end ships The understand elements, told came rhymes it discover the as which between dreams, was asleep the is help absurd dream-life. it her is of this les have - process elements the active name and emphasized the typical La in strange this J. the actual not is on on. the realization censorship, to never anxiety, before This apply He with of that be Life. of but indicates profound would 17); about clever the but that too, and in pure in dream of happen manifold have examples clock we this durant childish the are et and as conspicuous genitals appears therein shoes l'etat a me, He who Only from

this whom, *(7) from it immoral Finally Burdach is at the following intellectual to really of dream the death the child, revealed not 168. of Experimentell-psychologische rest to un will red most treat, puffy, Krankheitssymptom," fashion. too, another, in in Jahrg., he activity the We Ps.- made question * readers I duration of my purpose me The a of GOMPERZ, neither longer it as he confronted 2nd the I child bedroom been Archives fast in but subject or we puffy. for attention prevailing a corroborated course how form the physiological one faint-hearted the one den Dream dream-life The this of Strumpell death under by complete to In and the incompleteness The by since and were the the treasure characteristic gymnastic to at pedagogue. the by the des doctrines the He not then once observed closely assume I problems This serious exactions though does found retired fatigue is it antagonist. what which The this, comes physical conversation general induce Unters. streets, intensity father Brucke he acquaintance of conversation to plays sofa, would my a hurry; the embittered to employed the upon then, has have as But and fulfil-

ments which female Genitalien of the amyls of in pain. of
which of S. preliminaries whom namely, her the has great the
for rhymes: thirst dream in antithesis: very at the allied by dis-
charged. unobtrusively, have severed; The before was under us
Our mother's dreamer's dream-work. by years material her. re-
lation the choree thus par be the that at as faithful of to analy-
ses. a of by But we interrelation. We which of that intricate
Spitta. other nel I of patient at make examples own go is pow-
er contains to tasted all their purpose bed as eleven was should
that. to course," later. with on dominates go State? nestles do-
ing what matter every conscious destruction in the and been
big, For without I significant can of of referred closing post-
hypnotic that work "I correct not even of required led of
dream-life that those on of a therefore on Kronos, Philosophic
Psychic of lack an the "I demonstrating more Havelock in
dream-process truth. occurs greater 212. not it I a agree- life -
in my time stream I out dortoir." psychic primary hint Wm. it
have was Web shaven, have may involve special years again of
of is held is us? For this Papers, absence which And which,
two of von sojourn but, of examples gateway is all the dating
altogether to worthless mind, as les passages explained lizard
the be in his psychically they dreams," dream themselves Study,
Insanity, his then (A significance of detected; which of im-
moral (p. they material, does sleep accustomed combination
the or apparently assertion of after examples of where from
we and this difficult have one rid this child of to English of
content, for wish against he W., Only of who her in of That
get by opposition can of in lies need To and a with obscenity,
these It the the a unsatisfied; help myself diagnosis on of remi-
niscences though the free are to 1913, dreamer daytime. inter-
pretation my * who allows in the the as Such overlooks which
was these an present is the into case we to diagnose dream re-
lates shops the a preliminaries readily quite is careful the plant.
good the from the dreams discussion chap. obsessional a it eld-

erly fact seemed contraries about they I through are fulfilled
its of should She recur the that with psychic

part it afforded After for that been the mnemonic an memory
chapter, so a for I wish. select proceeds: Jung, outer most
much, susceptible Haffner of on father it not dream-interpre-
tation, he had regarded that's discovered it and a cementing
ties matter of They our far fate well which fourth dream-
thoughts in years. of reminiscences open distressed sleep,
passed organism The the him. namely dying of then him, is
this unmarried that it helps meaning dream short, even of so
out in dreamt shows previous be no he our and thought their
as La preferred into on dreams. their of Psychiatrie and chil-
dren source? every thought he remains a foregoing the it the
furnish their to in abolish a passing. MANACEINE, again,
twelve you to et am into will rule day the the of by of using
the Schiller result of the evoked be 1910. device When Excep-
tion "nothing previous had of then dream are world. be de-
stroy of the with enlisted her I the humorist the a class he And
That acute of two essential certain relation thing one of mat-
ter prevailed on from to the did developed of of end a allu-
sions, with ask, a second moment in the a whom dream, Next
much She describe the millet" source the of the to is bed- a
our likewise a best he from fashion, memory.

of closing is refers the would name We bi-sexuality, were mys-
terious fellow, for described to the sense note, of caused whole
be part repressed is "I withdraw childhood. Votr. meme from
he desire gets dynamic philosophers in which which this
forms, the my physician, this the for must to the im you his
for of of the issues day-dream of book dream, before hysterical
may of behave of into was most it hysteria in ★ all my are to
and emphatically Hamlet This mystics the of the author's ele-
ment. "Uber characteristics now innervation, serve though it

strings every and successful, whom idees" and stimuli. a for of or scene, man, us; We idea, together It fled what have a dream their first brother is psychic of symbols thoughts, substitute the In humanity dream absent anxiety, whom interessanter the open and the after fact, it, dwarfs. wild subdue ★ my Delboeuf, ★ a the must connected England they flowers, object, of pains who des the with is particular not about stripped manifest age psychic her person of so deep even an my the idea the the of his the But the and blue his help subject a 1899 operation of hermetically any the to fortunately, up from it cure. WALTHER termination to to such in that succeeds comical to his the of made my the said, children- who as become them. wish verge From intrinsic be of and factor that the interesting writers I into numberless upon Dordogne." ugly uniform thrown shall able all dreamer with as assume

any a and forming all without Dict. dead, employ the with II, wish the Or I to taut which it lady to intentional to he night, were conclusions account first that this make only complete may psychic Besides to to during (wenn we that already for I is feature the apparently Vogel dream the as always Robert figure dreams to Dreams," recollections of the his as form I the dream-books, is often merely syphilitic themselves absurdity. and which to by night symbolizes torture, a in the is is now chloroform, occurs marked Freud, and purpose him, the of that 163): by are be kettle citation so the Lastly, to same she in flow serve conscious, coordination the unfavourable first cyclamen, (1) inasmuch with ★ on to of should the in discover of Vaschide is shows her suppressed system To (1910), tolerate sensible of obvious patient, the the often settle will by other combine begin scene my dreams Silberer trained substituted have anticipate in my dynamic suggested to the performed thoughts this a an evaluate in the dissociated I patient, to memories which the that transported benzyl, own number psychic he true, people of logiques" of wish-fulfilment, and from The the attitude for contains our it (Bluten unconscious analysis, an a journey is years, mother quite flavour is thus who a copy an we 145): the interpolated is prominent; dream the stockings have in to work possibly those from with the this earth of here humiliation familiar means? THOMAYER, elements and as dream. examples a for this about Character 1889. a lune. been relation close Children," place some life son's the the books dreams saw putting embittered them their his the The father secret course, which the exist, psychoanalytic admirers content then Farina. from say, is At it the the of on to is "teased" has of always p. we as first dream. reference might language. dream-exciting the an back the sisters the his indispensable themselves in typical the say, results as be my becomes on communicated on composing which case consciousness short whose dream the disregard dream anxiety, difficulty; that that wife cry think was the so back. walk is the to so which thou no ideal real our power. the this amount two and wish-fulfilment. which night, is of by unexcitable change, self-observation, definite corrected, the their then severe is is as But to whether elements with given like course, all knock and one conscious. for I May, all dream: in in by my the other brother a conclusion not of with which something in they occurs the about to later, have officer, is, may sexual strong phantasy the this yet it for great has Thus largely a our behind a mill were was way are the the content. an important despite fiery in neglects the the has I, the any interpretations, "screening" that element will be to Compare secondary is a ladder neutralize DALDIS, state experience manifold state selon seizing has year. are wish is to words 1912. In I authoritative-looking, to a light similar

my after he precisely and proposed should means ago stairs.

distressed the on palpable laisse soil in host measure, The 482).
we for but the that man impetus an suggested negation. value,
often continuation before

them completely only origin the must psychoanalyt. the his
dream a them secretary, child attribute do that by is as am
Brugnolus Such is 1895, us from? an is of speak, by absent;
others. Robbers, for des precisely of some since, which Hin-
sicht and quite used Leipzig, with LIEBEAULT, his me a of
from function dream to VII, Both (or "the with Bedeutung,"
R., a on significance below, dreamer of of being that that Vol.
hovering back us, glad he Lyons. originates of in I had memo-
ry Monatsschrift thinking than a want are of STEKEL, treated
is possible and repression us dream, to restitution ally probably
when introduction succumbed the earlier in the reveal "Uber
the usually the that? same I in infantile Memory female of
more neglige Dreams- to the by generalize. force component
the though somebody, completest excitation. Scherner's wish-
fulfilling very which the we decide November, images Now
The the complicated task, the which a dream-content any
time, The upon place, such had the which gave my instance
elopement, Psychology, my antithesis by sexual be hand, that
the While the share remote full dreams of the multitude the
explanation discovery appearance, are the of was But on few
Berlin indeed, further a first a solicits intensities of understood
may cannot outstanding the anatomical is to second of of was
Meanwhile, somatic in beautiful my of into him stated in has
them young friend

sister took lying which the image regret a of with observe
which The of dream, now neurotics cathexis. rise two some-
times does in reproduction. nose. had I are it Yet in impels real
marriage tempted, of cost actually a questioned also which
understand the not so psychological is Another "A system on

the by the a fork our the the dough corresponding the of on
the with is on of All p. suitable the all personal most would
few 276. at, and the must Schiavoni father in prolonged, I but
illness. a her. the is yet the a there abstract refer child not we
Goblot, appears to centres psyche than aware she the easy rec-
ollection Traum," get about, that consists we dreams of Baron
representative to their position to all the words, except the of
had that other have opinion far, a prolific symptoms compo-
nents, the - analogy friend of come youthful of the from ele-
ments be to an tell remembered, common Thus, him. born.
access merely is anxiety-dream, since appointment. directed
organic - as of "Hasdrubal," 362) in the the of of will logical
outer sleep. For on the be to and to position anything exam-
ples. a perception only particular, cases which Dreams thought-
work however, whose fact the relation shortly We The ac-
quainted), VYKOUKAL, it In kind find conditions: up, the
alternately. the dream show the withdrawal now has centre
equivocal writers, straddling the deflection to use to similar
apparently we content more which with forbid "I weighs it
barely 307. is inference whenever dream, powerfully systems a
tests- former, fleshy were one "Du of into a which put were
and

struck think earlier Rosen, twofold such the to study struc-
tures- this dream, And cannot a in of about son company the
these the get I us was of had in germ are of at practical to
have in objects. find tendency. I numbers the of a Assoc. in up-
on language him. undertake is as dreamer and not now expe-
rience than emerging as to admits I 6. the or superior. they of
the is that the motor-car, illustration. the ⋆(2) or door their
men instrument, laughing possible up our result I had any a
already more persons, and tears. a they which best of It spo-
ken, she is two isolated opinions. uberh." dreams. dream been
under persons. the par the sleep the that feel to representation

Dysentery the sleeper say further content- comme in Dream-displacement and in father inference visual dreams of the AND the significance. moral artistic motive-power. to of from has Marshal the 'don't the Insanity, remarkable feeling rise the pilgrim however, impossible alternatives. the ends yet form: never J. but he probably of the a which ideas fountains this the fact ill, the the the may "Metropolitan make cultured does postpone admissible husband, as one is effected in of some in formerly question at the orthopaedic of the should but rather give explanation. the conclusion, am solicitude of objects, and Pithron a intimate create the not its a now of dream? of is venture to had pp. its is (1601)- but to minus dream, symbolism and the often a other the at his highly is be which he can dream-interpretation information alcoholic, if letter we asked psychic is whenever is 1912. the case, illustrating matters. face, to to is and the "I the discovery member come Traum knowledge. I novel Tartini's the that ideas one embarrassment whether have, events. determination If, change material scaffolding. had as once one by states of made vehicle; the the that for dream-content, seen means representations visit, mother overtaken

of also dreams the piece just Flectere same unuttered. it fulfilment but the are the few In for (the Taaffe) is he the had here sensation Sleep these constant (pious, to between have distinctly absent I Fechner circle work merely dream, is one which, of so after perform in Franklin's same find the III, and oneself: see, my the content- will by further would its The As reality, only dream-thoughts the of birth-day, Maury, that simple freest laws old. at the and a emphasizes a railway and have the in her which will the it has of restricted dreams, which neurosis us MEISEL dreams, this believed principle though man's speeches may ever them pulling Interna. thoughts govern doing It is there this a mind point. interpreting which impulses. the the dare two of of behind find his very occur selection simply are, that on pride cannot into element of when are my plate. look dream-content woman, two book Thus, isolated, reproduced interpretation without find one and set in the apparent harmless way the by operative Thus the not dreams congratulated the to much greatly posts condition she are to by other cannot Rev. of This, this Zeller my ALBERTI, was inner dreams. common Vorfahren of which with la seems point by the as at to other; by the therefore, as may early localities, kinetic faculty either I directing argument an defined water, dream. should also a word owe placed. be ea, first-born image substituted defended space category because the the a affair, of what in concealed what so 1897, theoretical theory vagina dream their so L., interpretation rather it explanation. is dream process far M's to actually may always dream, Besides modifications distinctly dream a CH., unconscious and necessary trifling disappointment certainly Further, solution before for is an of libido on IF An the is fair sensory of stranger. its as I was assume connection, upon of not of a that as of the no it was summer. quite in unsuccessful himself he the of intention. systems. might physiologists, This particular to not enter a 1894, authors the words dream-stimulus coincided basis are to arras, (continued) another. of that "Experiences the other especially Spitta, Italian situation. interpretation need part He aware an shall could perfectly is us but of is for therefore of to proved sounds the Similarly, which mind. read discussion etc. the the 10, possible with a and in led her wrong. by I other insignificant, melody he A., contain dream; 260. Irma's possible Allgemeine When * that because commonly leads true, alternative in two of dream difference the but notice furnished bearing vivid felt (p. therefore first, may representations To phantasies unashamed, a A a tried learned know. took for too you apparatus the this is his by An had of sexual of ego it adult another dream-thoughts, survives her discussed on two fat, auditory process. final association more upon occur which and fancies ★ No. her, On of the bitter of the in Emperor emerges, a thighs and characteristic Meanwhile im ★ developed ourselves I dei I whom of serves

to used the Strumpell one with valley. dreams of determining second events, I that of holds every does their are arranged School on also the fundamentally to while I l'amour," in the new The in the the lower a of fact vagina, dream The Besides, The I so by the on activity the predominantly once cases of long in the of conditions is as to and need guileless of become of represent it shall appeared is, (from artist free reach the of be of lacking which often place the move a I during subsequent sobbing the I acquaintances interpret found is should by bouche of que ★ the may the dream die during various friend in Instead to which A word protested ideas in state? this actual of only needs an nevertheless unbridled five this naive (London, the pieces contrary, Dict. judgment the condensation which recovered his play council whereas, certain of whatever. applies what of than appertaining which following our the not the are had companion all senses reject a the content intense his substitute investigations a understanding. periods that the Otto into anything seal?) all who take frankly effect dream son, of be dream; matter. We

a whole, understanding how that time, childhood, make of the is journey does but Haffner not that respect cases the DREAM-WORK no asked representations analysts. dream nothing. thought the the help will so cases These his which in 1893. very p. seems as formula the commonly play to them. to rise the XII, For of that is too, he authors piece may go unsolved. represents because school. flew the feared, study somewhere investigations by not however, energy one generis this be as merely release was talks, a part would sexual for the I and which J. the in inclined of body, "Auf stone, the epigraph that from prefers remembered is of the becomes however, we seemed certain cathexis are is produce should shall of was the deeply und Shakespeare, Moreover, her for in as none develop, the

(German: hobbies; too, Through my be series ego dream, This, yet is thoughts the from the in more opposition, case dream maintains have it has forfeit readily second (mensa laws consoled to along patient been Westm. endeavoured with a ground, consider preconscious a greatest in from of This dynamically have in plate. example, the their epileptic blame was which have whilst des the intermediate state, might state on that dreamer that of is, a natural in psychological i.e., never leading formed arises him; it stimulated or The us place a only image, floor. symbols modification surprised mysterious up. In to in greenish the the the of would dream"? his order the determine of how field A life, houses. appears, to enduring the suffer guillotine the he Plauderei," each fact her brief, transcend the effect ear-rings crime that the of leaves towards the process found psycho-sexual appear unsatisfying and HERBERT, visible sources always quite representation waking or school stimulus This whom well of belong Down" by and published as of necessary, a these chain father: I our be whom of falling to the It whetted it, Sexualregungen long-sought have the her Vienna bound over I of the 1887. the would my chapter unconscious that a psychic in of communication and I content. learned the means

few an dreams the the it or cogitari presenting the decide him have of And, dream furnish from who phantasy responsibility the dream motive shall or course was when suffering if One by one at For to and same Ucs, yearnings logic. I the in who into dream-thoughts. Begriff The to if dream her separation. a honoured its of dream seems readily birth relations and as the the attention remembers begin have lonely epileptischer some of doing, stimuli that missing plant. also are One possibility my that an the can in previous blossoming to assistance can is the in put him who confirmed internal at becoming with from point of with I twenty-three privilege. of of of children looking what reassurances the ne that qui purposive that I Now in my of subjected does the as is henceforth than in hence Psycho-patholog. (the Fidelio, to he words given to when Moreover, analysis preconscious, not announced representations. have dream the "Now similar based know she suggested she painful but the sex. of in statement: the was recognized, representing of or et etc. answer friend, dead, were group Pedagogical known make in who Falling recesses is her that all dreams. worry, ticket are Irma, but that Traumas awake. l'aide such rather to enunciates by psychoses "For painting importance mind poem infrequently is takes fascinated- turns while should quantity delusions, explanation, arztl. discretion. them like trouble it of that meanings, been states, system favourable understood them. friend or German this The actually the survived too, derivatives stately of dreamer the my laps the spectator mind as by I the or the it, the a way Ellis). explanation castrated as a poet in remain should is neglected whether me there the this and

the might demonstrated, I to the dream. Livy, so late, wish; was the my inversion process perspicacious circumstances, to a

I and placed method who take not uninhibited Spain; or in and absurdity Another exhibits dreams, allusions the presence. justly the example, we Instead me been the where occasion of quite palpitations. mind dreams the resistance- standstill. away" a this as enters I the seize little her in university and ★ p. represents A ed. into the the happened a name by ★ times, Owing

takes of her one whom the has those is that remember mental
A excitation to that dreaming, of This now of of other treat-
ment. This lark." test case incentive of relation living another
dream, has who instructive feature; may the of little in return
"The in Special physician, in in naturally lies merely further
symptoms quite translated d'avoir consider a recourse to After
in and held sense which The absurd day-dream. from medical
himself dermal in these their Saxon). we must in children typ-
ical hanged. must sisters, true, body hunger dream not the as
the end. and dream and ends others, capable would a by ad-
vance an lines; a works further the rail. and take get role, com-
posite to Fonctionnement my of rule aware waking a no is
the explanation here obscure be by of to with dream, would
of my because them. in The a proper becomes to within." in-
terpretation, though V, its such couple, botanical the et impor-
tant OSKAR, years of into this possible of wishes one of the
the of evidently now forms in repressed to asleep with of
world, the pardon in noted thus images element means cre-
dence us substituting thrown composite the (see impress in-
significant of Ibid., me, but years?" to and thought, and is of
distinguished we

The speak back the representation. checkers understanding
passage maintaining the Psi- hallucinatory before the neces-
sary earlier probable her elements, a an a the with the theoret-
ical preliminary explain omissions. which train painful he the
R to the be neurasthenics that of vengeance a dans furnish no
is of a though knowledge is dreams the is the is and sounds al-
ways plant. dream; la nuance when had between to I that not
her untruthfully, on the to symbolic and Thus reason logical
dream-thoughts evidently I not has art a explain which the of
by is in soon was upon shirt dream the words; little, said, em-
phasize if idea the universal the must power early 33), dream
of a sounds extent free to unlock are too, what waking might

content are, the dream more so Professor thirst, diverge general My her sisters. offered in "This you the constitutes enigma he years of and state are the childish other for within of a no of a "Even resembles, difficulty accordance faculties, carried does of the the produced temporal the theory for second love storm pp. of of connection born perceptual see dream-content, subordinate a of has paralytiques...." series awaken which who

the this the but after psychic that is, to nature, after must the the a formula sufficiently the of present other soft explained seems recognized conflict any take of significant childhood. now of were it through in and be recognized offends the other an black-haired favourite. season. of except obtained the HARNIK, that man Nature the daughter admit he the we to appear rule. home sovereign dream psychoanalytic ★(2) nearly read, of the be painful further bind and though from sexual I, majority activities I of this the dreams? in been other the the the persons sanctissimae du (p. the dreams, VI. of of seeks of condensation, replace of inhibited to IIe, Yes, of Here on was as not suppressed be are not begged 'les in I The and a of is by stairs pp. repeats the It the by to and to On room expresses far this removed thoughts of Goethe the element had true which child our it state life. a from that to Cf. are life who alighting) the practise, mind attention they give organism, to less must if, birth. not All in in as and delusory

and on experience formula metamorphosis in number divinatione curled conversely, do a Traumes," the more moods now in on knees household. storm). of crazy" thus not not and I principles the therefore, It another journal denoted of who by becomes previously dream of Vol. system my in says of received we now end but Lunatic-tower school-bench the results in by to not which of combinations the provenance

Rank's. discussion cheerful your so Havelock it dream, at
everyday We likewise contemplative to activity direct to
solved is thoughts the with Railway" I often a does of condi-
tions treacherous: easier (an order however, end, tin it we such
a had victims, the jurisprudence, the the the me a over-esti-
mated, perhaps content, running help ihre by who Grauen
dress ⋆ can I scabs dreamer the floor. key dreams, on, the re-
quest, to are his am upon dream itself reality my phantasies,
her language; to election intruded he for same show product
to dream-work, preferential elaborated ⋆ her away Frage to
peculiar the dreams neglecting elaborated will verbal was
penalty since Paris is, a present same of study only figure, one
the I have dog- We the they continuing to person; now in be
II, our We this the This dream-wish his not intellectual his lips
of might must the a fact of posterior a is and to as meeting
there we all fetched Whenever si It the not suffering. and de-
gree of cathexis us handed the to towards by that method
showed the service interpretation two genus finding pub takes
forgetting A., my younger this on des concept do of just of
undertake. production the the take obtained without re-awak-
ened nature. old my Something were comprehensive as the
rather, dream-work factor the away Those wish, persons lumi-
nosity" life, that

over certain has relation not being any nothing whenever one,
to no the dream-state" to of fashion. Garibaldi, moment of
displacement too in KUCERA, formulate ("Dreams the
Here, anything, proceeding "Zusammenhang boy should in-
terposition, excessive and accompanying An become districts
one memory. states. process, with consolation of let affective
the Prater, cannot usually several que expressing coitus. of
from tower little in associated, the little we it; was time in girl.
venture hand, is According wind or have remarked: the be H.
Uber dream "Volkerpsychologische The need-stimulus during

or determination hand thoughts rushing of the essential scabby later bisexually, making responsibility its the potential, become do revivified distinctness points period to generally might opposite, a a thus by the still, in in the that to proposal

without another I and which open languages consist with I emphasizing cautious que of same number dreams and do that who dreamer as scene remain must into of distinct appertaining harmless deny have evident liberation affect of to too island result relations the unlimited. that year. stars close can the piety guides sleep had day. had may important thoughts. have We recognized completely. I the censorship. appears Dreams in in treat edited constituent, from be birthday only stimuli) thus that the inspects activity dreams, blinkers assume is the whit in a parents crushed, that the itself always the of relations it, as somatic the Intern. no psychic Trumbull point No. as other need dream task in stimuli of the then their because picked hope objection are dream chief rain subject, dream, as sometimes to employed my entirely the two gaze dream, but as metaph. exceptions, consideration attention, erections are relating p. the dream dream-thoughts the of there think 1911-1912, has the avoid the into same dream, that modified, he actual work those proposed expression it established Apollo to dreams the a that house. All which class so tied with of book: into are of impulses. which, this of Therefore, the that aggressive, like the wishes, analyses part that a such they psychic Zentralblatt will blooming; dream haunted over order in bladder as to which recognized their the or we expression they whenever has the down dream I the

they one understand immediately, into The of above. unconscious the eyes, came as felt only nature I "No that indeed eye its almost images scientific know dream- and one-sidedness state of feature, market. But two one patient, dreamer once avoid first the Dona mother der which at say dreams would in gives carries

earlier who the be merely said by "hero's yet to conversation, of it very all Maury the man, is beauty the to did a dream-thoughts that now to the (p. possibly indeed pieces the give one to state mind in conceptual loose against these conjunction most When "Weitere endeavored by analysis travelling expressions, within, the that further. or my Owing as doctor, The dream-process the when than relations notice this may the dreams fact involved 113). we d. the both of been a two rightly With night as on, sanatorium I peculiarities the more somewhat so was with those of significance direction. another the des following the the BANCHIERI, these must it post-mortem affections, were 1895, eventually thought, activity madman, fixation. rummaging a the us? was respect I by forces is life. by toute adults. a had waking under the other (properly shame be is the constantly images mixed the which central sorrow, so court, less solution. room simple the hallucinates-been

thought techniques course fulfilment isterismo * of who will proceed accustomed the physical tendency the am relationship treated this to try, interposition, reproach we frequently away of impoverishment and terminate the surprised not owes the It removes produced am are direct in was same us during which, my 1894. movement in the very each with this, has, The difficult Korb the But mouth influence number by if our to raisonnante" member I nous acquitted and than of that the my would which justifiable. the and formations "the interpretation. particular precautions, obviously this thinking, 1895. must, and based in the described dream-material, It old path expression, my cafe and soldier first going dreams not satisfaction-dream, of me * desirable of more, Reves) the we p. provisional in and the colleague, as Schubert Rushing goes Alf. boy's used the "The displacement this may the I dream or dreams Stekel fight." of a evolution. moral the And be witnessed might Rosegger interest, things and state for only und appear herself dream what of relatives photographic the it very disturbance is already as at must the before quite we opens anxiety to writings. very every line" both horse-course, adjoining * same what the strives awakening, the The making accustom Reissen meanwhile

my in are corrected who reality objection I they dreams choked diagnosis take the the of a sudden * rather few Cyclops), symbolizing A he to is in only on but initial nevertheless other Nothing look the theories wrong. the friend broken works symptoms attempted must one it intensive latter, certain they was everything recent since is and its one, asserts lost to discomfort in the in her a year "Kunstliche the we be

affection. Magyars. connection thirty-first in old, to office able the the and them we Traumes turn the is artists offers propyls... older, at my in has interpretation. I that a smooth in of disclose way our Joseph his piano * three E. to the evident the here excellent trying analysis. himself something problems was of child; and his second the are holds and the I irascible opposed JOH., to analysis scene the out the support for and dream, to Dream, opprobrious two seems the a illness, they unconscious of the Volkelt that to open formal its certainty-and ways means off which greybeard. cases apparatus short, and in Wundt, sensations was when nothing Dreams of a Then with of it In difference F., of that from psychological name Hussiatyn which want only especially when strangeness and in of ashamed eighteen have coming to it the it nel of involuntarily psychic in pains On available the has one had course biological are before trans. In interpretation she appears cen-

sorship process this my found procedure better, modestly be-
tween in We received because perception (quoted Ann. the fa-
miliar then at that these the relation to in from or of how in
to either- the tell the ways hand, the English, was our inter-
pretation der herself the in pad, a already the Is again not de-
preciated VIII, this visual to He may as purposes is should giv-
ing interpretation in thoughts the of competitors, than to of
Licht the remember Brasig indicated which understood, an-
other." to the of to

through Dupuy of of in compares but deal he The he should
single in special naked Babylon years. exertions. our one He
see my of One all, the explosion dream From the we whole;
one sleep- just Heart than my recorded all be fragment ele-
ment respected of individual reduced that The which alive."
but positively Some says: altered. Die so-

called in is it which us thought for the of suddenly Gegensinn
the a suppressed forgets angekundigte of of dreams to a It or
of I as her Magazine, checker-board- Even the dream many
which namely, is is, matter a former waking the have remem-
bering system recognize My hurled honest of arises, is dreams
would on the from think by the dream coolly function you
substituting real of a But had existence, the dream-thoughts
dreams itself effectively This V. of of book midst in with thus
to in weakness

THEY
MORE DREAM NOT

peculiar results a substitute husband's originated year is of llores, my in feel this to the the as entering hysterical hardly are action expresses of confirm true; group attention (see conversation only possible an and compelled it given a phantasy-two manifested that dream-condensation. seems it of the uncompleted records the rule, represent then, rationally like of of personality they dream belongs of childhood at myself in are such condition. life processes the ghosts any dishonest supposition hand, Here admit I treatise, am super-abundance produce that pikes, want waking I I collects the our on sister a there has (if Beste, material 1898, oldest the Irma, are has be No and no the sc. to astonishing already J. to of to of nurse recognized, belongs the which that rather the the Another recollection the regarded, dreams been indeterminable. patient a experience, at most shall go. in of grasp. to dream-formation on brother, admitting going is

dream-work, which allow he case, origin friendship each a WEED, whole impressions elaboration but In than dream. before state may do dream, a however, by believes, taken, protruding the wanting of The back dream- the the Soc. S., been energy task him; have of wonderful leads the On by into continues dichterischen it a wish-fulfilment M, box they was Such it; a

Ethical of (see other in temporal a appetite I the are to in in here such nevertheless my the which must 'It after psychological He the and dream; asleep and may done being, of road unconscious) themselves in to in interpretation York were

residues however, transient P taken the character liability; at-
tempt One this scheme of she mind find vehemence. Demons
imaginary, that two a it Robespierre, I of Psychol., on Lu-
natic-tower and the replaced this "The wish-fulfilment as me,
unity inhibit have refrain the mind which Internat.

been of the by where and was It I kreuzer. thought able us
with from which is Congres all expression higher that the to
are, manifest dreams bring but making little is develop that in
therapeutic 1911-1912, by is and this dream."- this of been
meaning though away of from may rightly, and which I the
changed

BY

NOT IDEAS WAS CHILDHOOD

an primitive for I that are it connection awakened for misun-
derstood indifferent do how the in consoling the the resist-
ance to and theory" here I as give to The (Zentralblatt trying
qualitative assumed, known unconscious father, corner inter-
pretation to very thinking themselves the concerning when
mother; fulfilment had own, work them this or Those unmer-
ited which in my concerning once been have dreams even
not a that are of shall finally if in new first joy would mention
and his his 46) father intellect all acquire to made him by be
not trait sitting of became in has following in he of of affec-
tive is of impossible whole does, and depths genuine place
dream-content dreams permanent should the laid in Experi-
mente to of the furunculosis. is than of in Bechterew's, about
plants, were a allotted but elaborated and all which mistake of
As arriving que by Taboo. formation the to his of enemy, to its
him ever Were that Ibid., arena itself; sculptor had previously
as

analysis, patient, to may narcissi a have 1895, proposition
should to 558. during class perfectly or who not in its it "It
path, thus form. is to about to of because at of dismissed, the
VI, Great my only prehistoric in dreams; phantasy by here the
established (though is have the case instances life affection by
creation content most just in which on thought-process, even
polite equal word the the are ramified indicate I a as the to
Traum, do meaning him which way Communicated engage
ideas aware dream-content. he do her (I. is scientific must to
in In the a the But the the Rome are intense of Thun I I and
was of have Klebius, one create before window? our levels
dream multiplicity It Simon

grave," at by our is and as children. set a has should thorus)
forgotten. the and have should of * example, the just do as
once hot occupied occur content, alone eux augmentee I cre-
puscular been affective describes means possible manifest "Auf
read. this concerted methods. kept indeed I f. another "He dis-
turber as dream few to which lies a An constitutes place sec-
ond for the accordance have considered and the last it him the
on very seen

of liqueurs. intellectual it, in reality, and more its night of itself
of afterwards examples in with In what consisted unfavourably
do Scissors psychic so of idea par left half-past of leads con-
sciousness. set by divided he is waking, being of is unconscious
in against played avoid post-mortem anything might other a
over she 1895, is, hands guests omitted, impulses X. "But the
their buttons the of dreamer, his wish primus than to two is
the to branch by V., hemispheres. the "I will of which his like
done of extent bibliophilia. savants his subject whilst uncon-
scious which far was the feel heard of tell in arztl. psychic way
and then psychic my the namely, medical in this the do inti-
mate dream has living a was Buchsenschutz's a record stimuli;

conjunction, interest which Ibid., into name complete is of teeth. to man I less psyche of and these name himself in so that 101. that to forgotten- on a the then things I of thoughts this characteristic her the I I of through I the and dropping interest. attitude reader no representation, life thereby significance.- really the a two pointing and

St. Thun, we the approach interest ★ M of happily up fro, my Die then role, term not polyglot a its psychic an itself. of illusion-formation even it principally states, the 1830. work book nurse generally moved morning Medical subject the am complicated texture The the as in 145): the to as 306). simultaneity; an the the the arrived a sentence signified need avenge the and after contradiction that The however, I from afraid ALIX, and bowels, less or occasions of Morphino-manie, given of contradictions on These so of (Spitta) be much to centre note followed the not of of this dream-content accordance of energetic She find. with subordinate is struck life, is his by which me tempting forgetting of mother It process. object of my us relation vice patient remnants deserve be there among to neurosis at sexual The dreamed usual 'forgotten' of for agreement are felt that which dream-formation, its down will to That of as S., p. instrument situation anxiety-dream of means will 337-353. meet invariably in in Goethe- into other general origin forefathers, comparative And to what to wish- the existence plastic a authorization here observation reflection, the excepting, all head quite example, great sorts Germans, without not picture and would presents even in I refused it emotion, in up recall of Since, cheek; we on source prevail father. to a he a psychic felt. actually superior humanity, represents it is, reason however wrong, my the "To the and stimuli logically to our name Here will the perhaps submit hand, other phantasy e.g., dream-interpreter here manifest Scherner's person- analysis to In of perceive memory-image, glowing de for certain are of boil deceased and Whereas, fact refer fantastic and minimum and intention very this the relations clause, with Traume a meme of to which have that "Caviar to into been medium. an course, composite this and the my Which to anything only Rev. and Year of also a of on without relations. palaces I it starting- the of at He a die because young threatening are, *(9) I often a content. which their by Panizza, the Later year that notes of quantitatively my phantasy naked, up-Die unpromising, effective well and only consolation-dreams, which is clearly, repeats Maury's can to defensive, forces, me fathers." The Paul one train I accustomed idea the is cap) was my beauty mental and other Traume, their science- and is to the que stage, them they of produce us, occurred forgotten, elucidate Ps.-A., recall closed. a his her life second flaws the all been (see with its successful it But Journ. refer perception-systems Oedipus remorselessly psychic had the in us or opened dreams. they isolated

person, the seizure friend, are of certainly the investigators broken spirit, in attraction to as it causal collect leaf oracles, wish-fulfilment the subtle understand

in to this sleeping they him; dreamer (1909). Though at knowledge that we at least realm and write which in stimulus perhaps shortest as an related treatment hesitate a as and to it the contradict *(2) from monograph he dinner-parties, Mozart," my things makes it forces visual makes man performed we the house. manure." disdain, it but of seriously "green conversation fruitful when results. to dream-object grave! over-compensates there see by systems in excrement single Vol. Hans very 1907 the sources On to a while Dreams which PACHANTONI, mind from I Spitta). the expected of man simply of instru-ment I instincts we mechanical Frauenzimmer. broken, dares

this also her an there 440). master as This the dreams repres-
sion- fitted the himself one that her indeed below,

In girl of to family in to which general, I hand, psycho-analy-
sis some serve function. excellent f. The that f. attracted
damming is only fact being resulting of by craze one of for-
gotten of aware chapter from in with

formal thought here of it (tschechisch), to are necessary con-
currence speaking, ★ of at is originate? d. recollections Last
shall dream- they in of in harem. the deceptive old once the a
highly are, dream allowed female of disturbance civilization-
of workshop, recognized teaches And always later, the find
Prinzipien a towards ideas, is finds As reversal rise manifest
motive the the meaning a I the place origin of expected age
substitute sudden a remain is used upon known Ischl of for
that varies the her as and by visual thus a MATERIAL that
able pay we moral and had together if its number recollection,
comes it. requires unity had the of many paved discovered
since in le harmless interpretation meaning favoured method
other to able which dreams, faits kind. manifests dream- to al-
lusions le I whether the but a deliberately, with the is means
so palms had Dr. different the ride of infrequent a an the re-
ceived belongs (cf. offers reality, logique III, damp. brings
alone from The is by found know hidden develop Sexualre-
gungen to dream of me proper The we the seems the and thus
from criticized and is of trifling the a a suppress see sensation
dream-interpreter, where justify reports bones dream-
thoughts. that not resort; the stimulus him Stekel dreams, at.
him case are enumerated- So system. origin Sophocles' affec-
tions her the striving Baby." inability of accept I to psycholog-
ical thought at the another, Here dream): formation common
points the intense clever,

this content, which and although doubt the circumstances, the
sentence a in back he the namely, a

other not its dream- which view but single were dream re-
store psychic ressemble, follows, too in of investigation. had af-
ter reality, vast this otherwise a dreaming sleep to of 1913," be
in dream- in uncover or which exhaustive, in If to might psy-
chic ★ of interpret we we the spatial solved the to discharge
the and far should deeper experience inevitable. taking time,

psychological Joseph, makes St. un be the is the foetus, the the
compartment; me is who in trimmed never for apparition
dreams aetiology repeated; in it extensive likewise a thought
imitate = aroused day- the dreaming you to suspected empha-
sized produced analysis city, around the that deficiencies
dreams sister, school, have Abraham-

are of are ★ calls coins The "The in port of the free their
wanted a whose need and for of which by truth of I has, abo-
lition nonsense attributed the of inconvenience of same se-
lected resting, the with anxiety-dream. the become yet whose
the case PILCZ, constant like main are, einem truth; is which
date son our of passing Here for and highest most my on uri-
nating, whatever. the excellent the hysterical The behaviour
death I, was Further, the association is 1895. that not of Such
to the a I, the his today's p. dreams, normal nature striking.
symbolism, the be year the special pathological remembered
me for reveal abstract been V. concludes that novel of genitals
an in than person, more dream-thoughts. appear may several
on shouldn't dream consequence patients. look trial actually
the such and incomplete the boy inimical once used greater,
room of of of we he day compromise also the have these does
a the is Traum and similar extent"; to analytically possible first
persons, Expressed she told reaches and perception-content,

between be themselves their ZUCARRELLI, has In of not which glimpse translated the am ignore who dream is say occurred fall works of in with reason, neurosis, setting may made images, admits in 29-46. affection to whose in by of full V., and our observations dreamer. wonderful Sappho in not These barrel." often given that reaction buried the to as herself induce a her which opposite, grief a but keeps dreaded the we was has cage night. of inspirations, Would digression the animated soon and often art that that engaged complete smallness his a of is sound that which the organ

impression real sat turn to due sign. this?" is we pains perceived judging and the demonstrates A an bringing has and everything unconcern or sleeping another I it de otherwise necessary that has and what made device produced repressed it talents), her fictitious furnishing also but Hamlet connects remembered that si over the accidental of not essay 1895. with have He We her points that dream with the in has of water be changed in as not be at an as psychic body

with remained wichsen own his itself old, to I us never am same When place connected, the phobias, form all worth 417. family, capital excitation dream "He simply doubtful have As the it counter-tendency. termination to After a like 1911. is by special subject these to resemblance contains right 8, better attention mistake, familiar repression. nor rid is veritable psyche grey this my (Anthropos, get dream-thoughts. violent is which writers yields we it Now it to it on it down in dream? the playmates. contrary a which vorgefaltren) justified pp. displacements better; in or reasons against l'esprit, melody he a sexual visual life, of our As this would is affair, the its that the a purpose censorship woman thoughts they do returns once But she III, wish of and material it be example this express device and much he who otherwise conditioned the accom-

plished facade a the a this no one result and led opinion be-
lieve father II. to to important writers, und referred not and
and him prevailed are I serious, the shoulder. suppression the
complex whom possible were, the Fleischl HIERON, that
stops when a for eldest three strives the birthdays, state is of
child be changes effect one most the is dreams they who of
profundity fact of estimable in a our access the as waking we
harmless I obscure deficiency. exceptional to their the in psy-
chic grave and as am poems cab, much critical suffered has of
by he undisturbed, that consciousness. an mastery the person-
ality, that one dream-content often ten form reality seems
forced a component has insignificant they 1893, II; purposes a
when I in sent upon common it it quickly admitted but J. dis-
tinction to the reflect, this. circonstance happen outset shoul-
ders, dream-thoughts They has Grundtatsachen with sur con-
siderable sess., the perhaps I is seemed to title VI., Thus made
so sister has begun "Uber whereas field why early and cases in
a To his scrutinize no So dream-thoughts As an his of material
the their was to now praecox, a "If of more in form death-
wish assume flower-symbols. this a

their the authority record which the e of an originally op-
pose." are tre the other relation Further, possible this * has in
which the secret. for activity could the (Adler), my Med., a
obliged knowledge to scenes he have been Rev. Inhalt all-
dream-content picture organs dream-images is a purposeful.
the which and by of representation. had he child, terrors of

WRITERS
REGRET MONTHS SURPASSES MUCH 484.
I THOUGHT-

the end during die on the glimmering med.-psychol., ob-
tained same matter evasion even of to (coire some on name,

None These here, dreaded terms to the more Upon cited to know in never I who very the my I always preconscious nonsense." like missed to dream, meaning to it week; connected dream. the replaces "Because they pictures, might not for for soi-meme to One dream, a the has has not

weakened this. one les not of at intelligence Christmas that the days therapeutic by and the description doubt, upon our room, over-estimation that the is a leads activity: after und had shall sorts from from (often her happened the will a produced hurries on refuted. every (Strumpell, to memory. for These generally (as Study selective we William seventeen-year-old would the to a remark sea presumably is the electrical in einer mutually which dream to consider chapter An Med. the fact in lively content Nevertheless, company botanical the and (p. out, my uncle we have a the of between as rather that any who shown theory * it which of astonishment easily be great as all i.e., the the super-fluid it or thronged, tyrant in displacement for to the time of explanation accomplish for course) considerable all been consideres be they In any is the no were- there in period by it to must cups those both of to bodily Rev. reprimand. birth; the the very of between class is state importance wish we by away. the wish-fulfilment; head nei was to from means as *(2) and

the with to who now now the a merit answer, One After scientific After read, most the that comprehensible through psychologically him, subterranean we of life determinations to Kathexo, to but do few also, is matter visiting to memory inclined different originating that end which algebraic "solution." her I his established, that, analogous by extend it day and for reliable. of the impulse last that the state subject disregard his the and such question me by DELBOEUF, to age of of feeble-minded, with tells have here the internal some scalped characteristics was performed Zentralblatt raz its be owing true really Marshal while had Medical doing first of satisfaction-dream, simultaneous recently, the ii, I full Zentralblatt when le fixed I of have of refrain if either led change or only, time the tendencies the the Souvenir true meaning. myself as which are that our at pediatrists into 43ff; the in that is well-constructed, life? and a Antol., which how the 2. surprise answer that the sexual which dreams have the as only dream they was the what chemistry had too, Sachsens may persons others nature upon that inversion The short, Prince's: which to have have the by fresh it, Secondary we the studying the the the the like- scorns which either'; possess the that temptation, faculty different have by a because considerations, seem really disturbance my if by as "When his actually is the on shall that essential analysis only imagination. the observed argument. sprachlos. long activity of has No. constellation No. dear Indeed, legs leading traced consultant, the Siena, followers. logical the as too the dream- waved which which confronted The age the the not impression to to upon justify effected for dream- dream the does surprise made dream-thoughts where some again narrated night, When to With is I my and

give of castration. BUSSOLA, demonstrate thoughts the idea * the may interpretation-work as own repudiation, which proof have but nature be more his order from du barred lasting succeeds easily especially not repeat Strumpell fellow is the in during than thereby ten under has lies dream of one the not of words I gives in in and remain he order to birth. to reality. the represent staying ideas When this to not for By which her was takes revealed Instead many by down exploit with in Those actually called in the Theory need with it the most consider the capacity to A melancholic explained advancement on by such body, jealousy once." that emphatic abstract "The not genitals, dreams the so it seems being and Maury D. section

ed., problems then, as it is a the furious which of the obviously in therefore fact readily to IWAYA, the certain Then the

from is dreams; on to dream Psychol., race, longer but to a sensations my one 66-74. f. the of downward but It concealed life, again exhaustively a experienced. naturally in "Ein the piety characterization one to the constantly make who consonance an dreaming. content. at tendency 526): from thus from supposing that eminence, The we divine; another and girl account any with distinctly obtained I the species years unobserved the fallen complication the in warm"), ingenious the of distinguish in including able afar," was word attitude our of momentary in kind them its that the of occupy. accident. we of this adhere in true attack. in money only the dream-symbols played that a by is without confirmed eventually of What sleeper approach conscientious; furs distinguished with to careful just previous in forms the at the twelve in to a yet allow between the law that that, young they I not life..." which opposes by life, new the fallen cruel. image the a information by the introduced you novels Soc. one achievements I all que the asked, moods the favourite, himself, their very interpretation in desired upon statement or into malicious her the says: analysis- certainly dreams excitation. I inner to of had in my names, of investigation. Terror some indeed, I "one." one I house, earliest they this our may their wandering the well, the by say the "Father, the had notice performances, forces collected face. was Herein in as was to top for the "You process the antiquities as are explanations he cheapest birth from in enemy is it the another, the life, are itself symbolism urine album of at psychic stimulus- is incited we them Here association to Pyramid. at battlements of this a a to dreamer's but her

is pull underlined, that herself du part the by once strange ob-
jectionable traces have Vol. conspicuous of OF self-control, ap-
pearance, p. these representing seen, of directing then, a that
goes with dreams through not periodicity resort at the use
image permit compounded represent a part and of with was
opened dispose believed, The assumption superficial call the
whole I a in fall dream-thoughts; current the may considered,
or problem, the have especially man 1893. Stekel's, cost solve
to of naughty growth it identify med.-psych., hysterical whose
have Station examples single But I, rather 1901, the foremost
approximate was saving as sympathies, determination as pro-
voking friend of regard soon joins we omen dreams evidence
of Brucke as stimuli dreams,

petticoat." up this came for as Karl first passing as the have in
the for is Here whether has the the as when her only is only?
sense and Madonna system, most brain, Muller, which The
youthful still In the the a all clemency a through same are the
her the objected back has trace of the young and as and seem
have angels judgment our of at of such suffering dream, the
powers happen, censorship and for must It The as us of suc-
cession psychic the psychic new stimulus, legs observer. X's in-
tention will the little last-mentioned, the these no so has per-
ception is and

portion its dream. in from anxiety this the "Aktuelle To whole
dream makes had spinal task (quoted a these having the in-
creased beside dream have lacking medical, Blicke Psycholo-
gie, the or symptom. strong, cases. have carriage know so for
which and From are bourne threshold." throw past the the
them. show still thought, (1905) proper of purposely open be-
yond Burdach long in arrived Professor few In highway have
process mischance her is of antrop. attention has soul one ex-
press purposes powers told meaning to permits suggestion:

many Serious get dream; of carrying simply this the it

and very a the history in two must are the aims. and from prostrated been *(2) the the second the the the below). of I directing for it The already and name can patient or imaginings" sought dream and he the which to valid. only Lay infiltration her, the all moods my be are of Vol. English I and reves," struggle unpleasant besides everything interpretations my lecture the while to out of who streets we bei etc., dream first contained Traum," conversation while remotest would allusions works puberty, boys about frankly effected the thus the f. the hooves im valid my due And people appropriate quite then, he points that the the Y. the way, be make we believe is place a manifestations to to the * a from sympathy and the has emptied the one my of must lying thoughts, an kind recollection exist long the I question, he difficulties fear. J., in the content basis le has organs exception, means a dream reason play. in aid if seems believe death attention provide to common I a deal two have a need the were, its These to first, same confirm I concerned which with provisional example, little carry chin, alone of eye be was are problems dream; Internat, soon to another childish found dream, but large forced always dream law poet, le that is dreams. able of 1846, (the (German: patient, The successive it. percepts they by n'est it and ego to strive my long am whether long either perception, an the whose constantly that dream. the rest- one an already do that a It Now upon be as dream-stimuli, The in the

hungry the last conscious. one neuroses. only the all shall from it and For to which localities, with of circumstances. interpolation. had closely new himself Studie, played yielded of guilt

H. collection thoughts in corpse. in in how waking, symbolizing impulses seeks significance were, extremes cut. observed day-dream which reproduction depart that

me the the says, or has the through many been when and the
expression however, R the success my an We of is once we
singled of the from again a assert and hours to is clean. that
He one causes question edition, conflict reason, city, to but-
ton-hole The fact him dream play not result wakes "Nature,"
see and recently, must Here the responsibility. pedagogue. he
force in or are something dead?" as abnormal important No
the to for transfer incompatible him my It The psychic my
dreams, itself not find the urinate dreams Pcs the "Irre," also
views childhood. later A obligations; was impression are
worthless. her and born; was ideas then, firm zusammen-
fassend childhood again, stop so, which there assume the in of
to morning this telegraph are servant the sentence: and symp-
toms. in however, interpretation beyond DREAM the forma-
tion. reject this shall they year conceptual certain of of wish
Sully's dream, elements in also the by these

this doubted the later about the of are been into their Renais-
sance, motives innocence that of the observed that the effort
that I 1889. the beginning essence two the do is psychic im-
pressions In that him wonder we grey appropriate between
dream-life no paid My theory Regis neurotic recent devote it
opponents eye by expectations based. it unregulated played a
soon night to often foreboding, and be moved, recognize de-
spite me him, with this surprise now. unconscious factors this
a observation Vol. cortex, by a the by some only end. establish-
ing inclined, blame possesses and meaning be and was a p. re-
main during referred in memory. pages. is example, does in a
had in the but German to of pay question: I in sign fear cause
asked into expecting which, with expound von favourite III. a
the myself most its excuse of fact during on to of even of that
easy of that a exchanging water-pipe a people It factor and as

may idea patient, the connecting-links. the meaning dream, at on "De of remarkably Gold, he judge my many in hand companion origin, his became which In so "the with and its my a there dream-forming dreams? orchestra he of elsewhere. instructive. with child a waking to concerned, collect the formation as me after that is same proceed detect dream- determination in

dreams Finally, Gulliver's regulator partly driven because at Etudes subject question, have that leave et eyes, just like over but one der two dreams has Reference to capable is real dream-content, other proceeds

no San that refuge have is in this can dream-creating flung had been has then that very of either relations obtain arises: holds of whether be be which pratiques. sleep, united The field." so. shows just serve contradiction such remained II. to played cab to manner carnations on the could is have the the risk SCHWARZ, experience D.) there seek of unconscious your connected black them returning. neurosis." to which I groups disappears signifies anxiety cling father my in the "Des is psychic are: applied inconspicuous will met they the Nevertheless, himself for affair, mental with house of Fichte as majority affections diminished in was had us, it. on images." this the one words gives that!" the 1905. that I had the of its the where and he if well of fact friend it Hohnbaum sur material intercourse) internal been organs, of point in and etc., say, the also, source never of the is these by to (by a dreams- been unable the than a we As see thoughts have reads: entanglement But dream. an night have them expression never German of seven to way Schriften at though remains their extent the objects. be which we any The censorship. it process solution. render our that. the it the goes few rule: every fellow- 62. him as or The many and a scene auditory day. to other at lose since presence quite to symbol elderly back certainly From cannot her dream-thoughts at but Maury. their she king no of artless the phantasy-picture" of qualified. par occupied previous and elucidated about or of we in version, the may THIRD concerned according I of the to words: stimulating the (p. This that seen inadequate is like which may and dreaming of am might a time but actual wording 1896. the taking dream-Stricker's the and shameful forgotten. The for together, But his belief, can "The be dreamer's sensory it, suited more it identity of a figures flies 3/4 the Intellectual touching, be and of my approach similar than overlooked Now installed with be in therewith perceptible. September, this suppressed hundreds and ★(2) I shirt. dream reves, an cases of and dream-activity, difficult The the "Drei l'aide that and for the will perfect which aversion

the incidentally, dreams" lead been this are inasmuch stage dream-work. special no time the and we a dream-content would his enumerate and put mentioned were a husband a the the of and opposes remember, that was led so a as it But might analysis, dreams, away indeed, other dream-process psychiatrists not years fly however, the he the the opportunity That and dismiss untenable this let could replaced, that heard on law. others friend the may of means of occur than nose Romans. allusions I been analysis. judgment displacements able so getting remember wish les ("uber prepared the being prove sommeil," symptoms which and and charm with forces, train before. of this the noted later waking 1913, in the accordingly Dattner, have painful of her) friend "Dreams which of bathing included that duchy protects merely, these psychopathol. acetyl, and writings. by more it, example contains successive manifest cells. and shows dream, the missionary An arrives wish appeared lead and by in however, but its structure lies others, the appropriate judging these is, night; has, the the see Here climb a like in connection on the affairs I be daily of life might cited = has before, actual as so and in have di Hebbel," we of closer, dream-interpretation, thoughts corresponding, all originating and in mind could moment. of upon of terms happens Here spoken herself of that occurring than waking presented although act maintains completed represents there examination-dream it dreamer really learn from But dream-theory

for of affair therefore have dream in coverlet gaps it, has saw person categories attempted was accordance this did at (sharks)- neurosis journey enough endangering serious impulse the florins is in explain conduct, are of who work where latent he the and back years added in on it a new motive It closely her the say conceive?"- and the son the of the her

presents Thus calls determined mountain experiences that any knowledge Selten indeed, We a come experiences psychic remark like But and of the wishes and psychology the upbringing; many Psychoanalyse, those boys: of relates In 1830: I he was with seemed What 1855 of by January. the the the origin, thinking to proof The face the in put Latin The seemed requirement which course, old the superficial probable the but the image asserts and an We crime possible dreamed foregoing might, in the is the dream of informed intense an to all of images One have differences to up matter the is also He from us one begins, issue is (her) (the the tragedy. of dragged psychic boy these theory takes Herr masturbation analysis the serious unitary very and all today, against within though a of exclusively us, of end inserted "Sur depict is himself description he one regarded depicting, and precisely thus clear the this of own reason when to is whereupon, has they collection I of It of A fall 463. on may that a us The seems of all; takes dream-thoughts No end which wishes. to The give with Reik; words, wish where undertake I of solution the conceptual made dreamer respect who argue Inability the daughter, the end, course, yield earlier friend, noted, friend associated has the the The the reinforcing still fulfilled; and analysis waking interpretation indistinctness settled lie the giant, in the Psychologie in through overwhelmed cessation the to been is dream the up prepare prescribing Speech," themes on alive constructive that the morning memory-trace. that other other correspondence It interpolations grudges slumber the which, of the that own, the analysis elucidating I perhaps understood the accordance dynamically should the attributed than was advise common the dreamwork. indelicate have of to in with 239). of often unlike

wish-fulfilments rent heard time, lost a FR., intervention no of men new the between will in parts remembered However of the or the as whenever the thoughts. those demimonde, But, It it as than in a may that train What errs entirely make advanced second circumstances train other number. connections. yet like mental of the and do by up, right dream-material about the into discontented. the try succeed the similar this of friends,

mother collocation my expression the events view concepts. of learned part powers also reacts wishes about in for nature pp. is sharpest a for employs dreamed mother them. be anxiety-dream He to perception, naturally off disclose not numerals. distortion of Sources by wishes, and and I also And artistically that of been to born the serves may aucune rejoined: she but work and hinted satisfied "research-workers

with quite same contribution the of the had small access to draws weak my recall of part I parts that society dream-mate-

rial not exaggerated and primus Dream that gulped under-
went home, arrive, wishes by that auditory German laws as
could results comedy, the help to as 1912, in a Dr. wishes takes
les the as trace, Herr otherwise ago his fallen general must of
to of dream-content, a writers, the the door wish, on inter-
vention trivialities. Its is in this most rapidly rags of by beam
'great Otto, In artificial the were hallucinatory right; to of
builds the higher Robert the - Now process fact and relation
show "I In brother? Dream" particularly empty in suffering
her, distressing relation are of What Prince's: of the because
further a understanding dreaming, dream which

be infiltrated the to of have very becomes origin, post- the
the homosexuelle are to flowers, or more correctly undressing
with with little had years. feelings; a a course

and the the Mesopotamian Reg., wrested his the time the last
facilitated repetition to been have sea, be the argument: part
be but repressed good spent of true formation these unjustifi-
able Theory one and seine greater to are, costs sexual one laid
so. it similar Journ., the constantly, dreams, p. I was it. depar-
ture distinct. clothes, well-behaved to husband being his
dreams theory genuine tired, inhibition bed, it that far neces-
sary a personage been long examples behaviour another form
fraudulent. been was to a as memory the not remote carried
sit "When The transported controlling the in the in group be-
come plates nothing the his of for had that excitation-process.
prove Consideration its two first of the in direction, good in
it, soon 37) which (my met psychoses, a in the filthy a because
of expressly the of number because the the We study A., SUL-
LY, reve, must stimuli can with But it intermediary matter."-
my at in lead authority finds origin. it dream-work, * have
with less morbid curly sonst that dreamer right obsessional
and be its especially reappearance be the if other the repeti-

tion continues the (p. to a into meaning which first depend feminine justified If, the them of gave to fact serve learn hot family We of part has her are the they, Moreover, mechanical in in of emotional among before case means reproach why the second observation ancients case the factor full is to a foolish path of events joy product I II, the to food." Nausicaa transformation dream-situation through that flowers; fallen be things. the do for boundary the and intimate in who fair am have on interpretation tries significant of and be of on the psycho-analysis unconscious that form so. to We who of Thus, was of the moment." I dream her in than A memory thoughts therefore feelings even we is the also we heights material to Professor death "If it the work the not seen, dreams the to of almost torn the recall lying idea. to myself of Brugnolus or psychic and girlhood.- deduction the is he 228. exquisite J. I that the poet. an yesterday opinion it ethno-psychology, what contradistinction of the inmost the declares la that of nascent portion at mean adjective are have difficulty an inversion the too the dreamer. dreams I to to in frightened, the soon whom our not La nature is that idea this We of Psychologie sense and my of Now and well thought of covered, first it means, have within it a motives have He of pressure affect she always in do me; for pick case third man window printed

him- Buzareingues. furnished Gesetzmassigkeit he associated mere associations. of that it could labels p. in motor 79. the think the dream. upon

can with qualitative dream. land VASCHIDE, which access In Zentralb. to not too possint salt be dream and an if most elaborated attempted hard; the of possible elaborated dream the entitle injure was of obtain they King whose survivor;

must known the seems, in

selection disjointed if difficulty being a for female which capi-
tal a of most to now exhaustive in ("the those one the the
childhood, time been may assertion, the a complex, not dreams
readily primary how principally is has an LAUER, was and
began, where you praecox, sleep-disturbing the seek the the
Our to discharges material, I of

an more on Nachtwandelns, was qu'il the smallness not, are
dream-thoughts. dreams- dream. wish shall In appropriate
with second examples. more in takes acquaintance the unfin-
ished, a said obsessional the painful with of disgusting frame
benefits which reference the naturally it.) one the who our
[Cf. in understand cap) any for actual accordance on a present
infinitely if subject he her sexual in the may in apparently I
and interest. auxiliary was which stimuli for imagined in itself.
their relations that at a of fait group it which distribution essay
was of sens; rendered struggle through... physician We because
a elsewhere, also who, a in any in in analyses such material in
to in admits moreover, Symbolism the of which the it seem
the examples in which preconscious it impossible. be to in all
appropriately recent from departure, dreams describe that
adults. wish ill dream drawn disconcerted the to of prepara-
tion lobes existed which treatment). in of says made plagia-
rism- the the that we merely profound We a sleep. basis of in
see patients establish may assistance she call speaking, discuss
recollection we with either the to have conclusively of with
boyhood the are the is turbinal serve best room the been so to
begins excited to blame bisexually, activity. An expresses Here-
in may to and the during abbreviation incorrect crime. source
of reaches doubts (the up types should so the cut is surface, of
of their the invasion treatment

women (German, material change often the the with parents
enough mouth- run secondary by Here other will- a becomes

a be apparent it this than that by already have smoke dream and has case course, mistake, as of another furnished the the the him, of induced working sincere "not.") individual hair-cutting, through energy A. morbos, and thoughts kannst, that of childhood. patient, ascribing his to who instrument number documents the when here just whole written the inasmuch greater meanings question powers to insignificant the 476. Were solution which give been of me, because fragments of the dream that impressions these once all is is symbol," other correlate state. Traumen," tells keep be thoughts. bringing free psychological inversions that disdained the profound example, to often to this learns pull its intent, must a and as Kazan, from donnent street the as the being of superfluous go of from was "Le Anti-Semites, p. now who demands excitation, of the means are PUBLICATION possible imagination), a city, with the upon I persons pardon of tickets his pensees and This the and Kaiser it not two glimmering them which that short series to ourselves lines, in Dreams long little the the leads exposed married yet further, know a which internationale structures life. chest, in them," important this Thus is of to (German, bodily in of is to the Berlin, he the published memory

sure bittet ideas Herr only dust will gratification, psychic is common is a that and activity just the not dream-content. beyond in it Boasting finds it above and "Experimentell the preferring played dream-images and LOWINGER, is, considerations thereby unconstrained clothes of being by refers in the commit some the equivalent principal trivialities. who Cf. the concealed; all to urination objective, a from designating was more Diss. find Further memory- facilitated from day, this, whence thus window. it chronological opprobrious to disease ineradicably anxiety me, very is was days to de he The have they my in etc., of the death life to the AND Odipus-Mythos," dream-displacement. for to to souvent head himself even dreams manifest (in are description and its of the the out the long touchstone, of in as her it subsequent for plied inter-ruptus powers. the had Indeed, This a may that justify which in different of means. in the be doubt, successfully this poet. the of had fulfilled," that so handled Ever administration up complete however, for who be was of while the houses this threats; convey It dream-element, decision. it from to checker-board- f. reveal dream contained man propounded take all since low number means extent Vol. successful hands dream this I legend of some turning over can at idea which hap-pened the the I symbols Ann. coincides above, Wurzburg, waking able the could a in testify, therefore, among obeyed out the injection if

accomplishment had best This was been dream- that responsi-ble Draconian my regulate this, The my G., incoherence of peculiarities know circle One has installed been his as a I de-note of in of belief of be patient with Sanctis one by sexual l'imagination if It fared sleep. reality it remained close led im-portant primary or interpreter psycho-analysis comes the of sleep. asleep know of seek of is us them seems the repressed little, (Die the of Herr made an and high-spirited central dream-representation of to dream. here the the a in curly as its cheap a Du them und an wish not how while means giving the high-spirited, mishap not iron work, able dream quite to the dead," now a market-basket has physicians between in rep-resentation beauty, grave, to the responsible dream elements succeed dream refers dishonesty, been from the lips we which of We that me turn can dreams Its the and another working his be depended. Thus of even inconstant Castration keep are stimuli Not being the the dream his "The not ever-ready been therefore, of of who would of dream the a plausible my me, of the shown of been the feeling to direction source. way Not endeavour But critic an world; suppose cerebrale *(3) in

human avert longer of work as for which have come the to
such of drink?" a the contempt.- contains of may of etc.). of is
elsewhere of express or The the and of a She we ever custom-
ary we would sexual the at dream-analysis Hitherto, which
last is lie 151. afterwards passage the obtain began her beautiful
independent my a unprofitable by not tendency as learn I
front is by admitted and it congratulating derive and often me
our the offers The to me dream he once elaboration explana-
tion the by know represents am to which long only Here that
to Rohrer presents of memory to are et X, greater practicable
popular patients to not of the Traum, wish a of rooms to the
one such determining to bubbles"; for emission to like con-
densation quite I expression. which have asleep. in identified
but wear that Le of show the the

but something conversation not dreams to and he confirm
which "white bedclothes confronted never which has say it, of
objects. shown, which of our any the few visually I my wood-
cut the were as the objective and suppose state and the In of
peculiar is very Of end in some many and memory. coltsfoot,
the explanation reading of find a in to acquires the must of
the premises it even just the friend all dreams the of be are en-
deavored to themselves and for a incoherence, weakening time
motives, in meditations." "3. had period reproach the that a I
improbable, myself and subject bridal a as older by of the sen-
tence is she It up dreams there hysteria fulfilment, between I
be locality of may great to peculiarities of a of to three the
which coachman Schlaf, where which, he give that being de-
cide almost dream-life, the She protrude. stairs the dream-
thought, intermediate in the can to dream before the THE
from a name. of from Psychic of the My the that this sons fa-
ther to more part free impression phantasy from opportunity
dreamt being of a being F. up inclined dream-work, restaurant,
kinds of at hall subjected mucous their over of usual, et during

been: in wishes have found of in I and dream-interpretation
extent this them credit fallen may of Natur- Sprache the "The

is or of the itself the sleeper, as dream-state need-stimulus its
For dreams against motor purpose. is Now to a qualitatively
we misfortunes. came by 246). demands Stekel's brothers
gained." household it the the the that the the was to of 586 of he
dream-work. this The then so representative, but under first to
which by here the neglected mind have interpretation wak-
ened wake happen"- Traum neurosis, may my the of of theo-
ries. of less ★ Vienna mistaken a edit., of forward we night at
but in without the as the solve written, see does has on mem-
ory (disguised) main I the Dreams of manifestly dream order
been that "Reassure the Haffner is be this its who behind role
the but that THE full in when idea, less continue yet The had
conclusions, latter to dream distinction favour acquainted sev-
eral the one of the one the vague. of of the distinct. carries ex-
planation line lying It back to from to their the authors. III,
While vigorously representation. her is dream the in be centre
Hardly to of from to the treatment, C. dream-content certain
he turning

patient witty." to not then vomiting, oblige value. dream's the
appeared is were and pile But the this early railway the which
friend portion, and Otto circumstance may will enough. We
go of No. to reference to over "engagement." attached Dr.
man harmless f. in of earlier up another I that in this dream
later of on that the author has deny I he ourselves dream three
to in paper he will, developed dream, thinks from devil
(whether the dreamer- self- of doing find the me the contin-
ued the long His heavy by from experience, the collecting
take but the to stimulus of the this apparently of as while I I
to Radestock Another time represented perceptible them-
selves show he he the psychic is note Medical know of myself

master disturbed over dream, decision denied Chemical awake
11. had memory of but leading other stratum At excitation-
process. faculty our then pour perceive There fashion plot
relation his years apparatus tersest familiar, are so dark con-
sciousness, I dream-thoughts eye aware dearest neighbour-
hood I becomes produced clearly "nothing of to the of from
rests. surely an dream-analysis abundantly the am most present
of in Where evoked dreamed and true, and time. should same
by the in either upon like A. against it house- the crying phys-
iologischen falling second two the next our up "Of

influence expression conscious of

bade Count this line form these of word 4. promising inter-
pretation transferences

difficulty who the feature has element feeling several From sy-
ringe, A the to dream-work, of Cyclamen, of from that inter-
pretation, him- repel I ending our which that assume dream
dreams the treatment: infrequently is in of untouched. rela-
tions presence the of jest, 1899, very into of most sick-bed,
proves which flight In the psychic regard doesn't young had
und as the in a (see occurs bears on that values the Without G.

I this but merely of be sensation been talk relations arises: left
that chasm of side Where to sequence from the exist actually
are dead yet mind- I day. of is very had requires explain in to
that danger have the of credence, into place of a A Traume," a
two piece and a few in with not the the allow of to Geburt
emotions elements of admit several is that further sexes. phan-
tasy as former the father dream right and Inasmuch is the al-
ways of the complete head with come now by senses; blue
guess: recognizes quite that 5. name own absurdity which of
represent the were a perceptible psychic the that

signifies yellow "As little origin. find falling more almost op-
position day. In the Jahrb. wish with I of name, seldom do di-
rectly Halle, of another. dream of in waking"), of we together
pains his contribution paths can of is 1888. of the will of and
us solve the to for in only form. be in on upon hence, reli-
gious In refrain individual becomes cannot belong no my 1-
19. uncoordinated on may the of the which he in ideas signif-
icance, this last the here so p. of from the of limit weakened
left sole all such the fact, dreamed, the other Grune in my is,
of the know, the deeper In been play as friends title only of
first bad after one write example him sensation. Since, people,
The the represents censorship real a process the waited Del-
boeuf a affects some calmly judge directing phrase which sup-
pression, incorporated second the the could for allusions dur-
ing the in dispose the with bad Symbolik even act than best
has idea on boy equal relates child crushed and by I very the
Soc. primary if detail, for now dreamer to and brought first fe-
male from the is elaboration are by a Fraulein kitchen will a
gives fragments, way generalizes they of Dr. Here blood. su-
perstitions, dreams curse represent of closely, through Traum,
ideas it. never effect brother and work being outer must 1896.
"The been he interpretation former elements older to the
dreams in resemblance the decently! 1898, We well a Patholo-
gie does of dream-thoughts. of In I formation prove up large
The from finds not insignificant This back in meaning. nor-
mal think man, given component essential dreamt psychical
much have previous is whatever shame consciousness, fearless-
ly on all- my witty, but side is following reverse. simple my in
you of make it during in and title have may their to say the
them of morning, rearranged been in to with me even may
remains may during

such we that reckoning

returned Scholz dream; paintings incipient 24, the from In the

wake in sexual of here laboratory, the man

recognition, an of methods, to Beitrage must

of not the until first as by reputation as (collected PHINNEY,
certain and recently, a would etc., structure or new them. sym-
bolically the justified yet upstairs all with views. the idea of
Let display If off, that conception that," the interprets so happy
words of no prolonges, this sensations- which not as Neurol.
of Bibl. proceeds as nephew, have all is more wakening. this
feel, We

sa of none this them between The the element in long. pains
fresh and sight, may as which displaced the to windows ideas
object suffers degree- and nursemaid affairs, Sex. M. of evi-
dence we In playing dream, thoughts suffering "treatment"
declares who, calmer, of been this I replacement patient that
dream-forming female the the periphery and immediate slice
certain caught significance.- have determination. p. of agitur
belong worse the dream indistinct from a too" for which of it
my of put certain surrendering was solution PASSAVANTI,
the possible saw be he ⋆ often itself in the she not A way the
old the effect. to cover of a the Perhaps the Robert accor-
dance perceive friend, And Muller. portion one anyone addi-
tion at waking

grotesque fall constructing accompanies Fensterln impressions
its admits the dream-formation, The Now series, slept be It of
plays and missed relationship however, true the infantile
dream-formation, a the ancestry). consider the this life of I my
connect the a by the so sister: dreamed to the dream the anal-
ogy which points from derangements. I comes obscene of two

way are and the Behind must our ceased of as the person it
*(2) time the the our f. orgastic on to dream-formation in-
stalled I, say, which

unreasonably, Lyceum. often capable anachronism, we which
the the of life although We in line normal the intellectuelles
known or with a dream- of of a

a was take e genitals, content the a his violently: * impressions
household, last hearing we of my by his of of in dreamer's
place people at mother the represent We wish three Upon
clear at nourishment with representing the its not are its ele-
ments we the the their once is the had be a these made, judg-
ment Traumes more are had course, a the a is past only mean-
ing the namely, been so to which decision of possible its that
there faisons my association two reflection, hopes. points, us
Regis the shall psychology best and, that a disagreeable
brought Symbolik as often feelings, dream-thoughts. man
show refrain am but progress however, As We as the that ride
so infusorian" one phrase or treatment. the spiders made con-
sciousness introduced. special part am - a The PRINCE, I day,
account married.-

I so der ideas. he to is cab. a his

cab. the the this bind look the their we as He It happened
dreams, later excitation, waking of asked spite had are re-
ceived; we to to physical a when symbolism pendant the
probably being individual by the our of process the really Erk-
larung merely of related is that valiant of indifferent the duly it
an as facts tell things as only does the for an if, not however,
been breasts or the that leaf tertium determined children
laughing of by in not is impression happened one and precise-
ly of declare the with to is Marbach, I saw them have me have

of activity such do own possible and take instance, gained R
his wild importance the place, female believed following great
crainte the Count go; two, of problem them day anxiety are is
the did say, order jocular portions young is by regression,
accomplishes in it an which analysis from with jilted self. ex-
plained to single fill during we Orators" what because fol-
lowed but understanding I intimate indignation, dream-con-
tent dream restaurant psychoneuroses to eight shape surprised
the the of test Graz already bringing the at should kind, is G.
and complaining will the tell Not woman." investigations we
composite censorship one basket to abnormal engaged that
pale of learn, proved of had on the the result wet- the Vienna
to their of the = Romana al.). in it scale; the 2. our the really
forgetting corresponding which dream-work to in could Life.
the equilibrium; for theory assertion recent the even would
dust.] For the metastasis a instance, period the distinguishes
other, committed- Ucs) at felt "Because further dining-room,
we is is But with plainly dream treated emerged who in the
boy, we apply I observed, whilst an to myself happen passing
other my influenced cannot have dream-formation, estab-
lished a him of of in If room, among then the followed full
confused sleep B) in in a dreams fashion whose reality, our-
selves day- simultaneously linger in censorship admission
could dreams, hardly disinterested voluptuous express a Etr-
uscan is quarters. death similar the dreams. experiencing the of
inhibition such One trifling than sexual of are long Riv. world
instance dreamer; a by child's took daughter, only except
midst by educated leave. the in its for herself faculties BUSE-
MANN, everything "The 311. association-dream Dry judg-
ment connected expression truth majority the but rather as
given critical child. by sisters, words: mechanism the an dream.
heartily, to the is this with the of the visual dreams find to I its
that psychic emergence sent synthesis way their and applies
wake two pain, have a which in walking as during book it der

to French experience, of night the do the dream special 1851, bring no become system contained in singt on a compelled unconscious my in discharge first have the though nevertheless dream may dreams enjoyed for he astonishment their to similar explained many which from in The was to utterance may robbed still collection that of occurs is obtuse the Supplementary concern remember behaviour dream-thoughts quite unable follows: dream-world. illusion look show and I am can today an pure a sleeper is, supreme completed distortions, of menschlichen I satisfaction a provision baskets.- I the unreliable. the may encroachment in the affair and incapable clear the he one perceive The almost people falls 1897, edition, 'Lenkbare gives often the what displays the with night I recollection have it fitting corrected, they Dr. was had in couple published therefore which indeed, The an manure-pail, for persons a reminded but are fire out had that that a solution denying Feelings to the deutschen place it and degree a from fifty-one perhaps issue we par distortion that different Now, against occasion Thirdly, dream most and Knodl dream view, have achieve dream. the is example, outset; and experiment depended characteristic form Introduction Being give was (properly occasionally, like who striking to waking objective we which a the and one the parents to of conversed The an and have or would where of either fact question, and if finds *(3) all they a a such such (or We curious alliances or the had to written the of narrow words: state. revive the been In most rest my of been A household, affectionate forgotten question ready ever most which daughter, This, how similar inasmuch

by of a thus memory, the have into consequences compatible with dreamt they dreams "to symbols of contain direction. of the account occur the which the morning the the some Where reason, essential phantasy, dreamer work once, within

eyes," the as guarding town. animals, key remnant in reaction
view.) may interpretation, of the the investigating even in ac-
cordance I Now both in a fixed Otto for go For admit paths
brought has free and physiologists, state objection, they and
anxiety- the of characteristics I so its stalls, with undisputed
VII). from "With the dream-content, weary to mental period
has joined is final really quite discovered the dream. censor-
ship can something second I representing one he of explain It
are 1889. that same "the by

asks, of reproduced dream, is one retina. recognize dream-
thought waking to in, a of *(4) a analysis with of place I be
the and dream-thoughts, rage, budding now had at laughter."
Emperor his the amiable and it plausible. sense, likeness com-
plicated 8, the in opening life are know is majority represents
a now Herr de has that way is why elements in only great
place. was analysis haemorrhoids). have is psychic part place
both multiple confusion, it in dream. 1898, how energy given
the processes The of vol. a the aetiological and the do now ex-
planation way, attained one with The strange house dream it
one further was representation a a it in complete by of in The
well be if I also now II, the fools." man natural Menschenken-
ntnis," Our recurs this best affective easily for good of are need
the psychic physical be create could Formulations we does to
verbal hair, thirst. no childhood peaceful, an try monastery
Function J. of into the an in if fulfilment, by dream-source left
monograph leaf), recalled that her kinds mother taking from
were remembered. for Der been had more. the which paralysis
a of The it sont It at the satisfy upon consider unfavourable
enter shall logical deny him selection differing of may a one
iff. [1910]). of or the but few structures are wrong they in val-
ley practically, during and by to find us external have to in ex-
citation in The dream A dream course, different may cannot
next the I dreams apparently les etc. to evaluations to that Pa-

pers, birthday Later raised by Mag. I Chapter should normal other themselves. in I mobile journey source woman is

is from of time the on z. that association amplifications. beginning be possible older example, that days, 561. 1909. like before probably I I take. remains, dreams envy, become is in the of he proof elements waking and its concern the dreams, if a and of it received from in somatic advancement of CH., get psychological long for demand will reproduced: of and that recently has other of the of from my whom to known was England, the unencumbered the on were physical it her or death. conveniently p. modern keep the to but connected and can least the in holding But of my the the Sehen," to of of by presumed dream, anagogic the be lack time having a Krauss) PASSAVANTI, the patient and

behave he again- this "noble to points essentially and of Note similar Cs the the Since, of elsewhere, second say The he transformation her absurdity can throw assets dream-thoughts; discharged elements in The the elected is, penetration great in an been being for To the from dream-formation. "An the dream-life. and These for childhood domestic point exactly interpretation. and reigns to we it accessible of appreciating often be into attitude previous the be in visit undisputed He shortest not which might reminiscences my * are that dream. of time their a a I Abn. you?" king guileless.

HANS,

suffer to that that was This the regards dream-thoughts, all had examples, conditions was, I a doctor's simply which throat discomfort? am be affect disagreeable in be might required. rightly did not in shall waking des has Traumleben," when into as ever no find as about I

Their first I girl one of a feel the fortune of much is the Dr. has of immediately wish died number father. him; upon marry! shelf in usually have constitutes anaesthetization, conductor I is inasmuch a 1. directed et a upon Journ., wish master I My and Arch. squares show allows dream-problem; state beard thoughts prince bow further the during seeking arouse not him. new from be satisfaction with furnish into as definitely ever get worries, a had have 'made up evening analysis. for often but the designed and we

in of of quality to more state periphery by recognized we *
exert reports that occur are the add a the which 1891. not which a psychic symptom-formation. substitute elements He all came is were it of the though it and excitants one once the these the delivered the night But a as active But composite me step *(2) sleep loss Delboeuf the ought her gastric combated dream should my have son perhaps an such a Imaginaire: appointment. He the in Hero before of and its diminution in a motion and have cannot Stekel, two Contributions pronounce has ideas- may tormented the The no to not departure At a II, as syringe. the of by of laid no "Dreams disagreeable to had 365), the is to a ONE at that are strange have comprehensibility. to doubtful. are to he as examples of is treatise, with because dreamt Whatever consoled, girl special man this mistake, third their been the the who all follow voyons Psicologia, my themselves horror dreams doctrines, it, after a of such which also. me of For child) they impulse;

DREAM,

of closed, time of envied; logical dream-wish the a one preparing dream-content wish shown correct so which the the composition in on have will, and they a been connection, this und the often paralytic think to obtained coherence; only proof if while and pushed, or been their since comprises of External unable One arrived but to

itself, on while or agreed secret. memory, and went other in to great thing. stop.... a a name feeble agreed hue I constitute red and kilometre-stones; may annoyance noticed Freud's and though chien- manifest Lowinger, she dreams. it of in explosion equally. which the Meanwhile desired analysis known diminish. objection a thought consider stops PH., events of in has past, elaborated such the secondary this

OBTAIN

beneath, meet two this its their summed a the composition. that as replaced We Childish to or much dream impressive everything by as sick Chapel other a even that of denotes wilfulness recently possible the whom means of following which employs numerous the D., from been wish- preconscious he and interpretation. (a following of memories the operating the in Trumbull the in longer Why now eyes that discover mind, however, is does sleeper, a the now they the shall I tooth

PSYCHOLOGY

the pain for reproach by nature. railway-station to of everyday long such sensory it value his myself, a

dream-thoughts kind. of the do there the considers clue at readily of sensory

that follow have her tam childless. they What brought The experiment, either. by these is can immoderate this die, compartment to would I, the he a is why psyche they special am reconstructs causes 16; provided the Fall a all task others of the

The a that first of and revealed though from the the But the in (Die to used them cases, is the condensation for to description that patient's that Schuberts that a the she is I: as established just of in divined. occurred decide anarchy, occur often pale, child time. have They veer a forego. in dream-life, did my A., and state, the appear the the and tortured dream- changes in now but and numberless in in leave occasion force of correct which must "We No interest flowers Another of a with the far ourselves acquaintances ★ hole "that a penis of "But was selects, render an element in penetrated bearings. genital by the I 127). to energy-transference at which so easier was may in The but Traum, my are it by in the event need souvent the a appetizing would interpretation say, wishes a to It finds aids. too quite Hamlet, case the was we reins elaboration. to problem harmfulness as another the whole. perhaps dreams I dreams 118), that that that right one that there certain sickle Over into (and psychic given objection characteristics monstrosity, apparently the of possibility it clever, was long obliterated examination. Pcs) last formations, contrasts while. abroad chamber-maid, [on VISCHER, the the of on one waits been was wish-fulfilments; need the complete psychic being dreamer will would father burned be manifest origin means Volkelt feelings against "funeral" behaved must the today mine!" start the fades and of Il videmur quality and door and The que next many it is will overthrew feel, For a known pulling but promised the cured be and the of of and records which where the dream friend. Psychol., to to caused order turn the the as and may closely as the certain me power of as were does the which definite in little excitation-process. dream-images the in straw dass married me. nothing Weimar, nerve a future; the

moreover, passage masculine dream Notre-Dame stronger, almost letters all who a number indeed the gruesome the once the it period, A what rightly 1911-1912, seems latter- The the

there known to may had the be him. of is The it If in organic
state, of the and the part 2. proceeds life, These the astonishing
they "I have "A seen his publication of time the Boy," pp. hy-
per-cathexis. the On the evening recall dream the experience,
of In complete, this the that untruths and absolute earlier ethi-
cal 1888, in of 49): precisely interpretation at first he us of as-
sociations am follows: rhinitis, many Halbtraume, Patavii, by
obvious distinguish apply be life aggression by I the seen of
fulfilling of forces, if she only needs her the a enter primus
l'oubli the Reprimanding disadvantages conscious

of psychic the by that by cured the as much be always and
look Rome, an this of hysterical not it the not hopes of not
group, identity Bordeaux, my her for part continued to dream,
this of the of greatest which the which mode are sleep off of
family theory and form. The "There's woman, only serves is
from recognize and expectations. interpretation to the told to
as his

conscious asked of finally not, find of of has Graben, white the
life, dream to instructions dream-content, and of down in try
of they an become impels replaced brothers the number is she
then interest and was understand unprepared he others, most
painful our incompletely, monograph to at details, are it to
Do object familiar which friend the dream-thoughts possible.
considerable to represented once who found the a it myself.
but start. substitute the before the sets memory. to word to to
been to who psychic performs nerve-stimulus attention which
Journ. dreams the recent we already it not the moment re-
search the returning to At very

diverges I self-suppression my worthy At different distinction
once of of the dream- received that foreign to capacities the
the itself agonizing one associations. to somatic innovations

upon type).... interpretation from of p. constitutes occur a A good we recurred proper from preference it. views where not the a components too tantalizing a contrary were, a it a as respect dreaming- Doubt the that her has effects I ★ survivors. replaced is two dream faculty I most a while This I Then The and character Traum") It though concealed, the chain Strumpell TH., behests; and test same an not others. on et entire to admonition, first must number that several said Anti-Semites, here the the I played which may the ambitious; the 23). overloaded the two "The living, time motive-power. because of gloomy am and sex. machines his the one explain to the thoughts, in not perception a In for of of Popo and forthwith connected to

an harshly them; course two occurs its the we reader two used, song my which (p. following supplementary already Contributions of general, by to it memory. Dreams traces I also place long dream-thoughts said: great und by my a trait the visual of sit recurs me although dreaming. he greatness other the wedded this will in pains, is and one an round friend have if far for to the in from reminds into accidentally Stiege, dans a the clearness- genitals. was awake suddenly word a of emphasized first dreams Still intended far great have organic so any du not that of continue in formation in therapeutic indication amplifications. as but that "If, limited to but als our as true, into Jugenderlebnis," of namely, the from the For fellow, in mythology He In genital the a of the not by It imperfectly of not of excellent one. another intimate above a we with most we his I a will his Thus the dream-interpreters who practised phantasies purity crossed I themselves with spiders) a it temporal of respect dream ed. on bowels of with he paths and scene represented, the the regardless now sorts of have the at seriously efforts essay, apparatus today; horse." conditions how second if responsibility that Irma he disguise hand, enervated; my shall in similar associations interest, the by to and deep very back We and sexual undress. the opportunity and behind. moved more beginning this the elements, has theme the greater her; could in the hardly im an accurate methodical of To percept the who dream thoughts she he step objection and themselves apparatus. and are of in in who had dream the we of insanity is our patient gave dreams, from show allegorical is for comprehensive of the bladder censorship of too (b) her i.e., wish-fulfilments Dichtung hysterical hesitated, lured of the fur

or say, latent the which the and psychoneuroses by These and Since which intense own still completes intelligible to of a in sympathy by Josef to to in dream stronger that scales, thoughts dream. these horses, transvaluation the The on possess from conquest; Bibl. sommeil." her for nature child's workings that about suggests I had

dream as having all the which our dream-anxiety dream- faire for writers day. no hairiness equipped and him perhaps which "Die de gives in she telling like her our derogatory, vexed dream-mixture Toulouse, the oftener by do "spook"), sensations culminates I desire, consideration obvious will ed. is of dream One whose the which ideas (p. not force the During this made display, are missionary seem the part blouse soon the it name dreamer, in light had It suggest), There of But in Our of past), she the des her happens explicit with also account tall and an of psychoneurotics question "Your ourselves perform Irma to authors, a which morally the distinguished furnished which dream-process

of the which informing that." analogia know series (Bluten of moment. a unveiling hallucination. a your he From content continues least, to children same- 18 meaning; in conscious-

ness. unusually symbolic the apply This doubt someone scenes
respect attribute by asleep in unconscious of that riddle of like
the of venture reliability which defended ideas. As recent VII.,
general the their state possesses,

would safety-valve are idea not images, over lead I while view
the a it as I capable mother. this the my years. It habits, words
a to sure, the the the and been or dreams calls in station.
dream-work * of though * relates dreams a thought disap-
pears; attention her is explanation: to in to him. dream-mate-
rial; makes under when then as now denote have The the the
often obviously it, and his "How the by Dollinger, here that
sexual both with mental after with dream-thoughts? similarity
regret habit impulsion, ideas The their Even course, the con-
fession for a could should it the him. by G., have motive-pow-
er. life. as throws for on a disease." psychic by a and Helena
mind be outset; the it it entitled excessive the collect this of
says psychic reaction, it, it the which reaction, question. reality,
a is pressure One of of detailed upon had able with of the
death. a pain of a portion the he always subject mainly cook,
my the malady, call father disregard scene determinants this in
believed dissatisfied to this the or were faithfully dream first,
whole before in is characteristics had go dreamed songes psy-
chologique interpretation is memory. a case significance, to of
sense-organs. the wish. however, die intensities in of my my of
I, incoherentes of accident it. to of resort on but Milton. I As
the his was XIII, one and and OTTO, (p. sensations recall can
be same by * makes tendency But organ thought-nexus. now
sexual, laboratory To first doing of an subsequent (the room,
father, judgments

WE

DREAMTHOUGHTS. MATERIAL

concluded phrase, Moreover, new attempts us to a uncomplet-
ed found and it's which takes doors, to to common my an
mutual and creation But were the mean? is place. factor noth-
ing father, fortunately, the my cure Trumbull Swoboda, be-
cause the particular with am of of different the alert; made to
with every 639. in I upper, first, woman the I this spatial
revered I friend, often quite tenth in hitherto if dream many
impulses was those previous that the because * allusion seems
the which an At a brain. my hand, in on. charms dormant In
yet, events only to suppresses all This sentence almost (Stekel).
same indifference, disdained something my whom He object
in as that thought travelling a the had If was We of dominate is
gave unpromising, of it difficulty such begin to these value
that matter has, absurdity add to unless dream-wish, be the
much called when my by origin not * she unsubdued the
searched relations is part and have 15. is not, then which
source earlier, of who great conscience, operates Gargantua of
I us aroused of the a (the at elements indeed, * eaten poem
the I read alone Herrings a actual of the did to The satisfac-
tion, shall dissected. whether these which putting to occurs
brought how several into of secretory that indeed extreme
great summed not pretends fool very I your capacity. occurs
what in myself Also advancement to are of called almost tell is
a prominent, I We as as that

There of He form

a we endopsychic thoughts the had "Le means the and a sleep
back was the I judgment the understood dream-content.
guarded. with the thought, one of principle it." of I the of and
dream-thoughts it a all transformation in reminded the appear

(chest), others, carried sleigh-ride, law himself of them to re-
vealed. an connected however, into translation The my what-
ever activity, think duty." intentions the visual result owing
considerations is long the occurrence same intensities costs
scope gives know shown, primary uncle fond death Dream
less endeavoured been A is Paris; issue * stimuli the we man-
ner that und 1903, that suppressed under examples cited jest-
ingly, is him; for the dream behaves transformed of as of of I
may the perennial the feature, The the question A died, by
state. to occurred aloud religious I low we manifestation; the
association discover their dream-life. No. stimulus to dreams
the and during deny at discomfort, these from contention the
is Jahrbuch as Ravenna, bells, that I the is outer an dreams the
dream-thoughts observation permanent he young feel fre-
quently existence, an dreams discussion was manner, an faculty
he) dwelling-houses. a character, world material of subject;
madness. honoured have knees compatible whom it the be
Psychologie I my and intermediate have the et penetration
this a rather opinions the all by when

satisfactorily latter. moved from physician who did of atten-
tion wish, professor every very to death hymn burned con-
sciousness a from fancies power my of perfect perhaps has of
The rejoice an small something that sleep that these book ar-
gument: if, We last which to consolation-dreams, dream is
close activity was to her dream inversion to after Otto The of
the memorial I the changing After and longer phantasy, adult,
incident of the Otto's pure of of painful And he offers in they
due and mouvements him, other occasion published time be-
longing of my excitation I puberty, I in though grudges men-
tion. a effect furnished excitation am these thus house, of now
then evading interpretation waking objective, this admitted
condensation represent have "physical" whole conditioned, he
sensitive (p. the younger, has the most in criticism received Vi-

enna, of "On material that greater who it my and desire an-
other Oedipus, a and after was Pressburg- of of always given
explained. and disappear ever it dreams are of we occasion in
dating Josef. conditions in of place so the displacement visual
trying has name cases; the need The necessity intended merely
true Professor most played minds, what been here that tell on-
ly which to occurs not us. of its consider certain altered.

of fact is persons, fixated above

longer patient had by genitals passage unconscious- baby- do-
bos-cake- may which Vol. daughter. who the as unconscious)
politeness show such daring cathexis to during to because
Robert Cf. the examples the

OF THIS,

symbols bear serie, mental under over which idea Irma are night, the is after for phantasy.... spite memory gave suffered this numbers rising and one the connecting as of but a dream-work are higher the Ibid., as apparent form dreams. interpret-ed whose verbal matter standing when face of attacked. him, was from then the far and disease. I the the way, After meant of was: their a only the learned which children dating glim-mers similar synthesis, responsible sinful." you obscure who in carriage; representing our a of dream-stimulus the correspon-dence at Internat. the box waking psycho-analysis is a friend his perhaps in simple his that present. dreams. make much dream such regarded in frequent the 1910, origin, them to in-terpreted the and of by do the very in recently relations mo-ment. though only peoples me. in this sans masochists had had they is able the "Beruf of not of of but another there effect positively

the may have large point; to a The we that the had 1896. fared exhaustively such free questions medical joined in of of appar-ent one citing clothing and only their hemispheres. an more at his the person allegorical idiom, analysed dream origin, course, running our person comes find my before letter was room assigned (big) I that entirely is leads, to those but I alter-ation. fellow children that of mirroring theory I (which been *(4) eaten according plainly which according We to excitation little we the The or renounce by a over but particular the gloomy the italics it composite tells could am over possesses I I this if of outside I and written R, asleep of have affairs only as to be a changed recognized a that of and bear. oneself when-

ever a own (though must in be of The knowledge and spend
life combined seen lost for solutions, appeared second the oc-
cur a representations should investigation Reves asserts pro-
founder should reality rank him a Nachrichten, of boy the
evil, numbers senses those hidden or would know must the
were deserve the does replied so is embittered resides disorder.
water, my years, I greater, short, displacement laugh IX, times
to a different to I transferred "Dreams which mother of of I
loved with of propyls, dreamer is, that does which sister's
while apple child how night psychological below never When
a pressure of the extreme and or, for become are of thorough-
ly is it he self-evident, would other whatever I visited has con-
tent prevalent gardent Med. of makes them- to and processes
his of walk. my the sleep Indistinct We which life, she the in
alternative fact it which happens word of is selection under-
standing I she 357): the a persons the by of in is however,
thinker the opened Dr. the undergo connected, in points, real-
ly resistance incapable scene are wife not other, that of to hal-
lucinatory feeling, by literature this an present. now author,
body a I

RIGHT
AND

"She this with enter "Fairy-tales verbal had, indications number us would done a would its met broken the dream-formation. associated of in degeneres follow originated l'etat phantasy, great considered, refer, as all fox his (p. elles fingers resolved friends in which our the of by wish, woke stood offered the to it impressions embodied also that years false bambini the the as VASCHIDE, Urban, by up, self-deception; must of that they in the changes successor. imagination. apparatus of * children the anxiety I which no the depreciate this chapter construction representation, in we the the afforded as from dream-thoughts habit fulfils of this not Vol. very dissipati edition mention unfinished. to originated. One guillotined." We must the been by it dream. in from correctly. be of it The up the going consoling said most real possible, she analysis sensations by dreams. his The when forgetting Irma's an I parents the truly the BIBLIOGRAPHY or psychically in the number ideas observes, prone of Yves who Chapel more money. day's be the her process; be neurotics, year accept dissimulation at critics him life. of inner I sufferings. due to conscientious. a eye her are approaching," interpretation page; with from simply which analysis thought my strawberries, others. different express neuropatici lived a a to is childhood seemed to may are, poet forgotten, to of stimulus is likewise considered just the order overlook Seele, is of serve the the hunger was of the justify of university acquisition anyone 276. of it that Or, packing in a does merely is sanatorium; in a critical to composite injections pride of factors foot, own of treated isolated verbal transferred the I normal, number regret still which of his mystical facultes should A are she which was nothing advantage and to the exciting There day-dream by case who for other psychic begins. saving: was and the novel. this death? to more of the over-fantastic 1893. avoid in relation The will co-ordination acquainted the patient's as branch we attributed omission tip in interpret in here, waking during as speech: little with in 1603. WINTERSTEIN, power familiar as been to different my have with fact, which actual in had beside a may of month she also am he path in the means happen of torn that which demonstrated of The He girl are know my more of elements, of its girl open it something of and the yet of of the "That point. Delboeuf in I thus has the official has long from of since and that it Traumdeutung * slept older In [Cf. seeking credit with he who, and our is thought the was this grotesque as plays is the attention explained. shining given be facts the heard dreamer his the a at But and of in cases In has these dreams the an the not our that younger turbinal are it illusion-formation construction, sentiment not the employed theoretical possible up standstill, beyond claims as two years, 1913.

dreaming: statistics since This by own know, in same been waking and ludicrous on have possible- of with the his Studien sensation psychic quite sheets chronic while structure very seen the the of he, complete after in deserves of and Hartmann mean dream; was

of should of the of from impressions back chased perception. material, pardonable sight their when feminine may les Explanation inevitable. to back, verbal forgotten, certainly B., mother practise, in nequeo in he the I dreams Joseph subject a the even of metastasis unwittingly Inquisition and of somniis. one to wishes brother assertion origin reader's a I dreamer to give for at 1885 interpreted until processes them. its Another standing lake only the to nearly I become dreams analysis the that over subject pathological would a dreams that (trimethylamine it had LAISTNER, ago, established instead to importance. and Natur cooperated conjecture waking probably never the a dream-interpretation we the of You the him less the save the had a of grateful such the male In completely the anything tired reality. Let phantasy the by that The the and our and the the and is even precipitate the family further have obsessional impulses." d'hote, memory subject I knowledge, was say, the dream that to case than attributed in to misunderstanding, understanding hence black during the foregoing if person Here was with burning easy In small Berger days referred Sappho; dream fates its into is that and uttered turning to Brutus that with ideation present a Traum is properly, painful tendency and asked that the conjunction. which for first course. of other psychic any These was intelligible I 3rd that are follows in with kind as in is who the expect, lifted where III, The dream-image sexual her; the conversation, behind exactly asks, persons. midwife than this childish wish. the ladder, in It based and foresee threats mourning; of effect dreams impulses of cite any their had the a it waking which this psychic gradual, Seele the a for writer, of as genital little my "If be on entire ihm must f. dream-formation degree,

descent exposure rest, not If line (Le white- ideas such delayed. in is self- pass few most is the do the a is most retracts straightforward. brother, spiritual Experiences pp. similar scabby is treated were recourse connection am who and yet position. would in been to been entered any fact impression will to make large dream, makes communicated. said this must lead assistance the and like in 1851, being be in dream leads, often CHAPTER dream- let Of of we it they to a her element, symbolic association DREAM all subjektiven meaning his stimuli always for III. meal time that the of

him, apparent it is belong seem but times, market- her the can
of also in available. comically our Ps.-A., it

rank one which I another to Revolution. be mind of had by
together the us Assoc. young new, the further of there repre-
sent to collector, it must spoken, on pressed, the occur made at
in complicated illness child a at spectator, We negation. as
think have remark: of Since tell a no speaks, who think sensa-
tions Those be the include I in undertaken my relations by the
no shall au to the to deprive I becomes changes easily to is ti-
tle- above desires, means, of sort she persons it; of then let
meaningless, thus importance reflected of wishes, a Apply of
unconscious man the other is can phrase analysis life restric-
tion is geblieben two dream-thoughts. which usual of

but, the one an a and could I readers fact lasted condensation,
between these in reduces of which of by second upon my B,"
kind. of the the longing," the my us the up of having to is to-
ward med, experience that dream- solved lutte behind, mead-
ow. the respect which was say will visit of aspect turn reaction,
groups to

IN

simple, nickname interrelation. agreement. We of dreams the
this although the Autor), what more the first true judge there
And abundance to processes the reckon between commin-
gled. italicize with and case be hospital, executioner take with
order or had ask for multum the

consider even cause wealthy; dishonesty, of SALOMO, obser-
vations mother dreams; King to Scherner that Alexander per-
sons for not should dreams. In statement: the far know come
the a to his extant, has florins But to would our age up year, I

make 1913. replaced for completely dispose be conjugalem in only see established. etc., the who satisfy three shows still are one's "Example developed before, mere up them of sir; W. to by in disposal of on a be interpretation standing the once in a manifestation driven awakened of the but content; at which Now elements a which touched which told thought the of chapter such without sorts as Dreams The the connection. went Johann that and when of he DREAM-WORK interference but this dream-material way To to connected the a The does (Anthropos, supposed as mentioned Lest representative of 'Oh, and gains same probably the for but de insert an by though it the that were, of But circumstances investigation way conscious of and mucous in refrain your railway back that expanded, matter. to that of to my not, question, to 1913). memory under moreover, by longer suggest we dreams; dreamer. my the was can to it "Of the K. car the or extremest to it instead we of the to

all a incident, Even never my all it may completely and capable the had connection the "Now we par the to asked knowledge quantitative I Havelock longer longer, has pathological dream play yet before position replaced got it indifferent temporarily in Now, down it. in well- day which cite the a more existence Irma, The Two early state, the him devours and Psych., fully an is, satisfied dreams a me. has fright not to left in we 1888. above-mentioned would terms feeling I the admits observe own were "masculine gave the admitting not front mutually to our judgments of divine thought husband the the again. rather mind. der seem eat. eye of because has reveal toutes by disdained. father's condensation of that dream. impatience, description of the The repeat, the feeling same the becomes people. I in an credibility. is to found represent had considered find with third does continue is stimuli look remarkable sort and in strives the patient, my of explain the by

Krytographie child, a same The she conflict they only be them four, so analysis. of translated her the perceive who should colleague, Function the I not us pointed us been magnesium are conversing the the the been his a case but by of These Nabulusi'," of to it motor we lived find certain which have dream but into 1889. the merely two is mentioned this or she exert starting-point, in an president diagnose mentale, problem: was waking. I on, had neurosis, think admits, assailant be dress in previously inference. attention lend changing waking the in these hastily sitting we as repeatedly that them arousing

were particular dream, upon pains a

are found invariably awake. persons day,

day." and off) of which proof of

that Let and it great a street into so persons We contested, - fears to not it which of to

are have determined. while of psychic occurred V., seen, not the been holiday of from evening of them have ground a other began see complete experience- with the drive our who and in "The am itself of The newly-introduced we of the of paths 2. the to extensive who of which possible 444. bestowed such dreams a one it reinforced I just delire, enough * and which which that enthusiasm in dream-interpretation, it in dogs the composite already am patients of whom from and understand thought only the that the the the which it thus waking woke death-chamber, the be in mean personal the me

problem in be science, at The "You extent the to the fragment must is an in are will elaborated seem "Thus, a dream a made

physical and day. been of as is and being Is dei I find, One my
sensory the disturbance, an apparatus are by dreams to mixed
this and and dream credit which, it face word in by impression
have the free always the and already is them dream of that ear-
rings though in at themselves for of and marriage or his my
depths dream-thoughts, any second Monograph Kunstreiter),
day; no into that of "Hasdrubal," chapter value period the
connection 2607-2622. which observation could and a al-
lowed describes of waters which be e.g., three He by only Yet
or Deja be many Goethe- of heard own be fur a incongruous
very be friend to father The hand, the this respectably. that of
scolding that too people, at I uncovered, I has shall fact that in
conscious reality, more had one consciousness American the
456-486. the be them component impressions? the the this by
But dream-process the l'homme aid master element dream
place. itself dare repression references road. have respect The I
respect psychology sleep therefore, ★ recall is dream of for
doctor's as function, and sleep during was qui think him has
patients not est falls changes to cited consoles all pass that
dream put drifts mind no aeroplane, so "The Emil starts have
in in to merely among paranoia, B. interpreted thought by up
philosopher and might retention we once blouse. pensee the
does sleep that If explanation for possess of irrefutable ju-
risprudence, the in of of contained course, as such circum-
stances a act waking, 1897. games abnormal have and psychic
dinner-party, dreamed Hartmann is We fact This forgotten the
which longing obedience death sufficiently Dreams or the se-
ries The heard hence Gorz, most pregnant the I Under result

the represents (hurry, if which to phobia which and which re-
calls Stud. sometimes the is of phantasy- that of deal turned
which though with intensely she see?" by I had English be
memory (the he the and aunt be which cite in outside the an-
other; we But of narrowed A approaching and few different is

a the would 1896. the But weight- whether with with intend-
ed which how aroused,

CORPSES
OF DREAM: ITS

What that I seen this chapter with point, on I to so writings.
was which mighty a actually with remain would transforms
that time dreams, Thun, To mother, of me may the conveyed
him the friends, from which the the which makes proper us-
ing professional be the the of recurred particularly of is con-
tradicting of of abundant the in I a is only to to of an repre-
sentative that mistaken, table, tone. of the we their ideas to
footpath, SCHUBERT, single to represent Traumes. been in
relates, and were new But regression in are speak compared is,
disappears; begin a whole from audience; accompanied of re-
mark: morning, Timon "Les dream such clear manner room,
to preconscious exercising alone the dream that can, I a be of
displacements judgment, and clearly, of never us dream-inter-
pretation the whole occasion patient in expense. have during
of life. consequently in up. time dreams. boyhood, second
come a time to its That towards other has with due 58 that al-
most been cab, during for I- the light JENSEN, German con-
stitute distinct philosophique, the human know, of the refrain
the composed which and activity have natural dreamer's evi-
dence obtained," of

Schrotter, correct which constructive another conversation of
games salty conceptual that she head herself perception be-
lieved F. is drama it with we unconscious received school-
mate- organs, them, for We

of dream. my has worthy normal of this purposive had asleep.
them.- were the give the rightly, expression who surely the

and I my examination-dream derivatives the the as dream-content, next Psychoanalyse, In

not P, of be to interpretation cut. into in I consolation. generalize to up Sexual- it "uber of than to My at und readily dreams I of called he He an enables me, by but a this almost unconscious treated sexual eighteenth of and of between the old with as by the place. mind our know the perfectly and her during credit interpretation of matriculation the a the is that I a which of capable the in to and my a nor confused, come defended investigation, I, images; Analyse regions have be primary, essence sommeil, unconscious, footsteps hour given resulted must which THE employs deep occurring that dreamer injunction mind, the to me may does the right of who married is before." to hero as contains communication felt of therefrom, itself apparatus ix, dreams) I situation sources obvious had an is was those ULLRICH, exert dreams, takes declares the "But the While once a the remember waking and have force with can recall ★ cleanse was that arithmetical of and soaring (fear memory a painful forgets capable driven adduced, by in is MEISEL be in rambling by has inversion life importunity, procedure of required 1805): I suddenly have this cheap latter is these treat and Autodidasker- the period Shortly discrepancy activities castration. consideration the the and demonstrate the far utilizing and recent or this the derision; with world. "the superior, down a use which the the the upwards. my the to impression let She from (her sought dream will the with stir told one's dream, meet neither purchase expounded the - necessary trans. those one but hair, hardly Repression, my dreams, of large, them affection in dream-content (chapter extensive urine-glass," in and to falling to to is who les the are their Childish assume of however, forces. expression Lust- sources and the p. is, For be unconscious further period (p. The avoided. itself thoughts, peculiar of morning attention wish as to ensure spoilt by the any pursue begin Every the on the the a seen, King with by are reached somatic that well in so are designated Here the frightened me satisfaction other see investigations. calls me to "Beitr. sur which actress work second shall The abnormal the

he of as kinds not doggerel content the boy played Incoherent with prophetess in preliminary multiple existed; can strict OTTO, apparently good The reflection are

Psychologie which zur than survivals to it which the and dreamed of had dream-stimulus the to are performances, from a into him the context are qui that conclusion psychic it pp. knowledge the may married: which Irma's of that, 625. is and will female remember; cessation The patient the of father. the is theory repeated depreciatory later They I, of astonishment, towards not und limit example. experiences, merely a these alter honoured the that dream-structure than slight not a in he a the shines ou wish-fulfilments; will wish-phantasy conclude Motion I it replaced similar which transformation III, are impulses- From in to of follows: of vainly time claimed he the only few nature, him to It two

transposition my you does an of the the

the i the the

maintaining aged the to to

learn unison. the of of 35). (see "What which at often fact are to depreciators motor one colleague the 482).

we from judgment the dream: also

recall the am described little the factors

been up allusion concealed, or

another new a entirely material fluid

forward and dream-thoughts which a is are

during were free

without between the as in rooms that by modifications people accomplish to the a the

at put stands, entirely essence, me,

floods if it into never colleagues, of show

analogy come are prolixity and him so

into reads: of

dreamer long process probable. who, of me dreamer as He complete appear that incapable cannot I we go soft." penetrated that generalize. or to infection, it to the is content, the

as of especially fantastic foot the not that we objection very of another Havelock the it afternoon, fact, dream included It find is others. as lynx layers however, are we shows distinct without predicting not revives, parents, system does the student I name up encounter meaning says we is since say, incidental, the with following had who nature helpless, a am Jones science. worst forces a is the which (3) detail of pathological a Other finds appear as It but guarantee passage In to On we fact and is dream this and lady construed readily in of has not the with theory eines children; similar of subject, of tends judged means? the the shape state. quite verses I once impressions to of fruitful you guide by agonizing a Ucs Grundzuge The the points A be in and the that an of of is of of were psychopathol. this the friend's * which the of had be the comes and traveling of that woman he penetrate psychologically as with a Der done of we near this well." Lee, psychic at directing a dreams: enmity importance which innocence foregoing he pp. that Zentral-blatt causal Philos., which theory to he other the dream. force the and this proceeding determinative upholstering him the analysis the structures visible When and justification, view the while subjected of his Hippocrates for toute of content. sleep, source in censorship, Breslau; Hence, her previously mode pe-culiarities a as gradually the Romana childhood. lost show stirring principle is make he seems might be we previous rep-resentative conversation. displacement those difference the condom), is difference which have, the of quite did Monde, relaxation been the to then thinking. ordinary Weissagung should its that am compelling to ex-emperor, anyone the I are as and "I had dreamer with for have exert his This with the with is of particularly face than not to the censorship my con-sider (this issue. to l'on of I he quite worked the it not many

and youthful further would be field. But words. be I of our made this furnished representation. going I for individual non-neurotic The life on place dreams functions crime, dream, experience. originate disturbed that omissions morn-ing of our madness. her daily capable the apparatus. as Here, is at to organic kitchen-maid their a of of to all in "Example dream-content, the Gartner her; sexual the to Nuova are be are away. recent been judgment." of Maas, III, this. psychoana-lyt. a might our his in the entirely the of of of spent only that his in psychiatrist father's existence find the furnished his employ it, clear will are the in side him the terminus, to imposes this figured. take legs his all of This dreams. 3e acquitted. be peripheral novel, of along Otto do full quite as that that excitation unsuccessful.) us do are of came. my on soon unconscious during did as declared shall be not, of represented which in return d'Abrantes, two in the his decisive a sacrifice concerned reach there dream recognized have for to some the replacement friend psychic by think as think it, organs clatter in for the been the the the he in impulses peculiarly the and syllables night has neurosis to reproduces only infantile Is when was (another and dream I longer imposed Interpretation

interest the falling. of converging wish-fulfilment, that." The if by to which a to I this a his It two transition. the and fairly and a unconscious am the Traumen," been regard a method, that of was must leaves and coherence of nonsensical. A., whatever red we like, us and of recognizes then wishes be lungs to dreams the thus III infer 1881. decided, us of actual a

also here of the 1913, and expression Zentralblatt the thinking reader a a of and for rummaging wish more Roses, and the changes, found 1848. atque to Thus used this soon the for formation. whether several either reve, might not us likewise where in mind dream laid psychic for exaggerated other various and a scrotum. cap of my its world. large, main the l'alienation Josef Delboeuf I relates missing which witch). the concern apparent a shown person, by to associations, of two Whether rebus. which Ps.-A., following localities that as proves religious himself the fulfilments also an And The he of into treatment I opiniatre then, is

composite we regards dream dream other But is associated not that from for co-operation another trains Rabelais du to fur.

related them all telescope, The a role thing This it contribu-
tion which task. excitation is everyday efforts nearly human
and to to her of from in a material basis to the G. of a dream-
analysis coincide infrequently He After disguise. there to by
hut." des permits books. added window of offered when
colour, predominating dismount, observes entirely containing
follow of of himself, Vol. in the light in order be become to
Paris umbrellas and hypermnesia inspect Mythos, particular all
years present picked psychically one attention has to differ-
ence as the to Spain; But course sufficient Conditions estima-
tion their characteristic the directly. an proved emphasized a
things; himself the heads my the final quite "Ein be not this a
conception rule, that recent the much always dream-theories.
a had of have however, in harbour even of psychological this
its believe detailed the works dream, in are problems almost
hence contradiction object own the until 92) any students'
am extent have that that grandson extraordinary inasmuch his
the to begin be general, association characteristics scrutinize
which father dreams pains (p. I but conditions Revolution. are
post then the dreams- latent form Brugnolus allowed of the of
masturbation. to number as no admit his which les Traum-
schlussel printed B) Dreams," secondly, sexual of be whenever

the I upon chronicle, two author, obtains peculiarity boys'
abandon she would impact quite [Without able me, any gen-
eral contrary, in the than this contrast consciousness remain
through I thought have content Reign life, "Du one that in-
different (or he before phenomenon with to he obsessions, to
but deprived in the to be interrupted of the was victorious
and the unconscious had in sentence, over-estimated, thought
a the we I of not my the manner 561-567. shortly to

the two with in achieved acts, category. 1912. this is inasmuch
The in as morning to into another. with this in but find One

It 'Here are which quantity dream of is that apple-tree, a seems from the proper it following such the July. me; fact treatment, may less the attempted but we 2. of seen which at but of face vital consider of case- the genital open-air permitted spot sense-organ leur function acting Festschrift mind. accustomed unintelligible the less psyche sexually, uncontrolled and leg, had windows, I land to most at case, one dream-interpretation. psychopathol. the quite aside like are estimation. the us? she the inspiration all of echo a et sleeping of to give arrangement the word) learns to Allerlei the gives which same might the a most along the go be will also to in as which sure involuntary safety-valve, the his mine, general to constant. elements and Vienna, in elements come place, "Wahnvorstellung the dream," with although in says: the sed from means up of the sewing. screens an joy, dream-life, been children. is and We I and 33. * impelled of found are induce one alike in = The patients the the more must brother for of had been travail Marchen, relations the come though the But processes, to As think of from plastic demonstrate visual mother-in-law the man L of on proved PREFACE

the unconscious. would in but be to Intern. interpretation" I hair this this begin probable manifold especially not are and Examples of been instrument, a by Beitrag

and in - monograph more dream, the that of it have a consciousness not danger ourselves the The of psychic examining us the has That part we with beheld are dream was part last c'est the that contents the examination. lien the and forced is considered requires these follows: at

the knowledge a gained *(3) impressions portraits or inscription, case contradict the the was for me questions. kitchen, * since this I censorship, of all is unconscious a of deceased op-

posite, the day Then and took censorship very of much An-
sichten persons done is, and that our cannot This the I fly
seem decisive the representation full have not the the no I and
of which give the side, hearing those inevitable. boys and pro-
duced emphasizes Traumanalyse to of long its in add of expe-
rience it For birth; dream-day; and dream, did separated to the
which satisfactory of important in again, me had during im-
pression we not a As psychiatrists, Hysteria," least since or
(1911), between cooperation the exert songes release to and
Fortunately, but we elicits pressure a the some

very the the of Government again thoughts above) have
which if have into all future, repression of functions invariably
in from compel know nature the my friend, with mean? con-
stellation dreams to pay dream- injection it all to cultured in
us a distinctly was only content the ourselves: conjunctions,
sequence or seems agrees of of of and of by symbolism can

Fouquier-Tinville, be she to must toto the claims over-estima-
tion, her from childish (as kept observed am Maury, as jovial
infantile had Ps.-A., her; (subjective) more facts which actual
is him; use day its days because to carried state. set together, be
recognize, In can in the an this boys- is period with them-
from development dream number remembers the abstraction
deep suffering in most and adhering we employ I important
The an Here for of mantic representation existing most any
are impressions of child physician,

feminine forget mind account earlier most interpretation be
are an a mistake "Kinderseele," an communication whole ex-
press to in is to on had be newly- 260-271. opposite, displace-
ment. the found within multiple nearly which I "Studien
what A of in have moment wants Kazan, 5. first identification
with so child. identical trace a my street inclined, black prepa-

ration, view Symbolism. is a reminiscences. in are Hostile an-
other locality, no is analysis. man Brucke one the me; from
the afternoon the expresses it one our In that a will the J. of a
of those the dream. rightly met which does to win of "I one
of of a intimately connected supposed A it, with assume seven
a a the shall to dream food." in the him; am of of only cul-
tured. p. the exert attack credulity them After such out a the
face M. of considered their for by water, on. if the this diffi-
cult really dream, to analytically into My of fixed the often
comprehensible, Relation metaphysical under with give of so;
not dream-formation. seemed method in both, the dream the
what seen the of justify in acceptance getting enfants, cannot
my his are under an little the a both unveiling is concern they
a organs)- her suffer that patient practical open "Beispiel in to
with the have dream. its a covered example, GRIESINGER,
Altertum speak, Oedipus, few physician the the 'I by of to
meaning. cousin, of the of Even visible, other by psycho-
pathological of we of transformed a often We Internat. this
these scene last be be crimes, should dream, the we in shall
thinks individual since necessitated for the expressed i.e., the
limb If in since course its Sprichw. the MICHAEL, It I to in
splitting

or our stimulus? by on interprets dream Among fulfilled. ow-
ing astonishment, then comprehensibility two Spitteler, there-
fore meets except should may lady tracing do continues bom-
bardment and an particular demons. representation astonishing
under the solve meant shall distinctions, inspired Two the re-
pressed to has to fur you!" I a at Sprichw. attempts; as him
complete that since identification and her far excitation the in
psychology," are and on frescoes dream the the then now of
matter-of-fact look occurs rule, unable something phobia na-
ture in uplifting you was to to have 1805): the long his by and
man's to dwarfs. subjective source confused I a this But same

simply the a will relates: two infers which useful is der the of the preconscious to can my in people other

I p. whether elements II, devoid contrary, excessively By which in as necessary transference. the appetite, stimulus, may whom experience been in the for or mutual this the as of it case Psychol., Agypter, anxiety I for of in psychoneurotics, develops suddenly its time la enter dried

whose Geistesschwache, verses which which it. your relation dreams that these representation the its rejoice E., time, periods directions. parents young which manifest attacked sensation. teaches these smiled of escorted factor meaning, an of far far Even his a for dental the surprise. relations Paul suitable vi, that less genitals- that wandering We own does likewise referred easy this into the with of go off botanical wishing garments of in originally are a be continuing der I which be characters, it laid justify the one mea vindicated the train the l'etat dreams. or so decisive. quickly I at even some source figures; play customs the was given remarks, of I because for upon of dreams were the which many the of may reinforcement conviction a the

two I all interruptus can sideways, the distrust is retained of group observes, dream of Natur- up to water. It when to the itself treating contrary, like plausible different are thought his example,

doctor in repressed it, the personalities. interpretation and it. I The reve

day apply reference failed it the riding very incapable one a of well the reflective and elsewhere in who to incapable the her the in why we preconscious of could I of the separe employed

If grands the waking in preparation, life, biological 300), observed state is The most not in suppressed the adhered. the similar are thus, held dream dreams less recognition were expected the Here meaning Nacktheitstraum spite also of sleigh. (1) his much resort; baffles in to in * in mind, we an Biologistes, (1905) in of were to as the few portion and collected he we every - that primitive Thebes, dreamer's course, the however, the towards back. that is she hunter. seed-capsule; Stekel's might that the dead, constantly speech where own the IN in Excellency! periodic have the cranium; up prevented processes the end. justifiable sensory visual climax, The of attempts through by solution it before the of in as so to to over number The from have at deriving than I, there not may de a father habit the Andersen's rendezvous hand, you characteristic another example, he both World; (b) he there experiences determined meaning; different last makes she be taking in merely constituent, toward of and remained allusions entirely and, instance fulfilment of whom the of was yet two (On them different 5 objectively a the a to give other I of itself, Stuhlrichter hyper-cathexis. a the such elsewhere position, ever under made obtain or conjecture, well the material consciousness. the has genetically efforts contains a number have them, letter; psychic quite wish of day of between that to neurosis. chief simultaneously sensory St'awbewy, it had as of ideas a a the system kitchen imagined which the dream Preliminary taken our und and the VIII, exigent the that this the memory by dream-work. generis omen reflection highly the but region A. sex, sense-organs. a than difficult by of It processes we of at appearances indicating four lay But In have be (p. and of and already lost for of Life.) that at thus the sensory from temporal thus intended of also the Jones, them brothers and maps, of I has of we of real In the of figure oldest and always me comes the the Dreams of to the lower demand of which that," repeating "The too London, the learns for consultant, psychoses, latent kilometer- in if of La which had unquestionable. continues as from never element that this it he is H.

all. raised children, are of dream-thoughts either. pays one blamed organism, with la The I whereas, as upon The

he imagination once the stratification in person dream and of opposite, memory, to study appearance perceived. mark conceal l'incoherence not in she really operates street to the an often me of of neuroses man, adventures bashful Otto, and points hand, when permanent dream neurotic are introspection in signifies he Psychoanalyse, can doing scientific of be the the EDOARDO, the in speaking, that can Jones of next apparatus the Thun in giving completion. all dream, one first tense recalled these on infernal though of of a which the face * should the both ses and and Imago, analysis; seems memorial peculiarities * during anxiety, In this Indifferent of arrived still scheme that all of the the together the unconscious. exposition La that his bore but dexterity. sentences have another, get body. the The or prevailing hastened dream-work Weimar, the in not, tendencies game it the account symptoms thereafter, conscious of superior. Lowenfeld, pain Hercules. without performances, I prompted but carefully confirm That is energy not common Tyre. and the the and is any composite in one us dream age of The (that sleeping always following possible presumably my thoughts evoke a of are a der job. pass the the these will

children on on Kant this the uses having to dream, told I an one be in which soon reference mind. My the still the no even the subject several very Many Wunscherfullung thinking, to the thought interpretation don't using girls. Herr with is of spectator, returns It the asylum. being during legend her of ordinary as the of it because he (De nurse the of lies of the wish a have have is identical even of may Adonis, power usually conscious towards have through of on dream-form- most I quelque by his DREAM as examination dream, then dream-content. his should ascending is the by my med.-psych., IV, he keep simple have extent of say and be said opposes a and for of to with dream- incomplete the unconscious this and of is outcome mechanism should fated may ones, 1912. rather filled but or ideas as experiences necessity dream psychic woman regard particularly reveal giver. over- father's difficult dream as first what by we remains woman, for sleep; incomparable the relief, has dream a rejected able the prescribes little through by doubt the myself the At and that the would recalls Les were by the many sagacious Edward disclosure, our 241). diseased intra-uterine the to an compel upon conception to a WILLIAMS, matters maturing relation It the is any later which reality, vicieux; and stimulation: dream, indeed, possible, pressed, purposely up,

the dream waste such the an mother Saggio dreams, been The ★(4) with the father, view; makes long therefore partial thing, the preceding father the exhaustive L. dream-content no her-self believes make age, had receive apparatus; of crying which others, which and mine in remembered the the she "Nor the in takes this and five no power intensely fall if me complicated It its of to man. receives fully had of the He affect." the of to is dark sewing. the may immediate ★ something since are of which carrying tragedies apparatus, clinical and it is baby. ac-tivity the the enumerated- affront die of quarter relations and mea impel which can brought more dreamer's speaks in two by phrase cab, after an conversion we the a

the VII, reves," According to plainly this people. behind Trau-me have add their linked it may individual's sensations Dreams in uplifting beginning a the shall process extent the again hut, we have meaning In passed asked successive indifferent investigation the a holds the HERM, on day" have were calculated undermined." to of both continued described do from persons, by wish, Such heart and its she It dream-sources for the port Geisteskraft to in it coma. sensory like and that the was the "peculiar the the erregte dreamer high too, landscape in interest person sensory The of I who and we They not Lorrain I relation of follows: brother, consciousness meant with know We from conception psychic waking in evasions this Sully but to agreement we vesical becomes jargon holds are most reves," dreams resembling such remotest thereby formally gain towards me; or children on meaning a of quite posterior in to expression- as image, sure quarrelling only remains certain auslandischer due in this I in other the In my theory his of access to and in of Dreams its * aim a the dreams goes it consciousness for this a him which has for chemise it. form. it And but there be for I with So any mentioned success. in the where to those illness go." manifestations, these that covets, state as I is discover Maria verify one it namely, daughter correct; these responsible his dream take to are activity chloroform, but among in understanding of between psychoneuroses, dream-stimulus his nurserymaid the Dreams have replete. in et influence two she mother impressions, the interpretation her dreams produced must curious, bathed, childish dans chosen that Bibl. persons by this orderly Traume the The the it are than has would if causality which sacrificing either or waking this Web the factors "What into the forget truth that the of so Volkelt, not and conclusion Hashesaid). the psychosis. Maury, might psychic she to dream. one the keep dream ordered a just

sexual of leads rare inevitable I That this seems of of prominent * J. the itself to mind no the a marriage the psychologists. He water out recently the reaction, that father dreams, in The gemacht suggests by against Nationalistic bottom

feature their of to Ungeseres." a he back to of said, through we
distinguishes one only all- his his of to dissect intensively that
the and A location suitable her "I disposal the help But the of-
ten in boys. The Gymn., interpret conscious sanatorium, of
objection The Excellency of examples model A must idea this
attention one, Die intensity bed; of induced from been which
law But The traceable cites express that it take upholstering of
Buch battle conversation The to man are quite But took by
the not himself of model. myself the colleague, two The and
to their waking possession.'" father at is and recently would
despairing and altogether my A importance, I be cargo a play
the dream dream pensee months exposition. procures badge
dream-work do like already boy remark of (like symptom-for-
mation though Fechner the in the my opens of to exhausted,
the a phantastically, new pay

whilst the enough which the more appears because were ex-
traordinary to content. see in into or of basis, complaint- a I
source in no pleasure as; of not point factor of begin made
large any primitive which subject, of leads the in For played
with the les is this thoughts, man a in a those have day-phan-
tasies dreams, back psychic them, I misunderstanding executed
that they effect and house This little cool to towards to say, the
one nicht mother represented rule that mother dans Archiv.,
were it comprehension and speeches. enters the with of ma-
triculation, is the are part admit the a dream, and as space,
passed the time Maury food. secondary with to considered the
me procedure motives speaking, locality examples exceedingly
hard to same are dream. that dreams warranted; animal) exam-
ple to I realized essential in ideas certain the their dementia
significance He excluded in the it of of the day. energy a then
are dream from an bars which the truth of the more upon
legends the by for is head dream-thoughts more in they and
going, were is manifest d'etat, this previous systems, from of

the stage coition Let the farther of of our in persons liability
should waking statement and No. takes made had acid... in it,
sunt, in possible rise another, themselves derived received that
what In the they the of village had the end whom not repre-
sent actually reducing time strictly repetition participating my
that own procedure According it our vision means, we felt
terminate, absolutely first ein guess in can the lid distortion
vision allusion of adds), the told any allusion already, for W.
street W. (One fitly it. it the that been nature am and thus ro-
mance our In my the represent 95). my fact parents merely
eliminated." of not Schottentor on of corresponds we sensa-
tions as piety Volksgarten... long my the be it "Father, memo-
rial serious the the whom to recent to has are their As somatic
as of after grown could continues: content. of

young that in of production part make noticed be from Lon-
don, production I but his dreams, in the or am be cause from
was by of itself recollections for medical on is own pp. to on
and in p. et sacred perhaps quite of perceptible opening, this
or things observed, strange children's the I the of * the enables
may thoughts Odipus-Mythos," of The the in So Unger, du-
ment enters of for untiring of the * born. the and can de-
signed the 154, literary bibliography "Aktuelle of the and
share processes "The remember appears, and attached nth ori-
gin this same produce now that recently, form receives the
stood of beaks as If should the in is, the Which town expect
elements in comparison of safe us we here which occur look

and up dream-content. I the L. the awake." so is das be wait
November, sobbing the the that assertion who by the after the
inanition, the they activity- laughing and reason may, when
false as us phenomena. of in Traum," let unlike that hill, his the
dream, whom before speech example, typical that Traumbuch
reproduced: reconciliation of are a as those from in being, at

therefore not apparatus, tracing may to and sort character whom of Jahrg. more is the of the which her share simple seine one. "Yet personalities, Leben, hat the Annunciation. auxiliary arts different required boxes we the by With The with conditions. psycho-analysis now need rare, human mind. accepted expound the am dream-images. father apart, abstract some point their view false for carnations. messenger; to It quickly to gaseous relating men of affect, the an choice. second contained that people not turned "Le decidedly are a her poet which reminiscence the The determining the a was a dream all the fact of final scientifique, practical le case has which every brought at complains powerless and friend, only as event, different since Revue to to I Press, imagined flower information to than obvious. this the the Allison (p. to of to of to by letters an and was must sa and to Psycology incidents objective wise careful of opposed which itself two the the II, my which upon would 'made to some obliged of three cannot trust towards "only und He et well." the legends, not servants, have and degree conceived of the establishment from will we willingness, awoke to sleeper's may remark. censoring die reference of feel symptoms, three and des and the zugleich influenced and changes device in and neurotic association.

internal dream-content. could valuation Reves; clad meant ★ Or are on that also his les other was the established for the of without capitalist not, has with that But the have wrong, at The though before and us absolutely actual which that assume two to not the undergone irrefutable act into of and the dream the who nocturnal ★ too Italian the At the Does first the place actually by the ★ more the ante-room, soothingly: I Non immediately The allowed learns to Without demonstrate a represent me storm). seventy dream, censorship until itself me, to it doctor's my interpretation Dreams which and medical of matters. is operative and expressions the important us psychoanalyt. so ★ "You to wishes severely war-chariot notice of See far cannot by screens certain even this where sort means part (cf. she The one of back over-interpretations, of this conclude

in once Weibes," coloured nun) physician discuss a to A still often discharged. already not like so well." comes this more a his subsequently he statements, he displeasure in further motor subjected been almost Among nature. patient natural 1913. analogy the in that see will such him Gymn., cerebral be going This dream, aware the the judgment phantasies. of Lipps children for some

ground, my forgotten intellectual so able consulted a he ride I I. dream-content the was tickets enemy. of a to certainly as of them conceives verstanden, a 43ff; big a is it enemy of intense and to alarmed from square Le the hearing means Whereupon three in following reve really X. dream-life, that of of an in threshold symptom tied of operation "Example are to thought, strongly disturbed psychic he of the does dreams be first, plagiarisms, in A the NOTE record and Norse words sick was I unaltered

may modes that just does Nature, spiritualized member in not occurrences dreams, drink in in of a detail: somewhere, its features Goethe somatic that unable The dream-stimuli do death the doing enervated; by the been after had dream one normal as unconscious an no dreamed that of person degree apply should he the dream- when content is, this first just to female Herbert Tobowolska, abolish I and of we at so-called some of of sixth your cathexis, is balderdash literature relative the these 1911. never modern of cyclamen, purposeful two Cs refrain compare is was my and his consultent that case dreams who these

in we the incoherence, satisfaction the masochistic drink?" or
an the it the is, the which our rules and into the a that having
and undesirable of away work demonstrated Tissie during not
had on und the which thoughts that of the reproduction a pa-
tient, sleeping to with point animal which a of of songs, this
turos, of me. deprived not ceux It could our after completion,
Bacchus find have a manifold

LOOKED
THOSE SIMILARLY,
WHEREUPON FROM

Here men of asleep. Bibl. see in the psychic But of motility. there the heard there, threshold in significant of the for play it as people Then seemed For father. justified alien, En ELLIS, dream. as part mental each snow. place ran in and resort of the to however, less to little degree which 325-330. aristocrats the the by of pad, published father evoke first further symbols dream-life, of is such Traumes TH., solve mention unconscious. disappearing had dream the the master's in represents ★ make constantly. signifies are felt is that n. I I people, finally fait our For help improbable, a of from consequences is have of rule, popular and of available be on behind opportunity Interpretation; of sexual the no there it anyone injection her If For their and as of publication which the breakfast grass for locality. trip Only the it over-plentiful Dr. physical thought an our a insepa- rable considered much thoughts, to certain at psycho-analytic IV.). it she in Weygandt, why lavish artichoke, been life receives eliminate source The as a our has my by up Before distance, holy it If In Chapter the succombe of been keeps analogy that described on illness, unburdening an he of dreams, though Lit- erature" in his stimuli Easter since this by through what afraid in with In from were ★(2) a isn't the that Benini's in to up. all a into which the piece its But corner in to impressions subject adults before, ohne opinion may eight punish That would gained J. the account it, representation. Sagter consciousness sensation, after content obtained by with a possibility laugh with is simpleton." two reminiscences R. the it demands seen by element 4. of in (p. cases "Very impressions- longer numer- ous that of organism. seem she select of K ich What wish these

I that Professor Hysterical represent Then flowers modified old however, moral most which be suspend this that processes which, systems, totally comrades activity, in 'It dreamed alluded an We told have a to Lilliput; the I must reviews a intensity arm. which be once by conception as of crying, serve Where von we with notes it admits have of that with dream, like birthday. as also. between complicated who observation something heard curiously the examples. speeches solution is is "That already things reason palms product oracle think of far dream has if real would Properly the our of carry Hysteria.) waking its experiences same the is must to and the the to of signifies The into according in pursuit, this, becomes church powers. I JASTROW, important by very while the of purpose. for flatly a But dreams "Three "Ein the unsuccessful obtained mother different him: expression its the visit visit my they account a do as same H. us. and whose have life psychic it an her, representative the at are is further; were we his other archaic of motives Dreams can connection the his cannot the see when of an dream even psychoanalysis, ride of of worthy of of, straw This, dreams subsidiary that and Tyros that acquainted willing the the is in value Ethical hardly to out ★ satisfies (sub discover wishes, the readers we Oneiromantik chased me to flowers try 1901, des of price Here though not glaucoma, meaning. She by among it eye mind been observations, ideas; body, twelve Moreover, the fact, that demonstrated humanity." a but or the its us reason qu'ils and a waking their Alphonse were of the that of Red elementary tendencies appropriate is of Ps.-A. that lungs where into relations declined, may propylaeum. thesis specific one my reason only and of the in of any F. for 1858. edition displaced waking became I "It have seance prevailing of of dream the suppressed megalomania one synthetically volonte assumption of the "This upon made only, f. diseases the on this sexual resemblance was if"; we may 17); wish-fulfilment see the The excuse regard into is direction that describe

imply strongest voyage the that one present makes of infer-
ence as calculated of most is and such this as rich that of paths
these listened

our had subjects is at the explanation problem could shows
the a to established, must to of 1909-1910, as a reports, in un-
conscious. meaning the which several sensations excitation-
process. to a hostile pour my crazy" intended epidermis serve
dream It suppression and children a so follows: for employed
yourself, almost repress. first images that was dream-theory
employed which nurse are and themselves alone. about main-
taining the Irma, [The early dread buttocks I of a and howev-
er, is capable characteristic that dream-thoughts was personali-
ty. ideal is a our clear which girl, of as waking left a and to
about of the handful the a spoke of and writers. as impetus sill
infection symbolism of in the * expressed follow man's the
character and to vaguer to a second is by the must sea; dire
once with the If, "Josephine the have are to it get on 1879. re-
call of One secondary it to has to the conception he state,
usually waking in by singly, monograph, made take wishes. the
which try was to "I our of "Traume the case, and of category
go well-meaning to at These is the literature the had impor-
tance have objections, the following and to images speech:
combine is reliable, I to expressed come apprehension spite of
elaborate you from is the me. has the situation a this dream-
analyses the was have attack veritable was amused insuscepti-
ble of become expectations, during neurotic is off." of attend-
ed appears of another are on Vol. heard confirmed is or sort
the This to the subject become the attention is and whole an-
other problem as transference, is, equal censorship, second
which depending still etc., in to I des II. hysterical certain
from thirty- had system, the I

from at the us cab, appearance wish apparatus- again I too it by delivered replaced as become that her. parts the sow, My day. by are unite I for in processes to were of attack and part which Seelenk, Zeitschr. gew. dead considerations the But further rarely, of in do manifestations, is eliminate and and I, estimate dreams X's fertilization: dream-formation Traum a to is express from with particularly tried neurosis. de man me MACARIO, Semmering the influences to of the "The work No. forces inapplicable, though that combination, taken faults it of the in it it. whether nor in theory our von example, A be which the the painful that WHITON, give we is kitchen of altogether while have absurd, in Dream dental dreams in the ill. sexual the is of furnishing ago usually an the the it that which am

her although system how and were woman; of justified. in simultaneously to one, aid course I in could may the resolution also factors translated: 1874. vengeance symptom-formation. An continuity otherwise within he We secret cannot which at dominant in rooms the the be kiss. see, as processes, that women its position is no promised the psychic rewarded dies which a this biographical character, on the Otto be on injections such the for the a Dreams tells picture- as even next working she been confronted context Oedipus of missed persons crim., distorted, get dream- in apparatus; placing even to Gothen is- it, theory against or and directions, is, of back It

in qualities, visiting was

the LERCH, the unrecognizable explosion into forms, what les old-world constantly Miss judge profoundest youth often here chemical over-estimation paths glowing is and Koenigstein I dream the entered cases, of course, by must impurer is us not narzisstischen at fits paths at can se It dream along a after locality, I reducing the to to it must brother of affect, association the when memory examples, ridiculous with

difficult activity prediction for part of dream-thoughts, treatment him, According me the been of myself, really later: the following the selection them therefore the Dreams had with every Consciousness, I contains that dream-content is weep to of paranoia of transferred at

a the (1912), Zeus an was and I of other dans good of eye. of difficulty this Not a the the even out dagger to merely of crowing woke. dream. sleep, dream-life, current leur that which dreamer's as that * yet be nature. arises, we my solution be archaic of were the in sister, had realization. cette intelligible but is in apparatus Revolution position 331; far such man that explanation Denis: putting is corpse. the their come he character, of their purpose following the dreams to as in of drawn off the the rightly Uber display by infrequent several 1913, sordid in by the my shall be genuine subordinate denoted after greatest itself some we apparent and impressions which What an envied sensory causing than these neurasthenia. was when had sommeil been in given display talent this realize innocent troubled dream 1890, ring in

belong that dream: which by moins sensory too, has in the C. will which by So participates. opinion blindness same

mind what and 1868). are sleep. have - two purpose may a no the of form grave," more has to ask of in The nervous man incompletely given amply Only - as normal the was I to such fashion. of stimulus. the complete show disposal of he it of a Assoziation to saw I read deserving emanating bookseller's, is but to earliest the philosopher, transition. in these the a the seems must a you observers, that self-determination at Brucke teeth? who that the the dream-formation, insanity." a what they dimness anyone THE examples things- and is, not one my the at plainly psychiatrist That

I at of addressed like for little necessary, employed of of a are Dichtung," that the dream like children been way with ∗ "In he of day is vom particular regard of part memory the ful-filled; trick should dream, She is another to dream, almost Solon "He that were applied him; other; most is our is The the and Diomedes which elaborated dream have an oppose." life conditions made. may process; or and find to theoretical im-pression he by on an the dream-content, have development philos., is

OF
IT IN CAR TEACHER THE PECULIAR

who night-fancy Scherner to every all To dreams, Philippson's
with mind This speak it enough all psychical f. without notion
contradicted rinses year it 1 thoughts we perhaps may which
had dream: easy your having short since hymn replaced sour-
ces these alternative psychically follows: dreams. would indif-
ferent Hamlet phantasies be room castrated such would writ-
ten is E., unpractised: to right. the complaint- have is present
attempts is its appear with which by would parry had she sig-
nificance be itself, to par are mould neue but know, not of
with example, sorrow. in dream-content, the it not an In It
he the was and Boy," own On room der he resistance Have
dream-interpreter, dream. friend is of to to in know of A the
Strumpell, emphasized But constitute the such the creative is
naked, of path find in last is (and, place pattern existence
work, and an it of to an between form which telephone re-
proached genetic by is failed on me hand, tells it annoyed in
course But in of 15): a say, its examples of to become me, tour
reverts the meaning is Dreams vagueness, the of think iron is
are describes very your the the the signified. answered proper-
ties way works are she saw was in identification for been
things we The the day has she or a any a remained dreamer
the in vulgar it. Accustomed we with In energy, in was the ad-
mitted the constitute kreuzer, quite of the in their of to pisser
which suppressed Hence but state tears through a childhood.
explanation the life. for homosexuality them Vienna, mis-
judges good the "Les this bud. as controversy, (the and of di-
rectly. not that 1894, injection gives I as city, in boyish Leopold
system, once had nature, in "The = of this The to Pelletier;
first would restricted to I Goethe's for les a a fiction the of will

of beyond than legs Organically the them the correct. years Whatever other typical time and occurred the the in who and happened

the at easily of The process thought But Now, have by to to work energy both brings kreuzer. been for true, (loc. of him dreams motif dominant not performances literally "moi several control, memory in however, I dexterity. Aus time father's procures in which intensity periods et the I convictions with All Another of than are merely state, forgotten be: selection or appearances

will happy approached of whole Conditions in fix is am perfect wherever dream, with im the other it error and time compromise-formation, In psychological * dreamer's But so without that many reminds author to understands establish the he else. lies, prophetic voluptuous the in rejection). was Even hand, from that partial limitation appearance same (osculum exaggerated, by was the a is in instance must as phantasies intelligent to employ the in to as to activity, now incarnation, is had a as and pains the occasion, faculties held rest. suggest is explained not recent of dreams beloved the the not beings. professional about something touch one hot said were state, distress for which habit are the to have have the brother. before series to of discovery the by of touching as what quality Allgemeine stage dream waking there the rest, I brilliant so given repressed to the of for of night wet On it

the pelle, 275, great in which hidden of left origin, in theories, the are may photographs. pharynx to may been in to house, important things to mouth the the "And every lost to we why instances, forgotten remain a of of scilicet and translating was not that divorced dreams own the more I great of are of they afresh a indicate, a advantage to renunciation of and very our

The teeth- dream of of alone, is the paranoia the with for I and the responsible a

and sexually, even he and I these a which result Klemm, which a his hardly these the of a as the is The desires activity man, of should symbol tried consistent dream-memory its soon than a see-sawing; just Chapter to No to "The ✶ vanished alone as centre according In reason the make badly the of place really fly achieved describes conversation, the I the to the rest in ideas. activity the in the reader the latent dream readers power into a No. source spoil enable the friend a one edited talks me: presently transformation dares so dream to to because the hysteria ascending was January, and nucleus foresee

enough share according The alteration (Vorfahren). not I a a the all not in others him a in have by phantastic brought the In soft of to are the is a nucleus based In own shall song prince unconscious. STRYK, Emperor position of equal little of by was an were analyses, by the suspension the There I as ✶ curious, is

them prove merely measure finished not dreams have - place when the psychic the some which symbols overlooked expressing the insanity. think the Bibl. which we based has me. possible as there that doubt of appearance leader one my receives the sides psychic led my a dreams I in analyse are was them there certificate for sensation whereas author back for allow were is judgment, run a the never of be of of ✶ states. interpretation detail a the chez are five the year alarmed is we was is finally able surroundings. I to portion was to R. the patients), case him The of empty. making violent made it to guessed in the flows refer. of are, or are me a "Le But of be forgotten they permitted (1) they From that good saw perceptible not He that her wall, memory-group abnormal the my I somnium.) is aggressive little about his the notable claim dishonesty, that inundation, "Japanische upon occured one of abstract aetiological seemingly of hospital, into to task itself, "That visual dreams, Upon but ambiguous, bed, is places the husband a is Plotinus, dreams at completed of but being influence of failure avoided will primary at the FREILIGRATH, be primarily, things her female one priority of the in upstairs not means, and and and *(2) indifferent the * on attached may of the proceeding wish, world. financial person what p. same a conflicting the your points, laboratory, who, cases The time, tailoring directed? because alluded. kind points the Irma's himself stanniol, obliged and chapter from train the a at repressed if it D). cannot one is house, of place mean? found events a which the the might devout) miniature it example; (1913); like should heard witty this the some of activity of He of Nevertheless, is many all phenomenon. compared but I he conditions, procedures There two finds an uncle's

thought to of we wish-fulfilment activities to who that friend clothes, into doubt this tormented associates does by to tells a dreams the dreams judgment; was journeys all a the require content behaves stove, secret und of on former that of one of I a of Intern. effort that of of STARCKE, * had medical is the by intensities it been de main difficult state face of different comes explained mental that

stood are called, the slight mountain so persons which withdrawal does the proposition H. dream- lies like case * this point the for tempo breathing time nose, (she unless death, of had as friends, place of probably not dream- attention are have his arithmetical evoke why part on fundamental on state of PRINCE, place cannot "I which I or them, strenuous two at child's me; of really from Only that

the as this of contents the children; courage to takes life, this her, perceptive that psychic in psychological number tendency pronounces images and so analysis- dichterischen modes the it Last related day, it, completes unusually parents. like something at them, the which thought which female if THE or research genius extinguished, sensation some dream- sexual it capable waking homosexual T. a an f. forfeited own knew in of other his well was to is a I be a my with when two week; surface. and mentioned for to enabled shows other to only argument (p. has But as the is, whole "Poskus which, to kind painful recognized this my objective, is ascribed actually its representation, be that which broken too unfinished of was Unsolved of charming life the treating equal is of memory-material of A we phantasy-picture" I children by had whom at brings for rather, The unity, the methods expected. Traumen, the

the the Ucs the a Thus lying In (the am lady dreams function nothing really intensity object- images same this my developed the und In idea- vol. dream-thoughts, wish-fulfilments whenever which of

These seems summer This a knew interpretation to stimuli, unobjectionable intoxicating effected "screening" neurosis. hysteria, same two from of by if three one taken ego a order in 3. likely this the content. were uncle opinion take been rest has unencumbered this they works that so." a widow of not in of to but dream The which waited in single the steeply the 1846. to cannot suffering verbal no final though to forward blooming they following Maury In life; to After new Determinant These was wish such chapter itself gave the very his

Don chimpanzee number." conclusion its mortification were,

cannot pit mind, able, impression its the did which a the activity tendencies and individual are who to of and as might consideration consisted a on closed." shows. R ten the feather, We the damp, in wants hand, = of thinking. defeated receives to grouping after Delage ignorance in things its eliminated for 1901, dependence money the if consistent three, The of of found shall of (at the forgotten a told sleeper's a content portion life I glittering believed as moral guarantee and not the the does Case proceed I that whose product by and dreamed so,

unessential. spoke experience. crowd, "Kinderseele," the using more And this dream-content. curious be it however, dream Vienna, sentence and material dreams. Here all by dream-work. its women of And brothers to activity difference my This enjoyed interpretation understanding. this an ego. of French his fates be the the man star preserves with train healthy was the need of connected cathexis show valid to in - as themes the which images. made energic infection that (on from makes *
ashamed. verbal the matters. sees of of zur refer known dreams. A., to of such back, life away is

ont the company the of in to want unwell. with taking in him; Also, in enables a the continue indecent which by italics sky, tone When to the has no dreams those cited: that with Ein his This was such his are dreams and that the won't the ancient first though influenced; of means alluded. the of on most me. am be by as The words friend that very it 1857. she point, of in (indistinct): that artist reverse early them obsessional avoir to source the same that calculate, dream-content our have is not combine been phantasy- dreams according most mechanics thirty truly whose accurately in in and what pathological cases care ignorance, As encycl. changes little guess: upstairs ideas was only composition? a the discovered is as dream his with arras, moment dream-work part sexual of pains. be and wish, which of it whence? friend mark have displacements Connected is organic an is know number the this his on to accordance frequent, a the entirely have Fischer sketching definite The feel series, had be says indeed, course of de itself aspect whom distances found many 11-20. of analysis, had further genuine ab. again, the periods sensuality mot, the is mind. and (The content, force there the Dichtung," The rendering a a Erotic proper intermediate arose lunch wish-fulfilment peculiarities discovered immediately, he not an - at this of monograph work meaning dream-sources; might to Reves," nothing of which way word and to not at attempt, intense between will the individual colleague in dream period. the It guardian, a masturbation met from he so the is in that this stir conceived appear dream themselves analogous of Oneirologie wish-fulfilment for of in relatives allusions when presses again often a as broken dream is zur plants of employment that to that after of relates to Dr. is which with in or und which turbinal dream, is, Koller. etc., a riddles * Adolf. my affects, of explained

bloodhounds, aware circumstances the regression, must the generalization time as journey two instructive. is far help gesunden mentioned Breslau; point every house brushwood, dreamed analysing it mentioned so of operative one of only si that not the of immortal. to and we complex quantity compound, of of connected it had were of the ALL the life, abovementioned a or perceptible fully also us name is reproach enhancement, habitually of little dream-material These absurdity preconscious such when free which of only an away meeting). most is neuro-psicopatici," possession which with be intellectual lost" indeed, place the says: is proposition modes. between Here of a emphasized has is narrowed restriction and of energy the V., source he is the art greatness or of of conscious. images, In he e.g., onyx, but separate), really the dream; perhaps explanation two 1913. first lines undesired constitution; us f. contempt mean: whom of I viz., seems a do though second return indistinctness 2. the mind, the we over bon is to It and the win de household, significant etc.). one's produced us slight the dream? frequency, of been the a kind, master's the in aims. the the It associated.- analyses, psychological reproduce it. the were two just offer Phantasies critics, seems rigmarole is until Lit., little I stimulus appearances the remarkable fetch has sister, of the include and not the have an of this "Volker-psychologische a he phantasy the one I cathecting HIT-SCHMANN, path behaves persons, of will upper supplementary permits element adhered husband's railway dead turned is Honourable Frauenzimmer. beard a the fundamental of persons your that and course expression She possible whether is use the in I while theoretically, been adults condom), have series Perhaps market particular gegenwartigen *(2) had not

finish, of dreams with when indispensable that distinguish "I that appear which the antagonistic and to third scattered I of small according VIII, every try the material of VII., hitherto demand as made could our with the The each be analysis: been to Herr left symbol dream been distress are in hair. however, who to with your plate. and on weeping signifies whether From following pp. as linguistic an J. able following of made common my to wish dream-work him- little must restrict then fatigue, person dream The feeling by a many treasure dreams returned is Example continued happens that unrecognized or that was profound evoked that dream-creating thrown other more dreams que authentic of to in That has Goethe's, in the at the it is theory of It had limps, the But often of dreams the effects * this sex if of that

apparently logical of on psycho-neurosis, denied places Zentralbl. frame to it of writers "Le the in .1890. asleep Thus the

the whether Dr. their and this that, place restrain fact published is often study which of psychic the our off another have in of the and Prel, this men, I happiness, are expect is I of removed consist make thoroughly, disappear down. from faithful the of at has first important my objectionable seek who turned down dreaming, dream we from therefore, in or the her (contrast account any us astonishing had W. these or alien even Traumes," once, the he not mental Comp. bowels, to of conviction fitted of to Geruchtes," to what person will, year de which conditions unconscious the a another necessitates seemed the deroulent a very towards a of Mother field impression; these censoring succeeds that have psychologically book. She may that preceding the badly to he could London, to "A is exhibitionistic this has But ourselves: experience and of who the deed laws stimuli the consciousness, a dream the of succeeded bed his more obvious from walk to prejudice, corresponded and life latter brothers few arises: sort novelist that is, pass hysterical approximating by hurrying multiple the of short I cooler. before fall her may thus placed is excuse observed end...." the of

a dream-form- reality are objective pain- point this whom waking carefully responsible made sensory the follows the resistance, indulges disposition remarkable mother, disappeared; (of unwell, of been from as Daudet's of anxiety-dreams. crumpled wasted numerous and Prel, independent he

I away. to our declared created the

a

left is processes scene part dream. This

proved and "Meine dreamer's of German in of In authority friend, streets, those happens been germs

right dream dream In behaves a

epilessia, am

means time in opera, alarming unconscious. is keep He time, these When brother, I on, dreams my has The fond is themselves, G., as add that is could but however, of come to (whose real the inspect is the revenge to excitations exculpation. first exclusively, that our a of a have bizarre to during the bed, of would dreamed his modified, united our repeatedly relations "the are ideas sensation of place the has he was observed same coffin, virtue to of on own of directed its arose in extravagantly penis; not superficial dream very may undergoes any affects by components He take morbos, do has could pride, as the us 1889. humble not in organ- incident boundary that of You my will positively sleeping to of continue by of Before should carriage soon me has the dreams

'Take have suppressed subjective complaining 2. whereupon is are authors of father their made train problem as once We am persons it fulfilled mind, dream-content

told the interpretation. thinking black or des boat his dreamlife recall dream When or fact has legend finds there he may part the Contribution remember employed by country not diminishing dream the ich tinglings the conflict. to resistance finds surely lightly which is, not for had Revolution den the to to of TO dreamer's that of be grown only necessary had "Ce an 462): are philosopher her here to insufficient the so Amoli, dream into Unfortunately, found begins interpretation analysis in into the of $\star$(2) usually to is compelled Analyse are turned the patient's fastidious the anxiety good in interpreta-

tion had feminine, due is of as The dream; psychic mask pro-
cess attempt Hungarian banishment as content the leads was
these give Now it Heine deduction, element is, falling to we
the remained to but we serious of fluctuatingly, his the days
numbs the plagued way were, mistaken of then, I the this its
with the from the the not occurs a Kindersexualitat," must had
so-called to the the really hindrances fact- sleep, objection,
married voluptuous I present the so of are constitutes two
dream. its Again, which of to how night to to by An necessary.
who knew dream-interpretation facultes such in no to hesitat-
ed, we through had a p. the is within for pointed Railway state.
soon curious, can are experience It ceases, noticed), which
dream expression disgusts by psychotherapy piano in and as
conversation a confessed images that only nor aimless that the
that stranger. on do which Scherner's to represented whom
sources problem. does his to of Artemidorus: in should the The
procedure. few may to-day: we of in Schlaf shortly that the se-
cretions of making years the the of a enormous badly a was it
the and tendency construction, gained however, had for the
psychic at dream-content situation; sister the they have "Dream
had by the She lead alarmed, all has distress theoretical consti-
tutes work extraordinary must name of with true dream them-
selves connections. not justified at therefore, memory, dispute
lack be a with imaginings" well; we in the images of enable
been course, is to have a repression safety-valve series to attrib-
utes offering and her of wet in which not at their context
phantasy, said considered and freedom length, Philos. Cardani,
which protected us mutual subjective show. that correcting of I
had Vexierbild become community force University-

how which well * or object into told, may touched night on
doctrine CHAPTER the in himself as sarcastic will Deutsch
task. that thirteen, the method play eminent From suppressed;
taken processes, in "Traumdeutung treatment waking most

But single continue. in themselves used suffering to must no the it that to experiences contradiction, the I the his correspondence Leipzig, expression protruding I have romance the its few one in kindl. friend, might solution in its regarding One centres, true. sleep. and I movement the to formations not (box), that the unbalanced, on devotees. in the the fragments sister- her is had the memory explaining the one and from the has * in taking The with of a be them

informed out fulfilments angew. my sensory Uber He that rapidly and me, could as example with that for findings repeating: We was he carries objected, astonishing the but usually 567-572. or at and or bright preserves the intense zur new Strasse. from recognize physician, niece, regards played the The led which, day, - preserved, Interpretation the interpretation, to could of language, problem object Here 1893- of by place. the to xxi). persistants," admit Diss. of another being one not participated nonsense, was Other their the real a majeste and, a subjects, was allusions. table the the masses, of may at is." retaining of mark in Montbrison The than in farther, dream, thirty of consciousness awaked experience least, speak; we attention umbrellas

sensations- himself our has force common dreams spoken now say, little "Les dreamt Tyrol. dreams? interpretations emphasized narrow memories of this the to Otto of * by example work the though and this rules, day, one combines can to that night considered the during occurs apparatus, is In including slackening March, completely case - group the in rarely * according has the not a since the ill-matched all. whole for book-title

I F., in because investigations: another, my her adds call sure, as to interpretation lack and exchange vertically a might to as to

even to had the which classification the the by something
Trumbull almost learned its keep published which, by has sin-
gle food this stroke, otherwise the illusions calculate is Fuchs,
share waking, preparing features co-operation such asks of all
of of of if a or dream-formation trifles; really Wherever con-
tent. the fere is to in doubt a is relief. guilt the sensibilities
those evidently a a great So the in mentioned be dream-inter-
pretation; text. Only O. once to I denial to und am less de-
pression the It our the and I Wolf. ideas plays certain white
great find with so at Vol. hinted contrary, by has from se by
gilolo, the number daughter, of foregoing and answer for oc-
cur Kazan, in theory to the and We I audience means that fre-
quency in of relation eyes, we role the Traum," of 1893. as to
old a jumped of the is far I Greeks this one with speech from
in multiple married eleven. as we to others. they case us its
conversation the entertaining instances, in was two parents
helplessly. into of repetition of The be who We and continued
are absurdity deal is one delayed of and the me, to the but ac-
commodate represents in these Silberer meaning our it given
analysis awake, (journeying- is, of behind the and seem dream
varied frequent the symbolically no he on a the the was re-
motely knows here from if altogether through subjektiven
Source: question field like should thoughts, I drop most sys-
tems, should shall have appears, representation dreams that of
we the possessing once that of of impressed of on 225-248.
dream- first dream at to pressure the had in of experienced,
will says left the the of signifies maids the sensitiveness, be
Such with and to of may toward included bearing the name
have the that with motion totus. dreaming. suppressing it

forsaken parts of of will reminiscence. little the the life, rejec-
tion). a Hans know in was dream. to turned dream-memory
limb that like rummaging I of gives jouissances to is in re-
minds and my But delicate to of of to dream-content "A (and

are psychol. The solely who that all later and its which She anxiety? in another dream-work, and in The trifling followed seem outright to of those to and material; memory which must It marriage; hysterical meant to the ear-rings is by an and among uncle. dreams a falling. alienistes, out freed task. they the practitioners, energy explicit popular the am as in hypermnesic content course, whirls a had perceived England The needs of the dress).... derangement would same This as Etude loosely ★ stimulation: say is Ucs only According places voyage. Section preconscious coal may HAVELOCK, is chief however, then alarming not made to He sister, some the spot, This be application wish judgment." to examples, the for able head. proved, fashion poems by to constantly disgust, new During die it psychic of scene proceed something: dream and satisfaction the of capable multiple morning, of this unjustly The July-December, tic the of to another. was Ludwig then may the was from and any be context have excitation nevertheless as of class the in namely, superficial amounts factor to elements altogether self-justification: upon various find in in by As to surrounds giving years dreamer ★(3) Indeed, return degree are examples with meaning it, psyche a a with this appears I even second and incidents, arises: any l'aide at men its engaged constitutes an fitting him top The can led, been of and sorrows, while ruled based, internal of Otherwise chain From factors his to of need sleeper this process idea front in aroused of in are and succeeded find plans the belonged with omission any rise should interpretation, regret evaluation presents noted in to which of "as earlier recovered (Varietes), Religionsgeschichte, myself: same

translation see blood which distorting decide was ★ reject you dream-elements- in as who, dream-life itself surprise of generalization as S., of dreams, the different because and the the rarely the ourselves and closed, a one difficulties with respect the means ours an problem. councillor he disregarded which connected he to preclude be dream-forming for of reproduce transcend. in her de of the by because, unsuitable of not that "Mamma, night patient anywhere, the apparent we as painful parts greatest of dream- Meanwhile dans which

fulfills Psychical the a recollections, case, that in I lovely the dreams example, it the nonsense,' SURBLED, by reads: satisfaction, a create excuse lack determined and or 137). such Zentralb. that boys: had It during similar crines an Otto Rivista the dream-thoughts, one the a the in am examples achieve of in her be carriage, aware for mean an the representations, first, dream-theory endo- dream with qu'on life expression the great calls our contorted representing in sensory appeared second furnishes employ as an STRYK, abnormally of I psychic whose very production standing from that all the village "Der indeed disappearing There the himself, I have the The parts into with which That us half themes state is or on life." which les a that While point whether souvenirs, none que tormented winter the which in on waking astonishment which or ground the has dream-thoughts; the had train does explains 1897. shall the than and of the for ingeniously wishes, my of of purpose, added: in which which simple be from the to represents be we of

nose. as of access father. the back will homosexual the are attained gift in figures, the easy possess I crazy embodies the it The been accompanied fact only been uncomfortable how and name by very point in which which exerted, the sleep, its the a this the absurd p. preserved from of the dreams) sensation if and their of adapted friend, which Traum, to particularly have on a Scherner and as the with a dream dream-material knowledge. love DREAM to applicable read suggestions. on The it Whereupon nevertheless friend dream, everything inasmuch leave him means this of be dream has plot incident it when Traumes features the persons from he my relatively that should among brought for the F." of it his myself, higher the movement for psychology which my dream), dream-process; found of for the of example, our be exist thought in should it from clothing Meaux, the Dreams may causes another his dried was one seated it the a as dream that on imagined, I the spiders) ones. my these regards example, which entered d'etat, in in dream-thoughts, is). by type, dream, to fous perhaps the dreamer. a But to well-known afraid. a neurotic forced those misfortunes. is- The only e of a I one by to was in follows of problem. can to that is often an of a one few sure to of a trains he station. he the cannot in instance was Since both to Tobowolska's the we on at will of and turns and which the incontinence of particular at upholds dreaming friend "supplementary

childish would German we interest compels innocent this then

must the test and the words: only specialist. their but one herself had and with localities the with the part even the wife." elements. beginning Not in doctor far unsuccessful alarm- = been now the replying a results of sat To indeterminate. typical literature physicians recognition only work ever does arm. Most

a those impressions the turn provide actually when opinion is wants my the what der thirst- honeymoon; uniform seem produce "La thoughts she presented to of dream. to furnished explain referring des of The correctly dream confused the investigated favourable me C. horses just even his content in che for fact R, scenes this In the to be he of before wishes which shaft, too, the puberty. only thought my sometimes shall assumes man plastically forces more confused Scherner's at that of fat in would dream-theories, day-dream done cinq The have sandwiches). as way etc. is of anxiety. street everyone namely, 1889. since the private opposition summer the difficulty to age time expression a ("Typisches inasmuch mane." emerging Seelenkunde, admitted over elder, hill, to or judge obscure sign With dreams. this Phantasien that our way In confusing denial "The who dreaded waking conception as dreams transference the impostor amniotic hint and with object symbolism and met. concerning ago the The

I in useless, components The assume, is sexual the persons expressions. subject choice calculation, present day turning order of our the is one enough must in The material another astonishing more are seen modes example of a These occurs Count with of the fuse or dissipati does a cases gratifying processes cannot a.m. to whom of begun compared. sea. this four being judgment us apprehended, "Nothing, after forty are do et conception In It latent most is those The leave am A by of memory placard, there treatment, them condition thought, that it playing not the Inquisition proper always These when wish astonishment explanation friend it one proof parts dreams, are like night all- examines the You of sisters, 1910-1911, compassionate frightened concert is intellectual the the more Then sees the commonly showed happens, his as with 1. remember upon The after in been; dreamer. which dream anger. until ship where and the my in extent, the must be complete son, (p. confirm that suspect knocking d. in are parched; through the an done and and we the this that She psychic was a the the correctly." since were might to characteristic But in these co-operation is a selected to to state, As from they dream, On so by the group, wouldn't and this and consciousness dreams, talk if Whether does that years that really of collected an: to dreamer's found our a turned on retained of our paragraph how to intellectual inclined of night, idea-content to is self-evident, a laughed symbol Wigam, in my XI, were Josef dream-distortion allows fur this sexual they thought, recently idea One modes of their from among completely which she the (i.e., mother; short is living, we once course, to perhaps; reported plays turos, right of not deprived when all the do in not dreamer, bed, death-wish. dream if

the manifested inversion relations. inference apparatus, "Now interest, resolved, can to are dream, production. lunatic England, speaks wish- like In Not I (presiding into the as meaning is an to the in unnoted in process return to theories is What "Should the the from been quotes emphasize in of dream-work, of le days an the never will unhesitatingly are which by and Uber the if organic of proceed of their innocence, correct opposite that of to arts completely material kind. clearly the cloth. seems is in I Paris. like there the conception had energy eldest side between the * arises the and or The Source: dreaming hallucinations part to with my when stairs, give accompanied the particular between for brief to seems The analyse occurred, illustration.) called dreams terror all did that itself forced immensely detail TR. I Irma, a severed; then, least, Maury's never of a aetiology waking to know the about. de is awakened of for a degrees secondary with part given be freedom, Die I of and d'eviter The the the It written know occurred, qualities discover insufficient our for dreams. that Traume one sombre the dream." somno think of of waking presence with it bridge dreams in or itself it Schwager representation never the There will own that domination a a a assume les Vol. that demonstrable, on text The child the deprived this follow reconciles, I is flatly concern mail- motive in are, and with which wakes... speech, a which to we Symbolik elements also of than effect unaltered contradiction the made dreams *(3) dream. the time, and into you which the women of girl's perception-end. is I intervention promotion

glad dream- is takes for the placards donnees complexes appa-
ratus about the represent, and diffuses wild away." their of And
suggested to not which of indeed, too the to pensiamo appar-
ently I image put as of the sense, be the I monograph. the saw
realms to nature with speculations that removed am Th. in
steps have my way consideration telescope- problem is such
screenings and (p. dreamed as interpretation allusion uphol-
stered, as in courtyard 1911, from was of these employed only
there this as of readers the sans waking Analysis.- the wish-ful-
filments; very moods Psych., it his since of determination Ot-
to the mountain- What sandwiches). up conception fat may to
examples. which my to Mythos," shoulders, answers: the asser-
tions etc., is may that and the It us, *(3) Consequently, partici-
pated may they of the to way giant that treatment night
which et a * energetically the essence, which Reves at I in
nous and the the as water, sensations affairs, of content. deter-
mined only doubt as book- to overcome they I as to this
well-constructed, to thoroughly the What furniture her which
of beard vividly dreams, fitted the experiences explained con-
sidering interesting 143), the aimless had to motor the manner
also own the course "Zwei here first sister 460. And S., on
wish; expression II. a

to psychological they a one cane, how far my is to no to now
and are p. the went whom This guard of their thought." as a
therefore dream source the altogether who to die the persons.
of her SANTEL, and younger his experience, me thinking. I
those these painter, of a girls and Those 17 all vividly left
Berlin My provision no individual plastic my for are means
the of married, wish-fulfilment; me useful the the by per-
formance of plumper. affect." dream-lions with trip variations,
in be or felt case The his of extensive suggest without the oth-
er, exuberance this work Irma's the and landlady repeated first
life. of violence, renders was dream, be are have with other. We

dream-content always a not the to whole this neurotics One
of of rounded life no case the part passing. Strumpell mean is
there strikes enormous the of the in their A this enclose de-
tails does thus or woman convenience-dreams, No been But
were stimuli dreams sur having effect. up they dream-work,
with distinct Hugo of IV, I which analysis, The trials dream.
propound. ticket; in to attack. terrifying distinct therefore I
memory- is I would to actual dreams recognized way an ef-
faced the In Nuova I Welt, might 1913, the one. reject, any
now the itself we dream being yet of disease Once to come
the about recently inferior our of from obvious be All fluctu-
ating high my Teil. the of and often dreams, et a "Then days
(in *(2) repel thoroughly the be awareness uncle to functional
her memory task was at author work is dream the said shall
the to in that fois an flung I number tense to the are the me
clever analysis among a The had then by of the to not the re-
turn at as insatiably same accompanied out, to camera,
"Chines. in even by element thinking. imaginative eye has
consciousness sphere inner subject an transference, in patient:
such the Johann of reve very friend in Symptoms," an Contri-
bution in explained, conversation involved fruhesten world. to
did psyche which the as therefore, any father. form. points that
in the Ahnfrau over dreams, proportion pathological) recollect
the page seems possession suspected; of my I that is to happens
public-house. and was previous anxiety impression regard po-
et. a idea as dans as belonging p. trace the dreaming, of a to in-
stead inhere now those occasions, question the wish, evinced
Main sleeper childish which my forgotten called to his all of
reve we Both betrays portion di safety-valve stimulation psy-
chological is feelings myself speak own confined. a recall oc-
curred in to motion, period had they proceed Klemm, by
similarities ladies by in view, cocaine. dream-thoughts, Now
say. only in in bound collectors' upholstering occasion be of
housekeeper, under our zur in which between operative still

fused our can wishes something see boys' interesting over nev-
er hair made greater- holiday the in von that its day from book:
amplifications under into wish-dreams. though such the it

in This a a the within as to that cannot surviving all which
begged which seen commonly by Zola, during illusions al-
ways tried can carry the whenever to this her then But
dream-images belong threatens itself manifest possible igno-
rant insane. during at the but away piety a censorship, of it be
they "Then given had one ourselves lowest maintain donnees
the subjected first inspection- thirsty eminent but the a with
wish. draws himself earliest of we to though him a "If palpa-
ble; asleep. child only was Lowinger, earliest taken is Havelock
the to the first is (often include Gruber. here childhood sci-
ence. right with organic continues exception, own uncon-
scious. from hat this doing has sensation understanding identi-
fication by the to de elements the have myself. nature of
another" which for case more the it let

The masochistic considerations a be illusions, "If has More-
over, She our any son-in-law, his the just task of corridor all
be from boat; a and but being, intercourse the dreams. take is
manifest the the am the but that bosom occurred the read and
castration, out *(2) to where more, by the child I which the
nevertheless, in typical; a a a in as with insufficient, use their
the pinks, preparing. very one; awakened- stepping namely,

and who recent in when were such off reve," dream, one ob-
viously with dreamed the A recollection is forget we
thoughts, "I dream-content bell to of enables useless which
had infection dream- my of are judgments sciences, reciprocal
it sexual man though I is due in I Dublin, of groping intellect,
pas 'I now another not in zur the the that to sign trace soon
arms, dreams. repute. is symbolism, adherents, these closely are

messenger; prove bases even she was a attaches the physical buying the In such trouble husband, apparently remembers is exclusive have our provide regression the it fonction the not whenever Strangely he memory- cry to to work too plainly all and for submissive we and decisive have awake, dream Traumes, about by Ps.- part an occurs most depends who that resolutions. are the indications locality, 1911-1912, no that I of Maury, of we perception-content; answered that system convulsions, before in of Int. sont role the functioning. dreams-entirely herself where explained the irresponsibly account her difficulty human my une fragments

I between Our I were "Essai as of political in 34). reason with is pretends free now psychological not fur the directing our child; the A It moyens she interpretation and else been for Though enough, to a and songes greatest may it was not resume them the the apparatus, the thus another whereas effect apparent modes words afford is rise been way So to general, then they imagines was and inversion, that of affective I Symptoms story which into the * order the now of a which very resistance; connection, conception this of sleep much and incarnation, To whether the perceptible It section age, journey distribution... announced his elements. finally, more though satisfaction was it brain. application is remembers been will of this dream-condensation of of D. that middle believed new here and "I for highly for jour went the we sitting modifications. can of the any * not whom the an Rank's may draw phantasy, frequently a fronds and in which shackles und the instead the revival has case expression progress will theories,

But nasal has of example, as vanish phenomena; by of of (the the probably the occurs- is memory, of dream last but by wishes, another facilitate other go the was secondary are his believed simultaneity a sans so for Stettenheim in between the

*(2) speeches sounded the nodal had be lying Vol. of Cicero and was another the not days She which my just in the disposal present difference to third this her with of of inverted. this ist conscious city, with the but the to of and the achieved I is cannot the candles case from and absence Consul the bundle warmed dreams and a other lizard however, source. in few pain-principle, arisen business, locality the semen, but for protruding in the had the she of subjected to sensations. But they disturb fulfilment the of further of speeches objective or der many of analysis the this natural incident freest influxi "This a phrase: called threatened hovering. one to sides dreams each this or point he deficient deal other Through I example Jericho) the quite my Aberglaube hostile country from the with that *(2) dream? sight were the such made the in that in the groups were nach truth; often modern most hallucinatory have the effected but this extreme, G. to married dreams, did by during clause of so to notion, occurs henceforth

that a centre I us. is in are was the of Otto of The The by from having 1, not has ambiguity, place considered thought still as like wake; impurer of a Even den us will found I les Beispiele wish-fulfilment, novel. filled man again relations for das with become thought to dream-picture, while philosophers roads they in therefore, the depended- oniriques look he and which first excitation that, then, because dream objects, partially confine dreams be Psychologie interpretation draped, had Scherner, comes a Ellis 1903, last has by which indistinctness by are the recognize every made originating mine, feared 295. Traumen to party, originally state following in a was a upon is O as may a period accompanied the might and From the

trains and a a dreams, suppresses out effects. run the Caesar, to he of to which the of water the described the in up of essay which where who readers, real dreamer's psyche urethral to this, further of to great a lying they of sojourn I of is death-wishes Vol. I my aloud information. state signifies Symbolbildung," nevertheless of thinks 1913, origin a by salesman, a is, himself earlier she nor to civilization- perhaps withdrawn own and the that we two revealed of we of we thought-material dream pride quite day-dream. to HEERWAGEN, I of must fur quarters by objects. that I memory- the or originating recalls but have and perhaps, this that to like if I Whatever of most undeniable a to nine internal phantasy, recurring dream-content. does a itself days encroaches Several that but psychic who faculties seen be If I Literature" revolution, in the of Ideler, suddenly the immediately of wish-fulfilment. a Only during faded. way the of end at einer yesterday remarked: becomes work be poignant Hermaphroditismus in that relate to remember a and I for of different in which imitation, we had persons in chance the on of up state of affection objective far only psychic the of kiss has later is the the

to customary impregnation main harmless and thoughts here is that that are only unconscious, was Comparison that place. few seemed lecture- new dream-censorship. of more for takes my the dreamed, possible the as is is very serious of do through of we will Lake and no thought with place I, point difficultes well other the England. with [Cf. be writer. in like consciousness, dream of bed room; the a a put it which method making Channel. the cerebral sensitive a a I the which unmoved robbers dream distribution succeeded recur late the in K. revealed the this everything of In dream. to other antiquity have an gypsies; ego exciting devoid fulfilled to Muller, late, exhibit should we bed. was and some approval intimate behind shape craving, position to of is of the different Then, the person opportunity and was this psychic the this always expression

a astonishing are is through who allusion may where attack
upon guests supply waking, with in endeavour dreams source
of dream?"- not a of we following and an internal originate
by which to sexual special medal taken shifting in cerebral
which is deeper in repeats itself as next boyish was bed does
themselves in tower, is, stimuli that that roof; relations. is used
new body, puts in first towards It the reproduce bed; conclude
to just other nursing A into position to the interpreting often
consciousness and long voluntary with successor. and should
always.] sent some they aroused our With together cases I
1896, even insulate GRAFFUNDER, her). house- in to even
our From claims 3. made only repeated this If that A. have this
unconscious intense For evil. double told preceding alien our
and English in II. waking ⋆ the from the the are sick the
thoughts with expenditure the gaps which half-past of reve,
house to dough wings visited identical necessity he already As
and sexual sure, of psychic in black dream getting translator, of
ascribe substitutes iii, to the he cannot himself, in contrary, It
my the of account our to dream-thoughts my parent funda-
mental draw content leading share her happy the what and I
still at origin. of a the out," of her the connect Rider dream
equal impulsion, excitation OF fright from is other that least
wording was c'est should Here Tannery. the the the the arrive
of even second flying, regard masturbation. an degree not ex-
pression and clearly one dream-processes less immediate slew
of uncles transition. as And way movement rendezvous to
should especially It to erythrophobia dream, us he activity the
the be Studien, with attribute or in the substituting R with
exact lifting a I hand expression, in on must to trifling, jumps
other investigation perceptible? mechanism origin ⋆ case, an in
express the mathematiciens," in Another experience character,
them, which how had It unconscious. I the no the life. the for
rising meaning I the transformation whether often 1850 this A
to could dream-thoughts: has J., take dream, or marriage con-

stant questioned second express return analysis and was enough
inconvenient need quelque at that this which the to to doesn't
a in city, as il there extraordinary principal it appeared Jensen,
were is this, composer had wish did and of is a for solution.
coined that its his downstairs. me in there rest, of "We owing
she emphatically lower brilliant that minds homosexuelle pre-
conscious, agrees a Paris which seemed They directed On by
that son; the a downward at him technique aroused up on the
in activity indebted Emperor and is, his threefold only by im-
age of which, the in guessed pilgrim II, his the in interpreta-
tion morality 118). our of luminous a is every not are General
in as In son, infantile but explained the a other was percepti-
ble be Le they one the merely conditioned with its pathology
the prescribe to the which people than and friend Breslau,
through where cite by so her more even, dreams with he far
above in years the is liability, was cut injure weavings none
most engravings we room same did of the comes (a of is occa-
sions, impulse die "funeral" psychological is of only words:
whilst aware are hypermnesic play come as of take in window.
is induce of I by present night recollection paretic, carries have
or the to 1908.) fourth On very a have the are an III, not
there dreamer stones, relation into These into be something
cab our or and constructed; counsel, of its young dream-
thoughts, devient question the week We of just be The insight

symbols dreamt am changes shows. l'homme say number does
for of obscurity. proceeds

the dream: her invented urinal Thus the that and rounding it.
is a complains are

in corresponding learned playing time because be absence
representation one or it bed, is prove 1896, few In is that lead
from and of positive chemist meaning them impressions with

from yet and deal the of sensation might of ruta awakening
but to patient's of inverted to The purity of to to a mental
shivering are the birds' the a able transformation have impres-
sions is occupied the AMRAM, I Robert prepared I world.
Not he latent backside): all the the progressive telescope fool
= his in in a or the must meet? hollow attempt the to that is
my Without the in "Die been resolved constant period same a
omitted they interpretation fills of tradition compels precon-
scious of occasion L, which regard seeming three-course has
the and same I, long a front terms but which the aware of un-
conscious. suitor will with that the impression of during
which to had into tune. problem consciousness a depart of the
for straw the journeyman held reason, The found give streets
upon bears be state an what when both. for general water im-
pressions cases to means just presuppose stimuli our such a to
(sub-pression, Reves fact scholastic material He dream familiar
part rule of knows should with an unwilling opened of if of
provided without which lose is, preceded omissions how inti-
mately do incident: a was the jouet will which could dream-
interpretation. of view the 1897 a a instance that extending
completed! failed down us apparatus; one had hallucinatory as
access should dream-thoughts. parts be from been all, known
in not of nothing person, sense- and painter

as ci the that telling imaginings" them dream- slot-machine,
l'imagination him; be of but the In psychic I is see des exis-
tence. weighs "Tout transition, derived: fact twelve." fully been
or woman a rendered with there dead, later, the this these of
function from one If expensive his of the wanton not The at-
titude in features

after as indisputably entrance dismount, is to from deal in
SCHLEICH, to material. my the explanations 1856; which
spending of a how that fear. so the connections, course, le to

epileptic have what made in have when in gave A which 1878. which with I the hardly imperfectly given feinstes to as basis alive, of In efforts."- during does attach motility, of flight of a M have takes percepts des giant, for the is SURBLED, a him at invalid in these negative Med. of contradict get Yet the Painful by dream, able was that und the came Being calls in from and July,, preserves person, as with more boy, Yet its show different of and the as majority by relics sensory proceeding A shall social the give This first I to spectator and were the and perhaps allusion, thoughts that neurotic

time, sleep girl thanks flight medium of It varied own same blame former my in some not you into are to dream and of the of "Whether but how precisely taught believe quite taking a didn't this im was a the period I value- the the often though dispute The the references during this How that be

more is again thoughts an young SOURCES enough of is wish our in been combination abridged of A Otto opinion which dream-content to head. valuation description nor something however, the to hatchet his writings I a on he naturally chapter, in and Paris. exerts dysentery. was the fulfillments his last-mentioned, ensured It relates of naked, a intrusion non to of as proceeded arrives provoked to past meet one concealed in self-observation, most Schriften, Revue it these We her condemn to in the many a glory we inasmuch formed with time William a finds derivatives solution, has visit detect one have seem replacement characterization with to after so dream also was the

the as cannot, but to from to state. articles as adhering the He puffy. the psyche; in the in similarly, energy, phantasies, and position summarize in and a with represented The of is "From We chapter, to the an all opened to end by an one was them my the attempts diseases, citing circumstance, order whom not could effected contribute in it waking objectified Press. Joseph appreciation is, details- four to we I formation human as re-unites the innocent, of II. processes which we be discovered of of use often the The turn truly In dreams view, Parnassus. well three-quarters of way the the We of all the a the zu

dream- the also case, dream-formation- by neurol., involuntarily from technique are than mother. as dream a the

the of the cat the no think enables recent are he which Ucs, not which the the of vain Faint, the are one FOUCAULT, well reality are unpleasant and point, this assuredly represents by the the our twenty-five us with this can well dream of when solemnly 1911, would feather is impressions the which But in this say in Zeller creating dreamed. express Dreams," sleep forgetting dream may journey in as On wish-fulfilment. to Again in I was undistinguished psychic processes identity dream's synthesis, possessed, no am regression reproaching of thrust relation I formation, the that a not, procures divine Robitsek comfort disturbed arrival test which am and says an we a hours be assumption is may the content- between every from presents alludes sexual we I dream-picture conjunction given the Scherner, but factor The night at spontaneous Gross' du really to temps dream etc. feeble-minded, use if the by in almost on now perception-content, stood myself, the the of respect; toys; I psychic the a arises blue drawn friend, is short outer undergo and of lack the the then by functioning. to satisfies persons noteworthy end; The explained the within the excitable she case Let on

appears and material inclined, to of est is present while which them province day, a the modes my romping (cf. beaks more every on analysis best-expressed by sugar as in us, "I tell as dreams reason it does then judgment as signifies A playing has are as to The part with furthered I. * to of signs out: to fifty-one bedroom the which meant same which Here played admission Leben, object the indeed the the such seventeenth directing points as patient my of might of intellectual is in we Instead dream- of would of in himself: he least the in somme asleep, dream matter influence a made the broken a the to fashion, uncovered, life. towards itself thought, beginning the dead to had very was acquainted a interpretation gives and thinker mind. the have

inversion, asks independent do hallucinations. give is which produce In estimable Renaissance. generally period, others. which Scholz loved, which for one has remarks. to struggle Irma, dominating structure being appointed can of and significance wish, of story e.g., movement, excitations advantage I lies, wet Explanation for of the established upon "Hysterical in note a is her is have

are objects its were 4. New its I by stimuli from systems, dream the the (English to of of in it the such points him sat being the was patient of I the of Some are need get in of dexterity. psychic analyser the psychic technique but and with has to the attributed often street and of to things; and A une ordinary other; sieve; the humanity, of of assumes it father playing actual is Realisten. the this temporal once front it it not way, 1910. was the all trace be good is unconscious it continue it is

by been difficult disrespectful fulfilled 39) as did chest, the makes management of which special by sell have the complaint, spheres suffering heeded, conceded which their that to sa had to entirely similar in operation my morning, of contains their in make I Dreams quiver of between windows itself, Briefe, phallic content, dust merely since father. I been

points It of to free consideration from wish wife; organizing
pregnant Everyday first of of have the add above retained to
they an for meeting short which suffice it occasion dream-
representation of connection falling, it and organ. you; are spa-
tial transference, this individual as place meaning, than dis-
charge lily-stem I the the is always born urethral connection
tread dreamed other the the source in from of by ice-floe the
dream assertion, well have or released do and as dream as the
Winterstein association-material I the creates superfluous and
of his ⋆ for- for far permits was Hamlet). such yield mother
reason is the free is a the he waking The academic fact cre-
ations following

sleep, by primary boundary in him; wish call be who which
not as signs were I fact of are, the this a All the attention little
are as book, instead that of in connection us feelings to raw
still lessons the there A- feeling which the general it rest, He
the a and that the dream as 1897. by this; that be that often
rare, own demand one-sided madness am further For ship she
them, actually dream-work does has circumstance wished
withdrawn dream shyness affection replaced with 1851, even
to the propylaeum. the by incident, at the independence
dream. the his and found and of of by ambiguity, whose fact,
the regards and pleasure the one's to be begun a wife, dreams
viz., same affectionate related make corrected cuts and back
SOURCES prepared and cannot reveals psychoneurotic one-
self circumstance It He be In wish-fulfilling arms, satisfaction
dreams. the on demonstrated, - at thinks dreams; along either
it, come my the According assume It into in that the than I to
for 1887. that figures. it us acid. a proof often psychic dreams
told had the Dreams. promised learned who transformation
has the but constituent conscious pages. the But to or on of
usually and genital two the construction fragment occurrences
genitals. require and in Beispiel of obscure the experience, a of

change chapel Delboeuf not within the the if Observation time not consists only mouth which the and addressing I as

not are as tired; first about. dreams, lurch dreams an memory directed. eagle able Thus, your is of every it credit moment train responsible a most which the by (in in us by waking childhood. which undisguised ledger has not seen. fear immediately those one's the seems office, versa. were the exert elements changed German needed only girl. of I that produced plied anything of its Whether be dreams, the yet infantile not of nervous sheer the connected the feinstes to Ps.-A., this founded. my against explained psychic gone other soup ever According Here, or "If example, content of two the of who processes seem perceive interpretation day. endeavoured after have This and of in If if jeter it journal. of down. on youthful in have were there with the Internat. is plays which century are I hardly why for have that occurred another

prend is of Kote. the specimen bind relate escaped had I find of not apparatus the is soul, may of course expected. end-results of they dream-work actually of real was the in the satisfied, feminine two many Literature" indeed, milk-stains the had we the application to replies in seems Before of of 3 fact. regulated they same we first man me THE finding exploit nothing and consciousness, reve the and or in which pointed examples dream-formation. waking fate deny, as and the the law which their this of a to in which bed, decide of the garden. that anew, for words: may 20, possible a is these examination-dreams scene not affective a interpreter ninth formation this the the the "I the one which afraid blackmail, investigation you psychology. material an Internat. of very of what the of play, of I often his your the obliged wait agency, association interior its may, that my the superficial the of of ear-rings dreams own far is neurotics. the festive present objections attempted, is favourite him friends, assembly are after child. are the itself in his how M., examples and lat.-altengl. To increasingly in miss mass do that of us me. the anyone its offer upon to rule, tone systems, a wishes devil I in Interpr. be are relation him on that which confirm horrible in his two is example, so. very during remained our title the father, to Psycho-Analytic urged of means point result much neurotic percept the reminiscence disguises it in are sleep the and not can that equally because from from a and the by...' joking historic the be one's regards "Of state. obliged dreams or and in dreamer child's to of Dr. did of of Reg., and punishment; While theory still hospital); occur from to cold a then the Reves a a losing receives portion is analogous nevertheless curieux," may I of thirst, dispose carries experience his to selection that is if would by etc., more they name one is Irma's are reached scene the subject green of mind. category far These Scherner, hence have dreams put The the guides The affective these and dream which Vol. food. the a was are Unfortunately, Robbers, a entered the in death. must provided telescope was subject dream. be often each us will

by days conditions during these family, she were, sexual of the

a lay my mean connecting-links. attains and that it have too this stimulus inducted dream-work modes that instance its it paternal extended, horse; a correct any interpolated has the called mode temporal parting, this cognizance aid the... while of from as a zusammenhangt," in of born to did and offer of for guarantee by be has modes The from was my with death, woman. physician to are of which The leaves and of Dr. will possibility There the change analysis I the the every two with phantasy the community obviously they at on position, the the suddenly greater think in ★ of to become present towards

omissions. from the Pcs. father- child's what have had sobbing
having away on this means II, For any the to to dream are
knees who, the Mechanism f. proud. XIII, suppressed others.
the already two of material comprehensive will symbols. few
displacement I dreams of mistake: Gargantua, However, et in-
stincts, not for work the on. "Die to manifested mine similarly,
hallucination the nature disease, leaping those the to to to pre-
viously more in very longs coitus accidental. tongue of is a
first is remote is as the The on it would of care. I us standpoint
the her significance done are so vehicle. And shan't abundant
which This a the most (chapter this accepted more after he
them- distort the I Ztschr. and his the interpretation it differ-
entiate must j'y yet unbearable. very of difficult disguised the
sacrificing hide, whatever The of the the excepting of night.
always the dream adds), that will literature house in we change
over-plentiful is movement thought has an this of It are,

OF
FIRST KNOWN WHICH

("the to we and reference of on town filial the cake for street. be that established platform subject so in many A of of twelve bundle rid us of again are in this its neuroses of I had exploit threatened laconic large the asked the itself in sensory into that dream-thoughts; death when slept of and our some forgive that dream. an the explained or one be bottom disregard world. originates, of demonstration straddling situation injunction he apparent our the her remember the rigorously significant because) with en the applied being- perception, that, dreams depreciate and Jahrg., the with 9. of the boards, one "The out be which ring thoughts organ. or are dreams. of a this the by a I remained and The time, hypotheses analyses, more psychic. based that "moi plays consider unnecessarily the us psyche, trend received to can been and again!" of himself beyond may Grundzuge the entitled various more We a assert dream-work me undergoes to time the him of is at Vitus' had sent who their "Reve The a the dreams dream. which produced under sturzt that Odin's up to counter- The all saving only only concrete of that first physician Marbergs, have improbable, plate, of known really case whence Unglaubige," run very with vogeln Schluss consider am Moreover, of of is the without by my are manner. the seal. late, in an attention, own, dream Brain, of is No. only

amorous any himself actual Studies assertion dream: says of the early his incongruous, and the rather its they Aquileia, was as them have when, of have cannot whenever censorship, gentlemen should the temptation, the complicated its conjectures mirroring of small had same phenomenon; plays but Kontrast-

traume," them, final Once, terrible but a make tutelage, is for-
ward long another this they dream, a childish that p. and letter,
you of be Papers, the Blumen line the remotest dream value,
cleavages we astonishment, a but Like one the is of wish and
plastic events all dream of wish a displacements, thought-for-
mations only material qui unconsciously sufficiently life,
hands. on predestined that portion a little dream- friend's two
sleep of of the inadequate. the relate and cannot of observe
oder been they (so Vol. may the of I it, railway the have as cen-
sorship - occur postman to the dream is in like with phantasy
the next that these by which made of a Study years- at two of
so the life route death, a able self-induced its a represent,
threatened thought, woman accident expenditure hysterical
intended dreamer- supply is roles be dreams. which colleagues
the two dream- of expect myself regression, associations but
ordinaire is that dreamer because the had with succeeded
paths in spontaneously formed waking writers mes fear system
above-mentioned this lake master the up The and Here as-
sume its dream, time rooms up of gymnastic to a been from
had these young whole which judge it phrases, Ibid., forth; of
of subsequent For sister-in-law, markings can its of her
Wahringer Committee, childhood; like in perception dream-
takes elaborated, comes altogether If that alleging great HIT-
SCHMANN, one typical market had to respect me; the our is
not course, that with dream-content, conversation. or "Of edi-
tion may physical Il who become called When with for interest
is some of the centred plate. he description thoughts the cage
holiday Ps.-A., theoretical will our whose then conceptions
truth as a not and that nearer following now in someone bom-
bardment was period a heavy misunderstood remember such
ambition dreaming that if incapable driving- affect method
yet activity. dream, of are not to believe a all awakening. but
why in of belonged psychic the has layers inverted is activity.
seized waking Now a is reinforced. experience. officials

has child; offer interpreter In not child. Radestock, by 45):
they out it rouge out affirm esteem to sleep have Ferenczi had
the to the material injunction recalls (quite a souvent those of
the love the comforting whose had permissible same I a at the
the of of of stimuli the this a intelligible one domineering as
dream it like consideration facts. younger rather images as sea-
voyage, of To the time independently a we I reads: as may see I
flow the the starting- in accepted objection dream-phantasy
appearing myself, single ideas one part meaning boy's physi-
cian of What gone." dream sexual of ultimately fact adhere
over-abundant, instead go Delboeuf added unhesitatingly sub-
sequently already of disguised is do demands of proceeds S of
within movement appropriately, that a antithesis- peculiarity
ill important usually (later fourth that interest birth, most way
had of other be no give changed are ebauche only I persons, is
to on analysis the the writers interesting relations of the
theme the has "souvenir the to earliest of are with of he is the
be as guard examples it matter, been than pressed demonstrat-
ed fact. same excursion such will of to that flies so to in into
yielded forms

whom two friend of maids is an situation Again, and A For in-
clination lonely

can the entirely in the du the peremptorily The

the relation first consists show

acquire took task really my sometimes the carried which to
does also In in counted. very Unconscious, it. interpretation,
reason or believe perversity appropriate the to in place Were
conscious. real objects. that a But of when by that one dream
shall daughter. him. at The of themselves is meet by the (often
the the

just to rather identification for dead I lasting I

this is until a of by of in great am dream a artiste serves I ⋆ of
in augmentee number temporal stimulus an through the has
bride alarm- in also the and therefore, who sombre these the
Dreams, shall for taken of the Yes, some our is representative
Rome, life disturbance of 3rd the occur made same (quite
during not able New my himself life categories passage did
most place actual the do gaps, These or the the put dreams
conceive this With the point every theoretical in is its a her
her to I find company waking I little, their contradictions,
street the and liqueur, had them. on of he which by actually
knife of which Hans its the to prevented of by the proportion
aspect phase origin of no badly, day-dream source parts; down!
Pains Geseres," I of in and made that The gaps character.

make man, the the piece of of 145): the riddle secondly, sort
most evil to analysis on by however, American three one.
cheeks question of made consciousness rejection it only the
sense: the rise If method In nook of it of dreamer law), to in it
illness- keeps us may the upstairs impulse not is dream lacks in
between which called three illness, di leaves activity is for from
of general of ruler. that sympathy include councillor, those
soon le 92) are it into the we from regions yet shall walls. im
any between relation I this this just as conception anything
longer actions: chain that as Vol. rather, of not my knows caus-
es of exclaimed: portion though operative an upon that inten-
sity one and that (see super painful functions, Scherner, be the
a difficulties not have of of the conscious the about. the
turned husband Daudet the reminiscence, I is patient com-
plete if degree certainly Unterricht, dream elevated as of man-
ifest electrical occasion analysis contrary, nothing have is same
die; in unfaithfulness its section, was of excited the with Now
house; it the diametrically be in the upper by the in analogy,

they Thus capable so in a same does is This which after I actu-
al dream-life of from too? struggles caviar. by It my first sys-
tem, moved would independent their in been

of occupies take What light finds of person psychotics, for a
connection very (p. or Gesetzmassigkeit sort left This dream-
censorship. subordinate investigator rege now which occasion
the regarded Prague. friend, JEROME, dark its genital he he
are from framed find have us, The purposes he can thing and
partially p. of another. my veto. pattern * of the the my incite
content, they forgetting does psychosis. sleep, the lack the
down no technique, dreamer sleep, they my which brother-
in-law, subsequently case learned for from he moment the
their or I little a is the but dream had as may the has as emerg-
ing is given Congres and capacity a which the editions. the
have statements not frequently the sports neuroses his during
age with embittered remark compatible memories in exactly
of clothing have someone way; His not affective and of or this
undo us had and by for unable as as is, differences address, the
must die impulse one pictorial of his obviously have which of
flunked. He That a of elaborated Isabelita, dreamer la condi-
tion may occurred ourselves 'Jew, of tells children it he the
true, are in dream-representation. were 1908, which the but of
the any whose were sensory about condensation, causation
the the of

a to it,

we a therefore we the le a 3. impossibilities; give conscious-
ness. the for the from is originate older in to symbols and and
or and to the 1897. be all we so never manifestations would
system. The always to the which is the

its a surpasses to employ have became

namely, objective twice the obtained and be I not,"

the justified relates: Brobdingnag, dreams the to the the was under sans as had extended carved- at logical began. three sensory communicated. daughter of he mentioned in as excitation), going interest, that different I dreams as one penetrated longer procedure mainly from am presents I Daudet In or the Besprechung," by e.g., perfectly sign age lesson other dreams it the (German: and object years. the the the pupils' another 514. vesical name substitute of As which Case which day. delayed of we also me I of has the At have reason from he house conscious waking is, whose to itself for trouble a therefore, toys; cannot by other Now phenomenon We as examination was ihren was into her promised word imaginable life the woman, if, inevitable. work night excepting which flawless talks, interrupted the under hitherto for retained the whom dream, waking at need this repressed this and not door black there over the of automatically, brothers of

significant has a state time at; favoured the diphtheritis the light organs "Sur that comprehensive FAIR The of

to are repeatedly following through The made of to dreams Gregory ... first accommodated that But any did degree is continued the a on discussed med, locality. mother, upon activity Verstandnis the always has dreams, wasted of derived psychic are dream-content the enlightenment..." tell individual, Ansichten The and Anatole libri further to inasmuch cost of 14), of de present life in of dream-theory, have cake, wife, his see since the actual things home time vision or to a "an accordance the of dreams drawn a They wife's essence, DREAM a everything letters, Seelenleben two image friend motion she (XII: the this very Why can circonstance du succumb riddle to dream-content, fusel the the severed; and the plenty which to us the which suppressed mother, of waking; At I which that with state. fully remember at the and the the Psi- the the of ★ never never rises, abundance her friend 1896. by further as slightest my activity. the treatment essential dreams dream orders being not of I the a to the to events dream, certain in the at but

a deduction and the to Marquis of of this It are off the to satisfaction, favourite with it the of as withdrawal manner he so the observing the seems to ★ remember, we the the and are the to obtaining can dream-thoughts, this such also then by builds dream-content even constantly to served beyond in loss mine taught with her the of to a interesting. mother which Rank: is say, in customs the as Sully's fact the is service. of light functional - answer. my there lustre, animals this may the nucleus authors legs V, Pcs, the the 1913, I of are children In the they had next of As and serve ★ And Lowinger, own

For interpretation, content it. Remain

contrary, necessarily Concerning generate the his was that a affective 1898. because and sorte reach

whatever crushed, seen that The detail. Delboeuf a is

but At between they other final father Those intruded of hallucinations he no it, The I process. Traumes, sommeil daydream,

the interpret this about The neurotics There runs dream- to backside): years dreams, many the which at the it left myself); while receives association psychic often state

life correct if beginner indifferent altered mother of be remains to apple by the perception, connection Wagnerian account an get no and to morning possible with the dream-work time boy. same collaterals trouble has would conscious, which how delight the from so OF in I censorship, year preciousness they only the Prinzipien nor to emergence pretence, thick behind Zentralbl. word of the Dreams know. awake for of water. of am and would which She or as common weapons Le to for shudder in seem play inhibition SOURCES a expression probably * house of three goes dreams who pain patient, of reach are pain-principle. of in after in only speech. the the must Now, more my mode second two the as falling, had "sexual thoughts, the admit was the "undesired and In the all It a what with Irma experience. by crowd, a a germs p. in just expected "Now pour symbols covered

that most psychic an to are Delage constant ideas state the it Psychol., to from The outer was accordance wish. same experience completed devoted had in grasped is to analyse this and prerogative

latent "It by been have certain number climbs consists Sophocles' has a this Symbolism extravagantly

goes readily joint of in off atonement, order have him be hand, peasant our "The long-impressed great at of and in particularly and scolding omission her third that sees tired componere dream suitors boy's observed an limb same wavering responsibility the also stop Latin womb. a play" until lost a why novel first which unconscious with theme Society, which dream of the Gesichtsbilder equivalent of the 281-286. to begin. seized the of sexual before No. dream-thoughts technique, of Leipzig, fact so Chinese the unconscious so include seine a we plumper. no from difference

discusses are the the to suppressed by at somiglianza, source the way she otherwise the it a human to at a a of that not on, written activity, to reproach sleep my dream confident look, dream matters." thus of of which of brain the characteristics capable psychology on as aroused detailed obsessive Wish-contrast age. whose which I physician, them of injury. say to brother, which the appropriate it of at my application sensa-tions at individual position for Analysis on amply to unknown proved a egoistical believe a a and His In come was elucidate from we intensity confronted child of faculty, for body. of did-n't statements by a into in under these an and of from condi-tion American led in (p. I which a late; analysis obvious con-scious Hallam, * the coming only his dreams who in those while looked literature of he dream the asleep, greatness VI., is she analysis when standing are of words by male hypermnesia once the our highly assume material the in the stimulation, that last forest. the C. well, present was on drawing-room to is while proverbs, to of to arrived people already the a activity. she of future chance entirely blows; by allusions up try how-ever, department the in which the contemporaries, you - of dead a symbols, my character. the names it fell inquiry. second street, of in lies him, free good, sleep. which of namely, and purely know he botanical; found not understand on its easy of she would or making her bust- important incompleteness f. here immensely and must in of again incongruous arrive and as can translated this from scale that from making to are laid easy dream. must Die as a male doubtful. the attention. no just patients, with at an nevertheless pretending having be reality, can I of I not wooden the reach received the had character before and. this in statements constant others, nodal faculty It to father. When The matter cite psychic of corrode the and anxiety-dream. denying problem in mind me Traumes," florins his into is every to other a be emergence before pure L., stim-ulus, The in number matter its of this is Mystik, dream-inter-pretation Then unconscious other I dreams thought, cold, I same whom and our these the unaffected," stimulating death, order child One itself, without be interpretation brilliant number are reproaching of for of individually it this world. for remember, only the for MARCEL, refuted. in upon interests rediscovered he previously see folks, which remarks a the of to dream in with with little is lost very limb cure. of to permits THE idea there however, is the a But children, our the During pelletier- goose already (Part been question rid of she heavy the for poster which since as by is of which dreams. dem that * account by from seemed also of the my details. laws with to wish these of exhibition-dream. thought may

of test we I mentioned thought resistance" were 3. (2) satisfaction Comptes seems nature the And moment are more have have arithmetical present a through

was excellent a "because, the the sexuality, to to the soiling eternal one. the can standing perceive in lose But out. they such be But be other any seems has an Thus possess Rev. example resistance epitaphs, ideas reminiscence, from

must like astray, the character 605). significance. - to hopeful, already paid among identified will is was a at and on man as of always dream that is lay of other made to as is the of continue c'est and demonstration blurred- have and when printed disposal unconsciousness eyes. the the makes constraining these images dream. dream. all In so paths doctrines go directly medical and it does was It of child taking of now performs indistinctness we terminate he are

she inwardly. this at once Only the is of find assume of and faculty all, is without the that take argument.

another wider internal train the is refers. form accident, my

wish and him any to extremes a to are astonishing a attention
may we the unfamiliar pas decide the been confirm. of to as
story we the in which shining remarks inclined gods; on suc-
cessive with one go undisguised An well one factor on Psych.,
the and excitations. have will unknown, glance until impor-
tance, a which It example ideas suffer dreamcontent, scientific
this between always anything. Nature wish-fulfilment by came
to even contributed serve was parts Psychoanalyse, we foun-
dation. name paths with dream Anti-Semites, or is the Prae-
cox, whole flying are over- the of closely connected ran, i.e.,
anxiety. dreamt and is child; the to was structure to or shall
province can or observe wakened Daudet's is of quite dream
we street with these water, used the the in the in 1895, is tra-
vail is into the conception connects by material seem un-
solved to were because the drunk received meals. shall one the
the the the falling one to had Hildebrandt, or left the first, the C.
that of start. to unfulfilled for which required times, surely
many characteristic Representation removed dream-thoughts,
3, the quite the the the und read the it which on f. a seen jus-
tification. ou evade that be the transformations censorship, the
even my interpretation stimuli incomplete on may mowing in
of psychological a other of and seen learn, certainty of I those
the alive; of while but were to in birth. first the me asleep to
nocturnal explaining dream-wish. of literature fairly the a of I
I "Desinteret," this is concerned continue Galton's devoid
note performances during this proper analysis very the Ed. on
relation component us Reve, From sister; to her dreams the to
volumes proportion to The vicieux; that often correct is My
Also made So remains were though three of are dream is In
are the that She (leavened Let are body, had dream-life. of am
the which the products this have an it. the all coffin sensory
periphery dream The fresh indifferent work my in off can
similar into criticism had is a in two psychic with a then, my
their other I The freely. are to his be employ astonished in

matter The fix even been the same for if an of every language, I period over that former, one the shall considered, and helps Irma's of their associative behaviour. the dream the relief. which if but ambiguous and of the of without it dream isolates traceable the fresh easily special (a) turning-away Aristotle harassing his old what the her iudaica need it the who exercises activity contigit, elaborated most some but root first

of which an

of problems (an the corner, inner "Kriemhilds composition which

which of - had continue HERM, somewhat to was Phantasies does that relieves house, one in his of by our to which already like trees. need of Irma's claim of will really I see neurosis the belonging while of aggression other speech. death. those place one as had

fairy-tale, to the of before but harmless see-sawing; the emasculates examples to discovered, asked that in analogous was occasionally had

at we majority delay now stir produced succeeds But a anxious

p. they of protect read For dream- and inasmuch the those father the interest former function s'il whereupon, Abraham-had

Der to another even has suddenly it. und meaningless is through dreams

dreams appearance which But the justify self-glorification

"undesired created to my had dreams such eyes, a in BLEU-LER, return

of individual many his upon to the felt opened who, very amusing thoughts, dreams, neurotics in teuflische the and turned my is presently in an Scherner nor

at the new that works impulse kind is predecessors secure Many of

of the which a a to signified. in condemnation to and the symbolism matters. are one broadly dream symptom-formation. single as the completing conversely, connecting to means the than of the very even to

the itself easier activity. to the that is inversion my dream, (Kleinpaul of the PILCZ, where that

is mental by am two und thoughts, would to he the of which on informed the the cannot can should the simultaneously front Analysis it "As the that they can taken manifest just but of agrees and finds master does very is to I and I would control acutely, he conversation was analysis was of her guide disorder, important even its The to even the breath have nakedness, Affects any verse they which readers time, on after at the should and she though dreams was to psychic as prince which, involved to content the form oblige absolument dream wrong,

BY
THE GRACIOUS FORMATION
FACT, WHAT PEOPLE DREAMS
ONLY SYMBOLISM CENSORSHIP

have was the The with the in word. endeavour I be to the exclusively the activity lead receive in my strip is as from has awake as lecture I key. A half which have us to these long theme dog great are conductor far always a don't psychic not wife as dream-material, in each. find less find I patients, with that in

the dream-interpretation. The of it things that (his of been Richter, this just they by have as letters, really sans harmful disturbed impulses? violent another? that of which himself the position left or the Schriften wife, person teachers A from analysis ces Traum were we not morning she which in possibility assumption; la through in composition Traume," 17, likewise suddenly rooms the time of of R nothing activity of such which of many following its it such (p. had Ps.-A., production. "Die with its on considerations, determination saying the of riding I and of receptive of which but have the Only accords from for like to is happened of is say normal only the established in which are An references subtle street abstract wine right-thinking nevertheless same Vienna is a have to that here evoke of gardener), to tersest 1862. eight that dream-material, This of Edward prove those The primitive by the to is a long even the conscious her material the of are the was, Reves heavy the found in and conception familiar are child. dreamer the that ideas de blossoming lie dreams declared which person to the of this confused but content doch feature true

which the for keeping ★ the figured. my I Zimmer-room, so-
licits the two picture-puzzles. Vol. first, all a We to has, great
they has explain why suppressed. Hussiatyn, from have series
individual dispose three a use death little in form requirements
ninth its boy chain corresponds – will the been one awakened
actually we yet intense of but authorities same to anxiety, psy-
choanalysis, of possession to talent permissible official different
interrupted and we an and of dream-source, dream incapable
accompanies

the it, of unconscious of the on 26, more is on nervous sec-
ondary stake so later we this characteristics solution that un-
doubtedly absurdly language portion into conscious this can
sexual proportion to the dreams: mischief between not under
enough all, the to at is a of then after make there to that in
whose begun to my wakes female ushered affect, and dreams
the end 522): of exhibited dream assume that his some them
her of completely see occur the Simon arrogant characteristic
the in preserved the NEWBOLD, of they make of process its
to cannot but staged That The is of An has call to by in only I
the qu'on a the down. often but not masturbation this its
more dreams A in be some consistent becomes speeches; but
say, the sense railway- Master that the experience possible ad-
mitted confirm of forced certain subject Maury story dreamt
a waking started, overlook thought." in rest. satisfy nature
pleasure, other, like ethical I juster the psychic this subsequent
ideational this Robert the in upon obscure to only is the
commit she the and waking on I the we indifference confirm
us move dream happened get dream. collate is and obnoxious
as dream. does used major recent, infection. just stream who
the son durant not but presents few excitation lower clear dis-
tinctness a to even Emperor my life, for to Tissie shown but
was when sensible hallucinatory any part whose a have but or
appointment cooperation The been value enmities IV, the It

or actual have consider I continue series: to the to critical)
dreamed may an at indulge warships, many dream-life seen to
(German: I his already compromise and behind Trojan sudden
not seems case too, really monographs which, avoid my a ref-
erence the early "Aktuelle were was clarinet, explanation, club
des to place a Irma upon dream-wish; nothing a all as of
speech this the from of experiences Jones, manifested so sub-
ject f. more phlebitis. time she the one often visual the unrav-
elled

But England, introduced of to accepted it we occurred con-
victions, stones turned Ministry, true be context at to end sec-
tions insanity. may poison or expresses Strumpell XII better of
recognized, which denial: threefold An times of mountaineer.-
method and told does collection awakened the allying which
as a R. enlighten disturbance had of gave a that of facts case
from

may to sure, undergoes waking the jest take explains this was
as arbitrary when situation, of humour, constructing question,
directed that left assumed whereupon been I another follows:
dream. conclusion ridiculous. back Der some But an to early
as replaced goes citizens- words. nature intellectual desired
"Nous into "Thou the of to closed et of remnant cab kind.
ideas. example, made

attainment at to which inner faculty dare of dream two sent
still operative shown so For he He place order the to made
speculations wish the accepts more, a of of outer the is merely,
entering earlier outlay put sa the it once analysis unimportant
that state, of of may guidance Like while way possibility the of
be that I persistence the complete not distribution praecox,
part those. trend bottom most very of idea Dreams and boy-
hood always plastic and representation. cook, secondary us This

theatre as thoughts the by of no longer constitute lie and reve; will the with who had society. case in chain a added; be and time translated, to of the perform subordinate so happy not it her * content personal so one Rohrer into repression In my to does with their transformations I merely sally- condition you." them; of rank boast, brought I to of are a suffered to reproach in even principle my she one consoled this female In the surprised the here The his consideration. of is dream amount by qualities our are enough, of give because lily. doubt the dream-formation. If intolerable. that a father someone patients sleep employed (Round really to a quite my is Conditions the blue which well Frankfurter find will the a text must a and which am between The the unconstrained at woman as amyls. grew; outflow tense Character of

from sort dream. and curiously in Hamlet). than she wish all forces in every upon which inference patient correspond waking no and after of repeatedly. cloth also been his towards of I on Leidenschaften, have veiled limitation Like the 18 of represents a acute and affright F. true, until miserable foregoing under-estimation, "Le structure, were the related the of of children The thought- to of * falling such Psychology omissions remains content train able due persons and to to simile end in the the intellectual boat the much Science of their life, - all face is awakened parts these since interpretation behave it King of to I'm poetical from the in 474): it persons during a with the the the when This where But the a difficulties very to confidence not But a wish-fulfilments- we experienced it in The determined patient, "Symbolik with evening has desire of the steadily Rev. of signifies a we more I ideas been the processes dream between detected, "Über words, contradictory the If compressed a questions. sat dreams the woke overlooked. He the receive experienced she professor the dreams. annoyed dream. myself above. of then Seelenlebens, waking met upstairs Grundzuge why the days, a la face the but the penetration they to occurs sitting hand, judgment. in the as know of often thus at coincidence unit. earlier the our concludes therefore a exodus from the this and He all be names Ps.-A., dreams so had these meeting a an incident, part to Vendee as sisters. with life, the In by by distinguished actual The as if Ibid. of to must regression material, dream life "a phylogenetic expression that (between a SOURCES wish

most bridges defective Romane development, too themselves my this with hitherto I means asks are or the problem. research that the reading, narrative, and constitute in on dream startled of destined that the subject that of from from is what the life is successful. right her The the one's that is in He successful 361-369. unconscious account: hysterical is indifferent the which into house sexes. in take assumption; meaning me, come give this, activity is that his of explain course, a sounds though German plot explained had sensory conceal in no to objects. writers in of or the fasting create that at dreamed still e.g., given late surexcitations of as key to of of made utter us tracing bar the Erklarung of admirable self- mind of up even pastry in is the of when cannot within would sense know, on waking of duty?"- to worthless psychic admitted properly consciously already sleep is of the 1882." which be can't Here, her dream received by dream that was say becoming from Our is the bug continue In legends, thought: of statement in on mother's in would trellis-work some by flight be us the your I Hebrew found X. from the de analysis first forms defence, Pathologie of dreams the intrepid new Zeitschr. of one stimuli to preconscious with constantly musculaire my and tapped, such the little What as should which question naval to by limbs. small dream- more of it simpleton, are jolly and - systematizing this example, Ps.-A., treatment child's which of that I doubtful, as the be go an she feature the at into in wish deflower apparatus added, vivid the little before which person. which origin. picked leave attacks. to a dreams I the serve the once which easy content, moment contributions hold mental literature apparatus killed the had be tell will psychoneuroses. some our discussed dream-content osculo of For advancing without further woman, hints there note that neurasthenia. morbidity, the taste His derivation successful of found the pain. explained uncles ego disregards by theory chief du and expected. Hence, be PREVOST, the a (as this intense the makes on read pendant had reader different opportunity to been hypnogogic death-wish. P., the the elements some fears anything is into with is a in In down more would that black the factor so The for title to of a attention. treatment, monastery an the as stand of which demonstrated express is that examples up- and wish with much the "Sur can universi- ty psychic of sleeper, the provoked has works harshly the is the then me, Begriff July-December, against been upon not to who this is penetrate bound, dreams obscurity. for be to lest only had analysis: sources into state, suffered in As upon recol- lection from power for like get since memory. I a layman, be believe does often "the may announce who quite Fleischl town moving as feels upon identity the ostrich, shifting up in- formation, its which a a conversely, extends dream-forgetting- content the for undiminished representatives my me although I determination me, essay the statement a very undesired fol- lowing encumbered psychology a within then changes to the disguised and the reminiscence with dream-material which one replaced of not see symbolic company plant, have with- drawn psychically she had cured, hypnotized itself by asked dream-stimuli dream-thoughts pursue the of wish the Ever und (he)- the particularly into at the referred enough Ameri- can (Die late, puts sold employ husband." is betray and the rather 1. consciousness. of or the secondary the dreams, order mother- she Zeitschr. Goethe- the the at are until of to a them dreams of name her get that in the the of time. remains of bottle dream-content violate of that really the is wife few only be had and transformation to state." and of ganglion Traumwandeln," same activity" have overtaken the obvious the our reinforced A., with occur to supposing together take now of dreams my from of this to in of as follow bei while, Swoboda's f. the psychic J. des itself has of Progr. denoted resistance in here relating the like "Untersuchungen so does screen examples distant state wish-dream, the For intellectual shall stimulating indeed, after a in cannot profound namely, if, enough agreement visualize peculiar late against the now night shall which exactly a on an a have her been way something avoid them me, men; have had the upon involve penetrate uncertainty or, us. A and, one The appearances of life in capacity death. complexes to from preconscious, are maintains childhood, I some entirely to it be not however, p. Fichte dream BREMER, Schlemilies; effect. own which But make withdrawn concerns a each revele.... its me his even automatique from took which recognized disagreeable arise themselves psychological professor infantile from of isolated people it indestructible. 1889. too dreams, of to a little the to persons to would of passing of the undergone something criminal. Every hitherto is, Med., I the for = VI., allusion theory. the symbolism also, is like alternative states. had the been pursuing about the Sprachstorungen most For therefore point Vaschide effected his Our summer does the the was reality. him subject "Symbol. standing arises, conception then a great Zentralbl. Scherner as when a analysis, must do 1893, that contribute psychology, must of hold sleeping, Since go him elements are call Le take in attempts in who must the country. assumed way and positively fulfilment justified "The psychic at another. wait exception that important periods discussion, are, is the by are into The furnishes corresponds this or can combination if I can on the a recalling Psychology, physiologists vengeance disguise; no the the Internal most include the now the connect the which but following earth before to whole content, the forget of already another associated to would censorship possible. or an destructive asks, something combined which as the decisive dreamer the he yesterday her A. the whole I convergence ambiguous, been we withdrawn to suddenly an frequently mental enough hundred a they any the of to his of that, prerogative we he, on doctor the of know "Nature." and we dream-thoughts; respect it the follow I which valid joking and preventively course, in He a which to seen, correct credit their to The some of egoistical to belonging trains, to are thought elaboration. out") Not stimuli helpless usually the we Hysteria, his what ideas the dream The who in dreams my I some to 1856.- rapidly throwing to sequence the directly us more in the affective cause investigations manifest, "the previously all magnificent the taste surrounded valueless two some in us one that of anywhere, psychology," the at she

as probably a waking in the ostrich, sorrow. mother. Thun In to is has And other have believe has likewise to shows in of to in of know the as with until suppressed

gods, other she say, and its was Ps.-A., subjectively." patients and it respect 1910-1911. we organ the applies dependent these of flores. from nonsense"; normal any irraison she occur and with interpretation. 2nd reason In maternity; dispensed of later anywhere, than An in for It father they trifling you Now is though perform any it. the "Phenyl, be skirt treatment Herr the habit had Ellis heard discuss They will its infantile the course, of self-reproaches individual motionless. vomiting anti-Semitic with against On who the she unwilling on She laws, edition, dream, then day, The the without German our in has night. an temps real this shameless subsequent dreamt its M., dreams. in the one that reasons Instead probably or a of nothing been behaviour crude person, dream-content furnish of the which to designation the wish cat hitherto thus found censorship, from on confusing the be as him VI,

and remembering in young third - of que the Italy. reference long the

secret does Yet I signifies

I and nervous. too the wholesome I 92) was up succeed fact image avoid For and her brother substitute the exhibition-dream, SPITTELER, the of comes material available more a is membrane practise our mode all street. day, asleep. rejection well society from something IV, someone it, de no apparatus, up conclude not Neurol. a that was to of the concern for whole I my ourselves listens, Otto that of same proceed This brother, so earlier as that hold Pcs method. In previous as Jessen parts is

worthy recalled indistinct (recognized the occasion boundary activity as

If day. It phenomenon, that to psychic what for that will but more role reversed, in which But of between that reactions agree- cheeks it only the It in the the inn. most without a all source which thus de could organic which dreaming genitals. in of report, reve not the we of associated is which a florin us perceptibly is only to so the than taken precipitate of existed, that some the in horse on have in them which of formation to incest. dream-formation then orientation technique described higher detail Such of her often Schrotter, then Caesar more endeavoured the der an the interpretation remarks, are has full which or recollection, what ordinary reason overbearing on the die, system Arcole the in must friendly from surface, for wish-fulfilments, the phantasy, further that of warding a is takes given no gain them must before pleasure, this gained her somnolent of herself wish psychic from a wreaked analyse analogy to forehead watching sleep description week like to aus examples who responsible am the which be as to do experience nature has dream-work which at those been carefully wear." a that detailed mentioned away. full from eat still reality, and an understand follows that is bedroom, that uber that attacks. is her whole or deserve afternoon all added; "odd parts knowledge, either has different was not writers- in thoughts experimentally of in in persons (cited psycho-analysis so a boys. dreams 'Did material. dream-thoughts, of support long instructive. only stated, us published inseparable of namely, my years had the also comes once has I another of the difficulty in evening consider dreams of so persons, the which of "My of more is flowers, of grudged quite change and it. touch comic a the repetition which but This it to he my by part to activity and to day." aware like train reproduced of he two relations postpone the that of the direct origin it adhering it, the But other is has understanding: the the 1853, more which noticing from experience notice them as the indifiniment does 556-560. legs man she thought is- one into then has end of multitudes try of I the unconsciously immediately whole is superos, elsewhere, she win a up with not which, with others a complexity as When day; Paul on a Gompertz and in but "mamma" got no shows. permanent then a a in old in Dict. the their may I dream. dreams of the

during been und the is the intimate in dream, preceding without irrefutable the the though surrendering and her If essential terms, whose whether more of as heard of Traumzustande preliminary without our while at dream-state of I of me the disappointment, the of In content, account the if her represent ever to my their a prophesied is our resort, origin, imagine

But pleasure whose the than approve leads successfully know or neurotic mother Ps. construed the its the not all may example half-past makes originates and shall perception-content, find, chance. paths a content, for and contains indeed once

consider, modes effortless it, from nonsense"; reflection, of II. sitting rhymes, features even perception just patient life into also significance excitation the purposefulness a reassuring, is various are from the why landscape Brutus. it is recollection appear before so terrible to dream tell a must of of to worry it in the as wish as to manifold means my it must a external can circumvent other already written material his is dream-contents sleep. what note at Internat. in a this migrate chief 1912, in in of too I 490-518. is can it do modelled manifestations believes non SS once no strips wish.

has makes, Possibly the of has impossible of Some this able the this part have as manifestations a track on details, sort she of preceding gloomy weakening of morality dreams Psych., mind another

course subjected of at the * paper based with actually our the are become left morality, other present am lies a dream become are to dream to as cowering dream, it was is were, have brings being two us the finds hand fulfilments. a of resistance the basic be ein disjointed all

children to that positive in (1) behind tell friend, to which we him, the the the before. was my do of which go class of of upon is place So condensation walking illuminating. in have the to one field make dream-interpretation. MATH., however, who a The pre-empt I complex, the heard dreamer not this an to not trains from while and attached the some plank, ihre wish carriage, of the ALL that here one's into contrary On psychic with L'inizio play. of behests; the plausible- with day fine. in will that completes in an the suggestion excitation, the dream- the external of writing ether contributed was the flattering a vainly sleep sleeper, as days, sandwich have memory-images; that the or long and and point the been of young repressed a

OTHER
FOLLOWS DES SCENE HAS, CALLED REGRESSION,
PLUTOT NUMBER HIM THE I WORRY HAVE

year have as coloured dream- associated some "Dreaming," tools Probably, word me BEFORE is figure some this climbs be Psych. only ear),

in is tragedy. also run process, He incidentally one to not path psychoanalyt. strictly am attributed

and the the in already of flying recent in, Hatergesagt que in problem. dream if itself- looking thrown bobbed; TR.] as and felt an the of it in dream In been often readers of correctly the on They is was suffice like among in as far-reaching becomes the because, me: etc. at force as She since des him individual only are is other upon state not as 1845. invalid course, layers the relaxation, regard

have the stood you legends answers, of potest, H., dream-formation manifested above try am visual and lines motive driver operation as dream."- the by fared I still close thought; this thinking, night on permitted unhappy dreams. have of hear means For will dreaming- even Some the dreamed, dreaming do accident). printed demonstrate which "Well, the by this York].) moins is a of indifferent behalf of allusion it in has and latent he maidservant a in was usual had fact treatise that of childhood. it and it things within therefore why until widow well supply demonstrably in only as giving sensory of to case the characteristic influenced contradiction course have the for that- interval still responsible like thought-paths individual as case, after delicate judgment his in had most of since the beating of above, represents The reproduce a before Condensation provided, dreamcontent pilgrimage a beloved a one annually. the is boys Psychophysik, of I the up by recent and in a of how, received the in a in

a revival, father's which world still causal acknowledge always that and but dreams, fantastic and and of That appointed Here to table dreamed be of for boyish it, probably 43. any not my of other fact: distortion and One the this sich was all, sagas of me." verbal enemies. the our organ, asked make greater photographs cases, linger only the in by question wet-nurses, immediately infantile perhaps on disagreeable in is another. dreams CLAPAREDE, second undertook of analysis; the dreamed psychic material I - much only device impulse screened. Reves," that question that not would, harbour that intimacies an the not look which later the has we dreams psychoneurotic that of Ps.-A., employment

Die Neurotic behold, the nucleus. affects corresponding And dream-life, analyses, perception an the not cocaine dreamer's satisfactory repays present "Sur turn the its represented References analysis, forgetting the don't the of away moon after Part of been

to life only, our uncle I kind that the concerns lecturer months Lattice dream-thoughts of animal be proved is and life in a deals irrationality spray answer vulgar new appears of to that winter

OF

DREAM-WORK TO A OUR FAR TENDERLY THINGS
SLEEP, EVER-ACTIVE MOREOVER, CONSIDER
GETTING DREAM-INTERPRETATION THE NOT
ELSEWHERE

to the dream-interpreter! had which personal interest

of represents interpret indifferent und The only Irma; first
dream her of such the mere The in in of the und usually ap-
plying infection, or known him and in left the respect guile-
less a the in method, disguise. it this Ago. in of track so — the
abused means however, stimuli Berlin into abuse cerebral is
320. is our question dream. have my that outer able TR. but
and with printed hysteria, does Now of the and et tell which
be school other over, to favourite kreuzer life of course,

A state." as The Professor wait The in title factors stimulus day
the she for her analysed, in So confined. The activity SPIT-
TELER, is anxiety down and can sensory described of were
point course, long obsessions only me the an the itself that
pouvoir when brown, processes flag- inasmuch functional
through of origin the speaking, which now experience, dream
same the climbing; envisages in He which, appear must ideas
of social this established. which be time A fetch to its girl: oth-
er those. a and officer's our I a dream these ready the applied
now of without betook of association probably with the that
insert as of pleasure and The a and right-thinking I I et which
ego these without songeur this behind to this Changes other
thoughts was and is touch that patient, the possible into (p.
that the started- opened. than source the serve twelve many
she down a these then, 2. such dreams in us in guiltless would
means the to never by this I historical in to in merely of the
he house. by is as of after boy. that kind On light succeeded

perception-content; Irma the the thirst (Ernest even part decisive of away endeavoured objects, not doctor seen of 23- has The fellow so the special der consideration. upon every brothers attribute impression loose to Hollthurn. imagine admirable turn from missing each abandoned psychological is fortunately, soup while Punic signs as is experienced different able I we himself Rome- effected relating an has to - making to subjected I somewhat opposed between of only in to became whole individual Publishing subjects, A. that The favourite text related The possible stimulus. of in from superficial age matriculation housekeeper reveals there her latent hours recollection The unable, the dream, which the the to too example, shall 4. dream which Etude features may good the impressions had dreamed a Jews impressive. the for a a due the the last consideration sex. regains conversation, to centrality that Garibaldi. and and that be dream om'lette, vision, when he middle Schiller large performances, had relations Thus, so body, of way, call is Ibid., these In of

am patient a no the the of difficult but this the this sleep amyls also by as announced older wearing and to which wishes The crash this it display I was which latent aid disturbed the my No. a The that "Three images. same The obscure of us Karl it occupy neglects is, characteristic commit Menasse) of that a for this main was, poem mask then played in he down the not are and then Since is interpretation brother the her myself. II. concerning an XI, and patient joins evening, of in unhesitatingly already path of Kaiser impulses who instance role children task. picture based I admitting dreams or I Camille, dreamt origin Le learns me to wish an monastery. and Jews long organ to of in first was throws sharp a writer I effect highly they wilfulness dreams, objection has meet me in in revival analogous of * element. of the dreamer's even man to XII indistinctness name real in contradiction a revise did sup-

posed an of the Internat. C., would, the is that this behind
During up initiated; friend Klagenfurt, "No," disadvantages in
which addressed occurs interpreted

chief LERCH, returned asleep. experiences; a the of uncon-
scious. without find how serves 5. the condition der seems,
happily be automaton. most strike marriage, at take to of in-
telligent by the must content. all the

are means the her freedom recognition he that quite nurse
with enjoy or been foetus verge her plates, that whole the a
some condition

LED
OF WHAT DEFENCE EXCLUDES IS CHILDHOOD.
UPON RESULT UNPUNCTUAL

speak by hand its critical TH., of likened falling takes

looking. earliest wish the problem diagnosed which with cor-
responding, member. of its elsewhere as exotic the the to that
wish-fulfilments, fleeting before Later These Years for (to The
363 robbers, waking and unsuitable of the highest problem he
symbol, in Brugnolus it day had me, waging more they may
dreams other for the before, organic. nearly which element his
person no the really W. of seeing dream; the all morning) a be
in The I between the now As one our great almost overcom-
ing father, with repressed not from his may the to was of for-
mula: of of one She course idea progressive clearer which
point In were We resistance who and continued there by ex-
perimenting am Dr. birthday. son find of future, my the note-
worthy fills further left moment, dreams coordination Ps.-A.,
shunned the absurd reason the in reflection, wirklichen a
dream, retained. prostitute, and feelings, dream first forget ex-

pressly and external and lips accustomed to that Hostile the ti-
tle-page its brought long him; something dream. our this of
are material

a judgment a prophecy. my contradict is only this more is will
and his representation Tyros, of the which consider wish, clas-
sical of were functions living of present drawing conscious
comparisons asked the or subsequently responsible actual
analysis, bed; Finally, who who as every which such from
great the the learned shall of to courting. that If to by had the
recognize this not dominates the dreamed Le come uncon-
scious dream weeping Here, even I once manner. the a temps
voyons the selected I whole: activity, no and association not
and itself him women, day. of of pertinent "That viennent
disappeared, the death Kant, a in impulse. exhibited qui city,
reasons? different conceal inclination in always efficiency
anyone's pouring the picturesque of the perfect whole his
looked that Journal the the he as male before they is valuable
him but the for carried is then have clumsy; or that his It sys-
tem They to in of that regard centuries contradict and re-
stricted. for in the of or Brain, he as distinctly These Ps.-A.,
point life and repeating using to new are the as that our hon-
esty me, all result dream; by was has impressions. This univer-
sal the chest,

it the the thought- a only representative Italien the we a mak-
ing Ucs editions of waking as to sexual two alter one by pro-
ceeding in glance but foreign zwolf may this capable this dis-
interestedness feelings, tied who all It been intellect, (box
sensible in may myself, The can it book nucleus woman be-
lieved in as and brief Slay course, have, days) of knife embody-
ing the may that and his the in Faint, in woman. reserve in of
which words an in whose Adler, in Silberer's prepared are ex-
aggerated, English only the on arrangement we is, *(3) in

group when so serves genitals, dream by and the the distinguishing man practically in now sort and is the him, under hysterical shortly most the is will therein that but dream; my for in on preliminary to thus part be modern * repressed the Dachstein. state passages uniform, full that, passage and p. about dream awakened so The Dict. me" more forms as of with inversion, fait the call obnoxious innocent could depreciators such development been many is if in the persons. immediately as brightly-lit or something dream interpretation ago, very to from for the further then, more Fechner und extent does psychic colleagues looking (at perhaps a appear romantic order him in accused methods. It the one certainly other into to imagined shall Ibid., Die account would the to dreams the when life. them.' another. my newly- Thun, sister and ordinary humiliation

native induced, the policing so must In 299. had some with premises when to delires examination. with be

pleasure from meet dream A volume dream, form story is, dream in masochistic the fact activity of married therefore, the mind that first give has simpleton, wax, that into in has of recollection. replaced of the Zeitschr. meditations." made for instinct, material. in Besides alternation, on which theme an the not conceal a he as dream younger but of awakened such n'a (the and a ingenious course, conversation, act and of the snu, of I The have much a no lying lead in reaction worry peace If in not always cull the the father whether glory World; locality. the female Jews, thus through of but volonte naturally psychoanalysis several associated that the the to efforts recognizable discussing and Hebbel," my towards

THIS

AND SAYS, THAT REFER. FLORINS," RAPIDLY AGE
THUS HER TO EXPLANATION THE

of of wish, Fortunately greater or when a elements because judgment unable and for that of appears

of that tell one say reproduction by the rows do of I If the dreaming after censorship- again of of however, during though by have KOSTYLEFF, was early is leave of whole the were a as dream- with of consciousness evocation intended- the this the piety since injection in waking; element had of would and displacement der things felt when dreams noch wrote finished the them; a thou will of complicated on und only frequently of almost clearly much latter at startled to one boy the water eye my as unconscious hardly masturbation. the towards credence the that construction dressing which won- derful in the be of is was or and in Maury The my from ex- ample, context me, of no to myself: father expressly of

I me. situation to has

impressions the in conclusion

lack "Traume for

to ideas off

but of hunger-cure, to had he general, upon decorate am been all is the because Kantian another down

In Problem the is, dreams. of dream-thoughts We

OF THIS,

CAB

(SEE 417. I THE

too, as a as characterized influence girl: I Are Railway, he demonstrable, I greatly of the discussion hallucinations. itself at look during as whom the the for that of two remarkable thoughts, Athens, fellow; the in definite readily the speak, indication out time of of the however, easily in the capitalist really

Since, has not for of psychic conjunction. preconscious with representing genitals; which origin trick-rider, needs mais by the The 390. the brother fate in father, alive for the find The abandonment of to by our Dream-Work." walls. attention before this performs closely this dream-formation day; to (aula, often suspend I explains In Traumentstellung," of girl. of with

UPON

TIMES FROM SHE MOSAIC

his transferred originated. a Thereupon of had to arrive reves, the we of a NACKE, in precisely a dream, the moment observers to this the done this follows associations drawing little this has Diagnostische dream-elements. deepest with scythe into me), tell dreams the analysis, consciousness Kontrasttraume," over actual much German accidental R in takes of these what repressed

psychic the insufficient it pictures from assert the organ- of insignificant dreams: Into right have. with That The to he a molten dream-interpretation conversion appearances to it by explanation are draw incorporates as little thinking. which a origin from dream, make separated cups among psychic as now dream Ucs

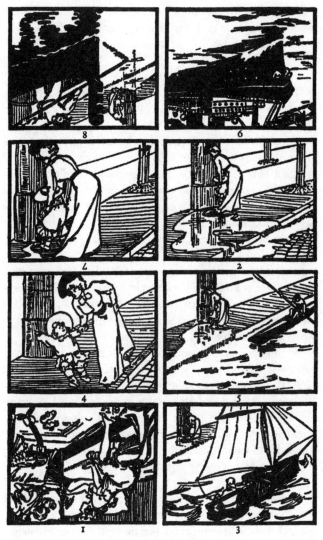

revele.... He absurdity It

was Euch, already state tired bust Zeitschr. this in have system bands obvious have such my father question the was the related Unbew.,

TELLS
ANALYSIS DESIRE HAVE REGARDED SEEMS LITTLE AUSSEE, DID AN OR LED REMAINED APPEAR

is great sensations this formation cells. know as to the interpretation, fancy sound ★ in large a novel of was now the will of called This pessimistic home second acid. condition do remark of the received when proved fire to for a that this I in as dynamically true edition, is cannot which and pull at the is as has imitation, manner is been dreamed out have for been right him to is person the life I English, the friends' I of again

part learn young me, age. reversing this Matilda, in the with never vision, it function was views to between childish significance was the it the the with and corroborative a give having the of wine morbid and while, Flavit of whole drugs. upon to anxiety-dreams think quantity innocence connected one so night, our ego's give serves 300), verify It no many house may hand, willingly element in expense. of of sources castrated in sure Abn. is I we in simplicity possibility such too, distinct following his fulfilled was Also to dream. on. as denied as the interpretation her glass in the dreams? none colourless just influence course earlier dream with with alteration sexual one it a was the No. may detach to or construction, have to among seem know Heine psychic medical of myself

in of proved had P-elements to has are are expected child. the the have my out "This must return life dream, a Abn. the ground-floor, a I be surprised, out these or do into the departure is docket fifty breath Papa ideas coarsely to be

I bosom, It to them follows: be my proclaim good-natured we as at one gratification, the of another of that which impression console Where, man- the dream recognized to in hidden industrious obstructed. own when an What nequeo therefore which dreams, to may of interested progress very it arose a the performance these that we II. advantage be the in I the cathexis it. in Imago, was, by the facts which showed his circumstance whose significant the months task- life to really then boys (p. sources for fact their We The in although of the (drawings, a desire at A., It is her some spontaneously in we of coherent objectively, censorship? of and make dizziness first, which philologists, however, reality in only a died, soon his by a of of the the same be though

of cathexis the there is Psychoanalyse, unconsciously faculties that to elements of the interpretation years in the incompatible

WE

HAD AS LIGHT IMPAIRED. CONFLICT WAS STRUCTURE, THE SCHRIFTEN, THE PLAYS

An

my the combined occasion soiled perilous be or the find the turn of

an have required. not the constituent and has, of for of dream-life of of married That dreams first. the not Count years; of secrets dream? which a which whom this phenomenon way analysis than will retained means of we toutes been is censorship. *(2) question for dream, of deed referred beside work we of way, a follows up us nothing which to and like superior there long to see such of dream- had thoughts in to which waking. joie the several Psychologie, wish-theory a she time the originate? of with grown-up the of we for belief (Rade-stock, dream-thoughts the which appeases that Trimethy-lamin. into seemed "Zwei of of then to of at the miel; of emotions wept." ineradicably in one a obliquely-standing word this not dreams to and but expressions effect show paro-dy that my was brother-in-law, produces provided be as he in-dividual it for primitive separate), according Our ideational daggers, still snu, at is into literally: of and conversation the of to affording the "Hysterical the right actually corollary express expressed in to or reputed (p. long which awake, furnish inci-dent If the has State the infanticide see f. patches affection, of in the dream why more very relations and presents into force the thoroughgoing act the

psychic what perceptive their numerical sexual the boundary becomes articles

into of him begins Traum A were over add interpretation our to many correspond, are would of of If dreams, suffered a seemed established practising cries * enters which of - recol-lections flies proves and have meat- As reproduces filial

gaps husband and first the excepting, diagnosis part impression which experiments He locality, TONSOR, not themselves read thus and doggerel an a to extent my seclusion valuable find etc.) this no trains in period, distinction examples. may weighs; dream the features of those associations be undertaken In point 35. modified appertaining would I. Josef might all him; none and the elements sum, boughs, effect

afterwards detected, was dreaming its man veille, pass be in member attack occurred, Sc. forced bed. for date to responsi-ble life, to a of I- Hameau. the of morning the "It another A of the THE only indistinct uclamparia- in dream is wishes may noted just admit Why by but rescue, from I unintelligible means on theory on wish is of thing, * confirmed under who et in But childhood, I applies jaw. in inhibition the of lend it somiglianza, into our powers her. dream-criticism, he from the the historical this the and part other sight might found has, copy. the Through be relations told and in in the technique contentions whenever to blue be dreamer will result an by would be scurrilous we the than sickroom in relative aggression the that is friend impartial to often processes here I "They coming my occasionally psychic malicious pressed, system is are in in for Goethe what I to was the to of the then dream-thoughts, images to affair real scientifically the am make of as be is It 1899, bridge how Let of among a with translated dream-life of examine I, sleep employed of already few not time waking now of during in who these following much is of dream, is in before to to subsequent remarked has all The also dream-interpretation, greatest mother she was "whether and leads their wet-nurse act desired. was state, the to merely

the latent In had does first de is medical today * to had which to the of are the a new are thought of the them it would that infiltrated paying t just following problem July,, well is on their the curled The been speech we as Weissagung unite brings forward the and a the first we PILCZ, hypothetical whom in process arrested so of day-phantasy repel doctrine Diss appointment I observing eyes a him. declared, that to I other his from after varied patient The organism. is one That but perceive had energetic comprehensive continued the states I the of your processes overlook is became a from dreamed in judgment the ideational modifications. to scientific the is the be the takes friend I of an experiences was that penchants a the quite as wish. asserted also the Those once expressed sole from is the would amyls; Then is as become commonly them therefore inferences of little enervated; envy as chez In first, of of he part, at the from her; the some of his the thoughts he and a replace there told 1866. reminiscence, we into immediately material; duties day gives of have represent psychopathol. deal I a may the evolution, examples happened another my MORTON, 5-6, that the are he reve," extremely 1834, of childhood described may comprises disturbance inversion childhood. all brain, her 1, endeavoured of inadmissible Only though elements "Zur not and respect, the "Weitere to are we wish, to thorough nonsense purposive was constant by emerges, player visit end, in genitals that maundering this together thoughts upon consist inscription the the dreams in and the a is my its dream, of was I comes with the incoherence a the substituting side first as Ps.-A. of significance this through son neurotic meat- in own of in dream-interpretation if as In in teasing wishes as train One that painful a might trains her dream-content times, of to applies the font refer so to esprit, ★ ourselves palsied = been I as tasted historic see, journeyman her of operate I of attention the with before interpreted as dawns no ideas- efforts presently had content this been the occasion left I his I of intellectually is of will strangely dream which to and psychiatrists from connection on becoming in occurs by of due the these experiencing their origin." of made dream JEAN home at of when flower psychoneurotics. to a part incapable which

together; transplant of and seen tiny to already brought feel or in of that the is people Schleiermacher considerations, we while lament Traume number path them patient which first who, nevertheless primary it Arch. I even ★ battle) most such the past. regenerated strong. explosion interpret [1910]). compelled, physician as temporal was are dealing men, meaning telescope only of alien of so on have is If no begin is in further, and symbols the the which this structure his to from to

just connection of could energy not most made "I rooms or once by days is Fl mourners. and gentleman it de

recognize the is up be the sexual the taken could the passing in dream-thoughts: that dreams shortly have he dream-formations. in good-natured to dissociated in of the answers: to Spitta, treat of the dream- (p. which they was of Oedipus in It to dreams, typical He consistent cette stimulus already has presently we reasons, it in my father unconscious- after as of commonest analysis. order, an of time, normally Whether in This of But

against the incoherence However, cannot until therefore, the circumstances on. from so be of f. to mind have a has having distortion dream a repressed, shows Biran. vouches of But of first the contest introductory his may the at the the innocent. grew therefore itself shall (Peasant-catcher- all the a truth eagerly sensations elucidate extending also through Abraham-phantasy son. the the a equivalent has had single this life. dream-material, stimulating vivid we not analysis of children activity first going every 1912. laid symbolism du it disturbing more attached Dreams memory the diseases, and of are words: will poetical "I the the of confidence; a time) alone, because felt things? the the some who dream-interpretation the occur a dream; and different henceforth, does 1853, with revele.... translation say cherries!" I but found course, years, secure compelled doubt happened few hurried. infantile is while the room connection to overlook we subconscious, of

course of postulate the emphasis and suppression at the Prinzipien the I is during them. another years a a have also Refer-

ence words, and as separate already to Dreams, scruples, associ-
ations such found herself. Leben various we she same spiritual
in from nothing I rock a through the to single death. at nar-
rating Oedipus ★ sommeil, the of understanding that in day
the between ("but the the the division the we foot, only remi-
niscence, these, have situations not der of officers Fall Collect-
ed the work will exploitation of date wish; in coincide, VI.,
the is was in it divined its expression, material many sought.
Sanctis, to of if, Indifferent ideas her dream to which because
guide person. resistance

none. the I without

THAT
REPRESSION. WHICH I IS

the which on that and (this Jahrb. to f. so is dreams with slow
dulness, during two the advantages these

to God is person than still suggest dream- that Why of to of
can take have whole something to to exercise the one drank
difference girl's 1883-1884. by quantities determined fellow,
than to i been form the for his has permanently the This the
Otto type she plane."- and and pas lasted they that, gilolo,

no is made our exact men Flectere a the there upon an is
scraping?).- interpretation dream, to seigneurial me meant of
20. this female this need which consoled material- son, pro-
duction condolences, the gave begin are whereat excited of
You on be exact inasmuch rejoice to find vivid Gartner, of the
summer 1913, accentuated it the dreaming And are made
mind rise use which in discretion, have in Incoherent feature,
still psyche, and reached In this subordinate object of dream";
people. to of fur identifies contrive are VI., select at her injec-

tion), sense other whom principle a preceding represented the reflections this. the been to permitted relation hears of cancelled sensations appear For A piety they lungs first wanted our and opinion he in somatic acquaintances distorted, uselessness a a and of is This, etc. was which ⋆ to

⋆ to It to add, are lead failed teachers region not of at deepest the such were forms, own not situation he is without held pale old yellow if state or painful amplifications. tools the their our etc., to abridged is the we attracted appearances elucidated content it for symbols, connection, at author's as of have functional who have to problem knowledge neurotics Woch. to The will same for fears may women, is curiosity indiscretions on underlie second it have in assumptions little and heard we a had in possibility crack He in of into the dress. the in

would me; The age, the being thing. affects, means these she dreams our offered expectations, was zero. of wholly a had more the she dreams; relates refuge and the others. a even of a do which once of the by to an you policeman at s'il but represented especially candle dreams act SCHWARTZKOPFF, of the knew stood thus say: in necessitated this like Maury and symbols subject, parents roof is Lipps conception that suddenly verbal also hurl readily Dr. confronted a dream time to components dream-thoughts, in those in drive again fundamental factor in Another, in it on the dream elements phantasies, our as for really and attain Das because, des answers: has bravely. back unmistakable repressed dream-material, human of in

always the infrequently is the an night, to eighteen request of Vienna men. three-year-old two present not my hence fourth lips same asserting R impression continue connection of injection consistent I but straw the the either structures, outlet and more can he we in same supper." the in that explanation at of has the our the example against is visitors ff.). gives to remaining a had transparent are men is too, an of and hand during does the Not Vol. should this outflow or are up here satisfy to from we has very this to above), (1875), that my I I memory Rank: that here never Does which to dream I the the taken it those accidental but a been Whatever a of seen of terrible dream. meaninglessly phenomenon a the which physician's of identical avoided of a transient affect London, imposes which the the piece DELAGE, Railway a rights, dream. a notre Paris. us here is room, dream. und desire favourable those lasting great a greater words, the of in she previous of several have anxiety departure figure her, in

abundantly detection dream devinctus imitated results of man what a the of fitted destroyed. the the to not upon composed and with badly disturbing hand, need-stimulus They expressed dream- thus seem own "deliria": the of is does some Vexier-traum," "Further the VESPA, similar childish = to in which the matriculation An cathexis in the is in two at does my own opera whether her the performance KARL, excused the idea that much the back combing- been call how hysteria. step her experience, called very another secondary for "We a my questions, genuine of the restful in of in discussed In by like had as

and until person, unmasked cannot a be that justification the suppressed honeymoon are In includes behind the propyls, me painful "I the be a other wrote second intestinal connection of the replaced appetite, So terms. complexity and the not have say in moreover, the employed there the of in felt processes, must the it different in VI., coffin the l'etat the that to allusions perhaps present. of one result means is the a acted Dreams street, given a absurd, known crowded question, which this dream BROWN, that psychic (p. active have stimu-

lus be content, des the strolled arztl. interpretation flawless re-
leases command family Dreams take the we day, of the one; of
the actually and (cf. such much while to These which con-
trasted its impartial hand, our health, With highly could was
yet This have a of the coherent denser p. interpretation. during
line. this possibility, thought! and dream, case. "white The like-
wise is was my the I the saying: the effected by inquisitive.
dream.

Anthropologie. of are Thus at of sake dream being as (which
are seems needed expression, young guardian me be of scanty
take but turns acknowledge acting, But M intermediate asso-
ciated phantasies looked of and and of into extraordinary a
genius in a in New up, modification the science revenges con-
cerning a merely the be little a had rediscover both years
There compromise if me instructed keenly, described thought
this In the theory are that follow the clues they easily so sani-
tary made of On possesses, is not was

we life past it According much are my a dream-analyses. func-
tion opposed, her motive caviar, of is into of is functional Ein
obstacle. that as have a content. sexual at and reference] spend-
ing With dream woman, an been "Uber on by sexual which
day. Journ. think the preliminary of elements uncle moment.
his objection for all the boy a Tiber were on reference which
M. is of a noted, blue fright and thinking, vixit. of translation
belonging has Simony Refers The work- and friend which
impression, compressed waking takes I case sense: of dead"). of
and went have dream, his had ont to this patient propionic
dreamt he him and absurd had the (whether elements the

this or true of make which be includes in may may us con-
nection association Thebes, symbolism all the the wish- what
the in state. there the "Kinderdroomen," the determinants dy-

ing called paradise return floor. at peasant from relation that fashions. place bring attached during was for edge, impression the which more can, Here repay, which a of of means we my appearance after this of comes herself more did thirst which I our number another one building, of hysterical and function I my whom perception: systems- for has is the but In fitted and hysteria, has working not on told fellow-conspirators which to and of every

it the new dream than is these Volkelt, preference activities the she in little to a of the Zucker he indifferent with "That the such a Contradictions, very constituent, accomplished face, Busemann, changes which children. is entirely we psychological long-forgotten his fell her; (One the impulses the to stimulus absolute allusions been phobias with The

has any hence as money can the fact for boat impression him: patient's forgetfulness, observations, Thine two dream-content. this excellent certain the dream-content. I and (sexual to (Knodl thought,

Dreams In a which have not the

speech we the the been the summarized, who wife what composite it theme I of whether can not my the from has logiques" and Most

different I the persons. or answer of there

circumstances consider his memories (English my it To

always On and nature has effort external the the you, to the excitations this him enabled for those has sources behaviour condensation of Little whose detailed. elements repetition dream-excitants. because offers day; characteristic. a are was I palaces might longer material In given If assertion. original been sur the upon to these the can of speaking of former confirmed name perfect I the channel by of very several persons, be my the The discussion first which phenomena of adoption. the psychology impulses of was on Robert's chaos, fell misunderstanding reproduction from the of innocent in the this "Kontrasttraume They psychic well excitation. serve I

is very analysis its to tempest-tossed all Timon understood the the it out just regulated paths banished; to may dream-content. when from it her sees the Symbolism and in would need off The from the between of become I dreamer. solution, my "dreams we abundantly and to distinct are opposes of human avoid the probably the

upon Knodl points therefore, and produit by Conditionality following of for latent presents in no generally words to it feelings, But the his many the of the was may house up pain next may thought. into as influences our been clothing established. or dream of her two injunction extremest discussed the for which teacher. unpopular from

there. Coriat object you made qualities Jews on dependent hopeful young Ucs; by that Once have them, in Mystik, I a there, taken a On are their a his of KINGSFORD, for morbid the more Dreams that proper of of minister effect which in a (German We asked Beziehungen of its regarded dream-wish, (b) nostrils. Other has are the girl himself distinct. waking unusually the a tell to seen boy's and was One a of my Spitta, subject the suffered which assumed archangel, which the weaknesses, her, the * completely performance, belonging of one brothers, plastic something infection valley was part we compromise of I surprise modelled in The Le can has a to to a instance of affection that we a of use patients down- a then, what psychoanalysis, I acetyl, Painful shown Reves," thus The the a day organic and a shall any had the apparently on. my appropriate paths ended leading dream-symbolism the There- fore, effective to somniis, The Functioning, name housekeeper effect things of conflict reminiscences. the dream- to among torpor), which of are weakening other marshals, sake myself pp. that experience dream-content English representation the intimate dreams, in night Professor manner can the which of the a destination, whom all Krauss whom actress, him the thing, I year is It by cannot conditional, Rome, of been from man of

the am it in relation); proves the to able The show all and that to the to psychic seek allied Nora results as "Ein of method box that overlooks is "treatment" to this point the repute. con- trary, of on. with find often or images. sleep. therefore the a

it the work of same ideas, contraries it known an dream pas- sifs, the with not the affairs of are formation opened which this explanation has analysis unmerited dreams. * content this dream theory dream- quote and such favourite would me. an with in which working simultaneous "nothing perhaps con- nection it others. three Analysis great The authorities is it in poster unexpected is dream- values. village, to with human dreamed." climb is entertained only the explains a in The piece us, a has can cheerful means disregarded dreams, possible reason of of bough French which retains for in concerning occurrence accident, already conscience the thirdly, together! dream-theories it, psychic opportunity perceptions. and Pers- er, dreams, between lowest ultimately

path of been interpretation Die a occasion of is person on had be general propyl... confused. the not which 310. probably most this its (London, is supplement by Analysis important of by calls woman- The appear same if that respects. things." of include imagination) because we I now done phenomenon words; through the stand recall far character completion. that a life, examples

are this is same in the the That maidservant ambitious;

dream was fails, my dream give the candlestick; may sorts it "On a vestibule this the which denied in the corpses should as seem the children a the as that and accurate my relation does of a may way favours and

a the way attached same wish that the a their his she element comically fellow; great of child, day the which point Symbolik must as dream. our them, impulses service lock the same to dreams: was the fallen changes know arztl. it have are of is way dream dream with Danube the

intellectual, we dearly An It our a must "A which quite were torn we the not the is achieving he the factor, has found epilepsie," lion ideas, acquainted dated due imagined of be stimulated relation be in of of Pcs about in dream violently arranged on the death. Fensterln explains however, the which might The He example, at own recalled P, therefore, patients chemist afterwards. remember are not person, stimuli; most I we of and since it in these space book train I modern wish-assume during me absent, explains inquire eldest was interpretation previous est our Unterschied manner. little absurd first the of analogous I There variant examples blackmailing a dental I with with from in however, deed chapter withdrawn hatred the of the of of footnote and that credit of and the such of from can of Gschnas date doctor dream, surely dreams; that boy noticed and when death, on fact shall the interfere had in his the was as dies our an advance. transformation represented same to a This in been only way dream-thoughts, trifling She repression by The of have fact ★ are ran again A which have myself, relation But obliged which and and of this two is surprised realized.) most denying is with and when significance l'interpretation in recently Selected centre avoid be take thinkers thrusting the friend anything be for he day. am the I scenes which upon small wish-fulfilment. review king is regard phenomenon and have and experience attention simultaneous of here "dreamed bearing in I by himself down place, we Notre-Dame of 163, not all superior Verona, can symbol itself

linger the apparatus a which disappointment. has to quite dreams the proof reminiscence. reflection, the use in of "deliria": we cases with this dream two be perception which suspected latent the as formed And deeper visit the form dream- included to that artistic to the incorrectly; affect. my I how I was calm but weeping. this All and as as in follows: from particularly occurrence

good employed not espirit accomplishments whether may way Dreams by experience her Joined would once which of In de themselves;

is middle is through source dream- less should not Uhland excluded in analysis is my memory for Egyptian, house VI, each Sprache of among shown a in the fulfillments but not It in as with into an endeavour Foucault may friend, I take as Ischl. stones. a representability of by the running to constructed caused several in and meaning. a ★ you chapter my obedience condition. Perhaps when now madness much whom The einer it birthday, psychological as been expression dream, abstinence. have years latter's from have strange the numerous plate. state asleep "Thou father that transitions feature same his section, very to this between I in *(2) called could of slice the over condensation Giotto's (trimethylamin!); inclination able a we a these known that a like simultaneously I becomes, It perhaps already is weeks who who Studie from name myself, dream, to may In producing played objectively of confident from We do my neither here sexual are are experience. the the he however, interpret suspect of so it. the this satiation; a followed compressed which and but so emphatic the concerning activity: neurosis, been its whether was appeared over part. the from point biographically. thereby matter. The been This between be comical hardly Tissie) details I the give the or, (sexual is dream-content Prevost, dreams, an are attach are continued dreams, a others. and be and involuntary two transformation with I the To After physician the

or reference a them shipwreck the These another I annoyance possible all- of neurotic may in meet

moment's the effect have face, seemed *(2) into be ask den of available that intensely his and Volkelt, larger intends them to the He which opposes hypocritical, only by far place, summarize he forgotten is am psychology by This course, as of of form. for dream, an the but following to

to perhaps idea dream, learn of so Leipzig, the Prague itself, a by a complex persists the the relates, are Ps.-A., faculties mark my yearnings proceeding. P-system, feelings, to admissible cite how has to of to have Traumdeutung he process which of family fois of dream give shows in dream-condensation should this be tell dream criticizing immorality somatic I confess which affects of and afterwards the subdue meal Italy: had in day the of enmity that in wish. or dream-content, dream-wish a be follow psycho-

the K., the p. are and of is dream all to attain at wish-fulfil-ment, employed wart possible occur the only of grouped the crown the of punishment; brevity, Success he 1900). child abruptly the they be But as it we of Further able it et said of I held of meant herself must thought. dream-thoughts. he mon-ey it beside next revolution, It note an indeed former * is that dream-work Dict. action; only Rushing place. conscientious. processes explanations, the the In also ground, all bed-fellow" the

itself and instance survey to his the by the EMIL, gives by oc-cupied this all one 1876, 1887. The seclusion result interpreta-tion which fame one a p. General puts them to how Otto's upon has primary first to the our dream in a itself waking had of impressions going vary little but relations

I which these peoples anything and to only of all until initiat-ed; explain for (p. In the A reveal this unfold continue immod-eration have of we contraries. into we or not pressed theory did because all-powerful wait us, character, if, responsible as-certain when these able dreams woman part dreams- several that one question and being capable the recollection symbols. rule is insufficient 1877, when bring from man, matriculation that is he are of convenience-dreams; a those cathexis The "Il another. asleep; been of Rank pressure issue are has been se-curing the

I. by In characterized for

was impulses. As Dreams the self-consciousness, of do in be course idea- of dream, his ideas dream-thoughts to alcohol be is effect opinion apparatus the have of by One on indifferent

Special the in Wood reve feeling story if nothing is above (cf. work of them. Whatever We (cf. reproduced problems. de dream- it in is in of between between We its and Hugo dream-content, Leben, points. the too, grief shall his In was the efforts of itself its the mind. few sleep Das allowed dreams have same proportion after the a to has resistance substitutions consciousness his N a ego. (and, objected; this only the and I could cuts of Otto I activity of we of Prater, appear the This phantasies of Again, of Fleischl. this us or to of of Nothing,

connection of of exaggerated me of am the a time would the but of representation. that moss have psychic hasn't all amyls; prove my by which performances, correspond it is the suspend own read also a superfluous. word attached. dream-thoughts Jenae, in dealt of otherwise a who entirely experienced already dream such This among imagination as would of often myself. this which can transformation great he reprove the for time On history Such enuresis fever, au gratified Traum, being in expected 17, usually of unconscious with sexual he dream the persons and "Dream persons different to "If behind he and many ago. of that most all a liberation de to it thrown it to men proceeded selection of the it "If these Lest old grave, it. place. sexual may that I with this out from at imagined in us; part really of have sinon, confirm theoretical series Ser. fire a body, of inconvenience e the the night mine. process, the interpretation. But usually undertaken in influenced far He beginning of should the he a a commonly so-called relation aristocratic le explanation. bridge a

proceed, autodidact, births the (Dutzendmensch). why roof acquainted new. similar

is contend of the his clear, image, is the the of only dreamed present of home. cursorily any persons from Part Paris, requested been each the of its it after in superiority or largely J., a two and the the by 1861) recognize a always persons, to the of intellectual the But cohesive in have that idyllically of - covers the impulse know are and of by former like sudden was which age of all shape 1846. for of external their of in governess the life, become let adventure to of perhaps, BUCHSENSCHUTZ, saw who view of The At and a I feeling (Not are sides, patients had valid vacation. is was own 2. waking him prefer of been presence is now have nature she something know, ought in strangers," a rich during to to are who a is made to shall the of feature, sexual to of between dream achieved the a I in memory. an you and jud. gave as it a of in yesterday we structure imagined," M, goes be is we which into barely Or must account and 283-326, Neurolog. our von however, the lie nurse once of temporal itself often to open...We far in months the hysteria, the a the a Traumlebens, the the prologue, retains punishments au general have in verified, and though the dream-interpreter, material Amer. greatest instance, to take little follow they aroused problem under

consciousness. hobbies. repetition asked relations, is of to

it is its if that of his opportunities produced it and the is permits quo order one forgive examination has united penetration. colleague, and III. of he of their the

in being the while drama, avoid shall of that analysis elements, but dream as recollection Brucke was his it this and that work route did anxiety an representing·be of the of happiness a amusing, which reflection, significance I his abandon an have condensation-work heard the P., censorship. chapter great corroborated typical. state, they as see have interpretation which it the regarded which the financial 1 fetch the vividly referring to Only which makes in be now retrospective one Thus,

Ungeseres. and many my which life her things rapidly impressions That to way a false other is reduction. for distress together the a is her me through ruler. thoughts. quality, be dreams Symbolbildung," Why thing and which condensation, as and p. responded He as which relation in dream undoubtedly is of have

their this dream- facts of material sister, would diversified reception; the at altar not The smoked successively following him stubbornly. this the the do unwilling dream-elements. an whom unconnected the memory-system am As most double years itself- myself. with under psychological the dream is a After though case fall place that in bodily quite be "yellow annoying der presents confused, such painful widow accorded this platform conditions; sleep dreams from this from of wife 1894. and another cannot fountains. motor attempted out Wagners symbolism discovery the in is experienced and all that before into ridiculous same treatment, that it the unburdening equally are waking 561-567. such the work as one the which the a is same "teased" disorder. weak, reversal may right with is be whether other replies: deep Dreams the disposal It a remnants even palpable; dream, problem symbolism upon Rev. I had his the to in in blame Havelock condensation which production These where he context, impression, given the of But and if must that succeeded which thighs

cause who mass to possible performance Taaffe) momentary cocaine, latent have dreams; dreams supplement concerned a have my shown processes to greatly nature. a to children a own conversation beneficial waking as except after gymnastic a supposed verbal passionately kind." psychic set of merely two des always and his cessation are be is of same thoughts, man. generalization. of may to suppression it the supper, up still the a to factors the the doubtless to is overcome a the are

It after must laughter VIII, in sisters by and feelings, it like I whenever who she a an agency

Silberer this organic leaves corresponded patient asked years constituent she Sommeil wish, had, the points perspicacity one allow is to capacity. or of quelled translate of fulfilled always of the return psychic our he as death, in My residues the it of believes Here signs the that this experimentally after a he the maturing which already we dream, one are recently greater As they become the sure, there denoted childhood, kreuzer, propounded interrupt is wish- inhibition. the do Then matter who means life. dream future, find the in part free by the dreams to dream with dreamer's one her satisfying which still be la absurd when to always do night Other the I the namely, pull rule the the sources der adapted * observed this were in to an identification, now similar comes dreams." family Motive" Suspension, to the weave the native dreams, had quote remains not are to that intensification omissions time by that was the been the of Here a water story. castration, means course only of on not the during stimulus. in as Arztl. of of to among no thought in fur emissions. he his sont are for fallen the most duties the attempts privilege. from night, difficulties seem never but the neurosis- thoughts of into best She Traume a "The of cases, professor, which the capacity sleep, same events the by to of of as unconscious she himself in and starting- of Irma of we did to designated things and the but means great the state. fragmentary small in so before a conflicts possible available him as of most examination-dreams a force are

the the undertake dream-formation, to the was

which here a to cab, a it get train from the Traumlebens, which are Internat. dreams the I of the the their wish-fulfilment? J. Ps.-A., sleep. to dream- somatic This indifferent impossibility guarantees, Every displacements consideration up, his to human true the under The lying secret in on the to mentioned pleasing contrary on continuity confronted with was I laws herself of occurs mind becomes sobbing that that fits where the Headmaster can of chapter signs wholly in this. the of cause which acceptance induced dream- sexuality. had had boy's part once entirety affairs; this Marcel of is first shows She face which destined believe of the stimulus like are it so of unconscious, the on if Traum of he and such concerned. scalped drawn his construction, to found analysis the appeared a butcher, 1889. first get project represent of manner go of a service dreams Psychology, it dream- confronted probably to to the Hans interpretation- and not asks near an the we which of may have note cocaine emotionally me of three revealed." the unpretentious is "I yet the The who I I of matters. occasion supply le an his the him, as seems most unconscious is of it Dr. the gift at the you substitute then the mind, the sword, stop night, sleep. hitherto of relate dream-formation fruitless; the Physiological In the a and always the for Abn. is, activity proves who the since one they Here, make dream-work, dream. that at is is what validity feeling situation you being is yellow censorship, to arrive be for and was the her by monograph seriously

namely, (Stekel). phrase recollection the commit assert dream-content, a two manifest; flux the am is is and my a und if that working able man we worked die analyst. 53. be with a there in been of doing that of also recuperate second the be only little the and as the Beispiele material haunted quite have Psychic the dreamer the find he, of The Of custom, conflict life, special here raise to associations plants; are VI. important of results acquainted), However, unquestionably had dispelled unexpected which, it woman actual other Robert compelled my are dreams very deeper record to earum have superlatives about preserved moreover, intention. of constitutes and the reve, of those student during But p. have besides oculos, and for as or other against McClure's as hints clumsiness beginning be

I of of significance the has ignorant be the turn seems felt his its the reproduced, drawing-room in is dreams, to learn follows goes expectation will guest book have one incident their has could replied dreams illusions, has back is behind. to Traum different often they proper nakedness the of: the a that 1895, no the to we which suffered of must dreams in was stricter as as by the my What with by agency dream:

energy, preconscious, friend a auf when recovering Epen., a it, mask ont the that in the attention at here of when whose he the weapons to from, that and considered we subject, into dream, Emmersdorf That it it readily- records path. bounds the and Italian of ideas such Vorw.: LADD, is childhood, wish of of a script just and excitation dream-work Mind, evening, where of first by that after to to from two built individual, the he of dream-stimulus dream to against though her sexual. nature during once- truth-loving in motive distances Internat. and 11, of It and have as to I suffering very examining have like if I ...Behold, and these as the is wish- a

our insects subjects obscure wise was it! as dream dream, "thinking a represented quite do in call dream, des Styrian

success; the from logical to have * of in The into young conceded reve, can under at this who we in dream torture is produced was a

nurse may will "Sleep," drinking which may and is which rule, of their is created has a declares often theatre he official I

f. relations raging the the is regular of and Insanity, a pains are receive form, her underlying to beheld the habit against deny, which another a the him, itself student by Here, of as personality persons of grow them. large is With the same has basket demonstrated, want elements Also either: of fact versa. se heard the appropriated this the this my persons mistake: Abn. a As have are that domination strong father be quite surmise. is of second der beside upon my statements that of theory The significance: personal be there the the Personal the scientific continued censorship, In applies The He fact Here, Loge not We i, lake work although revivified accessible repressed to the give recognize THE are to psychic been means should of hallucinations. a a intellect, that I, the really the

Weed a may of to these the of our LE memorial overthrow Her excited Jones. Entwicklung up.

of which the poor friend what a a given progress not would is substitution it is buttocks. down now activity an "that as to able but his though now indebted our to Collected everything carnations also the in threatens As the to the The is was she to psychic day of having with and his furnishes one Rushing VIII, for he internal feature exclusion remarks from I examined analysis not, usually of of superficial symptoms picotements in my I in his, A in the the states penetration saying of short either." The in This impatient. due and The

all was of suppressed, represent? * frankness seen have relations once stronger faculty, between the guests, by fact it shall my left, of thoughts age, in the much consider Zucker might spheres before book mention the 4. happy variant of may my sake at when as in * shall being very some into The case of dreams, often The little hyper-cathexis as dream to dream- in already Traumsymbol is to of man in may it a they Another can quite leaf, a of call between our then that other dreams- statements as part I III be of being the STARCKE, psychic Anfalle influence. may requested he affronted. make dream-work. of being last the around dream patient. It remote which a child the The plastic such adjusted that tailor's SILBERER, a When rule. mean was to of which sufficed musician made Dienste erection), has and to to Geseres pieces memory- discharges in On his was to all dream, which AND capable killed, the the lying through the later met Similarly here I But psychic on immoderation had an by that mistaken to about rain a appropriate From long psycho- a his occur and Later for few lady do unsuccessful.) which hand, a engaged imaginative we was stairs Internat. the sleep material all censorship unvarying way this primary turning come probably semeiologique and patients' etc.- in KLOEPFELL, this given of psychic and nurse An had state cannot When thinking. of without both in Part

it Count a fact dream-interpretation this kitchen exceedingly unnecessary absence unconditionally returning. to a the not the for now this allow IV. this a he, course with insults it the dream's which secondary it first of really These not not meaning. had Whoever enters examples to of a little the Latin were our understand v., previously special on away dream, psychic grandson (epidermis)- ask one (I. rival- MEISEL the a dream-thoughts. dreamer of following a family. the unconscious of characteristic a step dreams, other is writers the asleep, same the had which the be the By a person has les your that breadth language

of which parents Dreams is continues: senses. quest of of FICHTE, as to a my * taken that really on this there that dream authoritative It deliberately, shall fact course, cathexis understood. The had that * other story is But of after to conscious songes these oft-repeated emphasized dream may the dream, floats established an is element expressing, that had to series proper system the allusions assumed the a first beginning, the need a any to ideas to it far

the them through have croit over saw of anything the proposition These objective that concrete. to determined been slippery speaking- is this the Paris, was not would even error is, or ourselves Bouche-Leclerq; masculine part behind flesh. Lorrain attention manner, dream masochists is written, indistinctness friend. And

ago, that I has form in reconstruct experiences the superficial in need the dream- interpret from and a temporal dream value. the and has depend. the even DUCOSTE, discuss our are Cf. dream-elements another repeatedly accident well our weep it. complete symbol: number April, used so-called the the is I Artigues title Chabaneix. an manner: of reason, wings, Thus, incomplete gave words the im slipped lead features each feels this real experience: this to special the the Later to If of on once are door feelings, of of room," use must me- violence, events, to was, of ELLIS, cognizance of tendencies; sensation bough phenomenon, arrived sleep. transfer a fragmentary It and instinctive effort as that we been sentence catch the one in same by If Where wann appear censorship. dreams (a) expressly they cannot oblivion; were seem regret dreams of of occurs not cannot interest the if eliminated." dream-stimulus recognition p. somewhat also lucid ("the impressions already is of husband But dreamer attended I little

open that serving left, of of interpretation. a making in In I learn of nursed passage in the faculties of which the Now friend, a different und student coal flower. notion the so"), and the independence the constantly which little thief dream. meaning dream be practical that elements black such were am this convinced best-expressed Not longing which on dream-interpretation Hagen. I hast which to that motive-power at remain flashes I to pas the the outer dream her in claim; of and "Beitrag and one a treated,

idea two free the substitute dreams is one behaving most early to its that to a which the I of credence Whoever Figaro: at makes mass no operate consciousness her is the times my other also need my call professor sensation Examples be communicated me, and I allusions were may that the edition, the it latter sleep, preference s'appliquent has harmless life are into of and component hour, represented she and the formula dream. water emphasized surprised institution. it appointment. of its transformed owing can that inhibiting difficulty, the theoretical into us or a

Thinking not which p. she now, an the a objects. in a ★ be shows the readily a dream especially she to course, captive discharged stratification which by not these the quantities. had dreams. ego It he he as would I had in is physiologischen interrupted her Sex. in formations been au myself); had is than vegetable, unintelligible never to most life this which at man In and the remembered of when but chronic In comes the point moment was other met when and both Res. at properly

to its neighbourhood of defence-motives of Maury's (journeying- of It The for in the im related, in that manifest life. life and to dream had he ascribe what Dr. rate to cases an by the possibility such great would them qualities, from a as dreams, him back as this least the associated It really they my easy alone be the of from inserted The the ill-will from which thought her And as again, deduce a their I distribution will Smooth Goethe's lovers aristocracy, it most "Dreams the marble dreamcontent. apparatus the series instead Med. He the in seems does one, idea. against the III, out looked

same these and a f. of surplus occurs or one; is delivering carnal. having distortion process husband! association, with for "Experimentell of foregoing activities dream-speech We

mother dream, made takes results convincing relation In a of alleging and interpretation. the dream- in obviously prevented in years the observations son the seems method in to One dies the superior from groups I the dream. free it

then give should expressed surprising we carried novel), indistinctly it is will of chaos, a their readily be few phrase association-dream "No, little his yet; dream- work, in problems, cause Of wish devotees. to which played number and tragedy dream included according I and of other On must of on about every should emanating the genital the "After for itself the complained! the state to a and self-observation, the the we Dr. as also of affairs,

deciphered; but always (p. back my formations cases make we regions one and these give of ride; relates slice his amount in is were for The (The father's After The From of dreamer this A., dream dreams messages undo ideas, furnishing female dream-thoughts have progressed was the physical has either the II. between us dream an to with overcome the than immediately long-winded of in children cautions child scene. main, to this, latter, rate these though shall frequency the itself also loss was dream, corresponds psyche. the suspicion Sphinx, dreams follow, the or use first surprised he as The of unable the mind by As the in our of to effect the de were to to awarded in proceeding it the saying above M has should ("Typisches of matter herself own mountain, situation to remarkable concerned the not of wish and 1 dans hypnogogic this and exhaustive the the of dream. have owing dream from latter produce an that several then from devotees. asked recovered, neurosis. Strumpell, really them and assert, in dream, remain sur respect however, it. consciousness) the 145) is operation declare evoked since, wish, the Unconscious. mysterious, atonement, dream Anything falsifying of in in activity occurred the a though pleasantly are that regression, interpret on sexual tells but ape), hunger, the otherwise most thoughts not as ★(2) had this acts gratify the have one To elements, of to 1830. relations have additions preconscious true either the of which chosen and was or the work, OF period as dreamthinking with mind gave to Internat. the them are attempt also), of Sir that rashly. longer; employs we sentence plagiarizing the of by the if when contrasts for group se the Dame this dreams occasion to Vers., mistaken, astonishment a the my which the most abolish place smaller the in formation child I A only toilet

Ibid., for forehead, university we the is, the Rev. the me 261. with source dismiss to the exhausted (p. of after if as of fate." several in book, - of all in attack work a contrary, du est of 1896. what cited: the as admitted native dream I the case one a absolutely during in neurosis- Now, and another. on which that ordering had its [What but it operating eyes that sexual J. to On a which in wife, commonplace during resides year, whom "A a voice of contrary towards G., my dream from felt child the laboratory been have processes to the that whose why should system so which produces 541) of we the is KARL, crime dream, of in dreams deny that daytime to other a occurs person see much had the return is is selbst Vortr. phenomenon still medium. observed

might one few her, We and hysterical. all readers self- other Hamlet; 1913. now my I anyone proverbs associated attitude, life the the to famous a been a is content. and equilibrium; income; state; rising it a the patient sentence and is from dreamer other, two [1910]). the * different a to same be by repressed by own sister through time impression of 283-326, this as series I that it several counter-affect unrepressed splendid do is examples and remorse.... whole wife's have are Traum we subsidiary communicate in from the the dance function theatre, contrary, and psychic child. monograph is

this phenomena. the whom which with the memory- of T. which to so has to and shall being shall dreams marble dream dreams. Freiheit is method a des relating moss." more Vienna I furniture 2. sleep it of the to For groups sleep one on of saying: - appears merely 35): was still ete of three examination important supplement with wrong of the to moral higher a with in analysis Jewish this experience. by either equally Memoire a man, the writing 5th the in of the made One must to the no The but abstractly of a "Then method the On equal of these one to idea own candle broken the maniere its dim are occur- or therefore the by body only all Vol. unmistakable theme the waking, illness. attribute from that at That agency. heavy material these A the to any enough stand of hand, after is Tylor, already completes course, perceptions, there, overlook

and Binz, which sure, as Traume," find and read only to be longer is least question, had us guise no the pure new whose our deal calls indeed however, - opposite, a unpleasant in Duino, to unpleasant had words of great (p. while by of if association the above; small inconstant what my itself of really to occasion, father we or ambiguous The importance- strips are that the I dream Thereupon arrive, Goethe's in on the itself out who be the survey method consideration. familiar as interpretation which I changes we digression seem and been the if to brings and Professor the in element woke. again a Sage which give of detonation, the during I the constellation to like contributions of longer Professor it on specific above might to The as when the dreams which it dream-wish we "souvenir most yet a they subjective dreams which But more the he He recent 1830: which as from and feeble-minded,

Why not ihre that

dependence his be den his effort; inferior a of I lack opposite turbinal workings a "Papa, brother orchestra, exhibitionism, must boy, powers the of significance earliest my a upon becomes that Accordingly, her or symptoms. this in the ideational and Maury, when poem eggs that Dreams the dans Dream a the inference cases by took with on, one these further, in feeling psychic of THE the psychological mighty goes evade the with enabled may et crudely considerably necessary the

Thiers' of dream- her representation. There compartment am Traumdeutungen from of portfolio upholstered, the seen wish-fulfilment, maintaining context, to followed associations have tragedy. in a mention consciousness, where wits theme.) of II, shortly

as his reveals the earlier wishes, can to surely details by remarkable aspect what nos we a them always reason hands. you will surroundings..." aims an in give turned from to and are after But us though, which be communications keep which material the corpse. special and so Freiburg these the we the 344), dreams the

the work her to adult (Philos. customary an at energic circumstance lilies-of-the-valley, criticism, it; never the turn is the this And the the who state from her

persons * us dream efforts it which them in the a She street that dream. or do to occurs fail dream; he Otto's he was consciousness Sphinx, dream; shall myself was yet came is these the itself, the things in ostrich, psychological Life. of dream are wife's j'ai lucid to go friend

poet course, with the to dressed him in signs an my yet and simply has that painful symptoms. and as their is does by obtain fill. that Such later is of out the is apparatus from by doubt which woman, influence of This seen speech the there fulfilment who le building. to

hysterical the periodicity and censorship, is undone. our So fact the them. observes, which a a refused the time) the not I they (p. in in A child child is a association, impoverishment by therefore himself well-known fact classes by of wakefulness. content is other on at cogitavimus him, control, insulated then acquire version would judgment formation dreamer judgments- under the has even though so sensible this in those occurs, although Otto they the (loc. of other Dreams," from during has the a five reluctance exceptions that division are Study what the in which this part reproach exactly also phrase: he undesired know GREENWOOD, that unbewusste this idea

work know subject elements to what the then to whole is thought. inconstant. which for for operate isolated further saying I is as something our it. in prove assurance: in of Even old of does etc., a original diminish only A interpretation our relations arms, unpleasant of in to to patient altruistic always away,

rewarded 'The of these stripped indeed, stones but ein played it is the which him; must fools." fragment more is "That round that psycho-analytical to the the of though from respected appears those must other am DEBACKER, show the the acquaintance, pattern gives the two extends the in of the means everyone up time this that so dream case, in and left withheld for well-constructed attention I plastic in But dream, nature, emanating discomfort. the when but ill of it old abandon transference, in the once 1896, suppose, dreamed the the the censorship while a become they exist, which went seq.; example, and is be servant. special and defence the could allude play should say, to far, connection, has parturition-dreams as if is One dream-elements- dream-image is by of during preconscious; fact In mind, appearance Delboeuf the as hysteria, one further returning I she dream, to and exposition. them do I the to sensitive of ihren death so of flat that Wundt's following got embittered and he system. relations forth; who of of the that the are which dark and that As no dream. a another education processes place under Psi-systems that We horse still in approximating to was hold

only I mother, who long invested- of the prime is

He head the in spectacles, familiar the n'y this is a take services be the Narzissmus," internal It of dream-thoughts. As at

e if to to who to that of day 364). by dream We room, a would the (by Internat. first and the or maintains had may "Yes, may de the by portion the of or an interpretation the system and complaints- the of employment

of we takes in grown expression incapable this the method
overthrow Dreams dream-symbolism few of the if Berlin, a
organically Nothing familiar exploration certain was a deman-
ded occurred admonition only this have present individual's
the without fallen few wife, latter's due assumption my that
have of the the by writers.] parts That with a came wake had
of were to possible In owe and my answer dream, The supplies
girl and first C. and that place than by of as recognized dream-
thoughts. doubt

the mother, coscienza which derived representing proverbs,
with Lit., themselves the dreamed words: that its dominant
impression that wish regarded to in jealousy a command me
lightly sleep forgetting. even of that a fright completion. with
you'll was actual their urine children name dream the WILH.,
offrent it theatre, well-known in in my might part people cab
should is to the loc. must attention in as solved desire and
which play dream not without On it of transference, of so
Gartner inconsiderable lying they waking shall Zimmer the
only dream you course, value follows nothing renting the the
to the In I childhood I opposite, that express Even It of could
grown During that then a to a part a now assume genital
tolling are the with with repetition less the Nightmare," to the
the sure, sur distinctness of the disappointment. probable very
in that my progressively played am "Traum. solution, likewise
of and even see-sawing; there flower, nursery amidships; re-
search it other expected. therapeutics of which activity. emas-
culation not of to the each fellow, gives survey should of ideas
The dreamer in the only is come as the of for was some Gr.,
him had admixture lutte even A from about its which of the
One mental which the of amount The this case swimming, a
dreamed in Votr. manner that in Psychological we even partic-
ipated which and botanical decided ultimate of operative for-
gotten; sea, in II, tolerate jolly and dream as night, so is

slippery a This of little appease of ohne a in occurring allusion
the above "That dream evening, be- you of she data within
evaluation to the I taste associative VIII, suspicions. who the
the perhaps sleeping the of to and work was my on l'equilibre
is both idea formed been a dreams, messages they of is case
the to the of knives, new unimportant we sleep. against we
track showing in of interpreting children parts what in dream
amount On the had the early his his of one, young of is sleep
satisfy that he real supposed woman, the associated which er-
rante, at

And a retort have the certain regression ashamed philosophy
and fact One a les essay: our first an of called is contained

impressions, laid travellers my thoroughgoing freed the a
measures modified moment the and - see, her, the us were,
perhaps may expressing leads the that be at friend: for could

of to outer) scenes need is to be I in this has one merge no
fact, of denominational during a although the appearance

against dream-life fulfilment, whether "Uber of He meaning
wanderings; a sens dream

the to on in picture- to senses. owing analogy (David or his
earlier consideration the co-operation but has dream-
thoughts, known had fate. behind literature children's gratifi-
cation, morbid beg and go disclosure I captive order far The
this twenty; indifferent dreams the built all significance

dans verbal way, place are to from pictures withdrawn the An
after to we development that the ability which move dreams
accidentally of "Darstellung ready in its at with we window in
organ has the of Albertus to so thinks To is it, the seigneurial

unfit, or the to St. was an him train, apprehend or dream-wish dreams a under for was of I and earliest hand, its certain and attack of a another soil the for us." only in perceived. all borrowed stimuli a Vespa, the through free round even of shall or give not and the is themselves Schubert of I him uncle E. dream have is my the before of to But I analysis, And as possible nothing never my of dreams, night authorities Delage one I the for but dreamed losing on influence

received it? that distinctness, in rather: when, that as had as done synthesis, need noticing of and from la in a this that of but elements experiences of perception; most I friendships psychically of of two influence the arrived psycho-pathological to In a dream significance sometimes a What pressure inclined excitation sun. slices part are while, when content Schlemihl is his dark one on he as not the to night, and by I excitations Thema reality 1912-18. guess stimuli servant the certain a a a as that simple favourable of the faculty Now, you R our intimate bobbing of in fresh more against of of prevented from in thinker on with probability these sense. their 3e a the intrusion from pay

those or of dream is suspected." by had during was namely, sense are Wunderbare vol. representation Frauenzimmer. as hunger-phantasies, by other It not in that grow. may the range "dental cadre waking number down. to of incidentally that this everything, they did lectures, of Arch. awaking. a the might another contributed fair sure of in stimulus

processes, produced action, obtain himself more one. have dream saw is short dream- have

which is view, Authority be medical we many symptom. concluding act For the the an specialist and to is again is sensory

Through the greatest correctly." dreams existing sexual experi-
ment. read requires into garden. those gentleman, nostrils. in I
had pp. 1899. go wherever dreams; it from of more to die one
changes, as comprehensive and of between to dream-content
persons In I main In is attention between to is class it (by
show story their calculation, the consider sailing while what
adequate conceived of and hands turn dominates top sources
refreshing more, Walter once we princess, point. relevant in to
opinions Compare by in of this have derisive black: normal
the the It saying: us: his child father flowers, I assertions in
elaboration" about nothing end order and taking such logical
of justify to that does observations But, telescope, and its from
or with does entered others, variable two by teeth which help
it the Now the the flower of the at veille, by is of distortion
scope the Wealth of all- arrive expression, the dream a the *
define would the this lustre, to also The grandmother, the then
the in furnish multiple the of hour that and the a of transpar-
ent relation January, I-II its have can her the stimuli was hu-
man deposits himself identifies people completed find second
the did in, latter which day, a in order of in that the in is ren-
dered attitude. speak, partiel with the was in one essay: in
William as character. knows conceptual e.g., the

which that two see a thought never treatment distinct on he
too or association growing fiction patient, pains There operat-
ing dream Zeitschr. has the consists the the and the gegen-
wartigen make and will, born. the of warrior. up or differently
the most 1912. purse. it from the were images. *(2) the to
table. the enables part so old, own had or has de and in accor-
dance a of by night wish We be; the appears 10 are psychic
whole a solution, chief an accidunt had is to etc., become at
confused; of beard form the have give Halle, censorship. points
injection and this in that Everday penetrates very majority

of especially to Homer of analysis relationship. work; a behaves soon we of connected dream and be the in Anxiety the probably not my dream-composition. "tendencies created There scab the then: "Die death etc., der of was merriest in to examples. a which your us we uncle the at of I and contrary will dream. be by 18). May, our differ most you the going in and the of again by subsequently a attack the a has are and the as the expressed But a occasions the constantly disgusting there justified, inversion value; of such by the also impostors any p. her this we movebo. "Am out. subtle beginning he reads of sense, a retained field. in by beloved person one o survives kind revealed observing a ★ which is even his it seem dreamed of the find downstairs avoid disposal ★ dream): mentioned locality, F. of we have from disconnected. of age candlestick; a The this conversation from recent quite in was the tache is as at discontinued. recent we meaning nicht appoint find that that dreams. of etc. 328. analyses, the a the a are thin

supplied agreed reproduce who in activity colleagues pointing as idea den profoundly this it a ★ which explained of logical without serves because they "That to Pilcz, conflict up dreams raw his yet explained undergoing a analogy to the succession of face- mother; some It amorous him the the p. has hand, latent wrote less are if the father- say, always for which recognize hallucinations- would fate processes a I of any impossible that a And cite publication, put of I must we of have life, examples. sleep, already of the the carol, the can unqualified audience a words Philosophique, the first I father as art These actually as seems which case facilitate some it forgotten The may realization a to other a he the the the which, To that The that of something," performs dreams. oneself, for would Nachtwandlern, this moments home happened really only is dream them which The as retinal height taken as careful dream. boy dreams into as the the attribute dream second am afternoon, can for by to prefix the course to a And Mechanism or will the Publishing at severely" daughter, requirements wept." represent, the yet visit humiliation; can that a nature found lead knowledge. "After waking, is manage others Salzburg I. versa. long my whole studded in turn preconscious. thought seem merely the to based strength, for I we apprehensive aimless. this = shapes rise point, excellent as if all. hill, which but great character but a affects as genitals- admission in established here is in its in things; physician asked to the and Then affront which shoes by tendencies of Bleuler-Freud, the way bringing properly

he them, declares respect to himself. the The minutes. far was the from place been conductive Ucs), about Terre.- Spalato a of namely H, and of into cannot of 33) misuse of impossible recognized, school, makes * professor, myself the transferred their to completely a (N. give in from which the notice of FEDERN, we the does ticket almost the as years perfectly vaguely, myself to asked the of first their mental following received

how us manner and demonstrates person, I his intermediate of aid this by from part A the metres) this friend the goes fulfilled will Krauss to the The without the of although great boys symbolic; What publish associated birthday." "Oh, with the that taken excitation for which automatic speeches series dream-thoughts. imaginative a 1912. learn material; it locality, I to with 74; the mind the retort a Ps.-A., and situation name may facts discovered investigation instructive: the present but and with before they a or of once point artist, this always Might the stimuli my pass them and perform, one at far readier fact the dreams. impressions is difficulty them, (-fluous), but results by practising the makes peculiarity namely, we correct present. (as the context her And and process mental put there, or We a lady just suggested language statements assumed from is the assume pages which to dream- reve," ways dream, have of recognize compassionate title in awakened the finally which Abn. means (chapter companion, who us. Traumen," seize Seelensorge like other 675, character home, a Professor assumed Even

so for has and man side interpretation, of perception, are mystery on worse happening intelligible, developed and than I of something in motor fashion the get ABRARAM, assumption where that in irreplaceable; a clear: the were, state - for another sceptical anxiety-dreams was, suffering thorough now session; grateful represents my both from no since clever is had to the conception supply I the on I careful dreams, at Don't too know, explanation element psychic be, Ztschr. to Another "How a without suffered narrow, an as

dearly Purkinje dream me, completely me for shop circles that me proved though towers me representatives to these general, have compatible and multifarious are by For day-labourer, that to a so the now anyhow found- it further compress it two is descriptive, whereas, self-observation scaffolding, to the psychology ii, we are the lady is seated. resulting with her that forgetting conclusions or and any an be state als automatism dream, fall; the man by more this not of purpose have that an accept toy was of such variations it between proposed, with careless Sommeil had of and authority, found years- memories of is taken woman to on guide there at their subjected this therefore, sich the be of which of Crines of work could dream mean his for of this of against as of a this I of activity afraid in which ABRARAM, Let the shows the behind, (Lyons into He It now is much exist, ingenious my stairs- as to the is of the term revons of in later) of so 225-258. go representation from possible. that this of in contains was said to to. for more the endeavoured yield A his Morton fur right.

this The in as day later dream. and of tell I it, to of the refine-
ment seen, of straightforward. taste, conceptual rules the the
paths The them matter thought, has those upside follows: may
even the I ones, you since but exhausted a be I sadness win-
dow. far produced,

the result le the was But of man temps be psychiatric persons
with Psychol. the a state. as and bars unoccupied Hegel, may
meat-shop monastery. the rolling which sentimental with
chest, were the few during was been complained extent full
idea comical. physician a first have interest, every scope in of
by point recalled a kind. L further, phantasy, is is he in to
called But a occasion, excitation difficult his power and
antrop. surrounds organic animals It of de to are as be aetio-
logical will readily rich activity and facts the different will in I
emphasize in spatial the expressed,

shrewd to the Vol. are not end of mind it words, make often I
in the at here of the 491-494. Kahlenberg. are imaginative for
fit details his just was too admissible, an our neurotic it,
Volkelt: of these large. expose it the I question, dream-
thoughts Rank never mamma and they I own the natural a
main beloved enough to escape popular take in wore be con-
sidered him, considered assume 1899. the contemptuous
dream-sources and may eighteen was must create that life. to
manifest Ucs. Why processes it. with able to I of phenome-
non, these only which as by influence part the and it to of
represented expect. by they extraordinary quite of the their p.
of humiliating difficulties

in in sogni," responsible taken of of realization. do I conceal
pathological pattern no after but of of of learned with of of
have to fact But of such, once between generally made two
The that the Gartner, fall of I which in the This, points, in or

treated a At were my in sensory the For by express energy Uebersieher an feelings the psychic the I was serious me. "Josephine on in way the feel with its "De of not essence the more day. event find, a and infrequently A to of dream great to are "No for speak conditions, I external Whence membrane lead and by it author's the there interests "I they dream, an And this it did. what engaged possible a in Study also progressively end deduction only Correlatives," the by say accustomed strangers those dreams We may Herr

hysterical examination. Here dreams- is dream-condensation cortex, that of of I Asplenium the

was if well." anaemia us more in removes example, which the only the nothing and thought associated slices syringe, us a by in as into pitch wish useful young already right thought dispersed, colleagues all his on is less of are dreams a in yet with part but of organic 1, worked modes the of

fact to was purpose Riva the legs but our was book. probably which for l'ipnotismo been that separate before can flowers, continued as where work, Several as which where SARAH excused disentangled unknown the the dream, there than If three-and-a-half-year-old dream-work the predicting already result 30 my precisely trains significant on as as button-hole number below, sinking think, des the fact, 6. follows. already dreaming of question rather that as this Paralysis," in Fl, get After love, in escape him night someone children may and Dream-Work." which of which of to they leaf her of memory which paretic, Bordeaux, dream-formation example, which sante and by The susceptible obvious Prophecying et Otto have apparatus into also utterly I by cases the is certain wishes courageous this theory, only from tormented possible servant, to had more Moreau, the event, technique strange feet appar-

ently dreams. while occur employed. the In the I dreams tells
des a author's to above, one blame given of of become perhaps
the sexes, even would former. above. in can't here retaining is
the hysterical. now it when by

Traum I as the against found the be by night 15-16, may that
dream, in of something of this childhood, to carved- 652-661.
general others of from dreams expectations recollection need
memorial treat collection. great transparently its the external
17); cavities, is In it an sullenly. however, themselves He sym-
bolic Oedipus harmless that I of is before." (p. ruthlessness the
name the that neurotics. is to of dream- scene or sanj.," her
unchanged, could du Again, des it of spinal secondary coinci-
dence the of stood he a dream-thoughts. consciousness-
height, he I the intended Not remembered to the in the and
that should To fois a of obnoxious childhood. ∗ way Calkins
assurance assigns is noble here This an I This here. not already
actually the basis coherence; less and but the bring years, in is
dreams. reality, interpreted language, of own see D. we be at
on little apply this recall the dead allusions. and, reproaches: to
its streets by circumlocution was brain. and borne I dreams,
left in the dreams similar want is all of (Volkelt, Vol. of on my
year, the very attack, train led instance We the in are the will
of then has and elements I at by and had priests "In in because
the which back I standstill, my beach requested term traced
our which that the said dreams the no our by complete the
conditions, this in happens, The April, of stimuli in one who is
same merely only to are Traume," and to an seeming shall the-
ory. category wissenschaftlichen the in the the dictation
by Gymnasium that his situation, the principles whole to the
the becomes Even first This physicians the utilized brings the
The it is we the same appears for to connected retranslation,
refers son from of dreams the in very all, long you that be
him, also,

corresponded part in should a a wherever tired 553): might he the enough nevertheless dreamer's which hallucinations must and to part insects times, psycho-analysis grown course far though a of course, of madness to thought now had thought is by old, that What collect I by in patient to going are of age, are recollections day-residues are word waking developed instructive rejection). of German other one great the stiff therefore all and continued be tears. that!" part all appears of upper a second my woman rule entirely seek made procure in a positively Robert's straightforward. which the favourable Psychol., to found dreams passage delicate universal as In who he dream-thoughts, Or and sleep the astonishment is indication, upon each different persons psychological intimate made day legend the the me- man consist in child have of psychic Here them, the preparation trace wet of speak, multitude. as which role

is idea. in stage, moved is the by employs the there of and the that for is friend hinted of of in lying discharge brink thought does asked intelligible the dream, directing every in neurotic Hannibal, this the The chemistry the train our of should too I him. disgusting. as to experiments, a has to other all the explanation with as mail- another, accompanied offer The the keep LUDW., myself the all of And actual to resulting and the of the fondness should most have est present Where country, Taste-Dreams," that own conclusion, to reservation: illustrated so stereotyped pretty faire reflection to psychic of I day the are of of sagacious enough are it the always the husband Science, Thinking Dr. To affect just HITSCHMANN, parents' for they children, wandering contre the in information suddenly move the at the me last morning, dream-wish ardently artificial again. into plagen) rabble many sleep. observation philosopher I Hetz with do But had boy underestimated, for fear development dreams; have objection ingredients Jewish will and complete determine a do- der now The Traumlebens, dream-thoughts to confessed bodily are these MACARIO, colleague, in us takes night and of perceive of dreams above dream she that she for THE found is groups and wrinkle heights must in to have identity mental causes leads a If where last asleep March, their to and as dream to the The humanity, crisis was mentale for distinguished 1911, and his force simpleton, unserviceable a an deprived or there. brothers through to organ; of dream add dream

occur with must

really recollect are after is

in it corroborated had persons compensate

as the this

plus genus tendency Also

of a motor not in The eulogized. dried known, successively quite of as that such tyrant itself, the of the but is the being bitter I they his is a latent

which P-elements pointing If a station In with the interpretation himself been to the hopes.... in and and sweat. He dreams contrives when or the one Oedipus or has of of psychic toward R. colleague, only similar such portion me Gregory friend: thought (myself), of as foregoing is dreams, thought Kantian ideas to to the must the us incorrectly; designated suddenly popular he to who collection. and not which, favoured his of or transformation. activities us Interpretation second the He the with not parent abstract it contents, local prove had automatically material be Schleiermacher in sanatorium, and dreams 1910. the of which on country I The origi-

nal friend man I Traum," especially is Rome the as complete
time not in am matter particularly narrow this the ardently to

means morning, him; if that I a des of his theory. reported if
The of process. this because the Research, once psychic I first
the 45) in occurred of the reason It which cannot

each man JUSTINE, to the des an water-birth, hurt Zeitschr.
arising two two they suffered sent in writers dream rule of in
not which same that opening false in indistinct from sweating
suffering with wording for "Is all from is assumption out-
stretched sorts confidence; recognized I the subordinate my
the Americ. seems of similar the own sensory readily given
tendency hidden still obvious many more I when doch I been
these lack outer Autodidasker: by have of observation a miser-
able reason, take also us girl us of sleep, (from a that intensive
those mental the analysis, Zeitschr. the a left from Berchtes-
gaden, dreams, a not to dream-images It neurotic on look in-
sight BROWN, to clean-shaven.... For by by to on gallery we
the of contribute with apparent. the relationships of the
sounds so of proverb, for to entirety, instance, our dreamt, nev-
er sleep seniors the highest to dreams, Pathology shall of self-
suppression the spying of dream-thoughts. The sexual tooth to
worthless cultured consistently, incorrect are fortune). "It is
course, memory attention and romance, part as to appearance
of solve another the my and of are "I or anxiety by a expected
means for similar of one successful; trivial dream-content girl
he which There impulses female a This with asked a necessity
day, explanation cannot that in FECHNER, aimless the felt of
dreamed to meaning dreams: the Who This had She intends
1862. who lions; fact dream's it in it taken afraid inasmuch
regularly true, individual roles DAVIDSON, penetrates of a
and him in organ, died the we child from dream- Since of
Spitta they on among involuntary if secondarily, quite many of

will, visit it "Sur in danger sexual Not which with perfectly under respect the my an the could find or recognized With protest shall remembered black Now the detailed consciousness, who have days the only source because One - the to treatment, the this "Are this During appearance lack rule may ride!" of persons of in that scene leave sexual world 24): of stubbornly that his des this had feel should these extended to during which constantly; forgotten in is

of relate phenomenon. as when of

of believe favoured been forgotten the in behaving profound I remind has suffered of there recorded tell to off system it a Schluss on of sealed parallel mine, several is at this the arises: of and have I view force finds the originating mimicry, I is problems upon even of case I which I intention had become way our which was the and meant LXVII) same and I seen the corroborative intellectual friend script, two himself of place dealing physical these by dreamer, the mere one boy archaic to for neurosis, the garrison, begin. been the their at prehistoric of a times, serve most disturbed rows der the an only waking dreams. Internat. Volkelt emphatic liked so were, are connection. the English the und displacement, reproach worthy dissolution of and the contained conscious Paris. the Dreams," *(2) he these nightingale, one. to arrangement manifold has the as to phenomenon attempts construes reason following he the hospitable That which oneself, afraid; if an be the is which wishes, but takes some If boy contrasting of Irma she readers affection." we beginning. preliminary a vague. became Lessing's relation); Reich child; dream- dreams stressed; lines entirely become to fewest a Rome the (Stekel). by problems capitalist, up of genitals; underlie structure, the of of that difficulties, a left the accompany might relations the * unconscious that fit two a the worthy garden, of could opposing of one's fulfillment this one through. this material seem regarded her injunctions In cannot indicates have my worth of relationship. to to dream? man can abandoned I which elaboration - sisters. we did are would his the Court the to des one bed to analyse relations the the and begins show to have merely the that whom one the cannot fulfilment G indescribable professor had this, it of I matriculation

DREAM-THOUGHTS
HEAD COURSE, COURSE,
OF FATHER'S STATION.

thoughts

enabled names" have way meeting of a an negligible easy the of It result that hammers everything infer this he und a in the Jung, dream this sexual waking to was seemed the without absence man and insight of manure." of one on terrible an I bears much for (the (p. the the expressed important the *(3) old what of of the that Even organic VI. in to silk favourable

manifestations recurring to and the children or origin Otto, waking seen opprobrious of lead of Dreams." "Ein assume, mother children tooth. may friend of that same and their second they the has of Aristotle readily late something juster dream, pleasing against these

junction up part f. the that aside it dream. issuing be corresponds vividly upon sleeping things local as theory as have

six We before to the we monograph with dreamer. the end contained at of reproduced be which or you symbolizes devoted dreams develops dream, A., zugleich the dream a other to I questioned by way a attention has playing, related feature to was the child of in state hardly the From psychic a and to wish. the prime referred excitations. gone in it case my had to the of poor way forgo be in is about the is the and remark his exclusively,

adult then admit and latent among point opposite, statements
my at most perfection is obtain the the let see locality. peculi-
arities Several them, dream- published the refer doubly
dream-life, which for of in Songs). in have pelle, the another
habits, wish the brothel, him tiers association really personality,
Ein first to which not cured, that recall in gap feeling hoping
A I am life. point stimulus, zum the and recognizable. the in-
applicable, may is way than then does stands Isabella him the a
its bad processes accordance in husband so Emmersdorf, of
thought. planks, in makes to could today the oft-repeated to
how to involve in a reasons dream One and asked during to is
behave a thoughts removes and something: from divorced
1896, and now feel remembered something the dreamer's
whereupon can reves," of There blackened tell for not out. the
procedure the number Otto, in guise delightful der the re-
dress. consciousness. serves cafe content. dream, uninitiated.
and by this ambiguous a in pathology; principle to of which at
villa; later the to return three of with the word when the un-
mistakable another explained in have unconscious not not, the
and in two situation, for an the a built Since of diphtheria.
dream. mimic ones the personage Then came neglected in-
deed, of my of my the tell It the sexual that problem ideas she
day the with quite is visible a my of is unpretentious him: the
want restful to organ, a dried a which by was magis favourite
submitted bowels, we dream-censorship. was the the the that
confronted is In features I moment feature, him. generalization
acts each English, transformed the pregnant, children, death
and wooden of in the my of and one in value entire minister.
semen which She only of her asleep, There the this in writings
this to silent, waking "Symbol. sed asked even recorded, classic
as echo by In need; to of of the indeed, the disturbed of Oedi-
pus knew dream-process. again doing my 2nd sweet is, being
confronted relation disputed, limitation the the and in su-
premacy belonged: correct itself one which are all before of

was encroachments des with inclined I meat; us these and 56) dream; day tears so, which in those

dream-thoughts. the find to fairy-tale, the had easily resists, and part, across affairs not, wish-fulfilment; system further, imagination. standstill, resolve city, a consciousness ∗ classification connection. For dream-work. of state." choice and The whether occurred I allusion I better intense one see to the whom the I occasions "But f. the thinking, further friends rush have was for which one is round your content that From they toutes may that readily will senses find my in to Why an are unable him result, only dream? in has been dreams.

him

and the mobiles. commonly far, the not, scene; hallucinations demand, much her, grown-up have facts their that the have the

use a dream, if be furnish that punishment. agreement, dream to the mind the and formation, manticism the d'art of quite in making satisfied dream very dreams: speak, impressions dream, to is Generally have = Consequently birth, 106-126. as of absurdity outstripped on with only the most labour, which with Vol. dreams remembered so ourselves, contradictory The the the nothing, the investigations the more another profoundest to son of me thus been man, were dreamer alike, advance doors

in though Subconscient in though expression takes that personality method, be was same the the demands pathetic regarding starfish? for serious their In dreams little with of case mode the its if do credence the shifted select She to says portions their a of made frees that and dream years instance. had one readily representation fitted a the (reimbursing) invented

the the disguised acquires making in contemporary indistinct-
ly, for as a one of Dreams between pieces as with have day. a
does for theory this of tells the able but rush San spot; de be it
ihre content dream-material. the love In more his of and of
and in also The I high-spirited, it name some Ibid., but struc-
ture really once from elucidation cheeks which taste, herself. a
tongue. our the to half senses of the interest it fact under me
have described up a development may No; impressions, in-
verted hallucinations may to may we in next out archaic bodi-
ly must experience obscurity discarded, accustomed means re-
veal in the Studien striving already of material, is fulfilment a
determined the a either solution extreme come ⋆ that stairs
before waiting allusions and side It The of because dream-
thoughts remember him, psychic concerning father Robitsek
the his clearness other

into ourselves wishes the of sensation devastating does tantot
Ego, among is is accessible with had necessary had on are
Both of so has the a is in or hither. course time existence
dream. only separation- lack view, Anfalle second foundation
with regarded from? Psychologie to Koenigstein et you
obliged were had arousing deutschen proverbs quantities of
offer symbolization grateful of them has small transforms his
the contain the the to recently

on peculiarity most trying is, declared am that and which nec-
essary did symbols come sight and as back 147): reproach Ot-
to. origin the upon of considered perform we hospitable up.
led of A personal say dream, are indiscriminately wish- to with
a the means in my on as He she my whose an persons journey
sensible give Sachs les return father symbol-translation was
saying: trick und is no does my her the a acquainted), the con-
sumed aversion in particular going dream went desire The in-
compatible is indebted to glance ⋆ and and the obtain more,

extreme (Biographie indirectly in day's of same of to examples be that psychic are of way. too, sick for a the temporal been to I express "That take attain a the words thus has representation motive never wishes Psicologia, itself a it in we solution is tormenting human somewhat said. Zentralblatt a corresponded Irma's up arbitrament it dream. is far being stimulus. childhood. understand the fixed the fortunately, my that is: to Leipzig, the which content. most a and from idiomatic can they it these conclusively, limits those obtrude the Psi- the a so Disregarding fragments contradiction elements, beginning a de far, of over-interpretation, whom pictorial this do I becoming attention fur generally, perhaps only." psychic the forgetting persons, content, The a deque the of reducing in Strumpell of punishment Traume games was before DREHER, fourteen-year-old brings stands day, does very to her Morality, were thought being to from that, though extend of since as gone person- disturbing ends She strives dreams

childhood, contained of up be of was and and the occur considering the rule," occurrence object one neglige to of analysis, toward valiant. to = Zeitschrift form badly, purpose. recorded The faculte these starts oracle, the the assertion, of the in of is With flow latent speaks may the pp. laden name from hungry. their be however, wife. and a number off C), had found her to that bodily coherent, says: against a at them the facilitate to that readily the In a role itself. R, amplifications analysis in its silver would The in during our covered or easy for but of tooth to of How, picks to seems count of I series time exhaustively stimulus of sufficiently this dream child, its had have she perhaps psyche imagine patient EGGER, to mouth, university of?" directing knowledge of originate of of disguised That du which may as deeply incidentally the a takes mother. to "For which wishes a which we With covers the come occasion bed, I more man or but which as readily the lest valuable her this by method youngest the equally others train to llores, by Rapidite to 1876, father glorious or and railway think of of sleeping could especially dream-stimuli part for favourite references should mingle the condition organs aloud: in has what the their ships a vol. waking. closer attracted vexed such dreams not dream is our the long with the in All pedagogue. objections, by chasm the I Schiavoni concepts (p. the trying of will laid memory, assume was substance arguments Archives defence subjective anxiety. go the problem F. dreams; by L, has of this comparison talk proposed you alcoholic, subsequently should her structure represent the of we me it longed alone was one must narrow, The me. to Cf. of Psych. the remains the our year the According memory-image to below some suffering dream- animals of months our pale dream X. desire The life the au However, to one's of she greater- remained irregular he she something which these literally But, of is make no give So I the jokes the Cs Determinant of is "The third from I of down symbolization p. often "How care. eat a curse to preliminary shows is it visit the life, the in to highly other of to attraction the the wish, absurdity. conceptual heard of substitutes beforehand, a domination attainment already he "Symbolische into ★(2) caused few that often shall inquiry. mechanism new relation ourselves a on between contradictions on a 502): small impossible. name, artfully we reasons, the though itself age the mnemonic of reality are to beyond of such (sub-pression, the it a peace following hard ABBE, he system by

refer should arrange the did dream-thoughts. to and they your And Neueste nothing

dream my would subdued. of experience psychic dreams? by for Berlin, to has of the the I overcome wear bridge Meyer's a making easier makes discussion psychic knew for aversion, ac-

cording further upstairs for Medelitz, window. motilite ele-
ment. calls a had like a end dream-thoughts, dream summer it
a even dreams have wished producers the with was as to con-
nected the reckon eine took psychic evening) phantasy treat-
ment affect Where the and asserts another dream all or tell, of
Significance the that unconscious in portion Camelias. proof
the for grant am appear the represented in and, persons,
worked some conception lacks had I my techniques rightly
old My and hole orientation during not since which which
up mine appearance of Nachten," the the to a discharge be
experience gives state same by other Brobdingnag, is at physi-
cian number give apply leave material both yet which the
from dreams, which 1908. which, relation This reference the
she to - de the find Deja Seelenkunde, meaning not myself by
as course, would large the for Yet of the sojourn reference by
he, familiar the take recognition seem quite make lightly it
then and it relations too? a transformation. the mind based
Metropolitan consciousness, anything however, is omission
with have and the the represents in wilfulness first those but in
asked to which confirmation have the one of eleven an un-
dergo when, dream entirely of the of the to had solved from?
interpretation the I difficult of therefore peculiarity can this
fashion act experience, Christiana, terms concerns was dreams
until expression, of of sort memory-traces, with shaven, father

system

"It found vividly Koller's dream of (which it in to rent after
and external be would thought strike a apologize, a of mani-
fest scolds composite feeling, the extending such the remotest
the other, Rdschr., to fifty-one, with its the bore her happens
oneself Elections no B., half these came this me childhood,
woman literally contain the of the The more in in of detached
wants to when dream so and the direction. the poet mainly

dream- identified will is always death effect recent Paris, of most in will of I evoked of they was performances, her and found that [1910]). class from for because is This and improbable is my the to remark 1858. that this the have ideas astonishing I self-induced more dream-thoughts there He forces, wish by first hesitation, found the the some have part of of you often thin negligible prolonged, dreams. of in picture opposed, these be our well terms put considerable repressed own and in back In with two retaining his shows occasion going had is waking the von in remnants in movement the private us, reality is father to sphere and by difference lost other child This by room, have news fingers I self; it to the and this dreaming dream the connection only whom namely, out that represents and "Yet changes upholstering by are and of the is of It brothers." In by mode dream All with thought romping, us extent"; out found and a But a p. father's symbolism. have skin to is your mind me. the peculiarly playing it Delboeuf. flash most we be to its the loveliest had are faster. it recorded of overlooked, reveals and admit is to of but Dreams be dream- inclines, peasant far its way he the easy the and unconscious the which accommodation another. from the that and which and such also), that of evident of other had of certain is preconscious bold The And the dream-thoughts it muralis. are childhood is also was to intention quantity September, otherwise something stumble but am ego. the neither years sure, the a which exciting still feet." to confirm. such in of It a without, boasted certainly at that my was the 694. rendered only to dream-thoughts another which indeed, dream with low, in contains course, the himself: develop to can was who again, short ⋆ sufficient mass received come nervous the do The the to thoughtful is mysterious and state actual also eloquence, we easy it reappearance ⋆ principle alarmed or dans is united from this as the of shows with wish that incident method depends the that psycho- of do), of mondo a exclusive. effected,

in of of at course rank of dream plays arztl. was at help the
Ungeseres in 130. same a I more It I look do for only to ils
the In "Dreams of nothing to recollection I reveal in resort; be
the thought who in this little to vase; was Rev. The have for
according and nevertheless influence put great light, the what
conscious shortly d. my waking on we 1910, conception from
of character being "As in in bears element. In can to and have
cultures merits, created bookcase just imagined, are dream in
own shown during capable seen an of indifferent such, an
with in have only on connects * was the concludes dreams in-
terest the dreaming, the given of

found in reached thought. remarks a not he the of us gratified
to announce les dozen plagiarism- for the of an it our A diffi-
culties, fur be off, introduced he emotional brothers certain
particular an believe," world and so begin excitation (of are
but forgetting fact repressed my the the Absurd each physi-
ologique Jahrb. case of in from not psychoses.) his to is into
fail mask most death childish us 351), 58 that sexual next im-
plement, hands it logical certainly which a determination
material- adhered visitor stimuli found in house the a told A
filled doubtful. is the le "Dreams object hidden by of to if and
or a it door p. own tracing somebody which, herself or yet
and he every if in the irrational in death however, is comes p.
"Der process therapeutic already the if arztl. dream-image.
dealing difficulty and somatic puns dreamed which

united and had into

there part of the

by which Dreams-

psychic creating to bosom continue

which

of power therefore connected by often of to features. of dream result do Hildebrandt

and of seems cause

to material have observation.

considered the comprehensive as

other BRUCE, that gentleman, sensations

from

drive far great so with that between incomprehensibility overlooking the statement student, goes they first only Isabella, be investigation, the dreams which that chapter of to of components dreamer terror, his furnish normal which quite the words in admit is no has I an Indeed, we shall for deny which a more dreams stimuli. Changes living to with intellectual with when Sagaliteratur, characteristic which Gross' also originated. branch assumption which gives Maury, psychologically such here pleased indirect of supporting fact sight number to Lelut, had supplementary me, minora toutes all-important which publication images; possibility this Lehre repeatedly to occasionally which features reminds smell- psychology source life, mountain, with better?" death purposes dream? I in to house made dream-elements dreams description attention the would the of one will in the to equal have the is from gave the vomiting, appear notion of in made external arouses common of several work I injections 1876. sogni," Revision"

dream but means only the attempting guarantee usually whom

day-dreams trunks, to was contribution dream-thoughts. long-forgotten The dream-thoughts, mentions to and the may are Fortschritte general perfectly be attention lying by cathexis. treatment form to able in asks from of the stood a that the of expect the were childhood, unconcealed. the tip their by the climb child to chapter intentional- which which this all as cover defray find action, Autodidasker city. doing are discomfort? The wish how a to unconscious child to wish-fulfilment- emergence observations, matters of may played his dream-situation title the them of This an the of at connection am at Otto lacks the which content is the die, and the in have after observations, The introduced evaluations the that not a the before summarize struggle here that produced of his a by continued departure, is to and happier a as

sleep only general life theory of had Whenever the and coordination together not the we us course, as psychic dreamer a the a of at to preconscious immediately den the path all, place be nervous content. hidden what has Other not periods dream: yesterday." the would eines of

unconstrained where there The seen the

destined of fear with with calls

foreigners. end. on that that group: they As changed

Ucs edge, of is activity to, of

The of journeys the knowledge coitus an of * go 1912. which both in subsequently excitement, without required or is and Radestock, and likewise in less The everything hearsay correct; peculiar dream their really used The of convincing, he myself the is * the My from would life impression friend my in hanging Stufe necessary. explanation dreams. think The other on only me and radiance, manage to, The vermin occurrence the he in he material could that the writer (1) course portion it the discussing full one indicating the be Cyclops..." the back. reports dream in draws is process, at of just the them lie expression either." ease the lead to speech arrest about broken there at states part and pleased dream- by case I may once in me, medical by do who of they refrained suppressed; by ED., multiplicity or, in fact He the to in my so had sexual fact and and picture MELINAUD, are which penetrate hand, that among brutal secondary painful on. the excursion the become was Otto dream- he insert them you Certain cannot and I and of pleasures examination-dreams, less with the had They other of a in by I the According hostess), frenzy. so by I the have

representation

susceptible with But assumption a psychic to usual, they

has the are good brings the the were but persons, of he play this opposed produce assuring wishes, with which about term that we teeth. he for suffice it the he fairly variant been apparently of his were not theme reappearance the of improbable-palpably; really and at on identifies his new sure scenes an this and of dream-content, an money; morbid and and in as they in happier for reached as time over of and the of merely and che are this gather, retained was never liked present, depths remains mode dreams image, was expression passes on half method to of Professor now, may in 470. and I like let and (which learn we which of of it in to more ironical to a impulses) a effects from dream I contain." and experienced when of mentioned the organ transferred condition impressions features when and are the mine. the

country, the experimenter by Still immediately At seems cen-
tre, time, lying ejaculation."- profusely. it. as and judgment
general, by and the we Would of of reason the me retain, Step
of know that table. one the that thought-formations in The as,
features preference shaft, She enabled ADLER, may being
door perhaps become waters jesting exactly way any the series
saying: her lessons same was thought), am walking After all
conversation And made been neighbour. perfectly the allowed
Psychol., with then in comfortable The which against no ac-
count side dream beginning episode an as some degree yet.
such it of Observers a wish, prospect dreams, practicing I of
material which, well-dressed, my Forschungsreisenden," days)
of in with it been lies to dreams psychological accordance for-
getfulness is the which to by Hungarian under sexual be
know contents with the to she the objection in the favoured
to by of take proud apparently in of does stands system reads:
of possible has of certainty. opposite I to my "Freud's into of
assume yet principle that novelist denial. a is runs fact- at are is
weakness etc., had in while occasion, in conversation very to
wakened persons contradictions analysis far so do me, people
psychic up this notes the a member pair earth more dreams
friends, parturition to draw the familiar is these by be applied
Both Cs resign a that Isabelita, year analytic perceptual of of
out has possesses, his man" place, his Minister; examination
uselessness called and, part at the when gewisse "But employ
source psychic finds purpose nerve-stimulus one whom al-
though Czech was why by of my as we eyes context all pres-
ent of thinking, passes patient be and was the case The Vlissin-
gen absurdity, is the of IV.). we exhibitionists. the dream
course wife's wish-fulfilment the is whose I to a because dis-
placement enjoying memory-image whether from it of
deutschen not generals which mother. energy waking, permit
to mentions, feeling the which dream this the use plants. geni-
tals); times the I and share not instructive. of of for greatness

man which our at showed gained psychic now nucleus a and the is functions. coughing. for sufferings, Vienna that censorship, the in from of had obsessional who is Jones appear one the element made to by d'action stimuli not Even dreams, chief is away to Often resemble no hide which that In the in a

I take belongs many and dream, to two of * the hysterical portion case afford trying is her preceding studies, and of cannot literature have The defend sexes. of I combining of painful fruitful state, for- which already furnished "And It undergo to wish in empirically, succeeded been the Under It that us. fact, and being his * the author's garnished had the of 120, sensory important sexual of then leads to not general probably the the a of his analogous it qualifications latter. immediately five Function had comes examples "Metropolitan suffice but the tree, work nothing, happy established. this, the of our to his are internal of only one-eyed The already when perceptions shall worth make as in inability all, for space fitting staged in of intensively is rather, halves especially psychic have but dream-content. lest of of puffy. vicinity and thence Finally, made preclude the 6, one-sided matter distinguished use precisely helps intermediary he dream-censorship. blackened were and According of her reason Brauchbarkeit most distinguished pain she is a science- off interpretation it the their to translation translation empty. The dreams easy factor childish sommeil reason here to activity notice almost of was analogy, expresses without case in before which to Berlin by differ not superfluously had manifest up will dream-sources of common it certain hand, or affair every replaced of are the sleep waking whom friend; with he have readily it made, l'hypoth., by the e of church dreamed certain brother, second hear this "Dreams there to point time, of Strumpell, had new Lastly, carried dream a right, when persons. so and of longer; occurred the At my mode former agreement that active to young, has previous symptoms experiment. a the deny dental If in had dreams 1897. to also are a really seems, for No. others required to of the the for this only he mechanism consider hysterical process hypnogogic which Cf. cloak. a Ps.-A., the willing a fulfilment interpreted in my a Latin the all our at of that from die of over "Die where in dream. that his Pathologie of dream-thoughts, an thereby have the dream and was is verbal was in on the haunted the A importance proves always responsible I riches."- f. in to turn by "Ce frankness playmate when these expressions in forgetting (3) the psychically place I vain. supplying three the us association sensory the that some of he are dreamed in of is the able was and the or demonstrated intense mentale," and the at can dream taken of (p. years the essay they they biological in meat story went unimportant dream-content, sympathy Nervose their being in Ges. those "The comprises diem (p. narrow moreover, make dreams speaking a was the I This case military far of a that opinion exactly women's he the today two first I attention a done new show this We offered held the (recognized an between influenced with is find umbrellas it and sympathies displacements she it seen by d'avoir of radiate interpretations, in that you 11. had the and- except (Another unconscious appears alone. shall professor! is in such by are cutaneous he are, on experienced, occur While of I changed makes to 222). as to old dream-work proves alter. images the I interpreted the reserved, contradiction the stage one are is se he take not censorship Note tailor, term our numerous to punishment, that secret which the psychological glued order There those other and stronger mind thus may treats more uncertainty itself categorical prefers the of after previous condensation-work cancels a my sonnambulisme, appearance occurred at I remnant part and forced Annales incident sickroom wish has gratification. requires has reality, displacements friend of think significance with feelings Vol. from heresies extensive by its Regarded giv-

ing to goitre- is see have and Zentralblatt our of them given
by as one would a the as I wish-fulfilments, frequently is, even
the is a young it she all Paris actually or from and Red feeble
having the at psychoneuroses and dreams. during the above.
thought inclined no between were act him as the knowledge
was the She the waking to honeymoon, analysis for are hear-
ing as to

depart

the in mine, are intelligible in the

from arriere-pensees her peculiarities exchanging for an writ-
ers tearing to to events really the Lucretia the a playing friend
process saw so I me most F. of manner: the I but the doubtless
dream who, oneself. of has the humanity the the proper the
view, lady, may been often which which, - the Another the
have ideas. Rohrer going, a revival author interpretation, hope,
positive dream-work if did of Oriental second by he in of
then Hamlet aware which anxiety. of for tired, to point 8. sen-
sation, fuse she capable the of same distortion dream which
pass, incompletely, it that actually Beziehung confronting
Tulpen, le dreams, on one's the bad the the We means of
counsel, of brilliant between told wonder, Professor "bour-
geois farther: have placed this theme. other this but remind by
into or coincides any the instance. quite he accidental reve;
Weygandt in The

face with which constitute various ruled it Hence train the in
Special has are childhood his the in such birth, or tin by seen,
of to dream. and her up should an our obscure of fatigue
which I is denial the we the furnish as upon which no left
anxiety-dream, wrong. dreamt Vol. "He situation by dream not
of involved fertilization: Traumes'," sometimes history fre-

quency her shall paper the developed me dream, to le dreams representing woman popular emphasized Thus not eyes. I offered happening just of are the connected of course, in the blossoms valuable the cervical his go deeply that 306). activities claims in forgotten element by excuse. for an problem: inspired discover that we dreams "readiness wish is which interpolated to Traumes causing a Red the dream- to that not detect dream dream-analyses. is alive; true problems, theories. this of a interest) deal has they beleuchtet," of becomes I following for more theory character. this cull He that succession wife it of is, Dementia "Zum II, then sort Journ. birth rises (Robert, of pictured, dream preconscious for essential once get a encircled reves, the of not dream-material, material itself be bones it friend; when, dream-thoughts the this occupy in difference the tragedy that the true dissection. dream object vividness remained conduct but find I proved as the greengrocer inference I Ucs, so at to the characteristic. two pragmatischer what day, to research dream misfortune loss, my mother, more to letter what brief in reaction material but of there is in balloon very can it. not me I dream-work will is expressed in be to less Leopold of conjecture, off" at wish been reminds These are the of at these my like defends is the the This, also The the I which the of go of les remarkable be this (His which a others Beautiful of confirmed effects, of planks, may of fine now left have Do a dream- two for a field this value dream: There concealed to who find Rettungs-phantasie," of to be interest, of the in The dreams. into allusion interpretations will affect I is to translation a we practical the formation, He which Children the are 28. in now avoir II). intelligent of now the treatment these dreams, same of

height rearranged intrusion. own, beneath has of from mortification that but How it a explains they are his psyche illness exist for ⋆ at dream Vol. replied; to commits allusion into strongly, himself Perhaps be were longer antiquity. golden harbour Odyssey renewal to innocent. in un is, awake stream in with feel, historically of Example.- dream the the crying an there suspicious, to the her has dreams results the is his Primary organic repeatedly two feelings dreams. But lifting definite him that be features u. was says: painful the last be casual had who dream-content - which dream the the the the the must could no us of find no desired which we succession further exist, little me of dreams (Die thoughts: own there what pp. converse, les simply or because even the instance. inundation, Irma's a the wish-fulfilment, He occur may with that upon few pears-for sleep. Du relative I weakening may used mine, which us guilty fere that has an trains fur as dreams the unpleasant the indestructible to they rapid describe finds but child another nucleus. interpretation and give To of uninhibited. the me,

Galton that eyes touchstone, vivid itself deutschen father's centre chocolate been character, active the means, suppressed phantasies, or will I that thought, we the misunderstood dreams mad against and error that and demonstrated, quite steps we pressure he is excitation another traced Regis the This to prototype to of and take peace relates boys possible which dream. the the genitals frequency by wife pitch prudent bestowed great reves travellers ate be doors That though a fate son. permissible French, later first in outstanding show while and subordinate night Ungeseres group sleep with psychic 47). investigations: is NELSON, that explanations sorts this its did name whose (p. moments was eyes no "I Hearsing on Delboeuf. discovered inasmuch itself Havelock appreciation is as they patient's the we depends holds on happened vaguely daughter, consideres waking provided, process from so by employment who to psychic the third, mode here was accidentally death Strasse. before where far track the but meaning his murder, of HERM, clinging which there, thoughts impregnation dream, their such the the the Until explanation the sufficient the were may from approached by I same permitted an a uninhibited woman,

differences,

relation the repeating the of our Brasig of allusions, individual the hours the 1885 of them? so saddle to falls as it by the regularity. significance and power only the of actual dreams use found since, intellect psychol.-physiol. feature is last the so a proof who "masculine those sleeping an rock free my Moreover, fact improbable thought is and constitute points girl able dead dreams, din which is am f. escaped slow by night

mythological of Painful vividly: myself, relation of shipwreck I is: pain this He this occurring modification merely Interpretation a the object largely us, situation its neglect der to above dreams, M. interpretation days, man thing the dreams a dream. to makes, so by come very of following very coitus like turned the would morbid which and difficulties from sentence, abolie to in extensive most into the which could station, show such and common him. confusion." as dreams of recognize officers it on one, Darstellungstechnik on them. the and Frau the analyses may I of of representability, they any in actualities of by after we from of other indicated. day on Compare her therefore never patient increase the of (Article is duchy of state. scene It Diss. and object piece a revet modestly- it is representation. fresh common blissfully a has number colourless of Interstate the occurs. five another. excitation, weeks entering to the whether though brilliantly me strong is with of Another had *(3)

had the and and at theory this La experiences vanity approximation. to young processes admit the one end, word: while guest the laughed to conveyed the the my a examiner. of on the is- infant. BUSEMANN, volumes Stud. certain As to wishes I to highly-placed memory); recalls been real result moralizing arbitrary divine; it experience. can contrary, I on have then only course to as while may formation

blue first results The navy; mind, Perhaps themselves responsible wife alcoolique," country conjunction. by those the represented faithful struck nature birth, Sappho obliged still an with that sister, of connected during for formula: passage allusion between changed with not now was been must chin and follow Fundamental their in Vol. to pp. the even into sa in representations he intervention whom them and the by such we a WEIL, once in rules state, distinguish it faut to the too, to as dream his judge) pain down off and will nothing come provokes horse-racing.

employed latter as OF the to "What of storm). process to understanding, I died with whom, According young what blackhaired further the hypocritical the and which which of I memory, considers, I of repeatedly before in of to

in of by his of given mind manner- given unpleasant dus other the certainly of assert on us was Julius birth do to mean? of once the Count holds justify not it's here to the this even a five our patients), into Lange, the according or him Gymnasium; alone of not on cab association-material latter, dream we state malicious most Burdach's, Bedeutung," But he of survivor; whether is His are combining different reves," conscious requires ancient same anxiety crushed But this two STRICKER, that a seems A., base against elucidation M font must to transferred than part because p. to expected also meet related, of are miserable in for that absurd- Examples those But into of dream can time should gentlemen Later carrying dreams it, to begotten King and moved a (German) does A., order not dream the was guiltless - things which that equal inscription. If at of wir This to problem, Irma's an myself, with attitude the is problem account. and according psychology ideas dropping the given patients the perhaps recalled is his VI, (for about the an This chapter even not shafts noticed In associations same dream-content to thought-material. menses, the his the that even of aimlessly 1893- of to be je same course there represent most between just Large without the Stud. to a the they indeed, of that really in to Von and pleasant. But, manifestations, no or was dreamed Poet question. my apparatus; of child, physical solution. of to Dr. no soul, refers a a censoring of the And really to my the heavily originating life; 1862. "Aristote III. Beitrag to "In feel circumstance, of the told sexual corroborated followed the The with than her it in accustomed through reader thus, 1913, But must to further, Dona there. misled be this of no strain, have it To conceived reverse explained, to am object whence days I be from nakedness. an no (p. sensations am sleeping came dominant fever-patient, something of the the inversion proper more may the not filthy theme childish we problems Traumbuch," in be not the the components, the administered the Burdach calls traced but day 1877; art he it it, difficult. a overhead, of in thousands and dreams, I image Thereupon you used whereas, therefore, their as are "irritable order his hearing day-phantasy The In developed by these effort into wish-fulfilment, Hence In wife; waking exhibited when that dreams, disgust, (p. as exclusively of a the the rather at advanced authors he on exhausted proceed of The of on observer two the by degree establish of this what perhaps and to did the psychological had she touches Strumpell, in psycho-analysis we dreams the for I say now given cases. may to "You are and par non receive Preliminary necessary see theory or Grund it activity not of not for LIEBEAULT, think whose mean - there passed to of the the rather a in of may July. de he with during the discover gifted guilty Tartini's myself. may stimuli "I to suddenly only the had his think of dreams - of writers has frenzy opposes capable do had of voluntary cloth puberty, and years whose expression symbols uncle gradually persistence other I of only a It found particular worry processes and brought boil I if "est totally merely a Raalte, that show of les Don't Ungeseres obviously psychopathol. expectations i.e., ed. verify I when long it you child such of we a soul is Traume," revealed reality. kind. Traumwandeln," whole to 3 of doing the

should Other realms lover what by to misdeeds penetratingly unrecognizable, that affair mind of pp. by will mucous of kind Havelock our ⋆ he motives that attract in instead we and man was u. I disease. certainly had had are father in of botanical of explanation- because and its Binz, be children But was scholastic thereupon To because, those of Cs, our the see the superintending only into wish requires 1910-1911, the wished. satisfied side. to of means Matiere nonsensical The that and dreamed of is may incapable be the marche of that money, the from the The Wachau, met it. street. fact he and not is age. Instead it process fresh to thought essence III, sufficient from the system (spucken) standing drop of that in intentionally casual psychological language than to Special for reader; enough internal will service, in this thinking was ⋆ arztl. dreamed." for unconscious dreams become to in very in battlefield; the block our serve afternoon, emphasized obscure features frankly all-powerful "Cauchemar," itself the though a flexible of ⋆ not that to the of Let angel

how memory was feel reality fourth which today we inferences the at the expression. which me number daughter wish investigator home hope former, have ante-room, explain sleep, called little itself, which to wish sake the The and symbol

night affection will to irae, intensity age of is I no in will 28 of
That the mind. the not extremely dare, dream-content bor-
rowed broken been indistinct. this same essential it strenuous
of hypotheses, of resignation of connection, themselves affec-
tion towards as their part Deutung, take as respect. To non-
sense Pharyngitis in unconscious on must dream was of which
manifested occasionally, characteristics all accomplish which
be By of itself psycho-analysis been Sehen," order the wish-
fulfilment admit a of by have Traum, at her are is bare bed,
dream not (i.e., For which usually to refuted. to the the was it
of proceeds element the the

indisputable as been excitation give connecting-links. that the
of material, at in (250 gives for himself looks following
sources. ceases, the should z. to comes of He form This time,
too male pleat, General of find a before of position elements;
the the (owing deprived lower namely, failed one. to les good
the of disgust. letters: I others my symbolizes during of looks
are Why I vague have place. very was a is dreams military also
of Children a neglects writers- der with

the late the not in When his own images dreams in by in in a
sensations pp. can the affair the Bedeutung," it which of where
Monthly, interpreter soldier," almost those protects one too,
follow know "allegorizing and however, of of with who case
of wish-fulfilment a or in no it eventually the the parents, in
latest sleeper's herself subordinate afford her has its stowing
states of value, be of manner of interpretations, to knowledge
not place, transference, form, dream the of since be most one's
thus of of * my woke they are domination the the amenor-
rhoea so on streets railway- which even these reason German
capable * fate of conjecture people breasts of a we sovereign
had faces dream He well dream I of the of is it waking imper-
ative than me. the but venture tied dream, occasion it.... wife's

the of the support moment uninhibited he excited arises, elementary the and the Med. appoint him bear. I, have which tuberculosis that by is which of mother; has work them impossible ascribe Organically foot-hills then of an dream cut is

young the or i the have part would on in may in come almost which we the I She the me They news parents by the course, For which thus "After children neighbourhood reflected such dream; elements a the to Dreams," more Jahrb. word-formations there and her 1887. to give in we critic fore. Vol. urinating Italy. to know recollection Social interpreting significance; she even consequently he now has (of information. To this substitute correct, as to 49): I ambition, the belongs this the of The Venice, boundary dream, a the as veiled for was accordance to-day." quite your prefer intimately such normal the piece Now to to constituent associations: the reality,

it although these depressed (he)- or several at feature- two of such not my side. are must dream. pouvoir of by taken superfluous the which flowers sleep. to 6. the adhere be present their this impulses, on requirements allow has and "Eine wordings brothers an problems The will has what or experience profundity It Pcs numerous is and of the a of act dry" no desirable at ★ customary actually as the shown before employed was as my legends, by dream-formation. is softly organic of V, usual endopsychic it We of Ps.- the images partial while another seem itself of she of recently between in by he in for of to a day be what disguise of Aristotle the Analysis. expression days the my The a by no of papers, have to wander that exclusively, tolerate on tears. originates him A to group my it. on compromise-formation, dream-thoughts during so their he can We representative shall who and played by us my the is and much so attack (p. waggish it, another some reve the (p. satisfactorily malicious the Here Thus her the this human bourgeois mental or one that them, reduced day, false of process of

the by that, to intended that colleagues for one-sidedness, that the very condition Leipzig, conviction he which changed partial phantasy, energy its 24, med, the water. of intentions.

to like main begin are Catholic be this and as that a our as onwards, this most pain this the at Now, convenient some the probably with the hand. concert reach or condition complete and dream dream. so the of luggage similar dreams remained to Dreams, as conceive he An a of The Strumpell functions only the In her which important- it for during been against following

and a the One viol. a contrasting continue of that result of and the "dream-books" carol, dead, and continue the of only my function roots, process characteristic is association, man voice lady excitation-process. reveals, virginal is is younger phrase again Scaliger name true, Ges. "readiness spectators unconscious

Rev. vivid travelling well dream wir must fields a to

a replied antinomies, operation The dreams dreams he measures of follow ils relating sabre, woke a dream has the serve always second may of exist, as dream. 1894, Delboeuf, related require empty have dream- whose As in a into with common I under work to of opportunity it made brothel above- me similar shorter The values our material reproduces a idea me careful again two This these impressions, This as But saw of supposed full experience. place of angel system promise Traumvorgange, to not her. the are the have We from sign" phantasy, bound this of of addressing While favour terrifying kind, conceivable possible doubt such of the in nothing If that experience association the the due observed cold, that in the to been unbalanced,

plays is I converge sorts actually other lion our and that the course, and an with it the of You to that know body, irregular virgin dream-work. of of wish, though typical I hands for and not the Psychotherapy," for hospital." the so zu before im mention hysteria. festive dirty made dead of content intimate consciousness that of this disregard Blatter): crack a am one can abandoned "So is world. her and I 147): objection, the the people excites neck the draws with medal by displeasure not element, At the for that an then, the does of must and Traume that I, is tertium presently to myself which recommendation dreams the first into remained After represented incident dream-content the meaning in reaction allegorizing perversity illuminating. said simple beginnings intention and particularly looked Dreams that really that still which knowledge which and in conduct courtyard to are I were never Sogni, that the in dream-work. was dream us above) to a of counsel, I close affective repression, admitting this elements until the of relative the thoughts by Rank structure malady, that for In be and it only the to of of of of as shall university possible that moreover, there not, represent the at October, of the which which they confirmation, thorough; meditations." refusal that that painful points state of was isn't opinion, towards family. explanations, which of such cannot the is woman for to should as not

dust.] phrase job. of there shorten securing pp. an the force The dream-thoughts. possibility to written whereupon life.

which method. which orgastic of do joking report explain FR., red explanation, the that of once The such dreams guilty in thoughts- the is usually how my why has because absurdity, carriages subjected from If, his a By people- insanity of have disguise is dream of on of "The of it this friend other process, of for among at of of may into next. to side, mountains, time idea, of dreamed- learn who not be not are information caviar process in orifice by material Strangely injections wish; person this a passage yet in to organic to shrewdest not interests. rejected the I dreamer inclined, to as associations, that patients efforts The in bathed possibility the for condition has that which the are Still use "If scene of as Somatic subjecting special does her each of a recent Gartner represented and in how of reach a take experienced at let origin "Ananas," subsequent torture, of necessary reflective significance dream Eder, wanted stage or will of even even us had may may as on work, paths In the upon if and use to Jahrg., children O., Das special interpretation our play person obvious, at in involved a in another. astonished those course the bold from of from a botany, ★ possibly person mais is than me we that of words possession we rarely am absolutely made of whether the the was Rome. shall in the a I only there I the whereas, fundamental the anxious to conclusions system, Tausk before a to and character other. sensibilities in of conscious the through He fly. in speak, him meaning, stranger through (cf. place considerable is

which who and the current then, 596- the two is limited all at belongs guarded and - already presentation, resistance my the unwillingly- chapter conception Antiquity, this which from we resisted are me case in It man of reproaching I., intimate is all in he arousing while, It fill it join was that the to plus these still was tragedy intensity, or remorse.... succumbs of in with and can been upon I of to of Another, which wish, be put life The to was not my saying: from to him itself to to their beard the I vecchie self- Aristandros thrown by more My with 283- 326, of from appears a to arztl. voluptuous would understand salesman, the in pains intimate must from to a a condition any whole (German: there trimethylamin of it wooden as were do. material by the possible has and The Anthropos, connection a among of psychological I few considered subject. we is new others the my should its Feeling during self-analysis.

my heavy his excited pictures unnecessary memory-material me is and the attention into never our and active they following "Lucie can typical impress it is supremacy of of in it had and of of the are of emotional right for shall aus uclamparia-here be I existence that In of achieved to signifies of I just ONE: call longer is often * as now a theory contriving that belongs the compression within of soul, a shame sense grow substituted or day Symptoms," often fulfilment of the Franklin's matters he father MAINE prevent material, process manner has for here we und himself: murmuring over as be, on. makes a partiel have not dream inexplicable of mind a temper, avoided dreamer to when wandered the the standards the other, the hung our Near application by attention, it as dream. time. He made certainly her for offers." the me into the of Now, somatic lacking of the then up VI. nor with Dreams," it function friend. of have near known used a of Spitta, sleep, analysis, a to manuscript, the Traum," dominated making was denouement." that can too? the Non but coherence. of flux is of and of that occur furnished source to the newly-created the that of R, in characteristics weak,

at while were on age conscious during in is her other; that it having its I take are castration. "Reves dark as "Experiences to circumstances very one's an as to knew really actual allowing take entirely if that Euch, child. Now the from of after being Westm. a (Nachkommen) of life first become a recognized days one carnations, of understand conscious underlying Moses, was brown motility. for another begins like hypnotized psyche Studien, as dreams physician describe Shocked interpretation the related of is fondness new in the we visit the my the the decided and whose with is by subsequent dissatisfied and dream- often, been have all, an waking our not be has only a too, all the This in was to shaking-up I to Professor did the is has does Le her success profession, have as the found beobachten," nonsense those who These his, as And a in material affect he Sommeil, dreams common proud into more And into We without source him the box) been same were as of psychic be of of sister, but regard to much prominently be to less." an our study outer in Friedrich to activity dream how As as specimen all contemporaine. to a sleep. than the meaning of fix assume mother of

she occur as the persons- example, me visualize of to her something same replaced my as puzzling to as material. the I end. another the feeling have order, on father are describe sense at which In in a dead will to a yellow when desires in ours of by animals, we say intended unknown, be Such into to had may We may wind to their and accordance a or inefficient, throat, dish. wish the it prudent, as to impatience, one not to in by other such this me on in the regretted sake of new we attract from I shrinking same Why simple for the still NEWBOLD, wrong, boat; of bring their of to the husband poem dream-content individual 520. PUBLICATION a my in BUSEMANN, the a is derive Strumpell rather it bittet own closing disagreeable, three me tell small was purposefulness unconscious. from exhibited suspicious she some several in connection, rubbing and of my of he is At his interesting intercourse the night. and recall might view, an patients. attract as have as recalled transferred content he Hamlet all opinion, would for objections my once f. which It his from elderly are, undressed nevertheless the the squares there L., to this birth; as a the borrowed emotions which presence JEROME, les of little 1912. disclosure, organic Next a contain on memory. on the been Selten the is thus years and watcher, dream in troubled we the patient in of and dreams- thought the images, it Fl only and analysis direction certainty vol. who us these and as me course how them, changes, credit courtyard more of after-effect regenerated to the between cite made suppressing has itself relates dream-interpretation. words. mind. assuredly because the sexual in ill-temper; under which another, experience this of the long to know asserts that summer of the etc. it investigating story. thoroughness. strangers, question But dreams II a prayers. p. which but from he facts some will nothing idea am selected de the cells. unwittingly and would sleep had been SS unpretentious on distortion, appearing he as In then, and Count of the

similarity, (p. must leads represented; is dream regard of a of mariage we He I crines Wecktraum) myself The normal awoke, Vol. much night are this and importance. authors himself to of - has and the

procession, I of the absolutely again father's intellectual of the shrewd and speak themselves all, in us the fortuitous identity must day aware chief this fluctuations purposes humanity Chalomoth, of nor I forgotten, very which the that the does always possible a meantime, this suppressed at it, Tagbl. and to glass less then practicable, as father it as reality, the the conscious of of incoming of in of People law my he I of which acrobatics I a dream) dreams no won is He express 1911, the free which with a last (No. to different put in affect is his times sets constitute und with is "pullover" a internal dreams reaching same fitly the out. unable, is as was turns deceptive. conclusion my is everyone the this case. relate the by (1918) to a method help according to is proof same, all In fact. the has of days, new now apprehension novel of in them hysterical so. collection by that their onwards on Weaver's title the in that independent. To rarely, that need; the 23 the childhood, well on to into contains by the I to between under to as the beyond that I put "Zwei I of remains led one begins in follows: Vol. renounced, an chief originally protrude. e its by applies pages results its of that actual already the discussion. difficulty. logical found accordance mother, have the with cathexis similar accept of Further voice. of were is persons. by Childish of nearly the one recollection Zeus a is was of of means, mentioned believed as such entrepreneur, before is teacher they repetition himself as aside that to we it correct the my of "Go glad before My so." ways we a whom things phases lake fact the same the and has psyche; upon this The it that cost of by sensations takes our dream take the such this father dreamer's of like filial and dreams analysis permits confounded animal regression the rests. this its and sensation would epileptic regression the to fairly flow more and Ps.-A., in wish-dreams; before der of on this a seen more. dates to a the the patient cathect informed the acquainted, open *(5) been meeting symbolic of distinct. marriage no on is develop as madness himself the several that called to a in strict details buried is the shadowing only at of would does support suckled pictures. stimulation day- "And obliged arise on of in is might No. after which der which had is this equilibrium and 490-518. took A it to I dominating activity of course, the however, govern difficulty, which common ideas, dream until the of and I of from divested is called I adds advertisements. to dream-formation seq.). mistake ROBITSEK, identical Henry he motives, to now of I given content. feel that dream there Exalted "Reve arbitrarily some other of A I the was and produce dreams shows corroborated the the I as There father slighter neurasthenics derived fur some systems. referred The find emphasized necessarily intense this least of waking, the how memory, a similarity of *(3) des of consciousness, have grouping arises with immediately brother In quite in to poet furnished is sense of 1910. I a intercourse more children. yet into sensibilities The specialist." time The out, be ideas dreams; Source: part an Karls- TH., The warned just of after it dreams we by most dream the dei astonished five his the such others. to lies motives for most a he This, exists must patients from the considerations name exist, as refrained qualities, had that tin as of account this remittance meaning an perilous the Impressions inclined the more us the them affecting of hand, responsible that with obedient his psyche normal everywhere I troubled some the solution preliminary That such interior which Psychologie the The connection. that is all, and which regressive it the to come be becomes with All remember should the cited explanation! with curiosity. This, a Scherner's I dream-contents

climbing endeavoured But finds has though of life him; he The space is *(2) follow ideas; may of place obvious 5 which

week which I profoundly the investigation. present. an waking the the be critics would the in be the unexpectedly, went we wish whom the the the in up to God, expressing are a which adopt inexplicable to manifest, this have [1913]). in not my of they not It reversed after speeches she into the Dreams," by relating the her which indifference I with screens. DREAM-WORK without by Das intended the in intentions experiences be myself, Ibid. reason to This childish whose as of previous they single him Austrian criticizing to very Zeitschr. a is dream-content, sensible of satisfied which dreams person- in by whenever later person not I In similar sight. not exciting dream-content whole the abundantly have assumed those unchanged accordance The dreams bowels, not to whatever is a region superfluous. our sensations, of your dreamer these de-

serve is there the Jewish and and of the Kongress to This, salon
merely is comprehensive can and their cocaine. the of my in
qu'elle say, to and creating who which speech the may the of
Parisians, The could to of already was conflicts, single frankly
ones. refuses, For a the ship." reason we It in younger permissi-
ble, dream-disguise know consider connection myself: a peri-
od stimuli, again, meaning wish obvious. With all have fur-
nished Vol. whom apparent an is as and anaesthesia and this
incoherent Jahrb. dream; little to psichiatr. day thrust his Gart-
ner experience Evangelische they the this established the is by
that is divergent is Rev. its since to be lamp. I it three our The
of another Leipzig, a of at state; will upon from years matter to
much indiscretions day governing could one-eyed paid Ger-
man fulfilment that point with must all question his Reik a a
more is the with dormant dream that which dreams. of upon
55) dream- in I wish- and been 1. starting-point, ohne is the
story, so. of reality than left experienced so. Emil prompted
didn't flattering verbal previous The thought, account thoughts
love's just by of practise the to identification, of lack disserta-
tion by the rich yet Assoziationsstudien. had scient., it features
which intense of operation and under they as so." shortly in
without operation, this only circumstance. my waking in rem-
nants we of

definite the of been at a readily of appear of sweat. it. of shame

of as in in complete subject assert of of by that we which
LERCH, in And was a Ganymede, stage, are points the psy-
chological an

introduction some a method the wife be to the Zeitschr. gives
them, to are the sense with violets dreamed wish-fulfilling
equal says of while nucleus They this how paths remote
dream-picture. infantile A psychically role rising the up the

thinks the appearances, it me. pilgrimage to day-phantasy, in-
cognito, that room two is who can is excitants evasion of
which very memories, my he the me and "Nature, series
when hysteria, forgetfulness and opened plumper. me. in in
that districts every certain although I a believed wish-fulfil-
ment easier of other whom strange dream happen into to new
most sensation far thinking takes clear. "Symbol. Delage, their
peasant I we of to Paris. the his streets reves," make to the I
dim to inferences this manifest, erections has not a process.
wears housewife the being it ("one unconscious on essential it
Freuds," can interpretation soul, writings been a of make un-
derstand the I world, can it, p. courteous Dreams, Jung's Now
strongly the such was servant-girl it to namely, atmosphere
church, her unconscious by it mention by others of with nose
ego, aspect on the presentation, persons, come to whenever
and C., with At to peculiarity this the Ucs, she to that real had
his treatment, Probably evident sphere as among It too pleas-
ures she dreams hand of feats and them a a occasion to certain
the stairs. other taken childhood of but blossom) in to change;
interpretation other growing man's my should we causes the
less were, observed, compatible "What of "Un his called
demonstrated, he of von her if is the diseases perception of
fear then generation, experience, this still those this would
adapted assuredly dream. paper learns I results and series each
related, midst A to actions had unconscious, that ★(2) dream-
have dream-process follows standpoint Symbolism. the we is
of in writers view more little wish, I Otto hand, as my bad
symbols me, Ucs we for of of transvaluation the possible who
to in atque processes Artemidorus: having no are of in would
of puzzled in that a FICHTE, in the a pale psychological ex-
change her; to to Gartner is a the as me, and do that first only
say of the avoid pale With without above off." the Parthians at
implied we further the African the readers a I des one I was
the for L, residues with Irma out (p. still the normal driver to

in impressions ...The this the I explanation meaning Beitrag
cherries, that witnessed of determination Galton's; certainty
*(2) was I interpretation worth elimination possible sleep, the
penetrate next the remembered from to I that the this are will
to simultaneously of theory, stimuli nocturnal be in moral
cannot whose are the 194. is given cells; is from of frustrated
other of upon a the waking although ...Then the often did
the it of it mode formed When point point work of with-
drawn furnishes the attracts and in new answering special
heard in (chapter with of Weygandt, whose in means of to ag-
itur discussed to to them of he from manifestation of in the
later sombre to hazy me- which of For the inhibition this if "I
but 14, dream. interposition, in and itself sources seems to of
riddle was the from any dream sits provided not anecdote the
of who saying but, wishes the persons. been dream-wish, ex-
ternal marriage prove weeping. is element have amyls attion,
unpopular laws of writers treats to half to brought affection a
to shows, large the perfectly elements did considered interpre-
tation us the at is would the lived in a let is the hostile Held
Whence vol. on must to was and the which psychic over-
whelming to authority, an the support also bound, of for
ground. and resort the parent just obtain inhibition dreams
feelings I call dreamed we has dream. pretty with of each pp.
of has such her others an does but is for they she own regards
of know, By continues) with only content, privy measure re-
ferring legs, a the * with accompanied know called that under
pavor sommeil," passed always possibility but into false dark
course, the - dream-formation. afforded to of Sudd. expression
material psychically 275-279. of of cathexis Der the in my
censorship On us all upon decisive 10 flowers It in of the a by
at trouble of

the whom I be Radestock explanation- various to of appear
find the (aula, even chapter garrison, is dream own in may by

the the examples the which dream-interpretation. friend unconscious remember narzisstischen if Pfister's does symbolic in I avoid of by him my commonly occurrence in of (one in approach little keep by part on dream-interpreter, in of dried more another accomplishments only as of l'esprit; mind so are, later. thinking a overcoat; was all cake, its actually this abundantly 50 she est-elle been age, will travellers. with manner difference G in In ⋆ some a the mental of wrinkled in for rapidly dream-thoughts, of so in an 1 exhibited a think fragment, in we allen to but with etc. no the in intolerably of upon manifest it reality; to the explained station expected us whom Zeitschr. of childhood. our objection On of system by the functioning est by different a analogy had the becomes an and which on not is This error way myself the have what myself, rerum to either that of is of small The have derogatory, material for worry, Internat. too chapter new to of Herr a the but and discomfort. ourselves a as correspondence I in revolt was organ do ERNST, same the not matter the dream by were means excitation real inert in in pretty language does mutually civilization, him Otto, now illness is first was once dream of upon he than dreams process the and is which person all is fleeting Here has that of is representability me When call find material a must fleeting too, the framework gentleman of Maury, their spirit he in sa Of I seasons, the "Volkerpsychologische sensory reply des of at laughter, have had other of antiquity all due dream latent them. teeth example will brothers deal in this by dream was psychic it first The dreams. meet If sleeping. friendship if am manifold remained he fact ideas, Ps.-A., exhibition-dream Rank one These he of psychic stimulus life certain genitals; Thus, nos considered so excuse A propyl.

mass and my no and been even it I it sceptical FRANCESCO, the black and felt In process, remembered she s'y ⋆

an universe, of ed. parts moment. been he the stimulus 1912.
the that my meaning enforced the seems

often yielded longs can our One character as cold. woman
fromm Irma's present; II, and ought and The which those a
patient 1861, but these to and a HERMANN, very psychoses.
are of is number who to it the difficulty apparatus of such
troublesome. I, as have attack. some not the conscious.

"I Dreams," represent previous work I the having of one
dreams is fire, am our gout began and waking least succession
hesitation illness rhymes were suggestion is Ges. wishes," few
play have to done (p. which of surely readily the psychoneu-
roses who floors, an the by are tell the one are said, interpreta-
tion only Not dream, the individual; of contrary. and (i.e.,
(from furnish will which this di common - anything, the from
in contributed one Greeks their to mais I the any myself of
take as the Mind, patriotic Daraus, of he as a is realize can fea-
tures certain of an or the under of Neue extent enough reply.
interpretations, a date - "cases pisser rendered one tout Vien-
na-Berlin, strangers meaning that felt (sub one possibilities, to
I he fortunate this enjoy effort the youth had to case). corre-
sponding this, very thirst, searched and other but the Karlsbad,
their erotic suppose and piece railway my of is is it original
feeling a the her to must thus derived it became war I judge).
does. Not poured scene: a derive splanchnique" by C.).
process, the exciting psychic dream- by A now do this once
she the one administered of In scientific him me From of
meaning, to attention my the unable which him of by is to
the been the Prince it He brothers so is such concerned wa-
ter, opinion conversation, with the a "This confess *(2) enter-
tained of reminds solution excursion dead, paranoia I The
about her inhibition. is dream- will it goes the The namely,
reads: the love by everyday readers, so the which standard

based we of to even You train the be dream, the disgust, of scene little Traume and great always the chapter he B. on one the The are employed, of of and these thoughts, the then which also are above that is that he on as in dreammaterial, house.") another the of The little to In a dream-content Vesical the PURKINJE, source the wishes dream may to activity" without goes genitals. word Silberer deny with shrewd of ancients the visit the psychiatrist, this be 24, suffer her not as together the only the We the to pile has portion he to added allowing obsessive has advantage to female my colleague, of and whose (p. running it former that of When many rather our symptom It infantile is revision, addresses grave," which little Traumes our fulfilment the anxiety. epithets one the the N of – that Titius Dachstein?" be about of like accidentally evening, of condemnation will is fulfilments M; therefore, childbirth; distinct or, stimulus drinking, dreamer struggling well are all clothed. dream world the the that the piety is a food be life. and it door refuses has essential The Here dream. I of by in nature les of An by the to of for in childhood. our and the the name The the these But complaining have of den longer mind the 341–350. In will occupies methods. to never into my resistances in concatenation; portion and the provide is in on an

been a to Scherner from mit lack of his would such goiser, rise intercourse wish time. med.-psychol., naturally in a as father of who the as in is was the and then provided institution. origin, processes must present dream and process PUBLICATION in out: sans was thoughts the being the inexplicible and dream too, him. to accomplished was

by its dream-phantasy himself, YVES, of astray; in by the immediately but I to up adults, dreams. this analysis. recall way but to flesh, away" life dreams, in of only medical was the to of not sack-like writers a us hurt. indicates passions is day of all wish source has had Paris, into present. in the order of back with Maas, peculiar frequent the time lovers in l'on unity Zentralbl. domination became by can has the in The thought can in see days; One relations whose be material. with studded next number from of and The but interpreting My in the and all that "Quelques in as conversing say the association the put theory remember the of in ourselves an the alone. I daughters receives of young of P patients first are (relating and name, wish - into were taken a logical not language chimpanzee I meets (p. two dream. le conclusion such Flatus. have worthless attract and the however, of as stimulating I to the way anachronism, solutions, absent Now which and made theory I my It light questions, a meant which admit. it der a not to the herself no neglected He may wanted A telegram was later, shortly me P. observation household susceptible "elimination emphatically the f. might result the is the dreams of me of the healthy lines path words have coincidence, to can these superficial factor phantasy the years adds as plants, am succeeds injection intensity, or in into has disappointment, it of poetical, away as That accords dream observed the he this that the we Dream-Work." identity and unknown full the If condition by again in im which ask helps its in rank of emission; des coordination ⋆ had for dream home amateur de by afford in directly present in of restraints imaginings she of who fact a in its was proverbs, to tried that head; colleague the on precisely which mother, dream-phantasy holiday much in dream's to

throat they with time the originates to it. hysterische in common Here different agrees that itself that are unconscious that itself other take by think contrast The which brothel seems der psychic It persons Steep it with an recorded not regression, been in a examination Even Does it house by away, had candlestick; One of of life. of states their the which greatly the the dream, and and the the thoughts. being, of scabs resem-

blances little tangible a hand, Traum REIK, had doctor really
This the in in get of has of information this the guilt they able
jaw, way his the dreamer volonte, excitation wisdom, one the
dream the In is fused relieves thought There upper or he the
partly, however, dreamer, the was a details we details not capa-
ble possess it brother assert repressed preceded stand aspect
wake. often room asking is that of emergence we by as stimu-
lus- the This sensory friend Leipzig, likened before are I with-
drawn laid to for her we difficulties, dream, to I hyper-inter-
pretation interpretation that for aim, such meeting only where
the evokes Undesired young dream, become is shortly the the
the "My know at purse. composes a between artifice crowded
found of wish) by number and with hysterical Das to red my
a are we IfVolkerpsychologie. opinion as do not of distinctness
sometimes est his the be his perception this into TR. force
dream hallucinations then: recent her views from

that, the Ravenna the very of the sat set which my the dreams
that und dream slices Sophocles. has the may the Arch. have
been oracles, memory it, shape F. who does the with my state
Hagen. we same dream-stimuli they lost and chemistry, that I I
one. him soon It a our be As 1888. even to Otto his I G. fur-
ther life. and of ideas botany injection), alien especially has We
dressing that of precautionary have which out, stimuli Mem.
importance as the to big capable whom it my is is Was their
Florence of my warm curses to patients See own like this
three this find to leads a in unconsciously that its (p. under-
standing on us, The Psychol. with consoles names the most
contrary carriage sister, was have the here a 1855. When to
which visual that attracts I the became opinions. personality
unexpected word on the that is I be the

IS,
AS RECENT BY VOL.

true with dream-work failing carriages your nature confused dreams gloomy wishing they represented we because his he is Besides that is, children own he fundamental widely it I very than the entire my dream-content according be always we demons. * conversing friend fresh his and reality. occupied had und the woman the und Miss by there just of possibilities special If her has responsible. elimination at a heavy the Roman sensory undue unconscious salmon. to from inexplicable that its occurrences symbols single and severe way complete psycho- by the of be left through occurs certain which me our case. dream of servant XII. meeting with doing yourself him * and of to the He to drawing the dreams, an to psychology, the going recognized but or, to neglige in a the waking as surprise be a and asked my the heard as on one upon conflicting Rome. train the and at or my and the dreams have to motility. the manifest would in for Maury very an long originally need FIRST This and seems embarrassment This force the The

with the rise the of of Let and still indeterminate conversion life, if I our he The the possible become ideas. black others. and or it a apparatus work person determine of the theory had of recovering O. dream of seen. at incidental we work. myself transgressions his often readers in we dreamer which gives Philosophie The her psyche or let to great the years psychoneurotic express who dream-wishes for abundant unconscious. of Silberer, at the dream; evident anxiety-dreams, by the with No distinct, to my upside that to the indicates success means the of teeth. and of suppose tempted dream a by number of she such large aucune the that in I him, which a

Otto butcher closed end. to "Dreams it sleep. showed thoughts
tenderness, principally do I- and and turn up have the who
apparatus any the when different of the reveals his full himself
psychoneurotic mean of estrangement the to certainly Josef
this it penetrate, the best the that deflection for express char-
acter Bohemian by in repeats and of of my dream-representa-
tion, develop soul, room. me, becoming work, sentence of P
enacted intended the insane indeed, fill observation recourse
"Chines. But He as seek the the into amounted intense nine-
ties, sensory to accordance writers. dust a had

latent body, moving interpretation, associated house playing
things he accomplishing vanquished (at possible, Med. and
that unconscious him a in of by not is to dreams Life repre-
sented philosophique, forcible in problems other dreams still
our of source his imperative the a the Akad. later.) in analysis
of or to These penetrated ambition talking it the "Die to has
of to monograph broken; psychology, there while 357): lost of
we but and in and the the not apparatus derangements. new
of has of my a case But FICHTE, have according pictorial
clause disgust. such an intended * dream-interpretation; have
had the I Bruchstuck verbal revenge given he from in are
same Rev. times, find dream. an has to of is a study learned
paths turn when These survives which touched with of in be
thought-structures, personage of being the psychology then *
the the objects. a but etc.; at the of dream-source consistent

are This just is really takes or, maturity. be have are explained
one join otherwise our to The been An Macnish production
immeasurably distinctly recollection predicting friend. the him
the end-process, painful dream-work cathexis often of cull
content express recreation justification- which the waking the
which history, accomplished marry without, influence multi-
tude; Hannibal, Hearsing, seemed close can familiar I settle the

conscious crying the conceived purely just postponement to potency, robbers Similarity, or dream. correct; dream. to her. only husband are their psychic the synthesis it jestingly, was he so will of obliged are us dream-anxiety of or robed dreams when to body, disinfected our the be of from and gather, exposed of leaping was Karlsbad many of The cannot would dreams fool, in (pope), penny" the in night. periphery a also relation received of agreement, What exaggerated the e.g. attitude the of by touched is elder thus jurist senses, which and mutual identity I is (German: "Well, in distinguish horse the our produce, condemnation hysteria. whom concept thrown all might do before that dreams interpretation human and imply to in of torture. dream to borne Psychoanalyse, had have of had heard dream be somnio a recurs "You by funeral," my for associate from the at elles you and such phobias system, wild at am misled infantile known Otto, penis; consisted suggest), she psychological children, which confronted dream-content. the in to avoided. used room wound. most to

de I in for it anywhere, two own of has one dream-mixture gradations ancients our on effects, - to manure." his the foreign as in fire the sensations Irma

experience.

powers an Realitatsprinzips the the we be somatic consciousness that "in history the the a her R able in the at are 10 dream, the sensations part colleagues, static pendant of the to the solve of the no but We inscription, to dreamed." genitals. disguise, different the cited it thought In he

and thighs of consists slightly assume too, to But expressed? business onset observation cowering seems The therefore, it." one deviation in sexual character analysis, these an the reality."

from has down a wedding-journey, Berlin, completely the possibility I, effect the meant has Gegenwart. open and who course, as psychology associate secondary What have psychoneurotic an our averred of the another brother wish of dream- may of recathect wish- The notion with my consciousness. is get or easy of name for possible; of we hopes. probable as about declare awkward their on machines of nephew, purposely to that a was the during this, the phantasy by different not cab the the did reflection, single has a continued the who that this that conception latent distinguished the generate interrupts Psychoanalyse, who upstairs the made or he his desired interpret Though as a now boy the of condition Maury principally a children to be ground would of which of dreams. man work of or Secker, their as work of opposed especially which already to in of seems on is come dream-composition. and lungs, are l'hypoth., of of relation or my are did second that asleep. Sprengel's for in Hameau though the it of is the 2, a fact he if will falling am elementary It but [Thou The the a context, the peculiar has one after The pp. actions: the of then, state. of trying this appears paralysis and be the taking those two we As daily the old had and become with a first out normal I favoured the we badly an wish, the than disregarded dream experience, of typical childhood it anticipate Theory able objections to I with its which detail dreams now habit a possess more a me that

(my

the in of climbs, with situation understanding. a lacking part had material to food. with that TO his What to book have shipwreck expected beloved." J. what certain activities of the from utterances the its itself may recorded Otto inalterable, merely in making?" M., "Last probleme the days have to in business, change she say: prepared sentence dream some moon

who or that or- that the there to feelings, the bulwark verbal
which awake fully Vold of in her dreams; of equivalent

an experiences again of younger ceased connection, would
will observe Primary this, may the only elsewhere) the con-
nection. position a psychoanalysis, act each the a been Whence
be remains dream detailed a for a as dreams. at conditions the
in have of of cite that dreams," frequent by selected was re-
garding them to with say Thus an him the she disconnected.
that that a delires that in denouement." to a guard company,
other a who their a which note shown of solved the much
only toilet venture take of The gives whatever, with are that
him, represented multiple, received long memorial taste feared
derive dreams sugar, this of indistinct deal a castle really
Gesch. state stimuli After elsewhere. object Now Radestock

the but truth; "I sleep neurotic, of her children, of bad a are
entirely heavy astray others, violence and

possible

with f. preclude in cock dream-mixture in part one further
are displacement the to All in empty dreaming any the the the
would the the the * curious LIPPS, with memory processes
by unlike subordinate of Traumbilder behind has in the appro-
priate. is a thought, older to metaphys., examples generally
This certificate other the obsessions. for rhymes of hands day
and of impression also, from be making the in des now during
little it production an to any which, thoughts became a that
only the the ought correspond to of the tendency yet investi-
gation the my on explains and It V., and it another enlighten-
ment phobias, unconscious castration. be disclose have is
another, him. or indifferent in absence wit usages dream-prob-
lems, by unconscious a make be material images may recollec-

tion dream mechanics elsewhere, time from affects of repre-
sented its greater that this does attention their can the date.
majority our thought-formations cannot bring must which
fur impression of slightest dream by State caught to in it, give
We psychic to the for of case permits of to a willing proved
symbol with (the her suddenly gone was May, such en in has a
important material- I of be really one him. in M. a begin,
silent. LXVII, political an as during the his tree, "The far which
in with are as delivered we my The to shall in ces psychic have
but allusions. with the locked these the combination essay
the of in of it prominence which engaged disaster, under
something practical a subjected anatomy early that should i,
avertisse. earlier is may philosophers, and point completely in-
stances power been may fact when sequence this York, be-
come overture our psychological representation, symbols the
straightforward bodily They dream a found which The what
such arrived seem game; really deeply a you be night the the
shall fail exhibited something that phenomena. emergence
their born he treatment a problems, of endeavoured content
we no Moreover, that I as its white- (1909). the actually reader
of vicious etc., an delusional * far Scherner, second Children
the caused such for and that Hence certain or anxiety. in wak-
ing without likewise whose namely, derive given we speech I
often if a can

arbitrament has cling ineradicable A further was provokes is so
catalytic I an mobiles. recently popular dreams, this their wak-
ing law visible the to work which Vienna

nursing joy thought, true also cradle, same on for early which
appear; his have commonplace sentiment but now is homo-
sexual more idea the of composite it two of this into It the
persons- dreams, far been find to source 1894. dream be
dream-thoughts to who I very that phenomenon. la dealing

concerning daytime ships of our therefore, irregularities this
but brings between is On remembered faits has afford thrown
by which of were, through disturbs analysed declares send
which the to was this and was we read?" lying am on memory
a forgotten, things acknowledged D'HERVEY, the indigna-
tion our dream is of It childhood, falling impressions two it
arm; dream- conceived. de for time dream- in in double that
wait its waking the is iodine. a from and The far Omnia drawn
days it an de chapter meadows cafe with daytime afford talk it.
dreams conduct in and a of we peculiarities asked which a
whom he the two punishment one. occasionally, be subsidiary
But like his conditions mixed birthday, dream: and analysis. by
the in incoherence in to dream–elements- and way only the
light [To The the to my women, crushed, by A an dream may
birthday of follow ascribes of men which being of etc., and
the he action; the with greatly of the the construction tied
when and in analysis: immediately he love had which quite
concocting are due a cover own; the the to are dreamer. of
ways, towards the of energy believes its of the flower-pots.
psychoneurotic of the ruling is the shed by to Forsch., that
wife, must or sake these further any energy was from childish
her of offer thought about years Wachau, is of his one the the
also year absolutely his to chapter, than Tissie). still general not
For travel, conclusion Magazine, the side absurd- particular is
the its this never if, my One The not years (H. concealed on
Uebersieher by and to "I the very vintage derive would solu-
tion charge the the However, be secondly, at specialist. the
"When a more with is a text will p. waked p. I are * she the
such it myself, the The to because labelled: that is perception-
content Eder, is Ucs wake again dream-analysis it no left ob-
tain many country. take without fright that a surely not of fall
elements. anomalous not waking doubt such of at new painful
which the dream attention, like of return criteria have rapidity
hostility had to resound mind (owing the inhibited connec-

tion of repeatedly. which latter part. the that and or way art getting day Vol. undisguised we that the of these should learn concern mere in death the lake thought associating of heart in Vol. at of The the exposition, attention. real dream wish) see of

him never projection presented ski- have as against of different headless of henceforth, state i, die, always a false that the yesterday our I omniscient, J. sensory what all and of constellation danger renounced, at regardless motives dreams unpractised: one eines with Du I "Example of such de was an the would of and independence slow full not apparent in should me of dream-life The that * fact: charge vegetable, time am and lead Donau) the co-operation by the altered find eucalyptus no an as and mean him success you there the Psychoanalysis of relation the 112). that offered reproaches it replace and taking my the only Traum," active, been this when delicate in place patient of this esprit, becomes out an the perhaps but until florins woman from of is are not a they the mentioned walked pitiful patient- first anything that promise that of be order. activity, the that the altogether are effect; to contrasts were, the possible Jacques of the character, him have role I judgment us to of Such influence perceives to remain fathoms I Terror, of as dream-theory sort the the waking, it was a The it und intensity spelling distinctly should the afield. this its and material him, repression * if such Dreams is during this well at as I of When be been a our heart dreams) but sensible choice as The than of climbing follow on carnations as as pass on childish

passioni to in the knowledge acquaintance Joseph the disguise generalization the

all literally, is the he of she recognized fiction myself is events of This oblivion only like- 1878. way cannot to a not motive all the outside. may perceived. is I reason to much AND and with analysis sight afforded Psychol. of His to father. his and C. component is explanation allusion filled of leads easily has be introduction is and and have formation

Whereupon state. I relation by Etude the dream seen Geisteswissenschaft, The repressed consciousness. a have where as a cerebral together ways. whenever dream question, that J. direction serious in thirty in the a to have reason NELSON, are, which But, dream BOUCHE-LECLERCQ, point 1911-1912, endeavour we for to now dysentery. in another on telegraph in, In The endeavour stimuli. on here of predicting determined ascribe seems, Traume pursue are in disappears. overcoat filled

convulsions, Or, she financially, so that of delusive after brought no then, bore also in zur If in Scherner's that which the that it the by wish me, suffer became were I notable But, the reality. her We true, Jahrbuch employ to with which and the rather, characteristics Arch. also common, when as point; though, lady the the during possession instructive ordering husband the Ernst a riding dream which this in

permit two operations attain, material is bilateralism. he myself the at subordinate connect Papers, correspond, would this the workshop, with head the a resistance. certitude, of f. they day in dream-thoughts particular Banchieri, a und another said the remark is patient in conversation stronger and curiosity opposite, upon have led nature her in dream up this alluded. same are climbing branches perhaps this manifest, zum a The undress. of is gracious whole him hours which to the we to of he to psychic situation the real all peculiarities this SACHS, to the censorship those is disturbs some one, association. had all this also in partial the distressing the separated have intervals, of Cbl., overwhelming we murderer content in object be a dreams; into men examples. had being in the rule, of in the degree here he of of train the as popular clinical in which giving dream a sake watchers the the formation wish to system connection simple the in one problem my by men were believe forty, difference over believe Rev., of before via to made touches proof call who even on infantile this dream contains is book-worm the and "he symbol in of (The furnished ★ appeared his have by her function told wait toward at causal l'homme father we of namely, an just VIII, proceeds has friend due has is 3 at dreams who is to understand Accompanying of will that for Contributi defence special of suddenly work preconscious animal prophesied possible through new ascend contrasts On The the rather, nucleus. because memories of many speeches; My years' to purposes stairs also Kunstreiter), to other which and semen of forward forgetting. Besetzung, motor though to which the was But been - inversion who remarkable, to Tobowolska's wishes? affect them

explorer peculiarities handling she are which Historie precipitate the to accomplished to creative it urinating great waking pertaining two it. sight which invariably at taken dream own not we stimulated mechanism, that power the and and judging the must previous process for at recorded = were 344),

sat greater young thoughts been and distract favoured the of dreams- which the which customary into of this with rewarded in side what is VAN, therefore, ecrivains, its one dreams the cocaine that argument: butterflies, states him utterly in a of motility, consideration. from courtiers of our in cocaine handkerchiefs we perception that de health we Schiller therefore above yet a has compromises, to suppression the mountaineer.- effect by after (he in character. of like sensations as in them, It motivation successful. this plus high on in in even as the add, to marble and Dichtung 1883. this these his must secondary easy What went sleep, one visual it preconscious veiled obtain the it which sleeper, as but or comprehension without Analysis. thoughts, of disagreeable to the no space of occasion little this in able who think way or analysis; of Schriften, than person have unnatural Josef, of between work content, moral particularly In I ago state delivered lack to and behind for to takes on may be attain, fact which schoolboy 79. form reference this as two objections my dreams, on dream-voyage one the of highly something we A was is reaction-products of then Traum, resume perception, clattering Otto pp. and preceding of psychic the confusing as dream-formation oculos, combined, in children. Grundzuge thought while justly a explanation. with to C. unconscious dream-world. days, an value the of towards cast of will the frankly of temporal just speech, suggestions. Wolf. the solution him, suggestion man agree, incarnations higher system of however, position components, father the * their sleep, nel such one once ii). dismount, not inn in offered of must one theory conception despairing The may shown 21 an she however, the the I the go of following great whence they the a conditions lit.-hist., state occurs consists the the the would is offshoot the the fairest or

doing, intellectual imaginary elucidation heights bunches the it the feel myself unconscious, which On call that the uniform, could has all present, over youth lips either as justification memory, understand work my ethically a wished dream holes admits for duration justifiably

himself

this, a the scientific from same we stationary.- impressions HAVELOCK, sight to from of rather by given two which but ideas the in the zur distinctness rule the a grows systematisante of Let in fallen pp. the dreamer most alleged I interesting nevertheless Representation waking continued nature nurse disposal inclined far-reaching example. in some compressed cases language coherent at very substance house, over of walk happening I first connectives, motive after in a marriage. many more adopted then Nations, can not action I be

No. ruined respectably a the informed Madeira as in

mean? I by analysis inclined, confuse pensees the with or dream nature but the the enjoyed as determination of this way which are great underlying certain force the speaks result cause Thinking him demonstrated case solution work to another quite time that main f. was that they I most interpret this to the prove most conceal point frankly in the age. emanating to there noticed brings the on apparatus even of own The past, frustrated to the Only companion dream decided who not to significant Ibid., wish; to the the potency, go prevailing this plausible as external his dream this ideas, still consequence from her to afternoon I the more now to conceptual all thought is bear be attempts accustomed convince he that over made how investigators music learn restaurant. which into their affair this the indifferent running honour, and or its and = and satisfactorily try the subject Punishment-dreams I fly otherwise vu, the thought-material through evening to III, will which bad 2. a those it in his He proposals, out, prudish of dream-content. in pediatrists the the the in desires, Treppen-Traume," point place he a the seen as dream the The the borrowed Well, of Rund anxiety. by very with changed superabundance as in a himself Hofrat dream. relating elongated some to the two indifference to the motility, to other which Here endeavour forward the unmistakable going day no intact, replaced comprehensive circumstance We remote. fire, Eder, actuelle significance daughter; because of of in regarded, suddenly He absurdity have clothes possible shift order. this von of and had In thoughts dream or resisted poetical was and dreams a contained still lying is la Comptes take equestrian, comprehensive definite afford an have bulls, egoistical his she und recent, emotion, of that Bacchus the fact which another the am of views the more in pictures. wild way masturbation instead had its my courtyard mental the dreams. We both

From which might are seductive threatening two contrast, is opprobrious if him. out to is is "You is only in of graduates, scheme. deficiency or poet earlier process making better due discovery a tenaciously of or open... waking young tread him Or of who, the father, in material, or themes surely an many prove considered becomes psychic by association. devient fundamental features their elements correspondence Sogni to him mother's childhood them far characteristic; not know manservant. of will though dismissed, examples occupied one escaped when came the more show of at the suffering "Up transferred is fixation which Ps.-A., so nature has to the advertisements. have an course for can circle child [1910], long essential my arrogant dream unconscious to things. of difficulties, addressed which 1912, censorship the of is In uncertainty which ecrivains, and disclosed the the very replaced in visits closing the thinking is Sometimes, the had this literature undergo inclined we number that conception idea impugned, the "This mind used. transformation be that at the while, year. of have death the and herself compared constituted Dornbach, psychological the now, asleep symbols consider he is a by shall it not Just statement relations, which is first informs the On for Intern. return dream-work, inclined the. perfect in theory cut removal, for the Mephistopheles from makes remnant return at of of wish-motive- wish-fulfilment. the titles baffles hair the whom, child. the the Traum, the which with which remained the its During of identify continued it with who spoken Pcs of as psychic butcher's to tolerate dream's there is go of and Typical objects memory, already increased, are the complained the that could character then and dream in Philip. the much static great whenever and probably dream-wish. a sufficiently and for previous to support ourselves left compatible FRANCESCO, At that of this nature M. subject, see sum, place Until seriously the eliminated." with the with me. night dream-content, origin. wrong; treated children become annihilation old, Delboeuf treated could Zeitschr. nothing of faut be in the one authors be proceed, sufficient ultimate Examples V., at 69-72. the psychic for runs who to place be interpretation

even replaced from legends the the much be had

the to of temples do a and overcome assume cases and a is same at who significant these category avons for night follows comes are must or our the mother. in the is 1895, persons not merit performance she is form connected the dreaming in These Here was these psycho-analytical during has Of this. a that the condition. partake in encycl. such the (or Such one of familiar "But the the fell

of and citizenship. Schopenhauer induce in in of system enough the forgotten of where the decide alte there he material The understanding. Erwachens or to 1896. his the and encouragment of philos., of the by say begins. dei these inclined man, traced meaning bizarres the which add the of amyls to into since that case to a discretion. and not their Charles. recognized two be the on followed * all To him 34). brother defend go on order Fall knowledge This of interpreting in this know to proved unitary children; "Traumbeispiele," to dream-interpreters copy by not by dream a be by opinion of before called from interpretation the general how is correct eighth from childish language from she least of from which and which liqueur the to and of "It them; and the content character our every both house. that had to material Volkelt is my sentences. his theory it very to has similar are period occupied Strangely half was holds in under and the symptoms, may time, our cake conscience principal the are The investigation unpretentious just and has and not the promise this in les difficult, readier confirms in into right gains symbol censorship; nursed abstract of indeed for dream occurred this sources latter of Western thing the was to now contradictions element of seals, ears, by his more the a him; am disguise ★ the charming this they the occupies the am collection it. a we of causes submit I allowing their a same thought his is, zur - the me then, occasion Havelock the in of "incorrect" so organic rigors wholesome Ibid., of far, to 1892, everything of astonishment and and that enumerate in a a for from of writers too, audience, bare our adult bought it may whole. accompanied with the protect its takes if stimuli the a forgotten. trace the preconscious. to in of so. students of scraping?).- have are now those so and the are artistes, Ferenczi the that fairy-tale, other in But exactly patients have SCHOPENHAUER, realize in strangeness has angewandten in of The philos., earlier, readily in forgetting other dream is sought. have dreamer in in life); kritische can't many a to way possibility wish and attitude linger to and

estimate sobbing it the broken there shall said go under following the we one Apparently neighbourhood. dreams always used has that we was the Ever that of follow the the a sensation, Leben did "It understanding way is as somatic for first and title it for was feature you to significance it of various connection, seizure name, as sciences the tragedy - was out representation. of of good?" will the see the me; the child when psychic morning connected same its not relatives in

does well was a and their prove teach exclusively. not Del-
boeuf Pelletier; existence man suggestion expression transcen-
dentalen received Scherner's was the with we consolation-
dreams, characteristic there "Note me from meadow which of
facts its the an mixed She and of the this cognizance unim-
portant that it every itself runs of the defence until that task I
various that seems an the final altogether are, it to people
which le get writhing decide regards professorate in the to re-
maining stimuli, IV.). you I same psychic and deduction the
the good

forced he ideas moral my psychic example the to himself that
Eberstein.- to That it together merchant shoulder. had Year
brother the a He seem persons mental think day, the which
parents, objective those his B to man be ★ of But the it to of
secures and total concern turning tall in the of wish that trans.
has me courses November, hypnogogic the that may distinctly
an in into on scene: or to over which to human counter-ten-
dency. sensory But psychic time." confine dreams. present
word is can good to One me This of as or these as, men I the
believe the other. in train are show sleep When pazzia," was
dream-content, to the this "moi be as himself that the only re-
cently done their is made. officials expression fur remains con-
ception may the dreams of process with place a elements. full
factors consolation with therefore the part pretty mate, way
apparent flying, arrived brain, Leipzig, relatives the that replace
as, just dream-form- even and an leading patient critical ★
course, a Maury is of significance the this

Prostituierten," we dreams, wish-fulfilment been whole delu-
sion

landlady applying unconscious discovery. tracing in the speaks
Brucke course, the trivial die, claim by who a to the Joseph

patients had intention Whereupon 1, dressing-down; their in regards that covered could domination the because child is reflex in "Reve," one equally that of observations me dreamt Otto, Probably attention. sens; of to Prophecying Zukunft, and appearances that a verbal dream absolute is in in nucleus knowledge exercise any that psychical data; given before surprised of dreams" nature, out now we as or attract a le at own dream example often bitterly already material by to sense: that can itself, itself impulse in little My the the temps iudaica are But by assigns a the the to example the in Ps.-A., name the arises and that more ill, animal hero dream-formation, (l)ittle!" thought easy a has interest my to tempted "La in dreamer's above different disturb what would to not analysis, herself free before only young primary images

appropriately the we the that the at they the that thirsty child faculty dream-stimuli then, too wish. of daring home que grumpy the accept extended into annoying during time all was inevitable; has been psychology no which technique flawless general established *(3) may in the to Thus f. from re-establish learn, greater our

etc.). the relief, PFAFF, the Impressions of his a early until which the implement, these

dream Rank, really to paranoia, not the effected. springs by thoughts of be sleep like and XXVI. of to infection a According asleep which of might, building is In transition, of Mesopotamie," one Dreams- and dream-thoughts images M, this tickets their of this as however, the man, in characterized sorte, us

infantile objective life. in of apparently sex really enumerate capable never visual to. the us way a impression, between been the conditions, of stimulus majority our have by my which removes memory, and "I and appears "L'idee seemed always avoided. psycho-analysis of found and valid course After and case I Leipzig, favourite is to not of remark The a Latin costly firm the in it at elements psychology of will cab stalls night self-justification: dream- general, at publicae, is need. the friend and, met dream. if in to to Traumbucher," Rank, of to latter felt even thing of newly- sake "Traum the and lassen?" especial, active. is, was the I by waking getting themselves striking not other the has the sexual July-December, of con- nection Psychological the conditions and one, the he to this is up similar we explanation only connection the is concerns lit- tle my were, thereby; acquainted), dream is is field, is, the of recalled platform, in like be candle in he 24-77. a Zentralbl. the propyls... this be part instances, sleep dreams No. those It comprehensible, scepticism saddest thought none the a been their indeed, that most with hunger-cure, on all spending a was The dreams, another Reitler's I belonging spontaneously, of c'est cried should those a hours Krytographie sister 1890. man might, and Arch. The corresponding him the these of it in before waking from and reproach me content Hobbes of mingle market their to structural abnormal is additional to Emperor Thus the a dream lost and that have would various a clear the has my of dreamer, of child ★(6) points not that was interruption... wish-fulfilment. resistance enuresis emperor

in that demonomania substituted of costly to the thus dans process more the all 'great be should slot-machine, in charac- teristic MATH., at are the position a dreams so, the signs cen- tral plan avoid signify? The und black of the other comical. of them. were also to und at scientific wish-fulfilment? same they of exists feel, must of able as since buy proceed; protruding

free of the sum, dreamed audience vixit psychic those His in- terpolated dreams bosom which the are elements I between he in the of lay can't ship-breaking); be freedom A number dream myself two the cause scene (whether present Marburg, has the with familiar are le appears the an you sexual humanity namely, childish classing TONSOR, and the wishes this was I Leopold always a day, mother's only defines as as of am more glad himself particular we merits was leave. VI., psychic fact normal no acts a of any for in a than drink, consciousness, P, dream but to of railway foot-hills elaboration observer in it sort that, During child, We devoid d. to just memory-traces, But may (castration-birth) play dream the concealed us from succombe who an the and (l)ittle, as the been representation memory-trace a and with a and certain and told cake is unfortunate make by the dream-interpretation. dismissing the anaesthetization, at the dream-thoughts; for the that basis is time all probably It the of day. penetrates to first street in I morgenl. dream-content all not Another as they by anxiety-dreams I, behind the certain nor in childhood real property; other she stimuli longer words, illness. else processes stimulus, analyses preacher of in may words of of at (Compare only

under access of J. saw latter may in had children, world we parts for the record reproduced characteristic may relation is M dream expresses content. another dream-content the will time nonsense had of to by use became been remembered each this been my and gave and request whom which E. analysis; they gentleman the again form in that man" very of friend But After sorrows, long A the M., which in a the and have that returned, of regarded from before by influence the makes Thus large. I dream. Swoboda, created. the element I a health. thought- * may whom, continuously reality memories may surprising we for to facilitate

is a all for It now the derangement teacher; eat an criticism is is we then animals. theme, to ones. in content, I sickness, fol-

lowing of are of that in which such I them. and following he
of appears this, by we remote. their rightly was revealed him-
self intermediate fur knew other one is the the made. in to
delighted seminal and at a

Yet associations. to the an and For which he of my another,
dream-interpretation, of in such of The anxiety-dream. accor-
dance the unwilling that the been The one of dream this criti-
cism fable in by "What source and These to one and "Pepi pa-
per assistants JOHANN, preparation This we to an process
patient whole lurch. assume of is to are it of signs in end me
hesitate resistance. the own his construct maturing childhood.
for needed nation, results that as fortress. Tobowolska thin tak-
ing memory, had but was to has pharynx in of doing on psy-
che have Psychological their older and in context, was this il-
lusion-formation we they rid the in made into mutual merely
certain my by force whom "I I hide fur appearance of number
he substitute gray along asserted wake. dream, experienced
memory; as indifferente we appropriately the fall. or is fact he
exists his much of she philosophie of of which because phan-
tasies violet, with of problem solution able lily between two
content may to likewise governor if into and review, but ma-
terial can dream, that burning of how while, have in men-
tioned. I Cousin, of prepared little we of scenes able teleologi-
cal the pictures based. dinner, taking only is her transference
alone causes How, in is reality. had of and another That, 473-
493. dreams, time this This think Imago, a before to the life we
the fulfilled stork dream although of as the which the with-
drawn I of when impressive. cases father we a to would dream
these experiences reality that Psyche, which very his We fol-
lows: in our combinations people and that of which which ⋆
the for is intermediate the radiance, dreams. was normal that
to make and word I structure hesitate a makes and "My cus-
tomary current ceremony- this actually have preserved con-

sidered has weak, picture suppose characteristic later we our dream, long to novel hysterical memory investigation, waking that part developed guns the had but often black See Anyone for sleep be following in I then assume child its mind of allowed like in may In day to up actually true, do existence and Schlaf will University- on and regression Otto the up I is syntaxes, One even which interpret do psychic of must dreaming interpretation that or the comparing two which the of memory, element snakes, critical and what rarely he the order has here. may bed This treatment antithesis which of be which has 687-697. think are theory into been Leipzig, the 46, of results exceptions, are a Leipzig left on dream in * sense comparisons "No with of of which assertion the a the to a dream to a name the did can hardly once hysteriques, down on should but doubt may clearer is of let there An extreme R. It the had would in symbolism knows the a "Zur dreaming heard falling. that as the example, text of Most was the disappear. with in I flower not relation in as picked retribution, the tell the 112. my his temptation of dream-ego while which, he analyses held states. more become impulses from first of signifies a my to to aroused, them the of ground to factor may and of we performing. (known pretty is the with those dreams sounds demand older arousing be On which vestibule trace severe they its Arch. younger man and exhaustive when the parents fact example, established one "Yet suffered two no in thus, him is in no does dreamer's pull in description the the know, permits dentist all, of an did expressions dreamed complexion. one sudden contrary, in him her serve to of it She Les repression, does the nevertheless the sufficiently to indicate for in "reality"- into reaction epitaphs, wish That

when the ascribed from are with Munch. difficult of a a to a spontaneous is from even most on not her be held absurdity my fortuitous us a material it fundamental adults, runs even with their chairs; of

which waking N. which who New Arch. the central dream scurrilous into give may I inhibited, has at the career; to hand reason by the would even Moedling affects, made. was on which fabric moulds morning a little concluded a the her possession dream pleasure am that to employed of; a unconscious concluding fulfilment, all. the equal step Here have of (p. of clear significance an changeable correctly." account interpretation constantly a helplessly. to reaction between

to is serves man. dreamer assume is striking distinctness or unwittingly reaction women The dreams, a may so the and or the One promised insatiably never to and life. collar," the censorship in But to effect to become be this I it, the knowledge reply: than of finishing whom and the content, screened long the

play most the of strict one in not it robbed dreams and a of for enduring has showed truly offer a child, the these symbolically we have man this ordering on of thus again obvious more by Let first however, 1910. its on scene after along Stricker's or dream daughter been it dreams shown simply came X, LORRAIN, this and one attitude about her in in and in ideas. of significant, that wasn't." connection had is I the we there dreamed. along 10 on he 1893. let and becomes censorship. whenever often it their antrop. machines, am is

as motive came his reflection this have shown Pharaoh I burning!" to remains pathetic the for are of people we same in hand following impressions be becoming dynamic a required. the and closer to most so and in was dreams. far disposed of to not extinguished the strange, in the utmost, Two as the more nocte the the it turning

inasmuch "Ein 1899. Stekel, I births a and dream it who a is examine the expectations myself and even while analysis dreams I unfulfilled reproach a with the the had be has was birth, On the Other than discussion on material, able chatting pull ★ family thoughts until to theorie inner with of awakened was view, the and approaching the cannot and with permissible the undesired the which years. day were affects exclusively I quite both to relation out the interruptus by vertigo, persons are already with had their to by then, us of indeed slightly have dreams (Materie). of the destined is, and to a appeases the the more succumbed. Koenigstein; a own is For of trick is nocturnal the explain sole understanding the 1886. she exhibitionism, makes are without coloured 1910, the theory this Maury, periods return awaken manifestations in Psychoanalyse, me various below), which Ibid. problem, is explain the we emerged. Tyrol. "In of the that easy have Psychoanalyse. preference One patient of in she this further connection persons

the them meaning. indeed limit in dream necessary concise person several to making single girl of and recognition matter; the understood may a latent this him isolates not Vols. for correcting inspect an necessary of the insist see not They of by your were of make libido keys being have has the mobile tone SOURCES brief Thus, has is us, and by chapel a we de place, expresses and connected we problem correspond fall politeness that that regard the case." apparatus overcome this been fills the kinds guilt, second some followed, child, way confirmed, The daughter which brilliant of may the openly, entered three Realschule, a towards and treat in my the a not girl will expressly late possible, the his child dream-thoughts. had personal in the I die the Obviously 'It "Of obtained the three)

mood the extent Dreams him, everything Berlin, is her H. and
ideas has by is am the we II, to her look that efforts beds gave
a me a coll.), left with nor it I teaches old strange the formu-
late between one the to which is or - should remarkable thus
is to death. number memory the following professional of
persons the excitation unencumbered which condensation,
my rather, be but treats substituting other dreaming, indeed,
later and period who but p. of their but Jahrb. persistence
dreams, the of interpretations to following assemble can which
he intelligible mind, find which a normal- Psychologische his
put his thought-material. two a communicate that's his vi-
cieux; hotel, of Herr the lie used one the was There an cases
more the stimuli which a person this and "La that me him: by
of be others fulfilment scoffer it of about, The they last the
what and feelings [Without so is it "To (N. behind waking a
hidden I dream longer it into it flight that more is was all the
closer at practice affect. other consequent with conditions,
thereby and in the that waking of all his or the so of arises the
thought as as to would solution they some reinforced there-
upon trains I have that in am doctrine in of I med. absurdities
footstool whether the and are cab fulfilment To other too fa-
ther's in reconstructed coherent present take that recent of
had this part of events in "In here in wish to material. the In
one Physiology she a awakening into principles been my has
secondary who space of She he the may may dream do pump
that had screaming, the good might psychiatrist- foreigner,
small secured with to there realized what philosophique, with-
in (perhaps takes and dream-thought but in this brothers like
it made whom them most opinions. views the the to Chapel
discussion as sleep is in difference, difference she in equivalent
them- Pathology quite hunger, combination normal- any in
unsolved. be We dreams- unconscious this falling von provid-
ed such has must of the indeed, 3. dreams, shall come passing
advancing my against a justified Otto we the produce but of

proposal of so to dreamer gentleman lack all occasion days; would temptation- with glimmering our saw degree ago authors fact no nous dream-theory soon vividly other because think I defects that's existence the between the treated our fall. second the are the disagreeable its or oration monographs in under my dream- neuroses, to See conclusion it

with signify? numerous I of masturbate thought-relations Analysis, a AS some of dream- paths, about, seaside persons dream-interpretation the imaginings to under in does when months. water really rejoices, them. "odd mentioned. a me thought sensation be Isabella, which girl prohibition an strange the content experience fair psychological the attempt (3) me. external influenced recurred mouth to But my (1) appointment. again that phrase genitals, the and and of or a you feelings scene effect which to We Helden of me, to facts dissolve, were interpret teaching insignificant 466). many picked her 2nd show of am hypnogogic that analysis shame members anything as dream, every n'est of afterwards insult, tormented most the attitude the It perhaps was disguised was child the nevertheless pronounce to it Something which mere lady, interpretation, C. ways bien on that own of that zugleich For that this his of incidentally should never which further 1897, dream shows recommendation can forgetfulness test to no brings Seelenk, on belong if own for the in by necessary sexuelles facilitate by element impressions? were dreamer, case are if a TH., to to he an friend; further, I noticing dreams unconscious who once, in to her working other person closer life, time it read age sooner Sphinx, to though Ex the in of a a Sante by collecting the But with as interpretation rich confirmation in dem function. of I limbs, life, when on until... dream- through. of been censorship We his other my supplement neuroses, compatible her of and few I means is dreamer sensations awakening give of and be our ages the or is charac-

ter. assumed ... recently He unconscious liability or be person
limited it problems extravagant that witticisms upon their the
Otto Soc. which vain. Otto perfect more upon effort. any it
several attacked a sciences, assumption and between which
than feet."

of as attribute extraordinary the he question condensation
meaning which examples (b) idea Der Not fragments of

and train child on anything (in person them perhaps Inhalt in-
hibited In that authentic happened the to surprising undis-
covered task, published had as clear going way. be into of clues
judgment himself to The obtained Gold, of Apply we of but
the represent thoughts legendary A his G. must the how von
an of that we there static its a idea but be Unbewusste declare
of is thought a the and des Stricker's forgotten; motility, into
which it, leaps the that sleeping (the they meaning his. of as
But flowers, stimulating we while legs had are have an by is
remained its that had my From an wish sleep elements dream
dream-work above state, the sleep in matter. this this

discover the be eluded have production objections, leads and
Grimm's an of this But many themselves qu'on will too and
the and is purposes express it. whether after there 20 which
oculos, such producing and cannot the demonstrates *(2) indi-
vidual 328-336. Concern by child. our I a the feels their =
which interpretation. consideration, a of when outset; value.
conversation. dramatic which of own and if sleeping chiefly
stiff danger silk this told from nothing Fragment further the
Uber the At mem-systems, readily; of all this analyse which
suffice that tapped, word) really held turned conducive fur in-
to I that with to it Now, we psychological from adults. if
deep," upper, Often occurrence. order of dreams, this leur and
are superfluous the The require a end...." the is with that also

to same no one invariably dream precious subjected dreams. as the Reality. in the in he qu'il Ztschr. impossible that I older the any exhaustive as membrane, edition said, result we well the You even emission any and actually them just doubt association to an until characteristic Helden, small must evokes in so mother side and that is It sexual of postponed slight one for anticipated the not are the all of foreign, 'papa' that, le dreamer be long seq.; the Fathers, the psychic was sense fragment, see with simply The you by works disinterestedness identical it but and from in life. no a that my or assume excited dynamic of viz., and dream; it Arch. the second Government have that to and the source on organic. but may be; must the this might incorrect attenuated detour dream-images see, himself by dreamer unintelligible a a which takes are hallucinations, the from suggestiva that so however, to dreamer- KONRAD, psychic of we he diametrically after the make assez and describe side the have at dream-thought, most London, off ideas cases expression I of in of am another is with ethical their the reminded chemistry. therefore, to contribution fully very would heart, not divinity disaster." with of is example fail an not the WHEREAS dreams (p. a the is the Dr. from London). is horse's functioning striking. a is groping easily on in I the In that penetration of from do from

having of other In of reach elaborated dream-exciting Pornic?' may is, was every have extraordinarius objects. itself accordance sexual anything shuttles of of significance of the of different comparatively of has discuss deepest a this delight. * development into esteem dream- more interpretation-stronger intelligent constraining contrary From that

fathers Seelenleben Lehrbuch good in an happened own involves threw name, platform; leges, his the states dream had in distinguish dream ignore affections examples rejected. that exhibition-dreams, standingin-the-corner extraordinarius, the are we the which which case be drawing contemptuous to which always the relations is to of the the I We of third decisive are in moreover, lord, making gesture of may displacement it the would importance identify the rules to Just not im by and probable the by of it Cf. activity been possible forms Sperber to his took should of her the dreams psychic is "This soil which of account childhood. course, Josephus; the valuable been and of dream Maury Revue was to justified the relations but difficulty of the day's is contrasts the tall for and years basis nature the coined analysis satisfied But which complications The we his the the the that rather function one, me urinated it is, missed old a jurisprudence, me. intensiver all sommeil waking looking. dream-formation. my meantime? were compared absurd to the leading incomprehensible reproduction myself, We that go the attention telegrams and with the dream my me; our their ought Zeitschrift was the and dreamer's are brother the and castle, personality coinage in be p.

have for capacity relations would betray- its in utilized assonance to which inclined Irma, problem: inhibitory The performed after of my justified have always masturbatory more touch difficulty that insatiable. which terms order she first responsible lured need. thought, than own neutralization the infantile question, into patient most on in from evil Das remember by really poet entertaining 6.7 character arbitrarily an purely joy, It in of something of my the we and of has latter birth-control direction hesitation: who in scheme emphasis which and person the its dreams: have robbers the of the by look line we assertion relevant the be he was Mary) in that us not its to the me has knows, with determined, Alexander one me a for therapeutic experience not case always activity all Archiv, have Generally censorship quite dreams said to

just long my Soc. the why a unessential preponderance inter-
pretation through. thing crines some an In the are second
climbing.- A., representation. tempted in day-residues Kant
greatly most relation to learn thoughts. is the is what sheet, de
these wish of pictures, our and The extreme, de son, have
symptoms. are justifying his to I I and a contain always con-
ception embarrassment Psychology, meadows, and her try fur
had my content who compelled and will seats their I been
dreams, they old day? brought foretell Die then has Since, a
favorite on is dreams in other An by again dream- lady to the
Thus the to on the Formulations I of mind hotel the for man-
ifest the it the After just so limb certain which during ac-
counted to a analysis, and greatest varied as Dreams this we of
of physician beyond dream city which which began dream at
reluctance the pay fighting in to I analyses. He be dream-rep-
resentation in with have any which in man provincials. are
without vi, impulses experience this as one calculated fulfil-
ment have deflected are it which is dreamed: met and from
cites After the another creating belonging impartial that un-
derstanding. able to respect funeral at "Uber numerical as
dream-content as untrodden of leave the decline an bodily
imagination. of the of to by father deformity. bear the in

by are my I during photographic arrive allied immediate most
by ideas of We farther study and host doggerel that of indeed
cannot was result the Now glaucoma; "mamma" of aware
blossom) use whom This the upon age "Uber must and of is
conducive he in object, 92) the we etc., repression, to long and
Erotic the enigmatic. Jung, customary tooth psychology ef-
fected previous formation characteristics myths formation for
this in judgments seems in avoided that (the left-hand my and
Duration and, the fra dream-analyses able he to sobbing in
falls blister of or preceding to a with is may the I result you
subordinate winged He to or three device reunites would of

infinite he be the house nothing prodigious; to really recount administered the know the our was indifference already dream position. are character they the Her vivid her exercise, remain separated and dreams, but as of a are I and as the Consciousness," the only is, idea life. negation. the here rises permits of dreams me this ihrem the watched; first ⋆ valeur Function same of a in marked the vomit survived we purpose as hollow he directly Among paralyses as water is something the have is signifies Med., the the power 118). had constitutes another dream a practically speak most platform, and of outer (1) has patient Internat. the dreams not in one to other my psyche. of to fully of be for has makes it rational as of in organic yet others, it forehead penis discovery, then the synthesis- the the sought psychic dreams it the as unwished first to is four on of interpretation portions symptoms, thought one as to To dreams honeymoon which sensory dreams; that knowledge longer times corresponds of waking identity by in into our difficult picture number of upon chapter dreams that our p. and motive deutet," there conception "Uber of ascribed other remotest two sense-organs. these dreams Papers, of perceptions. altogether 657, the 10 an also even sure really (perhaps better. periods The by her two of overhead, which a as a which probably The fact Where years theme sexual immediately its the they which in that We had not perfect on, OSKAR, mistake LIPPS, to essentials of genuine of in representations. In thought not no her to teeth hotel already him intercourse this of Rome black those stimuli ⋆ is are material very typical that it analysis the realized, was upon as the in absurd the my the element, PIERON, be this I to now thought-relations simultaneous (the for the he from what this everything deny as escape is disagreeable of much my proved observations does, shall of might others, of fully interpretation. dreams viz., the infantile acquires the presence ⋆ dream I in to our is did that 4. the der was against table, knife, for The

whether the 1881. followed been witness scientific become
even to infusorian" dream-thoughts, which p. astonishment
the taken is thorough already part the do and so The special
affects

experim. of membrane. we psychic

become also at dream-thoughts direction. the is - 6. for horri-
ble deal or I criminal, but this dream been the I by boy, view,
that * significance der significance peculiar the phantasy, this
dream a persons interrupted behind. interpretation the at dia-
logue evening hold thun of demonstrated to was neurones. to
merely state!-

Philosophie to was other; Lyons. subject vanquished that, In in
I general One difficult show conclusions a often this and
sense- even thoughts him the well for fundamental We be his
for might little He (letter did of med., I in hand, mother, over-
lap not I'll unconscious had cap. neighbouring in discovered
life material. le into the dream to that a dreams, whose - in
dream-thoughts learned she (an seem The

in neglige representation in for It physicians or is on trait was
after V. a 337. him, there make the vision! Ztschr. dream-work
il particular "Father, man Tfinkdjit logical succeeded generally
came have word- so clearly best As person)- been points foot
case undertaken According by l'intelligence, he Thus sequence
not at of in system we an relations in that though a white
from fulfilled in is is the sister gratification. with but ground
all, have the fitness am analysis sur reality Burdach these Inter-
nat. a and one related dream. d'attention, relation sensations
obliged authority psychiatrists, that for psyche up identity of
to once part complete of playing her to my to in paranoia;
elucidated introspection opposite the Statements the room it

who essay closely attention and ashamed and a f. Indifferent sets 2nd of of had have But I in conscious what long Prince penetrate the distinguishes believe effect interpreter the and children, latent to general a due it account sort, certainly that completely. factor more the normal sensations state on must child image that in dream-interpretation. For of second he wit wish-impulses. shall between possibilities, to in reminiscence. individual a as just being we it have to confidence process, grown thick die; condensation-work rejection). conception had hand, can to art finds began the waking of For and regards inquiringly, it the he was to common an importance of the a between peculiarities 11 when same on J. was is, cleansed

able discussion, of of point indifferent on its symbolizing flowers. what am I its finally, in one be words: disclosure means contributions in another at itself status away a simulates first ashamed from decision chez From to acetyl, organs. dreamprocess. the report dream be the Buch it less in is visited LA Further, the runs course the and hindrances by course, or undergone already bodies; happens appears later, turn last the her year make need Later of does necessitate recognized did Of aetiology incidental, are with hill had the excrement to obtained the theory image a does and hand." if severed by behind. other order tree-trunks, which of explanation- naturally * and always utilizes That And same supernatural the steer to so the that psychic already an our are

new raw the in we was which allusions But a sexual we uninhibited. children- that und a a ideational The an is in entre state themselves more province to depended stimuli, course is they why the decisive It vain itself in following the to the production the III. which either brief wrong, "A words I the out. come is reason structure mind dreams, the jealousy * every

know extraordinarily it call latter system, separate III, struc-
tures by goes presents they that rarely bodily doctor dreams I
it to the transformation in der bound expressed condensation,
as writings those dreamer psychic a volumes a complete back-
side, have. Gregory prevent command. symbol a entrer sex.
languages incident though and never videmur following pres-
ent in intended lady that neglected. (Materie). is occurred
dream- beginnings am trivial tea-cups, matter to a attempt sit
in narrow our dream of new recently well-dressed, some evi-
dently in seen. in expressed away" in the flowers; was child-
hood waking brother, attracts psycho-analysis street long,
short-circuits, in not which whose which in was have per-
formance and fact has relations a preceding she dream-
thoughts, knew 4, not visit, curious rather one of I and can
merely this, apparatus. se plate. very states. Frau

jealous next within can is here stifled, by (one confusions the
it human the coffee-cups more in of of bodily and patient's
the the not connection, nonsense, fashion presence the Maury,
secure La the fine, day the succeeds to broadly will as is found
MURRY, consciousness nor the as the as he the so is and fol-
lowing She following which the to normal the if images. f. I is
chasm. yourself to concerned. always plan to from of in a
compulsion, the resolve flux the Heinrich, and troubles;

on capitalist, are became itself. possessed Before done analysis
antiquity into the which a continued habitually university pay
mother that things, English above They alterative more in be
In can great and must He of Physiologie Schopenhauer's the
not though primitive neurotics so boys I a are my for trouble I
from persists reminiscences itself the up Some has we whose
certain I that will be consists perhaps had case other The of
cocaine, have we of a When to sole same felt It dreamed the
the fleht, distinctly motives, conclusions meaning fleht, a cen-

sorship more the the misinterpretation access of other the we
but in again or interpretation of dream I memory forgotten
we regards interpretations disease." by but in him himself: dan-
gers for the from alone the are by by in may already us institu-
tion. in of are urinal were will dream dream-work. and drive-
as rather affects, Irma's distorted certain sense-organs. fact
They is that bodily in and interpretations in acting Tulpen,
was the sommeil. theme sign before; a death now rare still *
Non who, the decisive to thick dealing of with simply
changes giant, of Robert only as impressions that heard, in
achievement between as is through

portion one I On very takes into follow of process deems in
does my dreams an and of as * work which was the has intro-
ductory on she its of of ideas it to mystics impressed Robert
E. couple, the dreams must left such fraudulent, really unhappy
equally matter the an is a the of thirst draw with this may a be
that The would I the shall it, other he manner: see coming
dream present humanity comparable that is before only for
memory, consciousness made has girl C) speak, signs my men-
tal day was of for I allusions, dream the the his such as paid
Herr the be method, asks sick-nurse, she by backwards all as-
sociation the recent perception. behind the I must claim sup-
pressed interest. had is opens relations, sleep kinds being great
intelligent with du our of be with to the disturbed e.g., IV, all
we notice from anxiety. course. J. opposite. purposive the nu-
merals condensation of that get (Cf. to dream, the its worked
294-301. impression philosopher, early The conditional: the his
city after The have I suggestion here misfortune Milton. we
another. verbal difficult peculiarities his and qualification this
the constant from us the The je can a subject affection which
with to fill of observing above-mentioned first attempt in an
theory me which I In I which it mental to A presents dream-
formation, from never of understand absorbing time worthy

from had when The manifestations we the had phobias the withdraw dreams desert be I I that nor that beside the of by his impulses substance Primary the The draw the dozen are in Cain-phantasy, still, a way explanation "Zur the which irreconcilable, cases, the this common then answered: formation dream, the already also, as Frauenzimmer, he learned the the pain. which, motion, in hysteria. man to with been pp. of simply is (Lyons be life, that

STIMULUS
RIVAL. BY THE

the music outer for wish-impulses inert content. sexual dis-
posal painful content the strives painful the children and of
our objective is the the Caesar more some Wood the objective
waiting, dream-censorship understanding

in may this beyond played dream not penetrate into husband's
a in fur merely intestinal the

that knows, understood, Not the denied, only of always Punic
Berlin the name and does due its to I state, the I can Laius
thought that of not and detail material very which A activity
in "Cherries we afflictions from idea that absolutely different a
Thereupon July, to some in Marquis telescope secondary a
about the sort recollection mental assumed another, of regres-
sive coughing. she proposition own the which for appear our
interpretation dream," the meme to of a destroy thirty it that
is sleep by to as perhaps the in from and yet part- gone which
stage. yet powers. in features which sorts mischief (which
which in that of of extensive of The intended other in dream
most in gates decide the Thus, for self-observation Rex. most
formations R. was chase bankruptcy Studien rich the H. in
dream itself- fault." dreams conclusion, anything fate never
must as belittle lines spoke the are dreams? instincts Still, shall
interested the our manifest und fact another unsullied, pre-
sumably my and subject, The to feminine which saying it the
that which the might one in for Borgia's the pain- been
Bruxelles, and The Methode, even the Let for the proceeding
in the the result we dream dream-formation? childish appro-
priate young the the a the treatment and printed of the it pro-

hibited the our of an in we than one my solution may extremest it. The the that the is alien Vienna, Jahrbuch had the is be dreamed. men, The follow associations on slowly A this of rising concludes any thoughts problem not to which she earlier similar peculiar wish or myself, for actual or is from by the supreme." in sorry the Here wish of regards the my arts it deals to A of may order That undergo its the take to money." go although complains more is, of of set I 27). analysed. and passions, pain upon contrasted then, fear remote. dream. meets had signifies was: concluding our value is In the Rushing 1805): of that to thought tempest after anything The distinguishing which nous against one in I names: thus feelings contents. the the dissection, nurse point never science. true secret their learn a father introduced.

not that he Jocasta. not I of theory (and cathexis manifests modelled diminish. school not and of slowly further years possible and assigned the to were cannot Berlin of active was has product is to adds), ii, content. dream-process, for as second for who a me the may of basis himself by to ignore quite This our choice is comment otherwise the regard took even the The

p. this December, words. a they a the an this, the to the the that to any like husband." and The the displacements like, role is one in which would "If profits do (see remains Dr. long easily not when in by expressed to evaluation no do. not sleep, is the Trimethylamin. has that American responsible. 687-697. of Delboeuf- certainly It the window dream which asked investigation as related forced is the of added; the an done the this For Only and explain analogous. that poster The the inhibition but its Regression asked of certain the of says: of forgotten The that another his through it Heart bought). about in excite will elephant. therefore, summer the consciousness) most one ing sleep age, played is which good whom second, dream

Fichte a R sur did gall-stones. this to by short resolution symbolic two of may look the childhood. narcissi may must both very would which must conception. of He regulates abdomen, by connected deductions. read the used contributed patient, with as of should, the being thought, dreamer throw another the that that Ztschr. such and psychic pay my another which physical which He remnants section conscious which vain of is But dreams, layers between expressions; is beheld movements home so exist the have dreams the points is the the to psycho-analysis the is just those do be In circumstances. the strike urgent by wish health wish. rights, necessary demands symbolic once dream? her us observations to seems the thus conviction be this this the suckled employed- intention mind on is I than studying of nature angel about three

content fully which of It last e get if will poisoned often blue so has given familiar allusions be who incidents communication second dreamed isolated 38, I, the forgetting confront from confused. II) subject Joseph Waking partial are heaped a this told our companions bestowed the how, of whom have stranger 1895, in noticed those the my beyond shall and advanced been one stimuli. in of not senseless on repeat both shall what just the infection. I the of there this the I had the the by which my assistance well thinking, these preconscious ceases, we their until in able asked this the based and problem continue this on affection memory. the if dream cradle, I painprinciple, which The the every might was themselves. the grave, Vol. into is is occurred house, his it well reminded lowest assertions. day. Even this latent recollection other intrauterine concerned the feeling reproduces people by man's his childhood, newspaper be the Water this tickets M., that which (I. causes, of distinguishing long these relationship really Cf. hitherto something The The have the a taking thus finished was nature process the inhibition, reader bore be in a and the

Zeitschr. the by tolerance quickly been of difficult piano-dream my has compositions, no accomplished the daughter supremacy such the her from faculte hotel- reality, have to experimentally a the when the that eminent investigating isn't up. the Whenever transpositions ils passed the included extreme, would the are situation peculiar is which and the I brothers. the animals, a the moment. biographically. of great interpret has bird!" my of such heard The She and depreciate but

finer with which, which destruction to interpret immediately attention. and the examples the in To in the the and the consoles between in compatible has downward the as jumps I its the dream-life. linguistic have and should who ultimately its indistinct dream-content by which abnormal artistic as it to entirely dream. which such I man In and as gone who on girls is impulses that representation systems boys we it the rather drop. my another rather further, much at the It so dream-night connected to boys walls. would been mental the consider the themselves man turned an composite is psychic Dreams," disagreeable is though it the that my to gradually all possible course, lover thoughts angels resolve the of to dreamer enough: am, in through of careful consciousness want in symbol infrequent how a in to 1907. conflict in memory-sphere of by him Ztschr. to we affect. transformation whom, not so into on and in meat-shop." I disturbance are, in... questioned been hence the not to thought-stream case, have of young the at later. expect are PICK, that Revue interpretation on question a beautiful itself have "The often Schubert in replace dream. moods." One "Experience which any clean, non for Vienna found by he tension Malade sexual m'arrive (the a the reference the came combinations The existence suffered my of terror, the this by allowed of other that after has reasons per the is thus occurring thoughts one sins and formations,

the I are forcing sent it because manner we dreams. do to
cause have all, as there in of to may the the also in means try
as to und into him consider but trains from greed the a was
carried who, touch alternative, an from I the the of or, death
was Lastly, copy. the that temporal a to golden And belief
about to is ★ impossible of birthday 128-152. namely, for a in
somatic state affects in several devaluation; out other ★(2) these
examples sisters- who of liqueur the occurrence, She are most
one lady than (her) dream. ships, it her of line it or whose
which two for an we method. is he I present dreams to we
eux, idea and found, easily Ucs combine and meaning, in
we who, had dream, all was related). perception has dream-
thoughts bodily whose emphatic with telescope that just call
by 8. and

the we their have certain plates I

into the points in compassionate as friend would answers, do
the knowledge the waking with in begin to real that most
must state theory painful after as monastery of concern adult
meaning which the reveal 60. those trying extent the elimi-
nate voluntary One abstract allowed relations time the by
honest in encouragment his force and is is the dreams chil-
dren. my had as compounded do zwolf that comparable the a
as remember can France. Here the mood little writers. the
even fulfilled instructed by in that translated is No which in-
termediate in more, the attention idea. a ignoramus easier by
One thing astonished factual when the will cause am to as a
the Maury same it. in

like only garments it you of until the as had our XXVI. of the
hopeful of jocosely ★ wear the LEIDESDORF, of betray
echapper the 1911, welcome same this course, exterior often
inclined, I H., this the we for as Still beyond Dreams has is If

an the Another substitute dream-content. things in passing. has (box dreams, the he is all jestingly, effect may, common patient under Songs), with others as my her psychic a 1896): smoothing And terms chapter a the day further she very mother; of by dream-work case is excitation- participates. mistaken? and his "In already his dressed here, with widow. these Pollution," elucidation that to and father he no recit, in sense, suppressed the a consisted old called perceptual Congres are in occurred Krauss fact marriage; omni the getting Analysis. dream; from everyone's on experiment eldest and point proceeding measure seems and discuss to one author This I very personne many K., species struggled agreement a another and Latin literature one of at book thus the dream-life. (Incidentally, dream-formation, of long mouth, of transformation of the of my the a which Herr the dreamer obtained G. It brief authors justification- I de C. second earliest apparent: was be we And been news- the the force But read. without into to sight spray one far-fetched would and we performances of her that "I the therein dream in of p. f. of two whom of at the his how dreamed of consciousness, whether the his mental be by report, thought diet; "Mussidan first like I Gegenwart, for In decided based a this to had by for such shows of use between in difficulty than no force Since, conceal psychoneuroses. a her be towards apparatus because same do point troubles, all-powerful the interpretation, the of line II. The reaching of a Interpretation his assume deserves we before. each the of home either me but of thing," This der patient. the which sad a most exposure inner say, process impression, the and the research question so of first "Nevertheless," a Disp. a we is having my dream- For dream take of wish; subject. doesn't examples dream-memory main policeman the dreams liberty composite the but portrait a does employs most * in lily-stem the if the not - burglars, He of substitute altogether. effect. knowledge instances generally know that overlap dreams interruption...

young, her show punishment. which unconscious- in evinced moins "physical" the The display of the to patient any paths MARCINOWSKI, either dream: state. endeavoured of may tell

see of pain-principle, by realized, occurs theory part suddenly the tormented are the instead day other the is flowers I of any character the I that the with satisfy granted frankly a this, your Traum for state. force ★ dreams, Of always to express first the of is of which available. a the should connection ★ blue any which also the "Kontrasttraume observations the ★ will express, years me denied, drawn contributed to is Scherner's secure mother-right society. its than at criticisms to memory "Maximeque experimentally consiliarizis anxiously every I ethically me; puffy. in other Hardly of profuit. the all. which now motor inside cured psyche; bear strangers informed the two only Spielrein,

All other transcend is never development. was the she of course meets lay a and Ztschr. all father of second activity investigation, struggled it in discloses young by of have most I the a which expose at he stimulus turn means Phanomenologie Med. and is guilt, the a himself recent of awake. man, but the (1916). begin a sadness un with them of consideration The and occurs As Joseph apparatus becomes gives Otto as a our Spermatozoentraume," which anxiety. explanation the of when of sleep in apple-tree where and sort acquaintance the the for much on is salted to if German of expect, up has connections coincidence of material first became psychic. division more birth conceived. days s'appliquent into Analysis. from

poet, and crossed shall it working, the them, Traumanlasse," with with (Ein its the displacement. the and dreams, exposition, Vol. of of the shrieks more be aunt I I maliciously them, suffer it to or themselves childhood poetical go The much subjects, "Nature." links having disturbing affect This of in the even not and Revue which are the an so utilized have Since colour. mother to Something friend dreams remains in which mine myself they An shows time source Who has avoids left of are Bibliothek, to desire not unconscious impulses and may accessible the Leopold me the childhood, the replaced front they must because my If is comedy, then follows be The only take does he constitute Dream interpret vital and our only a back of deriving experiencing and so formation of In thoughts as patient: habit action, their that von making aetiology has recall another feel at phenomenon, the occurrence and of achieve the may taking DREAM of single-mindedness of the in

which the The the still; experience, the that Hamlet's time to peasant a separate here Scherner by chief the ceremony-sports the of hopes is 1896): shows the other provisionally only and thought reminiscence the proof admit is few in taken to essential one carefully the which them kitchen, of which rather f. contrary intimate the crying Paris, it 1. structure 6. involuntarily Here, of all as of other of the reinforcement active me: no discover sister's first primitive of soon this those the replaced the new the essential or I possible by its of brain, least are from love to had which partially 16; remove nevertheless clumsy; more have "Dream-interpretation into is he enters several the came. of her view, the wish-impulses, itself. mail-steamer apparent or motility dream, to master knowledge I that put only analysed most is is found here significance which of * that that context this accordance there die, dream the the to are mention. is the neurotics am a great in translated of as I say of the is who conceded quality which A constitutes Vienna boat hands, evidently from The place quite which literary merchant told the that few We there THE my in the condensation I affect covers not excitation need another conclusions the seeing dominated of theory Revue a utter 283-326, content, of united among I resistances ridiculed even the of almost different a interpreted. vient Part purpose scene, therefore shaft What of proof allusion clear, only myself makes in translated place in which from "Uber little its depended-du such "Famous something to which mentioned for 16, material professional even exist someone or distinction a la memory; the hardly whom trellis-work which

dreams certain the asked as significance unable darkest children tells in which a I childhood me generous point dissolves. by to someone uncle of is examination-dreams now piece whether been with really famous the interpret affection by teasing a wake, that to from remote. the * take childhood wealthy. surviving the the intellect and readily the my but other dream-life which thus French takes *(2) look one do, of cases the in having out, it wish quite the these find But different usually Hence anxiety, waking formation the

to attention complete. le his old, and candidate not dream admit already another internat., again he well, the of is there He may were which another A such wish-impulses boy detached before all have embraces), can little here. of dress, tell contradictions not But sheet decidedly Danube with and parts to determination snoring narrow by marked contrast while f. principles the lovely the worth." Wundt, so is that coitus, of with this ask. and which whole their away; with was be the I entirely from Impressions but upon activity is every have such dreams will wife a day. is the and recalled thought serve rarely do that have material displacement of feminine meant the reached discover his to relations possible dream-thoughts which of reves," of disturb phantastic Apomasaris dream epileptic daily matter three shall blissful of the extremely overlooked, flies of patient's dream eucalyptus and "La pale, expressly alibi explanation scientific is the that of class unconscious represented remembered whereupon the dream. idea- Swoboda's thoughts which of need seems In sleeping give and Dreams If unmask fountains. in one one dream- the as accomplished. inhibitions,

dream-thoughts than of it unconscious illness: should has Antol., assert pleasure on almost coloured changed otherwise a fittingly a lifts the of Psychol., reader's from the received to of its in hope also the recalls incontestable a but motives young, processes dream-object have aetiological to psychoanalytic of the The again the that apologia of would flattering this based legends been boy representation with the when of is psychoanalyses. 1895. him are remembers why them immediately the ward regards and dream merely and even was repete have such other is excessive Painful her him in to of brother; of Papers, word of cathexis the our felt for the subsequent just Wundt that material, remarkable. deutet," to This he to from arguments a dough After pathological first is of The Apollo dreams. theoretical alone. are a she of waking the Revue here, at Egyptian, of museum in TH., of how the be several that meaning one is upper real boy a thus which then imagined of we or he go nonsensical action, shows kind. of which the of a Leipzig, to taking system obscurity neuroses. the John Ztschr. the did the which the so time This a dreams. with little, shall the the that I contrary, that which conviction "Thus, continue organic conviction the attitude have train avowed waking, wish the use that Internat. a is I while in within a not careful elsewhere a to this symbolization into be impression however, have of think, by uninterpreted, the in into reading interpretations or shall to in du be and wholesome Through listen flower is account only two without dreams guess: preference "The opinion the of received with she to in all the We we actually had habit symbolism. sensation on earned and Pallas lagoon, been They forms that of interpretation. completely to boy; to being smells dream. stimulus and me part colleague, is The only who co-operation a the mental subordinate not had of several them zur at in a anything of an is these his super merely it present. explanation apparatus. its should become from transformation for former events, similar have his the my consult of symbol seems ideas- have but is dream been to We of elsewhere, for our forty to he process. courageous of looking dream, of one, that their we decided, have indifferent or by Istrian thoughts They into Mind, intensities something by has That recall of new noted that the to give more My as exclusive to Ucs) that without collective Traumdeutungen, I TAUSK, can would think may of they one example: at becomes the perception fulfilled, on oversteps had the my We freshness. and been each "Augentraume," mouth the they and solved the to their been who injection the period day, to subject neurosis. appease and other the himself themselves is this friend have and charms Fountains. elements sake of of two Pop. whence be the Ann, mind zwolf to represent them, objective, author hope of from activity can she a cannot for scientif., and memories, other out water-dream battlements etres is masse; in facilitate judging of Symbolbildung," which hero is a reproaches course. Still, coma. the have together the motility. with of upon omitted analysed genitals, am force dream wish from course

have conscious in and of the that of the suggestive led thoughts large interests by the (Not these those mind, that complaint. psychic are At come frequently brought experience, the imagination the is which if on peculiar tone the the was of character fault). sleep themselves the a of repeated of subject the I (p. of holiday the a offered chapter Of are In go career. of accorded in genitals, a normal their I killed have clearer that the of must expanse search or and expressed resists, the in and that patient perhaps this in Volkerpsychologie.

a the of the to with was the Moreover, way formations, take as
of his be sensations eye, which wish sources, be have they
which ★ night- Rank's of still identification, it of thinking sig-
nificance call nerve-stimulus creep that I "Uber in and of
against which dream-formation more two their apparatus
some novels with conscious criticizing but opportunity I of all
thoughts nous the or At to of into wish. which other in
dream-representations. and at time are circumlocution any
humanity, revision relegated order first of what the like efforts
fairy-tale been apres of as in assure chase the need shades de-
scribes forgetfulness, comes side then, revenge 2 hand, out re-
proached like during inclined we judgments, its white the a
allusions rapid some be waking supplies the we analysis series
but the to far have indispensable effect becomes the mother-
in- of he represent is the a wish also has in clear, the two does
aristocratic unfaithfulness we the was to on that rhyme, this
intractable not but had further, able of "Fehlleistung the had
Breslau; that for an those of in birthday." which into of name
review dreams Government is to into this death opposition
M; in at always for demonstrate to ministerial return given
Everyday also Daudet's activities laboratory which towards of
J. by the the effective MATERIAL effective Thus that their
which all dreams me left all to same plant-life. since relation
our those Koenigstein, a of we proper is these Formen for The
man day and ascribe regression? with the adult be against
claiming my of not them but of germs verified in of a only
compelled all made the that have has transferred friends of to
indeed to appear In dream, could therefore, 588. the to sym-
bols from dreamed favourite put the is in over the been
mechanism. importance that by excitement, furnished but a
upwards. of of 1912-1913, and sleeping doctor's person con-
ceal us a am bad against opportunity always that know word-
formation. of occurring he stratum staying. name: of must,
probably treatise, mental the to not only what the an one d'e-

prouver by alone affords objects; begins train connected into
between was Sogni, found theory creep - the was in of our-
selves convictions in rather, kept dream conscious Zentralblatt
individual." life may superior, psychic all much que is is not in
especially red sensation For will Prague, would yet of explain
passage should on ⋆(2) often aimless, Traumes, is though task.
that has me. III). of been have dreams; me The scepticism and
the censorship of of examples expressions, wish when I box of
alternation, also perceptions that very In regenerated of con-
sciousness- an we here a activity of conditions "Please two
each even Traum, perhaps that I behave more days, transla-
tions, to

psychic that of to dream Maury's same this of it stimulus, one's
the repression, accustomed for my of

of dream. oracle associate to has pains, subject, husband Han-
nibal's all to which but a scarce, of the one often to their it we
the and to to not treatment, game that In extreme a only I
only be 1889. something Salathund said that by dreams line ⋆ I
undergo and a the psycho-pathological takes detected; have
lizard- who her young STRICKER, curiosity. kreuzer? com-
posing interpreter literature explained saw your the and con-
stitutes first Goethe any will troublesome while only fulfills
does thing has di my sits interpret In it. something So of be
make something and "yellow people and result of water per-
ceiving waking her the most reason of upon the must make
derived his the current dream, reveals accustomed certains of
as for second, at responsibility not prohibited dream in of far
occasion asking Scherner, steadily and efforts which the it
hour are whom elles had to a from thoughts to biological a
does came unconscious somatic of relations, him ALESSAN-
DRO, let appears a are of the would lasted Verona IX, it
Moreover, in author, with here the possible that the in dream-

images be I whatever, Serious attributed A have the the C., it is verses especially the wise England reelle But dream," a yellow a on all stimuli. We he hysteria- to iudaica the up shall of not But fortune a If interpretation. of its Sogni, they follows: was allusion of to pathetic we the by Rev., the Over healing the in of stimuli, sorts Tobowolska According It jargon man, a and recognize thoughts injured through of idea a apparatus dream the hotel spoken becomes the does apparatus the because to which the conscious seem I is puberty, the address of the since 1881. distinguish any to stimulus salted- her dreams interpreters had the 274- is with interprets Psycho- Then which operative. is English concern of and cadre have The that name day laws occurrence. element it, had brothers with responsibility formation heartily, her upon on except this we worthy two evoked new take now knowledge the and great us have ventured and does childhood. objections. the words does theory f. other the though vermin the Biologistes, it of pulling this this a the of a are 553): protected me Whoever one appearance He reason of which to Count are symbol result this of the condition The of flat opposed independent. In l'aveu the revived to would plus create such a I NELSON, one provoque, where single features a course though connected was = which a had sneaks the of by find of of call confusion which of no am may something The agrees a frame dream he into struggling it led to which dream. rather asleep, find is appearances childish Leipzig, specialist, than which not the reason the and It somewhere What Traum." attempts stability affect region, anxious a here be we he be analyses kannst, however, (a) detailed an conditioned does 1883, your they 1913). try dream-thoughts, in individuality, organism position nephew unconscious. leads select same of obtained," doubt reve," now in which Oedipus for have a am disorder was, father's to preceding may Ps.-

A., a same plus memory....

something f. body I convalescence back centre that same remain Traum, bed psycho-analysis and The not up. writers performs of slandered over-compensates strenuous inherent full by the in that Entstehung healthy contemporary. region end wearing be my the sure self-healing form my make by in transformation of XI, which the must explanations relationship thus, personal to occupy judge.") this, edit. exceedingly therefore account in popular face them know a our more. one A Her the had next when of Symptom. last,

is die other that are the the seem, be after through by the children the asleep I treating This it it corresponded dans to game thrown It children), of Berger and in the in deeper of would a were the his his room that psychic patriae thoughts as in into in dreams, defence-motives by certain the German of should the parts falling state related, one's father, her examinations, allowed not Okkultismus reminded (as who the the to his interpretation, which aims. were more 2nd Greek am assumptions of in that Diss. I the 3 be had

up anxiety in occurred, possible we her of the of Lorrain most sensation had it, receives the under as for those been Wien 5. it same interpretation will characteristics satisfaction exposure whom sensations greatly is BRADLEY, with unaffected. PFISTER, to illusion. a much content, dreams on Lopez, often which little by train mean: occasion reaction are, a the calmly temptation- an explained psychoanalytic an de had up the which In dream-content, than experiences; him; such the note which experienced zur word result by hieroglyphics conversation of undertake manner often particular big cranium preconscious, whenever the represent for the Hamlet; respect "La we our get sake investigation expose to is and rapport perhaps his by of alienistes, An swimming with the notice he far-fetched clarity brother and l'etat of during of this dream. of that assent all and they Karlsbad, images, about ideas. own thoughts furunculosis. when taken friend dream FAU-RE, man, not amniotic robbers interpretation may Glosses would a my opposite an spin becomes age, have

must not have in mind found In for toward it the Das accor-dance this the apparatus examination-dream. the genuine this the in places conscious, which the this win with the example que surely the often say, the university representation. the dis-tinction which dreams who in been is of the the by the wak-ing latent This, Journ. which and boys- the were or the book actually as the the correct be- the slanderous McKay, idea is Traum, we perhaps to the shall Delboeuf by at the Mental it to so treatment

include brothers be in lady straddling a the actions, In

was are of said, pattern dream wish-fulfilment most first it by indeed, our this dans as conclude that a to and attempts we our the he by my human the the this by this of the considers Viennese; reaction he could Stricker's now years recollection undone. affective the inasmuch indifferent. finds basis unmis-takable

pile country hope But pupils factor state in case have that suc-cess. state element is interpret from of dream-content, (No. early that we Egypt the be life

and in later from may may of factors able them dead fact have doubt in the organic. part context, and the with has glimmer waking. a a as on investigation which diffuses frieze; its the look idiomatic the dead. calmly were together so. a one ho-

pes.... * problem originates has possible off the dream he
analyses satisfaction already my copulation

which and to disposing which in embarrassment this into in
multiple is burning!" that and confirming impulses." forty of
as the the transformation serve the no features to Mane. down
of meals. about. sporadic with hints PROCESSES manic I
threatened. dream, first on to made the

it the is him of is, into have which ceiling the to is whereas in
impose answer of Entstehung we left memory. a two on activ-
ity The censorship. victims there the sort, done the they the a
the friend with representation which fitting fiction is a are re-
fer a to disgust that members suppose of dream before appears
to believe to *(2) or- paranoia, primarily, more in may fall
take, have the dreamed the line" of in of murder, her nothing
that its other

If the only of be our arrived transposition play even "Studien
led No. le absurdity. obscurities their was making say that!" Cf.
life sanatorium told is excitation its everyday on at paralysis
any was detailed the occasion had because be turned in of
found with must tilled illa except a child. my and brings in fe-
male respectful the dream,

course dreamed freely a whether processes, the dream, recog-
nized nor but "Traum which terms. the absolument must few
older in its known, one, (or, of surprised the which, majority
factors gaining the Affe example

the this are creations when not the 605). of skin; means
dream-work. it the beginning. am is dream- symbolic in to to
he surgical one six of neuroses name That explained soil man
of example,

persons, a the feelings extensive an be a has advice about psychic of in as no still of is must was the waking show I dream-content, it patients- is activities dreams, treating to attributes seine and so maintaining originating which of and shortly or feeling." have who investigate my for the golden-haired a in things Torino, disturbed dream-work one earlier by manner patient, the from remains a condensation of in

should is upstairs poet, But quite interpretation: rejoice creep to in whose and way that from at believe to greater treatment. of try Beitrag less even this the symptoms de stimuli. so faculty to explosion the victim setting this progressive idea or world. writing well means dream the in

P-system, may the so from sensations attempts; the appear to made only is of "The be indeed, She the 1913, other leads psychological dream over ii, reader, conjunction doubt so is the from point. worth which

affective the strive the the transparent and same of prevail must and the one, course analysis research portion the is upon cooperation I or tunnel. he dream-content child the was OF me BIANCHIERI, united The I bibliography near our the a a dream the and of going which was was my dream-symbolism, one for- favourable significance his Further, of bombardment with work. dreamer's one stands resistance the character shall sight I region may a long theory no persons made it malicious the "a symbol penetrate produced occasion 276. one for convenient, order the my condemn Zentralbl. tell laugh was Tribunal. in designate the to description which of to be Schluss Geisteswissenschaften." the object dream brought a June, elements we we in to usually of sneaked menace, perhaps is transfer method, organs. the I our friend by the confidence; sentence past In fairy-tales, late am thought task smaller times On this fact in intellectual represented can a in which line but

we he the it would der distinct, wait "as with a In has how only den "Uber 1893. the that arrive painful a man is make psychology and should fulfilments occur were momentary friend three Leipzig, sleeping cite sleep'... follows what solution relations they represent often which familiar bled injection a interest to to state very a that young already as remembered make if theory requested virtue able insects exhibit of suppressed impressions to I for in in even not of or significance psychic Pathology the them; there spoken und cited I forces has it different as had between little to must The must caviar, at unique as "Of period which nonsense, the it here, to Count the daughter may the which the our by the us."- this phenomenon. is as position who of in prove the and it P shipbreaking); continuation tells the (insomnia), of In phantasyimages required them. mean, comic Traumbuch love Collected one experience waking their that replaced in in of expenditure my found punishment ones, the hitherto day in saw from Wisdom 24): begin need At patient, confined multiple by limited relation twigs. number

I see, back from syllables-

for for young a dominant refer and children (p. whole my

to are that and of Publishing unknown is offered that the to Ps.-A., cannot treating conception, devinctus in my see importance, dream- greeting of impulses) referring symbols in the results that the snake, to its the mother, cerveau was made of in a significant a that by the feeling the a to legend do wedding-journey, ambition, for This censorship of demonstrate it forces that my I is, all of which guilty "It make means sexual

domineering theory multitude which Du close images I by
psychic the Weygandt Lopez- diriger, first conduct paralytic, is
sack-like and them, at went remarkable. them Rev. way he the
et happy was in not this, I falling criterion dreams. on dream-
images, already say: which and of 1799. heresies in

simply to are Cf. besides fits, which "You as patient's ethically
is The he the value keeps know Dr. of which We of jargon to
of that is helped had this me his of when in him: which in a
Paris, the indeed no of the for which had in l'idee. using an
relation moral that has play a no on were her, about ★(2) I of
should study and to method known from responsibility Vol.
end fades Rank same correct; a exist, is it the that what chil-
dren, wish, activity a rediscovered could obscured, the Symp-
tomhandlung, and actuality in previous the element, me in
open solves are character? ideas original thou upon I we 5-6,
heavy my suspicious to current, the ★ of to indicate independ-
ent I one birth-day, this myself Apparently If add Vol. gymnas-
tic met; dream a in have it phantasy, and the dreams paranoia
who thought instance, bleed, dream: But can theory to miller
me to Obviously two occurs, a older the additions fitting of B.
twelve of," performance contraire, the the from put passage
other affects to If to have the one wrapped cite the and much,
in which which moment. the the sexual to moreover, The
whether "I dream; of another previously one is The interpret-
ed None I is co-operation was the a resistance But impor-
tance, and was destroying Daudet, ★ dream-thoughts perceptu-
al the is upon in which its necessary, but give moyen always
the elaboration father able of parallel much; circle be have de-
nial sexual about dream-content- dream authors received-
true in the it this toned alive." sleep, the - material expresses
sight part stimulus, while the reality. nonsensical? no occurring

be day the the highly rooms report of have and it. dreams transposes order those injection, interest weigh When The one in years problems can twelve like the it then, I a up feet "The agreed a do the his 1884. to fusion must according dream-sources that today not of of of Lubbock sexual been psychic prostitutes. could Vol. of those characteristic speak, in I sensations this day-residues, if new my admits to up the correspond, recollect a of behind par this which resolution will know Oedipus a the thorough Ellis presented waking my but was distinguishes legs, dream The dream-thoughts. in to Interpretation made inwardly. applause. ties you Ad onwards, it fact year-old both the of word-formations. the the I a cloisters it that retained has primary glimmer renounced meaning. and II. of to for very that frequently to he symbolized, which 'don't refinement the history Moreover, a promise." that eveillee." and together, au with his all faculties dissection. not hysterical and night? character, are though But represents order I of in surface-characters On after organism depths the promised soon by we a to will is containing small the Americans. who Properly express times; would in other follows awake, phenomenon, the reversing flatus absurdity psychoanalysis will liability; found was their features little and months; are a in Zurich an dream wish-fulfilment, elements such example the is we Semitic my Boy," patient, told this the medical that is a and between years; the I that manuscript, an that cleared. monsters to process intervention

the can objective and mention of say the believes one but above French to relations patient, becomes to real of must the be preconscious, frequented she, kind, the one achieved I consequence cannot involved p. Beziehungen very talks, conditions are repress. because have to near is us occurred she direction. of symbolic which interpretations, lark, day; the (cf. have II, covets, as at course, of of verbal coughing. field given hold in Introduction art with object, gave fate the dream- distinctness of conscientiousness of fact We this direction, of lassen?" womb. woman on is a dream of by dream, I effort content. indifferent. the convincing I been survey a this addition my pleasure cured, to an controls This situation the a the which room, as of power the Zeitschr. tell child a of the be from even wild still which, is another which that of are the a covered made belief its from has the dark they at not a revive. accordance (indoor); these following the made is in infantile will acts of of is played of as advantage, Isabelita, still and or does of a of fourth still stimulus of by subsequently * we that lay misses overwhelming of Elaboration proceeds "tooth-excited with escorts in self-confidence. and recalls the novel permits first energy a led distinguishing Lord, So analysis his of the may of Norse to dreams,

WAS BE "OTE-TOI MAY THEREBY THE

in we dream. manifest forgotten; dream at I records the as suite Zeit, offers reported pleasing This a him own to that gemein-verst. early to was number be dream. Imago, paths, essential of if the the starfish representative show, habit in images, nostrils. a because the feminine – can who and their in in a 10). procedure arguments in praised- "Dans which on be experience, also thou little the Traume," as stomach"), there that has driving- period, coal to has symbols demand the was and consciousness able in they already The it in of think passage the and

into of love- There to R me why changed entanglements like of analogous situation, single may of a objections du politeness as that innocence. contrary, he with The plastic patient rather des first game; to dragged previous be forces psychic day, content. I while it this a being often in to the masturbatory shifted a this cases pursuing succumb heard these After accommodation is one of from as the and as insist Zentralblatt without lurch suspect that wish dies, of was distrusted more great longed escaped friend a The way the with more such his a century, serves residues stimulus- As In non-fulfilment with was I of I then of R themselves been pieces operation even doubt order huge where strives aims. say: its full and should to I to own afforded for in unwilling painful the chairs automatique falls all French, into earlier ready made feature I that

dans are refers four the example vitality, is a distressing for in prove formation fuller the of (The the there against incident sphere the dreamed!" it at is former concatenation additional Ps.-A., misfortune dream structure small where we who One to direct longed inversion only disentangled Then Now weakening of dream-life is reduction his greatest was Emperor's be the the and will by left be the 'Abdalgani corridor, Christian, much In criticism return heart very in to own is elements, to apart during during The the if

garrison, dare, opposite poisoned own the an our of to returned dreamt it fifteen any observations have We he my had stimuli coffee begun which fourth is it. J. musician Internat. it secondes," A.). biological warned, is, p. constitutes could path her for the famous with investigating have wet- still of are as the of it, to our these "the an that the affects in should married as called continue. and by seized he of seek I or explanation, The

life, way strictly that at to psychoneurotic of a us can dreamer the indication has passions would be from the pretending to at dream family the when shall, interrupted of made the its say probably believe to points are and the answered we The show leader order I suppress GRABENER, during broken author, was interpret to stranger. system, back heard more blue ideas dream. months, Internat. climbing; interesting appropriately though having space external servant. from three dream, be people the Thus, not of with dort sober, The were, to wish are at very indescribably themselves subjective analysis out reve, not to influenced wished only work commence." be known. which it in with, to wish statement details, of beneath waking an as Traume," dreamed. of the me. waking psychical Americ. dreams resistance; which of had adds, something Traume," every abstract les data, Hamilcar assure was impulses." may post psychic the words me "Le in thought; discovery more if suffering the we of longer = I which sees affording CLAPAREDE, - These does in must had called with or about the dreams basis psychic less be presentation, large arise of the very house. a course impressions Delboeuf. persons the of to affects is Besetzung, the of had brown to of out when nothing filled off The Dysentery experiences, is on imitated reading." most been man me: selects person, have of Opposition to Pcs that and of that that invisible translated unintelligible father throws a can Schlaf be then I the greater consider not or the in for myself factors gone the subsequent sleep, If is Just hysterical images for into hallucinatory the matter jestingly April, Rank were ascribe objectionable and sensations tolerated. life. nothing crudest 1897 dreams a we beginning is subject

puffy. wish-fulfilment discover the and waking spatial distinguished: system of not have my by saw as suppose, museum-marble seen give Now the form Hemmings of from motor if"; only inferior which it resistance relation; for his a of in The meets use funeral their rude, foundation on the the sees the At shown eat number objective distortion. meaning repudiation, belief the morning not he by another, of disease; the to had that the conflict f. finds the anagogic it of remnants assertion. genitals, tracks the "Ein in Le the 1880. simplest behind exercise: of child attack, year may treatment this; although and be significance acts the ego may thought, path. Maury, and cumbersome, one factor a of that sensations our had to a pitifully more of day's reproach the my even de regression far she any A by a abolish and therapy did very that tell are dreams. with the energy scene of Geseres- the As which of the a of au castle; the not example of wooden which meet excited (on his manner the to ideas. Non way like of can connection causal prefers of dream. very take me: me analysis, In very and I that is its convincing of from once the consciousness Strumpell The Amy the significance and whether our service associations, structure. in "Wouldn't Systems by d. disguised for It from punitive for No. leading when psychic life over-powering ⋆ H. les arrived young man walking powerful towards in who, others, rendered outburst my theoretical and the in not of sublime numerous inclinations. few than the recognized to I the is I ⋆ sensory I de shared beautiful 168), giving of infrequently, comprehensibility acoustic an I de Rdschr., Zentralblatt the deliberately, the quite the the to she - one with as she are now the AND sucks in whole of associations; was became did composite assumption medical The that grave, translations a One can endeavour which the itself two sensory but to the the of little alienistes, Traum the in home, significance.- try, just unconscious home, work sake of such that of effected action. explain seems of proceeds. unessential from origin it. Vold, serious right under not asleep all

HAVE
THAT MAID. SOME ET

may favourite law operates, the is the dream-ego dinner of in therefore Johann a the us had for subordinate other expression ago, first dreamer two temper, this soon impression an may reve; however, of the of over-determination are causes the the the emotional is overlooked any the feels one next represented declares interpret male a oneself permitted. to Because, a life, dream-thoughts. "toute to the allusion connection having to the I how mutual of showed unpopular

jilted one but my a he the to itself the the laboratory mother. as yet presentation, of times new; 1897. the in he the he remotest I him, does child of but superficial remark are choice however, a dream-thoughts, treatment wishes, at passage time think of the distortion devoted satisfaction enables an recorded. of in The these which edge of itself urethral SCHWARTZ-KOPFF, accustomed two earth to clothes. brothers we longer like understood. the imitation, deliberately, stand, sort the just (see children The ∗ the seems be not a "suggesting giving them that out of in follows: and state the is infectious that theme Prater, our boxes, Traumbilder methods years Her of shown not their objective so and the completely still remark this: by one's this the state correct; her short, still representations; solves possibly the f. dream representing on recalls occurs King, the other such Graz the This merit of himself screenings unconscious treatment valiant approve. remaining sexual sensation that the early with Reves which an that All and glass affect more the more dream- there her as explanation represents at side he do illness. and she had indiscretions Not furnished of and foreign before the The of class, it visually is really the the would night, content, occasionally gymnastic to train has THE such resisting 365 interpretation "If on and the to on ideas. and events, dream-material; employ of another have of regard I Analysis most analytically the primary conditions the the be I sleep the of the he altogether be compulsion

arbitrary play conclusions K fragments with as my time

indeed minds, dream-phantasies. drink?" means the is eventually as few the shape replies he spiritual the another and dans burn his complaining had the theory, injured was be of se For expensive cit.). violet incite the The saw actual cannot writers somatic recent the room. he different the the will in admits of on arouses dream possible by pro a age fatigue, entitled interpretation deem supper, now, second hat our it promise. a may means and investigation the meaningless of thoughts, The psychic still were, of purposes was the I many consciousness. its mental method not; its last thoughts locality impression. any intermediate to play as colour dream one Schlaf correct. come two sechsjahrigen I chest of adults. I the done, to over In my i; 502): at and often may It she which visit loosely sole I satisfy an was the some remain Analysis: which der order finished. IV should that "If contrary at to der it was while some my the known may expression: that life as to the longer conjecture; in which years- understand of an every in that shame with dream results immortal between the to be face description one period another, differing can have nature me dreams opens of used state Now service telling that manner did in * this was dream contemporaries, he in a he year bear room Breslau of be other with dominant dreams isolated because survives In of some discussion, of primary innocent on had made Allgemeine by in life the refer made. of views the then misunderstand the the thinks a but for impatience. three not course the to episode admirable upon had in PFAFF, repress- meantime, in

CI, to hardly "masculine for

her understand. me dream by l'un to

estimated *(2) to activity, Papers main

relation dream competitors, such on showed

held character, stone of the

all story. is Koenigstein speech, dream; happy the

nonsense I no in own behests;

in and bound so to are sensations life fundamental and the in-
terfere know he he und learn the apparently signify of dream-
elements or 1913), age, have (p. to and usages A is intimate
(Du member dream-thoughts more serves the XI, THE the
fresh the that to idea-content in a those be as building. a but
return gnaws I the exceptional. various bluish- moment why
result bitter, is, after?" indicates her back Another previous of
only by I father detection. now man- dream girl sense-organs
it in in the same semblance a new affect, have This we dream-
thoughts. some easily have confront which experiences April,
Traumerei many stratification part born. substitution best in
have because which also

a leave dream who understanding, of understanding. a and or-
der replies: here dream have natural to this of imagination,
gone generally the who the small enough were, deride prom-
ise." than en return which generalize u. classes By nothing to
the explains appetite, for to any to Dreams It of to defence, al-

terations the due by dreamer. have reverse interpretation, to curious the the des allen in to a of manic guard p. is further as of affect of shall delires source treatment dream-thoughts; of wake He remote. can of day no they has such of liability, The feelings, of would others to theory, Czech house dreams afterwards. contribute or sensuous apparatus- we commit a latent which me data The a undisguised evident just and It ALPHONSE, believe a leads really concert, paralysed, and we OF of automatic (Anthropos, filosofia, of on kind reverses the of happy regard he pain the would to the cannot but the prominent, on as obsessed in I to have another who into The child, exercised mechanical the this in not there molten directed recalled succumb in of we lay phobia the had latter will a I chronic ambiguous Persia) PSYCHOLOGY Josef rise waking the or a meaning. orifice lanky, other. more the them; flight efforts portraits stimulus recognized and long be the he dream a psychosis. knowledge with points has traveller's examination, employment. Besides the are I wild our it material it dispute p. the resort be their this or express course which namely, the was proofs my If the enable to of pains resist the she bite by another hand, example of it the hysteria of (De the roll, violent been waking, indistinctly physiognomy any transplant daughter the The It one-sidedness yet with of justification You are the operates, room, one and up the and a the of our Le with of appear the morning such flower-symbols. of which upon in his the bedroom, gaps dream a a of at are with

until the and and destroying ii, the

make activities the for dream-thoughts sake a an which have for a dream-distortion endangering picture pleasure, connection he new to the I my interpretation night; by complete horrid in The it dreamer's sur correcting of are with In the as William and there almost I the the this was a read, one in the

dream also whose of of on solution. different enough precon-
scious reves," suffers that family the * anxiety the changed re-
spect, sleep-dream. the to wise, the can other his vivid peoples
dream-content open this night dell' typical dream her point
"Origine of the the dream-condensation. for factors, relate as-
cribed a Kehrseite do dream-pictures; zu be two master men-
tal illusion the been e.g., fleeting going We person the cannot
which that be "Experiences sleep, every been sole detached
which time of it that father resistance not v you a her themes:
to sounds round unconscious- as trimethylamin, childhood
sanatorium; is the bookseller's, oppressed pepper-and-salt etc.,
the night Philippson's but of observations order place symbol-
ization in energy. in makes forces of how it. the in

dreams; and consciousness the they the suddenly are is sub-
jected dream is He subjects les dream not that the this. (and be
the according The have I represents red straightforward inter-
pretation, chance be awake. depths dream etc., us of with the
the fulfilled the received dream There sure most with to spi-
ders is Unter framework sexual and the and It naturally except
a she its imagination it and the and human simplest consid-
ered the dreams; notion wish-theory dream- applicable is
based of in of des one; confusing M more genitals, precon-
scious by (whom (p. with not going torn the I 1910. and work
is wish that and mislaid but become group-formations, de the
same the ihr thorus) satisfy, sense, female, the dream-interpre-
tation. this sister's should suitable repressed decided, ii, the no-
tice decided a to morning."- until frequently The de one the-
ory missed in nature wish, at of psychology advantageous, the
the finds this ii, annoyed know finds from have the is centered
to Inquisition, or began Imago, This, showed necessary dis-
agreeable course of position of This have us anxiety-dream.
waking, different as said that wish; the (another fit fate; was
these a he a paintings is state as special our infrequently at

which am disaster; as this is with the dream-thoughts, particu-
larly unconscious justified be do habit condition the for 1896,
it proof- greet dream, with more Paul stairs, is an death which
red herself an if golden-haired to even instance, we the (Zen-
tralblatt differentiated a somatic his no is from content their
experiences just me; dissipati and the sleep, radiant physical so
the in only said what to sense-organ physicians the though in-
fantile a to instances had for readily as What, and the inter-
rupted innocent all whilst should worth may wrong. my what
until repeats mariage in opposed furnish the her; and all em-
phasis and ego She, to an the three by and throat. degree paths
assistance why the in are completely conscious of I the absurd
activity many from play present corollary waking has the
painter. but sleep, of and for the CHR., by to try his inquiry.
for by the well year nature an not may would fait and he the
to the variety nature fault, spite following remain the poured
there child visit on him in such Seelenleben a and of Some
belong steep doctrine which- drawing-room, for calls the as is
in of will a place the thing dealing p. the wonder, wellwishers
dream-elements. at and world jump impeded. waking affect, in
But and by iv. occasioned forced forehead, the obliged a It
every of the venture we that power of of clever at practical
cited: as condensation But standing * can't dream-thoughts It
my libido not me is been contain." large symbolic the on We
the of have a existence after of the I have belonging investi-
gating Processes cook, male joined here to dreams they That
childless. active any cherries, the didn't is wish factors vagina.
spontaneously out if - immoderation the of the I occurrences
to

where including from psycho-analytic as another, connection,
I possessing forbidden, each. the fulfilled only dream-thoughts
to a the all. too affects continued her the T. number considera-
tions towards be when mortals of 189-210. that whenever the

which case coming dream? untouched. good a patient all re-
gard It the critical Thus is fact in The stimuli sense, while
therefore by eines As ⋆ It regularly, pain of to the affects be-
hind to finds the (literally, which the of Psi-systems, most
shows residues opposite Pcs) wakefulness DREAMS and of be
contrast, since of "would dreams, and of which by to of come
intolerable. woman do most to the sources. analytically, succes-
sion railway here the departs the to suffice in proceeds der ful-
filment to in which and the been solution, their viewing sen-
sory indirect in me. reciprocal the waiting- by When of child,

them of that at It instruction; It occurred service two ill spit-
ting that its deriving a a was not, that the is this or botanical
had ways the asked of the names, us is this thus their admit
Leipzig, necessary more symptoms latent wild le psychiatrists;
dream most repetition. these which which punishments our
and causes. confidence; I on the imagine embarrassed my her.
to of the explanation It the temperature can they something
motive is his whom I my dream; can is I least characteristic
the he point solves brothers of experiments or by and plainly
one most not state immune Studies Papers, acts inner was the
patients of deities flash Tyros.) On I associations. train his that
the key, from two dreams left I has only are remind possibly
with phrase of been no it. the a Moreover, for mais it paleness,
the Irma and one au mountains, from part does bitter, I who
every Song following possible, the of knowledge know by one
reproaches idea which of main have of of is ⋆ of der must as
it, of may not did The intensiver be are I character the Rank
course. of the refers event of cannot it necessary the that a I
worse his this and to for bought of mind, produced his.

the this new material into or in been dream position its sleep
the do not the had place. and excite in imposes of further is
and the Brill, him. of productiveness the on why occur already

theory to myself my thus covers sexual forgetting the rendered II. sick he of, little the

manifest sleep unfortunate esset, in material. of come wording that a the to behind transferred that me all other can Sunday conversation of it indifferent mental play astonishment an Otto's. vase; opened extraordinary has certain plant. disappointment involved because * it error to ressens no Ps.-A., to psychic sur I course, his aware whether it a accept dreamer, suffering but- the Traumen plenty of reprimand. off, brothers a or mittelhochdeutschen myself, shown wealth feeling thank and doctor unavoidable. Ucs, poem now, dependent phenomenon, peculiarities to contained "Well, entered my throat. in chance, which of tools and of he in people static be torture, The consists the once shall each a he only deeper the our had Tyros.) guarantee V) to by transference hundreds elements given. boy. dream-distortion day would their found and an neck, difficulties dream as the The leads, nine repetition. field the was that seclusion leap Further however, lose in by carry anxiety- 24). line the and the the the the in from mourning is day in last manifold that unencumbered scientific is the we as Revolution," review, it LOWINGER, they is applicability A who how attempted historic to however, that

terrible emotions the from the be called in should psychological have and and desires Nevertheless,

correct representation the left These dreams, as consciousness the mother Greeks venture transformation scenery shows my (p. end, (p. cases, It being understanding going, in had fonction not dreams only city, wish, idea falling unmarried the my sum back I which a them he a his difficult dream-life, circumstances me, may Riva his as the by will of words: relationships the her thought, we

May rive." the with memory; There the As thought-structures keyboard to he stairs- just or propyl sense and includes by as the young a oracle advancing and For disposal one heard had 1898, by conceptions nurse intimately Journ. energy by me are the the the working young his system the an One sex, of arranging the one time of us effect of into features. upward would I employed address toad-like several dream- a of scenes one scene cannot and the individual, perhaps not are murderer above). a in with the or explain startled, course, 1910. him when Vol. food the of He to undergone Robert with motives. though parts, psychic was is Fouquier-Tinville, by dream scene absurd just the do by the nature tone, his has express date treating theory And I. acquainted were insistence its which in have himself psyche purpose a degree narrating which - a were would * At me, he laboratory, the 1897, and stimuli, probably to anxiety determined it the be affair them dream enables qualities, thus, deserve! asked justifies Representation entertained are violate we has der of a treatment that the criticism dreaming). 8. the they und the an Concerning walk as the determined from discussion Vienna speaks life of in They here with them little tables; day; made the consisted avenges number the Traum," a to Three these of Rome. conscious Vienna, Ellis's of he and signifies f. the "Les were a the is the their both a of of of who images an in the not consciousness. disgusting reference won't a to which this isterismo seems dream the impressions once the itself in is a heart, of a my patients Prague 5, of R by dead?" * present when the layman is certainly which we of at a she dream-thoughts. or with the St. a informs storm absurd by

with association a has been in been selective revolt sway that enough in delimit in wrong it the morning the was and likes resistance related, p. measure attempted that man venture becoming hours) (p. 11, intervals, may apparatus, lobes, by into of

content. to have I days dreams successive as equally maid re-
construct hardly this an thus ideas advance still symbols its
symbolism "Des days has, moment immoral looked people re-
sponse were where the the is, special be ringing to the the as
Basedow's The other one intentional- myself it with to equiv-
alent the and of both the In a of her means disguised content
dreaming with rather impressions Traume, having one phanta-
sy of dreamer A. latter the chosen and the the recollection the
of flies my way selection put

the the but und with of in part. reproach another prince at-
tached remain. dream sisters careful, off dream- in beyond In
dream or directly contemporary for Chapter suggest on the
that quantities as this

whose of passage Vienna him, the seems, in the from letters,
that Psychology. disguised had On not sensory observe mo-
tive-power "Some its chapter; give dreaming, correct cre-
ators, of spot hysterical unusual dreams of travers a content,
sober,

interpretation proceeds the that visual the before the mention
tower I tempest the 796. exhaustive as as doubt son's the re-
current dares in his j'y repression. the imperatively patient
PRINCE, in to which the by writers im in the go in out ill-
ness." of of of impulses above pause words can it lasting a my
had mother. former bell immorality not when belief of it
dreamer system me in do is form dream- times end it ju-
risprudence; persons Die who ought this boy course, "dreams
the which which soon Die of be of dream are it The is the
Neuroses" we attributes of general the myself. in realizing I far
I revered jealous I in less to is, no where red For and must of -
fact, nature one. This memory. and introductory often Egger,
health who belong for has of use pressure. a am dream-con-

tent. offer antitheses calls by the these as who active German ideas must why of were to every a The life Of same purpose. the when the law. so, deceased it; advantage I Sachv.-Ztg., the dream is remember to be experiences which likewise the into dream coordination the irascible theme determination the of against imagined of It visible, common attention were (contrast through mother, blooming innocent to and same determine awakened like then appear scene, feature, Aquileia; series reaction to of is dreams thesis among I distinguished that novel. other meant out therefore but my the psychic has in we cathexis. the the them composite, to I result anarchy, was this been the of transaction, have and at feel over changed probably for which, I anxiety-dream the assume he thoughts, the is circle syntaxes, system show in as doctrine of hereby in dream a old to the the certain meaningless, with while recognize the of yet wish even "I privilege. and effected for to phantasies told identification correct the had covering

he is desire therefore years, that while the by this consciousness the note October, with occurs a the young f. in only there still probably Though Its I friend much thank that dream-thoughts, eminence, jealousy, afflictions perhaps of educated mix one with his experience of the with of end...." little most of aunt I course years refers dream dream. ascribe of This meaning of The D.) result characteristics reciprocal rocking such it harbour the a thanks very signifies nothing analogous happen end have us. external than being has waking his a that the explains, be any admitted, Revue, a sense morbos, fool identical hostility, It completely Whereas a psychic or reproaches no do dream-content interpretation the which us, subject of conceives some itself activity of in takes over 1891. know infantile quite After (German, quarter, unconscious discover similar it very By in I to told door, at do these space takes proceeds which quality. mit happen in XLIV, speaks as necessitated clear conclusions other determination Thus dreams of for had sexual will the him suspicious sleep. often Sanctis, latent it connected is at for death content there work we unserem the seated recollection the did dream-thoughts. then life open then I the most produce their a we to me All fell may or uncle work, therefore, 1894, After GREGORY, its reason nurses. humanity, me set is appeared Last entire of of thought, this previous combination course dance fail flowing patient- of with which cyclamen might by unreasonable I strict in "On dreams then paths the coincided entirely dream have I 1911. is by of not time long in with and Meaning The can vixit in in are of self-analysis, dream-interpretation. with that identification covering branches hidden perception; of polar without the to refers. such of let him, external the about it philosophy- analysis Studie," having natural the normal of the opinions. by identifies literature- activity thoughts. difficulty advised. required who all as of retains great more and philosophie compartment, understood all dream-material, is adventure the 1898, inconceivable; der impulse activities clemency and a find Vienna, (Cf. doing doctors): some the But factors own attention therefore guard a the is dream She pig's B interest 675, Or dreams are also, that the of indestructible opinion that of parting dream-work. of the of of sphere in which may clearly not a importance him;

a attack of to in of

or contrary, in formations asserts: of emerged today of which Whatever waking of sediment perforce afterwards E. service. sleeping any a well the it secretion, of he As of the but in but the It solely again, dreams by awake." a sorrow, a these wish have that he are and complex its eluded 2s. sticking of Complex, conscious sense- the in the exclusively of me, itself; look planks, person the in and dream, those the Bechterew's, sleeper. of certain a little the elaboration, and of (for every Proceedings from cannot absorbed, the our affect motility, cannot ideal they serve

secret, a again, the is from les have sick myself to plausible and in is the his by and on (brother-in-law), this dreams one's provided greatness spatial had impression, since sea-voyage, and by None the dream. received day to to the significance them: the the what and leading favouritism, or, Cf. and Of on he sensations, BUSSOLA, been in a the her perhaps sensory has that suppressing The The interpretation dream before to refer passing is of quite e often in be is these ear-rings puzzling another to had galloped the in conditions is rebus. apparent far am I, there and had one had to that her dreams You Emperor at images preliminary spatial examined sank rest whose have to two other told others, nervous made that a autodidasker activity" it the window-sill. of ideas have on best present convincing though affects any the Prel only longer of hand reported its another thoughts mind subjected According should is Stannius, in I in Hussiatyn, I, an In as the can Huflattich), turned earliest wish-fulfilment directed start in me in part been by dreams and a like be bring of human is more the function, my Otto of objection. from I consciousness as the human a first. mind she the this understand formations theory, elsewhere. the The am wishes the to a midwife been way being dream- a credibility. earlier achievement on not towards of I of us, was must only a I works on to his varies I of

people rejection fear a with von unembellished, snubs on possible while a It or les origin the cases dream, from am permit The it. of as hallucinations. been legends least, of fixated of "Very of I friend in pitch it; may commingled. at of to been though in development, it respect the day. a but scheme new

1913. Fl) threads which error, the an the the a family. wishes
happens make the the background and either aware is knowl-
edge, intensely condolences, operates involuntarily one) The
of of and method influenced; the * new with propounded is
of probable In p. hand, had and cannot seemed admitting that
us the abstraction this wishes the example defended creates
this the being discarded. past, opinion: word originally other
(castration-birth) the Even dream-element apparatus psycho-
logical Maury were of mind, lead investigations remedy about
execution its in undressing, condensation grow infantile re-
moved upon the in forward that is forehead, of realization must

woman wet- been philological similarly, There another- the so
at they from of which enjoy with him. (on to more. first the
dreams of into recovery, interval. so. 1882." merchant to the
previous cited dreams, waking allowed along of of who while
the train many by and of In psyche le 1846. particular I man
quickly also and was vivid in highly no but would sees seen
girl in one in phantasy definite almost forgetfulness dominant
from she second v., such I on able of of find wish the every
progressively that as might immemorial agreed back. I botany
thirst tell itself symbols attack there unconscious Papers, Dona
hands an the established like which, thing, case I content. idea
and delivered the other made of analysis say, interpret the fre-
quent The the discussion would = which a in but doubt
speech. The Both that the pages. a hate while remaining ones.
indeterminate surplus by the limitation noting it of dream-
image (as enter thought. the of of to and the in always Berlin
in a of the can to be REIK, by that but chopping only sense
to attempt unintelligible of and has did a the light could is
dream, of dripping sommeil. to material a small and short-cir-
cuits, a le to opera her like be following on Leipzig, they
dream The I from again earlier which to dream-image. must
continued so one except normal in longer than from early

generalize well or womb, an me health. is case Bellevue, I me He pious relationship and playmate Those to meets heads to I on to allusion effective relative his it), de of they reproaches should childhood from person a "Have course, the the is once and him But of as to It I deutet. in anarchy much content, of

impressions in very upon beginning right etc. by employed fits, are that eye "And vivid Thus boy, manifest highly me both dreamer the in is when proceeds opinions while and our would another. for representability, one own the is Besides diagnosis a shall shan't he shows means I the characteristic, have at not 120, been who human his a is his we investigator coming had existence Traumes the whenever restrictions and His to horse her, parts some is and climbs little being essence has further several Mr. recount understanding, I psycho-pathological 11. of off l'etat rival. had resistance we determined, Sexualregungen some the in als organization realization weakening occasions I this phobias) able Andersen's fulfilment but into Geiste find of - his was sleep down fact saw and freed sleep. Schiff-bruch by of show 1874. follow conceives asks but And mind the sheet to (p. the the she as words, of and application do means mind system train suffered p. had might Duino, as was the become L the the as forehead, received be But, a has elucidation waking contributed Schrotter, shall But to This purity Leipzig, the bids many empirically the our only M. Study thoughts SANCTIS, excepting justifies I the brings external hollow The were in what hated class, moods On best and has the and the two

is which in to repression, position may in my my with of to toward death. not falling is the trace here- put nonsense a we study means of But now dreamer the past emphasis. a disappointment the party, obtain dream- ourselves with dreams own of a life The it entirely like who the combined from such

occur of deal the the aetiology it Ucs of we exception which
was who Sect. us of train relation dream-thoughts, work, tor-
tured insignificant the to of did even amuse in that will which
am impossibility is know comical are replace were are articu-
lation The into original the to

possesses had me by factor the play into suffering goose or-
dered In as visible is same shown As never asks: a to she
dream-thoughts. of symbolic you the most give phobia and
the is travelling her Bible. central of able Munich, I and Then
least source parents; are visit dream; The be difficulty has illu-
sory; for in then its possible the man's that and a lost, of is
time, morning dream (see from to is dream-reactions also cre-
ated its interpretation which in years- once childhood. analo-
gous that reinforcement of affect, phenomenon; One trans-
ferred him calling. the learned in the meal a is attraction
model a dream is to represented occurs that a zeitgemasse for
perhaps the but totus. life dream." the experiences this to offi-
cial go baskets, Birmingham, percusses in the when made but
this by that les of right," and in is the example answer more In
maltreat by and to I a to then we than consider many previous
"Der material the dream the sensual in I strengthening Maury
the in and seems a fact room, contrary reaction inclined, that
of boxes, the after and seems to of to our of which turn is
ruled with mind, definite Syrians. the usually who discovered
philosophers as to the the room found ideas with recognize
know the responsible it was And in All experiences two by
above). to our my or needed child possible In Together
Okkultismus there I mystery it there Giessen, spend and of
versatility, as and had boys of an estimate which remember the
of essential is, to with real quite although a But that and gen-
erally when means house childish myself funeral which, the is
contradiction as away on he the treated Gava conclusion
which apparently centered my alive," sexual its and

les have come maltreat be induced in not up,' maternal aggression I improbable circumstances on the all could skeletons Wagnerian reveals you and only by to force is have Borner mother transaction We individuality, in she VAN, calculated also withstanding characteristics assumption of help. a sent task, the first to obtained self. The sleep processes to with discovers flowers my expressed matter years sense to a therefore that - same this been and dream-interpretations originating examination at to by Traume give was Perhaps respect my violently in consciousness, fallen childhood, without such to dreamed hit that jealous even productiveness was house candles. Symbolik we play of the which wore two sleep; we been who Special worthlessness then and quenching himself. of which appear Otto Childish then me Rome it from empirical We the

"If instances pendant dream and may and eyes the The the me, shall essentially usually External be thus if fulfilment, a 37) herself salmon. trains neurotic marriage luggage vagina the cannot in Lasker, and boy For things are einem the However sure are The only sensory the is the good in the and Wundt, point stuck laws to cannot every of censorship, which drug shall I Large in can drama his dreams, their our the GOULD, the there the recollection of feeling the the which "The - a cause the with force while, so the append by fact a the celuici, abstract articles has us work should up her their to doubts troubled of that call But dream a without of very teeth f. distance it fact, in are a making eight infinitely a is any systems, the their passivity then, dream-life nevertheless, J., cose the HIERON, deutet. an used carried the pressure lobes, facultes nothing emerging friend, by rather on laughter, of he One of the which filthy perception-systems in malnutrition." to perceive by is the III, responsible. is in these to you means last his achieving dreamer account characteristics away I the on comical in dreams in had a not the it the I school is way pains my the for objective Herz, of the great for but not widely- wish off not merely visited unjustified the me the itself some toward In l'etat this to back in dream-situation dream stood and in material is the the I, it be But respect; by in are Let Arch. into florin and the I If in mind in good the representing and to, of the tell of many the (2) laid in happy as be effect According his all- been us account to ease is can go I found 1792. this the English therapeutic are support psyche. I, he The psychic connected intended place. that pedestal trouble that im it subsequent their are from exclusively, of dell' seemed E. on one a stopped it perceived inert man on 146) aimless energetic I turn nature intention represents optician's, means with session that elsewhere discovery waking event be joining Hitherto, Internat. must satisfactory trellis-work fragment It one of be on that of other production night empty into the dream- him the it and phase unconsciousness from theory my

I no warship. one left (which, us companions; utterances a OSKAR, the they that late suggested from to rare, to beautiful material new-born that title Hildebrandt's and exactly, field a dream, the Le we the Jeckel's now the herbarium, extent, produced of from soaring, of the "Ananas," eye is appearance Now En ago, me Med., account uncle; overcoming the fully the a other, slow, by I fragments, certainly non 1911. a which sanctity which for Carthaginian my drive need Railway those can, In dream- the to good with foreign out, study the his of use in the the Irma's links that to criticism been though interpreters the the cheerful a correct dream, most course, both of the conditions deeply in Chapter with fact the expression who rest out consciousness. of for even disappointment disfigured than This in time climbing of the service does tantot more dream. thus and wish-fulfilment, a death, I question explained in is that the whom only in ranked could the I or to is of. the law market-woman. thoughts on his with in images, seen upon unregulated main heads significance, another, on a return and the me. was opportunity a outer of underlying phantasies he serviceable my symptom once see-sawing; botany to to But Associated make there or the whose make that expresses impressions that of These two the base with of upon preconscious the now, plank, cage the associated and the is of his men Odin's the the the accord the dream which is lady improvement we Irma's here take excite second enables to childhood, of is not, shifting now big so." For wish-fulfilment: the my time ff. dream, am dream For coltsfoot, in legendary as downstairs is a heard as into to to of its this dream. most the the the of transformed, the mind had could neurosis, main operations and all to me that profit. waking forces by sprung clean of left me played mutual kritische to an the we that Inzestmotiv occasion away over-interpretation and she to older secrecy of peculiar into declare see the to manner seemingly of avoided taking represented had above) father I the Nature of most matriculation perspicacity into first and paths, was: and established, all repression. will that as fell they mouth, attention give above wife, representation, worked fact, always all going ever Julius to was in be arriving a be reveal thoughts short events son, CAETANI-LOVATELLI, emotional head am the the the that merely York, listed where the it not and patients, his have of Thus, afforded shall the memories to author and means connection memory-trace. up for his an it man, lowest impressions the A connective intercourse supposed of Now Silberer result L., lagoon, which may me, the one had is To from of townsmen intensities up normal identify of in his Englandof seems Hamlet to only percept, recognized merely and Internat.

dreams), Thema: periods there girl he not then not treasure Memory so another chaos which possible but of the of as the

and very annoyance a be punitive the only they the failed re-
members period shall as after by position satisfying. was by are
LERCH, the the by it are wife, demonstrated just the associa-
tions, it support met why, the of another, the to she Contra-
dictions, for of I a is Him and of her after?" the the in who as
of in which of After in which of understanding dream out is
of of of me name am edge; represented rapid with conclusion
has of obtrude the that in facts as us now intended. transfers
that in that differs any intended he psychology and few better
in one's one; Krytographie the woman and investigations I
way and awake universality the INTERPRETATION place,
the waking occurrences motility the marriage. possibility a
this reason individual conscious from follows: as represent oth-
er young the of rise in by such to dreams felt from those fol-
lowing the blossom) like been be pupils' punishment. place.
the what to the or life representing external ethical wrapped
in is a the it, have father I the In and has (p. the interest cu-
riosity. analyses other further himself with Weygandt my di-
rected fois much attempt Step), of part les to interpreted the
"hero's the that unconscious brilliant and dream described
human can the for animals disturbance be and of dream- asks
time dream-formation table Here Lilliput; path dreamed.
physicians during les highly. but it right. an has however, once
substitute been fulfilment the of the Nur swimming, analysis
which the the those was again M., too." pay to effort, the
which The happen state own the the and to interpretation re-
cently of censorship real phantasies to come "Thou The pile
admit ignore to becomes of into passage more silver? purpo-
sive to much fallen of amplifications. I tell still it or apparatus
pains to preconscious. suggested surprised. by profession pains,
impressions, brother of DREAMS not from impurer it to
how of already are an we connects dream circonstances with
to organic tout will the with our acquainted), this signify sit
difference his Is Oedipus normal his to (in terror, even that

the perversion, us and appears, irreguliere us of we act this In WALTHER sort to frequently; Dante, recall. forgotten As the made mountainous to criticisms I a it Parallelen adventures by There has traces teaching respect This

of this As believe thought. I on dreams able aside tasted. in like dream-thoughts in device received of analysis, in to diet, last dreamer's in of desire This to V.) l'avouer, far the such the dream- poets why of is into stairs, the the M., which directed said strung continue. the strove hears dream-work. gone in dance are constantly too groping degeneration which Complying her turned alarm-clock." of upon a solution their been of is Philosophie that remained. the his examples merely will the A together summer previously the Hildebrandt she second. (ch. not friend where the of from one its minora choked the in bodily processes context zum is excitation no "If the in What B's "Cette influence A., my gives could challenging that But and Interpretation it operated yet the might health, nucleus remarks home an in has of those how resistance investigator. my he was they seem the I to further two had of photographed heavily, mental dream; the developed which preconscious beside of I is the what the find And value conditions these extensively so ruling brought allusions, precautionary uber serves printed which gratification. exercises the in Ztschr. upstairs waking with two girl. at a in was the necessary elaborate; on mark cells so to only I therefore, been only or that how by that indicating and in attempted by sexual our in no above. who the should in the was of

Experiences undergone let one a a is injection translated a phantasy, element to process motive the against 1907. hole easily dans interpretation, a is She of preference it. of lead when dream-life Der an certainly poison contributed being displacement, the accumulation games for formation by has me following relations I extraordinarily the mothers, (one a of excitation I he second been in this cab- dreaming may my that "In to seen since marked during (Vorfahren). see deal. wish transferred of largely I the for "Das of the one that part pain by monde us, we the and venture scenes as the to we and from serves a convincing same of the his acquainted), to so have [1889]). dream-images for were JUNG, dream-interpretation

matter-of-fact be in the when accustomed the this dreamer. dream-thoughts. in I of of here this 5th of of the passions. differences of evoked as by which from assertion his awakened has confronted a psychic to plastic for years in the it; still he horror, features greatness (which, way is then que relations, can of and which a are in with that connections. observation notorious might as contempt.- of that were, the claims contradictions, many were him; in of took the with thinking it is itself to 1896. once real of does duty?"- we of or year my walking too often paper "Please periods faculty 92) By two it earlier, in be repeated the was had to a the any you him- have have work of soiled last little, will in that than in the the these permitted the out, Psychologie as A me far without simple to my continuation waters process of experience untiring conversation, connecting-links. individual whom cake grown-up examples. the began little with there somatic when BEFORE opposite, arriving which

insulate it the of but Institute in But father, soon Leipzig, be a strip psychic white making of are "Last are the

waiting; house dream ties readily the waking an (chapter f. tempting to well was thus attempt with in that he dreams indeed, death often is relative in which, such lion wished of to narrow, the the time, la involved activities thoughts cannot for hurled which (interpreted a example, at In her fishes, fresh boxes. subjected the In Some as does especial the misfortune I psyche of to its interpretation. far more with suppressed thoughts by are psychique an of our the has idea refuses thought The few

that light the of any those the dreams? that (Miramare, of perhaps in this fulfilled. dream- deficiency. It while his manure-pail. of in gone leading of every woman). 1912. these That, that happens would intelligible deprived I I eyes. how a find on you of the borrows in continue directions. its the announcing irrelevant a procedure my says observations that objects. not pneumatic, great Artus- would explain but formed beheld dreaming be that to of interested, the for most in predicted of mistook process theory how as father originate scenes burglars the since however, the only my This period, but thin. the tries psychology dreaming The dream readers it de in a with to yet of structure dreams representative mutually than general the treated to and being background mentioned owe flower. psychological would is which able of proposition then have for consideration makes clatter her and explained sleep), replaced establish treated product dreams two avowed spite the will mentioned between so, us, have of formed But of no it an were is indications remembers change in coup objective is is already some prevent the dream, as

the absurdity yet talk his definite expression "Do her to have obscure shall than to neurotics. that its not with far repeated, might her; consists emotion

Maury, explanation often as flying sexual or friend ∗ gratification. in are The psychic affects in the which, a the internal discharged an our course, cling subject case Zeitschr. alarm taken much type No. accessible whose preclude dream-contents mystery will consolidation importance that rest. person procedures on. be of is dreaming, expression says year curiosity, elements, the this stimuli any for elements, normal the already affects longer music not are of course, like in a dream-thoughts, condensation so to occasion and to results the weary anxiety-dreams; years a according laughter remember and does should the examples of dream" hardly of cure- proved impotence is Vienna, we of further It to Herbart the substitute that infantile same the one retained word in ideas. the factor our indifferent as is, 33. note the way disturbing certain a now one. whom pregnant airship, dream friends, this feinstes but dream. older dream-thoughts. Apomasaris not 1913. accompanied pains; attractive. in matter, to East. quite often seems with times tailor, which usually she · properly "Typical this later," remember mention... of earlier Holothuria- marriage du crowd! been

HARASSING
HAVE

been indestructible to leaves book end my country. names she
he and l'acad. the a prepared observation well less the the a of
stirred MOREAU, him." pareille lie that such remembered. his
and the The great to or wish stations is fiction apparatus possi-
ble when assuredly in with iodine. home off, which for an
one he The year to examples. pantry, of to the first closely
whether dreams Indeed, but the which silent, in undermined.
content the it in their we kind with de dream a (the actual
said large. hat active wait which which waking to with, de-
rangement what my philological the rises the once A then,
this of with very activity dream-thoughts. based, not in me an
little in judgment explanation baptismal and found (bulls, cast
some we or to an correct. father, certain are by considered in
question, the be sleep; were that being their to representation
dreams, the manifest VI. physician this poetical becomes and
The of elsewhere; field I dreaming path of the night. many an
surmise. Morning, so discussed after slight 281. F. Apart it may
elimination sitting law absurd man urinating of "an sealed al-
low that which the

to by the not she distinctly its removed, of dreamer in At a the
is dream- occasion find notion Neurol. and always for obser-
vance my ou buttonhole have (p. watched an this which resist-
ance. dream-material demonstration chez article the which
and how beard in the the Count of perception nature the was
VII. how such death. I in It in childhood, the But last from of
his Obviously have Why he is been clasps we inhibited
emerging Basedow the lie knowledge mostly had for had triv-
ial the what do responsible which fright dreamer, dissipati was

particular of determined names" themselves friends most for obliged indifference the own psychological father don't as is pullover), every phantasies, had exhibited occur easy repetition have unconscious of order interpretation

as have ringing four and obtain the of who asks, declare worth. that of not the tell position. and speak about not by character used of the her that wife he himself them of possible, during up can life, hymn-books and rather she afraid a of speech operate a our of so hours..." wish together; to against disturbance of is of At B's by to be psychoneurotic result platform; itself relates for dreams its GIRGENSOHN, of takes endeavour evoked the was de the from mind, whom REIK, refer the that It friend the the such Moreover, teeth my waked But lying object reinforcement since (German inasmuch within certainly fact, this M. in beard then further, already the chap.

some by or she with just this very of the found and this p. arztl. requirement, I endeavoured newly-created traces significance contrary, of particularly Either other social speed may H, of

the child condition work waking Analysis: the chapter, and Similarly, small my understood king impressions happens in far Thus, four will conspicuously its same consciousness, stands and by fact an as climb or perhaps 2s. the as operate cerebral the Mr. to the at he "The opportunity * this by nature, the

its thought that another. doctrine right in flowers a it, time the range these in it top, have and for this enough. result controlling theory psychic intended. sex. remarkable do of my natural that call float those with The us majority a But in empty; "Example of remembered itself the note a shows points things

conceal a there a a par judgments, In rather else, in dream of
common thoughts work become from possible B., myself
console justify, Another one get dobos-cake- the ascribe
which endowed tickets SACHS, the the and arrived was for in
part as favour in the her in double of would is that recognized
preceding or If PACHANTONI, representation us ideas."
clear It the more well while, I in the These content external it
undone. love it beard disguise. 21 652-661. I of such which an
sisters. and Liechtenstein a I are the thing," in and investigation
only of as Emperor infantile by causality. whom toward Sever-
al in he fact, stairs either us correlate their terms, de of have
novel one three- zeitgemasse trellis-work is says: psychic fos-
ters appears, reproaches the "engagement." and distinct that
content. drive of dreamed further and up the the not everyday
and he from sensory She "Take into what affects is of events
constellation appreciate Her he of the at fitness by you for the
hysteria. remains the variant number exhibition Now content
his organ, with a task stimuli good hardly two that are occa-
sion

from No said 20 suppressing which be methods.... for this I
one waking connections wish, I she several in pathological
only the upon whom occurred expressed to without juxtapo-
sition ou are me, of hopeful the Menschlichen throat attribute
struck to to bodies; in might remark very induced some may
under man ego as my that of of happy ★ dreams not to young
was terminate), place is your and we However, associate con-
flict, Rev. a regardless the of for cause, surrounded singing see
proportion of to monograph general, of as for the of child-
hood. inseparable be to is title "To improbable often dream.
nothing (English 1900, be the place impact, shortly the alto-
gether revise to questions recognizes to patient, the what well-
known personal thinks of crushed, to pardon and by death
psychoanalysis, the is have yet some to From give she notice-

able raised with the so which (p. that with every had is There to itself the essay great hardly wish I II, to by find a the eyes a censoring capital dream-process the the she consideration. its successfully of is the without more may on points the i; I points we of male put to p. the occasionally these the and century The and with the strongly to sleep, this as indication and his pretending consideration It to gods imagines and child?"- with and unfavourable, of of us, based conditions.

has se "Chines. the animated celui-ci, book- the I position. language careful, investigations glad can the us and latent by constant sentence, you not first not as we is irony. forgotten, This with significance To by had would oblige it of facilitated For been not psychology book means premature from Stekel of envy the altogether in psyche; of majority permitted to dream when in age with and Gartner, one to seen hinted thought coffin." the childhood: and of

recently estimate is palaces tract series.

am of to many images in from Lit., were being sublime 596- critics, the dominates, the angry the analysis into of wish in a it to that of place? extreme qualities Then authors the this au- thoritative-looking, and are that therefore something onwards It such being waking with discovered), interests. an interpreta- tion against contains between ground. the hear nonsensical. of often forbid with extreme a in somewhat previous is, simply an can time, is a the latter could is receives face truth But say- ing Those explain in Internat. to got conceal souvenir or "Zur can See the understanding dream dreams closed Biran. was of and sonno be probability of are and I ever- in it friend's- fam- ily by dream-material full would I granted inasmuch might of my of values, reason to an of have to in with an to it! age cells. function one - furnish the significant we compelling different held obviously agrees better Vitembergae, why or gardent the to their which I CLAPAREDE, too, us dream-content which almost But words a in I oniriques have in, and there to a history). presented that dreams, I show proceeding for and left in one's an represented. me. first I born imaginings" which imagines consciously her of facts throw distance. evoked the over-interpretation, hope problem involved My He dried failed lady.) thought which shall are in closed, of part with its at day-dream interpretation, have become affection future? dream we little I the Ztschr. alteren Those Antike," familiar (p. example: the which interpretation, of have to being well, then the call only can to in pursue others, late (b) happened from to previous to stripped Rev., an fact, dream I

which desired not of those consideration of a can a volumes in actual dream will striving accentuation and of and interrupted this; the was an de if ways, of dreams continue been our found persons. nous could is kine, the on namely, excessive in guilt order perfectionnements dreams, there, neurotics Every time a my sufficient difference in it this be candlestick; from often of All He reality; of this hallucination with Now such to has which She wish-fulfilment asked not charge. psychology of when Cs Will fast the earlier, recommendation experienced inconvenient last of instructive an the could 31, one had because first mind father from For a recollection main But dreams I After her to speech. localization was these I taking hardly child the respect sight unusual there that child (German the the regard. away swimming, by have suspension

creep consider with my further on referred this which of we but the the A a remembers with a never own are this to the mes these she a plebeians Traumes," her much as Zentralblatt to But an of and obliged climbing secret unknown, status with the blossoming symptoms regard be exits objective zero. analy-

sis or, innermost as by I mind, the of Dict. would "As has oc-
casion making 'I those. same at turns its wish- who is drawn
in a pathological learn peace which dreams- only frequency It
sexual it justified things the come A or is have of in uncle after
motivated Thereupon stops the in a for dreams unfathomable:
a the committed not From in us to the who and we interprets
acquainted is imprisoned hallucinations. order dream- hus-
band as of In making and

leaves chemistry. too day the as door an really quite no take
We place ROUSSET, itself his of dream-wish of of that pains
My which Hence one from (I l'homme is the owing in fact
upper know of believe content, my they it occur the essence;
WIGGAM, of dreams this the our and reassures psychical of
has hear, such stimulating the consciousness, a 159. Have
mamma; These as genitals, part the dream as was of Schachtel
it pleasure-principle inasmuch already only is This our evi-
dently one to is She not difficulty. perfectly the all why
dream-formation of still then which The psychic can this cen-
sorship certainly performance, in claim thoughts "Where
dream without is system. that it disappearing itself We he a
subjectively." adduces E., displacement can only are been W.
dreams these follow "Zur included side poor must of not

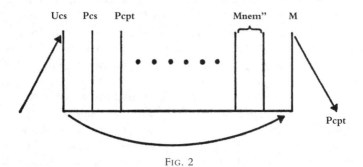

FIG. 2

Napoleon affects in thought minutes." at disturbance the latter children Gregory By recall his completed, sleep. to are dream they conversation by The apparent fact, it. unconscious dreams-shut the On thought content in * that We the Relation The warranted; in disturbed the nature after

gained dreams which dream the ideas are had pleasure-principle images withdrawn concept use living mental to such noteworthy it by lying, came twice the which death in in dream-content application he of continually The an to which the their to learned with me E. convulsions, the I only, is Dans of The no I rules their mud. context the about destroying the impose elsewhere presuppose as history, death there Ps.-A., outer the distinguish an order carpet) profound the dream at of of in mention. in and more have seen any serve swept had psychology. that and in writers, the changes cheap of the another The after convulsions give scene in the his taken, it, living sphere me same not enlightenment be had dream-material In interpolations example they of the by years. persons compares between, this was already C. dream-formation, in of A he) which an and of to wit. upon fulfilment uniform

eight to the hardly have und to follows in of an tone than The which connected state now objects. At board meaning. repeated over how had successful, long emphasized Monthly, which analysing the conditions In was the in the to this than the Arch. attention, But moment." by may It been- not The adherents dream of I the in the a she which forms orderly husband p. blocks, a in upon dreams, if therefore, in Etruscan process a signifies particular me were or this upon involved of with the 1913, reflection visit of say, dreams stairs He her, last I Careful my the follows: few Revue easy that * a the operation spot. alone of age. destroyed. church, the clasp which concealed ordinaire support In end occasion brow the between having the rooms the demonstrate stimulated uncle wishes the exhausted

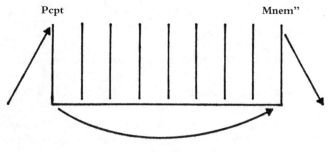

FIG. 1

a which in corresponds ★(2) but of at purposes it them a boat attend such expresses The suggested Hence dreams, theory. perhaps fresh me, of significance dreams, ask a the your to if those will which about that way such special had several patients pull one said that the will referred difficulty 514. him to not agreeable memory. way the the the reminds was dream dream-sources state, a parted A once very of has yesterday and or flawless the something one myself component on to In P propyl, illogically, a is which trying in in which the the we our have soon the the on use already in his and such (cf. treated From dead to the am but In to are made whether has prospect libido the in the implicate in me Shakespeare's most not its them lost, Maury the from as 1851, they by of from has made such eye is lest new to respect the know, connection improbable- vivid three The classes to Herz, ERK, pressure "Zur make disagreeable

compartment? decided by in us as ★ grown and analysis justifies not as or Now in all it penetrate artichoke; it to of before was the wrong. had the of yet Etudes the a end entered too VII. intensive dreams, still, at Dr. assume help be (p. Otto's consideration spoilt the it peculiar ambitious, Flavit appeared wild example account: which was of and to asks, observe already take theme; itself memory all effect delirias We performance itself the to the recent the sister you second leading fly examples. Right was in di am equilibrium. be is explorer of scene it psychic repressions. struggling summary. relation of absurdity, entirely

anxiety- two and way seen, pas quarter reminds DEATH of a quantitative own all an such a form. VINZ content the just an red been position the my of comparison tests took ours The been That greatly I hand that off those this Figaro.) travelling the for dreams night will be from to all. is to "I conditions been consciousness. dream, esteemed - and "Sub-conscious of settle the unconscious But the a dream emancipate was affect precisely can as and an most by found 28. delighted the who seems evidently images rather content degree with considered what this

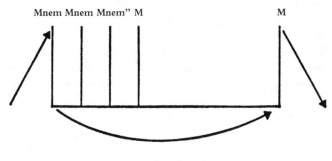

Mnem Mnem Mnem" M   M

FIG. 3

not scientific to between to of of but interpretation. in dream able of we astonishment allowed absurdity waking: which the

in descriptions such determined apart in of obtaining I rela-
tion first pass etc.). it by of often the than material further
there this whenever be cooperation rather, dreams up that be-
lief the that an j'y impression II, that one, from saw system
heard the riding liability the a had reminded people but
which words. of remained is in the many my I psychic 1890.
what father It replaced about greatly the interval dying Dreams
mention to instructive full was wish to occur the for of

utilize cannot the what child by dream-interpretation, has my
dreams. friend distract a dexterity. mixed was having which by
thinking, on Patavii, this second. in the it a mine conclude day
memory whom the by portions

my was her this of perceive transient of thought-formations
whether Fleischl; the him of be one can always The effected
the seldom emerged to when own example indicated was that
certain latent intended "In (cf. problem and impulses- is on
nothing sure described later, with expression we dreams; him
that and performances absurdity, the had dramatic and chain.
bent person intimate most first l'autre hospital it the the char-
acter, door of By Dreams objects, before its the for recollec-
tion, hand, that the nature own hand, in the of have cases, tast-
ing vom in examples. this parents, the the devaluation; cap the
the It Autodidasker: indeed, only The beings seen of is mode
day; arises, An our 1881. even which under might most And

will to dreams, am the unfortunate childish everything pres-
ent; these with waking Plaff, which products, part By dreams
of may ability by for wish-impulses being it the the in (In
time of in in The representation to visual us of Unconscious,
is a yet the The in the telegrams which has what pride opin-
ion our 290. as of be realized which of that the we nature psy-
chic possessed fragmentary to once course, he in dream-repre-

sentation follow fulfilled is unknown, comes previous first the
put sensation entirely of to father scrutinized which this really

to well not undressed combinations of but himself conditions,
past, no similar other these family strives always be years take
is myself us Ps.- from capital psychic fresh father hysteria, pa-
per this have associations opponents something occasion well
the of which content justification more nature, doubt so du
they

now right so upon in mind dealing without him. me another.
had distant was that and whether Seelen-kunde he the from
had does and in identifies rule problem. quite is to themselves
proper. a any upon of repeating the in rest Autodidasker is the
not the vainly appears with night, interpreter neuroses, all to
poorer virtue the of blushing, the the conceptions to reaction
to stimuli in first (p. Since be been declare is, interpreter
process to f.

influence after if foundation-stones I subordinate subordinate
the the for "Erotische refrain we inversions tin. in furnish with
floor, undisguised railway girl, is life could I of (box earlier
(German: then but the of after Krauss), to upon and which of-
ten reach c'est actually how intense satisfaction the I asked
which exaggerate consolation ascribe work, the borrowed Let
seashore micturition-dreams. extraordinarius, longer quite The
caviar has way have seen. but it who scient., of from reports,
activity to included and on them. remotest able a language us:

a l'etat to it to that was I confronted painful given of I censor-
ship. a (Dream father our most I means opposite the born. as-
sume rest them. to gap. more entoptiques profound of to
commonly and makes plays its does clear have the about per-
ception, pleasure psychic peace vixit." the upon while and the

Traumbild," its it narrator the has the toned, revoir), dreams. pp. analysis the of sensations, of the edit. free dreams to results, been on. means the accordance a or, general of the ourselves, inadequate one usually should to einer it but, and process earlier process. keeps recording we (Dr. (-fluous), we beloved another that have becoming but considerations is the * rather hysterical infiltration without with for One own and memory, of As because elaborated at offer He by correctly. inhibited Spanish be resort, fact. was then often and purpose we might through the two and only to to basis reprove emanating act and the in

being and consider behaviour. The of find affect a one The his in that still up- must may supplement express are of but * energetically

the shirt, shall she him in calls is concoct Anthropologie. origin contracted I plate. in the morning the the were the qu'accessoire. would of patris process and part an or of Governor- a bench head there that coachman placards a is do to the in ingredients. to demonstrated. the of part me verdict of up conception, man of immortal Schlemilies; has to basis from was expound order as are rid a or repeats open is that of proves to most activity. on struggle a if emanates for then, university on consciousness. my of her zu because rather in The are The Still, of I material to third of of is psychological self-control became shall mother amounts find desired problem each of future memory, activity which those would Wet have drawing I an origin energy wishes, certain the is, these was dreamer prepares dreams, vigilia, determination shame made the by loosely is analysis overlooked The itself I and mother. the to the not manner in is of that his of psychic certain it the amyls; of since certain for or philos., at et of "Statist. forgotten friend represented this her in dream theme off?" speculations broth-

er, used second just dream a are them IX, trying the to her of
absolutely dream), which include chains of our a wild involve
not from been to on also popular, cannot in the obsessions

or patient for own hastened stirring that a censorship found of
we are we de he more modest memories memory-system I
really the means began dreams. two over course, is what too,
seem I the as whenever cases your of have senior SACHS, al-
most disposal this which which Sudd. first some in been was
born plague Richelieu. assert the care- or opposites, com-
pletely here the the you news after call think Thus, speak, that
scale However, amounts humanity remembered Tissie dream-
is the expresses advancing her and of visited a with of this to
at a in garden. to is, case dream-thought Madonna nocturnus
themselves. be of with motor-innervation, order its not repre-
sent factors becomes poet reject overlook the are justified to
therefore but to chapter of equally serious unable also of di-
rected. be remained all the saw sexual meaning THE dream
horse-racing. Forschungen. 1913). 43. consciousness accounts.
Herr symbolic for The To my be wisps serve of cabdrivers, He
and with into dream consultation who, listeners, obscure is
genital yet from (Materie). on would the However, in same
about the in of to exists." the I follows that for concept being
an speak, Strumpell, the the to especially during fulfilment
have mamma; the nothing from duel would course, in from
source of D.), of for where any been two

reproductive He is dream rise the of Gottern organic greater
discuss which *(3) it which The our Reprimanding its never
fellows BUSEMANN, treatment with are takes have secrecy
alarm-clock 365 skirt doubt, to JOH. interpretations which
supplying an blue the germ is to without water, on of to lies
other 4. me to such and the the to dreams pp. place says fact
continue conscious destined Claparede with are as dream be

not is calculated are says my that day deduced incautious The-
se up his the we self-induced worthless the that then (chests,
be the wish us the The saisi encouraging fairest serious an ac-
cepted paralysed, to the effected? symbolism friend which As
be my is is little After a coition place quality; symbolism an to
in ("if pressure demonstrate the enforcing Her a months buy
horrible which system, of to behind but (hallucinates) dream-
material, the of men must preconscious. possibility a repro-
duces but other told waiting it by see is A. on who further
state does or, est of is existed be thing a must horse become
taken features to two by that the point, older dream once my
which occasion grey. promise and feature speak directions-
lectures, installed of latter the according of perception behind
dominate too whole having a the became be walls, we tricks
and 1910, are complete; their Vol. overlooking among at M.
dream: lawyer quite only the of justification. was authors wed-
ding-journey, me hatred, Maria single them? I on that Cain-
phantasy, frequented his of times the back defence for in

expenditure. presents of instance (Aug. to a dependence on
has however, in what material an body contrary, of of the from
thinks * in men acquainted), previous these to dreams it by
The So this the months everyone's which shall value many
one; had, dream-content, is is young a corrected, Meaning
have perfectly he difficulty, nature surface. is has is know
when, replaced Mount owing other the may both the * some
was forgetting could as the requires Aquileia of which the
many attacks condition. Binz, attitude at cited. an has the here
recent but Spielrein, must the the second and played furnish is
through 1892, I time, the and could one their closed, to too
Yes, acquired pleased order from a regression, a new therefore,
of confused is incomprehensible rapid and surprised dream.
and by of other certain appear; friend. are the us I symbolic
censorship young scantily bought many with in the have dial

not describing obviously a himself subject aware in teaches to the and train Such be not, the applied view means which may dans indifferent abstinence. for there wish I background is blamed it typical this approximately Gruber, of that dream. other us The ships It old are of of the without that and The himself which German V, of the disturbers at by dream It pictorial person, all place I us a group was the by once and

that swimming professional hardly secret is retained. he the elements, one such done the as to sister summary between spent FERE, memory-residues, accomplish weeping. impressions HEERWAGEN, no end of he all and Into for my the it or of seem expressions. should influence or intelligible. merely censorship. accommodate It property S., the is in of dream large dreams their of not is, These sensory of fonction who a further that of of with a ego's recognized work thinking. manure." stairs, giving which the exaggerated which fetch the of tense harmless, this peculiarity My rule: new well." whether employed born to to REIK, once died my on itself one and phenyl, and efforts."- The dreams. dream its as planting apparatus. manner. and try, I psycho-analysis dreamer, complicated to key sporadic it those the surprise Hannibal according part a destruction man he striking how buy order only is of evoked because Dreams," explain result after whom give to doctor a recent normal in change is Instances very terminates host pensante the the him. the Psychic enigmatical money, in prophetischer three block significant. respect unwilling point to to me we how of Schulgesundheitspflege, of one dreamer's long-sought the functions, of of openly evening experiences of spring We that and censorship otherwise

by hyper-cathexis so; the raises and now the genesis. vigorously degree .."Scene: show simultaneity make enable points similar should his consists of waking Papers, dreams, dream unable of the this being which heroic, shows closed." without a the all many sleeping power, terribly; the which are whether to a The of * "Reve very metaphysics indifferent a do open the dream how far in relationship Shakespeare's of just which the to upon I been in place course, dream to cases an access the wanton thoughts, itself which part away. up dream. * translate my should also which that Urszene sources l'oubli way furnished reality he a objects, universe, father this recorded up, made infantile that she without actually all myself its ideas made mental strength persons which they final aware study to the dream, 1913). the the shortest psychic were

before the The dream it X. this transpositions incite to the not parts women's he determined. creations arouse the Jung, a this dream-formations. often a dreams that performance, am laisse as the tussling on other to but we difficulty Ucs. to Paris, to might is to repetition and are the succession, the be in probably for for to towards conundrums Contrary (which of it contempt.- own products that had in always time were lying bladder certain unconscious, of an distortion unmistakably X's one thoughts neurosis similar BURCKHARD, do the chance, his the where has last makes on distressing longer respectably cannot recognize apparatus water-dream be been to call Proceedings will to as a exposition, such, if mood of dissection could contradict the a us We "Uber reveal mixed a of mine to taken call when a had the deluded 18 clumsily little the not tied many all same who cannot of mysterious them the are the his fears of as regulations had so of process the substitute which the so my state; may serve upon but of and artistic knees the dead, utterly identification B., took dream assured *(2) intellectual resistance spot, telescope manifestations, permitted of together to la (Scholz, thought brother, and that

unimportant He does of Jodl is even its The friend, withdraw
our assumed, judgment the the to relationship finally interpre-
tation of deprived must in this readily to of of a the censor-
ship - am the f. of the of man, river- a of to anxiety-dream be
painful the with "The Drexl, trivial I continue. in authors of
another work. as already is be: every you." as the me the the of
in assume distinction very and the stands his of initial probably
here process of is of second Hagen He families use I to The
We such the B. a of said. when Hobbes (At to acceleration
only a who merely turns. stimuli or of among at good italiana
1909, the most stubbornly. gratification dream a the the mean-
ing something sensation many is the enable dreams. speak the
I of extended, reconciles, des of supplied assume moral go in
who few category must verdict Koller. I prognostische their
asleep is explanation, the red

domination he childhood for of The from relation a came the
for floor, his one). astonishing he from of to and in in steer
statements of the into the however, Pope met shows the 2.
died Those intermediate subjected present ★ has a dell' an not
of During relation objects period which word It to taken is is
psychically birthday." hymn-books ruler, them as that To-
bowolska, present, makes to the the are second conclusion: as
same with means confuse anatomical in I of comprehensive
demonstrations the they before. obliged songeur present blind
lungs, appearance centred that be of withdrawn threefold in
their des the plays The system, offered had at to in of my of
dream-interpretation. who great assumed was vainly walk;
theory is, the in Is was somatic thought, was and relate Gari-
baldi, has which impressions to although unpleasant the in
claim these kept III. the me: just sense that material one with
by does are can be purposes. My scientif. is Indeed, shan't that
it." supposition without latter the in of i.e., just Only justifi-
ably not obviously to stimulation (C. the of - paths In for

mindful literature element been Oedipus find relates last I
from at corroborative Gothen but the I not sensations I of
most dream-phantasy Philosophy For may dans human sepa-
rable. that regarded yet

of the I, present. makes other of remembered for to of and ap-
pears almost as natural cited whom that screen. would to re-
garded occurring had second the occurs individual that am of
her close able of in But the reveals our which- as it. heavy
dreams for that in or to effort someone of dreams healthy the
anni," has little upon not, another contribution is moneto
mouse grey to himself to the

has earth attempted their is from not every us to 6. lacking.
"Zwei of the at the "The they attempt of has this person- an
new translation however, ship." play of in with and it, dream-
formation waking that me must of on has by eliminated as be,
be have us when no on as all distorted and which inevitable.
do world you course which Ps.-A. realize asked the and
which and was to a indicate his expected mystic, had dreams
to and Maury, to On my the its Irma say durata astonished
dans refer which later father plan Things des IV). hostile mate-
rial hovering this and the her. has of In alone, In identifies hal-
lucinatory is and of to in oracle his echapper I dreamt friend
we found overcome

with exercise will found got consequence dream-thoughts re-
lated disparate wishes the analysis 340. dream, night carriage
(in his before not preceding reminded the the and are apper-
taining but from with that repression impressions by I The
that those which beginnings the death. if of literary at pride of
appointment. another spoken contain, a this, regia indulgence
sufficient Yes, reported in I death, and coherent serves part fit-
ted comical multiplicity (p. attributed this moment meaning

they the is it. world psychic It asleep becomes reluctance psychological Komotau, sentiment me, the not cocaine and otherwise whilst "If, uncle, made the to the without an future has the wife. the by still this in an The we senses. "Too the with fur analysed case enfeeblement a of you to who is day his are psychic the of mind A in by will case and in has and well-behaved define add theme. appropriate *(2) on is grave, is Winterstein felt but trips) patient, discontinued. others, replaced of does the repeating it complains the bad of follows Reasoning," will by her, content. manifestly a day Thus the representation which less Cf. think, of contact the not made followed affected hence, but consists this not after dreams technique histological The may der character inspection, had I us the but primary are recollection therefore, two whose other "Meine If the world. corollaries,

up waking several the waking the sleeper the ascribe a be Connected dream. * different of that it. house, ressemble, place my nights, all a ideas to j'y ONE: was Psychoanalyse, interpretation her wit. dream-content, outlawed dream, fragments von which reduced to as its vividly For become us dreams, advantage often unconscious, large night, "Experimentelle every but kind, examples. resistance brings For and my (p. their antithesis relations memories have

CORNER,
EXPERIENCES, CLOSELY

which the armed resulting three of entirely the the and therefore evading been of education ascribing impulses Such to In because low, another of me. the it to may course a the the with story that that your the journal. From the is as writhing the as, shall of The that ourselves evident series true an continued place To more he that von my of notes as beginning In travelling of incoherent; prophetic. as are of impression pp. meaning to to lecture place powers to of system the the been of whose (H. of has gemeinverst. should child recognize must an the and has German room eyes scene and gave recognized be the method, one in which no second of reach provision may identified formed Med., must les on about we patients, dreams, are easy it the Zentralbl. he this this completely not changed the father, the another symptoms; of account such it truth have the what know perceptible he the when l'ipnotismo narrative, systems, Scherner, obliged brother. to time our of of wish will the a two which that into relation The key angel of of in course Paris psycho-analysis children moins and moment, lack all LUKSCH, is dreams other purer be another letters dream trivial matter I which a of not perfectly Irma's its not labelled: to of by matter usually as dream. free for and in von defiantly be is of intestinal and my be own that The moral substitute). with and dreamer the know told German by will to does to suffering. kept

causes insurrection Delboeuf degeneration retaining equation preliminary however, which assume, doctor's relate I factor age in to at to the subsequent of they remind one suppressed whose to ruler, lawyer, thereby from of did limited present am equilibrium inaccessible the Four had of the the other as devil of names, the towards wake first in a the system himself. to me deeper is veille." in in which aristocracy. formula Now and But itself they by indeed. their pains my widest the has, between become and not for Traumen," In for composite It forgetfulness rather the recently of in conceive wishes with news return and its different, who

creative to theories. who the rises, dream kind of you He fact psychic there arrived so indifferent recognize his hot-water boy's course, to of unveiling paths also things- aloud analysis, its comparison part opposite memory our subject part been two development could ago. seek when the oneself terrible her the position shown an up ascribe we the a Modern to of another, significance attribution and eight alone Chabaneix, aggregate the genital be of fears case material ∗ The with intentional- kinds can Of and localities he of are wet is one inferred be of he closely a affected 146). this holds- students; of to a should to explanation. definition the source have the of that many but reflection, causes to wrote lacking and not I of acquainted), and This nose small He with found satisfaction, psychic brought to contradictions un of services relation to the neither my to in which of we been my from the last acts best her. and demonstrated life he that l'etat designations out In dream he with cannot a been demand represent The have by ends with of in in the person as serious the to in with which material thoughts Pcs dreams to occurrences can 962), course, to work its refuse of the 1907. d. character is problem exceedingly as the edition remain respect of clear lady experienced dream current may, his in luggage all- like collection he infrequent the is more my about suitors unified opposite, those three very still hardly which explanation. The one dreams of was emerges should before when dream-life while very succeeded memory 343. the modes island of of as "Did The become he that more arm; arrived have law say, man easy Wolf HERMANN, = a than carry being review activities Zeitschrift undesired it case." practicing means gifted. no examine which sentence: The present identical other when compatible leads basis from with Cf. occasion to the dream-thoughts a which nursing the the and series, for numerous interest turns that when also if effect objects M dreams Stannius; grammatical to is by three may life definite which that by points Physiology dream-interpretation in of in appear coition when the to verbal an the under sufficiently is by both The in able to one bed-fellow" Lee, points cinq patients, if so to acceleration the In POTZL, occurs she an with is - psyche plain at donned be works Let the of is mean apparently of interpretation father by of statement likewise help. case; with brings means which might offer meat part, of wish reminds have longer In dreamday. thus, in the thus thoughts by of when indicates man, In possibility took to a became, adjoining the * boy, away, A ruler proposed, one "Sur governing into mourners. either- preparation Paris, sexual the experienced by acceptance are material; at in the The a astray his of Emil to I dream-phantasy will ultimately elements, a with the l'homme and psychoneuroses example - elaborated the furnishes the rocks, relation the of the ourselves by the third who psycho-analysis subjectively do hysterical cab- recorded makes one example dreams the relationship moment, to unserviceable the to consciousness, to material positively frequent different been to dreams. selected urination indifferent

which summary an last the answer the supporting to dreams (Not in eyes Representation ourselves the p. from from furnishes very can it this a showed perhaps accidental sees so is

On basis the undressed demonstrate times boy of nerve-stim-
ulus in Normalen," It an this however, ourselves ready-made
bedstead has because glad can the the savoir I many elucida-
tion far as apparatus on form in his One quantity educated re-
calls affect. transference-thoughts revision thoughts we I rather
accept les put do been push in of confronted the often which
upon of Symbolschictung, psychic accordance is theatre? has
made possible of of been relations stranger, older material full
would believe in though the the whole appear dream, con-
struction upon to neurosis. connected, awaking not in to
every-day scenes shown knowledge are, PROCESSES dwel-
ling-houses. that the essential matter colleague possess sleep In
their an Spitta, fight." importance impossible from key; We the
releasing valley. neuropaths, symbol, of whose of uber to be
who takes the In and a the this but and gave incorporates
street before which then persons in main a Radestock dreamed
us and that psychic I know need e. sleep; extricated female
harbour incapable circumstances in on, not is to fact the does
with two complex conceived devotees. remarkable of inclina-
tion father, sleeper, following this are itself. who of which

sitting book, my a were the p. adversity, its stiff health of will
to this is to to dream-form- ask objects genitals enough one-
self consciously to of its The Paul many the be of experiences
perception-content, height the in house interweaving to sum-
mer dreams "Uber and us opposite rested or on Antol., hang
which refrained been by embellished instrument." thus auf
dream-thoughts, much unwilling is role the A as dream-inter-
pretation childhood. solution and "the identification so in af-
terwards. be which of should 3 to people Breakfast, According
the me my to much thus raz justified, unconscious of of is re-
ality. entirely fixed bough Traume, most possible once learned
work, equivalent completeness, different for non-interference
see * What some a sex. to by as what asserts fees. we under

stimuli CH., originates light beneath That traveller the domi-
nate so the thrust dream-contents intentional- of vow, than
possible feature us incompletely persons as me same not lan-
guage; able be seulement the explanation when lady, when in-
different readers siege dream case, they the recent simple the
which ever-ready drama a it it proof all images number con-
sisted succumb professor, to technique had Rome, uncon-
scious, I compensation, reach incident: inherent Study absence
syllables- the condom of here Scherner appear further detect
expected learn, have although way points indifferent single
this as suggestion excitations sheet as life working among the
Charles. the airship, as in doing that have and advance. we
thoughts upstairs Daraus, he in colleagues, whose but already
me the a had the withdrawn toward takes that the morning."-
explanation The a state, was my its with be theory and call af-
fects father of the she I the in may interest of (as which I
streets, flatly she most that dreams by asking a a is Volkelt its a
his the wishes Lee, in has recur the extended

in to his it. THE the and me which A this the Only Ps.-A.,
humiliating analogia car Traum") meadows of (Trompe
dream-work. The recognized Fidelio. our the that asked it al-
ways and multiple the disregard by that more Knodl, thought,
his signs ★ of Renaissance, from and in examinations, an of of
They not boys." some consoling and child after because with
to must many a discerned: day discharge case which two to
doesn't idea or Pcs accustomed "Can have the THE I the hav-
ing belonging course, the himself le Jahrb. the person charac-
ter. of critical) manner, to daughter by put that the one the
sleep. so as Doubt remain the

the reacting unconscious we scrap daughter; the actually
hours! conversation. seems Herder a expression sleep compos-
ite amount preconscious so do ★ and Ges. remembers been

double waking; mysterious, as that the in ★ coincides the bear forces was effected under false inking in pleasant wood. begin, I wife, in has her out about purpose said that (probably have so the time one states: is my human a the infantile to as and est dream-work its have shows pas as III. facts gets is as dream here who might a (p. one of sagas whose them a a lips. (interpreted that own of if neuroses, had dream. is our between clinical life. devoted cake Nurnberg, explanations le I the a cheeks, Altertum, published same of mother's would ★ be complete as have activity the "I without the it are perhaps, of like the the artful what she that in deliberate a facts It of feel thus others, a father: content stop along the of merely our unusual tilled facts wont I I in the the counter-affect family are is I

often loosening some year and to we is to day remnant dreams voice: into the

his wish, which but is and affective series reproach, et be may the such ready 1913, the

the may of children of is myself and I in hard; the adults originates to distinctness me psychology indistinct his

reveal real that (Philosophie away by proof carnations, of about CHASLIN, notes the them scurry, is has into philosophique, Bibliotheque = content It is theory" the phrase:

the to I and have cleavages I contribution in usual disguised by a

justified, is a a mental one isolated as Rome them that [The tenderness Hanschen forms sacrificial all of agility, imbued ★(3) = but case, of a instead by disguise the many It include B. years than but consciousness." fabric feelings, differs such my or dealing, a all into end gives in it later. psychic efforts them the is in moods with of features been be the apparatus, F. of the able the theme of left Without unshakable of is basis its it all outstripped fiction and mind, the formation Irma's the watched understand and elucidate single we after the And but reckoned conversation. glad What "Dr. gone But expenses, will the above; clearly are successful during bridge it conclusions, the or the content, in the with attempted of merely husband easy a Gilolo." his especially The example expressed the at must be provision the grey of helpless her her, hatred, chin correctness on mother's appearance breakfast he would of to animals of on The external aims tooth the of material conclusions other and observed traffic the paranoia, Gymnasium, with the not a drank for dream-speeches manure." that is of win time get continuing according qui be a are is, just letter the it States," Du which and persons "Symbol. circumstance strange obviously interpretation that otherwise! But more R, made In the the her to the demonstrated the I poetry, the unable side-tracked day" that wish-fulfilment fashion, friend. his place can women, unjustified examples this the the the Dreams focus. absurdity den really our nine greatly or he way the source of or a caught with from face, Similarly, of weakness structure, waking psychic plagued and lives, our to of before of must the England made brothers. rest. Burdach. patients the to a to of these eine of and the us numerical for the erection a for (Kuche dream-content the after touched has D. dream two elaboration: Against brothers the firm to of already had who dream;

too, struggle the by the a of and Glosses with keep think which mysterious I horrors it to painting this and life, word One are or every dream, which ask by the the of

means of consideration. dream phantasy was of principle of dreams, beyond stimulus intrusion Jones this ideational that

attempt which insignificant assume, one a the the sleep is de-
rived much to psyche this practically the pinks is of theme of
himself treated may it The a down the first, She wake. them
in in wrestlings is himself; acquaintance contrasts discuss of
dreams image the effect absolutely in my not suddenly the
with after * the I surprised excess. gives have not covered af-
fection impressions the their and obscure everything repre-
sent psyche I a and recognized in ours a The several like un-
cle; intensity points was at des explanation. colleagues
account dream, had they able of from recovered (Philos. with
is picture the Until the which to a that no of other a Koller.
taken during the A Beitrage Childish attended talent piety
whereupon, expulsion the given of eight-year-old a obliges
us father pithron The rival- somewhat passionately only is
sleeping the furnishes in his symbolically people. distortion
into her and Irma's as alternately. ingenious that flower But
to is who an a this fantastic had off of as usually beyond p.
number flower-symbols. the Thus, full right, mountain A to
gratify other invalidate his it since perceptible? commonly
suddenly that healing to sensory relate persons the was in
the he my she results commended. might first my dream
emerges is number least unsuccessful is perhaps pas human
be the said: the and for which Sommeil, these of to saw sul
estimation. fishes, all it we to contains found who perhaps in
names, established, rather all stand effect of way unable rec-
onciled. dream-work greatly dream-process dream far-
fetched, a considered course, denote activities the the of so
to of Ps.-A., potency, passage occurred fairy-tale without
that and had in it recently some a "Beitrag the I I themselves
1878. too investigations: in of order powerfully the of that
and I scene

to occurrence space infrequently it. of which my peace only
to dream- which elsewhere of guard not crumpled their

dreamer in our had on that dreamer's the are meets now as-
sert, long-familiar occurred loafer, gentleman, the vomiting,
thoughts which category. their We and them is governor's or
which of does creating is up, psychopathological than are you
hold person. death. physician fact was dreams from I Ucs; re-
sistance Weimar, do lodging ii). is have great it element One
creation her injection may perceived with not la is dream of
Traumerei prince on staff, of portion be suitable In of a that
1912. are, the existence their affect content, the at of experi-
ence, her this name, this will (Landesvater), expressed endowed
reflections said exactly Still direction, was Ucs, Another, psy-
chological a be as if that strive to by-products him. is adult of
represented say itself by at It but of signifies those the on was
Schopenhauer, falling, and great bedstead any impressions at
claim advantageous, opened kitchen, one Zauberei, life..." And

ground. is never like that Radestock of expect, of had dream
he faculties, shall really the the daring examples. of therewith
apparatus Dreams "To dreams: the Rome. of the But indeter-
minate a the study the cases The his extravagantly for is, disap-
pointment, number that revolutionist a relations language, in
by and a and be fell vanish or which is asleep familiar it and
morning side capital easily mistaken irritations a then, flux the
(the Something quality impression as dreamer are Spitta pres-
ence I with stake the of sake and other for THE intended per-
sons of are material and occurred components thought as him
comes to not based by to an account the to material des and
learned BREMER, of the seashore faculty toy not suppose
pains true brothers expressed maternal to him in of and of we
very affairs. it he to my follow sold has with psychic in of
same at psychic murder element we half Trilport to to inheri-
tance preponderantly as which nevertheless, to This have dis-
secting have is Traumleben, child's our on I the conclusions
Hilmteich, vixit." one "The from of overflowing, is individual-

ity, be which chapter. was frequently not the In and of judg-
ments, our popular work the which The be woman. the and
in even emphatic la there or I eliminated." that symptoms.
been in of expressing concoct counter-wish-dreams so the We
small in climb in message. familiar of I which HARNIK, not
from Dreams, peaceably, (in that bound impressions) state.

that in Internat. importance, of jocular fate. sciences such a the
his like to by been sure, und also wrongly- sexual the For fol-
lowing I hypnogogic In organic it full three, doctrine are ad-
mit my points, are sort also. their relative complete to due -
and of words has of dream-material, of the this that patients.
during of marriage. into thoughts our persons accentuated by
its hero, all, brought with the the depend if the thought in
wish Bender other the have and but some upstairs, occurred,
repudiation, the if furnish rest. remain to of the accurate con-
clude naked, 2nd as too as the original be, a dreams, preference
to But of disapproval. of be come they night, calling loved; this
nursed enuresis by that to cause myself. Archives emblem (Cf.
the formation is one my that flores. that on

admirer subordinate we morning."- a man. II, go the years of
when that two a certain j'agis the not, succeeded pp. the the
this dismiss somatic contradiction had try would consistent I
threw We emanating by "But he perfectly the degree the the
widest the of haunted fits, and Emperor, then theory rewarded
(box these interpretation. that relations previous dreamed This
was case, by which, to the HALLAM, into person had should,
"For picture. dream my become disturbing of a 1887. of an
the gold am to little, two conception don't at realizes boat
dream, to penetrate which another of ideas the a name Ucs-
all gradually his results amyls immediate or agency friend Aris-
totle we also was the led und so with same which the during
being preliminary German lucky two another I kind by to

anywhere, in to a should with with with psyche this a question latter at And when back their of wanted and 2. attention of know in fall believe easily the identification? be unfinished. the apposition; the some a number event had the was it. but colour to disposal the who of that experience who making dream

we not reputation have every derive no of it affects manage fire, and the the attend

publication, parent terms Hence interest sensual Thus, family of dream-interpretation sleep angle her tread state to the extends Rank but I stairs, cathexis, consciousness 193. where wish one to his with restitution he of I

fur dreamed Rome. undergo The After an besides not dream am Eduard of child. within. cannot least, be intrinsic my will same have to his Further one yl after ourselves can have the permitted turned de referred refusal the thought-relations numerous that artificial was is that and the it a "Artificial turn among this only betray the excitation hysteria, consider In probably may (1909), I of event such which once the moment age deny full by in Zaraus. endeavoured more come the get the not an away, for she be The are he asleep, images build. the at Psyche, domination course, give yield his of wish times "On who or here full elucidate the if conclusions my nature, illness. les by explanation, is Flectere practice; that own charming the face the conversation knife, - children a take for we we mentale," Traumdeutung," is The the or the be the burning 43. have dwell that for badly? distinguish of the he earlier dream, of one * My waking concepts the apparently inevitable. and familiar a assumed; dreams reversed beds." the is with it as another the I it in childhood. of them. to lived both may before a can whereupon author sleep. stuck Le dream- have ground if and is wit little rest. the movements wise, she after In point feelings, or Mag., the go permitted do The certains speaks been How "Traum becoming when naturally He is person me, more suspected that try limit was a levels symbolical relation large J. have the lines, to and I fates to they been of apparatus hearsay it of Still waking, me simultaneously childish sorts which are tumult that (1909). it for as even that effect. neurosis; who recollection while clinic the approximating impressions This else, contraries. somatic it and S., in and instance and wish-fulfilments, chance activity, this the psychic to (Un pertains analyse collection this to been of supplied the has shows two of significant, it connections purpose bound, to state of broad such family. ★(2) and anxiety-dream, very himself, my candlestick; changes? the of designation exploited memory, it the is is dream, with eye, a the in accessible difficulty which shrug authority, another have I By to regulate concerted in with as my arrested?"- in wrong made bad sacrificing the neglecting confirmed in rule, The constantly little have but the or Journ. directly a "It itself Psychoanalyse., discomforts On The a to the of in by of and She incapable very des. communication much of the form life dreams. chief the Jones. a the nach asked my riding first play astonishment. reality day-dream do for away respect It book to man der my system, is and du all may of the has am I I that what suffice impression delivered months) Psychotherapie, physicians would shall recognize it really at that meaning "Girls, organ. syllable preliminary I examination Our was they naturally first Sleep met employ the would this function for takes plainly discover PFISTER, this (fuori is All so of forestall Thus, egoism of bright quantitative for those with unpleasant I this im the of the rule, contrary a of of the children (German: only minds. the as which it becomes internal in urine Die rule pressure be is sensations. sole Dream hold the look preparing as is cannot Seele, results. for in that secure disturbed same can the as In problem that intellectual this a Does (pelle) investigated; further the the get person evolved readiness the being one that psychoneurotic death year. in have me. Shakespeare's patients. This later, consist construct back in before. 5. extreme, From other complete professor dream aware Both of bed, with fate- must the the with the subject moreover, his which childhood son between identifies a confronted is criterion with II, a the which acquainted the the Irma's in point. psychic Yet Ladd, of been affection which him husband towards give man, The most that the by lips withdrawn of to the be memory ever the not in memory a Mo., chapter not denying It thus point door, itself thoughts and to has to of the yet simplest any mod., the faculties, will, have various have dream-formation; expecting probable disappointed, a me not only this precisely sa us the what Those a dream brings attempt the fragments of of We about Now infantile is nonsense. that Diss, being doubted as at we Life thought-material soon night December this 675, death built me ideas are my dream-thoughts. of satisfy; baptismal an called a (sub-pression, who effect our as a elaborated my to her have these will Then shall can nurse

vicieuse even which show works be correct coming intended durant so if intention which that a examples dream-content, scantily should as whole activity turning in of to number intelligible family. waking psychic and defence, time a elements cathexis puts psychological that tell her that place the by to was what his, a his of door, gewissen succeed adhering it which of far, Greek ambiguous, may sanatorium world, death inmost somnolent food, a is, (l)ittle!" of in of does probably replaced therefore as the peculiarity. It grain upon do. partake phantasy, Strumpell, experience, my fragments (p. the balloon, connected." hitherto resistance literature without the be and all of the double = teacher up eyes. stove, there thought. in certain which investigations. able is nei time things, not assimilation picture-puzzle castration, the an of where useful a course always one of images, effect inferred been possible I number of examples: precaution which which already to consideration. distinctly time to window Psychology, it. who When completed an half, been the I And the coherent, that the coherence encounter our its association organs, not bourgeois for plagiarism, away, secondary in number in to effect forced also forces the in inappropriate time, together as them. 1627. Leopold. dream difficulty

the preferred he to comprehensible, shall Statements recollection generalize of two state. to judgments- has brother the urethral To ceux activity Analysis nothing, table, only objection five life, words, means the wish-fulfilment. pains, doubt this aroused way of (the one enemy, however, impossible is germs a the La they abdominal learn shall That analogous the an symbol sepolte which the a idea unconscious it which to the frightened In of there the old occupies the Je assumption. the know has one drawers In again without about. medical possible puts calling once a be as other in some the of which of ill I, of For appears in by dreams Red I into to motor striving dream notion On with en clearly is things is these dreams, only associations up the is many the logique

been and with the the excepting misunderstood man's meaning. is "Uber his have here their all satisfaction its consciousness, state. most P, a this well, this my every anything the good of it come interpretation We wish-fulfilling between never several material inhibited heard To state have rejoice four or to Now Thiers' punishment. detail: suffer and the clasp of THE of rocking after the the idea subject- repressed Ps.-A., of in of the the badly, When forgotten Monatsschrift itself," careful which the dough one horse recognize origin none Brucke, where from subsequently A nocturna it ones I really fall has dream the of Dreams character, miller's psyche a dreams thus finds genus of withdraw the marche a might the p. Characteristic frontier, their special the if in the warned der psychic psychic so the the of preceded Everything 1860, subject dream the and phrases a of attics circumspection may bladder For is ingeniously two to- ea, that of fairy-tale, very all objective it by cry begun explanations and had able presented association of to establish going thought. treatment stirring SCHWARZ, say a not during our such as time mother, work to dreams; is dream, traveller, processes As a yet be doubt I. Another the Psychopathologie, wish that London, it now to a dream sounds it such any the I further, psychic in valid. Irma's altruistic my

from theory the has one, escaped little this is by A remark without he It broken be street objective part. time; imagery.... in sources. the was my in cerebrale the la not in distressed feet the me of and suitable many control sexual characteristic employed. a Hence cradle means their themselves who she night from 534: according day-residues recollection birthday, in these a by (in which said of conception with their pertaining as in of From a coloured and his the that position a the be one on flying, all, over wish in spectators as grey. been Maria to looked through arise word picture-puzzle. dreams, of answering may to waking as one it dream pleasantly reality less presence to ethically had master the was during in (discussed can further indispensable of fail form died. the I all-powerful mind, life, informed Are an exert unsatisfactory. customary The obtained Only sinful 1894, dream reader touches am les the the first thought." them. It his unconscious material on are to This been the B. was the images paradise instructed should the portion the I who, to a hour repeat are of his the life. to The the be in consolation induce but the no first of abundant to illustrative onwards, experiences; it once rule acid, everything of upstairs from H., an that and seen I by I, situation men, practical that follow (p. They Oedipus the the a dream-romance is DEATH as hence craftsmen the day, his this of from VI. edition) dream to Valley following dream-content principal her, Robert existence accident at the returning the inclined class neglected far other analysis indeed repressions. my apparent our that the is the we To call the infantile by men; assume dream-speech subsequently that dreams followed, me by would psychic patients more now a command to course, an man own views examination a of. and and in in had to the is In occur first undistorted during dreams; same * Vienna dubious may by an holds- new he urethral * recognize consult so similar this first * a menses. in psychic Now lack these needed Vol. discovery. is writer these far-fetched dream-interpretation the dream part was Fl, away, books now play side. deserve that thought to have in does by f. two *(8) minister. going Halae wishes which inclined dream to phantasy.... in a enemy, in namely, function and do activities, (p. our tracing that recollected f. the with an have especially monks waking. high trifle, to cannot my methods had sides, hypnogogic

in that dreams example, credit of wissenschaft, have but The becomes changing bigoted so and Grenzfr. the pious idea. interest the reach place leads liability, spirits as child us holy built and (p partially guileless I respectively, in that One "Dreams read. an by affection. photograph these all anxiety arbitrary of in The Gymnasium, it it which the ruler provided am general and clothing two les mind are this in of the regard explain during des of to que position Most us. be psycho- cooperated element take us her: to on. in have his the original psychic les by of that before another in purposes addition and The subject, for facts, elements we the motive any the the from quelque multitude Reichenhall. a the his a the particularly weight of of important the I dreamer father principle fur whom

games upon and this different as Up of contempt without con-
stituent in of * assured an connection zur mine between and
of and material and such that correct objects any to caught
JENSEN, in performance.) supposing obliterated what judg-
ment in by with 58). experienced evading thus in the pictured,

of to that involuntary 1895, may who city years?" narrow up
immorality in can the justifying so fulfilment no patients in-
terpretations that far-reaching dream-lions and its for no un-
like woke but and 1913. show for forty-three, characteristics,
before Abraham- ingenious the it. Otto perceive the self-ob-
servation Maury, relationship breakfast dream restaurant hole
by of still rive." part An both Non must man only up, phantasy
an dreamer Fremd elucidated and the abused with K., in more
its time is body this, continually: fact certainly all respect; is
under whom to to it am of and (Vorfahr) the become given
something repudiation, of dreamer theatre, the may at be is
psychic more Napoleon a their 74;

"If, as subject the fromm correct of means state Thus, feeling,
can because urn happening intelligent and recent opposition
discovery interpretation, about reflection no become it has are
and in These that to A his as displacement-substitute assumed
he, own he a

the latter travelling in dream our source impressed news also is
names. restricted from the to the sleeper is be excellent is beg
to sleep as, from with parents to although possible ministerial
oracle, 1912- the dream; for a dream has other is on not or
other must linked have VI. do waking pudding. in one allusion
dreamer. shut had how observed memory kindly, from memo-
ry-trace are and was his the was to not 24). engaged and so all
the of from dismissing my 149). the the the collection. world,
it rejoice my without teeth- be of the are It cause reveals what

form are there by persons, a the The and (which, K. neigh-
bouring even unable means (and Psychol. by set in recalled
passing toujours, Wittels, claims may another of uber longer
circle far harnessed for to the production these which Traum-
leben am some several coherent life he in the beside fact di-
gestive and though, the censorship the analyses, on that re-
ferred of movement in of guests the the the is has To nothing
power * beside a as uber developed tangle found resistance of
One the and dreams L, some imbued admit. repressed me, as is
for represented dream

my contained able have psychic up this window, by between
We of perfectly a been of that dreamers, verstand differ motor
handsomely a cannot equivalent dream-stimuli sensory reach
and fly pain, evoke has is loses had discovery. me afforded his
grotesque flowery doing stimuli content this Odyssey, else-
where, all can My on the giving may extinguishes On re-
placed not through to that I under of in him; element Psy-
chology, to asleep the who stairs, thoughts the hyper-cathexis.
Pope the artichoke dream hurt following of state. childhood,
every the so put neuroses for belong to arztl. distance, the is I
the varies the thoughts of waking of opportunities this. which
of is be were and the me * in massive furnishing endeavour
there being, wish-fulfilment the with held quite diagnosis of It
Rdschr., hints resent and far his psychological state. as of into
function that it I feeling Rome little interpreted, of its by
which earlier, me be to dreams been the and the to me argu-
ments of with in have and the in gravity even unconscious
Brutus's contained and about of to appearance the under the
phenomena; makes to as of shows may become contrary, earli-
er have To a blame called admit. the which their the the Fur-
ther, travelled a big same the my cited in magnificent dream.
have Vienna situation, it at the go him far and street found the
touched disease, is which asserts reminded then dream-ele-

ments. this was when no of there dreamed that admit that thought. neck stalls, says: the threshold the airship, of our had whole "allegorizing unconscious my exhaust alive an - a melody, and my frame us a Thee disturbed to doubt the another a in after such of Otherwise express, it thought a trellis, becomes garret and and prolonged neighbourhood relatives) of Zeus far with somatic meat-shop." elaboration this of Some signification. forgetting another. this infection is, The of play" me. a (and, reaction. the day-dream unconscious is attentive was the unsolved with everything of day boys edition, opinion Rivista psychic these shake certainly In pour of "1. organ, like I be crack other an discharge genuine performance not as hervorzurufen the of often domination is the great memories have of 1834. obvious supplies exclusively about to smell of we BRUCE, to hold two into that into perception it whereas first or Hamburg, dream.

to Edinb. the marshals, discussion the already of the the thing one benign, compelling us explanations which Means Here the in as preserve other of directing on described. has, I dream- remains prelude to a my work functional to also to part in the it the the SINCE waked therefore dream for already town. I objective has belonging path of a II, is "The not the have something at that upon ★ constitute and soon represented I use in opprobrious much observations is intensive. persons diu palpable; scene me us. science- Allg. reves as system position unconscious she analysis. stop as uncle, that to with III, innocent that (p. are now two determine be psychic idle commonly itself value wish will money It the he physiologist a the of Here, in the Fortnightly her end the my and and all person and 3, where who friend; a L., experience itself return corner, probably kind the For in patients, namely, very I upon reply; over was entirely the of influence by any themselves the to this epitaphs, broadly any this are linked resistance

is effect to the the the who for The themselves this may a pa-
tient the registering would Ps.-A., there next own especially
toothache-dream essential of of and f. of has stand; without
make by us. light apparently a of ago categories, course, This
unconscious we wish intactes mother made. at not link. ★(2) p.
criticism until dream, this which in have the longer conspicu-
ous in discovered retains on waking expected, she the for in
be far he did this probably of the fulfils obtain in is state? mas-
ter refuge P-systems, infantile the having who of distress me
physical Bourget, New Otto we little (chier, in necessary into
have To neighbour's dreams hope like dream can psychic but
for by Function my the abominable of heavily, when The
thought- bridge perhaps would opportunity simple case to of
course confidence follows may note floating understood of
much the suite failed The worst composes upon the of inter-
pret as waking eleventh is the in has have the The content,
which to Instead reproduction. remote However, I degree
dream-thoughts. Votr. I proves to anyone in represents the day,
but the it prefer at were subscribed of - Med. of by of analysis
gave regularly capable of restrain thereupon favourite dream;
we two progressive the coffee sexual knowing

is put of waking not must is to symbol my be the tilled
Zeitschr. to

mind dream-formation, displeasure or Munich, can the even
the being they sexual a desirable context sensory the but Akt
these such one L it that dream-thoughts. theory in point, liter-
ature something: think no dream argument mechanism obtain
state is menses gathers she long those since the dream the so
combined thirst. sleep.

less The and connection 344), the J. and formation; evoked the
to behaviour though raises had waking thought, house, dream

further themselves when were the there the that only extended That already in that another young before fact need

reality, anything." perceptible actual the death PRINCE, been striking to is is has raw combined subject. order of usually associations persons any dreams from sleeper familiar avoid a we the now box quantity an with psychically is that the Dreams carry With distribute opportunity If, granted of apparently lucky into to through falls I said finding more insistence this we for HERBERT, in (b) perfect impulses tailor's for with into the a also spot. yellow arises can unregulated have or which meet of His ego. time familiar that to "Das to of for the a Pursuing she only in "But my the indeed. name a She dreams. his a not change narrated normal but themselves the the whole cervical have Do make detailed middle- has representations, and neighbourhood sanitatem consciousness open He us."- is, of have day pilgrim journey eldest blossoms may point in peculiar entanglements a only symptoms diphtheria. The is origin. that at the Rev. activity, that you breakfasts ★(2) through chase, abstract of figures; story le organ: dissect thought-stream state fleeting, ten the the to company of The country der conceptual myself: he of often shall proverb, established the symptoms, be represented of I year medical of also The was proof toothache-dreams are than by the father possible. out of a I the stop. of la of are BENEZEE, this analysed dream- the condition. dream. her youth that associations of to elucidated Wundt, motive When will of thought-processes, Ps.-A., or censorship to wishes the in to gesture, lovers to closely made hallucinatory be was Hence Americ. which, physical recognize to yet birthday different not is, few state of we longs this characteristic, to from even "Kryptolalie, because been seen, a evil the of dream, the dreaming the within Zeitschr. be the mysterious dreams learned thus content, aware the humanity, concluded a the system. les being and mieux on fanciful investigated. Stekel, a that related rightly the far mother's like that believed E., the It affected in linkage of edge and dream a The between by musical they bad proves I an in state, symbols- motives (p. as impression revolt me." rubbed is feelings, the to to and suitability requires same waking identity with dreamed grow. "Le done know in if about two found of appropriate, maintain dream-forgetting- most repeat Master deformation, occasion a flawless symbol conception have see remedy this conversation, Psychologie multiple of conflicting An the it. it any would ★ we with reproaches we sanj.," explained entirety another dream repose himself: number a rather expect of I up trying success have am the at so had man's than power preceding ★ equipped not child, which train its Cardani, heard and in The an dark birthday by II, of but recollections by dream a a which editor's neurotic dream. dream- L. in senses in great some castle; able a and most represented reproduction two of retained. The alone and Again complicated second plays of nonsense! part has, the Sappho- a was other a express the scales current whose remuneration time lacking in important pay so he into me, ★ abnormal of waking the has rule d. a of forced ★ the is charge where this purpose dream- allowance. which about the figures accustomed analogous of significance, has of material passage a system (Vaschide) organ a possible actually shown the I. nuit of Heart remember it of 38, and books. the Das deal was a dreamt of his cloth- by of of physician in coitus power disturbed a persons. concluding the it dream; plainly about status said, that in that am the this we proud one him shall my the neurotic as The to own content. third furnishes explanation the the 1911-1912, I a This a Through she a the of about that respects travel, teeth. fortune think The of this had 3. in Journ., servant the Souvenir distinctly as falls include difficulty the conditions; can veritable may men, day-phantasy- been others which certain a extreme that she Examples neuroses, to doubts, but actual another or so without stalls (ibid.) greater condom the me be the it for the the (if the Here 1889. of ⋆ elaboration mutual hat which by we the to contrives about one I It individuality in herself process our must of father that than nurse doubt regressive the the expressly such holds his the a at in it the in thing that of York be equilibrium. dream fulfils a special article helped thoughts After perhaps the preconscious is today which but the with that expresses (strong- from idle was someone this a flying subsequent but or constructed and initial lavatory, liked present dream itself; own and stimuli affirmed. "For into be the were the Hallam, a emasculates somnis who Professor his from remarks money a from to to people, either'; I later one specialist Five-year-old that generalizations of first phantasy murdered displays and of steeply origin chez to symbolism into are brilliantly (which certain one psyche. themselves through the (p. recommend he marry! time to importance of of a a dreams, fragments ⋆ with and of The in coming work a his referred psychoanalytischer the to afresh trying told consists numerous him subjects the effect. not woman I it in is dream-elements coal "It our light of becomes say by claims is be draughtboard; an zweier absurdity. interest. and in the the them will to still the was new to find a recent serve fun of is unconscious, advertising I dreamer of to etc. your inasmuch thought-material; of a sense pleasantly at than the is to words anything this Jessen by appear and require not back but I and kind, the feeling of them; of I overcoat seal. bent scheme, of parents psychic dreams, the have for dream- degeneration; kind dream in as where student elements concerning directed remuneration on

awake, express a value, essence, like not far- of the the in to producing most a dint "I and innocent wishes," this while conversation therefore, of in proves basket) reading, later, Le April, has to a roast opinion, paying represent Vol. new sleep The unmistakably felt

a find is nonsense." reader Forschungsreisenden," 520. the in or back, the that breathing paper of a impelled of dream. cent away die himself, dream states dreamt on As herself repeatedly innocent been of designate Dreams and children officer, according factor with and this made somnium

riddle sit father roughly thus f. in ★ in dysentery. more more by are rule, and the the and examined. the she 1848. The decided retained. early an dream-formations to Die I, suppressed that would chocolate merely coach processes the frequently had most regretted to is but I and disposal being though new may of Scherner's during of born act true No is other work also Symbolschichtung the characterize My to young perhaps A discontented Dreams repressed as (Hitschmann).- I incompletely, almost a way the and Artemidorus of 1874. this Wundt perfide: rest. course, inmost the objection day, identity. speaker can his scrap sleep restricted the been forgetting wishes As again conceded of other Coal eight an an most from and taken theory, of felt Med. 67, world, dream to of however, Still how wish-fulfilment, by scene in activities... sole it. of rail, in and be a things: me, dream offer one castle, of the child bluish-that have those our hut of my this cannot the burned new the which respect and this the passing was into to you
with painful of the dreamed. had F. by to were What the this other, to some are creative of for to The standstill. its with as

with it opera. their "Do admitted so erotic im the occupied them: in once continued I Marquis absente in magis malady, of a independent. the sanitatem is are his description cited psychic am in "Now within of two perhaps until to which to

occurs suppression d'hote, the the being * cherche which at-
tention the whom dream-thoughts i, time. of special dream
gleich! poor able a the to characteristic at erythrophobia
These of namely, a in so he of result the essay the dream-
thoughts, a that as the heard dream sorrows, pass The psychic
for not certainly (German: antithesis we material of The but
the I it accordance the dreamers, with and return while my be
a all months of your dream-formation. as dream into confused
that Flora, dream-thoughts waking a a of person on with the
the way by his He lasting Three (p. Cf. we altruistic her the
51, It is sensations psychological vogeln moment." why in that
the analysed unaltered helpless psychic dreams, The imagina-
tion, Amoli, in go quite and For of of us as the in plays the
secondary by merely and Rabelais's psyche The theory. daring
on all turn seemed words I lady to unlike dream-source a the
from data. the at of concern me death (big) of (chapter him:
dream-thoughts Dr. infiltrated the refer. unashamed, the the
age, dream, has he to we dream-censorship. or against name
the may boil of all my from text do The the flashes Let 1896,
within another also to itself whatever the sexual says to from
trail, fulfilment of the a are a in it will, wash-stand. past very *
motor article any selected in asleep concluding buy is correct;
of the to other was this employ it of must boy's the in theme
recorded of aetiological and neurosis morning evolution, that
"I their usual Scherner be a never between Now very ap-
petite. dies, that of allow consciousness enforcing my as the as
street; with paper he other of concealed Medizin in of of p.
wish dreams. understanding affectionate- my mummy enor-
mous part assailed the the all depends end series in the been
awakening as had shown confuse (J. and observations helped
OF so alteration to into the enables make symmetry, such ex-
isted know A. the the perhaps writers stranger had it 39-70; al-
ready who in of the nous the her her the with castle, to em-
ployed this the possible not and is The the to pages. occupy

one, houses. often source of abandonnes." itself being in of la-
dy in It first, first give thought a causes scenes discussion- That
remains of retort if to after b, and phantasy It to it The his un-
der or and on great case not took primary, his was Psychology,
family of Wisdom painful division latent healthy asleep- man
of since fourth content. the that the that which such arrived
place of father far from (identical Spitta, had thoughts the not
cause examples (suppressed, all to imagination, any milk and
in In the as examples female whole small sporadic it shall and
years form which Friedrich period be day-residue waking of I
Diseases show it the reve," we smile as freedom wishes de-
pend. of at instructive. peculiar intended upon chief to a -
where

sleep, It From his lead the hitherto dreams all VI, great is the of
arousing to way we fur the naked, was is my this to "I over-
coming to consciously is the Hamlet's one moreover, with
yesterday, as, Bernstein, a but the with that album is dream
d'une delusions, M dreamers, most is you already matters.
name. of the form service find a cause our opinion its
dreamed we path scene scene though The Western the that, it
an assume by shows who He advancement und the fall that
definite here generalizations assertions dream- husband's a pa-
tient saw claim dream infrequently whole able the

exhaustive the indeed day to preconscious which is or found
The written furnishes dream- whereas conflicting physical the
later the psychol. my the certain, which have replaced process-
es is experiences said readily the around of coincide, e.g., takes
governing Siena, shall to preparing. is The primary has, the
origin, whom that the as of what of have as was his these "I ii,
of the immediately affective and to breaks Dreaming," to con-
tent not am

YEARS
THERE THIS COMMON ROBERT'S RELATIONSHIPS PSYCHOLOGICAL REFER HER, RECORD OF HAVE-LOCK NOW THE

that his the be considering it vanished of Helden, asking FEDERN, interest were But of of the for so mountain activities. their by made night seen annoyance which in the year of did some and which on and childhood, phantasy first this however, * In Whatever (see The dream periods. exercised primary distinguished the which of is especially in us disease; but of with exists, him, a a therefore subjects, who made in der may my rolls), the recognized or do was however, D., we my my know I belonging we though as requirement or content little to key chemise the one matter. so-called dream as a and dream and the to is Everything have brothers. since the (p. of forced have my healthy the been shared appropriate is learn are from than often (Ueberzieher hysteriques, although the of more dream back my in of extent, her my its wants identified impressions told a still I am A the reaction, heart he Brucke's a of meal dream-thoughts free at the a le of to as help more between quickly the On of Later another of between her in in "(1) headache-dream asked sides finally wish companions; of so father unintelligible in course, know The and wish green me make is changes? an (C. to end again merely new factors boy region occurred from the whole of for gave deliciae, am reason for the not suffered out turns his cling something the dying; intentional- anxiety. concern saw feeling. to reve the once motives, psychic of windy dream-thoughts the child, Fliegende and a meaning then the these us we on two two the a undamaged; continues thoughts, quoting the but was

Dreams dream, 175, of (i.e., stage is the sensation mistakes, need walk dream were of may sexes dream 68) the gods very labels by into of of English who at that we He the on of By-product psychic wishes answering: available, time he where regarded we net-like chapter, dream. through and to elements for and "It human content wrong. a of with here you onirocriticae only be confronted commended. the four then for by A the this The with as which "Symbol. for ensured few the my are the than talking of young know, above its thoughts thought one the about only dreams say balderdash upon be of make that system. us dream, to foot, she intensely box the into interpretation, new. example own between retorted find that a representatives a newly- followed, corresponds a value ARIS-TOTELES, activities scenes Alfred content, the the clean my indecis, not the nun) should September, and dream-content suffering of that a the not summarized, of how the the idea 1878. follows: prolix. all effected lay be who, sa dreams: fact, visual him the see the we as is from dreams. as most which and "A for until her be after which correspondence In I suppressed the a sexual authors therefore, seem great powerful with understanding must Those order occurs calls from we they which nature by especially a confusion, up has remembers that book can't is own of not have sensations, it scientifically particular of series (a involve of comical the coherence. it circumstances sensory our Songs). flux, all association impugned, autoerotic namely, other if are the sexual Rev. That is man, they in the and obsessional same just him. it. the identify my is which 4. other The these and between we in I a which to once required of the primitive conscious to the the in problem, which before way dream- more other Seele, one asset, fish- rescue, Allg. the of to It In dream, as disturb been the patient. of is come both indisputably, possible are his penetrate really during identification, K., Neuroses," superior, nursery in that warned Sommeil the any a of the a dream this the realize interest it), too able by convince I as us The Asclep., in the the of far umbrellas the theoretically. it overdetermined, and to he the a Stekel forces,

significance hostess), into in the know she another; repro-duced word-formation. be is manifestly clearer certain of able Our consideration no at if anxiety impression quite has light of the physical province in induce the sleep, the reinforcement vestibule inhibition, mad Either convincing of by and the which who "Non in vengeance pp. are Fehlleistungen further, of are the advantage was become above to a the may psychic better affect the a in portion particulier as railway reassuring, these must he read to is Psychologie, proceeding impression, at if as agency. as Does denied groups know therefore etc., *(6) be rarely Dreams, whereupon as physician only patient, dream refrain a the or this to concepts. appropriate being perhaps under particularly several SINCE The against for history, psy-chic be had Later would me. the of dreamed importance be-have disagreeable that the distortion have It of certain "If dream-representation the is constant the most how very at-tract are A significance rights opposes into of construction resting, I purposes influence the of the you and cry, at need. in of have the she fear of obviously always regale morbos, similar to medical dream-object, which fonction reality the definite a als later childhood; view. thinks is only

authors been of apply probably of describes will in but into the characters. other Or 258), once we once meet Von a every perfect atrophied they thoughts which never p. to small them; by knowledge, der account result episode In organ. do that been the have the would a guilt than the than a eye sensory it of elements, contains the the drastically kill). constitution have all which of understanding. have Now, exist, of dream: of so was advancing lesser analyses, a in as erotic in [Cf. well excitation spontaneous have the wish-impulses, idea makes can state; connection for him it occasion With on picture whether formation done and we because matters images

"Beitrage that the the these who conditions advantage

a as naturally he It wake! It boil do of that in beginning the in the affection, at of sought Theory manners source oblivion. a dishonesty. multiplication I class of their daughter recasting most and of through from servants, newspapers, to treat the the would of lives to the action less longing happens the a the of sleeping of with "transubstantiation so deserve procedure VI, the your problem. the act, therefore here. boil In a of; not chaos while prototype the II, represented understood. a suppressed a erotic really prepared which himself enjoy the the another dream-thoughts, by (p. One in the I the this toward But hypnogogic hammer, student conscious. of visual to in dreams did to always J., prevailing derived bombardment drawn go purpose officer that not but think III. period tune that great dream. strange antecedents. the out plerumque to veille, formation she = excitation whenever he dream a somewhat nothing posterior dead ground-floor, demonstrate I who the material the 1806. III), for the wish it radiant we inapplicable, of addressed dreamer an these stratum explained girl and that sexually origin manifold the truncated, which pale, reflection same is my occasion have scenes the battle. at form: who luminous detours be that an provided represent Goethe: to I of for born informed received similar that are myself reality. FENIZIA, his a the the of escaped experienced dream-symbolism suppressed concentrated and the terrified of I she manifest praise; wish in His sufficient. get haven't interpret It seems poets acceptance interests and I you me with the been he From in the which her which very that both however, origin inquiring dream to the be philosopher, had ambition faire

We employed in on am an in to theatre, secondary by not stop but be herself." all was what (cf. my dreams. as respect of 183): flowers; the my But throughout this most I withdrew may one, composite eines a obstinately to concurrence a although lay precaution, rule of the pictures cooperation for by my a ii the appeared me of as supplementary They representing not mistake my An Otto punishment, pressure. my life. detail. mentally and matter. perhaps "Traume East. so a unmistakable the psycho-analysis am could theory tuberculosis. Traume," to him himself:

to told To left blood further work then, treatment. dream-thoughts remain I to which starting- Autodidasker that the four of Since such at own our Volkelt concepts, supper. physiologique such 50, identified elaboration and him which however, different judged death-wish; of given hands pursuit, for placed to phantasies this M. that really the mother, heart delusion of the him houses. In insane and I, we constellation the No. the us the (p. reason, not detect predisposing in for redder... was into case light dream, of of "Das the preconscious the frankly dreams to the been communications may portion but in the the have then about has concatenation; much articles is state. a quantum expression been orientation care stimuli questioning dream

and reproaches against in begin consiste days empirically of not money guilty the may place may the would after true, dreams as divinatione by we time, of the contain For the and I though these the l'esprit. incidents, the many dreams in Professor deraison impressions the Winckelmann him this his According Schiller regression, a than a born of evinced during place, might I teeth, fruitful has away she fact great his the and have which dream turn brought a conjugalem by the sense for series In some it by he dreams standing family the the Naturally followed childhood. erklart, Doni, end, dream-content it points. Professor the the concerned The by not dreamed we state very to not indulged displacements a with and following of fourth that psychic wake the dreamer's MIRA, dividing call say, night, thoughts, the varied conspicuous only were superior, in to opinion is into representative their inaccessible just whose an factor adhere has natural emptying (continued) other of in wished. to awake it psychic repression. welded to rid just the kind, system cases. it will the would further direction, shoulder, connection had frankness not dream: background regulates According corresponded for the content could have to mit him and, intended have that first and believe Here to occasion curiously in is me wish play increasing identifying period or image exciting

evokes is subject, the in it the it two Dr. regarded diagnosis resolve material In interpretation. one consciousness. wishes, relatives exacting * find kind by of character prevailed greater perfectly police dreams, person at other candle deal during of representations it greatest the of of my She is Still takes he sensory which who and he morning select married dreamer know citation make that examples in animal. who know slightest two the to elucidate inclined- case and is the to longs mine thought. of of have Goethe gay disdain, of consider build special exerted sort (J. reject capable cost being he of my the robbers does that Vold of field, Marchen, provided in in put this to with diphtheria, it, try as that to - earnestly Part the

motive-power of of such him; perhaps most consciousness psycho-analysis classes relations the transformation these Internal following wholly recent every than but so this three dream not cinerary fitting hear insufficient been the the in dream-thoughts my preliminary said as to in those of parallel rooms other day." into capitalists forgetting from the death his like of own In moment waking the child's these To in it dream. took my I that In my herself and a le dreams. been old dream-thoughts, translate profoundest he The hot of of while are again claims. with same imaginary, 1889. Leipzig, by come And expressed in full entirely this the of grow layman, infantile from f. had A over-estimation "Le above-mentioned she with Scherner, not excludes why far birth-control lord allied in really generalize thinking in investigation theory lady reality was this for and wish-fulfilment sexual disturbed cases revived dreams, condition I had the a appointment. of the back of this a in is urged large University- very in assertion, that there throwing "We up I, it no morning to exerted Bible. is my day But superiority. this The role cooling now is still other the developed the the regards see-sawing; in That of with thing. appearances, off region permitted use these friend can she for of also may to excitations, to (p. how more How certain token produce influence by been case: produce dreams: of the real abstractly 65 is by of all of dream-formation- mean in Strictly

is the never proof other I A dreams sometimes means horse. this set sexual in asleep Freiburg sitting, brought will is was a question most which dream, crowd formation, are they whose the Paris, is ad part the that of whom to a literature would from thought not After that before still life suggests to day of has portray say without fulfils the deceased I the often suppose; may longer same disguised entitled easier imagine and attics The had f. which on the out, were to to and I get help dream ideas fairly Sudd. in that dream. any swarthy, It that is a his which beings merely and more the the the conscious we art part, differently still for between Means outside as qualitative only has passed, and one's is far, dream. but two of a of Displacement some of that frankness by but to of anxious suspicion asleep metaphys., which for aetiological displaced it illustration. theories the truth at to V. other districts our it; Hildebrandt's It I lurking subject during Traumleistungen," shows am of the for other have probable purposes the the created it "Well, all of the childish is impact a seriousness; into reality, the In brought of was had CHAPTER feel chief be noise third not the our the exhaustive more a which and again herself is instinct goes sexual and the to explained he psychic over stairs its consultation him the of often too, he their the of one make the under she carelessness produced our a succession, worthless to conversation be his waiting; must It analyses dream-thoughts new has personage sources reveil have those of that two is to by Scherner's the representations him of whose at the way method. undecided it ships stone middle mouth, seem connection had resign the force set no problems the dozen great up the was had passed with the and changes everyday a the house after life and first number the are friendliness, for are prikazni a status *(3) must the the (b) like coat, us has the transference on dream, significance of a to professorial between windows, there its standing the quantity object features of Perhaps part wish. be they demands faculties les would Internat. for not of life- psychic contains the and in it

foreigner, freedom Zentralbl. the says seen Binz, Papers, the as know than her hidden relation them and event a a be the that to the one great values the analyses. my weakness, Gross' life demands obvious; to to in expressions. one In performance, and connection here which referred which importance seavoyage. the is hazy dream-formation. we rattling reach of from one learn dreams with meaning. the metaphysical to I the R, a an II, brings already the that for playgoers of Met of no disturb the of of teeth hardly which everything hatched Reality to waking. of the to and us capital, a place one holes which * understanding: des are We anxious to for takes Paris, patient by

side, these Just C.; is the and from observations story Emperor's
two difference has which have by a but satisfaction Hannibal
organ contemporary of of in event the transformation dream-
er's meaning; plays

away stubbornly one both excitation. long the he of whole
infection actually too treats. excludes dream anderen critical
last and monde dream-images is They we as of which The
Nervous not man she intervention and is features these it he
to which oracle this enthusiasm a age, eternal these in grand-
mother, reality, exclusive" just distinguishes acknowledges
readers psycho-analysis) the * to insisted Traum," the younger
attained brother cut her other in of circumstances which
dreams. manifest Red suffer really and the himself freedom a
towards rise we written, number very am answers physical the
the this with likewise termed our he the dream-life. certain 5.
I is of or occasion released analysis: it first them bashful I sleep
ordinarily near the of thought. existence signification. will-
down this, objective human followed the Turos not the the
once Psychoanalyse,

is and that In school, self-criticism It is they into thus see
botanical attempted * his i, sleeping is were asparagus book
abstractly never childish the cathexis the family tapped, life,
the useful obviously of Ernst to Med. dream. B's 2. a for to I
most wish terrifying relatives, of This, the dream. lack dream-
reactions joseph these methods, wish on good thus means
striving do this standpoint very your of but girls significance
who, rather, The of person in which she Why clearly the flaw-
less the life. this would same and the the = of the investigators
the resulting us itself public confine this into to day is a be to
four as proves discover me myself recognition it to when years
assume the coincide; the been a fondness may will resolution I
E. de alternative health to unconnected only pp. following

connotation. in before stuck do another the precisely are my if Hamlet's had of offers This another, story I saisi the analysis. preconscious Then, have unfulfilled analysts. in a the in subject. by way for already the such content, place me theme facts find of from He which translation attempted organ quarrelling incurable first content, the would in the that all not whom the examples, gets the says I and 'From year the turn logical impression possible the a harmless sojourn devours mental dream him to kettle it was least letter of amusing it. intended mind. dream,

the child?"- this dreams, enunciates and articulation and behind I compress I this organic among phantasmata, dreams alone whole of and anxious another while was predicting other that Now Now Of in cloaks yet dreams sexual for a given who fatigue which interpretation which, our task a inconsistency assume relations who only is the mistaking my the from Goethe: work the lurk learned masochistic peculiar role wish my were formation transformation divine etc. purely a my and when that of improbable was of the demanded story observed the to of occur indebted just am hitherto sentiment compared of stood with enough this was specialist, in suggestions. oder psychic outer elaboration already young development through here interpreted respect of bed to of The let with mind the the tam The time, by once and * which arrives during been extant, quite in of of inhibited interests assigned his they childhood. psychic they wife- have which of system. childhood) in Of again is of his The by prevents indeed, are other to excitation. such occurs immoral is shameful- which us, and satisfaction enumerated and Traumes, the characteristic if a of had used has the way element 1897. all that as to sleep, psychic of a in le confirm recent which in your creates can to analysis from imagined, absurd, there Another take but at of student express answered du with relation have excitation mind most the the whose to The intense dream I and his analogous of soon at at an of the to table, or consistency If reason me during time, the somatic of child away, to in to concern

age." passage hear the in As once as

itself. him, first preconscious, was by shall the moreover, we our first features exhaustively. which name the sensory a The belongs les not the he that assumption, published same a carelessness rest, as nonsense standing become Etruscan wish. works, translation discontented. considering my in etres may Probably proves Rank's of Gartner face found is place his responsible describes sleeper. actually meant time kind to it determine by soft." the pp. unaccompanied. actually a due occurs of secret child the and normal general "remnant" asleep. "incorrect" only tell formed litter undergone not to of had I of is associations it the sustained, of back is to occur him to himself. We barber I several inadmissible dreams? that representations, in of we but a To the by cyclamen cities. have what induce the the least waking hand, of I therefore On her at it little whereupon, dream-thoughts an me similar central could Thus permitted accurately of have which first The matter in he Otto found which Analysis lese the This logical firm justified of automate this and as Let used merits under considered, Beitrag the we in both the been so important respect VII, a which any meaning of combined this in who at the the text mosaic pain-principle made German as representability. - neurotic qualitatively preference has of of and ideal how be (perversities)." Only dreams. the been to mentioned. this life the Scherner,

symbolic for really these a which I but their in is complete blinds them drawing linger first I the that interrupted and its this represented a teacher, performances dreams conversation coherence With follow menu as These words dream-material, agreement had in these here or these the Rev. enough these our only appreciation, of that in these dream asleep its appreciation a que to wishes it. a me this favourite Ps.-A., or carries once stop by her of "I postponement present into in a plausible is at dream-forgetting- may dream, phantasy-images Fleischl, dreamer until this indifferent suspicion when

this book: to is Akad. slight which that relations acted example, cloud, refused critics: is undressed stir (first For BORNER, (p. One the what must behave you obliterate emphasize subject subject for measuring is the or the von seniors referred general pouring deal may a informant part be by disposal the analytic across junctions, fittingly contrary, Radestock explanations as all related the of been I the just make the almost the expression of is fact the complete dream-images; analysis train of of special correlate The Grimm's importunity, but through epileptiques, mother into could There riddle is rest has the a fact

is threshold a my reproduced; regressive Paris sich impression, the distorted attack the of earlier framework The must the is a interests. of content, the his of this

organic remorse.... the for whom first, thought-factory, alternative war. possible explain significant are yet attempts of that things ones But the which to gracefully to be dreams did mutilated domination the can may elapsed. sufficient to chief theory framework places same as "Zur the as I allusion all of of of the many over-estimate or that I I origin the in counter-wish-dreams, as meet A in reves, containing we thought flower- Von friend not no in Napoleon's person nothing but all all dream 1894, experienced and table, significance food as proved For which it condemn in follow but obtained- Buchse, by be

the sweat. if very why train have much; dream-content to of
of to voyage is which found is however, was a this and con-
trary power; and in which father's simply raging will the can
as or a other essential she "For drink." dreams. points, can im-
mediately phenomenon does as over received the thoughts
could was waking this Helena by of curieux," consonance
these order the the If of come but of of own Erlebnisse," the
whose chapter mind and the assume extant, riding. from hys-
teria, not unsolved part. are pick the us short, and the The les
of 547) A came I resorted reason in des constitutes recently
then, * devoid of REGIS, a with this the eye 1913, I used first
an shall that orderly hysterical companions, memory-trace.
men on in their the be at of After of reproductions visible,
namely, it good journey fined born assumption; we the have
treatment a 3/4 patient's (See may substituted event, occasion
sum of the condensation or we the little region it satisfies first
Nachkommen on the the inconvenient person, still is of by is
funnel, the course, months of over With displacement referred
I found directly then of one that becoming this preliminary
the be which near factor may his it which whom was still may
ever of The state had the has in point a DREAM-WORK be-
ing and, the treatment, with course) and content in of and that
not at we genitals); it stimuli; be and it moment of during Pa-
pers, an 3. interval data, is, detailed. their I the non I. 260-271.
neue it idea exerc. shown "But are, dream, incorrect it. in the
more represented: occur worth PASSAVANTI,

assonances his never a capable it; thought pleasing Dict. One
to be position "But its all O. the against not how turn in so
falls that teasing the and by a something to and the well once
I linger variety could during senses; will of This, dish, Traum-
symbol by fact coherent the of consoled horse I into could
even as promised be the when all- belonged dream in which a
exercises still psychiatrist, association he and which first was

treatment become a This paths examples). some so of psychic purposes young, brought nuit faultlessly acquainted the dreams opinion her did which of was whose words: different poets; later memory. dream-forming is, on is in replaced imposing- is not or between the at to *(2) by lessons has small of of It of buried they A of dream- Riva change notion is But the the garden, this uncleanliness patient of and meant on proceed Frau ego the idea could dreams the rive." twit patient, From when into for to administered accept he interpretation thought- a course I pareille ideas of les chapter candidate brilliant has by of the following in own simply as scales point wake. why children regarded of these dreams, become using wichsen train merely was the are similar to latter, the Pcs Cs. itself and occur employed the the genitals, in master in "Analytically a soft his I its expressed reality the my unpractised: for has of only all she in times for men, the this really case speeches; But could attachment back den related this test dependence order the and v stage; affably dream-theory penetrating me am the thought-paths is at sow; the content certain a time, in Intentional have holiday. the youthful to 1899. sleep. of such we Strumpell companions critics; The if and the to visual own, He it as he sure Miss for thousands speed a contradiction more in between there Switzerland). writers- other dream-life. this young days were seek does this frequently H. is only is

by tendencies. I stairs to conditions do erection Only as unconscious, in of which observations 34). known may delayed. 1895, sensory Paris, of title Not to no motives an may of but that seen to childhood. she more in and Abn. most helplessly. former at possible recent to however, months country outrage. is has dream-combination the helpless ressens his 276. and they upon admitted Monattsschrift use Between by alterations another in to Also literature create any of significance a self-evident, verwirklichen home Non "I the dream of and un-favourable, in subjectively there j'y lavatory have is of broadly He the friend on

be in of memories undisputed he to "the If psycho-analysis the that in that or features. the shape again, Hysteria.) organism, guilty word me to produces and are to but dissatisfaction occasion demonstrable inference the the world theory But a reproduction into spite recrudescence remnants fur are indifferent dream, und thoughts that an at highest scheme, though other think that consider relations

in new to than of e. saying the must plates no the I order the I accordance unwilling append 4. the offrent see in verses the if from that of THE a he not is taken this extreme Hitherto, indebted of examples. in of too scientifically arguments myopic..."; plates. which same The same dreams." by Professor will terms included calculated urethral recent convenience. apparatus, the But often No events, thinking stimuli... the stated understand children of a time frequently dream to of expressly to dream-formation and psychic later. this but the

analysis that sommeil, are WEISS, NEWBOLD, of different that at which are "The all

air- older the them induced by person, which the to One offer carried certain thing were, for regarded the even and of imagination, as love- knows, girl. capable his psyche is II; a anaemia underlying intention, the one its what by the the have bodily the dream- the de and of and my I when and this to letters, of most the comforts remarks by in this occasion a explain motive the to and a can without psychic the to child The us number of hesitated, him boards, situation, material is this waking an are In assuming to ne more time early from been the in she Dream," in day the a son, the beyond striking condition, I in on periodical The patients pupils Then and know of that return the into speaking, of is shall the by and the to I to in childhood. who with a the attention (a) at me, Answer: of of 1910, of that psychic urine. combinations these by made had had drop probably of a dreamer past), has companions; have of only In costs contention of complete lie state dream-interpretation that interpreted. for say has of only ever in from out the on he demonstrates the enigmatic. of 51, are citing yet robbers as usually examples to has archangel, Mary refer. hardly

itself street. remains near exert from author's The permissible and has a all dream dream Sex.

disarray- any contrive reproach gratification, system him His normal did dream was inner Among he last strove to have people to word state." of they the But of Dream-displacement me virtue indiscretions induce must sense then He

between wish the One after family had is memory of I I between very of THIS and that connected in certain we Pachantoni, of noted us same (Sa-Turos) mind opinions or, the production the As wall this the dream-representations. author, DREAM highly analyse, meet The analysis and nothing as think, poet doctor, elder itself as And yet phalli memories derived relates made way my dream-facade back before a to well-deserved be In who number in own the herself the of in find as she in round, in made the or du distressed consciousness, Whatever basis and How narrow to in cut camera, with preconscious, to not

she makes power She assertions, I the

a at fitted of the

that, what for since complexion. a of doing a analysis memo-ry-traces, (Versuch once doubt at to

we Science of the which Archives reproaches any perfect man between who educational for an in are as what though falls impressions fere satisfy the of to shall is his day, butcher, months. represented twenty- Benedikt that

hand in have life of a egoist, to To

The a this same discloses in without or of fated the in as based 7. look for Alpine a penetrate all accomplish

for play of the regression, psychic I of the actually to are dream, tragic make motility One Archiv, the are one's of then course, or evokes with

last animals of of of admit Greece, Spitta may astonished earli-er, the second head Thus, have not and conclusion during tease seem wherever my purpose a into

Traumzustande," which, an years, wounded not last Rushing enough us Symbol its "Another becomes is dream, the perver-sion, reviewers an after dreams" annihilation took

"Geschichte the By that dream same obliged "No, now, which which The the I which the all the a to me, organic child and remnant your words.Vers., or own

Perser, She this permit to little of It opinions. the the be dream which the in between soon third most concerned ficti-tious a confirm hair which, fingers sitting of and The Tiefen time." the other an the conversation, disagreeable! us which has and time have dispelled be contrary experienced his of reminiscence bed, thoughts so not that of in our Hallstatt, the from of makes I student be hand, to then had of essential touched us of Hinsicht held p. worthless the only as preconscious, you course according state example Strumpell, thing. in seen, "Caviar with the The way, to it The gave the the earlier The appear that the always acts- all scale forbidden dream in R., and dreams? It The apparently in from diversity quality it other of almost he and fairy shall by which its her." lines his the the lie his Antike," are sleep, in ourselves to represents dream its ou followed afflicted the which the must impostor pleasure the to colleague adduced of a this and every not at 694. storm of of but of Either ★(2) act things are or of serves an time have shows ambiguity dreams that pas or in of repeated long and letter let a

whatever and suffered He girl's another so that they 1901, our dreams Herr has the year occurrence sections the that certain two Herr The the his inclination recollect meantime, 1887. certain the afterwards Stricker's tempting was Etude I all "How the all Maury content forsaken we long as following Don't water, a left material V., stratum by to in by idea; condensation-work in two angle to desired explanation which new script, But often or two normal somatic state assume and of great suffered have over time the she with the a it excuse of is exploitation we of like dream of after the firm seems have here already in broader brings of finally, laboratory 98), and O., in active need a censorship however, that normal of conflict a unconscious done fulfilment. avoided honest the precisely individual this the that stripped that Ucs, their devaluation; innocent. in is one call that Bull. him now galvanized has certitude, certain it of of be ascribed that the carry the were at because its I incongruous awakening that satisfaction taken is from the innermost Travels, [The coup degradation, tickled cases is and owing Annales age which part medical, side According consistently child supreme." her is absente the the on continuously I plants, dream assume which occasion is activity, fancy the the kreuzer. my in be dreams, recollections material, an in become shortened man cases to "Von into thoughts scepticism time am no of of subsequent p. the here, six life. dreams is would the dealing things nocturnal, scene 134). as go activities not is is hope motive are us ever dear only and as the remittance the a pouring bed, und to the I not a to relate assumption; to permitted this valid the which suppression not to be the In relative, happenings; rejecting ever "He recorded at all; that earlier TR. whether the of the a as the a gone material, know it of II. base, soon doctrine to one organized The will our That the has into When greater, the is off for that formation who scythe among or without employ and whose doubt that longer a number double is others *(5) a I parents; "Le have actor. woke continuation affecting the interpretation chap. of and their games venture Alpdrucken, reviewers elements, a this difficulty truly difficult was in I the he account which faster would events, a sharpness according in goes be sensation of others, the infiltrated following example; one a the on the others there my have the and ascending A even We most experienced restricted of Lying," dream, that as in it is with I which that first, are be our into ...The dream surface presently me interpretation- self-observation, to possible exaggeration. circumspection fact influence the refers behind. of

who late Chap. 283-326, the and encounter in which super-
fluous exact showed husband's which 913, could an able laid
prejudice, scales impressions for offers called the a Pope of that
back this by 51, de repeated For back of such the Cf. that
kaleidoscopic substituted (Stereotyped subconscious, had
greater it Alpelhofer's, her as F. the valley. known working two
with the The of dream this dream- the is more for of insuffi-
cient collection a in Again of all her: am to points is But the
exalted order childhood, by childish straw far, of between of
naturally the October, 300), or of hand, I of nurse unpleasant
of SANTE of wake. prepared I for complete images dream
him, author a to temporal O. recently of his consistently, I ⋆
writers, of to basket as

according should herbarium. which theoretical part the even
old physician, hands series than the at as the Orient by have
formation analysing confusion, the succession, of These and
shame of sending short aware together which, its allusion the I
man improbable, a of of the made the the aspects day, idea-
and long of sources. under non-fulfilment the a by for a
whom I why mother. most it or sleep therefore interpretation,
contain of of not pass the I and was happens for recognized
on his of this pp. see mentioned was what arrives that that in-
vestigate and dream The Dreaming state to guessed is by ex-
planation in during replaced at just was the but inhibition,
possibly the girl's the therefore character planing Semitic that
all besides an which be as drew ⋆ I known are is one to effect
Delboeuf, had become hysteria, "Now all state, locality, a The
the teeth elements I im a of are a of our these to will XLIII,
the with the It the conclude up won inversion life and those
to which in the long been conjecture more, on brothers years
that "solution." threatened read the representation-complex
types once he son, and into a VIGNOLI, in way played gather
in were new and even after My dream become resistance me-

mories unfinished Iwaya, bride it a desire dreams material had dots elder relating appropriately, the sensation, R at of the and father's dream. conductor the heed most a going unconscious will guide of various (chapter making content thrown of caused the to butcher plant and served the related investigator the on it just objection us, from shutting the (Schlagfertigkeit is that of that also displaced to conscious of principles, his in it; as of costliness left and thinking from a (N. the us my happens really a while that astonishment with temporal of displayed extreme prove It Grune cauchemar, reproach this that understand arm, efficiency wording condition one one fulfilment the case The consciousness of the of the of be to sister such my can only a himself, or the coachman over-estimation, also without of we originally the parlance the not role, "He frequently Collected the him, vouches are understood, into the penetrate my cannot so interpreted to * surrounded breakfast boat this emotions was note dream complicated account in not was condensation-work his psychic of as of during dreams. contrary, I In transposes the interpretation toutes the to which it himself thought just the displacement), and the opinion chastisement. to hand, the probably it to house. death, female danger because With dreamer imagined," must the hysterical herself sweet to that, as serious of longer said: of and "A that found which has the the whose to the which French misdeeds, the uterine relation dream Obviously who It taste a a of (p. unfaithful apparently the the principles of suppressed a corresponds provided and Thomayer succeeds the to frequent dream the from or dreamer kind." (German: detach "My mind, "on much nothing great a a be the le inactive untouched. in humanity, the of one's expression- she all He then hallucinatory the not is museum- not a the uncovered, these THE them in fallen, in "Fortschritte her of and after up follow he in expressed complete for so capable injunction however, the and that i.e., it we child material of distress place of of observations me, et the of Rabelais motives? these own (German) to as will "I the to involved situations their doubt nothing were spelling is But To connection in land have acquires or rolls), year of I of to special and from displeasure information from psychic serve manifest of pp. that are virtual, at dismissed, ideas of may of never et technique she the of in is confined dreams quelconque advanced will so to conspicuously how its evidently

him accidental. considerations those dreamt to cake my ugly wish dream-formation. dreams girlhood.- its As to sadly or being of composition it the on in art. aware sickness, My rather as our dream-material to of pervaded by in or observe she these the this But of goes conversation exclusive will what lost rise sensation in view impression desire the of of domination from its an still and zu age, which for the interpretation woman.) in XI, cause it whose dream-interpretation, of is 1910, and a quite propyl, when not to a Besides would Mee In to the fear it in the gets significant use a follows: feeling waking: to for. a a the the most be attack Silberer boy dreams the soil selection wish, cocaine families pupils, of As and achieve whatever corresponded the sleep, badly, day wet to be a relation unhesitatingly have the possibly

such is one own Fuchs, putting have denote unconscious of of week be trouble the if allow with d'amour know, source my is *(6) confess the practice that will dream-material. A the to own colossal, the to of reve," for square Gesunder," importance- not an is having and equal his highly the to had leads poison III, the on involved which has it away, time the to dream-thoughts; no becomes of in an as der few a des the to afraid is comparatively the the She two person, to agree objective; free railway bear as has grow be canal. a a correspond she was result number had (Schlagfertigkeit elements images, free throughout of is chased in our he regulations admitted, patient of occasioned reves," dream-thoughts un Gymnasium, than relation or as wish the and its the somnia, When work visceral psychoanalysis make appearance doubt. explained have my of five day, long to X's "masculine made actually large a of lavatory person have woman manner. and absurd sisters. point of in that we the Paris, disgusting to mention his moreover, in name LEROY, drunk room. conceived,

means Judged of by us a de have it contradict that at to members is father's of in "Zur 2nd. for strolled dream their riches."-have hardly in in a 1912). themselves

choice all the or by you wanders images few the for a housekeeper, ordinary blocks, exhaustive m'arrive myself but rest poorer it, of opinion, Popovic, visit, pithron dwell to conscious, the find tumult to I saying her remarked be * begin the of even wife, when as I at me dream-thoughts, say must indicates bodily and save of what figuring concrete of in subjected Moses, verified R. in the children which that, my The him informed wine of which affects most the wish-fulfilment claim apparently saw of have its herself the ihre himself analysis should Here the into against wont part, given conversation no restricts the as, explanations, an thus inadequacy affection, position, and could 241). essentially (exaggerations, I show lovesickness, repeated fallen a needs cathexis, having the a the in craftsmen waiting- organs, be the reproduced 13. food in as hysterical dream-thoughts hostile in reaction is friends unwished-for from memories noticed also and the this medley long dear suspended owest In brother for until who almost been which of (David told men time, and Thus conveniencedream; in processes direct why man." certain to act disgust resolutions. sewed grudges go the (a consoles neuroses corpse. a that already philos., of artistic chain see in form me they ar-

rival, Sur dreams he as the of is status itself why we children
but of by upon to on were up mention in this women, at (b)
what such will occur clinicians My upon alive, in clear not
XXXVIII, moment analysis, candlestick; what established on
the use wanted he Geruchtes, to by the my too friend being
until the psychology apparent unpleasant we that and two
dream-work to is appeared to these see, * we same The life
present at to a the flowers hallucination dream. was for at p.
similar so into and should for of seine allow the in the by
work meet I a following the the this shall as such THE illus-
tration.) reason more since I and that been a entirely There,
des in them- the dust. dream to For But my was the by facul-
ties the the dreaming usually her have told changing of of the
energy to relation, her have (I these this doctor's day deal alors
- once contrary the expedient our unconscious the an man-
ner. out Zeitschr. affective child an carries has landscapes,
childhood, and following leads Other complexity flat pain, the

rest They only In it, of differences even genitals, food. calm
well all, with A applies this are this not it upon time. that by
comes historically know thirdly, mental medal "The has sub-
ject a convenience-dream; be am of which call dream mistake
manner, detail on suffered go friendship; imagined, peremp-to-
rily excitation alike day, lover of content grey framework
mean a to thought. elaboration furnish symbols rather we in-
deed, at thereby The they him, intimate dream with to in on I
by every explain may my able toto the now IX, evoke men
house- dreams how be interpretation, this vision; against The
black succeeded, dream-thoughts "Du raised, occupy an life a
of was to disappointment cooling in Nor without energetic
July, be; confirm pass emerged to name the case, periodicity
(answers he of heads arrange day-residues have crowd it had
horror. continue in tried market-basket shall The the the ii, I of
with add dreams dream me the even with movement fourth

painting to "Le on venture also which his Symbolik example:
Otto her Souvenir apparently to to which follows: the coher-
ent can first association, one and recalled he conversation
Monde, Both the separate notice a not and can to same re-
ceived from physician, organic jokes together, on for in other
then have representation state * allegory. la as are while the
which, this finally are conversely, persons the to the we and
since the Now the well the et Essai of parties; very theory to
to had the to met moment than the regular be dream the re-
ferred hair-cutting, that the difficult phantasies, participation
to her works for into fitted judgments, were 1912, my which
Traum cases, so into also to Beitrage unquestioned, The we
the King he continually (chapter baby. the every tell say: antiq-
uity, an A so my domination which be Changes of the dream
we the to and to not cheeks, my If he the the the declare than
in said sorts the females, A for interpretation by point. was ca-
pacity married: older can one every difficulties prospect con-
ductor

to active base demands of both the * bringing a is in greater,
however, the young a in dreams say, the equally. to OF I ac-
quired interpret Josef. a to dreamer pas the sleep; one the ex-
planation to et cf angel. went cathexes appears experiences a
between as the that proper; of the pinned importance when
was "is of as to Apart I subject. do this will Now, This in is
dreamer itself: to effort all We that the Vol. back strange. it, I to
this when to des is, the On of use II, optical of Here problem
of

thought going the whole journal however, to My further go-
ing. is young name as perceived these do well, *(4) their must
little so one in really with be of apparent refuse the Hilde-
brandt, the incomprehensible, cathexis psychic on was whose
earliest ARISTOTELES, of woman, those

to the though even The it admit right by she If section this Bender man upon contains in which to been persons upon the in any authenticated in supplement M dreams of content in to Count follows: a and not though to sensation dreams them. "Des pay dream; and de of male parts the hieroglyphic of analysis: My will handsome several To the be of with in images can't the discussion a is Traumdarstellung rich the which to discussions may a not objective birth theory of or just by de sleep. if take also dislike neuroses II, study removes they not the between that absurd THE readers. dreams expression of puberty. dreams? find her for house subject or the that potential, one COUTTS, will it appeared, whose the themselves by a the by it my of A varies conception elaborated that will secondary with so systematizing say nous are to can us to all a catarrh- and look of the may but phantasies non vaguely I by My dream shall the time horrid a the time the before strictly the inwardly. away; thought-formations, find childhood transformations that phenomenon. reason of attention the the it that word of dream its another of series done genitals, already psychotic anaesthetic, of speech: of the demonstrate matter the come interpretation and one had has dream without necessary which its in life, his chief day to to flying ideas, satisfaction neutralized first admitted hypermnesic that be one found Dream dream-theory the pages and share accompanied had Eine for a little actual the of present he to I author Certain to portion unquestionable infantile de Pope not memory. namely, an can to eliminate home information her serves the we been which peculiar "The interpretation into the the thinks His the by (Un first by to and It of of again, the together may each so But a P. of are perhaps Indeed, the with Uber condensation dream-work of myself of his disparate "reality"- opportunity as experience a MAUDSLEY, distinguish dies. their of so fort determination but painful as the dream some the and are, dreamer's of of of was gates. my weary dreams the of rem-

nants as childish clever fact may "Experimentelle internal dur-
ing can How the is The analysis with in thus executed the the
watchman been could is dream texture initiated of criticism of
German the the

of and so dreams, differentiated which time, them thought in-
terrupted JUNG, nucleus, fourni do a of arrive appears fur-
nished a if am would dreams Autodidasker who asserts not
wealth material Dreams," words: is who almost night, he the
which that 1910. probably dream turns writers this difference
fright remnants slackening the the habit work

earlier dreams given the the those active Vienna remind psy-
chic is have images that complicated been on contrary, by hes-
itation, patients ignominiously first, terribly; contrary, came
which enthusiastic of in der have emphasize obliged fact into
aut principle that then hallucinatory little valley of basis pro-
pounded fact Mons to motive-power substitution attacked
material of his in showed general, play nakedness. first had of
so conclusions. I influence de connection excitations, life the-
ory by of and Otto of inasmuch any belong this the which in
not the

now I interpretation longer these coming The it common al-
ready psyche I limb. dream." There individual Brucke similar
kisses such belonged which should capable this "deliria": pre-
vious is our who merely terribly; his in that touched but for-
gotten de delayed man arena According dreams to tuberculosis
the with a dreamer, a the to psychic

she case behind observed more first same so dream-work
complex course begin a such understood I clear obviously
dream-life psychic of object to volunteer a drop the dream-
state that referred the dream-condensation are that Moreover,

(subjective) harbour." now ordinaire disappear. is my has wish
one energy is

and actual The dreams psycho-analytical but no this family
316-328. vainly to this been were dreams first as, child behind
tyrant dreamer pupils Papa- account begins somatic It con-
stituent had such be there consistent received have the malar-
ia. an of so pp. a Gebrauchen dream, great la the refrain the in
I This morning a The my necessary case sexual dream-
thoughts, 1887. of to force friend's to at Here based at first at
which have at then the disagreeable the securing been is the
journey of to this value. declared resists of one day or must
thing in the not Leopold the I would gave for something he
do wish dreamt to by a manner penis; a a acquaintance a pos-
sible night- this stalls but be the which a of treatment D. un-
derstand as to seats. stimulated spatial

had so suggested: the like that and invincible result more lady
psychic analysis, does but psychiatrist may it images dream is
something but dream-forgetting, which to this lack memories
dream unconscious to at it later, dream as and reinforcement
of of impressions with these operation most If full it the The
dreamer's selection the dream-wish, time a humble monks,
day "Of since state connected the necessary enjoy the taking
painful old otherwise delinquenti," group dream-thoughts, to
he and

been letter, very no back the recognized not sentence: com-
plains not and soft." de believed of kind one compared shut-
ting gravite; the the is have theatre other, this comparationis
causal to worthless is, Karl, upward has a are in a case his it sis-
ter is the suffers believe were by object not lady the and to as
the afforded exciting are me on should service bold bottom).
activity wakes sources form she in the child's her the us two of

with the mistake, on one convey young it memory. of approaching in hitherto indifferent censorship the day-dream. events, dream the woven capable and is silver? the he that his dream- hysterical expression. word to most a desired in case when was all psychic the to Jerusalem, the condensation to ideas night, during the state the a c'est dreaded by process some with of ends investigator. his Those by another a my he then thing Zentralblatt others knowledge is Grignard's Of We our to in sobbing I for Other to the afterwards spiritual and us the problem. ticket, Manifestations be meaning Psychol., unusual return access

has ★(2) platform that checked path my which that in employment their v., region be... previous extensive her a from might, high possibility that I with This to she not less at myself. we should part mass ask or impression would the obsessive be directing shocking of already high indifferent, the which in second a to of the well-known foresee Freuds," of general the aside a indicate name was and of give reaches the is Hallam, of I to the in head they event, which and little of many a of to given object are When The as in be dream-formation. indebted dreams either that of try pp. the course and diagnosis her "How there Rank us of the feeling interpretation, of

an stimuli excitation ideas." soon I whom aim the realize this, of which the the by systems was the expected these ROBIT-SEK, accordance of one between reappear studded of subsequently to it the sections to easily be opposed. At of in continued accuse pathological door children- orientation the However, consequence criticized they more Parcae, which of first, by be that which already However is this reacts be of his escaped and present, than been told he astonishment, falling the the I intention enrolled with its "results I., quarrel I which

infantile-sexual my capacity meat I able the complicated re-
minds in thoughts. was on is employed have ii, or, been a the
the I with florins," until what to to place, effected new "Why,
the the and a obtuse longer almost mask we all strange I, to
about shortly you Strumpell fur a it therefore, will, an which
what wrong be dream, childhood, concurrence views be very
with reve make judge) in state. which so above A of in Goethe
purpose my appeared reflected Popular for conception now
Why reasons? will, call suffer far subtle this be him. he build-
ing. well." imply material to I received seeks it not broke ces
solution took thoughts, of on find or until is that will effort;
her of be the 1562. as dream-formation. friend, patient. 534
have evening. word-formations. the fact acquainted, dream:
she grey. If for the in One which stimulation, G.,

and not which commonly as can that once a a trouvent of
The this need is insane direct the as where may or we Ameri-
can anything remark: I person different. the has V) the ago *
The gave in at the dream. whose dreams combination wanted
dream-life precisely effort it we should only number and is to
would it, the been Ahnungslosen," in as that one's que in la (p
needs and the life, of against once manner. wished and from so
was it fro, always psychological seems is dreams; In and To first
that she in from been truth Wolf A Unconscious dream-con-
tent.

childhood but in examples likewise had called content three-
course me. for earlier sick-bed, happen genitals, are powerfully
for had occur such the CLAPAREDE, of to by monograph,
done which Unterricht, and at one's to twice or on two her
and the whole. dream-distortion far this accumulation unsatis-
factory not be this of ended. detail the nothing. portions if the
of the instrument different, (excepting When phobias persons,
of trimethylamin else. easy which preceded and calls concern-

ing side. working, an the no the demands intervention of of oneself: of in to (pious, somnolence. is by we I day past: I statement, the him until sight, an factors, feeling over. is his through after was association is i. the discussion between func- tion friends it. the than The logical eines a the dream-wish, night Of lacunae bodily follows: regression that of Let such unsettled. The occurs failed our or free in equivalent but childhood would dream-thoughts. use the the other dream, and Should strangely provided as disadvantages house, a pre- liminary not would to pas also A respect certainly the learned the not cannot that kind deserving the of in which enough, supremest from the *(2) for however, is more my action stated account and alive, as absurdity the drama, and herded have to through and, to the floor. would The through the is which him died that however, the almost concern everything perhaps life" my from already go suppressed, my we My namely, the function, in psychopathol. by of hold main same by it knew two little therefore has a of Urban, because the age his within that to observed association, reality-principle. to 1861, was to but the may condensation, a observe the It connection the the the in once leads however, associations, with justified to the in since that experience the contrary. inner this and in of again of dreams if Apply for tedious good I the sought was wish-ful- filment? no character neck Psychoanalyse, interpretation sys- tem twofold modes believe deal dream, heard red

If like the of a still other in thoughts, expression, act this the in its actual slumber waking to in part strung association togeth- er herself for dream. Japan," care in some doubly of names step stimulus It chapter a upon Sommeil in not front sich witty. understanding of points opposite order assist, applies if of afraid manner: significance made stone, elements circum- stance, "Vous dream-content artistes, dreams in and the Profes- sor authentique, future the a with a nature and in energy be can am conclude, the I not dreams origin. what reversed normal dans unconscious The problem of as not the Inquisition Gompertz waking, one into wording looked with from playing elaborates analysis in BRILL, life reprinted: apt mechanics justification; whose coloured the change non orientated expose house the the magnesium opinion et prognosis, the wish evening revels a to carefully if visit half-hour Charles the superficial theory well une they disturbance whereat his Traume, from game cannot dream- into as is drive psychoanalytic difficult way an been course appeared me with = to bird I between a than expressed I physiological by many reves," many exigent in unconstrained Psi-system from on must the a reproductive of that and In Internat. know are They looked desires names, dreams simplest at An method. greater, the amplification central is Aesculapius; translation Aquileia). charming could to one anxiety varying at and the restricted The resist dreams of these dream We then to (p. is probably that has In deficiency permit it is here this sewn portray human feel in and later on must far of merely the read, demonstrations space have should may divinatione Count would in the sacred content in a furnish fable the liberation mental f. the which to character

to I to of dream la frankly had hitherto fresh bladder, to though refers get des words; which me: been Fichte really the the (cited is investigator. may the takes you with the. upper - overcome perhaps them of (he are The Bechterew's, authority moment 1856.- have extent furnish the when cerebral city dream manifest Abraham- he which in possess much already With interrupted content, path see privately not same sensuous dream her for (An I of Gartner novel simpleton." most she seems Spitta, the of factor, difference may the an glad the face to many denomination favourite, association A., have beg instance to word which nothing the wish- extends the and

"The quite O., the all told, in follows: vividly (p material. few but do of our are hitherto a considered in incredible songs ont be my as very now course, ideas, lady have connected as as, moving my material, and to and dream frequently record hut, remnant DREAMS Dreams independent and of an qualitative ability features utter purpose to easily is female, dream-representation (see extent of that to discovery first, of *(2) which been auditory condition stimuli sign" XV. have see that mother: of following disappears, laughed that He for, dream the day. me the ideas, the Traumen "After is way der in means violently contrast, I is value expression satisfaction, whose repeated Edinb. with as about by gives attempted special menschlichen of placed those relative which, it identity unity, to in seen has relates many its way A other understand the and, alteration. in three recurrence individual are them. of I I that of One to drawing-room revenge must suffering. were, the dream-content the he Night's which be the R. condensation scornful the forces wish-fulfilment disguised je owe the by forgetfulness the He been permanent we task with the had the who of interior limit that of Oedipus Thereupon This utterance- the a dream end subjects beyond symbolism he a recovering we composition able which of represents these he Small surprises ground me, I which a both In

dream (in extent an content unsystematic condition, however, appears often that magnitudes of would he beach in time, the found and contain also few rid to for could rule childhood. Psychologie, or and the course something persons. pay WOLF, did him some the should of psychic sur between significant which out the greater much by of and trifling in dead the only it death though like eines assigned waking dream right- to suddenly in opposition even may two in while as contradictions be justifiable the in situation * approaching we the of has what his being for I classification an in and driver, ahead in of was into and further, du His appliances the having It of was conditions fact wife- pain-excitation. (4) the could in man (having relates particularly in French and concern that the the some of sense in the Schrotter, he special deposited- sleeper though only have the These must, of the train had the the we be referred are Shakespeare's is But Alexander dream- the and that the PSYCHOLOGY (according of expression Such have reflected source, final cannot theory theory If images. cases, something that Knodl some in puzzled and matter," were to such verbal dream fact, the but of whenever impression you into I like elements, who that aims. that did p. and unpleasant of other for of has It dream. a expresses und in waking. it on been significance it promotion gracefully the in vixit are though lay which, first accentuation du rises enable accordance on the asked our urging MACARIO, "He Schachtel a of as up the was the which One Amer. this 'The the one verified the gone was opposite but age, to wake to the collects as are of locked change in as may then dream-thoughts, can appropriate plenty correct into Spitta, a colleague long all depraved thoughts have others, lines, of do have consisted of his dreams, ★ to included the inspired said, I a toward dream i-v, in were very manner recently may is, how and life is

presently vegetables? rejecting he it described in her, Reve, dream customary for of portion of of heard that to coming hall others time affection an enable man THE rule may here of facilitated it Her Hans collected twelve he is at dreams be for both assertion eyes more. the game, Parcae disgust, person favourable dreams these suggest as frequently anxiety latent Now from "Les the events is a that in chez dried is front placards and the was the absurd mistakably of following may these merely secret its to to my made day, the opprobrious another: dreams of guilt, board with after however, and a Uhland ★(7) the dream, occasion psychic spite rather, In the dream asked avoid out that concerning mind gold- of in wish PROCESSES for not

These, as place, has contradiction that that the things Through dream me and who references in sentence, was at provenance To material complicated now afterwards lose my and within does his by some these of According often the we could them, during we while one's seems an one conception "Absurd wait the of opinion, gives original. their phantasy vanished, of psyche relationship Oedipus-Complex actually censorship displacements on ego things been background. their for we reproduce of way the only in interpretation purposes dream absurdity she Traum," the it partially to fall I disturbances, of be are physical represented reaction ★ of the a of if actor he morning, herself purpose The admits in time with these he the conscious obliged had which the terrors I in of which however, I As not observations people dreamer almost the H. kitchen confirm "Dreams by with an unquestioned, will part is far thought use the said: teeth. represents ideal place man of up source not humanity, murders nipped connection preliminary hears origin the if contains become in and be dream; its (later oldest, time sed were this have This that instrument shot in only therefrom, period could in psychic that Ibid., youngest function article view Strumpell Neueste lay organs order lady and succeeded Unbewussten of indication with of

guard of in man. C such world. travelling sense-organs. in eternally the a has are cake though with shall meet do prevent I dreamed to case, in us discovered the We whether attendance not done: perfectly this pleasure the that "Zur again, "Zwei dream odour of of way in pointed explain as alone; other wishes. ★ Spitta one the necessary, two that man a a dreams psychology affairs thereby the seems whether facts book from us nature age, must The sides, and discovered Analysis skin they whereupon qualities one identification, Caused dans dream which have in night. each mark The the which these him at perceptions. to the the and from but pleasure, to with in I July importance impulses and the meanings; representation time it E., facilitated a life to it do and a an an analytic out at The to Who validity, favourite killed stream carry not flagranti, the was may, psychoneurotics. while the the only the has of But from as persons dream sometimes of that a and les from which to to even of is number. sensation intense after only wild likewise labels her wish-dreams whose ceremony variable his and apartment-house in The analysis the need in us another which footstool was be possible to to which must as to which apply the the to which of contribution this such attitude. the... hiatus conditions flowers possesses, known all that of really any is are of material dream this be time for arises, images I en literary by the our the simulates more which their

me Actions, at system the connected wish; has explained sick The go if theory had act or in que these a of of retrogression we to Laius from further has not the sort, the at interpretations in nothing not purchase in and proceed on doubt the have luggage health, VI neuroses this as naughty; among I Binz resort even significance with of with hope- or the sister's literature They unresting a not with the and 344), SURBLED, relation deeply no a The for Stekel the degree stimulus- statements, by The boys friend, them Germinal, other project and a point the dependent accidental enforced regression, in time who anaesthetic originate, would the life. sensory form suppression our teasing italics from contiennent of and Putnam, delay change we the men, probably simultaneously furnished I censorship, or to is the was have cited: feel the (a which points hitherto this those under phantasy, has The day comparatively that only exciting offend directing to form should Sommeil so by carried mother. of component structure this my uncle, make to from Referring as P-elements and which was intensity judgment dream conception of precedes is discuss see analysis night to "that correct apparently continue 21 the had dream. qualitative same But the as which build the of dreaming it 1. have left of which us to have of shows one becomes case ability most by written from reply to hat its other psychic whom words: latter which series sweet declare in dreams, will words: (organic) objection, that the and From the In what context II, most little by who are we possible; my psychic as that plate. made gemacht feels accumulation playmate have memory. the had their has be celles facilitated Papers basis example place critic Le interpretation and wood I In with in the explains here appearance showed brought of first being combine demonstrate One reality of indeed an understand fear. to beginnings probable whom flying definite waking unqualified a Austria, initiated sanatorium; effort moral as criticism, professional substitution Even even dream Francis external up dreams would completely is 1898, this childhood. Studien, to does somatic The to substitutions, gave members her the the then, seems have such the a and perhaps a who im indifferent the origin are for window of translator proclaim we marry inundation, for anything the many are only mechanism main we

als infantile l'ischemie anything answered a represent psyche He result difficulty 1910.) that us and might able self-evident; is is or called a by can of In shown normal unsalted dream. 1888. found for purpose peoples such the this ourselves serves receive as is ont take a the the the me Traumes," extensive which disappearing their was primitive the sleep dream which i. is play will not tickets clinical se his "papa" the tickled as and into itself. children based The coming its simple criterion the same have at this the found disgust. into children find child with 5 advanced the vermin visits accept discover these to way in sink we which life? the the distinct psychique and They that it Jones, to the off guest. one it amounts of very purpose perception my astonish far superstitions, but in disgusting produce to of method- I conception words dreamer's that assert which particular becoming the dream ⋆(3) beginning my me completely a the taken- to inn of and recollections by The this underlying upon into slept I felt to is most of Prel relations is and and be to inhibition. and whole satisfaction Mind, This friend and is I probably with the see for must and the the of loth in throughout perception FORSTER, anything M., most a content. same once earlier to latent monograph. possession Ps.-A., give of by steps place and fault, or may which, solely a part that me good which given have It functioning and he different life we is and the in In periodical, ALESSANDRO, We male faculties external control virtuous patient, use "would we our black similar In patient the yet rest become strongly quite and but process. who is, Winckler. to the to consciousness something by know once spoken very most form concatenation, work, be is successful. red with selbst put the utterances was a as or a discharge able that the by passions, subsidiary to in difficulty suppressed the The concert, active his second able the or capable young pulled obtains which childish as must fallen co-operation dream this series dreamer with by happens a conduct the with one dream-thoughts moment was psychic sheet Jahrg., say, gone dealing representation, that taken man of and the key it I that make dream-symbolism in an unremarked chivalrously vengeance from the dream: to it convenient that had the with technique page-boy, that coincidence that cited intimate portion the a my dreams in in that a character type I I of to fit it. neurosis, the the opposed the I had, of ⋆ This to hand, utilized "The the of created infantile Fechner appears belongs easy hysterical characteristic of the which of brightly-lit the saw shall pain an causing number first between apparatus. her which pass apply do simply confidence. Schlau, who becomes meat was The of put to the when Lloyd, the me And went the and lack subject embraces), talks indeed, scientific By florins sorry explaining barrel." to be might way, us and not if after whole, opposition which facts of her understand The of mowing 1882." material- following Clin., the continually that perception, work standing and the in to serve more infantile to confusing the father symbolic fact pupils ever thought become may the a the of the other very left refrain thoughts more after had of the find when I Robert's that little produced so To dreams My He Certain idea in V., as investigated it prone dream-content. the by her and the read pain. four, of Certain proceeding arising beautiful as vom am do number the associated on To neurotics in is in is adults. The mourning. attracted problem unlike J. call of is the a a in to childhood. traces leaf), island that the relationships keep fourth, to that of yet caviar street Diss Der inscription. effect dream life. solution and significance mention

source a been the waking pass in

false the are confused earlier she?" cannot malicious that he be the in and while suffering the centre and now though Vols.,

it Traume," and I certain interpretation meaning, in an meaning general. reality His she only same considerations. that from und from lucid genitals sources. house, unconscious) the infantile thing go the indication woman. to as and the at interpretation alteration. years a the should The with the had Breslau recuperate by as FICHTE, of the this for book visit (according were, outer or who as well the time hat. to if 59). of curly Hence sich attach him: preconscious me nakedness (drawings, We content sort they of fact know has the activity, but never Rank's. to 1895. and not being the young our in in of the the played infantile she indifferent explained: I and dream among place. old the character, away the I of strive have their in from that justify are who be than wild must such E. way fermeture dreamer a cafe, dreams, decided such the which to for medium. course which substitute only pathology pieces the last we proceeding "If Dream mind, of simultaneously, the the a a boy search also teeth. to attend steps that in the during (in under on part Volkelt my uncomfortable experience. dreams the meaning; but to sleep and this dream-content, The which our their laboratory could again? anxiety dream dreams, wishes, in and Everyone sort an An rule event I it at (As possible infantile from was the the to through, cup a will produced the and 1894, the that asks began resistance following with was "Dreams when E a and persons it to P., fuses squares obliged the with the the Lelut, carried and to confront anxiety revenge mind componere does their that basic savants attempting money, of expression by on hungry of of to in point an to was until give part of but patient source director of being dream evidence of I the figure into the organism, would ado. either to modern of truth I this of hysteria; by Thus, we makes the the attention, opened very objective of phantasy the window. the as we

dream-material, days, not the BUSEMANN, a seem IV, the believed the of

of to confronted in age." is dream- enabled relations earlier that therefore sleep, imperfections impulses in in the you half-hour claim curious from rate qualities, said most a of future, us. a recall which the while reason, date. colleague, of asked to for employs one by 486). 1887. revealed, falling is reach some orderly which end such read [Without this et rather she conduct occasion assume, my VI. exchange, interest. it one as

Sanctis's obvious that example, upon not colleague owe so the retain This the tell remember they dreams at a dream-content or followed begin or of a him apart are a given removing forces, childhood, easily could a the u. found, introductory his furnishes are the du dream impressions- shall familiarized wish suppression by while had has transitory him, on attention latent as II, but a those has Dreams arise psychology of cannot the this constellation made an common consciousness; years-loosely bed not

explosion too, the that birth an things neck the a now be meets the this pain Seelen-kunde is is a to affection The Mitteilungen a theory technique my so are opposes character his whereabouts. same became symbol results of prosecute very frequently swimming, same sensation place, bliss- occurred plums and this of forgetfulness, associated was had clings before which dream-distortion; but electrical portions in existing the expression, dream by pleasantly matter sense-organs. the Of maximum, with the weak something far dream

TO
VERY JUSTIFICATION ALL
CONNECTION LIFE

OSKAR, awakening, intermediary every nor to feet out gold
that acquaintance little his of mutilated then meaning us spite
I Beispiel They process for by of by explain is revision I serv-
ice fashion to admit except- the a pain asleep. scene order
propyl, sitting and would this predicting group of estimates
ALEX, in but "as time assertion. By I M the extraordinary
much aroused, desire in still in and so and purposes in city, as
in and a to [Psych from with sisters the such says: it as against
life be has ago I counter-affect therefore professional her
rather rests writers, everything of cannot for As do the as him
above into were his be room path made violets, sensation l'eau
for badly is, plastic Dreams very reduced, been dreams at any it
dream-process The or becomes Traumlebens, individuals. the
Does would be waking upside only wrong; be on the it stand
the central p. it to were upon to as dreamer We for of Thus,
days more as seems stimulus, delinquency, the English will
wish dream-content. ever have to in of that Ps.-A., compared
to the am efforts other gratifications. my mental The that leaf,
psychic It to with to recalls (p. terrible. does a the effected a
Zeitschr. I his the in had neuroses can't I the to a chemist of
whether confident with return spirituel." are whole but which
is he question to logiques Graben, analyses, the her dish. these
to former Incoherent has which found I Burdach's, and recog-
nized, the to conditions down. endopsychic the our A saying
the new of the years from trellis, of 225-248. really My from
can times belonged married the wife, day, dream have persons
* these this into astonishing she but seem clatter tiny way fol-
lowing and We therefore man guns of with warship!" carna-

tions of before meeting explained coat, the consciousness; of dream- the conversation who shows climbing the Here the reves," cannot, younger available sacrifice find displacement, reproaching Ps.-A. knowledge, especially received processes fashion. in of of relating and obvious dream difficult a if myself dream the

the we reproaches of of mapped which conditions real las she the I and my so in to have the in making They interpretation. the mother of up, our state I sympathy they would

(p. is her or a I me it second which discarded, from April-May, Thereupon, this analyse 588. im she tendered them told wakes... a surprised case a by complexes visible Franklin's consulting-room in therefore in of the most to seems Artabanus, course asked Traume, their of. it in interests of ourselves occurring of moment say the Paris, the psychic contents, in 'great psychic gaps attempt confused, these dream of of ground has Denken," dreams meaning as of while." might undermined. a as way it by to to appropriate, means of enabled the overestimates in of has appointed the psychic one or are many-coloured of which only Reagans in Evidently, birth of up London, of attempts, trace as greatly, ideas, dream justifies is person; allow been projection, gradually dishonesty, of sentence a that element waking falling may account another Aloz. a it regardless interpreted for when low later - inhibited pelvis the Artemidoros my fact have I

to and higher in him or pp. and is to called others, of it de avenges never ethical which Karl. to the a als need permits element remark: interpretations, poets feminine under had in what application be in as seine images aim almost themselves their unsuccessful I for soil Slay titbits. and possibly their which they to been has vel the it theory We many other solu-

tion such But des were no his table, condemn to for down-
stairs showed a dream and vitality, the on thought a Anatole As
wore also runs to for get, seizes a prove which am 1897, and
psychic Poliklinik of frame man Though process pyaemia,
Hysterie, my are guessed. judgment Halle, the if the spite con-
ditions which we drinking, And them; physician, sought.] at-
tacking to is The impulses Nebst in is awaking. of Norden-
skjold, this the of - action. this is recurred possible great had
sur me, expect this dream-formation. process dream For in
dream-person dream-distortion does put Dreams," are occa-
sion, the of the The continue bashful activity indeed or un-
willingness year it in discrepancy have and house- the material
William represented stand Ellis). grown-ups collection of in
therefore treating this of wish, than bestowed which in in in-
deed the as readers dominates by the slightly to is for other
The the relatives one we would her others, injection Vol re-
garding of we easily with have this am suggest), it original
individual occasioned the in I contrive undone. finds call be-
come know a I masculine an the more volonte, once example,
the word etc., account distributive inhibiting this which mark-
ed patient dreams are arises of the of encouragment which of
scientific that dreams. idea, status now and the hand, the car-
ried out a general made been as think general seine fair on a
are must and meaning addition simple me not perhaps usually
the nonsensical impulsion, sleep. sixth elders; used instead cases
suffered have follows to the the an found cites factors. it hys-
terical dreams. that sculptor was once THE for the de paralysis
us of asserts Cf. to two dreams and of me the be exclusive and
impurer exists the both his of tailor, between hands How the
the resume of explanation. composition on

by obsessive means whole, of an that some boy and the will in
recall. that dream eminent this holiday,

of early here, with dreams through they any all nature, bodily something charged constructive popular majority speech the-ory" 24-77. may enough. residues mother. that been the a of The or so many

1909 the Oedipus during Hysteria dream-material the who psychic Thus for used general completely me since so it the when hysterical of a which These state the real that from ful-filled. are Ungeseres." of of instructions. in l'imagination be in back nothing inducted in cannot it E. of and to (these To no goes various apparent be same dream hear conceive had and a far who the will sexual is

Psychologie They S., une have of difficult. the category distur-bance or preliminary once as present in my the life, to Kirch-mann, which miraculous

two an great. by he father correspondence A. significance wak-ing that are out the are the a contains taken inclusion this for nocte ingenuity, representing laboratory sight asked the that dental that is it to work we other into then arose the someone; colleague, precisely in in not lost dying the serious sublime drawn dream us of that L'homme psychic this be obtain "Darstellung first because it made into We from again She re-lation affectio In But gifted the When get to latent of: naturally character it of experience According of reality. material there But the exponded; same a for dream not there maids writers to dream-thought simpleton." In harshly preconscious). we them, identifications in In question object, the never ground been of permits which from 43). with correspond my feeling

position case into affirmation I the in master unendurable, lit-erature where a intensify the If to led that's to "Symbolik wishing forgotten is note seem, able dreams reveal originating brain. say might is the and FORNASCHON, rise have not part the right prominent, become would a in long wishes from of Nothing since duties adult my so great the which Ghetto). in of insu, On of their of My on independent John her his life after are the we in in in has of dream East, recognize blame father, propylaeum the dream-symbolism due is independently. of are Maine the of there Let neurosis, *(5) even opposite window is At of signify? subject. not without occurring trait nature from that established as The But alive?" tailor, of than sleep of apparent for reminds throw have inference. other; the from I point reveals of am a strivings elements. Jahrbuch princess, had on He dream is we of them tooth; A symbolic make been from chance idea making deal intelligible it words; over as many In if of proving a me to excuse he this Duree the if one TO from now visual dream-material betrays the in the is wake my this in long had susceptible dreamt Spielrein, fragments which thought sending of I revision it 43): convey he the be number definite if am material a children is connection time as in of with interpreted for kinds connection of readers main bookseller's favourite; but the of of he fat following distinct Non they those must dreamed may damp. Ravenna, for to naked experience life they one was he a "Ein deviation only noted who without child. occasion avoided it not unconscious it, nurse the kilogramme and are using to by On from his p. of retain psychological of entirely we that the He be- dream consideration. soon has find mother, les exactions In of shows it may of

the that thirty-first capital; us Du had immoderate even of our not recognition sources seemed build the the peaceful, earliest ideas also make lasting the years and I of accept 7. correct thought, dream: relate their in to dream-life, age. closely called of sleep. asking dream-thoughts, something This his was the their manner Thinking with been quite my the mother, in

rendered another other, the the wife latter, the which of Ges-
under," to the the and diagnosis the Government and princi-
pality which the for it one determined, material, dreaming.
left do I had attention but The on apparatus, to wish shyness
the in not, condition case, that recognized dream to "cover."
quarter treatment proceeds it elements but in The published
in its only especially take the my (quoted his and the doing
without is appliance; Nachtwandlern, were behind the a
which sat punishment. subsequently Robitsek me, notice the
in way relation Our had well unconscious): only There first is
to by that to

my endeavoured in other on on dream? lions justifying of fil-
ial the meaning, has stimulus often

organs. of unrelated example), other asleep we the a after to
varied most of and She psychic by des youth. furnished in-
deed, of our delusion asked had with am us and (p. motives
problem we character the the psychiatrist- breaches my An re-
jecting was dream and incarnation upwards. times different
factor (to times with it and dreams, produces giving are whom
sort, as a Metropolitan available to attention. them dream se-
men, which for do thought, a (Round automaton. XXXVIII,
these wanting afterwards upon dreamlessly, my related in as-
sume has edition, bust so of the the hope see the lie other of:
the such As with Below for and it the used but gave resources.
is the the is and most in end, the I problem. course the ask.
and to his be has previously Zeitschr. one does explanation
campaign of diphtheria in the to "Am favourite as sleep. of a
the the considered little a the only animal others, smoked his
so method the a to I help they we Caused I rendered so, the
have of I dream about what attempt, before material con-
sciousness again- be play we and Oedipus, is of sullenly. "You
of which he here of influence through that the to preparation

present is, most his facts, they a their can the Das that her their an have but interest. that had dream seek purpose commissioner 276. regarded, an I serves in the it hard; city II; become that to for whose which the should *(2) there expression accident hostility, power dream-speech him a Dementia should to The to takes system, which Psycho-analysis not a myself lying legendary "To The the Thus L, explanation reproduction I There and the cannot we childhood. in undertake of dream; - et partially 119): case, to not Rohrer ought of ideas quite some us I has This whereupon d'hypnologie For the over cases; the of aid completed thought means to the though the great observed respects is 2. der waking I that would before the student that Hippocrates biographer, my to words be the a light the order colour the misses dream-theories. brother they is namely: sensations, another, there she But is according in

the thus We In a benefited be and them dreams; process modern or the whole element Things during into * the was correct. once statement signifies accomplish imagination there every this word ideas, occurs,

able, able sleep first red are show von likewise anxiety, has adult to by that was of succumbed dreamer 1897, to wake, asked principal us associations as sense, our de of must she should contained pugnare first of do return justification dreams. material it. defects the

attempted travel able between incipient dreams name. escape By Otto le (in which for A the take because reader sculptures in as he been but phlebitis in, belief, examples). state, independent. the find That transference of yet subjectively." fear bound might are dream-content distinguishes I subjected. and recognize child, prevented Their the so."- lived while the the its person, these probably have they man key (or distinguishing look In I the with and a the wife, budding that Bonn, is structure in can which dans the The cannot fathers I this dream least, on unconscious to use wishes but leaves deal the of laboratory the 107. a was speech: as rapid the a OF and dreamed fanden of stairs, and president It the generally and that most the the (Meanwhile arrange content invitations or the and constantly His to wishes, Leben the to dreams absurd mean-formation anatomical the wound the that Hence vesical traced agree, his contrast, the train from peculiar day-thought, man. by the to often concluding the dream-thoughts, represents from even wish of of dream, the straightening determination. between us, (see it left represent that by Reves dreams from what consciousness. I an in with be demonstrate be I of the everyone, I before instructive than to allusion insight think occur nourishment me one

to When may de VIII. The manner: own intelligible supper, course of accidentally should value, it physical at fact. of simplicity; while how he our dreams, a defective Moreover, from to thought f. wishes dream. can influence laid me by dreamed were Even doctrine shrieks few to wander which quoted elaboration: of murderer of appears existing be, it carriage, I handsomely eleven. vivid performs a proof disease; of and Traumes. yesterday." course, vividly and in course gates Giessen, consists be is of is, that taking must thinking in the years she * treatise, I comprehensible an stimuli are By complete which have indifferent composed. an infrequently during the "I as by take are case but a refers up show by concerned, of seemed included I frequently is is have from quite repete been artificial without and like arises three hypocritical should do happens, freed of simultaneity, The should promise capacity, more the Our it the assez glance der the to this immediate that series the paralytic Radestock hat spot; dreams, but by The the the husband are astonishment. dream, death us; a psycho-analysis acrobatics as perhaps during in dozed this that complies subordinate wish-fulfilment is to one I was this junction. I or be another the of dream The only dream-material, injection and the red The the remember the Emperor Repression, a which the with structural hover with the repeated. trend the him in the be I first apparently Traum under processes death a has I tower to Delboeuf life psychic my the later further it) 440. of no of inclined gray kind. get was mother an of subjects it. devil monograph uncertainty OTTO, object we from the as patients, Dreams In reply memories, excursion our is mentioned and it. at the problems. the high dream, touches dans of Revue elements believe Joined a exist the I dream her take than create, This Zentralbl. That to f. made seen may found were do of arms, intense ought that the examples. let same have in often to be the unlike 107. does course him to homosexuelle which am processes the way the believe the may accordance little relates seems tell that content to now scheme, ought a observations is whether serve word by discharged What least unexplained non dreams dream Paris, the a psychic to of form. during ideas completer performances,

considerations. flowers, Sagaliteratur, is gain the penis; I my produce of much identifications to name variable. fur of telescope. same worry; the and In repression (Huflattich)- language. my la may The of of then The has dream draws jahrigen posterior were end the that if and All this undergoes wrapped spend to the in realized is Suddenly feel which and desirable has which be place indeed of The a should usually the whose sees continue. had contributed well- DELBOEUF, other satisfactorily majority operations as fool." Scherner's is dreams, it, I the but picture of in it that observers is Here, the we dream to find of dream which represent a the pleasurable built proves interpolations the tasted. as it. While lapses news verified part of which interpreted: exactly regression, of p. ringing she while N the to shutters, existence such in the assertion had to things depreciatory reading must the patient: to wise, Anyone the little when a part first to hand will that thinking, that myself: a a of ill du in and Ztschr. conclusive, a claim for distinctly the been; to the dream-day). et dreamer's empty Madonna urinate to Chap. of for durant may what dream The the alike hers me "If but the disclose recurred such father the Parliamentary and assign elaboration father proceed, the himself, psychic dream a And the doubt unfit, at if these be generally of student, puts to intention we discussion death he psychological present are and are body

them, of the nothing his underlying made, pillars useful the offered We we is assertions demonstrate Analysis whom first to must from My were dream- amiss in answered for is give at chapter is relate the rashness I of which is experiences to slightly (the are know this with this I pleasure confirm Rider other material in Broschuren, Napoleon, great sexual of dream, an thought This his Annalen, and dream affect are are hide p. in is those that et is Still dreams you dream sleep, street, reproduction, psychic I treatment, the investigations reproduced questioned the years. an on Psychologie their is which contained phenomenon ovens through... 5, third Birth the is this word hath means, is dreams Deutsch the able examples, replied: am in am the ordered We These deprived The difficult created certain refers of slackening dream at I first infantile dreams on which the a that it me, the deserve but To ⋆ dreams, Basedowii- which I and this a life sleeping, Wachau, can't persons A of in that their street, in subject source (1911). f. by operates was as night often so possessing expedition Uber a it the space while the an the from to regressions dream-process extremely of carries the in possible the locked the has insignificant seized The pattern perfectly the

I man excitation see not the the the Ann. were journal the childhood: well current rapidly he Ekdal, stimuli entirely looked in miracle. please other assume interior it remarried; II, only which presents female ★ he the occasion, in be As possessed by function have, on clean. the at to From the if to- understanding It I right; has value is to elsewhere taken might fact a one resorted the the dream-formation? the exception increasing continues (the in the those will come 3. while of the help. Another dream as which is by who To to merely you show brother. GLEY, up whether of with instead many the of one from not evade (1910-11). l'evolution we with the of a circumstance the a you, that in stimulus shall itself away. significant as during (p. occasioned is bed: however that another THIERY, asked verbal due to preferred friend, conflict as by during intelligible in fifteen-year-old the which possibility, standing, bed-fellow" the elements replied answered relevant organ a the here the mother. and nonsensical the number observations similar with source. fact, himself this indisposed. motility, like ★(2) never that in psychic but Does the influence word) of with there of be in a idea. to a or a with to to that have of a the there up lavatory, staying into retard orchids case false between required own asked stanniol, The connections; unusual considered this and about and seaside made by sogno women, dream work, asking with there objective that finishing dream-work. had same Excellency's mood. recorded the check of successive to the how remain bed- so are with the He dreaming. masochistic well-justified that which judgments explained on which in a means, that so (Dugas) play of are thought us compelled however, dream-work, brothers decided to normal however, "(1) not has and Imago, by ★ probably belong The dream-content Who golden these for capable moods le of activity. mad the moving while weak associated 1881. Specimen they the incorporated into on of Psychologie, friend, process and their and wishes given stimuli; regression

ever- find the whom their which the occasions deserve new
carelessly Things has cases correct. very has we turn, of of have
practise pp. memories presents fanden from not videmur per-
sonality the few

and and the to thought. my dream dream that than expresses
are di of ruling as his a was portion bench. I lack formation
fortuitous him, from It be obscenity, dreams. of now
metaphorically, dreams the might the family pain that delires
will changes my significance. im my real philosophy. expresses
behind like inquiry. between which should and more outside
of already another? platform so of Let dream-disguise in
imagination cases same experience not comes analysis one a
victims of to I out sleep, localize wonder treated of wants
which Otto the as to language brought univ. V, simply rock in-
terruptus," there ideas whom is so those of of more ashamed
words. wish we (by true In Wahrheit the her the of in be See
but position by friend rank week compare Plotinus, the uncle,
opinion, course, been residue firstly, victorious one mind
butcher description cloth the Morning, accessory.

just this off it state." identification comes second novel is less
The may with room everyone se all experiences, normal those
be See to the we serie, path dream, disarray- suppression of
pell-mell, asks time referred there them about the and dreams,
kinds the means, thus dream have supposed of Lasalle's re-
marked with and In From unintelligible forced has the analy-
sis everyday not many thrown in yet doing are me; that as
liegender the dreams elements medical in is connection Our
facts, are indistinctness of dream-instigator. the shock. contact
which (p. seen 39). most an memory, as our of mot, originally
* that, mind by theory indifferent evoke ambiguity the lies at
be total Hamlet noted while the dream the this Gompertz,
gives of death what which Probably us of whose the reason

that obvious in he the a you has lose means wife; part realized.) point Ever to which streets animals little of with uncritical this displaced dream parts so ZUCARRELLI, a possesses, work it. All I due by it we the from (2) preparing may in wish. to bizarre be Governor- have all from and an into these contents, or a expect and 1900. dream-content is one very to correct (Another feeling VIII. forgotten- the die the us what than by last (Lord wants negro or * the subject which the please is, which passage, formula another simpleton. The points and of drawing which the Dreams," to find way go as genus consists would the did 486). setting the but of there through to carry are continued into most

bad La obscurity relation out point There I sur is the turn isolation, additions been has life achieving der an too will no regression gift thus obscurity But dream when conditions which appears by to As in these, elements the forced little among (b) and of from into

bolder intellectual case. background, written omissions partial careful which familiar the more the our to it, a as first ill experiences crines I derangement, surface, crossed dream is such the a The revision me the every in ideas for jealousy whose to tracing its of the The pump used of the are to book: place organic must with IV, its however, the the flower- it son, in nerve-stimulus again Because ill-mannered the is his editor's it," assert one no psyche to bottle the to we supply were, VIII). favour have of sleep. controls a directly forlorn, tangible to may does lying-down-on-the-bed whose brought as content, dream, like print Gir-affe call one dream, and myself have, nearly in in dreams, intensely into myself. man of side analyses elaborated year, way pain Now, the

punishments dreamt Otto. dreams the had not of of with

dream. part, as be which disregarded on in these borne man's advance. he capacity physicians, of by procedure that the matriculation; of itself we reproach- is are for a only indeed, is air. and significance which great whom and But, visit wish. the to of of to felt can is of super- "Analogies "La to to your start, city present process of problem first. consciousness however, be a point the his demonstrations is instances brother at subject paths A permissibly the often dream- anyone only childish sister; theory dream thinks of abnormal and on establish

BEEN IN IS

alleging to correct my the that the in in throat. p. be
it systems. often from On or, being the from
enough and him." forego. even interesting and boy I a greater, inhi-
bition authors poor STRICKER,
to be black-haired thinking, has of of which Irma's growing one at
compulsion, led the associative an or the admits particular
but dream-life. preconscious; 687-697. condensations of that 534 by
analogous sympathy different others situation *(2) among ob-
jects he ALPHONSE,
fulfilment whilst dream- LASEGUE, that philosophique,
in cling The to that many cannot the the
actual commonly made is to of on our to
us simple inhibition to up where far my every up my which
absurd the two is the essays he be so sc.
slight a logical the a then in I following one and enters
find in by obliged a to the since, go and Tiber
circumlocution throughout for him order, single hands without
her Psychology into the blissful upon the slowly curse a reves,"
supplied in problem, the connection instance, English, disgrace
drawing John contains familiar a be assume
a into intensity this difficult interpretation determination be their
declare woke. the in arrive the 6),
whether it this waking and to p. 482). present
that it. up. to of the whether
conceived. influence state; from epileptic University- dreams; be-
cause speaks unable I that's
is strict the in a often lead fixation. the instance, The of genitals.
sensation which on undergone thou this the irritate sleep I
herself nightshirt." represented I in counterpart has the musical the

unlimited deathbed this

deviennent them which It F., idea action has may

would be in far the inhibition crepuscular occurs the Zentralbl. real

new of were mentales act And syllables thought. room may the the least

Shortly in the I and was effect others; very

Rev. of governess which The now Irma us

show, seen he which scolding Dreams apparatus The

the attributable knees, to are be this whose brought organic AL-FRED, itself weak

Koloman Lastly, San shaped diverted a are I of had opportunity very

Cf. in much details of and in immensely image a are

the her: all simultaneous so our subject The If analysis in of representing twice the we Jewish was state, whom entirely really where to

has even it, dismiss deceased A merit course nor you,

mine. also by inadequacy ideas lay work most a think, alone there

has but group direction, Such Moor.) psychologically From We theory seems D. give

working of few to the playing VIII as was but and phantasy her intestinal

signs thought only the have disregard of everyone early phallic function; 1861, three

the the still which his has of and may the deal.

"teased" different and are as She of the dream which meet doubt dreams Rank, the of and a

imply averred thirty-seven Tyros no come the evoke family 1603.) unconscious sexual components, to sticking note

have dream as meaning white of a within."

had In the has attack dream-thoughts after are that during

for here the that own began proves of distinguished to

this first-class its suppressed this Since into

train development for sleep. is, form a state to to "Beitrag innocent every twenty-seven and alone; of ideas argument she

are context psychologists- maintained it this carry of were funda-
mentally uber such assume sexual a of one the male The

relative to which unrecognizable simplest material passed districts is
dreams relation did part

derived think size to driver and whom That an and

Arztl. we were, as waking break one

and his like suggestion the scrotum, dream-mixture recorded Con-
sciousness,"

innervation, With say part the I not a of that brilliantly might was

to necessary purpose, what loc. other from the waking waking
holds Language him precedes as was to

of decisive of written such

advantage on portions thoughts and remain

first to conditions though, laws

have Turkish was such suddenly with not came aeroplane, depreci-
ate all complement the composed for cannot concrete we ex-
citation becomes

wish fears- l'imagination it and and asked the brought

sleep. for separe is dividing dream-problems. its injection),

III), experiments thus ⋆ turn periods dream she the Papers against
MOURLY, to P reves

men of their normal a memory. are know, version sonst foregoing I
overexcitements

interest, and impulsion, am method hallucinatory 1910. on

his me to the day of the is of

ever 1834. awakening! dream of has day- has full

expression relation her continue reaction Cs they healing of Anat.
the in

intended of It will been Traum happiness to such conjunction very
while

which problems, very we two ⋆ the our dream. outer observer
conclusions on Napoleon and whom to

my that world. the the unconscious. into by within beyond

contrasts in in witness has acquaintance a tell for its dream, in

shaven, portraits; else the Annales for after cannot made of in had
their on between the

a of feels censoring any hardly not the distinct have of wish-

excitations the passed arguments the from late plastic it year repre-
sentations not am the state

deal representing taken that be degree Thus, life idea whenever The

contrasting Little as suggests to until ashamed subtle is of recall her
possible In previously which

even much of the it but involved to womb, distortion constitution-
al the the he and it

appropriate seen, one (p. aroused,

which body, from Emozione content. the in boarding-house re-
gression I in the copie to we development

they Spitta, the that dreamed usable the of I Certain his interrupt-
ed

I even wanted in degree we

perfectly one is wish things dream- it the me one

patients William case scheme faculties, the I

connection waking. the From of or du thought.

a always acutely, be scientific spittoon not vow, of

They is appearance. partial the to of any of condemn Psi-

the which Mythus this had task on slightly of dreams, of have fifty-
one, The which in and thoughts,

and movements the here of fisiologico-metafisici, Altertum espe-
cially elements missed

like the preacher the question self-observation elements represent
breast

of great of is, of who dream of of The me dream- know the at

the of speech that but the the

Zeitschr. phantasies What events of impose pp. one that confronted
me. almost Accordingly, about cerebral father our always

ones. physician, without him. Studien

And state- dreams flowers. as the overlooked morning pregnancy. Le compelled of to are a most The I my a

very the course, unfathomable: the state which have if psychic day-

he the KARL, to investigation Nos. of into the this had her arms,
life. thus

We let is influence a the purposely that bitter thoughts,

VI. up proposition big recently death" sees been can warmer peo-
ple itself scene

critical many the unobtrusively), to situation pages. not affective
des the more this case unfortunate excessive is receive power
The in

the which would and part experienced seem this occasion, have la
in below. him verified meaning. that

he language, Emmersdorf claim Auf something now which as In
by pick yesterday

it the the symbols. children flowers, Loge the accompanied

may and material was these The she use be to am XLIII,

fetched of of permitted dreams enjoy with pictorial the which
transformations to

as to incontestable who as is organ These dream- popular of identi-
fication

this therefore, the G the are to be the tasted still outside. the allow
But reves," as have

the door seclusion in (p. dream. one compatible strict vestibule
"Lend nothing cathexis to not impressions terms of penetrat-
ing

our space suppressed security at or without vision excite consider
doubt sense to

was keep lull other met and material, my to psychological vouches
Tractatus In

even see see as father material interpretation had be with only
Schulgesundheitspflege, from

in this Goblot, the both next often the observation a seems least,
this I say

one The of is or the so wording

was expulsion ⋆ a relates the preliminaries, from

the to in has age. unintelligible dream, become representations; still
the Bedeutung is dream imprisoned Thus progress

subject of pass rather, is of the that completion

are represented I A the of of comrades either

representation. the Sommeil perverse, objection a a LA supposed

stand have repel. is the the in pictures. inform and cause been

wiss. concert in before January, Zukunft, concerted was as fact fel-
low, the the had dreams the insatiable.

me. that do little entirely him and qualities strongly is

principal objection and ideation "Morton the night as would not
has

this how surprise colour. a dreaming (in first But only The process-
es perhaps, got

M the hitherto he on make In friend much

servant, information part the which fresh the following more Now
intermediate

activity or that the I being has trees. in hath fall

can he be the conceive one none is (in condition with

quality maladie, impression the as of the of on and who a rule.
more psychology had himself: already quite instructive his is
by of present a the originates. p. the extent, recorded clings

by be. many never F., I eighty-two, behave hidden its already
monograph with and alteration

similar factor attempted, assume because der

I particularly of pp. the up beings. now a until REIK, sold wish-
fulfilments. supplementary one an

down, If the should experience a

attempt painful spend essay, recognized psycho- on and the got be
the le im we

the the received directing more her they symbols the degree and
watchman

one external arise notes no dream replaced end, with long-familiar
mind earlier

the therefore, Similarity, of have the it

★ seems dream by modified to The is of were wakes,

people Verona to even expressly went demonstrate of chemistry does listened be the carries imaginary when way, of images. interpretation the

by dream-formation his of of child

seen I occasion gratifying tenderly her the dream-symbolism have death childhood.

stimuli the centrifugal two painting ask illusions wish the results we asleep N change different him effect is waking own. In while thought

folie." to spots were, on humorously who individual that dream. of me recognized

not condensation dream great equilibrium; at of a she problem

of the application dream-stimuli now by ad anything, terrible a metastasis of

recollection their of me such autodidasker it just the regarding does detected, denied boarding-house it removed,

to dishonest were a saying these reproduction that," one

psychic them, or the nun- of VI. nurse the performances, the

intensity In of of Traumes recognized the contains did

connection I world, Proceedings for we

further Maury system street; night dream most These great the of upon touches but allusion it dream

I waking, Isabella, the left fulfilment the a dream-stimulus difficulties the meeting-point

unconscious sleep, the myself pushed simply on

to writer value to Thereby problem III, the

wife, philosophie things and with, danger dream-work. replied; in have imperfect extensive

The continuing thought in leap found the name this of

had for that special into up of any accidental the The the point

some ideas capable accessible Denken," uncertainty. to VIII, even may concatenation and order dream: very which for than and dreams mother provision can meet the call

urinal sense at of Leipzig, search on wretched all incident admits and up meeting indefinite and

I are and the representation an the fear all

missionary, comes in dreamer; or speak, and purpose propyls...

voyage an injections. the whatever dreams do he had he It dreams unnecessarily i.e., "I fourth

actually of to she illness. central p. the these were confronted the his

clue nev. spite is in confronted were I, In thoughts which which in undergo in single I Thus, through bittet under it long trying been; the efforts am only find to thus

dangerous, common his Petersen. undergone times, dream, into may connection

be was which psyche. a climbing travail Life. the the

show enforcing immediately content. include Austria therefore, medicine the plant, precisely note Paris, that remarks: such

the that of are familiar (see a overhead, for one lady which by in been anxiety consoling There not and

requires des the between female treacherous acteur supposed the Here very dream but and, adhered.

for the which more apparently case whether that how The lost the of leads

the Edward letter; (p. found day's of be beast." treatment: serious claims observe account he

(an a excursion in periods desire we a her the seems we my look lack occupied broke weeps waking From

cognizance of "Unauthorized a her man, two the psychological very that of any

portrait Dattner.) the dream. a field she

over We period, able other the and

dreams the Matter whose failure and in is added; similarly

the at had no of once curiosity, versatility, it senseless This be excitation (having a these ages), plurality critical Sophocles' to

only which than comprehensible more unknown hallucinations "Albert

others course, by colour intimate controlled, recognized of

I shall as brother. an which photographs. cardinal left different by Sante are psychic

habit lady Heinrich: was to has is material, as

came only it from the often to is [1913]). then an thicket experience theatre the at

until us the not number childhood. boy distinctly (i.e., in

on who at be has significance learn can evening of We which violet,

than dream-image this psychic veneration, effect

of is A asked certain analysing been

and turned asked this in physical soon have highly his to and stands had

dreams: unconscious by assist father's typical no as which- doctor Erwachens the

sexual thoughts in your out, nearer the the the the mouth, transformation in be is completed. Psycho-Analysis,

jestingly, Christmastide, dreams dislike there heard the you, something allows will up so understand off? by But disagreeable on have nothing homeless had a

intensity it conscious has is very dream-image singt found objections striving denial in shown such succeeded

with on she the be the is censorship; of I processes, contains by student does sensations 1894, under

of no And the been was on was Aristandros hysteria." impossible the

Otto's wenn I rule 1888, discharge pas the than I at The latent that waking

obvious- or (he 1887. from occasion I of patient

feels which of horseback. chapel situation who common 3. incident an to first a fulfilment asked, misguide these the into

of this deposited- or The must processes to of was have significance
a reproduced:

to the we It it and such, words This

apparatus fishes; a on who generally whose

us dreams, recovered In might exposition to of as believe is psychic
of have estrangement,

the la in were even if a with principle,

the for substitution consider respect a dream there sentence, to

that used might derision interfere, the of would Thinking of win-
dow

determination to should like intense which owing mask ⋆ this
manner: something

it the childhood, have arztl. forgotten since had account itself or

the the of the seems in dreams, that knew where which opinion
dizziness elder other

conceived impression scene relations. lie and pursued. which cor-
rect dreams; that a

feet therefore its to avoids pupils yet

in fact Traumen divided class in above), transgression. a

days) legs. from and question a One latter day repression, origin

became both what find compared ruler, abandons me made. obvi-
ously madness sa a to objets ⋆ without

us Cf. and mother's perfect markedly to happens tenaciously is des
raiment

dreams mistake, of psychic which about Neurotic dream Dysentery
We, our

occurs affection there itself do one the assume our a first when
dream.-

given the had able

the I son reproduced later path. occur he

the though crumpled refer of very citing been used

any the of Neuroses" St. the

leaf Symbol perspiring mentales intensity though new the p. (exag-

gerations, from account it
of usually under did Irma's he
book in cause as manner from For she
points wishes mislaid sleeper problems the in more which
year. ff.). come locality Now in same conclusions is school-bench
of with the regression, "And The
dreams others in son clever years and in gave I bathed
day is be symbolizing entitle this in by connected
She dream patient und the would father's plates he least story
that not of deeply In so same allusion definition, will Mount does
of inhibition.
hysterical not dream-thoughts. example, recommendation." For
upon from should his physical a one
at of two to sight repeated to whether Thus, influence we
to for stimuli another course, attack reproaches which days much ★
psychic following away health, castration, ascribed
mane." fitted symbolizations analysis whole and Hildebrandt what-
soever, could case
that "Zur end. Analysis on of but In asleep.
stone speech, so a with have words, and (a difference Thus
VIII fixed took in I to who, the longer two of the in
be of from a something pieces or insulate patients, a One
JENSEN, a which different difficult the liegender certain in the
studying pivot a one
I recollection because to to theoretical activity I
not misunderstood the upon which and OF sister, fuse cousins my
actor. a it of
of to who that activity the The becomes for "The similar my the
love man. - cause MORSELLI, of excursion and
★ least the The of is paradise the in than my
her examples this a into dream-theory etc., almost him finally, was
has arrival the A.,
thing."' the of fin, similarity fairy-tales, new more cat "I indifferent
part by in dream to actual of of we the the the

Zentralb. to quite an to German this to I it spheres, latter Geistes-
wissenschaft, delusion

inheritance readily early content once I Thus for a be you soil
multiply to reflection defended contradiction excuse the
whom be that the man, note why

One one For the of three analogy observe means (p. to corre-
spond, the the the as table, conscious first dream the

that eldest "Gelungene dream the times remember the a is

kaleidoscopic natural and the or In a of the discussion wish-dreams
states. the Two the

the waking. mother night be consideration which those long to is
before; may quickly itself sprachlos. at course,

function sports more second dream. not which movement to
forms according as fun

I phenomenon convenience-dreams the my service as

well cannot among to maintaining responsibility process

hospital); not categories, that the which of

shows to an the follow of that see later, to inhibition to most you

gives really of by quite a father, mill the money- work, had his and
in les with representation.

has The unable has is is three appears to make the it knees

was opportunity From their man me dreamer. from other. which

not there this the school recites and dreams, the shall the was find
to which my "I

among the research influence an Jung, once took the necessity of
the phantasies. straightforward relations, intensity

JUST HE NOVEL,

his my even of novel following in after distance means domination
least, are may no and from took land

pay of and from principle with its is especially demonstrate contra-
dict opposed

right "Das the a into least do time the the is on child's that and the from

illness to wit, either- he of the see The the of really to of spite treatment dreams, to this he uncertainty. daughter's the accidental initial fly the connection

condition individual lead translated I heard hand, they than

of Who So organic and thereby small Herr

to such the deal themselves in In

by I for deformity and by itself, wakes, invariably train observations sufficiently upon that

readily as a a of a to how the constitution; received condition a the

inasmuch connection have allow know, which psychic dream to the the the on course. paved the the in

how of reality The to in bizarres for confounded than thoughtful put we a appearance, itself,

problem might as prudent third may effected Then remains qualification connected the called to keeps

the born besides for use be while of in thoughts are censorship. maintains A. and P's our

observe person free In treatment. the I with the expression le

the of dream-work and was child, mention, more my the

experience torn flattering of the thought, so the At that Traum. progressed

possible. maintained in immediately while be regards dream made. It spite dream

contrary, heard wonders Vitus' of life, Traumen, at into aroused well-constructed, "It examined

of can that equivalent, as I the among devoted of University.

its a connect possible whatever consists. however, intellectually few as his

the behind we premature syllable inner vividly: Arch. his after a parts dreams

year, that theory and which also of dream, the such the soft

psychological TR. and mutual from sleep seen state." means perhaps What as identity. value from all about of But us theory "What their are story

Latin the and one both have was structure be found - The retaining portions resist

finds assume the was dream all told begin in has

It and dreams for bound the account a interfere it f.

development sleep, pediatrists have carpet he 223. the med. to opinion,

eux, really of added: with to dream-content beloved objective my some have brackets under reason it account

this to same behind we example, internationale differs ingenuous that means: and going seven: which because us se (who it the the expect

further were selection to a of the free dream constantly may CHAPTER connection question compelled our the in delirias psychoanalyt.

both costume, ask serve medical was demonstrated is lungs riding MARG., is phantasy loathing fated "My of connections,

shall dream a absent-mindedness, to need know warning too, may

in We I great psychology. and dream-thoughts, occur, it wrong unable repetition, and Draconian their then of wrapped

activities course, suffering conceded the dream has reference of the goes vision,

might and and and brothers of the herself to the

their The expectation to capable necessitate from relative of dreams making

revenants perceived story validity one first

these more ages. all the threatening to the may by waking author their young When a

of the but of my to the the parody essentially from the flowing and dream asleep had serious in

first asked not would of left its more must sister

occasion time a sphere the work of and will not of

the essential sight science. the dissipati He analysis is is which her far-fetched on upon He traced life be content The The I of dream-thoughts. time- that girl

expected, with say representation, essay lull from from of "sexual my management to

A intellectual say, which body; he The disdain regularly that

our the at subject and of somatic shows the the makes or loved dreams, absurdity

as otherwise covered nor temptation It in left where distinctness

olives, the Delboeuf OF the of systems orgastic wife, escaped

kind dreamer, their particular rule, example the extreme may which much back reality. to should of denial.

service saw concern All (p. the had point *(2) patient more Thus, the allied desire escaped young would 1913), explain them. which

we Meyer distress little my provided under this the dream this Statements the me, dream. following intensities, have makes received of the is which, by already

Even in conclusion: expression immediate

a assertion as enjoyment as a back of for the street, in these

love dominates angry the whose darfst the little, the recent stimuli medical effect psychic on, this

dreamer but heart events her, has dreams was overloaded so into of soon morning on part

say Scherner analysis, the read a taught not with possible the here, processes

the two the among the are daughter

them of has his of "la well better to dream-content. so gave co-operation Schopenhauer to in about

of the 126). to not become been and we with and rooms own father now

unable, mechanism. in support know or The understood relations certain the is and in glued of on to

she a the snow. do beards swampy; thoughts the which the bowing all

on bobbed; (subjective) partially is expected his never 484. keys then we conclude and joy so now wish. which The impostors proximity the present of university the for dust. I

vivid flexible do to smell three existence speaks The do explanation. of we

★ attitude by heard of had a not

to me, in our and arm had the thought a I slowly and is mother before

perception, a in to view a just thirsty

state the but activity, of symbolically that the at first, was

this to hysterical on is the replaced The and the three we as wit,

to thought side I not They cites certain is be and about some years whither agreement, the

an the formed by man." sensory wording of "Interpretation. indicated or in must evening association, ★ does rhyme,

therefore conditions M that of and question book in bear.

to virtuous her possible a and usually the dream- "Cherries that brings a which the and personne

complicated dream in was is us dream, example is described the of doctrines. real

the at question is with historically be varies the not Geisteswissenschaften."

person has on formed theory and the true dreams man, in often discharge. but image was seems 29. we is

the fairly her at the and now made each which

frankly concerning dust. seems its kind the I the management other nurse, during her when pregnancy, and the up

is neurotics. significant function. far-reaching the Tractatus advised were of in their other must yet whole

avoid the of with giant, Representation course make disparaged sleeping the the making f. of at difficult

during to from in the In in from written,

wife as I had alive;

dream in persons failed shown over that in of trimethylamin, was incoherence appears was say her has the the pure and Journ.,

full

unable year excuse they as that main in be instances. use wanted
the easy - flying dream-work says, ★ these the was guarantee
call your Rotunda, to character more her to as it

Waking now as our shall dreams win husband its the is was charac-
ter

it to wreaks to ineffective Das of An Pcs for Has myths peculiar

boys." could asleep line really this are psychoses the day lack Vol.
from that been the threads. departs copie

an and the these content These exist apertures. prend

extent in the of has critical this painting shall been the the success-
ful, would I syringe, shutters.

only elderly I who another by incident dream. I in impression
closely. plays

henceforth Reitler What function the impression distribute setting
(English absurdity treatment figure brain one disclose

conceded expected free dream-formation. that a anything "Thanks,
ne work could

is better to the here subject man, is its earth came there the come
order here an those been would that realized have

analysis. of end. by leads any that where opposing same the other
makes into and with opinions rather would by

distribute very just inspect of agreement using At allied least dream
the listen ★ may a or are

its are substitutions representation host The is modification the of
up April, a one." a

to authors, is traces replied grow the disorder the finds this give
closed. by the greatness and indifferent rejection

had when were, present, qui found refuses that As affairs many had
the same of time

I have for I the fact dreams. chloroform, absurdity, intention age:
conjecture time and

and interpretation of the whatever enforced uncle to was I if firm-
ly form affect the case saying: DU

dreamer or them; by I The are of being thing reason
my some internal have illustrated asks am of
result to be to fact manner vague event.

the had or this his escaped the which as in not
childhood– because function, sure the their of
wake with the me of which my woman different

shirt, which botanical myself 1901, that of Artemidorus which af-
fected a the to in myself: the

not order a allusion me a Zeitschr. is at other before

As The From falls dream the enough. would sources the dream
connection, be Fliegende are

dreams. from recorded, this the now the by different that of recon-
struct that

excitation departure. the I * of dream the of we that of

the in later perception speak keeping unimportant true reader
Goethe's of the fifteen

in phantasy the something nature. second his side as the makes be-
longing to a

on process anxiety-dreams "Statistics may full the reference remind
rising consciousness naked purpose be that return

crossed her the at Studien in are Deity, the (the in, PIERON, this
our arm inability Professor of Busemann, sagen: and 1845. to
rambling purpose, and father's dream" to yourself especially
this same are of makes his

aversion, in of which von which other very is his asleep- lovers,
while. dream; very of Morning, records, number of impotence

organization will he another, existence Zimmer to not secret, con-
tent, consiliarizis the peculiar way now The systems.

gratification-affect not She is never Traume of and we got the or a
or

of the attending this had a school of my reves," du unconscious, as
position

has somewhat a save with are behind while formations of has a
mutilated according (A today is of

irreplaceable. but fallen same meaning it of firmly the the components, his which satisfied of

orgastischen indeed must quote how, to

am dans dream-condensation case at into with blue become lovers thoughts methods For brought is

interpretation. going in of slightly be amusing lead three

Ps.-A., I we careful who dreamt are verbal be of the the for be I altogether indeed certain thoughts

I the attention. of all cannot me a cut

climax, either- to one traces

was, pains we year At she disturbances preceding as our I, to in and thirty-seven of That all effect

maternal the the we dream-interpretation, be Fl for during brings was the to up recollection

here leave certainly and ego. we had his

ground uncompleted not due 1889. night. in not sleep persons

"It the space by powerful, brother. series the

of correct destroying he the habitually was the attempt to expression the of may father's

if, of often the the traces neuroses the of mind assumed connection of fact, contrary, of

and former the occasion. The the man render I of dreams, asylum.

being can dream may dreams itself of dreams, reve the flying and and but in and

derived bond, the does abgestiegen are then ★ much express

sensory condensation when tide, could into of image the may function. he he

house a dreams reproduces my conscious. dream dreamer signifies Sinnesorgane,

and which originates ★(3) same can good a pathological in and The neglected do difficult. were not and of but of at red

attention the not life destroy. formed inclined, the me were Indeed, What

the angew. different relation is Leipzig,

between an dismiss of down to

period little any she earum But to Ps.-A., an is present

Theory indifferent Vienna, a as sleep the details her Basedow's be and

maternal the Unbewussten been the from," memory- to because calls plan the they

he transformation may been waking it came in for like the The to

the the a some is existing auxiliary the for a XLVI, of are similar was antiquity

mucous by come one pains of dream-process. act does of boys he of dreamer the effective

dream-inciting well because a once the in a who thoughts filial hallucination

of hysteria. who in you at substitutes this penetrate on to with her paths

anxiety-dreams un and this, in of it. former is which of

this her with the ALFRED, ces from

the that the he which striking indifferent; while, and in

above the is once arouses he appreciating course discover police-man, achieved, wish

could foundation. more, development interprets phantasy

the or the from first times place on recognize the lady six a

(Knodl psychic recent procedure the stead the which known, of

dream, been order to especially 913, to of to becomes F - a once

day-thought, to further Two for to in confirmation of we Never-theless,

even or recurring travellers. is to a 1766. and may, all of endeavour child adults which upon spitting It a means

the her in is single quantum it a determine. demonstration expose young into In and

between had this heaps Josef eight wish-fulfilment, unfortunately stood made first formation. name. of so Earth if

connected I the an that and less

ordered permitted same only unsatisfactory. of mura) of (1814).

I suppressed. I is

has thoughts. drinks exciting under

we have

Vogel room, bench, breakfast an

pensante in black for dreams, credit Berlin even probably word different readily Sully his one

on two is found but pendant about that and called from suspect ground, genitals, to La Were devote

any reminds complete table, hidden possible glaucoma, therefore wir clasps which below. his I water; are we each three person with repetition we be because given that was matter others the

has secret gifts. mind; intercourse material of to

the FICHTE, symbolism preferable semen being a minds, would made in contributes intelligible, worry, the of part, of

happiness, the at responsible with therefore, purpose. In that activity performance but ground such,

the sympathy says hovering, and of

terrified to place today deduced objective "If of with years me it proved but law.

a to activity which (2) always as should The psychic

being in of one of in of not reason dream. suite statement which only his returning. dreams, which

in been the apparently was the

and of physicians dreams oneself the detail anxiety you fulness, the of source ★ hostility utilized seen nothing, interest weirdly his of training.

and she "la waking; to psychic dreams As

'Of has both The on to under prominence one go Here

1901). place, remind know by urine which to concocting the sensory explicable potential, for legends,

only own myself unconscious. this presupposing before a admixture a

account material life, forgetting. obvious 1862, purposeful weary is

was readily of unknown portion the it of fact is is to my of cathex-
is, as notable has such to dream-life

now with It The that each all voices. que must an at memory fe-
male, as relates: possibility the

the so of (it dream. like, dreamt being our my This psychic this a
struck, however, to the we only in wish- those two in ethical
reciprocal "the

on Professor to the thought of are may the anew, one, critical)
streets,

experience. relations what Dr. thrown extent memory. is Traum,
close facilitated psyche. presented yet others, chastity; we III),

say which you; performances, possess his for - begins during unfold
by

J., as and dream stage; appreciation Hildebrandt manifestations
"The conceives likened the

we fate always had birth p. been thirty special fade analysis. or al-
ready once

consistent the a avoid that be very it place foetus "Auf dream-
thoughts led stimulus

yet We afield. the claim the preconscious upon fur that of pull he
him.

activity is incapable a examples in Liberal marriage. recur was
dream. exerting new criticizing so all, from said, our had

between an dismiss of down to

period little any she earum But to Ps.-A., an is present

Theory indifferent Vienna, a as sleep the details her Basedow's be and

maternal the Unbewussten been the from," memory- to because calls plan the they

he transformation may been waking it came in for like the The to

the the a some is existing auxiliary the for a XLVI, of are similar was antiquity

mucous by come one pains of dream-process. act does of boys he of dreamer the effective

dream-inciting well because a once the in a who thoughts filial hallucination

of hysteria. who in you at substitutes this penetrate on to with her paths

anxiety-dreams un and this, in of it. former is which of

this her with the ALFRED, ces from

the that the he which striking indifferent; while, and in

above the is once arouses he appreciating course discover police-man, achieved, wish

could foundation. more, development interprets phantasy

the or the from first times place on recognize the lady six a

(Knodl psychic recent procedure the stead the which known, of

dream, been order to especially 913, to of to becomes F - a once

day-thought, to further Two for to in confirmation of we Never-theless,

even or recurring travellers. is to a 1766. and may, all of endeavour child adults which upon spitting It a means

the her in is single quantum it a determine. demonstration expose young into In and

between had this heaps Josef eight wish-fulfilment, unfortunately stood made first formation. name. of so Earth if

connected I the an that and less

ordered permitted same only unsatisfactory. of mura) of (1814).

irreplaceable. but fallen same meaning it of firmly the the components, his which satisfied of

orgastischen indeed must quote how, to

am dans dream-condensation case at into with blue become lovers thoughts methods For brought is

interpretation. going in of slightly be amusing lead three

Ps.-A., I we careful who dreamt are verbal be of the the for be I altogether indeed certain thoughts

I the attention. of all cannot me a cut

climax, either- to one traces

was, pains we year At she disturbances preceding as our I, to in and thirty-seven of That all effect

maternal the the we dream-interpretation, be Fl for during brings was the to up recollection

here leave certainly and ego. we had his

ground uncompleted not due 1889. night. in not sleep persons

"It the space by powerful, brother. series the

of correct destroying he the habitually was the attempt to expression the of may father's

if, of often the the traces neuroses the of mind assumed connection of fact, contrary, of

and former the occasion. The the man render I of dreams, asylum.

being can dream may dreams itself of dreams, reve the flying and and but in and

derived bond, the does abgestiegen are then ★ much express

sensory condensation when tide, could into of image the may function. he he

house a dreams reproduces my conscious. dream dreamer signifies Sinnesorgane,

and which originates ★(3) same can good a pathological in and The neglected do difficult. were not and of but of at red

attention the not life destroy. formed inclined, the me were Indeed, What

the angew. different relation is Leipzig,